Exploring Latin: Structures, Functions, Meaning

Exploring Latin: Structures, Functions, Meaning

Volume II: Clause and Discourse

Edited by
Lucie Pultrová and Martina Vaníková

DE GRUYTER

ISBN 978-3-11-133268-0
e-ISBN (PDF) 978-3-11-133295-6
e-ISBN (EPUB) 978-3-11-133303-8

Library of Congress Control Number: 2024943406

Bibliographic information published by the Deutsche Nationalbibliothek
The Deutsche Nationalbibliothek lists this publication in the Deutsche Nationalbibliografie; detailed bibliographic data are available on the internet at http://dnb.dnb.de.

Cover image: © Martin Hundák, © Faculty of Arts, Charles University
Typesetting: Integra Software Services Pvt. Ltd.
Printing and binding: CPI books GmbH, Leck

www.degruyter.com

Contents

Volume II: Clause and Discourse

Section 3: **Syntax and Semantics**

Section 3: **Syntax and Semantics**

Concepción Cabrillana

Lepidus vivis: Semantic Content and Functional Gradation in Secondary Predicates

Abstract: On the basis of an initial analysis of the syntactic and semantic status of the constituents of the plautine expression *lepidus vivis*, this paper aims to confirm the hypothesis that there is a correlation between the semantic content of the elements of a message in which a Secondary predication appears, and the degree to which these elements are necessary for the message to fulfil its communicative function. To this end, the Predicate Frames of the verb *vivo* are first established on the basis of lexical data and cross-linguistic comparison. The analysis itself, using a corpus comprising Latin comedy and Augustan poetry, identifies and describes the main types of contexts that can be found – more and less assimilable to those of a copulative nature –, and shows the conditions under which the Secondary predicate can denote state and/or permanent quality as well as adequately fulfilling its communicative purpose. Among the conclusions is that the loss of semantic weight in the predicate in fact drives a more necessary lexical presence of the specification provided by the Secondary predicate, whereas this need is significantly less when the verb is more fully realised from a predicative point of view.

Keywords: Secondary Predicate, semantic content, Subject Complement, communicative function, *vivo*

1 Introduction

This paper fills certain gaps or pending areas of research in the field of Secondary predicates (hereafter SecP): specifically, those contexts in which SecPs appear with *vivo* as a main predicate. The most significant variables in this study are listed and described in the following section, based on an analytical approach to the plautine expression *lepidus vivis*. Within this framework, a particularly important aim here is to explore the possible correlation between the semantic content of the elements that make up the message in which a SecP appears, and the degree to which these elements are necessary for the message to fulfil its communicative function; addi-

Concepción Cabrillana, University of Santiago de Compostela, Spain

https://doi.org/10.1515/9783111332956-023

tionally, an attempt will be made to identify and describe some features that characterise the constituents involved in these kind of expressions.

Thus, in what follows (section 2) we will propose a syntactic and semantic status for the plautine expression (*lepidus vivis*), this serving as a starting point for the subsequent analysis; we will then present a formalisation of the Predicate Frames (hereafter PFs) of the verb under investigation (section 3), which in turn will allow us to undertake the analysis itself (section 4).

2 Framework of the Paper and First Approach

In the section on "Adjectives functioning as secondary predicates", Pinkster (2021: 781) provides the example which itself figures in the title of the current contribution, and observes in a footnote[1] that examples of SecP with the verb *vivo* are very frequent in comedy and (Augustan) poetry; the enumeration in which the specific example appears exemplifies SecP which, in Pinkster's words (2021: 780), "describe(s) a non-permanent or transient mental or physical condition of the entity to which they are related". A first approach to various conditions that facilitate the expression of permanent qualities by certain SecP has been made elsewhere,[2] specifically with verbs of stative semantics. The question arising therein led to the need for a comparative study of the situation with verbs from other semantic fields, which is the goal of this study.

In this more global task, verbs not only with different semantics, but logically also with different levels of agentivity and dynamism, should be considered as central. Although in principle there are no special semantic restrictions on the verbs with which a SecP can appear, Pinkster (2021: 779) does point out that such SecP are frequent with "verbs of standing, moving, finding and perceiving".

Hence, this type of predicate is common with verbs located at semantically, syntactically and aspectually distant poles: from mostly or partially stative verbs, to much more dynamic and agentive predicates such as those of movement. In the space between these two poles we might locate, among others, the group of verbs that imply an intermediate state of sensory or intellectual activity: that is, verbs which are generically called verbs of perception, or indeed the verb which will be the focus of the present study.[3]

1 With references to Heerdegen (1913) and Hofmann (1924: 81); cf. also Pinkster (2015: 206).

2 Cabrillana (2019, 2024).

3 As for the verbs of "finding", they are in principle omitted in this more general research project in order not to widen the field of study too much, which, among other drawbacks, would make it difficult to compare results.

But let us look in a little more detail – albeit briefly and before developing the core of the study – at the expression included in the title of this paper.

Certainly, the interpretation of a given Latin text by one translator or another in an attempt to identify its function (syntactic, pragmatic, etc.) cannot be a criterion, much less a fundamental one; such a criterion could only be one element to take into account, especially from the point of view of the overall semantics of the passage and/or of the work in which the passage is found.

Accordingly, framing the expression in its context is essential in grasping its meaning with greater accuracy: in the scene from the comedy that contains this example of *lepidus vivis*, the young Lysiteles, Philto's good son, tries to convince his father to allow him to marry the sister of the wild Lesbonicus, who has squandered much of his money and thus left his sister without a dowry. The *adulescens* Lysiteles bases his argument on the fact that they will not themselves lose their fortune through the match, and that it will constitute generous help to the friendly family of Lesbonicus, which is in keeping with the principles of virtue preached by Philto.[4] Once the father allows it, to which his son reacts with an enthusiastic *di te servassint mihi!* ('May the gods keep you for me!', PLAVT. Trin. 384),[5] Lysiteles asks one last favour: that Philto himself ask for her hand. It is at this point, when Philto agrees, that his son utters a very grateful *lepidus vivis*:

(1) PHIL. [. . .] *dabitur opera.* LYS. *lepidus vivis.* (PLAVT. Trin. 390)
'PHIL. [. . .] I'll attend to it. LYS. You're very good.'

It seems beyond doubt that the idea to be conveyed here is the one which has figured in translations and dictionaries; it would not make sense, or at best it would lose almost all its emotional force, if it were to mean 'you live as a charm', instead of placing greater emphasis on Philto's quality ('You *are* a really nice person'), which rather than being fleeting, is a manifestation of a property that Lysiteles wants to show as being permanent in Philto and which, in the way he

4 Cf., e.g., the latter's intervention shortly before the scene in question (Trin. 280–312) and the reaction to it by Lysidamus in Trin. 313 (*istaec ego mi semper habui aetati integumentum meae* 'I've always considered this to be a shield for my youth'), or the crossing of interventions between Lysidamus and Philto in Trin. 355–358 (LYS. *deum virtute habemus et qui nosmet utamur, pater, / et aliis qui comitati simus benevolentibus. /* PHIL. *non edepol tibi pernegare possum quicquam quod velis. / quoi egestatem tolerare vis? loquere audacter patri* 'LYS. Father, thanks to the gods we have the means both to sustain ourselves and to be kind to others who wish us well. PHIL. I can't deny you anything you wish. Who do you want to support in his poverty? Speak to your father boldly').

5 The Latin texts correspond to those in the Library of Latin Texts at Brepolis (http://clt.brepolis.net/llta/pages/Search.aspx) and, in some cases, to those on the *Musisque Deoque* website (http://mizar.unive.it/mqdq/public/); the English translations are from the Loeb Classical Library collection.

reacts at that moment, is simply revealed once again. It would be incoherent, then, to present this reaction as something isolated rather than as a consequence of what has been made explicit previously; more than incoherent, it would also reduce the effect of Lysiteles' growing enthusiasm that results from his father's acquiescence in a decision of great import, that of allowing him to marry a woman with no dowry.

We might also consider the data provided by Ernout and Meillet: in this dictionary, s.v. *lepidus*, redirects to *lepos* (*lepor*), in the sense of "grâce, charme. – *urbanitas elegans et mollis ac faceta; unde homines tales lepidi vocantur*, Gl. Plac. CGL V 30,17. . . . *lepidus*, fréquent dans la langue de la comédie, est rare déjà dans Cic., et à peine attesté à l'époque impériale". It could be deduced, therefore, that a habitual way of behaving is implied in the meaning here.

On the other hand, Aresi (2016) makes a reasoned, illustrated proposal for the meaning of *lepidus* as a personal characteristic, as a way and/or style of life – mainly in comedy but also in Catullus' poetry – or as a type of (liberal) education, etc. This way of understanding the term implies that it can be seen to convey the possibility of a permanent quality, although not necessarily so. It is a meaning that is certainly receding, until in Apuleius it has practically no other sense than 'funny'.

However, I believe that the possibly stable quality of *lepidus* in this context is not only due to the semantic content of the adjective, but also to the stative connotation of the verb and its somewhat desemantised condition, in the manner of the copulative *par excellence*: both aspects are compatible and combine to produce a construction which, if not fully copulative, comes very close to being so.

This is not an isolated case. Let us look at the following texts by Catullus and Terence:

(1a) *sed tu insulsa male et molesta vivis* (CATVLL. 10, 33)
'but you are damned awkward and a nuisance'

(1b) TH. *Num formidulosus, obsecro, es, mi homo?* CH. *Apage, sis. / Egon formidulosus? Nemost hominum qui vivat minus.* (TER. Eun. 757)
'You're not frightened, for goodness' sake, my dear fellow? :: Get away with you! Me frightened? There's not a man living who's less so.'

The expression in (1a) is part of Catullus' jocular response to the request for some slaves, supposedly his own, by Varus' mistress, in whose house Catullus is visiting; the joke is made possible in large part by the atelic state attributed to the verb and, equally, by the permanent quality potentially carried by *insulsa* and *molesta* ('blandness' and 'annoyance'). In fact, there is a great deal of coincidence – this is not uncommon with unclear or disputable examples – in the consulted translations of this text;[6] the one offered by the online version of the Loeb collection (trans. F. W. Cornish, 1913) is unequivocal: 'but you are damned awkward and a nuisance, [who will never let a fellow be off his guard]'.

In the case of (1b), a scene is taken from the conversation between the *meretrix* Thais and the *adulescens* Chremes before the appearance on the scene of *miles* Thraso – Thais' lover in turn – accompanied by his troops, so to speak. The elements present in this exchange of questions and answers make clear the copulative notion of *vivat*,[7] this time in construction with an adverb, something quite normal with the copula itself; it should be noted that this adverb is, in fact, co-referent with the adjective *formidulosus*, which is used in the passage for the first time with *es*. As is well known (cf. TLL, s.v. *parvus*, 576, 53), *minus* can function as a comparative adverb.

This initial discussion has introduced certain troublesome issues: the possibility of *vivo* functioning in a copulative way, hence with the capacity to express not only a passing form of acting but also a more or less permanent state; its semantics and possible verbal dynamism; the problematic border and distinction between SecP and Subject Complement (hereafter SubjC), as well as some of the respective characteristics of these two functions: their (non-)argumental nature, their semantics and the word classes encoding them, their temporal anchoring with respect to the verbal process with which they appear, their eventual pragmatic focalisation, etc. Consequently, I believe that at least these issues need to be addressed in greater depth with regard to the examples discussed.

6 Cf., e.g., 'you are as downright ill-bred and disagreeable woman as lives' (Ellis 1889); 'but you are stupid, tiresome. . .' (Cornish et al., Loeb); 'but you're damned tactless – a living nuisance' (Lee, Oxford); 'mais toi, tu es malencontreusement sotte et importune' (Herrmann, Latomus); 'mais toi, tu es terriblement sotte et insupportable' (Lafaye, Belles Lettres); 'pero tú eres terriblemente sosa y tan fastidiosa' (Dolç, Alma Mater); 'más tú eres tan maligna y fastidiosa' (Alonso G., Aache); 'pero tú eres una tía aburrida y pesada' (Fdez. Corte and Glez. Iglesias, Cátedra). This is also made explicit in the existing commentaries, where reference is made to several of the examples given with this meaning by the OLD: Ellis (1889: *ad loc.*): "*vivis*: an expression of common life: *Mil. glor.* iv,8,10 (*si non mecum aetatem egisset, hodie stulta viveret*); *Men.* i,3,19 (*quando una vivis meis morigera moribus*); *Trin.* ii,2,109 (*lepidus vivis*); *Bacch.* iv,3,3 (*inlepidus vivo*); Cic. *Att.* 3,5 (*ego vivo miserrimus*)"; Fordyce (1961: *ad loc.*): "for *vivo* as an emphatic sustitute for *sum* in colloquial speech, cf. e.g. Plaut. *Trin.* 390 (*lepidus vivis*); *Men.* 908 (*ne ego homo vivo miser*); *Bacch.* 615 (*inlepidus vivo*); Cic. *Att.* 3,5 (*ego vivo miserrimus*)".

7 This is also the interpretation of Barsby (1999: *ad loc.*) in his commentary on this passage.

3 Verbal Semantics and Predicate Frames (PF)

As a first step, we need to assess the semantic potential of the verb in question, and then to determine and formalise its possible syntactic complementation patterns and the other variables involved. Likewise, a discreet typological comparison with other current languages might shed light on the semantic-syntactic behaviour of the verb.

3.1 Lexical Description

Since this lemma is not yet available in the *Thesaurus Linguae Latinae* (TLL), I will present data drawn from the *Oxford Latin Dictionary* (OLD).

Table 1: *Vivo* in OLD.

1.	**a.** To be alive, live; *vivens* (pred.) in one's lifetime
	b. (w. cognate acc. or sim.)
	c. (in exprs. indicating a person's, etc. length of life)
	d. (in oaths, asseverations)
2.	(acting as a copulative, esp. in affective contexts) To be a . . . being (or sim.)
3.	**a.** (of things, usu. poet.) To be animated or active
	b. (of qualities, emotions)
4.	(of visual arts or its materials) To live (in illusion), have the appearance of life; (sim. of inscribed words, i.e., to give the illusion of a living voice)
5.	**a.** To go on living, live on, survive
	b. (in valedictory exclam.)
	c. to live in the memory of men
6.	(of abst. things.) To continue in existence or operation; to live on (in literature, song, etc.)
7.	**a.** (in an emphatic sense) To live in the full sense of the word, really live
	b. (pf., in valedictory or sim. contexts) to have lived a full life
8.	**a.** To sustain life, live (on food or by other means)
	b. to make a living or support oneself (by)
	c. *de lucro vivere*, to live on bonus time, be lucky to be alive
9.	**a.** To spend or pass one's life (in a given manner)
	b. to live (with a specific purpose, for a given person or cause)
	c. (w. cogn. acc.) to live (a particular kind of life)
10.	To spend one's life (in the company of a person, in a place, etc.)

In a broad and general way, I have marked in different shades of grey what I understand to be the basic different meanings, leaving aside variants due to various contextual realisations. Accordingly, four meanings can be proposed; although most of these are very close, they imply certain differences in the predicate frame that they are able to establish. In terms of what is basically of interest here, i.e. the presence of (non-)argumental elements with a SecP/SubjC function, the possible predicate frames would allow, *grosso modo*, the following options:

1. 'to be alive, live': $A1_S$ (+ $A2_{cogn.\ acc.}$) [+ SecP] = **OLD, 1, 3–8, 9b–c**
2. 'to be a . . . being (or sim.)': $A1_S$ + $A2_{SubjC}$ [+ SecP] = **OLD, 2**
3. 'to spend or pass one's life (in a given manner/as someone)':
   $A1_S$ + [+ SecP] / $A2_{SubjC}$ (?) = **OLD, 9a**
4. 'to live in a place': $A1_S$ + $A2_{Compl-Loc}$ [+ SecP] = **OLD, 10**

Abbreviations:
- A1, A2, . . .: First Argument, Second Argument, . . .
- cogn. acc.: cognate accusative
- Compl: Complement
- []: the constituent in square brackets is, in principle, optional from a grammatical point of view
- Loc: Location
- S: Subject
- SecP: Secondary Predicate
- SubjC: Subject Complement

As can be seen, the frames tentatively proposed, and with some elements still doubtful, include basically two monovalent ones (1. – except if there is an internal accusative –[8] and 3.) and two bivalent ones (2. and 4.); important to note here is the fact that all of these are susceptible to appear with a SecP, although such a possibility is very remote in PF 2., as is also the case with *esse*.[9]

If the data provided here, both semantic and syntactic, are taken into account, the following hypothesis can be proposed in general terms: the greater the desemantisation of the verb, the more likely the existence of an argumental SubjC (e.g., PF 2.); also vice versa: when the verb is realised with a higher semantic density, the

8 I do not deal here with the debate on whether this constituent is always an argument; cf. de la Villa and Polo (2019).

9 Cf. Cabrillana (2010: 232–233) and see exx. (5)–(6).

more likely it is that the element that may appear is a SecP[10] (e.g., PF 4.). Subsequent analysis (section 4) should reveal interesting data in this respect.

3.2 Cross-Linguistic Comparison

As a means of shedding some light on whether this situation is unique to the Latin language, or has persisted in later languages and the heirs of different original families, let us make a brief interlinguistic comparison. In this section I will show the data available for the English and Spanish verbs corresponding to the Latin *vivo.*

3.2.1 English "to live" (Data Base: VerbNet)

After grouping the fundamental data of the VerbNet Database, the following basic meanings and complementation patterns for "to live" are distinguished:

1. 'Exist (during)': $A1_{S\text{ - Theme}}$ $(+A2_{Loc})$:
   "Elvis lives"; "Herbicides persist in the soil"
2. 'Lodge, inhabit, dwell': $A1_{S\text{ - Theme /+anim/}}$ $+ A2_{Loc}$:
   "Cornelia lodged with the Stevensons/ at Mrs. Parker's/ there"
3. 'Exist in a certain manner, mode, or style': within this meaning, a series of so-called "Non-Core"[11] constructions can be distinguished, in which the following elements may appear:
   - 3.1 Circumstances: Circumstances describe the state of the world (at a particular time and place) which is specifically independent of the event itself and any of its participants
   - 3.2 Depictive: The state of a Resident during their residence
   - 3.3 Frequency: Frequency at which event occurs
   - 3.4 Manner: Manner of performing an action
   - 3.5 Means: An act of the Resident that enables them to reside in the Location
   - 3.6 Time: Time when the Resident resides.

This list coincides in many basic points with the proposal made on the basis of the OLD data, although it does not offer a definitively clear position as to the status of the component of the third meaning: on the one hand, in the definition of the

10 This would be consistent with what was presented in Cabrillana (2022: 98–99, 106–107) in relation to the processes of copularisation undergone by different Latin verbs.

11 Those considered "Core" would be the ones listed in the immediately preceding frame (2.), i.e., Location and Company.

VerbNet content, this term appears as part of the essential constituents ('Exist in a certain manner, mode, or style'), but on the other hand it is classified as a non-core element, on the same level as satellites such as those that would express Time or Frequency. At the same time, it is worth noting the distinction made on VerbNet between "Depictive" – restricting this function to a "Resident" S – and "Manner", to which we will return later (section 4.4).[12] Finally, I think that the two comments made on this construction 3., which I reproduce below, are significant:
"1. Could be either a general mode of living or a specific set of experiences. Syntax Includes: NP1 – LIVE (ADVP) (PP) (**NP2**);[13] NP1[agent[animate]] LIVE (PP)
2. Location, as in "He lived a thrilling life at sea", can be omitted without changing the meaning".

Abbreviations:
- NP: Noun Phrase;
- ADVP: Adverbial Phrase;
- PP: Prepositional Phrase.

Let it suffice for the moment to draw attention (i) to the possibility of the A2 ("NP2") being encoded by an NP in addition to an adverb or prepositional phrase, and (ii) to the fact that a locative element is not obligatory in this PF.

3.2.2 Spanish "vivir" (Data Base: ADESSE)

The Spanish Database distinguishes two main groups, the first of which is the richest and may contain several possibilities:
- VIVIR I:
  1. 'Existir como entidad biológica'
  2. 'Habitar u ocupar (un lugar)'
  3. 'Convivir'
  4. 'Llevar la vida (de una determinada manera)'

  i.e.,
- TO LIVE I:
  1. 'Existing as a biological entity'
  2. 'To inhabit or occupy (a place)'

12 The fact that a constituent with a Manner semantic function can have an argumental status – especially in such contexts – is an accepted assumption: cf., e.g., Pinkster (1972: 81–82, 1995: 36), Ricca (2010: 130), Tarriño (2021: 410, 413–414).
13 Bold type my own.

3. 'Living together'
4. 'Leading one's life (in a certain way)'

In essence, this database seems to recognise the existence of one monovalent structure (1.)[14] and three bivalent frames (2.–4.).[15] It would be difficult to give an account of all the variants that the database proposes here for the meanings collected, since it presents the general information as a whole and considers a good deal of additional information as arguments. However, it is instructive to note the frequency of occurrence of these elements, which obviously do not all occur at the same time:

[−] Clasificación semántica y potencial valencial

Tipo de proceso: Vida

Argumentos:

				Frecuencia	
A1	PAC	Viviente	PACIENTE	659	(100 %)
A2	Sustento	Sustento		28	(4.2 %)
A3	LUG		Lugar	315	(47.8 %)
A4	FIN		Finalidad	5	(0.8 %)
A5	MAN		Manera	201	(30.5 %)
A6	COM		Compañía	42	(6.4 %)

Figure 1: "VIVIR I": General distribution of constituents.

For the second group, restricted to one meaning only, the data are as follows:
- VIVIR II: 'Experimentar (sensaciones o vivencias) (ligadas a un periodo de tiempo)'
  i.e.,
- TO LIVE II: 'To experience (sensations or experiences) (linked to a period of time)'

---

14 Meaning 1 ('Existir como entidad biológica'): cf. http://adesse.uvigo.es/data/verbos.php?diccio_id=3943.

15 Meaning 2 ('Habitar u ocupar [un lugar]'): cf. http://adesse.uvigo.es/data/verbos.php?diccio_id=4968; meaning 3 ('Convivir [*sc.* con alguien/ago]'): cf. http://adesse.uvigo.es/data/verbos.php?diccio_id=4970; meaning 4 ('Llevar la vida ([de una determinada manera])': cf. http://adesse.uvigo.es/data/verbos.php?diccio_id=4971.

[–] Clasificación semántica y potencial valencial

Tipo de proceso: Sensación+Tiempo

Argumentos:				Frecuencia	
A1	EXP/EXIST	EXPERIMENTADOR	EXISTENTE	132	(91 %)
A2	EST/DUR	ESTÍMULO	DURACIóN	140	(96.6 %)
A3	MAN	Manera		25	(17.2 %)

Figure 2: "VIVIR II": General Distribution of Constituents.

It is interesting to note that the constituent with the function Manera/Manner[16] appears in both entries and that it is considered as a possibly obligatory element by this database in both cases. However, perhaps of greater interest here is the high percentage of the explicit presence of the constituent denoting Manner in VIVIR I, the richest and most comparable meaning to that of the Latin *vivo*: after the omnipresent A1, it stands in second position in terms of frequency (30.5%), behind only Location (47.8%). Yet, if we look at the specific scheme of meaning 4. – 'To lead one's life (in a certain way)' –, the data, as might be expected, are far more categorical:

Llevar la vida (de una determinada manera)

[–] Clasificación semántica y potencial valencial

Tipo de proceso: Vida

Argumentos:				Frecuencia	
A1	PAC	Viviente	PACIENTE	177	(100 %)
A2	Sustento	Sustento		1	(0.6 %)
A3	LUG		Lugar	9	(5.1 %)
A5	MAN		Manera	169	(95.5 %)
A6	COM		Compañía	1	(0.6 %)

Figure 3: "VIVIR I.4": 'Leading life (in a certain way)': General distribution of constituents.

16 With my typographical emphasis in Figures 1–3. Concerning the question that the SecP can be assigned a Manner function, cf. Pinkster (1972: 122), Nichols (1978: 330), Schultze-Berndt and Himmelmann (2004: 59, 112–115), Himmelmann and Schultze-Berndt (2005: 11, 14, 32, 36), van der Auwera and Malchukov (2005: 411), Schultze-Berndt (2017 [2016]): 21). As for the question whether or not such a semantic function can have an equal role for the whole predication, cf. Himmelmann and Schultze-Berndt (2005: 7), Schultze-Berndt (2017 [2016]: 20, 29).

In sum, and in a very synthetic way, it could be said that one of the common denominators in the data from these languages is the recognition of structures with an element, more or less obligatory and depending on the concrete verbal semantics, which describes the way in which life is lived/exists, is inhabited, or is spent.

4 Analysis

Let us now turn to the analysis of the corpus used in this study. As mentioned in section 2, Pinkster (2015: 206, 2021: 781) notes that the use of *vivo* with a SecP is frequent in comedy and poetry, especially Augustan verse: our corpus will reflect this, in that it is composed of the entire works of Plautus and Terence on the one hand, and those of Catullus, Horace, Ovid, Propertius, Tibullus and Vergil on the other. The number of examples found that are susceptible to analysis is close to 165, not a huge dataset, but which represents approximately 32% of the total number of occurrences of the verb (512x) in the whole corpus; however, what is of interest here, more than a statistically robust exploration, is an individualised, case by case analysis that will lead us to a finer description of the characteristics of these examples, and from there to the relevant conclusions. In what follows, we will deal first with the analysis of the main types of contexts (sections 4.1–4.2) and the most significant features involved (sections 4.3–4.4).

4.1 Contexts of a Copulative Nature

First, we will look at some cases in which the compulsory nature of the A2 that indicates the way in which the S carries out the verbal process is clearer, and the equating of such a process to the copulative meaning[17] is more appropriate.

(2) BA. *At tu ecastor morem antiquom atque ingenium optines, / **ut** omnium hominum homo <u>te</u> **vivat** nusquam quisquam <u>**blandior**</u>.* (TER. Hec. 860)
'And *you're*[18] still your old self with your old ways, I swear it. There's not a man alive with a smoother tongue than yours.'

17 This is also the interpretation of Goldberg (1999: *ad Hec.* 861). On the similarities and differences between the proper functioning of the copula and the partially copulative nature of *vivo*, cf. Cabrillana (forthc.).

18 Typographical emphasis added by the translator.

This text is situated towards the end of the Terentian comedy, when the courtesan Bacchis lets the young Pamphilus know that all the misunderstanding with his wife has ended well. The speaker uses a syntactic quasi-tracing in the structure of the consecutive phrases – which, however, is not apparent in the translation – and which, in this case, is constructed without an introductory element (*morem antiquom atque ingenium*); this type of subordinate clause is the form of expression used by Pamphilus in his immediately preceding speech, where we can also see the use of various lexical elements (*antiquam . . . obtines*; *semper siet*) which refer to permanence in a state:

(3) PAM. *O Bacchis, o mea Bacchis, servatrix mea!* / BA. *Bene factum et volup est.* PAM. *Factis ut credam facis; / antiquamque* ***adeo*** *tuam venustatem obtines /* ***ut*** *voluptati obitus sermo adventus tuo, quoquomque adveneris, /* ***semper siet***. (Ter. Hec. 856–860)
'PAM. *(throwing his arms round her)* Oh Bacchis, oh my darling Bacchis, my salvation! :: You're welcome. It's a pleasure. :: Your deeds speak for you. *(stepping back and looking at her fondly)* And you still retain your old charm! It will always be a delight to meet you, talk with you, have a visit from you, wherever it may be.'

It is not reasonable to suppose that Bacchis would respond in (2) to this intervention by Pamphilus with less intensity; in fact, there are also lexical elements here that underline this categorical idea (*omnium hominum*; *homo . . . nusquam quisquam*). On the other hand, if *blandior* is dispensed with, the presence of the ablative *te* cannot be justified, and an expression *'There's not a man alive than you[rs]' would make no sense. Additionally, if *blandior* were understood as a SecP, the resulting construction would not be possible from a grammatical point of view, nor would it make any sense that someone *'live(s) as (a) charming (man?)'; in fact, Forcellini's lexicon (s.v. *vīvo*, II, B, 2) includes this example among the cases which are said to function "Item pro *esse*", i.e. with a copulative use. This is something that we could also confirm by applying the test that Happ (1976: 287–290, 413–414) proposes for the identification of a real SecP, given that it is impossible to paraphrase the Terentian expression – *ut omnium hominum homo te vivat nusquam quisquam blandior* – with a sentence of *sum: *cum blandior sit, homo vivit.* On a final note: whether one chooses to translate *vivo* with a genuinely existential or copulative sense is more a matter of choice on the part of the translator, a choice which is not affected by the adjective *blandior* being made necessary, since this necessity is beyond doubt.

(4) MNE. *Petulans, protervo, iracundo animo, indomito, incogitato, / sine modo et modestia* ***sum****, sine bono iure atque honore / incredibilis inposque animi,*

inamabilis, ***inlepidus vivo***, / *malevolente ingenio natus. Postremo id mihi* ***est*** *quod volo / ego* ***esse*** *aliis. Credibile hoc est?* (Plavt. Bacch. 615)
'MNE. *(speaking to himself)* I'm unruly, I have an uncontrollable, irascible, untameable, thoughtless mind, I have no moderation or modesty, no sense of right or honour, I'm unreliable and without self-control, disagreeable and graceless, born with an evil character. In short, I have what I wish only others had. Can you believe it?'

(4) is the lament of a very sad and discouraged young Mnesilochus at the thought that he is going to lose his beloved because he does not have the money to attain her. In addition to other interesting aspects, I would like to underline what seems to be a clear parallelism in the speaker's enumeration of the characteristics of himself: in the first use of a predicate, that verbal predicate is *sum*, and without appearing to make any semantic difference he then uses *vivo*, this time, among other adjectives, with an antonym of the *lepidus* discussed above. The summary judgement of the message – *postremo id mihi est quod volo / ego esse aliis* – recovers the existential-copulative *par excellence*.[19] Thus, in this case, a transposition that would go from the level of the qualification of nature with *sum* to that of the form of life with *vivo* does not seem to make sense; in fact, it begins with the use of qualifiers with *esse* + *petulans* and a series of bare ablatives and prepositional phrases in what is quite a successful *variatio* of constructions, and closes the expression with another set of adjectives/participles – *incredibilis inposque animi, inamabilis, inlepidus* . . ., *malevolente ingenio natus* –. In short, everything that the speaker says about himself appears to be conceived on the same level: inalienable properties of his nature and way of being, as the phrase with *natus* expresses and as, rightly this time, the translator takes up in the final part of the enumeration: 'born with an evil character'.

A clear example of the ability of *vivo* to function in a copulative way is seen in (6), below, where there is a co-occurrence of what I believe can only be interpreted as a SubjC and a SecP, something that also occurs with *esse*, although rarely, as in (5) here:

(5) *nam* ***sola*** *nulla invitior solet* ***esse*** (Plavt. Cist. 310)
'usually no girl is less willing to be alone than me'

19 I leave aside the particularities of these dative constructions, which are partially dealt with in Cabrillana (2016).

In (6), referred to above, I understand that *privatus* would be the SecP – i.e., referring to a social status "as a private citizen" –, whereas *beatus*, on which the ablative *te rege* depends, is the SubjC – i.e., in the sense of a certain way of leading one's life –, which is necessary to complete the comparison established by *magis . . . beatus*:[20]

(6) *Ne longum faciam: dum tu quadrante lavatum / rex ibis neque te quisquam stipator ineptum / praeter Crispinum sectabitur, et mihi dulces / ignoscent, si quid peccaro stultus, amici / inque vicem illorum patiar delicta libenter / privatusque magis* ***vivam*** *te rege* ***beatus****.* (HOR. sat. 1, 3, 137)
'In short, while you, a king, go to your penny bath, and no escort attends you except crazy Crispinus, my kindly friends will pardon me if I, your foolish man, commit some offence, and in turn I shall gladly put up with their shortcomings, and in my private station shall live more happily than Your Majesty.'

Without being exactly the same case, (7) also highlights a further important issue:

(7) *carpe viam, mihi crede, comes, terrestria quando / mortalis animas* ***vivunt*** *sortita neque ulla est / aut magno aut parvo leti fuga: quo, bone, circa, / dum licet, in rebus iucundis* ***vive beatus****, /* ***vive memor*** *quam sis aevi brevis.* (HOR. sat. 2, 6, 94)
'Take my advice: set out with me. Inasmuch as all creatures that live on earth have mortal souls, and for neither great nor small is there escape from death, therefore, good sir, while you may, live happy amid joys; live mindful ever of how brief your time is!'

The verb *vivo* is repeated here three times, which is significant in itself. Certainly, one might think that the participle *sortita* does not play an indispensable role in conveying the core of the message; however, in the two following constructions featuring *vivo*, which are juxtaposed, it is precisely the presence of *beatus* and *memor* which allows for the distinction between them and the transmission of a specific meaning; in short, one which qualifies and completes the verbal idea.

In addition to examples (2) and (4), there are other cases of a similar type in the present corpus, some of these with particular justifications.[21] This does not prevent them from also occurring in other types of prose texts; let us consider a couple of illustrative cases:

---

20 I do not understand – as would be possible, according to Pinkster (1995: 184–185) – that this is a case of two Secondary predicates.

21 E.g., PLAVT. Capt. 828, Cas. 135, Men. 908, Mil. 1320, Rud. 520; TER. Hec. 300, Eun. 1031; HOR. epist. 2, 2, 157; VERG. Aen. 3, 493, etc.

(8a) *Quod si nostris consiliis usi essemus neque apud nos tantum valuisset sermo aut stultorum amicorum aut improborum,* ***beatissimi*** ***viveremus*** (CIC. fam. 14, 1, 2)
'If only I had relied upon my own judgement instead of paying so much attention to the talk of friends, whether fools or knaves, how happy I might have been!'

(8b) *Sed et Theophrasti Peripatetici servus Pompylus et Zenonis Stoici servus . . . et Epicuri . . .* ***philosophi non incelebres*** ***vixerunt***. (GELL. 2, 18)
'Besides these, Pompylus, the slave of the Peripatetic Theophrastus, and the slave of the Stoic Zeno . . ., and the slave of Epicurus . . ., were philosophers of repute.'

In both examples, the expression of the verbal process could not remain with the sense that the speaker seeks to convey without the adjective *beatissimi* in (8a) – *'If only I had relied upon my own judgement . . ., I might have been' –, or the NP *philosophi non incelebres* in (8b) – *'Besides these, Pompylus, the slave of the Peripatetic Theophrastus, and the slave of the Stoic Zeno . . ., and the slave of Epicurus . . ., were' –. Even if an interpretation of *vivo* as 'to spent one's life' rather than 'to be something/somebody' seems possible, such NPs would be necessary to specify the way of living 'in a certain way/given manner'; in the specific context, then, the expressions to which it would give rise would be devoid of the intended meaning. Both examples are again noted in Forcellini's dictionary (s.v. *vivo*, II, B, 2) – as in ex. (2) – among those texts in which the verb functions in a copulative way.

4.2 Contexts of Ambiguous Nature

Taking into account examples such as these, it is not surprising that cases can be found in which a definite interpretation is almost impossible;[22] in a certain sense, these might constitute "bridge cases" between both possibilities, that is, they allow a copulative interpretation but also a "vital" reading, so to speak, with a meaning

22 Cf., among others, Himmelmann and Schultze-Berndt (2005: 52): "Obviously, when the first verb is semantically general but not completely devoid of semantic content, as e.g. the positional verb in 'The man lay dead in his home for three days', it becomes difficult to distinguish between copular and depictive construction", or Schultze-Berndt (2017 [2016]: 16), about the criterion of omissibility as entirely unequivocal: "this criterion, however, does not always yield clearcut results". The position argued by van der Auwera and Malchukov (2005: 399) is also noteworthy: there would be a gradation between the copulative structures, the constructions with depictives, and the cases of attributive adjectives.

that is partly more typical of *vivo* than of *sum*. Such cases would exist in the gradual space[23] that mediates between one meaning and the other, something which is normal when semantic notions are in close proximity. It is worth recalling that *sum* and *vivo* also share a quasi-identical existential meaning.

However, one relevant fact must be noted here: both in a copulative interpretation and in what we have called a vital one, the second constituent can almost never be omitted without the construction becoming ungrammatical or what I would rather call "unfunctional" in the sense that the speech act does not fulfil its purpose, i.e. it does not convey the desired content, which invalidates it as a communicative act in itself. Let us look at some examples where this can happen.

(9a) *at felix vates, ut dis* ***gratissima*** ***<u>vixit</u>***, / *possidet hunc Iani sic dea mense diem.* (Ov. fast. 1, 585)
'But the happy prophetess, even as she lived in highest favour with the gods, so now herself a goddess hath she this day in Janus' month all to herself.'

It would certainly make no sense to understand the text without *gratissima* and, as an inevitable consequence, without the element that depends on it (*dis*):

(9b) *at felix vates, ut vixit, possidet hunc Iani sic dea mense die*
'But the happy prophetess, even as she lived, so now herself a goddess hath she this day in Janus' month all to herself' (?)

The superlative is the key constituent that allows us to understand what is said below. In short, whether we make a copulative reading of the bivalent *vivo* in which *gratissima* is a SubjC, or we opt for a vital interpretation of the monovalent verb with a SecP, the superlative should be present: it completes the semantic content of the predicate in a way which is necessary.

(10) *cum tribus anellis, modo laeva Priscus inani, /* ***<u>vixit</u>*** ***inaequalis***, *clavum* ***ut*** *mutaret in horas* (HOR. sat. 2, 7, 8)

23 I refer here to the gradualness in the semantic density affecting the predicate in question, so that its rate of predicativity can be more or less intense. The term "predicational" can be equated with "denotational", in the sense of Lyons (1977: 207): "by the denotation of a lexeme (. . .) will be meant the relationship between that lexeme and persons, things, places, properties and activities external to the language system"; cf. also Goosens (1992). I will return to this issue below (section 4.3).

'Thus Priscus, who often attracted notice by wearing three rings, but once in a while by wearing none, was so fickle in his life, that he would change his stripe every hour.'

On (10), it is precisely the presence of *inaequalis* – an adjective endowed here with an intensification which allows for the rare absence of an introductory correlative element – which is responsible for and justifies the existence of the sentence which follows. On the other hand, the translator has either needed or wanted to resort to a kind of paraphrase with 'to be' ('Priscus, . . . was so fickle in his life, that. . .').

4.3 Semantic Content and Functional Gradation

Naturally, there is no lack of cases in which the SecP functions in a way that corresponds to its more or less *canonical* definition.[24] An example:

(11) *milesne Crassi coniuge barbara / **turpis maritus** vixit et . . .?* (Hor. carm. 3, 5, 5)
'Can it be that Crassus' soldiers have remained alive in disgraceful wedlock with barbarian wives, . . .?'

Although it is not possible to say that the omission of *turpis maritus* leaves the content of the message in exactly the same terms as when it is present, I believe that in this case the issue is related to another factor, that of the semantic density of the verb; in fact, the presence of the bare ablative *coniuge barbara* already suggests that we are dealing with a case that would be included in entry 10 of the OLD (cf. Table 1): 'to spend one's life (in the company of a person, in a place, etc.)'. The semantic content conveyed by the verb in this type of construction is denser, providing more complete and specific information – i.e., 'to be married with' – than when it simply refers to a generic 'to live'. Thus, it could be said that between the degree of omissibility of the SecP and the semantic density of the verbal predicate there is sometimes a certain link. If this hypothesis is correct, one would expect that what has been exemplified in (11) would also occur when we are dealing with a meaning involving a location, as in entry 10 of the OLD mentioned above:

(12a) *quaerebam, sicca si posset piscis harena / **nec solitus** ponto **vivere** torvus aper* (Prop. 2, 3a, 5)

24 Cf. e.g. Pinkster (1990: 143, 2015: 30–31, 2021: 777–778).

'I tried to learn whether a fish could live on dry sand or a wild boar, against his habit, in the sea.'

(12b) *tamen illic* ***vivere*** *vellem /* ***oblitusque*** *meorum* ***obliviscendus*** *et illis / Neptunum procul e terra spectare furentem* (Hor. epist. 1, 11, 8)
'yet there would I love to live, and forgetting my friends and by them forgotten, gaze from the land on Neptune's distant rage'

(12c) *territa sorte dei per opacas* ***innuba*** *silvas /* ***vivit*** *et instantem turbam violenta procorum / condicione fugat* (Ov. met. 10, 566)
'Terrified (*sc.* Atalanta) by the oracle of the god, she lived unwedded in the shady woods, and with harsh terms she repulsed the insistent throng of suitors.'

The omission of *solitus* in (12a) would alter practically nothing of the semantic content to be conveyed;[25] in fact, despite any issues relating to metrical needs or stylistic elegance, with the first S of *vivere* – *piscis* – no SecP appears. Something similar could be said of *oblitus* and *obliviscendus* in (12b), where in fact, and as seen in (12a), the translator is forced to place this information between commas, as an addition without affecting the core message; a different question would be the informative contrast that might fall on the polyptoton of the participles, something we will return to below in this section. Likewise, the presence of *innuba* in (12c) enhances the meaning of what is said in the *fugat* clause, but its omission would not render its content excessively distorted, incomprehensible or obscure.

I believe that these are cases of true SecPs, where the greater density and semantic specificity of the predicate makes it possible for them to play a less crucial role in the transmission of information.

Conversely, when the semantic density of the predicate is lower, the need for a SecP may be clearer or increase. Some examples:

(13) *Cum mihi dicebas: 'Per ego ipsa pericula iuro, / te fore, dum nostrum vivet uterque, meam.' / Vivimus, et non sum, Theseu, tua, si modo* ***vivit*** */ femina periuri fraude* ***sepulta*** *viri* (Ov. epist. 10, 75)

25 To be more precise, it would perhaps be necessary to add that the sentence would remain grammatically correct and also semantically clear, but the communicative intention of Propertius would be slightly altered: the poet not only wanted to convey that a boar could not live in the sea, but also that this would be quite unusual for a boar. I thank one of the anonymous reviewers for this suggestion.

'then you said to me: 'By these very perils of mine, I swear that, so long as both of us shall live, thou shalt be mine!' We both live, Theseus, and I am not yours! if indeed a woman lives who is buried by the treason of a perjured mate.'

The value of *vivit* here seems absolute, i.e. it would in principle be a realisation of the monovalent 'to be alive', but without the specification of *sepulta* the expression is meaningless ('We both live, Theseus, and I am not yours! if indeed a woman lives'[?]);[26] in addition, the semantic contrast between the fact of living and the way of living-dying that the SecP expresses is added here.

(14) *indignatur amans* ***invitum*** ***<u>vivere</u>*** *cogi / obstarique animae misera de sede volenti / exire* (Ov. met. 11,787)
'The lover was wroth that he was forced to live against his will and that his spirit was thwarted as it desired to leave its wretched seat.'

In (14), and without any additional information, it would be practically an oxymoron for a lover to be outraged simply because he has to live, but not if he is forced to do so against his will or in a way he does not want: *invitum*.

Similarly, in (15), if *viximus* referred to the mere fact of living, the full significance of the idea would be lacking; however, the accompanying *innocuae* pertinently completes the message and provides the necessary semantic and pragmatic contrast to the earlier *patior sine crimine*. The translator's use of the same term ('in [utter] innocence') and his faithful reflection of the initial position of the verb on both occasions (*Patior. . . Viximus. . .*) is significant:

(15) *Patior sine crimine poenam /* ***<u>Viximus</u>*** ***innocuae****; si mentior, arida perdam, / quas habeo, frondes, et caesa securibus urar* (Ov. met. 9, 373)
'In utter innocence I am suffering, and in innocence I have always lived. If I say not the truth, parched with the drought may I lose my foliage and may I be cut down by the axe and burned.'

Together with this requirement to complete semantically the more generic content of the verb, we must recall the possibility of the SecP being focused and thus pragmatically motivated, something which is coherent with the previous phenomenon.

---

26 I understand the participle *sepulta* as a SecP and not as a possible part of a NP *femina sepulta*: despite the metrical and stylistic constraints that could be adduced, the semantic and informative environment, and the position of the participle, make this advisable.

This is an aspect that has been partially studied in previous works,[27] and for which there are often calls for further research. As far as this aspect is concerned, we might mention here some of the examples previously cited, such as (13) or (15) itself; let us add one more in order to show the possibility we are seeking to describe: not only is it necessary for the SecP to be present to complete semantically a somewhat desemantised verb, but, at the same time, that SecP is the bearer of a focalisation; in this specific case, the focalisation arises from a clear contrast:

(16) CLEO. *Hic vincet, tu* ***vives miser***. (PLAVT. Cas. 403)
'CLEO. (*to Olympio*) He (*points to Chalinus*) will win and you will live as a wretch.'

In the text, Cleostrata, wife of old Lysidamus, predicts the outcome of the raffle to decide whom the slave Casina will belong to: Chalinus, the squire of Lysidamus' son, will win, while the overseer Olympius will lose and will always be unhappy.

4.4 SecP Expressing Manner/State

As a final criterion of analysis, we now turn to the study of a feature that entails certain problems, in terms of the very definition of the SecP and also its characterisation. Our aim here is to verify whether, as is usually accepted, the property encoded by the SecP (i) is transitory and whether, as a consequence (ii) it cannot express a state. First of all, it should be noted that, in this respect, poets show a somewhat greater freedom here and use adjectives that denote a permanent quality, such as those expressing size or substance, stative physical condition, age or a certain socio-economic position.[28]

This question was partially dealt with in previous studies[29] focusing on its application to verbs of an eminently stative nature.

The basic difference with the predicate we are discussing here lies in its lower frequency of realisation as a stative predicate, that is, in the possibility of it functioning as a more agentive predicate than the eminently stative ones mentioned above.[30] Nevertheless, it is not difficult to find examples in which the candidate term SubjC (see 17a–17c) or SecP (see 18a–18f) expresses more a state than a transient quality;

---

27 Cf. Pinkster (1990: 162, 2021: 819), Winkler (1997), Himmelmann and Schultze-Berndt (2005: 18–26, 67), Cabrillana (2021: 511–515).

28 Cf. Pinkster (2021: 782, 787).

29 Cabrillana (2019, 2024).

30 Consider, for example, the possibility of understanding *vivo* in the sense of 'act like'.

this is necessarily combined with a stative rather than a dynamic meaning on the part of the verb. And this in turn is consistent with Pustet's (2003: 85) reasoning when she refers to the parameter already established in linguistics of "Time-stability" as linked to the greater propensity or not of a verb form to undergo copularisation, so that the greater the temporal stability denoted, the greater the probability of this copularisation. Hence, it seems clear that in (17a), and looking now only at *locuples*, we see a NP which can function as a noun and which denotes stable economic position; in (17b) and (17c) we find, respectively, a semantically related participle and an adjective – which we could perhaps understand as denoting a subjective evaluation – and these are employed with the intention of expressing permanent states of life:

(17a) *magna minorve Foro si res certabitur olim, / **vivet** uter **locuples** sine gnatis, improbus, ultro / qui meliorem audax vocet in ius, illius esto / defensor* (HOR. sat. 2, 5, 27)
'If some day a case, great or small, be contested in the Forum, whichever of the parties is rich and childless, villain though he be, who with wanton impudence calls the better man into court, do you become his advocate.'

(17b) *Qui fit, Maecenas, ut nemo, quam sibi sortem / seu ratio dederit seu fors obiecerit, illa / **contentus vivat**, laudet diversa sequentis?* (HOR. sat. 1, 1, 1)
'How comes it, Maecenas, that no man living is content with the lot which either his choice has given him, or chance has thrown in his way, but each has praise for those who follow other paths?'

(17c) ***vivite felices**, quibus est fortuna peracta / iam sua* (VERG. Aen. 3, 493)
'Live and be happy, as should those whose destiny is now achieved.'

On the other hand, among those cases which we might be inclined to consider as SecP structures, it is not uncommon to find examples in which the intention is to express permanence in a state, this being possible again thanks to the less dynamic meaning of the verb and its more atelic aspect. I also think it might be said that, in addition to expressing a social role or function (18a), it is also possible for these SecPs to denote a kind of inalienable property (18b–18c), a generic manner (18d), or even a subjective evaluation (18e), where the quality of permanence can be reinforced by the context (18f):

(18a) *Quas fabulas? Non, inquam, patiar praeterhac, / quin **vidua vivam**,*[31] *quam tuos mores perferam* (PLAVT. Men. 725)

31 As we know, *vidua* seems to function mostly as a noun; this is attested by Ernout and Meillet's dictionary (1932 [1985], s.v. *viduus*): "se dit surtout de la femme veuve, e.g. PLAVT. *Curc.* 37 *dum ted*

'What gossip? I'm telling you, I won't put up with it from now on, I'll live as a divorcee rather than tolerate your habits.'

(18b) *ante meos oculos tamquam praesentis imago / haeret, et* ***extinctum*** ***vivere*** *fingit amor* (Ov. Pont. 1, 9, 7)
'His image lingers before my eyes as if he were present; he is gone, but love imagines him still alive.'[32]

(18c) *nam qui cupiet, metuet quoque; porro, / qui* ***metuens*** ***vivet****, liber mihi non erit umquam* (HOR. epist. 1, 16, 65)
'for he who covets will also have fears; further, he who lives in fear, will never, to my mind, be free'

(18d) ***Vive*** ***pius****: moriere; pius cole sacra* (Ov. am. 3, 9, 37)[33]
'Live the duteous life – you will die; be faithful in your worship –'

(18e) AM. *Quo modo?* ME. *Eo modo, ut profecto* ***vivas*** *aetatem*[34] ***miser*** (PLAVT. Amph. 1023)
'What do you mean? :: I mean that you'll live your life miserably indeed.'

(18f) *Aequam memento rebus in arduis / servare mentem non secus ut bonis / ab insolenti temperatam / laetitia, moriture Dellius, / seu* ***maestus*** *omni tempore* ***vixeris****.* (HOR. carm. 2, 3, 5)
'Remember to keep a level head when life's path is steep; likewise, when the going is good, to restrain it from excessive joy, Dellius; for you are sure to die, whether you live in perpetual gloom.'

Space restraints now oblige us to move on to the conclusions.

5 Conclusions

It has become clear in this paper that *vivo* can sometimes behave as a copulative predicate, and not only as a verb with which the usual SecP can appear: the analysis of the Latin language itself, as well as its comparison with equivalent predicates in other languages, serves to illustrate this. In such contexts, the deletion of the

apstineas nupta, vidua, virgine; ou non mariée (correspondant à *caelebs*, cf. T. L. 1,46,7)". Examples similar to (18a) can be found in PLAVT. Men. 727, Mil. 1417, Capt. 318, and TER. Haut. 388.

32 One of the anonymous reviewers suggests that here it might be possible an AcI-reading of *extinctum vivere* instead of an interpretation of *extinctum* as a SecP: 'Love imagines that the dead is still alive.'

33 Cf. also, e.g., PLAVT. Truc. 418; Ov. fast. 3, 427; PROP. 2, 30, 19; TIB. 2, 6, 51.

34 As noted above (comment on Table 1), the question of the internal accusative is not addressed here. Examples partly analogous to (18e) can be found in PLAVT. Amph. 1046; PROP. 4, 11, 45.

element which might initially be considered a SecP renders the resulting expression ungrammatical,[35] so that the constituent in question would have to be considered, from a strict syntactic description, a SubjC. Although not necessarily linked to this, a further affinity has been noted between the copula *par excellence* and *vivo*, namely the frequent possibility of this verb expressing State and not so much, or rather not always, Manner, and therefore that the quality denoted by the adjective, participle or NP used is permanent; it is, consequently, the combination of semantics and verbal aspect with the meaning of the second constituent of the structure that allows for this behaviour.

This fact is partly related to the de-semantisation in the predicate that usually occurs in such cases, so that the need for a particular specification by the SecP increases very significantly. Our initial hypothesis, then, is confirmed: the loss of semantic load in the predicate leads to a more necessary lexical presence of the specification provided by a SubjC or a SecP, whereas this need is significantly lower if the verb is more fully realised from the predicative point of view.[36]

As might be expected,[37] there are cases of difficult distinction between the function of SubjC and SecP. However, beyond the usually invoked test of omissibility, what has also become clear is what we might call the "un-functionality" of the expression arising from the omission of the presumed SecP. In the surrounding context – an element that can never be ignored in the speech act – its absence would deprive the corresponding expression of meaning, so that such a speech act would be unable to fulfil its function. It is more than a matter of a relative semantic difference between cases with and without SecP present; rather, a case of the necessary presence of the SecP if the message is not to lose much of its meaning or to abandon it altogether.[38] At the same time, an issue that cannot be overlooked is the fact that SecP are also relatively often focused, or carry a contrast that is often essential in the speech act.[39] In short, it seems advisable to abandon the consideration of pure syntactic/grammatical omissibility as an essential criterion in the characterisation and recognition of a SecP, since its application does not always guarantee this identification.

In addition to extending and diversifying the corpus used here, there are still many aspects of SecP that require further research, and which will necessarily be the subject of future study.

---

35 See exx. (2) or (10).

36 See exx. (11), (12a)–(12c).

37 Cf. Pinkster (2021: 779).

38 See exx. (9a), (13), (14).

39 See exx. (13), (15), (16).

Bibliography

Data Base ADESSE: http://adesse.uvigo.es/data/verbos.php?sense=3407 (accessed July 10, 2023).
Data Base VerbNet: https://verbs.colorado.edu/vn3.2.4-test-uvi/index.php (accessed July 10, 2023).
TLL = *Thesaurus Linguae Latinae* (1900–). Leipzig: Teubner; Berlin/Boston: De Gruyter.
OLD = Glare, P. G. W. (Ed.) (1982). *Oxford Latin Dictionary*. Oxford: Oxford University Press.

Aresi, L. (2016). Per una storia della *'lepiditas'*: il caso Periplectomeno nel *Miles gloriosus* e le sue risonanze da Terenzio a Apule. *Argos*, *39*, 142–171.
van der Auwera, J. & Malchukov, A. (2005). A semantic Map for Depicitive Adjetivals. In N. P. Himmelmann & E. Schultze-Berndt (Eds.), *Secondary Predication and Adverbial Modification. The Typology of Depictives* (pp. 393–421). Oxford: Oxford University Press.
Barsby, J. (1999). *Terence: Eunuchus*. Cambridge: Cambridge University Press.
Cabrillana, C. (2010). Praedicativum and Subject Complement. In P. Anreiter & M. Kienpointner (Eds.), *Latin Linguistics Today* (pp. 233–245). Innsbruck: Innsbrucker Beiträge zur Sprachwissenschaft.
Cabrillana, C. (2016). El estatus sintáctico-semántico del caso dativo con verbos estativos latinos. *Emerita*, *84* (1), 145–166.
Cabrillana, C. (2019). Sobre la naturaleza de las cualidades expresadas por el Predicativo con verbos estativos en latín. *Graeco-Latina Brunensia*, *24* (1), 17–28.
Cabrillana, C. (2021). Constituent Order in Constructions with Praedicativum in Latin. In A. M. Martín R. (Ed.), Linguisticae Dissertationes. *Current Perspectives on Latin Grammar, Lexicon and Pragmatics* (pp. 505–518). Madrid: Ediciones Clásicas.
Cabrillana, C. (2022). Procesos de copularización en la lengua latina: precedentes semánticos y factores incidentes. *Glotta*, *98* (1), 78–112.
Cabrillana, C. (2024), Expression of (non-)permanent qualities and coding of the Praedicativum in Latin. In C. Cabrillana (Ed.), *Recent Trends and Findings in Latin Linguistics. Vol. I. Syntax, Semantics and Pragmatics* (pp. 151–165). Boston/Berlin: De Gruyter.
Cabrillana, C. (forthcoming). ¿Concomitancias funcionales en predicados (no)copulativos latinos? *Latomus*.
Ernout, A. & Meillet, A. (1932 [1985]). *Dictionnaire étymologique de la langue latine: histoire des mots*. Paris: Klincksieck.
Forcellini, E. (1940). *Totius Latinitatis Lexicon*. Padova: Typis Aldianis.
Goldberg, S. M. (2013). *Terence: Hecyra*. Cambridge: Cambridge University Press.
Goossens, L. (1992). Graded predicationality, semantization and BE in a Functional Grammar of English. *Belgian Journal of Linguistics*, *7*, 53–71.
Happ, H. (1976). *Grundfragen einer Dependenz-Grammatik des Lateinischen*. Göttingen: Vandenhoeck and Ruprecht.
Heerdegen, E. G. F. (1913). *Das Wort* vivere *in phraseologischen Gebrauch bei Horaz und älteren Latein*. Programm Erlangen.
Himmelmann, N. P. & Schultze-Berndt, E. (2005). Issues in the syntax and semantics of participant-oriented adjuncts: an introduction. In P. Himmelmann & E. Schultze-Berndt (Eds.), *Secondary Predication and Adverbial Modification* (pp. 1–67). Oxford: Oxford University Press.
Hofmann, J. B. (1924). Syntaktische Gliederungsverschiebungen im Lateinischen infolge Erstarrung ursprünglich appositioneller Verhältnisse. *Indogermanische Forschungen*, *42*, 75–87.
Lyons, J. (1977). *Semantics, I–II*. Cambridge: Cambridge University Press.
Nichols, J. (1978). Double Dependency? *Chicago Linguistics Society*, *14*, 326–329.

Pinkster, H. (1972). *On Latin Adverbs.* Amsterdam: North Holland.
Pinkster, H. (1995). *Sintaxis y Semántica del latín.* Madrid: Ediciones Clásicas.
Pinkster, H. (2015). *The Oxford Latin Syntax. Volume 1: The Simple Clause.* Oxford: Oxford University Press.
Pinkster, H. (2021). *The Oxford Latin Syntax. Volume 2: The Complex Clause and Discourse.* Oxford: Oxford University Press.
Ricca, D. (2010). Adverbs. In Ph. Baldi & P. Cuzzolin (Eds.), *New Perspectives on Historical Latin Syntax, 2: Constituent Syntax: Adverbial Phrases, Adverbs, Mood, Tense* (pp. 109–191). Berlin/New York: De Gruyter Mouton.
Schultze-Berndt, E. & Himmelmann, N. P. (2004). Depictive Secondary Predicates in Cross-Linguistic Perspective, *Linguistic Typology*, *8*, 59–131.
Schultze-Berndt, E. (2017 [2016]). Secondary Predicates in typological perpective. In M. Everaert & H. van Riemsdijk (Eds.), *The Blackwell Companion to Syntax* (2nd edn.) (pp. 1–49). Malden: Wiley Blackwell. https://www.academia.edu/28947962/Depictive_Secondary_Predicates_in_typological_perspective (accessed July 10, 2023).
Tarriño, E. (2021). Adverbios y partículas. In J. M. Baños (Coord. Ed.), *Sintaxis Latina, I. Introducción. Sintaxis de la oración simple* (pp. 398–433). Madrid: CSIC.
Villa, J. de la & Polo, J. (2019). Internal complements in Latin: more on their semantic, syntactic, and pragmatic status. In C. Cabrillana & Ch. Lehmann (Eds.), *Acta XIV Colloquii Internationalis Linguisticae Latinae* (pp. 453–463). Madrid: Ediciones Clásicas.
Winkler, S. (1997). *Focus and Secondary Predication. Studies in Generative Gramar.* Berlin: Mouton De Gruyter.

Silvia Pieroni

Ablativus absolutus with the Perfect Participle: Grammatical Relations and Diathesis

Abstract: As far as we know, the label *ablativus absolutus* was introduced in the 11th century by Alberic of Montecassino to designate the well-known Latin construction. Thereafter, the term *absolutus* has become a key-concept in metalinguistic descriptions, to refer both to the fact that the construction is not governed by a verb or a preposition and to the lack of coreference linkages to the matrix proposition. As has already been observed in several studies, however, coreference linkages between the nominal in the ablative and the arguments of the proposition are not ruled out. In particular, when the absolute construction includes the perfect participle of a transitive verb, its agent – in a wide sense – is fairly commonly coreferential with the subject of the matrix proposition. Starting from this observation, this paper questions the diathetic character of the *ablativus absolutus* with a perfect participle, both when the structure is transitive and when it is intransitive, as well as the related issue of the grammatical relation of the nominal involved. Some common assumptions are thus challenged, such as the passiveness of the absolute construction and the subjecthood of the nominal in the ablative. The paper concludes with a proposal for the description of the Latin *ablativus absolutus* with the perfect participle.

Keywords: perfect participle, coreference linkage, diathesis, subject

1 Introduction

This paper deals with the syntax of the *ablativus absolutus* (AA henceforth), focusing on the constructions with a perfect participle. Its organization is as follows. Section 2 presents some grammarians' descriptions of the AA. Section 3 deals with the AA with a perfect participle of a transitive verb. Firstly, it tackles the issue of absoluteness, that is of the coreferential linkages between the AA and the finite proposition in which it is included; then, it discusses the assumption of the passiveness of the AA and the related assumption of the subjecthood of its nominal. Section 4 provides a syntactic account of intransitive AAs with the perfect participle, by

Silvia Pieroni, Università per Stranieri di Siena, Italy

https://doi.org/10.1515/9783111332956-024

referring to the Unaccusative Hypothesis. Section 5 concludes the paper with a proposal for the description of the AA, both when the structure is transitive and when it is intransitive.

A secondary, but by no means marginal, aim of the paper is to illustrate a case where the metalanguage has conditioned the description of grammatical phenomena whereas "it is impossible to define the elementary entities and constraints of a language by recourse to its metalanguage" (Harris 2002 [1990]: 1).[1]

2 Grammarians' Descriptions

The AA consists essentially of the combination of two elements in the ablative – not governed by a verb or a preposition – such that the two elements enter in a predicate-argument relationship and cannot be dissociated without disrupting the whole structure.[2]

Few impersonal cases consist of a participle in the ablative alone, as in (1). Apart from them, the argument relation is fulfilled by a nominal (a noun or a pronoun). The predicate relation may be fulfilled by a noun as well, as in (2), by an adjective, as in (3), by a present participle, as in (4), or by a perfect participle, as in (5).[3]

(1) [. . .] *eos* ***sortito*** *in provincias mitti* (Cic. epist. 8, 8, 8) (quoting from a senate consult; see Steele 1904: 317)
'[. . .] such persons [. . .] shall be dispatched to the aforesaid provinces as by lot determined.'

(2) [. . .] *quod nihilo magis ei liciturum esset plebeio rem publicam perdere quam similibus eius* ***me consule*** *patriciis esset licitum.* (Cic. Att. 2, 1, 5)
'[. . .] because he would have no more chance of destroying the state as a plebeian than his kindred spirits among the patricians had had when I was consul.'

1 This research was carried out within the PRIN project "Metalinguistic texts as a privileged data source for the knowledge of ancient languages" (2020).

2 There is a vast amount of literature on the AA, in general and in Latin. Among many others, see Bauer (1993); Coleman (1989); Keydana (1997); Lavency (2000, 2001); Milani (2001); Ramat (1994); Ruppel (2013); Serbat (1979). On Cicero's uses, Steele (1904), cf. Steele (1902).

3 In the selection of examples, Cicero's *Letters to Atticus* will be privileged. I owe many thanks to Francesco Mambrini, who extracted for me the perfect participles in the ablative from Cicero's works available on PROIEL and LASLA. Extracts from Latin texts and translations are quoted according to the Loeb editions <http://loebclassics.com>, unless specified differently.

(3) *Memmius autem dirempta coitione* ***invito Calvino*** *plane refrixerat* (Cic. Att. 4, 17, 3)
'Memmius, having broken up the coalition against Calvinus' wishes, looks a very tired horse'

(4) [. . .] ***illo imperante*** *exhaustam esse sumptibus et iacturis provinciam* (Cic. Att. 6, 1, 2)
'When he was governor the province was drained dry with charges and disbursements [. . .]'

(5) *Iam enim* ***obsignata hac epistula*** *noctu tabellarius noster venit* (Cic. Att. 13, 46, 5)
'I had already sealed this (letter) when my courier arrived after dark'

Though it is not frequency which will be investigated in this paper, it is worth observing that the AA with the perfect participle, relatively rare in Plautus and Terence, is by far the most common type in classical times, as shown in Table (1), taken from Steele (1904: 315) (see also Dalbera 2022). Within this type, transitive structures outnumber the deponent ones (Pinkster 2021: 387).

Table 1: The AA in the Epistles of Cicero (from Steele 1904: 315).

perfect participle	present participle	noun	adjective
430	171	73	67

As for the structural role of the AA in relation to the proposition in which it is inserted, it functions as an adjunct; therefore, if considered as a proposition itself, as an adverbial proposition (Touratier 1994: 655; Lavency 1997²: 195; Pinkster 2021: 389). It goes without saying that distinguishing between a nominal adjunct and a subordinate proposition is at times difficult, not to say pointless (Longrée 2014; cf. Storme 2010). Consider for example the passage in (6), where *suspenso animo* could in fact be considered as a noun phrase, though *suspenso* is not an optional attribute. Thus, the noun phrase could possibly be treated as a predicative complement:[4]

(6) ***Suspenso animo*** *exspecto quid agat.* (Cic. Att. 4, 15, 10)
'I am waiting in suspense to hear how he is getting on.'

4 The possibility of considering some uses of the ablative, among which the ablative of quality, as predicative is suggested by Pinkster (1982: 250), e.g. *capite operto* in *Invocat deos* [. . .] *capite operto* (Plavt. Amph. 1093–1094) 'she invoked the immortal gods [. . .] with [. . .] covered head'.

In this regard, Guy Serbat (1979: 353) wrote that the AA is "un syntagme en voie de se transformer en proposition" (cf. Torrego 2009) and claimed that it is precisely its origin as a nominal phrase that excludes explicit anaphoric linkages with other constituents of the same sentence.

Be it as it may, the usual absence of anaphoric linkages has been traditionally formulated as a rule, that is, the subject of the AA should not be linked to constituents of the main clause and, specially, not to its subject.[5] In fact, the term *absolutus* does not appear in Latin grammars nor does the related concept: as shown by Scaglione (1970), the term *absolutus* with reference to our construction[6] first appears in *De dictamine* by Alberic of Montecassino (XI sec.) (Maiocco 2005: 1–29). Here follows the passage concerning the AA with the perfect participle:[7]

(7) *In ablativum absolutum preteriti participii fiet conversio, cum verbum quodlibet accusativum regit, in quem non fit per obliquum aliquem reconversio, ut: "deserui seculum et ivi ad monasterium", deserto seculo ivi ad monasterium.* (II, 15)
'A transformation (*conversio*) into the ablative absolute of the past participle will take place when the verb governs an accusative, to which we do not turn back (*reconversio*) through an oblique case, e.g., *deserui seculum et ivi ad monasterium* "I left the (secular) world behind and went into a monastery": *deserto seculo ivi ad monasterium* "having left the (secular) world behind (abl. abs.), I went into a monastery".'

Alberic's *De dictamine* is a schoolbook. It gives instructions on how to craft polished Latin sentences. Among the techniques which are suggested, the *conversio* 'tranformation' consists in converting two coordinated predications such as *deserui seculum et ivi ad monasterium* into a more varied and less plain structure such as *deserto seculo ivi ad monasterium*. As Sluiter (2000: 395) remarks, the term *absolutus* "was there to stay and can be found throughout the *artes* of the 12th century, a period in which grammar was dominated by the concept of *regimen/regere*" (Copeland and Sluiter 2012; cf. Weston 1935; De Roberto 2016: 115–117; Eberhard 2017).

As for the implied shift in person, the observation goes back at least to Priscian (Bognini 2008: LIII):

---

5 This absoluteness rule, as shown in many studies (Moreno Hernández 1996; Molinelli 2001; Greco 2005; Galdi 2016; Tronci 2022; Cotticelli et al. forthcoming), loosens over time (according to Serbat 1979, in correlation with the evolution of the AA into a dependent clause).

6 For other uses, see Mazhuga (2005).

7 The text is taken from Bognini (2008: 7); the translation is from Sluiter (2000: 413–414).

(8) [. . .] *quando nominis et participii ablativus verbo et nominativo alterius nominis cum transitione personarum adiungitur, ut "sole ascendente dies fit" et "Traiano bellante victi sunt Parthi".* (PRISC. gramm. II 190, 20)[8]
'[. . .] when an ablative of one noun and a participle are combined with a verb and a nominative of a different noun, with transition (*transitio*) of persons, e.g., *sole ascendente dies fit* "when the sun rises, it becomes day", and *Traiano bellante victi sunt Parthi* "When Trajan was conducting the war, the Parthians were conquered".'

Before that, on the background of a comparison between Greek and Latin, the grammarian Diomedes had pointed out that, when a perfect participle is combined with a noun in the ablative, *ablativus et pro nominativo accipitur*:

(9) *Sed in hoc praeterito tempore ablativus et pro nominativo accipitur et intellegitur pro infinito tempore, quod Graeci vocant* aoriston, *et apud nos est in participiis, veluti singulariter audito hoc verbo respondit, pluraliter auditis his verbis responderunt, pluraliter et singulariter auditis his verbis respondit, inventa veritate tacuit, peracta oratione sedit, viso fratre gavisus est et cetera quae sunt similia.* (DIOM. gramm. I 317, 11–17])
'But in these past tenses [the participle in] the ablative is taken as a nominative and it is understood to signify an indefinite tense, which the Greeks call aorist, and which we have in participles, e.g., singular: *audito hoc verbo respondit* "having heard this word [lit.: this word having been heard], he answered"; plural: *auditis his verbis responderunt* "having heard these words, they answered"; singular and plural: *auditis his verbis respondit* "having heard these words, he answered", *inventa veritate tacuit* "having discovered the truth, he fell silent", *peracta oratione sedit* "having finished his speech, he sat down", *viso fratre gavisus est* "having seen his brother, he rejoiced" and other cases like these.

As explained by Benedetti (2021), Diomedes is talking to Grecophones: by *ablativus et pro nominativo accipitur* he refers to the fact that, since the Latin participial system has not an active participle in the perfect, a Latin AA with a perfect participle may lend itself to render a Greek *participium coniunctum* in the nominative, i.e. related to the subject (Knapp 1923; Kruijer and la Roi 2018; Benedetti et al. 2021). By making this observation, Diomedes in fact reveals to be aware of the

8 Priscian and Diomedes are quoted according to Keil's edition (1857–1880); translations are from Sluiter (2000).

linkage between the notional subject of the participle (for the sake of simplicity, we may label it the "agent", in a wide sense) and the grammatical subject of the main proposition.

3 Transitive AA

3.1 Coreference Linkages

The pattern described by Diomedes, in which the agent of the AA coincides with the subject of the finite proposition, is common even in the most canonical Latin. A couple of instances quoted in grammars (Lavency 1997[2]: 195; Pinkster 2021: 397) are (10) and (11). A few more instances are shown in (12) to (17) below:

(10) *sic est locutus* ***partibus factis*** *leo* (PHAEDR. 1, 5, 6)
'the lion made four portions and spoke as follows'

(11) ***Hac re*** *statim Caesar per speculatores* **cognita** *insidias veritus* [. . .] *exercitum* [. . .] *in castra continuit.* (CAES. Gall. 2, 11, 2)
'Caesar learnt this at once through his scouts; and fearing an ambush [. . .] he kept the army [. . .] in camp.'

(12) [*Cornicinus*] ***abiecta toga*** *se ad generi pedes abiecit* (CIC. Att. 4, 2, 4)
'[. . .] flinging off his toga and throwing himself on his knees before his son-in-law'

(13) *Memmius autem* ***dirempta coitione*** *invito Calvino plane refrixerat* = (3)

(14) ***Confecta Britannia, obsidibus acceptis,*** *nulla praeda,* ***imperata*** *tamen* ***pecunia*** *exercitum ex Britannia reportabant* (CIC. Att. 4, 18, 5)
'They had settled Britain, taken hostages but no booty (tribute, however, imposed), and were bringing back the army from the island.'

(15) *Ibi dies quinque morati* ***direpto et vastato Amano*** *inde discessimus.* (CIC. Att. 5, 20, 3)
'There we stayed five days, plundering and laying waste the Amanus, and then left.'

(16) ***Obsignata epistula*** *accepi tuas* (Cic. Att. 12, 11, 1)
'After sealing my letter I received yours.'

(17) ***His*** *ego* ***litteris lectis*** *in eadem opinione fui* [. . .] (Cic. Att. 8, 11D, 3)
'On reading this I conceived. . .'

The frequency of occurrence of this type may even reach 50% of the cases in some texts (60% in Caesar according to Hoff [1989: 407]; 45 cases out of 100 in the selection from Sallust and Livy analysed by Kruijer and la Roi [2018]; cf. Maiocco 2005; Dalbera and Longrée 2021).

It should be emphasized that, according to the traditional description, these cases do not conflict with the alleged absoluteness rule, because the perfect participle is passive: this means that the grammatical subject of the participle and the grammatical subject of the finite proposition are different. However, it is at the same time clear that the observed linkage strongly relativizes absoluteness (Remmelink 2002; Spieralska 2021; in general, on the coreference linkages of the AA, cf. Bolkestein 2002).

Furthermore, it is worth emphasizing that, though the perfect participle is traditionally considered as inherently passive, its combination with other elements may produce syntactic structures which, taken as a whole, may or may not be passive, as example (18) shows:[9]

(18) *Gallia est omnis divisa in partes tres* (Caes. Gall. 1, 1, 1)
'Gaul is a whole divided into three parts'

To make the standpoint more explicit, if we consider the AA as a composition, as it is, and diathesis as the relationship between a predicate and its subject, as it is, the passive diathesis of the AA with the perfect participle of a transitive verb, though a commonplace, can be questioned. For example, in (17), there is no doubt that *litteris* is what is read, that is the object selected by the predicate *lego*; but, as for its promotion to the subject function by means of passivation, evidence is not that certain. How could *litteris* be proved to be the subject?

9 As a matter of fact, structures such as (18) are considered as "adjectival passives" in some frameworks, as opposed to "verbal passives" (cf., among others, Wasow 1977, Embick 2004): see Rouveret (2018) for an application of such distinctions to Latin. However, put aside terminological divergences, the point here is precisely that structures as (18) differ syntactically from verbal passives that imply a notional subject different from the grammatical one.

3.2 Subjecthood and Diathesis

The main tests for subjecthood in Latin are the nominative case and the control of person-agreement in the finite forms of the verb. Both of them are unworkable in the AA.

The passive character of the AA with the perfect participle and the subjecthood of its nominal are thus assumed mainly on the grounds of an analogical argument: as *litterae lectae sunt* is passive, so is *litteris lectis*. The assumption is that non-finite clauses function exactly as finite clauses, that is, that they must have a subject exactly as finite clauses have (Haug and Nikitina 2012; Nikitina and Haug 2016). However, this analogy lacks a detail, not a minor one concerning our specific issue: it lacks person, which is precisely the element that syntactically proves the existence of a subject.

Some additional arguments in favour of the passiveness of AA with the perfect participle might still be invoked. The strongest is the occurrence of an *ab*-phrase as in (19):

(19) *Tamen conceditur, minus honeste nunc quidem violata iam* ***ab illo*** *re publica illatoque bello quam si olim de ratione habenda impetrasset.* (Cic. Att. 7, 17, 2)
'Nevertheless, it's conceded, with less dignity it is true, now that he has committed treason and made war on the state, than if he had been allowed his point about his candidature earlier on.'

Yet, *ab*-phrases cannot be considered conclusive evidence either because they also occur in structures which are not passive (see Bruening 2012): e.g., with adjectives, as in (20), and with nouns, as in (21).

(20) *Sed hoc a Maurico novum non est.* (Plin. epist. 4, 22, 4)
'But surely this is nothing new for Mauricus.'

(21) [. . .] *reum Publium* [. . .] *fore a Milone puto* (Cic. Att. 4, 3, 5)
'I think Publius will be brought to trial by Milo [. . .]'

Moreover, the agent of the participle is not bound to be expressed by an *ab*-phrase and may be expressed otherwise.

In (22), which repeats (17), the agent of the participle – the same as the subject of the main proposition – is expressed by a nominative inserted in the AA. In Livy, the insertion of *ipse* in the AA, as in (23), is not uncommon.

(22) *His* ***ego*** *litteris lectis in eadem opinione fui qua* = (17)

(23) *Romani quoque imperatores L. Lentulus et L. Manlius Acidinus* [. . .] *iunctis* ***et ipsi*** *exercitibus* [. . .] *ad sedem hostium pervenere* [. . .] (Liv. 29, 2, 1–2)
'The Roman commanders Lucius Lentulus and Lucius Manlius Acidinus [. . .] also united their armies.'

Even if *ego* in (22) might in principle be considered as the scrambled subject of *fui*, it cannot go unnoticed that this type of scrambling only occurs when the nominative subject is the same as the agent of the participle.

The person by whom the action is carried out may also be expressed by a *per*-phrase as in (24) and (25). This, again, is a pattern that is not confined to passive structures:

(24) *Scaurus* [. . .] *obnuntiationibus* ***per Scaevolam*** *interpositis singulis diebus usque ad pr. Kal. Oct., quo ego haec die scripsi, sublatis, populo tributim domi suae satis fecerat.* (Cic. Att. 4, 17, 4)
'Every day up to 29 September, the day I write this letter, having been voided by Scaevola with reports of bad auspices, he (Scaurus) has given the public its due at his own house, tribe by tribe.'

(25) *Qui enim potest aut deserta* ***per se*** *patria aut oppressa beatus esse?* (Cic. Att. 10, 4, 4)
'For what happiness is there for a deserter of his country on the one hand or an oppressor on the other?'

Finally, it is worth emphasizing that in most cases the agent of the predication contained in the participle is not relevant at all, as shown in (26) (Longrée 2010):

(26) *Me vero* ***teste producto*** *credo te ex acclamatione Clodi advocatorum audisse* [. . .] (Cic. Att. 1, 16, 4)
'When I myself was called as a witness, you must have heard from the shouts of Clodius' supporters [. . .]'

This hints at a stative-resultative value of the structure, that brings out an adjectival, rather than verbal, behaviour of the participle. Consider (27):

(27) *Itaque nunc,* ***consule*** *in carcere* ***incluso****, saepe item seditione commota, adspiravit nemo* [. . .] (Cic. Att. 2, 1, 8)
'So now we see a Consul shut up in goal and one riot following another, while not one of the men [. . .] lifts a finger.'

All of this is further confirmation of the description given by Mellet et al. (1994: 309) of the Latin perfect participle as "un accompli non depassé", indeed more sensitive to aspect than to diathesis (as a matter of fact, it is a verbal adjective in **-to-*; see Meillet 1928: 155). Joffre (2022) has newly returned to this topic (cf. Joffre 1987), by highlighting, besides the adjectival and non-passive uses of perfect participles, as in (28) and (29), impersonal structures such as (30) and (31) (see also Rouveret 2018: 249–250 in particular). The comparison of the latter with existential structures such as (32) makes the nominal character of the perfect participle quite evident, and nominals, as such, are insensitive to diathesis.

(28) *At senatus decrevit ut* ***tacitum*** *iudicium ante comitia fieret* (Cic. Att. 4, 17, 3)
'Then came a senatorial decree providing that before the elections a "silent" process should be instituted'

(29) *Inde domum cenatus, ut sim mane praesto Miloni.* (Cic. Att. 4, 12)
'Then home after dinner so that I can be ready for Milo in the morning.'

(30) [. . .] *illo die quo* ***auspicato*** *comitiis centuriatis L. Murenam consulem renuntiavi* (Cic. Mur. 1)[10]
'On that day, gentlemen of the jury, on which after I had taken the auspices I announced Lucius Murena's election as consul to the assembly of the centuries'

(31) *Huic ita* ***plausum est*** *ut salva re publica Pompeio plaudi solebat* (Cic. Att. 2, 19, 3)
'[. . .] who (Curio) received the sort of ovation that Pompey used to get in the days before freedom fell.'

(32) ***Erat*** *enim* ***spes*** *propinqui reditus,* ***erat*** *hominum* ***querela***. (Cic. Att. 9, 15, 3)
'There was the hope of an early return, there was public murmuring.'

To summarise: the passiveness of the AA with the perfect participle of a transitive verb is an assumption for which no conclusive evidence can be produced, as there is no conclusive evidence that the nominal involved is its subject.

10 There are no examples of this type in Cicero's letters (Steele 1904).

4 Intransitive AA and the Unaccusative Hypothesis

The next step we need to take is bringing into consideration the cases in which the AA is intransitive, which have not been considered so far. It is well-known that the perfect participle in this case belongs to the deponent paradigm:

(33) ***Cosconio mortuo*** *sum in eius locum invitatus.* (Cic. Att. 2, 19, 4)
'When Cosconius died I was invited to take his place.'

It is also a fact that deponent structures have a strikingly identical morphosyntax to passives: among evidentiary facts there is the complete integration of the perfect participle in both paradigms. In order to account for this morphosyntactic identity, it has been quite uncontroversially accepted (since at least Benveniste 1950) that passive and deponent structures have a functional coherence. To quote only a couple of specific proposals, among many others, Mellet et al. (1994) include both within the hypernym "diathèse interne", which means that "le concept verbal vient recouvrir le concept nominal sujet dans une adequation parfait"; as for Gianollo (2005), she considers the domain of *-r* inflexion as characterized by the coding of a de-agentive situation.

From a strictly syntactic point of view, both similarities and differences between a well-defined group of intransitive structures and passives is captured by the Unaccusative Hypothesis (UH, henceforth), first advanced by Perlmutter (1978) in the multi-level framework of Relational Grammar and by now a widely accepted hypothesis itself. According to the UH, intransitive structures may be divided into two subsets, defined in syntactic terms to describe purely morphosyntactic differences. One subset has a final, i.e. grammatical, subject which is the subject at all levels of the clause (its syntactic behaviour is identical to that of the subjects of transitive clauses): this is the unergative subset. The other subset has a final subject which is considered to be an initial object, i.e. an object at the initial level of the clause (because it shares properties with the objects of transitive clauses and with the subject of passive clauses): this is the unaccusative subset. Thus, the common trait between passive and unaccusative structures is that both have a final subject that is an initial object, whereas the difference is that passive structures only have an initial (i.e. a notional) subject different from the final one.

The extension of the UH to the description of Latin is not a novelty (La Fauci 1988; Loporcaro 1998: 191–199; Benedetti 2005; La Fauci and Pieroni 2007; Pieroni 2011) and goes well beyond Relational Grammar (Oniga 2004; Rovai 2007; Cennamo 2016). Under the UH, the deponent morphology is a manifestation (not necessarily the only one) of unaccusative structures. That is to say that, on the one hand, *Caesar profectus est* and *Caesar occisus est a coniuratis* have in common the fact that the subject of both is an object at the initial level of the proposition; on the other hand, *Caesar profectus est* and *Caesar occisus est* differ because the latter has an initial subject different from the final one, whereas this is not true for the unaccusative structure *profectus est.*

Back to the AA, we shall therefore observe, in agreement with Oniga (2004: 292–293), that the intransitive AA with a perfect participle perfectly fits the UH. If deponent structures are considered as unaccusative, the nominal which combines with the perfect participle in an intransitive AA is its initial object, thus fulfilling the same function which it fulfils in the AA with the perfect participle of a transitive verb.[11]

5 Conclusion

The Latin AA with the perfect participle may thus be described by the very same description, free of charge, that holds for Romance participial absolutes, which are its direct descendants. In Romance, participial absolutes are in effect one of the tests for unaccusativity.

The rule for participial absolutes in Romance is given in (34) according to Rosen's (1997: 187) formulation (2 means object):

(34) Participial absolutes in Romance
"The verb in participial form is accompanied by a nominal which [is] its P-initial 2"

This rule, in fact, still leaves open the issue of diathesis. Loporcaro (2003) has thoroughly described the lively debate about diathesis in Romance participial absolutes among those that claim that structures such as, e.g., Italian *ucciso Cesare* are active,

11 We will not discuss here cases such as *Sulla omnia pollicito* [. . .] (SALL. Iug. 103, 7) 'after Sulla had promised to do all [. . .]' and *Vix cuncta locuto / Caesare* (LVCAN. 7, 329–330) 'Almost before Caesar had ceased to speak', but we nevertheless observe that the medial diathesis of *polliceor* and *loquor* suggests the hypothesis that their final subjects might fulfill, at some level of the structure, an object relation as well. The idea that "[i]n each case, [. . .] the Middle morphology signals the absence of the external argument in the structure" has been also defended, recently, by Pinzin (2018: 11).

those that claim they are passive, those that claim they are sometimes active and sometimes passive.[12]

The analysis of the Latin AA with a perfect participle would seem to hint at the further possibility that, from the viewpoint of diathesis, the construction – at least in Latin – is underspecified. Although the perfect participle is labelled as passive by a terminological convention, in fact it certainly enters the passive paradigm only when combined with *sum* into a periphrastic verbal form. Otherwise, when it is simply combined with a nominal, as is the case in the AA, the passive syntax of the construction (i.e., the subjecthood of the initial object via the demotion of the initial subject) is not assuredly verified. To rephrase it, the perfect participle is object-oriented, and so are the constructions in which it occurs, the AA among others, but in the latter, there is no evidence of the promotion of the object to subject.

This does not exclude that an agent of the predication be involved, though it is often irrelevant. As has been shown in Section 3.2, it may be the same as the subject of the main clause or a different one. This interpretive openness itself hints at the hypothesis that it falls outside the relevant features of the construction.

For these reasons, my proposal for describing the Latin AA with the perfect participle is the following:

- the relevant condition to define the syntax of the AA with the perfect participle is the requirement of an initial object;
- the combination of a participle and a nominal in the AA is unmarked for diathesis.

Bibliography

Bauer, B. (1993). The development of Latin absolute constructions: from stative to transitive structures. *General Linguistics*, *33* (1–2), 64–83.

Benedetti, M. (2005). Dispersioni formali del medio indoeuropeo. In L. Costamagna & S. Giannini (Eds.), *Acquisizione e mutamento di categorie linguistiche. Atti del Convegno della Società Italiana di Glottologia* (pp. 95–119). Roma: Il Calamo.

Benedetti, M. (2021). Il grammatico Diomede e lo strano caso dell'*ablativus pro nominativo*. In M. L. Aliffi, A. Bartolotta & C. Nigrelli (Eds.), *Perspectives on Language and Linguistics. Essays in honour of Lucio Melazzo* (pp. 31–49). Palermo: Palermo University Press.

Benedetti, M., Logozzo, F. & Tronci, L. (2021). Ablatives Absolute in the Vulgate: some remarks on the Gospels. In A. M. Martín Rodríguez (Ed.), *Linguisticae Dissertationes. Current Perspectives on Latin Grammar, Lexicon and Pragmatics* (pp. 263–278). Madrid: Ediciones Clásicas.

Benveniste, É. (1950). Actif et moyen dans le verbe. *Journal de Psychologie*, *43*, 119–127.

Bognini, F. (Ed.) (2008). *Alberico di Montecassino, Breviarium de dictamine*. Sismel: Edizioni del Galluzzo.

12 For the vast amount of literature on the topic we shall refer to Loporcaro (2003). For a diachronic consideration of participial absolutes in Italian, see Egerland (1996).

Bolkestein, A. M. (2002). Anaphoric ablative absolutes in Caesar. In L. Sawicki & D. Shalev (Eds.), *Donum Grammaticum. Studies in Latin and Celtic Linguistics in Honour of Hannah Rosén* (pp. 51–63). Leuven/Paris/Sterling, Virginia: Peeters.

Bruening, B. (2012). By Phrases in Passives and Nominals. *Syntax*, *16* (1), 1–41.

Cennamo, M. (2016). Voice. In A. Ledgeway & M. Maiden (Eds.), *The Oxford Guide to the Romance Languages* (pp. 967–980). Oxford: Oxford University Press.

Coleman, R. (1989). The Rise and fall of absolute constructions: A Latin case history. In G. Calboli (Ed.), *Subordination and other topics in Latin* (pp. 353–374). Amsterdam: Benjamins.

Copeland, R. & Sluiter, I. (2012). The Ablative Absolute Dossier. In R. Copeland & I. Sluiter (Eds.), *Medieval Grammar and Rhetoric: Language Arts and Literary Theory, AD 300–1475* (pp. 314–338). Oxford: Oxford University Press.

Cotticelli, P., Dahl, E. & Zivojinovic, J. (forthcoming). *The resolution of absolute constructions in Late Latin: The role of non-finite morphosyntax in alignment change.* (Paper presented at *Latin Vulgaire Latin Tardif XIV*, Ghent, September 5th–9th, 2022).

Dalbera, J. (2022). Le participe parfait à l'ablatif absolu dans la narration romanesque latine. *L'Information Grammaticale*, *173*, 19–27.

Dalbera, J. & Longrée, D. (2021). Ablatif absolu, ordre des mots et figement lexical dans les Métamorphoses d'Apulée: une étude contrastive à la lumière d'Hyperbase Web Edition. In A. M. Martín Rodríguez (Ed.), *Linguisticae Dissertationes. Current Perspectives on Latin Grammar, Lexicon and Pragmatics* (pp. 249–264). Madrid: Ediciones Clásicas.

De Roberto, E. (2016). Assolutezza sintattica e discontinuità referenziale in italiano: le costruzioni assolute nominali nella storia dell'italiano. In A. Ledgeway, M. Cennamo & G. Mensching (Eds.), *Actes du XXVIIe Congrès international de linguistique et de philologie romanes. Section 4: Syntaxe* (pp. 115–126). Nancy: ATILF.

Eberhard, K. (2017). Völlig losgelöst? Überlegungen zum sogen. *Ablativus absolutus* und seiner Behandlung im Lateinunterricht. *Forum Classicum*, *1*, 17–24. https://journals.ub.uni-heidelberg.de/index.php/fc/article/view/44760 (accessed 3 August 2024).

Egerland, V. (1996). *The Syntax of Past Participles. A Generative Study of Nonfinite Constructions in Ancient and Modern Italian*. Lund: Lund University Press.

Embick, D. (2004). On the structure of resultative participles in English. *Linguistic Inquiry*, *35*, 355–392.

Galdi, G. (2016). Remarks on temporal clauses and participial phrases in late historical texts. In P. Poccetti (Ed.), *Latinitatis rationes: Descriptive and Historical Accounts for the Latin Language* (pp. 651–667). Berlin: De Gruyter.

Gianollo, C. (2005). Middle voice in Latin and the phenomenon of Split Intransitivity. *Latina Lingua! Proceedings of the 12th International Colloquium on Latin Linguistics. Papers on Grammar, 9 (1)*, 97–109.

Greco, P. (2005). La subordinazione participiale nel primo libro della *Historia Francorum* di Gregorio di Tours. *Medioevo Romanzo*, *29*, 3–71, 161–210.

Haug, D. & Nikitina, T. (2012). The many cases of non-finite subjects: The challenge of 'dominant' participles. In M. Butt & T. Holloway King (Eds.), *Proceedings of the LFG12*. http://web.stanford.edu/group/cslipublications/cslipublications/LFG/17/papers/lfg12haugnikitina.pdf (accessed 3 August 2024)

Harris, Z. (2002 [1990]). The background of transformational and metalanguage analysis. In B. Nevin (Ed.), *The Legacy of Zellig Harris: Language and information into the 21st Century, Vol. 1: Philosophy of science, syntax, and semantics* (pp. 1–15). http://www.zelligharris.org/HAR.pdf (accessed 3 August 2024).

Hoff, F. (1989). Les ablatifs absolus irréguliers. In Calboli, G. (Ed.) *Subordination and other topics in Latin* (pp. 401–424). Amsterdam: Benjamins.
Joffre, M.-D. (1987). Le signifié diathétique du morphème *to". In *Études de linguistique générale et de linguistique latine offertes en hommage à Guy Serbat. L'Information Grammaticale, 34*, 307–315.
Joffre, M.-D. (2022). Les fluctuations diathétiques de la forme en *-*to. L'Information grammaticale, 173*, 5–11.
Keil, H. (1857–1880) (Ed.). *Grammatici latini*. Leipzig: Teubner.
Keydana, G. (1997). *Absolute Konstruktionen in altindogermanischen Sprachen*. Göttingen: Vandenhoeck & Ruprecht.
Knapp, C. (1923). Is the Ablative Absolute Necessary? *The Classical Weekly, 17* (2), 9–10.
Kruijer, M. & la Roi, E. (2018). Paradigmatic Possibilities as Perspective for Absolute Constructions. Exploring Linguistic Differences and Similarities of the Greek Genitive and Latin Ablative Absolute. *Mnemosyne, 71* (5), 799–822.
La Fauci, N. (1988). *Oggetti e soggetti nella formazione della morfosintassi romanza*. Pisa: Giardini.
La Fauci, N. & Pieroni, S. (2007). *Morfosintassi latina*. Pisa: ETS.
Lavency, M. (1997). Usus. *Grammaire latine* (2nd edn.). Louvain: Peeters.
Lavency M. (2000). Syntagmes à l'Ablatif en latin Classique: conditionnements et valeurs. *Latomus, 59*, 819–841.
Lavency, M. (2001). Syntagmes à l'Ablatif aprépositionnel. *Faventia, 23* (2), 73–85.
Longrée, D. (2010). Ablatif absolu et effacement de l'agent en latin. In F. Daviet-Taylor & D. Bottineau (Eds.), *L'impersonnel. La personne, le verbe, la voix* (pp. 143–156). Rennes: Presses Universitaires de Rennes.
Longrée, D. (2014). *Demisso capite*: Ablatif absolu ou épithète détachée?. In C. Cabrillana & C. Lehmann (Eds.), *Acta XIV Colloquii Internationalis Linguisticae Latinae* (pp. 361–372). Madrid: Ediciones Clàsicas.
Loporcaro, M. (1998). *Sintassi comparata dell'accordo participiale romanzo*. Torino: Rosenberg & Sellier.
Loporcaro, M. (2003). The Unaccusative Hypothesis and participial absolutes in Italian: Perlmutter's generalization revised. *Italian Journal of Linguistics, 15* (2), 199–263.
Maiocco, M. (2005). *Absolute Participial Constructions*. Alessandria: Edizioni dell'Orso.
Mazhuga, V. I. (2005). Die Begriffe *absolutus* und *absolutivus* in der römischen Grammatik (1. bis 5. Jh. n. Chr.). In T. Fögen (Ed.), *Antike Fachtexte* (pp. 171–190). Berlin/New York: De Gruyter.
Meillet, A. (1928). *Esquisse d'une histoire de la langue latine*. Deuxième édition revisée et augmentée. Paris: Hachette.
Mellet, S., Joffre, M. D. & Serbat, G. (1994). *Grammaire fondamentale du Latin. Le signifié du verbe*. Louvain/Paris: Peeters.
Milani, C. (2001). Verso una definizione di *ablativus absolutus*. In V. Orioles (Ed.), *Dal 'paradigma' alla parola. Riflessioni sul metalinguaggio della linguistica* (pp. 373–389). Roma: Il Calamo.
Molinelli, P. (2001). Absolute structures in late Latin. In C. Moussy (Ed.), *De lingua latina novae quaestiones* (pp. 473–484). Louvain: Peeters.
Moreno Hernández, A. (1996). The ablative absolute in Late Latin. In H. Rosén (Ed.), *Aspects of Latin. Papers from the Seventh International Colloquium on Latin Linguistics* (pp. 471–482). Innsbruck: Institut für Sprachwissenschaft.
Nikitina, T. & Haug, D. (2016). Syntactic nominalizations in Latin: A case of non-canonical subject agreement. *Transactions of the Philological Society, 114* (1), 25–50.
Oniga, R. (2004). *Il latino. Breve introduzione linguistica* (2nd edn.). Milano: Franco Angeli.
Perlmutter, D. M. (1978). Impersonal Passives and the Unaccusative Hypothesis. *Proceedings of the 4th Annual Meeting of the Berkeley Linguistic Society*, 157–189.

Pieroni, S. (2011). Decomposing subjects: A hypothesis on the controller of the ablative of the gerund. In R. Oniga, R. Iovino & G. Giusti (Eds.), *Formal Linguistics and the Teaching of Latin. Theoretical and Applied Perspectives in Comparative Grammar* (pp. 133–149). Newcastle: Cambridge Scholars Publishing.

Pinkster, H. (1982). The use of the so-called *ablativus qualitatis* in the function Praedicativum. In J. den Boeft & A. H. M. Kessels (Eds.), *Actus: Studies in Honour of H. L. W. Nelson* (pp. 247–256). Utrecht: Klassiek Instituut.

Pinkster, H. (2021). *The Oxford Latin Syntax. Volume 2: The Complex Sentence and Discourse.* Oxford: Oxford University Press.

Pinzin, F. (2018). *Stuck in the middle: a morphosyntactic analysis of the deponent verbs from Latin to Romance*. Doctoral Dissertation, Università Ca' Foscari Venezia. http://dspace.unive.it/bitstream/handle/10579/12877/956151-1197504.pdf?sequence=2 (accessed 3 August 2024).

Ramat, P. (1994). On Latin absolute constructions. In J. Herman (Ed.), *Linguistic Studies on Latin: Selected Papers from the 6th International Colloquium on Latin Linguistics* (pp. 259–268). Amsterdam/Philadelphia: Benjamins.

Remmelink, H. W. (2002). Inferring implicit first-argument participants of passive ablative absolutes in Ammianus Marcellinus. In A. M. Bolkestein, C. Kroon, H. Pinkster, H. W. Remmelink & R. Risselada (Eds.), *Theory and description in Latin linguistics: Selected Papers from the 11th International Colloquium on Latin Linguistics* (pp. 301–316). Amsterdam: Gieben.

Rosen, C. (1997). Auxiliation and serialization: on discerning the difference. In A. Alsina, J. Bresnan & P. Sells (Eds.), *Complex Predicates* (pp. 175–202). Stanford, CA: CSLI Publications.

Rouveret, A. (2018). Sur la construction latine *ab urbe condita*. *Bulletin de la Société de Linguistique de Paris*, *103* (1), 215–265.

Rovai, F. (2007). Manifestazioni di sub-sistemi tipologici attivi in latino. *Archivio Glottologico italiano*, *92* (1), 51–64.

Ruppel, A. (2013). *Absolute Constructions in Early Indo-European*. Cambridge: Cambridge University Press.

Scaglione, A. (1970). Ars Grammatica*: A bibliographical Survey, two essays on the grammar of the Latin and Italian subjunctive, and a note on the ablative absolute*. The Hague: Mouton.

Serbat, G. (1979). L'ablatif absolu. *Revue des Études Latines*, *57*, 340–354.

Sluiter, I. (2000). Seven grammarians on the ablative absolute. *Historiographia Linguistica*, *27* (2–3), 379–414.

Spieralska, B. (2021). Relative Absoluteness: The Case of Participial Clauses in Latin. *Philologia Classica*, *16* (1), 90–99.

Steele, R. B. (1902). The Ablative Absolute in Livy. *The American Journal of Philology*, *23* (4), 413–427.

Steele, R. B. (1904). The Ablative Absolute in the Epistles of Cicero, Seneca, Pliny and Fronto. *The American Journal of Philology*, *25* (3), 315–327.

Storme, B. (2010). *Sicilia amissa*: syntagme nominal ou proposition subordonnée. *Revue de Philologie, de littérature et d'histoire ancienne*, *84*, 119–136.

Torrego, E. (2009). Ablativo. In J. M. Baños-Baños (Ed.), *Sintaxis del latin clasico* (pp. 211–249). Madrid: Liceus.

Touratier, C. (1994). *Syntaxe Latine*. Leuven: Peeters.

Tronci, L. (2022). Les participes parfaits dans la Vulgate. Influence du grec, diachronie du latin. *L'Information Grammaticale*, *173*, 28–37.

Wasow, T. (1977). Transformations and the Lexicon. In P. Culicover, T. Wasow & A. Akmajian (Eds.), *Formal Syntax* (pp. 327–360). New York: Academic Press.

Weston A. H. (1935). The 'Ablative Absolute'. *The Classical Journal*, *30* (5), 298–299.

Liana Tronci

Latin Constructions *sum* + Present Participle: Pragmatic and Syntactic Evidence against the Periphrastic Analysis

Abstract: This study deals with constructions in which *sum* and the present participle co-occur and investigates them in a broad corpus consisting of Archaic, Classical and Imperial Latin authors. According to scholars, these combinations especially occur in Biblical Latin as an effect of the translation from Greek and have to be analysed as progressive periphrases. Scholars also claim that in previous stages of Latin, *sum* only combines with stative and adjective-like participles. The goal of this paper is to propose a different analysis, which takes into account the syntactic and pragmatic features of the sentences in which *sum* and the present participle occur. According to this analysis, *sum* and the present participle do not form any verbal periphrasis. Besides the copular constructions with adjective-like participles, there are two types of constructions with true verbal participles. In the first one, *sum* and the present participle function as predicates of complex constructions, i.e. presentative and focalising sentences. The second type is an expansion of the copular type to verbal participles. The usual coordination of the participle with an adjective in this type of construction supports the hypothesis.

Keywords: progressive periphrases, presentative constructions, focalisation, Archaic Latin, Classical Latin, Imperial Latin

1 Introduction

This paper deals with constructions formed by the verb *sum* 'be' and the present participle as they are illustrated in (1)–(2). Against the scholarly consensus, according to which *sum* and the present participle form a morphosyntactic unit, I propose

Note: This research was carried out as part of the project PRIN 2017 "Ancient languages and writing systems in contact: a touchstone for language change", funded by the Italian Ministry of university and research (MUR). I would like to thank all the audience in my talk and particularly Simon Aerts, Nigel Holmes, and Hannah Rosén for their questions and remarks.

Liana Tronci, University for Foreigners of Siena, Italy

https://doi.org/10.1515/9783111332956-025

a different account, focusing on the syntactic and pragmatic features of the constructions in which *sum* and the present participle occur.[1]

(1) *deinde exercitus ibi* ***est*** *locorum* ***sciens****, sed mehercule magis strenuus quam felix. nam magna pars eius avaritia aut temeritate ducum adtrita est.* (SALL. Iug. 85, 45)
'There is an army in it, too, which is well acquainted with the country, though, assuredly, more brave than fortunate; for a great part of it has been destroyed by the avarice or rashness of its commanders.'

(2) *itaque probe definitur a Stoicis fortitudo cum eam virtutem* ***esse*** *dicunt* ***propugnantem*** *pro aequitate.* (CIC. off. 1, 62, 4)
'And therefore, fortitude is correctly defined by the Stoics when they say that it is that virtue that fights in defence of justice.'

Grammarians and scholars note that the constructions with *sum* and the present participle, though being attested in all stages of Latin, are very rare in Classical Latin as compared to Archaic Latin and Imperial Latin, and grow in number in Biblical Latin, particularly in the Vulgate (cf. Plater and White 1926: 109–110; Hofmann and Szantyr 1965: 388; Haverling 2010: 491–497; Pinkster 2015: 544–546). As I said, these combinations are analysed as "complex verbal expressions" (Pinkster 2015: 544) as they are considered to be either verbal periphrases conveying progressive meanings as compared to the corresponding simple verbal forms or adjectival-like predications. According to some scholars, progressive periphrases grammaticalised along the history of Latin language and especially in Biblical translations under the pressure of contact with Greek (cf. Dietrich 1973; Amenta 2003; see also Bentein [2016] for an analysis of the corresponding Greek constructions in the framework of grammaticalisation).

The goal of this study is to propose a different analysis, which accounts for the combinations of *sum* and the present participle according to the syntactic and pragmatic features of the construction in which the two verbs occur. I will argue that *sum* and the present participle do not form any verbal unit and, therefore, are not associated with any specific semantic value. Conversely, the meanings they convey depend on the construction in which they occur.

The paper is structured as follows. In Section 2 a short account of previous studies is presented. Section 3 proposes a new hypothesis, the research questions,

1 Latin texts are from the LASLA database. English translations are taken from Loeb editions with adjustments.

and the methodology of this study. Section 4 is devoted to the analysis of the data and Section 5 to conclusions.

2 Overview of Previous Studies: Findings and Problems

In this Section, I present a very short account of previous studies, referring the reader to Tronci (forthcoming) for a more detailed discussion.

Previous scholars have acknowledged the existence of two types of constructions, one with “adjectival” participle (which was prevalent in Archaic Latin) and one with “verbal” participle (which was prevalent in Biblical Latin, particularly in the Gospels).[2] The “adjectival” type and the “verbal” type would be different from each other, as in the former, the participle has a stative meaning and is usually contiguous to the verb *sum*, which functions as a copula, while in the latter there are no such constraints (cf. Eklund [1970] for an analysis of the differences based on syntactic and semantic features). Examples (3)–(5) illustrate the adjectival type. Note that the coordination of the participle to an adjective in (4) and (5) provides further evidence of the adjective-like function of the participle.

(3) *Carthagini ego sum gnatus, ut tu* ***sis sciens***. (PLAVT. Poen. 1038)
'Just so that you know, I was born in Carthage.' [Lit. 'Just so that you are aware (of this).']

(4) *sed dux atque imperator vitae mortalium animus est. qui ubi ad gloriam virtutis via grassatur, abunde* ***pollens potensque et clarus est***. (SALL. Iug. 1, 3)
'The ruler and director of the life of man is the mind, which, when it pursues glory in the path of true merit, is sufficiently powerful, efficient, and worthy of honour.'

(5) *sed quamvis* ***egregia illis vita fuerit et carens fraude*** *non fuere sapientes quando hoc iam in opere maximo nomen est.* (SEN. epist. 90, 44)
'But no matter how excellent and guileless was the life of the men of that age, they were not wise men; for that title is reserved for the highest achievement.'

2 See Barrett (1909); Marouzeau (1910: 37–39); Löfstedt (1911: 246); Plater and White (1926: 109–110); Lyer (1930); Hofmann and Szantyr (1965: 388); Eklund (1970); Piras (1989/1990); Amenta (2003); Haverling (2010: 491–497); Pinkster (2015: 544–546).

Unlike the adjectival type, which appears to be less difficult to explain, the "verbal" type has received more attention by scholars, who have argued that, on the one hand, it does not seem to be typically Latin and, on the other hand, it was the source for Romance progressive periphrases. In fact, the combinations of *sum* + present participle had an uneven distribution along the history of Latin language, as they were very rare in Classical Latin and grew in number in Biblical Latin. Based on this observation, scholars have argued that the verbal type spread in Latin under the influence of the Greek of the New Testament where the verb *eimí* 'be' and the present participle occurred in the same combinations as in the Vulgate (see references in fn. 2; for a corpus-based analysis of the data of the New Testament and the Vulgate Gospels cf. Logozzo and Tronci 2020, 2021 respectively).

The second aspect under investigation in the literature concerns the issue of continuity vs. discontinuity between Latin and Romance languages. In Romance languages, in fact, there are verbal periphrases with progressive meaning, e.g. *stare* + gerund 'be V-ing' in both Italian and Spanish; they are formed in a quite similar way as the Latin combinations under scrutiny, despite the formal differences consisting in the auxiliary *esse* vs. *stare* and the present participle vs. the gerund. According to some scholars, the sources for Romance progressive periphrases are the Latin combinations *sum* + present participle, which are therefore interpreted as progressive periphrases as well (cf. Amenta 2003 and references therein; for a critical discussion, cf. Logozzo and Tronci 2021). In addition to this, Coseriu (1972) argues that the distribution of the periphrases in Latin as well as their spread in Romance languages provide evidence for the fact that the construction arose in Greek and penetrated into Latin as a calque: "wenn ein Faktum im Griechischen, im Vorklassischen Latein und im Spätlatein, bzw. in den romanischen Sprachen erscheint, nicht aber im klassischen Latein, so ist viel eher die Annahme berechtigt, daß es sich um einen Gräzismus handelt" (Coseriu 1972: 141).

There is a consensus among scholars that the "verbal" combination *sum* + present participle should be analysed as a verbal periphrasis denoting progressive meaning. According to Hofmann and Szantyr (1965: 388) *sum* + present participle denotes "das Zuständliche und Andauernde der Handlung", while Pinkster (2015: 544) explicitly relates the periphrases attested in the Vulgate to imperfective aspect: "[t]hey correspond to similar periphrastic forms in the Koine original of the New Testament and serve the same aspectual (imperfective) function". In her study on verbal periphrases in Greek and Latin, Amenta (2003) investigates *sum* + present participle in the framework of grammaticalisation, arguing that the occurrences of the "verbal" type in the Vulgate show several imperfective meanings from habitual to progressive and this proves that a grammaticalised progressive periphrasis existed at that stage of Latin (Amenta 2003: 103–123). As Logozzo and Tronci (2021) argued in their study on Vulgate Gospels, this analysis is difficult to support for syntactic and semantic reasons and a different analysis is possible for accounting for the data of Vulgate Gospels (see Section 3 for further details). Building on this new hypothesis, this paper aims to address questions regarding the functions of *sum* + present participle in Archaic and Classical Latin and whether these functions underwent changes over the centuries.

3 Hypothesis, Research Questions and Methodology

The reasons questioning the traditional account of the combination of *sum* + present participle are mainly two (Logozzo and Tronci 2021).[3] First, the traditional analysis pays rather marginal attention to certain syntactic features of the combination of *sum* and the present participle, namely (a) the relative order of the two verbs, i.e. *sum* first and the participle second; (b) the occurrence of certain nominal elements, i.e. the subject and/or a locative complement, between the verb *sum* and the participle. These elements disrupt the contiguity of the two verbal forms, thus questioning the assumption that *sum* and the participle form a periphrasis. The second reason for rejecting the periphrastic analysis is that in several instances of the Vulgate, the Latin translator rendered the Greek combination of *eimí* + present participle by the simple imperfect, thus showing that *sum* + present participle and the simple imperfect were functionally comparable in Latin and did not oppose to each other in terms of aspect. As an instance of this, let me show the translation by the simple imperfect *docebat* in (6a) as opposed to the literal translation by *erat docens* in (7a) and (8a). Note that all three instances come from the same Gospel.

(6a) *et descendit in Capharnaum civitatem Galilaeae ibique* ***docebat*** *illos sabbatis.* (VVLG. Luc. 4, 31)

(6b) καὶ κατῆλθεν εἰς Καφαρναοὺμ πόλιν τῆς Γαλιλαίας. καὶ **ἦν διδάσκων** αὐτοὺς ἐν τοῖς σάββασιν. (*Ev.Luc.* 4, 31)
'And he went down to Capernaum, a city of Galilee. And he was teaching them on the Sabbath.'

(7a) ***erat*** *autem* ***docens*** *in synagoga eorum sabbatis.* (VVLG. Luc. 13, 10)

3 Cf. Logozzo and Tronci (2020) for a syntactic analysis of the comparable constructions with *eimí* and the present participle in the Greek of the New Testament.

(7b) **ἦν** δὲ **διδάσκων** ἐν μιᾷ τῶν συναγωγῶν ἐν τοῖς σάββασιν. (*Ev.Luc.* 4, 31)
'Now he was teaching in one of the synagogues on the Sabbath.'

(8a) *et **erat docens** cotidie in templo.* (VVLG. Luc. 19, 47)
(8b) καὶ **ἦν διδάσκων** τὸ καθ'ἡμέραν ἐν τῷ ἱερῷ. (*Ev.Luc.* 19, 47)
'And he was teaching daily in the temple.'

According to Logozzo and Tronci (2021), *sum* + present participle form two types of "verbal" constructions. In the first one, the two verbs are not contiguous; the verb *sum* usually occurs at the beginning of the sentence, followed by the subject of the clause and/or a locative complement. The subject can be either indefinite, thus functioning as a new discourse topic, or definite; in the latter case, it functions as an already known topic that needs to be emphasised. Depending on the different informational status of the subject, we are dealing with presentative sentences or focalising constructions. In both types, the verb *sum* and the participle do not form any morphosyntactic unit, as they serve two different syntactic and pragmatic purposes: while *sum* serves as a focalising marker pointing to the element to be emphasised, the participle is the semantic predication of the clause. In (9) I provide an example of presentative sentence. For the simplicity sake, I call this type "non-contiguous" verbal type.

(9a) ***erat** autem non longe ab illis grex porcorum multorum **pascens*** (VVLG. Matth. 8, 30)
(9b) **ἦν** δὲ μακρὰν ἀπ' αὐτῶν ἀγέλη χοίρων πολλῶν **βοσκομένη** (*Ev.Matt.* 8, 30)
'Now a herd of many pigs was feeding at some distance from them.' (Lit. 'Now there was a herd of pigs at some distance from them that fed.')

In the second type of "verbal" construction, *sum* and the participle are contiguous. This type correlates with the adjectival type and can be viewed as an extension of the adjectival type to verbal predications, due to contact with Greek. The aim of Latin translators to be as faithful as possible to the source text led them to translating literally from Greek, thus reproducing Greek similar constructions. The observation that the verb *sum* appears to be inflected in all tenses unlike the former verbal type, in which *sum* is only inflected in the imperfect stem, confirms the relationship with the adjectival type. In the latter, in fact, *sum* appears to be inflected in all stems. Moreover, in specific cases (e.g. (6a) above), simple verbal forms can align with the Greek construction *eimí* + present participle, which is never observed in verbal constructions of the previous type. The use of *sum* + present participle can be understood as an attempt of the translators to be as faithful as possible to the source language, even though this construction was typically reserved for adjectival and nominal predications in previous stages of

Latin. Through this approach, "true" verbal periphrases were formed; nevertheless, they did not diverge in meaning from simple verbal forms. An example of this second "verbal" type is illustrated in (10). In addition to the Vulgate version in (10a), I also give Old Latin translations in both European (10b) and African (10c) versions. Note the different translations (*erat praedicans* vs. *praedicabat*) in the European and African versions.[4]

(10a) *et* ***erat praedicans*** *in synagogis Galilaeae.* (VVLG. Luc. 4, 44)
(10b) *et* ***erat praedicans*** *in synagogis Galilaeae.* (Itala, mss. *a*, *aur*, *b*, *c*, *d*, *f*, *ff*[2], *l*, *q*, *r*[1])
(10c) *et* ***praedicabat*** *in synagogis Galileae.* (Afra, ms. *e*)
(10d) καὶ **ἦν κηρύσσων** εἰς τὰς συναγωγὰς τῆς Ἰουδαίας. (*Ev.Luc.* 4, 44)
'And he was preaching in the synagogues of Judea.'

Based on this approach, this paper aims to explore the usage patterns of the combination of *sum* + present participle during the Archaic, Classical and Imperial periods of Latin. The objective is to investigate whether the hypothesis that has proven successful in explaining Vulgate data holds true in these earlier stages. If substantiated, we should observe instances of *sum* + present participle serving as markers for presentative sentences and focalising constructions, in addition to the adjectival type.

This paper seeks to answer the following questions:

(a) Which functional values does the combination *sum* + present participle convey in Archaic, Classical and Imperial Latin?
(b) Are these values consistent in all stages of Latin? Are there some functional changes over the centuries?

In order to answer these questions, I searched for all occurrences of the combination of *sum* + present participle in a broad corpus consisting of Archaic, Classical and Imperial Latin texts. The texts investigated are those of the database of LASLA.[5] Data were extracted automatically by searching for the lemma "sum" plus the

4 Old Latin data are extracted from the edition by Jülicher et al. (1963–1976).

5 The database of LASLA (= *Laboratoire d'Analyse Statistique des Langues Anciennes*) consists of the works of the following authors (in alphabetic order): Caesar and *corpus caesarianum*, Cato the Elder, Catullus, Cicero, Horace, Juvenal, Lucretius, Ovid, Persius, Petronius, Plautus, Pliny the Younger, Propertius, Sallust, Seneca, Tacitus, Tibullus, Virgil (see https://www.lasla.uliege.be/cms/c_8570411/fr/lasla-textes-latins). I would like to thank Francesco Mambrini (Catholic University of the Sacred Heart of Milan) and Margherita Fantoli (University of Leuven) for their help when extracting the data.

grammatical category "present participle". The query filtered several instances in which either the combination was of the adjectival type or the two verbs do not form any syntactic construction, e.g. (11a)–(11b).

(11a) <u>*primus*</u> ***esses*** *memoriter progeniem uostram usque ab avo atque atavo* ***proferens***. (TER. Phorm. 394)
'You'd have recited your lineage right from your grandfather and your grandfather's grandfather, and remembered it perfectly.'

(11b) <u>*quis*</u> *illaec* **est** *mulier timido pectore peregre* **adveniens** *quae ipsa se miseratur.* (PLAVT. Epid. 533)
'Who is that woman coming from abroad with fear in her breast, who is pitying herself?'

In both cases, neither the two verbs form any predicative unit, nor have any direct syntactic relationship, because another predicate, i.e. *primus* in (11a) and the interrogative *quis* in (11b), correlates with the verb *sum*. From the pragmatic point of view, both clauses consist of two parts: (a) the predicative unit, i.e. *primus esses* in (11a) and *quis est* in (11b), which provides new information; (b) the participial clause, i.e. [. . .] *proferens* in (11a) and *illaec mulier* [. . .] *adveniens* in (11b), which provides the thematic information of the clause.

The type of clauses such as (11) were excluded from the analysis, as they are not relevant for the topic of this paper. I wanted to present them, however, in order to show that the co-occurrence of *sum* and the present participle might give raise to different syntactic combinations and, therefore, investigating them is a very hard task that requires a multi-level analysis.

4 Analysis of the Data

In this Section, I analyse the data following the chronological stages of Latin documentation, from Archaic Latin (Section 4.1) to Classical Latin (Section 4.2) and to Imperial Latin (Section 4.3). At the beginning of each Section, I also provide quantitative data.

4.1 Archaic Latin

Most instances of *sum* + present participle in Archaic Latin are of the adjectival type, according to Ernout and Thomas (2002 [1953]: § 287). In this type, the verb *sum* and the participle are usually contiguous, e.g. (12a), (12b), but they can also be separated by an adverb that denotes the degree of the adjective, e.g. *maxume* in (12c). *Sum* and the present participle can occur in both relative orders, i.e. either *sum* first and the present participle second, e.g. (12b), or vice versa, e.g. (12a), (12c) and (12d).

(12a) *senatuosque sententiam utei* ***scientes esetis***. (SCB, CIL I 581)
'[. . .] the Senate's decree, so that you may be informed.'

(12b) *ut tu* ***sis sciens***. (PLAVT. Poen. 1038)
'[. . .] so that you may be informed.'

(12c) *quoius* ***cupiens*** *maxume* ***est***. (PLAVT. Amph. 132)
'[He is lying, embracing the woman] he desires most.' (Lit. 'whose he is most desirous.')

(12d) *minimeque male* ***cogitantes sunt*** *qui in eo studio occupati sunt.* (CATO agr. praef. 4)
'And those who are engaged in that pursuit are least inclined to be disaffected.'

The participle can also govern genitive complements, as predicative adjectives also do, e.g. (12c) above and (13) below:

(13) *Non edepol piscis expeto / quam tui sermonis* ***sum indigens***. (PLAVT. Rud. 942– 943)
'I am not looking for fish as much as I am in need of a conversation with you.'

Distinguishing between adjectival and verbal type is difficult in several cases, as the criteria are not clear. Scholars have considered the semantic features of the verb such as stativity vs. activity, as well as the syntactic criterion of the government of complements. Both criteria, however, are not striking, as, on the one hand, the meaning of some participles, e.g. *cogitantes* in (12d), are borderline between stativity and activity; on the other hand, adjectives can also govern complements in genitive, dative and ablative. Therefore, with the intention of analysing occurrences without any preconceptions, I applied the search query indicated above in Section 3 and obtained 6 attestations, namely 5 in Plautus' comedies[6] and 1 in Cato's *Liber de agri cultura* (see [12d] above).

6 The relevant passages are PLAVT. Asin. 620, Capt. 925, Curc. 258, 288, Rud. 943. It is interesting to note that the automatic search returns the passage of example (13) but not that of example (12c), presumably due to a different labelling of *cupiens* (adjective) compared to *indigens* (participle) in the corpus of LASLA.

Two occurrences in Plautus' corpus, hereafter in (14) and (15), are certainly of the verbal type. In what follows I provide a syntactic analysis of them, arguing that they are not verbal periphrases.

(14) *quia oculi* ***sunt*** *tibi* ***lacrumantes*** *eo rogavi.* (PLAVT. Asin. 620)
'Because your eyes are shedding tears, that's why I asked.' (Lit. 'Because there are your eyes that shed tears.')

Despite the translation of *sunt lacrumantes* by the periphrasis 'are shedding tears', the two verbs cannot be analysed as a verbal periphrasis for syntactic reasons. Here, the verb *sum* governs the dative *tibi* in a typical dative of possession construction. The construction is peculiar as the "possessor" in the dative case *tibi* denotes the holonym with respect to its "possessee" in the nominative case *oculi.* In this type of dative of possession construction, the noun phrase that denotes the body part must be determined by an attribute: without the attribute, the clause (*oculi tibi sunt*) could not have any meaning. Therefore, the participle *lacrumantes* functions as the attribute of the subject *oculi* qualifying it, but also serves the purpose of fulfilling the meaning of the clause. It is an attribute syntactically, but it is necessary semantically. Instead of the participle, one could find an adjective or a relative clause. The verb *sum* functions as the predicate of both the dative of possession and the participle. The fact that the participle *lacrumantes* denotes a non-telic action has encouraged the analysis of the combination *sum* + present participle as a progressive periphrasis. As I have argued, however, this analysis is difficult to support for syntactic reasons. The durative meaning, which is rendered in English by *are shedding tears*, is not due to the alleged periphrasis, but comes partly from the lexical meaning of the verb *lacrumo* and partly from the syntactic construction.

In example (15), the combination *sum* + present participle occurs in an *accusativus cum infinitivo* construction. As in (14), the periphrastic analysis, which makes a consensus among scholars (cf. Pinkster 2015: 545), is difficult to support for syntactic reasons.

(15) *tum isti Graeci palliati, capite operto qui ambulant, / qui incedunt suffarcinati cum libris, cum sportulis / constant, conferunt sermones inter sese drapetae / opstant, opsistunt, incedunt cum suis sententiis, / quos semper videas* ***bibentes esse*** *in Thermopolio, / ubi quid surrupuere: operto capitulo calidum bibunt / tristes atque ebrioli incedunt: eos ego si offendero / ex unoquoque eorum crepitum exciam polentarium.* (PLAVT. Curc. 288–295)
'And then those Grecians with their cloaks, who walk about with covered heads, who go loaded beneath their cloaks with books, and with baskets, they loiter together, and engage in gossiping among themselves, the gad-abouts.

You may always see them enjoying themselves in the hot liquor-shops; when they have scraped up some trifle, with their covered pates they are drinking mulled wine, sad and maudlin they depart. If I meet them, I'll drive the barley-fed farts out of every single one of them.'

Two predications converge on the verb *sum* in (15). On the one hand, *sum* governs the locative complement *in Thermopolio* in a typical existential-locative sentence, which denotes the place where the subject is. On the other hand, *sum* combines with the participle *bibentes*, which denotes an action performed by the subject of the clause. The two predications co-occur in the same clause and no one could be deleted, as the locative complement is the pivot of the following relative clause *ubi* [. . .], while the participle provides a relevant semantic information. One could question whether the simple infinitive *bibere* might occur instead of *bibentes (esse)* and what might be the reason for this being not the case. In my opinion, the participial construction *bibentes esse in Thermopolio* and the simple verb construction *bibere in Thermopolio* would fairly convey the same meaning but the former expression makes it explicit that there are two predications, which share the verb *sum* as their nucleus. The construction *bibentes esse in Thermopolio* focuses on the fact that they both stay in the liquor-shop and drink. As is the case in (14), the verb *sum* and the participle do not form any progressive periphrasis in (15) either, as they do not form any morphological unit and fulfil two different functions in the clause. However, the durative meaning, which seems to characterise the clause and is rendered in English by the periphrasis *be -ing*, is an effect of the syntactic construction in its entirety.

Example (16) below provides a comparable instance. The only difference with respect to (15) is that the two verbs *carens* and *fui* are separated from each other in (16), and this makes clear that *fui* combines with the locative adverb *hic* and *carens* is a secondary predication.

(16) *quomque ex miseriis plurumis me exemerunt / quae adhuc te* ***carens*** *dum* <u>*hic*</u> ***fui*** *sustentabam* (PLAVT. Capt. 924–925)
'For freeing me from the many miseries which I endured until now while I was here without you.'

Summarising, there is no evidence for progressive periphrases in Archaic Latin. The combination of *sum* + present participle was used to convey different types of construction. First, the so-called adjectival type, where *sum* and the participle, usually contiguous, function as the copula and the main predication of the clause respectively. Second, a particular verbal construction in which the verb 'be' is the main locative predication, while the participle denotes a supplementary predication.

4.2 Classical Latin

Unlike what scholars argue, e.g. Amenta (2003), Pinkster (2015: 544–545), the combination *sum* + present participle is not rare in Classical Latin. In my database, I found 35 occurrences, which are distributed as follows in the texts: Cicero (8 occ.), Quintus Curtius (5 occ.), Lucretius (5 occ.), Caesar (4 occ.), Ovid (3 occ.), Pseudo-Caesar (3 occ.), Sallust (3 occ.), Virgil (2 occ.), Propertius (1 occ.), Catullus (1 occ.). Each author makes a different use of the combination *sum* + present participle. This is an interesting point for my investigation, as it shows that the co-occurrence of the two verbs served different purposes in Classical Latin and was not at all a grammatical device. In what follows, I discuss the relevant uses for each author.

In Cicero, there is both the adjectival type, e.g. (17a), and the verbal type, e.g. (17b). In the latter, the verb 'be' governs the dative of possession (*illi*) and the attributive predication of the participle (*madentes*). Note that the participle is coordinated with the predicative adjective *compti.*

(17a) *eorum autem alia rationis expertia* ***sunt*** *alia ratione* ***utentia.*** (Cic. off. 2, 11, 4)
'Of these again some are devoid of rationality, others are endowed with it.'

(17b) ***erant*** *illi compti capilli et* ***madentes*** *cincinnorum fimbriae et fluentes purpurissataeque buccae dignae Capua sed illa vetere.* (Cic. Pis. 25, 2)
'He at least had braided hair, a curled and well-oiled fringe, cheeks moist with unguent and bright with rouge, that were worthy of Capua – the Capua, I mean, of the bad old days.'

In addition to these, there are also constructions such as (18) that have been not yet analysed and therefore require further discussion:

(18) *sed videtis ut senectus non modo languida atque iners non sit verum etiam* ***sit*** *operosa et* ***semper agens aliquid et moliens.*** (Cic. Sen. 26)
'But you see how old age, so far from being feeble and inactive, is even busy and is always doing and effecting something.'

In this example, the participles *agens* and *moliens*, which govern the direct object in the accusative case *aliquid*, are coordinated with the adjective *operosa.*[7] The three forms, i.e. the participles and the adjective, function as semantic predicates of the

7 According to Eklund (1970), the government of direct objects in the accusative gives evidence for the verbal function of the participle, in addition to the "active" (and non-stative) meaning of the participial form.

copula *sit*. There is no syntactic difference among them, except for the government of the direct object in the accusative case, which is only possible for the participles. This clause is interesting as it shows that verbal participles could occur in the adjectival construction in Classical Latin. It also signifies a broadening of the adjectival construction to include true verbal participles.

Historians also use the combination *sum* + present participle. However, while Caesar only attests to the type in (19) (four times), other historians, e.g. Sallust and Curtius, explored the construction in a broader way, see examples (20)–(22) from Sallust.

(19) *nonnulli etiam Caesari nuntiabant, cum castra moveri ac signa ferri iussisset, non **fore dicto audientes** milites neque propter timorem signa laturos (esse).* (CAES. Gall. 1, 39, 7)
'Some even declared to Caesar, that when he gave orders for the camp to be moved and the troops to advance, the soldiers would not be obedient to the command, nor advance in consequence of their fear.'

(20) *his difficultatibus circumventus ubi videt neque per vim neque insidiis opprimi posse hominem tam acceptum popularibus, quod **erat** Iugurtha <u>manu promptus et</u> **adpetens** gloriae militaris, statuit eum obiectare periculis et eo modo fortunam temptare.* (SALL. Iug. 7, 1)
'Beset by these difficulties, and seeing that one so well liked by his countrymen could not be put out of the way by violence or by stratagem, he resolved, inasmuch as Jugurtha was quick to act and eager for military glory, to expose him to dangers and thus put fortune to the test.'

(21) *nam quae ad hoc tempus Iugurtham tutata sunt, omnia removistis, avaritiam, inperitiam atque superbiam. deinde exercitus ibi **est** locorum **sciens** sed mehercule magis strenuus quam felix.* (SALL. Iug. 85, 45)
'For you have taken away everything which up to this time has protected Jugurtha – greed, incompetence and arrogance. Next, our army in Africa is familiar with the country but, by Hercules, is more valiant than fortunate.' (Lit. 'Next, our army is there, familiar with the country')

(22) *ita amborum exercitu coniuncto, Marium iam in hiberna proficiscentem, vix decuma parte die reliqua, invadunt: rati noctem, quae iam aderat, victis sibi munimento fore et, si vicissent, nullo impedimento, quia locorum **scientes erant**.* (SALL. Iug. 97, 3)
'So, after the armies of both kings had been united, they attacked Marius while he was now departing for winter quarters, when scarcely a tenth part of the day was left. For they thought that the night, which was at hand, would

offer them protection in case of defeat and would be no hindrance, if they were victorious because they had knowledge of the locale.'

The three instances illustrate three different constructions. The first one in (20) is similar to (18) above, as the present participle is coordinated with an adjective in a typical adjectival construction. The difference between (20) and (18) lies in the fact that in the former the direct object governed by the participle appears in the genitive case, whereas in the latter it is in the accusative case. This discrepancy arises from the dual nature of the participle, encompassing both nominal and verbal characteristics.

The second example in (21) is a typical "verbal" construction, as the verb *sum* is here a existential-locative predicate, while the participle denotes the action performed by the subject of the clause. The adverb *ibi* is governed by *sum*, while the genitive *locorum* is governed by the participle *sciens*. The comparison of examples (21) and (22) shows that the lexical meaning of the participle is not relevant for the occurrence of one construction instead of another. In fact, the same participle *sciens*/*scientes* is the second predication of the sentence in (21), where the main predication is the existential-locative *sum*, while occurs in the copular or adjectival-like construction in (22).

Turning to poetry, in Lucretius, the occurrences of *sum* + present participle are mostly of the adjectival type, with the exception of the following two examples. In the first one in (23), the verbal participle *coercens* is coordinated with the adjective *dominantior* in a construction similar to (18) and (20) above. In the second one in (24), conversely, the participle *stans* depends on the copula *est* as an adjectival predication and is coordinated with the past participle *suffulta*.

(23) *et magis **est** animus vitai claustra **coercens** / et dominantior ad vitam quamvis animai.* (LVCR. 3, 396–397)
'And the mind is more potent in holding fast the barriers of life, and has more dominance over life, than the spirit's force.'

(24) *porticus aequali quamvis **est** denique ductu / **stans**que in perpetuum paribus suffulta columnis.* (LVCR. 4, 426–427)
'Again, a colonnade may be of equal line from end to end and supported by columns of equal height throughout.'

These two instances are interesting when compared to one another, as they show that adjectives and present participles, on the one hand, and present and past participles, on the other hand, appear to be equivalent in poetry when they function as the semantic predicate of the copula.

In Ovid only three occurrences are attested, all of the verbal type, see (25)–(27).

(25) *Sisyphus* **est** *illic saxum* **volvensque petensque** */ quique agitur rapidae vinctus ab orbe rotae.* (Ov. Ib. 175–176)
'Sisyphus is there, rolling his stone and seeking it again, and he who is whirled, fast bound, by the circle of the flying wheel.'

(26) *signum* **erat** *in solio* **residens** *sub imagine Tulli; / dicitur hoc oculis opposuisse manum, / et vox audita est "voltus abscondite nostros / ne natae videant ora nefanda meae".* (Ov. fast. 6, 613–616)
'There was a statue seated on a throne in the likeness of Tullius: it is said to have put its hand to its eyes and a voice was heard: "Hide my face, lest it should see the execrable visage of my own daughter".'

(27) *nox* **erat incipiens** *– namque est meminisse voluptas – / cum foribus patriis egrediebar amans.* (Ov. epist. 18, 55–56)
'Night was but just beginning – for the memory has charm for me – when I left my father's doors on the errand of love.'

The former two instances show typical presentative constructions: the verb *sum* functions as an existential-locative predicate introducing a new referent into the discourse, i.e. the subject of the clause, whereas the participle denotes the event/action that concerns the new referent.[8] This type of construction also occurs in Propertius, e.g. (28):

(28) **est** *Phoebi* **fugiens** *Athamana ad litora portus / qua sinus Ioniae murmura condit aquae.* (Prop. 4, 6, 15–16)
'There is a harbour of Phoebus which recedes to Athamanian shores, where a bay lulls the roar of the Ionian Sea.'

The analysis of *erat incipiens* in (27) is more difficult than *est fugiens* in (28) for several reasons. First, word order, as *sum* and the participle are contiguous in (27), thus pointing to the periphrastic analysis, and non-contiguous in (28). Second, the locative meaning of the clause in (28) with respect to the temporal reference of the clause in (27). In the most trivial interpretation, *erat incipiens* is one of the earliest instances of the progressive periphrasis, because the two verbs are contiguous and the verb *sum* is inflected in the imperfect tense, which usually correlates with background information (see discussion in Bortolussi et al. 2023: 296). However, it seems to me that the reading as a progressive periphrasis is neither consistent with the contemporary occurrences of the same construction, nor suitable for the

8 The adverb *illic* in (25) provides further evidence for the locative reading of *sum*.

elevated style of Ovid's passage. As English translation also highlights, it is better to analyse the passage as formed by two predications: (1) *nox erat* 'night was = there was night'; (2) (*nox erat*) *incipiens* 'the night was at the beginning'.

Summing up, in Classical Latin the combination *sum* + present participle occurs in two types of construction. First, the adjectival type, in which verbal participles increased in number besides to the adjectival ones. The frequency of cases in which verbal participles, also governing direct object in the accusative, co-occur with adjectival predicates in coordinated structures is evidence for the spread of the adjectival construction to include verbal participles. Besides this use, *sum* and the present participle occur as independent predicates in presentative constructions. In them, *sum* functions as an existential-locative predication that introduces the new referent into discourse, while the participle is the second predication, which predicates some action or event concerning the subject of the clause. Neither the copular type nor the presentative type have progressive meaning.

4.3 Imperial Latin

Among the five authors considered, namely Juvenal, Petronius, Pliny the Younger, Tacitus and Seneca, the latter is the one who employed the combination under scrutiny most frequently. In fact, out of 22 total instances, 15 occur in Seneca, 3 in Pliny, 2 in Tacitus, 1 in Juvenal and 1 in Petronius. The occurrences of *sum* + present participle in Seneca are all of the adjectival type; the participle is usually coordinated with an adjective, i.e. *pueriles* in (29) and *egregia* in (30) = (5).

(29) *pueriles* ***sunt*** *et* ***aliquid habentes liberalibus simile*** *hae artes quas* ἐγκυκλίοι *Graeci nostri autem liberales vocant.* (SEN. epist. 88, 23)
'The arts which belong to the education of boys and are somewhat similar to the liberal arts are those which the Greeks call the "cycle of studies" but which we Romans call the liberal.'

(30) *sed quamvis* ***egregia*** *illis vita* ***fuerit*** *et* ***carens fraude*** *non fuere sapientes quando hoc iam in opere maximo nomen est.* (SEN. epist. 90, 44)
'But no matter how excellent and guileless was the life of the men of that age, they were not wise men; for that title is reserved for the highest achievement.'

In the two following instances, conversely, the combination functions as a presentative construction:

(31) *sunt in fortunae qui casibus omnia ponant* [. . .] / ***est** alius **metuens** ne crimen poena sequatur. / hic putat esse deos et peierat, atque ita secum.* (Ivv. 13, 86, 90–91)
'There are people who attribute everything to accidents of fortune [. . .]. There is someone else who believes in the existence of the gods but still commits perjury, reasoning with himself like this.'

(32) *praevertor iam ad consulatum tuum etsi **sunt** quaedam ad consulatum quidem **pertinentia** ante consulatum tamen* (Plin. paneg. 63, 1)
'I pass now to your consulship, though there are certain events relating to it which did in fact precede it.'

In summary, there is no evidence for the occurrence of the progressive periphrasis formed by *sum* and the present participle in Imperial Latin. The combination is employed to convey two different types of structure. First, the copular construction, in which true verbal participles, also governing complements, replace adjectives and/or adjective-like participles. Second, the presentative construction: in this case, the verb *sum* always precedes the participle and denotes a existential-locative predication, to which the participial predication is added as a secondary predication.

5 Concluding Remarks

In this paper, I argued that *sum* and the present participle, though being very rare, are attested in Archaic and Classical Latin in constructions with "verbal" value. The combinations in which the present participle has a "verbal" value are of two different types. The first one is the result of the spread of the adjectival construction from "adjectival" participles to "verbal" participles. In this type, the present participle co-occurs with adjectival predicates in coordinated structures. The second type of verbal use of the participle is in syntactic constructions with double predication: in them, the verb *sum* either functions as the existential-locative predicate of a presentative construction or serves as the pivot of focalising constructions. In both cases, the participle functions as the second predicate of the complex construction, as it denotes the main action performed by the subject or the event concerning the subject. Alongside these constructions, *sum* combines with stative and adjective-like participles in copular predications in Archaic, Classical and Imperial Latin.

The results of this investigation clearly show that the analysis of *sum* + present participle as progressive periphrases does not hold. Conversely, I suggested analysing these combinations as conveying different types of structures, according to the syntactic and pragmatic features of the clauses in which the combination occurs. I have also shown that the distribution of *sum* + present participle in Latin authors depends on their own preferences and stylistic reasons. Although the occurrences are too sporadic to draw any conclusion, I noticed some preference for the presentative and focalising type in poetry and Archaic comedy, while philosophers and historians preferred using the copular-like construction.

Bibliography

Amenta, L. (2003). *Perifrasi aspettuali in greco e in latino. Origini e grammaticalizzazioni*. Milano: FrancoAngeli.

Barrett, L. C. (1909). Two notes on the Latin present participle. *Transactions and Proceedings of the American Philological Association*, *40*, 18–21.

Bentein, K. (2016). *Verbal Periphrasis in Ancient Greek : have- and be- constructions.* Oxford: Oxford University Press.

Bortolussi, B., Logozzo, F., Sznajder, L. & Tronci, L. (2023). Kontinuität und Innovation in der Partizipialsyntax der Vulgata. In R. Hoffmann (Ed.), *Lingua Vulgata: Eine linguistische Einführung in das Studium der lateinischen Bibelübersetzung* (pp. 259–328). Hamburg: Helmut Buske Verlag.

Coseriu, E. (1972). Das Problem des griechischen Einflusses auf das Vulgärlatein. In E. Coseriu & W. D. Stempel (Eds.), *Sprache und Geschichte. Festschrift für Harri Meier zum 65. Geburtstag* (pp. 135–147). München: Fink.

Dietrich, W. (1973). *Der periphrastische Verbalaspekt in den romanischen Sprachen*. Tübingen: Max Niemeyer Verlag.

Eklund, S. (1970). *The periphrastic, completive and finite use of the present participle in Latin, with special regard to translation of Christian texts in Greek up to 600 A.D.* Uppsala: Almqvist & Wiksells.

Ernout, A. & Thomas, F. (2002 [1953]). *Syntaxe Latine*. Paris: Klincksieck.

Haverling, G. (2010). Actionality, Tense and Viewpoint. In P. Cuzzolin & Ph. Baldi (Eds.), *New Perspectives on Historical Latin Syntax, vol. 2* (pp. 277–523). Berlin/New York: Mouton de Gruyter.

Hofmann, J.-B. & Szantyr, A. (1965). *Lateinische Grammatik. II. Lateinische Syntax und Stilistik*. München: C. H. Beck.

Jülicher, A., Matzkow, W. & Aland, K. (1963–1976). *Itala. Das Neue Testament in altlateinischer Überlieferung*. Berlin: De Gruyter.

Löfstedt, E. (1911). *Philologischer Kommentar zur* Peregrinatio Aetheriae. Uppsala: Almqvist & Wiksells.

Logozzo, F. & Tronci, L. (2020). Les constructions à verbe εἶναι 'être' et participe présent: *status quaestionis* et nouvelles propositions. *Bulletin de la Société de Linguistique de Paris*, *115*, 191–239.

Logozzo, F. & Tronci, L. (2021). Le costruzioni latine con *esse* + participio presente: perifrasi progressive o altro? *Linguarum Varietas*, *10*, 55–77.

Lyer, S. (1930). Le participe présent avec *esse*. *Revue des Études Latines*, *8*, 241–249.

Marouzeau, J. (1910). *L'emploi du participe présent latin à l'époque républicaine*. Paris: Champion.

Piras, A. (1989–1990). Criteri e limiti di accertabilità della perifrasi con *sum* e il participio presente: dalle origini a Lucifero di Cagliari. *Sandalion*, *12/13*, 63–97.

Pinkster, H. (2015). *The Oxford Latin Syntax. Volume 1: The Simple Clause.* Oxford: Oxford University Press.

Plater, W. E. & White, H. J. (1926). *A Grammar of the Vulgate*. Oxford: Clarendon Press.

Tronci, L. (forthcoming). Preliminari per uno studio delle costruzioni latine con *esse* + participio presente. *Linguarum Varietas*.

Anna Orlandini and Paolo Poccetti

L’évolution de la négation entre double négation (DN) et concordance négative (NC) dans les langues anciennes et modernes

Abstract: This paper investigates the evolutionary path from Classical Latin, a compositional language, featured by a Double Negation (DN) structure, towards the Romance languages, featured by Negative Concordance (NC), a non-compositional structure, combining a multiplicity of negatives with a negative meaning. The key point of such an evolution is the positive value acquired by the “N-words”, developed by the Romance languages. The core change concerns the system of the indefinite pronouns, shifting from the quantitative value, typical of Classical Latin, to a qualitative one, close to the “free choice” indefinites, in the Romance languages. Moreover, unlike Classical Latin, where the negative force of both negative particle *non* and indefinite pronouns remains unchanged in any semantic and syntactic function, the Romance languages balance their respective negative force, depending on the semantic role of the indefinite items. The negative force of a negative particle increases when an indefinite pronoun plays a semantic role other than the clause subject. Synchronically, social variations and informal registers of Latin as well as adjacent languages (such as Oscan) evidence for NC structures, that are consolidated by the Romance languages in their diachronic evolution.

Keywords: “N-words”, balance of negative force, semantic roles

1 La double négation (DN) et la concordance négative (NC)

Il existe un bilinguisme interne à chaque langue entre une langue logique, véridictoire, compositionnelle, et une langue a-compositionnelle, en évolution continue. La norme,[1] issue de la fréquence d’emploi, permet de classer un phénomène comme non-marqué ou marqué en diachronie. Toutefois, en synchronie, deux phénomènes

1 Cf. Coseriu (1971).

Anna Orlandini, Centre A. Ernout, Paris, France
Paolo Poccetti, Université de Rome 2, Italy

https://doi.org/10.1515/9783111332956-026

(marqué et non marqué) peuvent exister à l'intérieur d'une seule langue, même si avec une fréquence inversée. Ce que nous essaierons de montrer pour la double négation (logique, compositionnelle, non-marquée en latin classique et vice versa exceptionnelle et marquée en latin archaïque et tardif) et la concordance négative (non logique, a-compositionnelle, non marquée en latin archaïque et tardif, et marquée en latin classique).

La NC est en contraste avec le « principe de compositionalité », qui pose que l'interprétation sémantique d'une proposition est le résultat de la somme des sens de ses composants ; ce qui est, en revanche le cas de la double négation (DN). Ce principe n'est pas respecté dans la NC, parce que, dans cette structure, qui cumule plusieurs éléments morphologiquement négatifs, un seul exprime la négation. Par ailleurs, la a-compositionalité est plus naturelle et fréquente dans les langues du monde, si bien qu'elle est connue même en ancien indien.[2]

Le latin classique est, en revanche, une langue compositionnelle à double négation (DN), c'est-à-dire que la présence de deux « items » négatifs fait ainsi qu'ils effacent réciproquement leur charge négative, engendrant une interprétation positive pour les éléments quantifiés. Le latin est une langue de type V-NI (verbe non nié – pronom indéfini négatif à négation incorporée, ex., *venit nemo*), alors que la plupart des langues romanes sont de type NV-NI (négation verbale et pronom indéfini négatif). En latin classique, *nemo, nullus, nihil, numquam, nusquam*, etc., sont des quantifieurs négatifs à part entière, ils engendrent à eux seuls une négation propositionnelle, selon les forces illocutoires de base déclarative, jussive, interrogative :

(1a) *Nemo venit* 'personne n'est venu' décl. : $\sim(\exists x)\ p$ « Ce n'est pas vrai qu'il existe un *x* tel que *p* »
(1b) *Nemo audeat* 'que personne n'ose' juss. : $!\ \sim(\exists x)\ p$ « Qu'il ne soit pas vrai qu'il existe un *x* tel que *p* »
(1c) *Nemo venit ?* 'personne n'est venu ?' interr. : $?\ \sim(\exists x)\ p$ « Est-il vrai qu'il n'existe pas un *x* tel que *p* ».

Selon le grammairien Diomède : ***modus soloecismi*** *fit per geminationem abnuendi, ut si dicas* ***numquam nihil peccavi*** *cum debeat dici* ***numquam peccavi****, quoniam* ***duae abnutivae unam confirmativam faciunt*** (gramm. I 455, 11–13). La règle de la double négation qui engendre une assertion positive semble ainsi être une norme du latin littéraire d'époque classique plutôt qu'un emploi naturel du langage, qui peut présenter deux négations ou plusieurs négations qui ne s'effa-

2 Cf. Viti (2011).

cent pas réciproquement selon la NC, par exemple, dans des textes du registre de la conversation, en latin archaïque, dans les dialogues de Plaute et de Térence, ou en latin tardif, par exemple, dans la langue de Pétrone. De son côté, la DN est toujours binaire, elle opère sur couples d'*items* pleinement négatifs qui interagissent entre eux ; il peut s'agir de la négation propositionnelle et du pronom indéfini négatif, mais aussi de deux pronoms indéfinis négatifs. Selon Ö. Dahl (2010 : 14) la DN est une structure symétrique parce que nous traitons avec deux termes également négatifs, alors que la concordance négative (NC) relève d'une construction asymétrique parce que seulement un terme est un marqueur négatif et l'autre est *quelque chose d'autre* : « traiting one of them (= negative markers) as a negative marker and the other *as something else* ».

Alors que la DN est binaire et opère entre éléments quantifiés pleinement négatifs et donc sémantiquement symétriques, la NC présente une structure ouverte à plusieurs items négatifs, donc sémantiquement asymétrique, à différents degrés de force quantificationnelle et de force négative, en relation avec le rôle sémantique des « N-mots » dans la proposition.

Il n'existe pas dans les grammaires latines les plus connues qui se sont occupées de la négation, un travail enquêtant sur les facettes multiples du développement diachronique des quantifieurs négatifs du type « anti-additif »,[3] tels que *nemo, nullus, nihil, numquam, nusquam, etc.*, en relation stricte avec l'emploi de la négation propositionnelle *non* dans une structure à concordance négative (NC), c'est-à-dire une structure où les éléments négatifs peuvent se cumuler, mais un seul est opérationnel, il engendre le sens négatif pour la proposition.

DN et NC ne disparaissent pas totalement d'une langue au cours de son évolution : elles y sont toutes les deux présentes, mais avec des fréquences inversées. La structure non marquée est celle qui est la plus fréquente dans une certaine période dans l'histoire d'une langue. Nous analyserons, dans ce qui suit, des contextes où une forme, presque disparue à un état de la langue, peut re-apparaître comme marquée et contrastive (c'est le cas de la DN en latin tardif et dans les langues romanes, cf. 4.1), ou bien une forme qui commence à s'imposer (la NC) peut apparaître au début de son parcours évolutif (c'est le cas d'un contexte osque, cf. 4.2).

---

3 La fonction de « anti-additif » (qui signifie qu'on n'y peut ajouter rien d'autre) employée par de Swart and Sag (2002 : 385) exclut les expressions signalant une petite quantité qui ne renvoient pas à un ensemble, telles que *peu, rarement*, etc. Selon de Swart and Sag (2002 : 385), « negative concord can then be analysed as resumption of a sequence of anti-additive quantifiers ».

2 La NC (« Negative Concord ») et la EN (« Expletive Negation ») entre renforcement et affaiblissement : outre le cycle de Jespersen

Selon le cycle de Jespersen, les négations se renforcent et s'affaiblissent dans le temps.[4] En français, *pas* participe activement de ce cycle. D'abord il entre comme « minimiser » pour renforcer une « négation plate »,[5] non emphatique, telle que *ne* préverbale, ensuite, par affaiblissement, *pas* perd sa valeur emphatique et se grammaticalise dans la négation disjoncte *ne... pas*, qui devient à son tour une négation plate. Ensuite, *pas* se renforce pour devenir une négation unique postverbale.

Partout, l'évolution diachronique plonge ses racines dans la synchronie. En effet, la fonction emphatique qui donne lieu au renforcement de la négation « plate » est un fait pragmatique du discours. Mais aussi l'affaiblissement s'inscrit dans la pratique discursive, parce que l'emploi fréquent d'un mot, et à plus forte raison, d'un outil grammatical, est la cause de son usure, comme l'avait déjà observé A. Meillet : « La première et plus importante de ces causes consiste dans le besoin qu'éprouve le sujet parlant d'être expressif, de bien faire sentir sa pensée, et d'agir sur son interlocuteur. Le fréquent emploi d'un mot, par le fait qu'il imprime dans la mémoire et en rend l'usage, pour ainsi dire, automatique, lui enlève toute valeur expressive. »[6]

À la différence de O. Jespersen, qui avait privilégié l'érosion phonétique des particules à l'origine de son cycle, à bon droit A. Meillet a souligné les raisons pragmatiques et discursives, qui ont été, plus récemment, mises en valeur par P. Kiparsky et C. Condoravdi.[7] Sous ce dénominateur commun, chaque langue suit des parcours différents.

---

4 Comme le dit Jespersen (1992 : 479) : « On obtient ainsi une perpétuelle oscillation entre l'affaiblissement et le renforcement de la négation à laquelle s'ajoute la tendance à placer la négation au début de la phrase, si bien qu'il lui arrive souvent de disparaître par prosiopèse ». Mais aussi Meillet (1948 : 139–140) : « Les langues suivent ainsi une sorte de développement en spirale : elles ajoutent des mots accessoires pour obtenir une expression intense : ces mots s'affaiblissent, se dégradent et tombent au niveau de simples outils grammaticaux ; on ajoute de nouveaux mots ou des mots différents en vue de l'expression ; l'affaiblissement recommence ainsi sans fin ».

5 Pour la distinction entre « négation plate » et « négation emphatique » , cf. Kiparsky and Condoravdi (2006).

6 Meillet (1948 : 163).

7 Kiparsky and Condoravdi (2006).

3 Évolutions des structures de DN à NC en grec

L'histoire du grec permet de saisir le parcours de l'évolution des structures de la négation suivant plusieurs étapes, marquées synchroniquement par la fonction emphatique qui met en œuvre les procédés du changement. L'origine suggérée de la particule de négation assertive, déjà connue du grec mycénien, οὐ(κ), rapproché de l'arménien *oč'*, remonte à l'expression *$*h_2iou$ (k^wid)* littéralement : « dans n'importe quel temps », en tant que renforcement de la simple négation de l'indo-européen **nē/ĕ*.[8] La grammaticalisation de cette particule qui aurait remplacé, avec une valeur négative pleine, l'opérateur de négation hérité, se serait, donc, accomplie avant les témoignages du grec mycénien au IIème millénaire avant notre ère.

L'évolution de la négation en grec se déploie sur trois niveaux : le grec homérique, caractérisé par une structure à DN, le grec classique, qui a une structure à NC non stricte, le grec moderne, qui a une structure à NC stricte. Un point clé du passage de la langue d'Homère à celle classique c'est la réorganisation du système des indéfinis et, notamment, le remplacement de οὔ τι / οὔ τις par οὐδέν / οὐδείς. Chez Homère, οὐδέν / οὐδείς ne sont employés qu'avec des fonctions emphatiques,[9] aboutissant, en grec classique, au rôle des « N-mots ». Ces pronoms tantôt gardent leur force quantificationnelle négative pleine (comme les indéfinis négatifs du latin classique), sans besoin d'autre négation :

(2) ἐπεὶ καὶ ὁ κακῶς πράσσων πρὸς **οὐδένα** τῆς ξυμφορᾶς ἰσομοιρεῖ (Thuc. 6, 16, 4) 'puisque aussi bien celui qui ne réussit pas ne rencontre personne pour partager sa disgrâce' ,

tantôt, ils glissent vers la fonction de TPN. C'est ainsi que la NC s'impose, permettant le cumul d'éléments négatifs :

(3a) βροτῶν δὲ τῶν ταλαιπώρων λόγον **οὐκ** ἔσχεν **οὐδέν**' (Aesch. *Prom.* 232) 'il ne tint nul compte des infortunés mortels'

et la naissance de la EN :

(3b) ὠμὸν τὸ βούλευμα καὶ μέγα ἐγνῶσθαι πόλιν ὅλην διαφθεῖραι **μᾶλλον ἢ οὐ** τοὺς αἰτίους (Thuc. 3, 36, 6) 'reconnaître que la résolution prise était cruelle et grave, d'anéantir une cité entière au lieu des seuls responsables'.

---

8 Beekes (2010 : 1123), s.v. οὐ.

9 À ce propos, Denizot (2014 : 82–85) distingue deux types d'emphases, notamment une « forme renforcée de la négation propositionnelle (*en rien*) et les formes non adverbiales de la négation focalisante οὐδέ », incorporée dans οὐδείς avec le sens de « pas même un ».

En grec moderne, la structure à NC stricte s'impose : la négation δεν, issue de l'ancien pronom οὐδέν 'rien', est répétée indépendamment de toute position syntaxique du « N-mot », par ex., :

(4) Κανένας δέν ἦρθε 'personne n'est venu'.

Le grec classique semble beaucoup plus libre que les langues romanes en ce qui concerne l'ordre syntaxique des éléments négatifs dans la phrase. Comme l'a montré C. Denizot,[10] la règle acceptée par les grammaires,[11] selon laquelle un « N-mot » suivi par la particule de négation positivise la phrase n'a aucun fondement. En effet, la tournure la plus commune οὐδεὶς ὅστις οὐ, ayant un sens positif, repose sur deux phrases distinctes par un pronom relatif, par ex., :

(5) καὶ **οὐδενὶ** ὅτῳ **οὐκ** ἀποκρινόμενος (Plat. *Men.* 70c) 'il n'en est aucun auquel il ne réponde sur quelque sujet que ce soit'.

À la différence du latin, le grec classique admet la combinaison de la négation assertive οὐκ et de celle subjective μή, qui se retrouve dans des contextes emphatiques, par ex., :

(6) Ἀλλ' εἴσιθ'· **οὐ** σοι **μὴ** μεθέψομαί ποτε (Soph. *El.* 1052) 'Eh bien, rentre. Il est certain que je ne te suivrai pas'.

L'on trouve aussi le cumul de négation dans les subordonnées introduites par les *verba timendi* et *cavendi* :

(7) **Δέδοικα**, ἔφη, ὦ Σώκρατες, **μὴ οὐκ** ἔχω ἐγὼ τοσαύτην σοφίαν ὥστε Χαιρεφῶντα ποιῆσαι πρὸς ἐμὲ οἷον δεῖ (Xen. *Mem.* 2, 3, 10) 'Je crains, Socrate, dit-il, de ne pas avoir assez de sagesse pour rendre Chéréphon tel qu'il doit être envers moi'.

4 Le statut quantificationnel des « N-mots »

Selon les calculs de la typologie,[12] les langues de type V-NI (comme le latin classique) sont très peu nombreuses et développées dans des zones contiguës. En revanche, le

---

10 Denizot (2012).
11 Cette règle est reçue aussi par Van Emde Boas et al. (2019 : 648).
12 Cf. Haspelmath (1997) et aussi Bernini and Ramat (1992 : 205).

nombre de langues à structure NV-NI est beaucoup plus élevé. La négation cumulative ou concordance négative (NC) se généralise, en perdant sa nuance emphatique, dans les langues romanes : l'italien, l'espagnol et l'ancien français :

(8a) *Non viene nessuno* (it.) – *No viene nadie* (esp.) 'personne ne vient'[13]
(8b) *Non dice niente* (it.) 'Il ne dit rien'.

Dans cette structure, la première négation, la négation préverbale (italien *non*, espagnol *no*) s'affaiblie, elle fonctionne simplement comme marqueur de la portée de la négation sur toute la proposition, engendrée par le quantifieur négatif post-verbal. Le cumul de négations est, dans tous ces cas, une redondance afin que la valeur négative soit immédiatement comprise. Cela répond au « Negative First Principle » de O. Jespersen, réformulé par L. Horn (1989 : 293), qui pose : « There is a tendency to put the negative element as early as possible in an utterance because the contribution of the negation to the meaning of a larger constituent is particularly dramatic and the hearer needs to get this information as soon as possible ».

Ces énoncés ne présentent qu'un seul opérateur NEG au niveau de la représentation sémantique. Il peut être engendrée par la négation préverbale ou par le quantifieur négatif, selon le rôle sémantique de ce dernier. Par ex., en italien *nessuno* dans le rôle du sujet et en position préverbale ne nécessite pas une négation pour l'introduire, il est « self-licensing ». En effet, en italien, les énoncés, où le terme à négation incorporée est préverbal, ne nécessitent pas une deuxième négation :

(9a) *Nessuno viene* 'Personne ne vient'
(9b) *Nessun dorma* 'Que personne ne dorme'
(9c) *Niente lo spaventa* 'Rien ne lui fait peur'

ou avec anticipation du CoD :

(9d) *Nessuno vidi* 'Je n'ai vu personne'.

Ce dernier emploi est plus fréquent dans l'italien central ou du Sud, en sarde et en portugais, mais il est perçu comme incorrect en Italie du Nord et aussi en Toscane.

---

13 Signalons toutefois qu'en milanaise d'aujourd'hui, à la différence de l'italien, les quantifieurs négatifs apparaissent seuls, en position post-verbale, sans besoin d'une négation préverbale, par exemple, *l'a mangià nisün*, it. 'non ha mangiato nessuno', où *nisün* est le sujet de phrase (cf. Vai 1996 : 88). On peut dire ainsi que l'indéfini négatif en fonction de subjet est ici « self-licensing », même s'il est post-verbal.

Il existe aussi un troisième type de structure (N)V-NI ; il s'agit de langues dans lesquelles le pronom-adjectif indéfini négatif peut ou non apparaître en cooccurrence avec la négation verbale : l'italien, l'espagnol, le portugais, le catalan colloquial, le vieux slave, l'albanais, le grec du Nouveau Testament, l'anglais non-standard, l'allemand non-standard, le géorgien. Ces langues admettent la variation exemplifiée par l'italien et sont dites « langues à concordance négative non stricte » :

(10a) *Nessuno è venuto.*
(10b) *Non è venuto nessuno.*

La présence de la négation préverbale est en relation au fait que le terme à négation incorporée soit en position préverbale ou non. Mais ce qui à notre avis est fondamental, c'est que dans les deux cas la représentation sémantique est la même : ~(∃x) *p*, c'est à dire : « Il n'est pas vrai qu'il existe un *x* tel que *p* (=venir) », qui est la représentation sémantique du pronom négatif dans le rôle thématique du sujet de phrase. Ce qui prouve que la négation préverbale n'est pas toujours un véritable opérateur de négation dans de telles structures, elle commence déjà à subir un affaiblissement.

Certains pronoms indéfinis peuvent ne pas s'affaiblir et d'autres, morphologiquement identiques, peuvent être interprétés comme des TPN ou des « free choice » (de la classe de *any*). Certains linguistes appellent ces indéfinis morphologiquement négatifs « N-words »,[14] en français les « N-mots ».

Le problème du statut quantificationnel des « N-mots » est vraiment crucial dans l'interprétation des structures de concordance négative. Notre hypothèse est celle d'une évolution diachronique à partir de l'emploi comme quantifieurs pleinement négatifs réalisant la DN, en latin classique, à un emploi qualitatif comme quantifieurs indéfinis génériques (ou « free choice ») ou quantitatif comme « Minimiseurs » ou comme « Termes à polarité Négative » (TPN) réalisant la NC. Rappelons que, selon W. Meyer-Lübke (1890–1906 : 778), la négation cumulative serait à l'origine des emplois « positifs » des « semi-négations » (les « N-mots ») des langues romanes. Voici la vraie clé interprétative du phénomène de la NC : les emplois « positifs » des indéfinis qui, dans la négation cumulative, gardent encore une morphologie négative mais qui ont affaibli leur sémantisme négatif.[15]

Dans une perspective plus fonctionnelle que sémantique, plusieurs savants qui se sont occupés de NC ont fait l'hypothèse que la fonction focalisante soit à l'origine

---

14 Cf. Laka (1990).

15 Cela correspond à l'idée de Giannakidou (2000 : 90) : « Of course, the extent to which NC constitutes a problem for compositionality depends on whether we taken *n*-words to be semantically negative or not ».

d'une telle structure.[16] C'est une hypothèse fonctionnellement tout à fait plausible, mais elle ne nous donne pas l'explication sémantique du procès évolutif. Celui-ci prend en compte principalement la « positivisation » des indéfinis, comme le suggère W. Meyer-Lübke, ainsi que le jeu alterné de l'affaiblissement de la négation propositionnelle *non* et du « N-mot », en relation avec son rôle argumental.

En latin tardif, l'affaiblissement ne concerne pas le pronom indéfini ayant « le rôle thématique du sujet de phrase » (grammatical ou logique), qui garde ses propriétés quantificationnelles ainsi que son sémantisme négatif en position préverbale et aussi postverbale.[17] L'anticipation du CdO en position préverbale (italien *Nessuno vidi*) est rare et zonale. Tout autre pronom indéfini, même s'il garde la morphologie négative, doit être interprété comme un TPN ou un « free choice », selon les contextes :

(11) italien *Non l'ho detto a nessuno* (français *Je ne l'ai dit à personne = à qui que ce soit*).

D'une manière surprenante, la possibilité pour un indéfini négatif de garder intactes les propriétés quantificationnelles et le sémantisme négatif ou, en revanche, de s'affaiblir, semble pouvoir être indiquée par l'échelle hiérarchique d'accessibilité à la relativisation pour un SN, formulée par E. Keenan et B. Comrie (1977 : 96) selon la Figure 1:

SU > DO > IO > OBL > GEN > OCOMP
où > signifie « plus accessible que ».

Figure 1: Accessibility Hierarchy (AH).

À notre avis, l'accessibilité à la relativisation et le rôle sémantique du sujet sont intimement liés. Mais cela assure seulement que le pronom demeure négatif et quantifie existentiellement dans le rôle de sujet. L'accessibilité à la relativisation, maximale dans le rôle du sujet, assure seulement que le pronom négatif est tel à part entière. Un pronom morphologiquement négatif, dans d'autres rôles sémantiques moins accessibles à la relativisation, aura une charge sémantique plus faible.

L'échelle de E. Keenan et B. Comrie (1977) nous prédit qu'au pôle à droite il est possible d'avoir seulement un TPN ou un « free choice » (lat. *quisquam*, angl. *anybody*, osc. *pis*), alors qu'au pôle à gauche le seul admis est le quantifieur négatif (latin *nemo*, *nullus*, *nihil*, *numquam*, etc., osque *neipis*, italien *nessuno*, français *personne*,

16 Cf. Viti (2011), Giannollo (2018).

17 Ainsi déjà Horn (2020 : 11) : « quantifier negation in subject position functions as 'more negative' than that in non- subject position ».

espagnol *nadie*, angl. *nobody*). Au fur et à mesure qu'on se déplace vers la droite, le quantifieur négatif s'affaiblit et la négation propositionnelle se renforce. Il faut donc postuler un basculement réciproque entre la force négative de la négation de phrase et le pronom négatif. La force négative de la négation de phrase, en cas de concordance négative, est moindre en présence d'un pronom négatif sujet, mais elle est la plus grande en présence d'un TPN. Ainsi dans un énoncé tel que : ex. (11) italien *Non l'ho detto a nessuno* (français *Je ne l'ai dit à personne = à qui que ce soit*), le pronom négatif dans le rôle IO (italien *a nessuno*, français *à personne*) est interprétable comme un TPN (italien *ad alcuno*, français *à aucun*) ou comme un « free choice » (italien *a chicchessia*, français *à qui que ce soit*).

La série des indéfinis en *any*, tout comme les TPN du latin (par ex., *quisquam*, *ullus*) ne sont pas quantifiés de manière existentielle (∃x), ils sont des *variables sur un ensemble* : *x*, *y*, *z*, etc.[18] Pensons, par ex., à un énoncé ambigu tel que :

(12) *Je n'ai pas compris* ***un mot*** / it. *non ho capito* ***una parola***

Si « un mot », « una parola » est quantifié existentiellement, il a une portée plus étendue que la négation et l'énoncé signifie qu'il y a un mot précis que je n'ai pas compris. Mais si « un mot » est un TPN, il renvoie à une quantité minimale (« pas un seul mot », « non una sola parola »), il sert à renforcer la négation, tout comme un adverbe (*du tout*, italien *minimamente*), et il ne peut pas être quantifié existentiellement, mais seulement être représenté par une variable libre (« un mot, n'importe lequel, una parola qualsiasi »).

On pourra rapprocher « l'échelle d'accessibilité » de E. Keenan and B. Comrie (1977) de « la hierarchy of negative items » de T. Espinal (2007 : 55) selon la Figure 2:

NQ / Minimizers > N-words > PI

Figure 2: Hierarchy of negative items.

qui représente une variation décroissante de force négative et quantificationnelle selon un cycle négatif. Les vrais quantifieurs négatifs (tous les pronoms à négation incorporée du latin classique) ont une force quantificationnelle plus grande que les

18 Dans l'approche aux « N-mots », les positions des linguistes sont fort disparates. Selon Giannakidou (2000 et 2006), il s'agit de quantifieurs universels non-négatifs, alors que pour Zanuttini (1991) de Swart and Sag (2002), de Swart (2010) ils sont des vrais quantifieurs négatifs, interprétés comme ~(∃x) ; selon d'autres encore, par ex., Herburger (2002) ils sont ambigus entre la valeur pleinement négative et celle de « items » à polarité non-négative. Nous partageons l'avis de cet auteur, en essayant d'expliquer quand et pourquoi ils gardent la valeur pleinement négative, et, en revanche, dans quels rôles sémantiques ils subissent un affaiblissement.

« N-words » (les pronoms négatifs non sujets du latin tardif et des langues romanes) qui ont une force quantificationnelle variable et moindre et enfin les PI (« items » à polarité) qui sont des simples « variables sans force quantificationnelle ».

5 Cas marqués

5.1 Un exemple marqué de DN en latin tardif

La double négation (DN), non marquée en latin classique, devient plus rare, marquée et contrastive dans les langues romanes, alors qu'elle est la structure privilégiée de l'allemand, de l'anglais, du néerlandais. Le latin tardif évolue vers la structure à concordance négative (NC). Toutefois, la lecture selon la DN pourrait aussi redevenir possible comme forme marquée. Il peut s'agir de textes hyper-correctifs, souhaitant imiter le latin classique, tels que, par ex., l'épigramme suivant, en hexamètres :

(13) *Mortale cum sis, genio bene fac ; quod erit cras, / quaerere ne cures, fors*[19] *est incerta futura. / **Nil** tamen **haud** spera : varia vice cuncta feruntur, / cedunt laeta malis, cedunt mala tempora laetis* (EPIGR. Bob. 42,1–4) 'Comme tu es mortel, profite de ta vie ; ne te fais trop de soucis pour l'avenir. Ce qui viendra est incertain. Toutefois, ne perds pas tout espoir : tout est dominé par l'alternance. Les bons temps laissent la place aux mauvais, mais les mauvais temps eux aussi s'effacent aux profit des bons.'

Il s'agit d'un texte très construit, voire artificieux, comme le prouve, au vers 3, l'emploi de *haud* avec un impératif (*haud spera*), d'autant plus que *haud*, qui normalement nie un SN, est en voie de disparition en latin tardif. Cet énoncé peut recevoir deux lectures. Une lecture mono-négative selon la NC : « Toutefois, tu ne dois nourrir aucun espoir », mais l'on comprendrait mal l'adversatif *tamen* dans l'enchaînement argumentatif du texte. Il est dit que l'avenir est incertain (*fors est incerta futura*), mais l'on conclut par un message plus rassurant, confié à l'asyndète adversatif du dernier vers : « les bons temps laissent la place aux mauvais, mais les

19 La voix *fors* appartient aux codes, *Bob. Munari*, alors que *sors*, conjecture de Speyer 1963 *ad loc.*, semble une *lectio facilior*. Suivant Nocchi (2016 : 266), selon qui *fors* est « la *fors* imprevedibile », nous gardons la lecture des codes. Par ailleurs, le *ThlL* 6, 1, 1127, 83 rapproche *fors* de *fortuna*, comme nous l'avons fait dans le cas de *mala fortuna* (SEN. epist. 13, 11) quant à l'inconstance, la volatilité du mauvais *sors*.

mauvais temps eux aussi s'effacent au profit des bons ». Il faudra donc envisager une lecture selon la DN, dans l'esprit d'une reconstruction classique.

Le *topos* de la non-inéluctabilité du mauvais sort est bien connu :

(14) *Habet etiam mala fortuna levitatem. Fortasse erit, fortasse non erit* (SEN. epist. 13, 11) 'Le mauvais sort aussi est inconstant. Il peut se réaliser, il peut ne pas se réaliser.'

Et la suite de ce passage : *interim non est. Meliora propone* ('pour l'instant, il n'est pas là. Envisage donc des éventualités meilleures') explique que les conclusions (« soyons donc optimistes ! ») doivent être tirées de la *probabilité* que *non p* : *mala fortuna fortasse non erit*.

Il existe aussi d'autres textes classiques auxquels l'épigramme renvoie par *memoria docta*. Il s'agit du premier livre des Odes d'Horace, notamment carm. 1, 9 et 1,11. Le renvoi mot à mot des termes *cras* et *quaerere* ainsi que les structures de l'interrogative indirecte et de l'impératif de sens négatif (*fuge*), nous dévoile tout de suite la source :

(15) *Quid sit futurum* ***cras****, fuge* ***quaerere*** (HOR. carm. 1, 9, 13) 'De quoi demain sera fait, évite de chercher à savoir'.

À laquelle renvoie ouvertement la proposition : *quod erit cras, quaerere ne cures.* Or la traduction de *Nil tamen haud spera* selon la DN, qui positivise et engendre une litote avec l'encouragement à « ne pas perdre tout espoir », fait pendant aux suggestions qu'Horace donne à Leuconoe (carm. 1, 11) lorsque, face à l'incertitude de l'avenir (v. 4 : *Seu pluris hiemes seu tribuit Iuppiter ultimam* 'que Jupiter nous accorde encore bien d'autres hivers ou que notre dernier soit celui-ci'), il encourage la jeune fille naïve à cultiver un espoir modéré, mesuré (vv. 6–7 : *spatio brevi / spem longam reseces* 'tu feras mieux de réduire tes lointaines espérances à la mesure de notre courte durée'), un espoir de courte haleine, sans trop d'illusions (v. 8 : *quam minimum credula postero* 'sans trop te fier au lendemain').

La lecture selon la DN, grâce à la litote (qui est souvent réalisée par *haud* et un autre élément négatif),[20] permet d'envisager un espace moyen entre espoir et désespoir, mais où, malgré tout, il y a encore place pour un peu d' espoir, si petit soit-il ; ce qui nous semble cohérent avec l'esprit du texte de l'épigramme entier.[21]

20 Cf. Magni et al. (2017).

21 Pour une analyse exhaustive des *topoi* philosophico-funéraires liés au thème symposiaque qui sont à la source de cette épigramme, cf. Nocchi (2016 : 264–267).

5.2 L'osque entre évolution et conservation

Parfois une innovation peut apparaître comme marquée à cause de sa fréquence relativement rare. Une preuve d'un tel procès évolutif semblerait fournie par l'osque. Dans cette langue, l'on ne connaît pas de pronoms négatifs à négation incorporée (lat. *nihil, nemo*), mais seulement l'association NEG + pronom à polarité négative (par ex., *nipis*), ayant le même fonctionnement sémantique que les NI (fonctionnant donc comme *nemo*, quantifieur négatif en latin classique). Or, cette langue est balancée entre l'ouverture vers la nouveauté (la concordance négative) et la conservation (la présence de TPN, morphologiquement non-négatif tel que *pis*, cf. lat. *quisquam)* :

(16a) ***Ni** tagat **nipis pedi** suam* (Rix ST MV 1) 'que **personne ne** touche **rien (quoi que ce soit)**'

Il s'agit d'un contexte évidemment marqué par l'emphase, parce que normalement, dans cette langue, les interdictions ne présentent qu'une seule négation. Ainsi dans la loi de Bantia :

(16b) ***ne phim** pruhipid mais zicolois X nesimois* (T. B. 26) 'il n'aura pas le droit d'exercer le pouvoir d'interdiction à qui que ce soit durant les dix jours suivants'.

Dans le texte osque (16a), la négation initiale *ni* se répète dans *nipis* engendrant une structure qui s'éloigne du latin classique : ***Ne** tangat **ne quis quidquam***. Le redoublement de la négation *anticipe* le résultat roman : « Que **personne ne** touche **rien (= quoi que ce soit)** ».

La négation préverbale (***ni** tagat*) se cumule avec l'autre, et s'affaiblissant, ne permet pas de réaliser une affirmation. En présence d'un pronom négatif dans le rôle du sujet, la première négation (*ni*) n'a pas de véritable force négative, véhiculée par le seul pronom négatif (*nipis*) dans le rôle du sujet. La langue a eu la nécessité de réaliser d'abord la négation préverbale, le plus tôt possible à gauche du verbe,[22] ce qui a ensuite engendré le cumul.

22 Selon le « Negative First Principle » de Jespersen, reformulé par Horn (1989 : 293), qui pose : « There is a tendency to put the negative element as early as possible in an utterance because the contribution of the negation to the meaning of a larger constituent is particularly dramatic and the hearer needs to get this information as soon as possible ».

L'exemple de NC dans le bronze de Rapino relève d'une formule emphatique, du style familier, comme chez Cicéron en latin classique. Cet exemple de l'osque confirme :

a) que l'indéfini (*nipis*) dans le rôle du sujet demeure un quantifieur négatif et fonctionne comme *nemo* dans le même rôle ;
b) que l'indéfini dans le rôle de l'objet (*pidi*) n'est pas en soi négatif, mais il peut entrer dans une structure à NC, légitimé par la négation qui le précède.

De la même manière qu'avec d'autres phénomènes évolutifs, les langues sabelliques, et notamment l'osque, semblent, une fois de plus, anticiper les développements romans ; dans ce cas, l'évolution vers la structure NV-NI, mais la langue peut aussi garder une certaine conservation : le deuxième élément pronominal *pedi* n'est pas un « N-mot », comme il arrive en latin tardif et dans les langues romanes, mais il est encore un véritable TPN, tout comme *quidquam* en latin classique ou *anything* en anglais.

5.3 Structures à DN marquée en français

En français, langue à concordance négative (NC), *pas* garde intacte sa charge négative et entre dans des structures à DN. L'énoncé :

(17a) *Il n'est* ***pas*** *venu* ***pour rien***[23]

recevra une interprétation positive et emphatique, selon la lecture marquée à DN : « Il est venu pour quelque chose ».

En italien, la même phrase :

(17b) *Non è venuto* ***per niente***

serait ambiguë entre deux lectures : dans la première, selon la NC, *per niente* est une expression adverbiale, alors que dans la deuxième, moins immédiate, *niente* est un pronom neutre négatif ayant le rôle argumental du but. Les deux négations se positivisent, selon la DN ; l'interprétation contrastive que l'on obtient sera ainsi : « il est venu pour *quelque chose* ».

23 L'exemple est de De Swart (2010 : 176).

En français, la même phrase sans *pas* a seulement une valeur négative selon la NC :

(17c) *Il n'est venu pour rien*

où *pour rien* a valeur adverbiale (= « il n'est pas venu du tout »).

Une norme grammaticale demande que *pas* n'apparaisse pas avec les « N-mots », tout comme avec la négation explétive. Toutefois, en ancien français, *pas*, en union avec des « N-mots », recevant une interprétation selon la NC, était possible, comme le montre ce passage emprunté à Molière :[24]

(18) *Ne* faites ***pas*** semblant de *rien.*

La structure NC, la plus naturelle en latin archaïque et en latin tardif, se maintient dans le passage aux langues romanes. Le renforcement négatif que la structure NC présente au début, ainsi que l'affaiblissement des « N-mots » sont les moteurs du changement linguistique de la négation latine.

5.4 Le développement de NC marquée en anglais

La langue anglaise dans sa forme contemporaine est une langue à DN et possède une triple série d'indéfinis (*somebody*, *nobody*, *anybody*), elle peut témoigner de ce cycle de renforcements et d'affaiblissements. Le moyen anglais présente une configuration selon la NC. En 1500 par effet d'une restauration visant au latin classique, l'anglais devient une langue à DN. Mais le cycle continue dans certains contextes de contact linguistique, comme pour l'anglais créole, qui présente les formes *nothing not*. Ainsi, par exemple, dans le *San Andreas Creole English*, une langue à NC, on dira :[25]

(19a) *Nonbady no waahn daans wid Taiga* 'personne ne veut danser avec Taiga'
(19b) *A no sii nonbadi nowe* 'je ne vois personne nulle part'.

La NC est engendrée par les contextes marqués, réagissant à l'enseignement scolaire. R. Jackendoff (1998 : 36) cite le cas d'un petit garçon qui se plaignait : *nobody*

24 L'exemple est cité par Bernini and Ramat (1996 : 174) et repris par De Swart (2010 : 181).
25 Bartens (2013).

don't like me, et malgré toutes les tentatives de sa mère de lui apprendre la norme anglaise (*nobody likes me*), il persistait dans sa faute plus expressive de sa douleur.

La fréquence de la négation cumulative est plus élevée dans les variétés diastratiques sub-standard ; par ex., dans le patois londonien, le *Cockney*, dans l'anglais américain des états du Sud et aussi dans l'anglais afro-américain, dit ebonique.[26]

6 Conclusions

Cette enquête nous a poussés à réfléchir sur un phénomène intéressant : le bilinguisme interne à chaque langue. On doit penser, en effet, qu'une langue n'est pas monolithique, mais soumise à des tensions internes.[27] En ce qui concerne la négation, la DN appartient principalement au domaine de la langue logique et la NC au domaine de la langue innovante, mais les deux structures ne s'effacent pas totalement, prêtes à réapparaître à phases alternes, réciproquement comme phénomène marqué de l'une ou de l'autre. En revanche, l'évolution est uni-directionnellle : elle va toujours des structures la langue logique vers celles de la langue naturelle.

Bibliographie

Banniard, M. (1997). *Du latin aux langues romanes*. Paris : Nathan.

Bartens, A. (2013). San Andres Creole English. In S. M. Michaelis, Ph. Maurer, M. Haspelmath & M. Huber (Eds.), *The survey of pidgin and creole languages. Vol.1: English-based and Dutch-based Languages*. Oxford: University Press.

Beekes, R. (2010). *Etymological Dictionary of Greek*. Leiden/Boston: Brill.

Bernini, G. & Ramat, P. (1992). *La frase negativa nelle lingue d'Europa*. Bologna: Il Mulino.

Coseriu, E. (1971). Das Problem des griechischen Einflusses auf das Vulgärlatein. In *Sprache und Geschichte, Festschrift für Harri Meier* (pp. 135–147). München: Fink.

Dalh, Ö. (2010). Typology of negation. In L. R. Horn (Ed.), *The Expression of Negation* (pp. 9–38). Berlin/New York: De Gruyter Mouton.

de Swart, H. & Sag, I. (2002). Negation and negative concord in Romance. *Linguistics and Philosophy*, *25*, 373–417.

de Swart, H. (2010). *Expression and Interpretation of Negation. An OT Typology*. Dordrecht/Heidelberg/London/New York: Springer.

Denizot, C. (2012). La double négation et le tour οὐδεὶς οὐκ ἦλθεν. *Revue de philologie, littérature et histoire anciennes*, *86* (2), 65–90.

26 Labov (1972 : 773ss.).

27 Cf. Martinet (1975), notamment le chapitre I « Diachronie et synchronie dynamique » et Banniard (1997), notamment le chapitre 1, 7 « Prototype de la métamorphose ».

Denizot, C. (2014). 'Personne' et 'rien' dans les poèmes homériques : emplois de οὔτις et de οὐδείς, dans Latin *quis/qui*, grec τίς/τις : *parcours et fonctionnements.* In C. Denizot & E. Dupraz (Eds.), *Études sur deux interrogatifs-indéfinis-relatifs* (pp. 69–88). Mont-Saint-Aignan: Presses Universitaires de Rouen et du Havre.

Espinal, M. T. (2007). Licensing expletive negation and negative concord in Catalan and Spanish. In Fr. Floricic (Ed.), *La négation dans les langues romanes, Collection Linguisticae Investigationes Supplementa 26* (pp. 49–74). Amsterdam: John Benjamins.

Giannakidou, A. (2000). Negative concord and the scope of universals. *Transactions of the Philological Society, 98*, 87–120.

Giannakidou, A. (2006). *N*-words and negative concord. In M. Everaert & H. van Riemsdijk (Eds.), *The Blackwell companion to syntax, vol. III* (pp. 327–391). Oxford: Blackwell.

Giannollo, C. (2018). *Indefinites and negation in Ancient Greek.* DiGS 20: University of York, 20. 06.2018.

Haspelmath, M. (1997). *Indefinite Pronouns.* Oxford: Clarendon Press.

Herburger, E. (2002). The Negative Concord Puzzle Revisited. *Natural Language Semantics, 9*, 289–333.

Horn, L. (1989). *A Natural History of Negation.* Chicago: The Chicago University Press.

Horn, L. (2020). Negation and Opposition: Contradiction and contrariety in logic and language. In V. Déprez & M. T. Espinal (eds.), *The Oxford Handbook of Negation* (pp. 7–25). Oxford: Oxford University Press.

Jackendoff, R. (1998). *Linguaggio e natura umana.* Bologna: Il Mulino.

Jespersen, O. (1992). *La philosophie de la grammaire.* Paris: Gallimard. London: Allen and Unwin.

Keenan, E. L. & Comrie, B. (1977). Noun Prase Accessibility and Universal Grammar. *Linguistic Inquiry, 8* (1), 63–99.

Kiparsky, P. & Condoravdi, C. (2006). Tracking Jespersen's Cycle. In M. Janse, B. D. Joseph & A. Ralli (Eds.), *Proceedings of the 2nd International conference of Modern Greek dialects and linguistic theory* (pp. 172–197). Patras: University of Patras.

Laka, I. (1990). *Negation in Syntax: on the nature of functional categories and projections.* Doctoral thesis. Cambridge: MIT.

Labov, W. (1972). Negative attraction and negative concord in English grammar. *Language, 48*, 773–818.

Magni E., Orlandini, A. & Poccetti, P. (2017). *Haud* : usages et fonctions d'une négation perdue. *De Lingua Latina*, revue on line du Centre A. Ernout, Université de Paris IV-Sorbonne n.14. http://www.paris.sorbonne.fr/IMG/pdf/dll_14_magni_orlandini_poccetti_haud.pdf

Martinet, A. (1975). *Évolution des langues et reconstruction.* Paris: P. U. F.

Meillet, A. (1948). *Linguistique historique et linguistique générale.* Paris: Honoré Champion.

Meyer Lübke, W. (1890–1906). *Grammaire des langues romanes* (trad. A. et G. Doutrepont). Génève: Slatkine Reprints.

Nocchi, F. R. (2016). Commento agli *Epigrammata Bobiensia.* In *Texte und Commentare* 54. Berlin/Boston: De Gruyter.

Vai, M. (1996). Per una storia della negazione in Milanese in comparazione con altre varietà altoitaliane. *Acme, 46*, 56–98.

Van Emde Boas, E., Rijksbaron, A., Huitink, L. & De Bakker, M. (2019). *The Cambridge Grammar of Classical Greek.* Cambridge: University Press.

Viti, C. (2011). Osservazioni sulla negazione cumulativa. In M. Lasagna, A. Orlandini & P. Poccetti (Eds.), *Attorno alla negazione. Analisi di contesti negativi dalle lingue antiche al romanzo, Linguarum Varietas 1* (pp. 13–25).

Zanuttini, R. (1991). *Syntactic properties of sentential negation: a comparative study of Romance languages.* Doctoral thesis. Philadelphia M: University of Pennsylvania.

Colette Bodelot

Ita ou *sic* corrélatifs de complétives

Abstract: Alongside their standard use as correlative adverbs referring back or forward to various types of satellite subordinate clauses, it is generally recognized that *ita* or *sic* can also serve as preparatory devices for A.c.I. argument clauses introduced by *verba sentiendi/declarandi*. However, besides these clauses, whose infinitive construction leaves no doubt as to their argumental status, *ita/sic* may also refer to non-constative clauses introduced by *ut/ut non/ne* (+ subjunctive) or by an interrogative term (e.g., after the verb *facere*, or verbs of ordering and of asking for or seeking information). In this use, can *sic/ita* always switch with endophoric pronouns (*id*, *hoc*, etc.) and do the clauses they relay usually take the hypotactic argument position or do they tend instead to retain their independent status in paratactic arrangements?

Keywords: *Ita/sic*, endophora, argument clauses, structural ambiguity, parataxis

1 Introduction

La vulgate grammaticale reconnaît un emploi standard de *ita* ou *sic* comme corrélatifs de subordonnées circonstancielles, parmi lesquelles notamment les comparatives et les consécutives, sans ignorer leur rôle occasionnel de cataphoriques de propositions complétives revêtant la forme d'un A.c.I., après un *verbum sentiendi/declarandi* (Kühner et Stegmann 1914 : II, 1, 719 ; II, 2, 572–573 ; Hofmann et Szantyr 1972 : 359 ; Lavency 2004 ; Pinkster 2021 : 35). Pareil emploi est attesté en (1), où *ita* et *sic* entrent en concurrence avec le pronom neutre *id*, déictique textuel à l'accusatif qui demande à être saturé par le contenu d'une proposition jouant le rôle d'argument ou d'actant par rapport au(x) verbe(s) :

(1a) ***sic persuasi** mihi, **sic sentio**,* [. . .], *non posse eam naturam quae res eas contineat esse mortalem ;* (Cic. Cato 78)
'voici ma conviction, voici mon sentiment : [. . .] un être renfermant de telles facultés ne peut pas être mortel.'[1]

1 Sans indication contraire, les traductions sont personnelles.

Colette Bodelot, Université Clermont Auvergne, France

https://doi.org/10.1515/9783111332956-027

(1b) ***Ita*** *enim* ***scripsit*** *ad me, sibi meam commendationem maximo adiumento fuisse.* (Cic. fam. 13, 24, 1)
'Il m'a en effet écrit que ma recommandation l'avait énormément aidé.'

Mais, à côté de ces exemples, où la construction infinitive ne laisse subsister aucun doute sur la nature de la subordonnée, *ita* et *sic* ne peuvent-ils pas aussi relayer des complétives introduites par exemple par *ut/ut non* ou *ne* ou marquées par un terme interrogatif ?

Pour répondre à cette question, nous avons recherché dans PHI les occurrences de *ita/sic* entrant en séquence avec le verbe *facere*, les verbes standard *imperandi* et *interrogandi* pour voir si ces adverbes relaient, en dehors de propositions constatives, aussi des propositions volitives ou interrogatives. Si tel est le cas, ces propositions revêtent-elles la forme de subordonnées complétives ou gardent-elles plutôt, suite à un agencement paratactique, le statut d'indépendantes ?

2 Le cas de *ita/sic facio*

Si nous choisissons de commencer notre analyse par *ita/sic facio,* c'est que F. Panchón (2003 : 359) a relevé trois passages de Plaute comportant cette séquence. Se référant à Bennett (1910 : 228), il constate que *ita* n'y fonctionne « pas comme un vecteur d'emphase, mais comme un cataphorique annonçant la subordonnée » :

(2a) [. . .], *eumque* ***ita*** */* ***Faciemus ut*** *quod viderit ne viderit.* (Plavt. Mil. 148–149)
'[. . .], nous ferons (en sorte) que, ce qu'il aura vu, il ne l'ait pas vu.'

(2b) *Satin habes, si ego advenientem* ***ita*** *patrem* ***faciam*** *tuum / Non modo* ***ne*** *intro <e>at, verum etiam* ***ut*** *fugiat longe ab aedibus ?* (Plavt. Most. 389–390)
'Es-tu content si je fais (en sorte) que ton père, à son arrivée, non seulement ne rentre pas mais encore s'enfuie loin de sa maison ?'

(2c) *Quin prius disperibit faxo quam unam calcem civerit. / Ita paratumst. ::* ***Ita*** *di* ***faxint ne*** *apud leonem hunc serviam !* (Plavt. Poen. 908–909)
'Bien mieux, il sera éliminé, je m'en occupe, avant qu'il n'ait bougé un seul pion. Voilà ma combine. :: Que les dieux fassent ainsi (pour / ;) que je ne sois plus esclave chez ce léno !'

Apparaissant en une « structure intersubjective » (Bodelot 2018 : 192), *facere* n'y est pas « désémantisé » (Bortolussi 2014 : 128) suite à un processus de grammaticalisation. Dans (2a–b), une interprétation de *ut/ne p* comme complétive n'est possible que lorsqu'on interprète les accusatifs *eum* et *advenientem . . . patrem . . . tuum* comme proleptiques.[2] Du fait que la valence de *facere* n'est pas saturée par une telle anticipation artificielle du sujet de la subordonnée, on attribuera à *ut/ne p* un statut argumental ou actanciel.[3] Mais pour artificiel qu'il soit, l'accusatif proleptique, qui représente, par exemple selon H. Pinkster (2015 : 759–761), un « pseudo-objet », y interdit la commutation de *ita/sic* avec un objet revêtant la forme d'un pronom neutre, comme cela est possible en (3) :

(3) *Quos pol ut ego hodie servem cura maxima est. / Nisi unum* ***hoc faciam, ut*** *in puteo cenam coquant ;* (PLAVT. Aul. 364–365)
'Morbleu, les surveiller est pour moi une tâche très difficile aujourd'hui. À moins que je recoure à ce seul moyen, de leur faire cuire le repas dans le souterrain ;'

Quant à (2c), il est ambigu, car *ita* peut aussi y fonctionner comme un anaphorique transphrastique ; *ne* y introduirait alors non pas une complétive mais une subordonnée circonstancielle ou une proposition indépendante juxtaposée après une ponctuation forte.

D'autres contextes semblent plus propices à une interprétation complétive de *ut p* du fait qu'une orientation de *ita* vers le cotexte gauche est exclue :[4]

(4a) *Quid properas ? placide ; ne time. /* ***Ita ille faxit Iuppiter,*** */* ***Ut*** *ille palam ibidem ad<s>iet, /* [. . .] (PLAVT. Pseud. 923a–924a)
'Pourquoi te hâter ? Doucement ; n'aie pas peur. Fasse le grand Jupiter qu'il soit ici présent en même temps, au même endroit, [. . .]'

(4b) *Quin* ***ita faciam, ut*** *<tu>te cupias facere sumptum, etsi ego vetem.* (PLAVT. Capt. 856)
'Bien au contraire je ferai que toi-même, tu désires faire des dépenses, quoique je te l'interdise.'

Que *ut p* complétif puisse intervenir en séquence différée avec une subordonnée circonstancielle est montré par (5), où *ita feci* est précédé d'une finale ; la seconde proposition en *ut*, de statut argumental, est incidente au seul noyau verbal *feci*, tandis que la première l'est à l'ensemble constitué de la régissante et de la complétive :

---

2 Pour des études ponctuelles sur la prolepse, voir par exemple Christol 1989 ; Rosén 1992 ; Halla-aho 2012.

3 Pour une interprétation divergente de *eum(que)* non comme accusatif proleptique mais comme véritable objet de *facere* et de *ita* comme attribut du même objet, voir Taillade (2019 : 176–177).

4 Nous avons exclu de notre étude *ita/sic factum est ut*, qui peut représenter le parfait de l'impersonnel intransitif *fit* et non le passif de *facio* transitif.

(5) ***Ut** amantem erilem copem facerem filium, / **Ita feci, ut** auri quantum vellet sumeret, /* [. . .] (PLAVT. Bacch. 352–353)
'**Pour** faire de notre jeune maître amoureux un être bien nanti, **j'ai fait qu**'il s'approprie autant d'or qu'il veut, [. . .]'

Un autre cas de figure, non confiné au latin ancien, est celui où *ita/sic facio* introduit une proposition au subjonctif à sujet identique. Si causativité il y a, on peut, en cas de relation « intrasubjective », tout au plus parler d'une « autocausativité » ou « causativité réflexive » (Bodelot 2018 : 181–182).

À première vue, PHI en offre un assez grand nombre d'exemples. Mais à y regarder de près, très peu d'énoncés présentent effectivement une complétive annoncée par *ita/sic*. Il faut ici encore faire abstraction de toute une série d'énoncés dans lesquels :

1° *Ita/sic* reprend, comme en (6), au contact du verbe passe-partout *facere* une prédication précédente, ce qui en fait un anaphorique transphrastique :

(6) *Quod igitur fecissem ad Urbem,* [. . .], *feci in provincia. Neque **ita feci ut** te ad meum arbitrium adducerem,* [. . .] (CIC. fam. 5, 20, 2)
'Ce que j'aurais donc fait aux portes de Rome, [. . .], je l'ai fait en province. Et je ne l'ai pas fait / n'ai pas agi ainsi **pour** te mettre à ma merci, [. . .]'

2° *Ita/sic* est extraposé à gauche dans la régissante alors qu'il appartient de fait à la subordonnée en *ut* ; dans ce cas, on a affaire à ce qu'on appelle une *traiectio* (Kühner et Stegmann 1914[2] : II, 2, 614–615 ; Amacker 1998 : 139 ; Bortolussi 1998 ; Bodelot 2016 : 8–12). Un énoncé particulièrement intéressant est l'exemple (7) de Caton parce qu'il présente deux éléments anticipés dans la proposition régissante : d'abord *viniam* proleptique, qui fait attendre une complétive, puis l'adverbe modal extraposé de la complétive, *sic*. Si l'on fait abstraction de ces deux figures, le premier énoncé correspond à : *Facito uti vinia sic curetur* ; ce qui est donc cataphorisé dans cette séquence, ce sont les propositions paratactiques introduites par des impératifs en *-to* :

(7) ***Viniam sic facito uti curetur** : vitem bene nodatam deligato recte,* [. . .] ; *susum vorsum semper ducito,* [. . .] (CATO agr. 33, 1)
'**Faites en sorte que l'on soigne ainsi la vigne** : palissez droit la vigne, bien pourvue de nœuds, [. . .] ; conduisez-la toujours vers le haut, [. . .]' (trad. R. Goujard)

3° La valence de *facio* accompagné de *ita/sic* est déjà saturée, comme en (8), par un pronom neutre, relatif de liaison, orienté vers le cotexte gauche et jouant le rôle d'objet ; la subordonnée en *ut* qui suit revêt alors le statut d'une circonstancielle :

(8) ***Quod qui ita faciet, ut****, si cupiat uberior esse, non possit, habeatur sane orator, sed de minoribus ;* (Cic. opt. gen. 9)
Littéral[t] : '**Celui qui fera cela** (sc. ce que fait Lysias), **de telle sorte que**, s'il désirait employer un style plus riche, il ne le pourrait pas, doit bien être considéré comme un orateur, mais de valeur moindre.'

Mais des fois, en présence de deux déictiques, l'un pronominal (*id*, *hoc*, etc.), l'autre adverbial (*ita*/*sic*), il peut y avoir ambiguïté sur l'orientation du premier :

(9) *De hac re mihi satis hau liquet : nisi* ***hoc sic faciam****, opinor, / Ut utramque rem simul exputem,* [. . .]. (Plavt. Trin. 233–234)
'Sur cette affaire je n'ai pas de savoir bien net : à moins que **je la règle**, je pense, **de telle façon que** / à moins que **j'exécute,** je pense, **l'idée suivante, à savoir que** je mette en balance l'un et l'autre genre de vie, [. . .]'

Si *hoc* y est anaphorique et renvoie à la situation de dilemme mentionnée, il sature comme en (8) la valence de *facio*, et *ut p* ne peut être interprété comme une complétive. Pareille lecture reste en revanche possible si *hoc* et *sic* sont tous les deux orientés vers le cotexte droit. M. Lavency (2004 : 85) parle dans ce cas d'une accumulation pléonastique du pronom et de l'adverbe, qui, en sus des nombreux exemples de complétives véhiculant le même sens en l'absence de cataphorique, illustre, dit-il, la démotivation sémantique des cataphoriques.

Des candidats plus sûrs au statut argumental de *ut p* après *ita*/*sic facio* en relation intrasubjective semblent être :

(10a) ***Ita faciam****, ut frater censuit,* ***ut*** *uxorem eius huc adducam, / Cum ista ut loquatur.* (Ter. Phorm. 776–777)
'Je vais faire, comme mon frère m'a conseillé : (m'arranger pour) amener sa femme ici pour qu'elle parle avec l'autre.'

(10b) [. . .] *dixi ei* ***me ita facturum esse ut*** *in eam partem quam Phania rogasset primum venirem.* (Cic. fam. 3, 6, 2)
'[. . .] je lui ai fait part de ma disposition d'aborder / que je m'arrangerais pour aborder la province du côté où Phanias m'avait demandé de le faire.'

Dans (10a), la seconde proposition en *ut* peut délivrer, par-delà une comparative parenthétique en *ut*, le contenu d'un faire évoqué au début. Le même rapport peut être perçu en (10b) entre *me ita facturum esse* et *ut venirem*. Mais, dans les deux cas, la double traduction proposée, avec ou sans « s'arranger pour », montre à quel point il est facile de faire glisser le sens du **contenu** d'un faire à la **modalité** d'un faire, et d'interpréter *ut p* non comme une complétive mais comme une circonstancielle.[5]

Force est donc de constater qu'en cas de coréférence des deux sujets agentifs, les exemples certains de *ita/sic facere* cataphorisant une complétive en *ut* sont encore plus rares qu'avec deux sujets distincts. Cette observation est solidaire du constat que l'agencement hypotactique y cède volontiers la place à une juxtaposition paradigmatique. Ainsi dans (11), où *ita fac*, constitué d'un cataphorique et du verbe-vicaire *facere* à l'impératif, embraie sur une série d'impératifs indépendants de sens plein qui suivent :

(11) ***Ita fac***[6], *mi Lucili, vindica te tibi, et tempus,* [. . .], *collige et serva.* (Sen. epist. 1, 1)
'Fais ainsi, mon cher Lucilius, revendique tes droits sur toi, et pour ce qui est de ton temps, [. . .], recueille-le et ménage-le.'

3 Le cas de *ita/sic impero/iubeo*

Pour *impero*, la construction avec une complétive en *ut* (Kühner et Stegmann 1914 : II, 2, 221) l'emporte, contrairement à ce qui se passe pour *iubeo*, largement sur la construction infinitive. Aussi existe-t-il, dès le latin ancien et pendant la latinité classique, des exemples, certes peu nombreux, mais parfaitement clairs, de *ita* annonçant, à côté de *impero*, une subordonnée conjonctive de statut argumental ; ainsi en (12), où *ita* semble contribuer à rhématiser le contenu de *ut p* :

(12a) *Pseudolus mihi* ***ita imperavit, ut*** *aliquem hominem strenuum, / Benevolentem adducerem ad se.* (Plavt. Pseud. 697–698)
'Pseudolus m'a ordonné de lui amener un homme vaillant, dévoué.'

(12b) *etsi Dexippo quoque* ***ita imperavi****, statim* ***ut*** *recurreret,* [. . .] (Cic. fam. 14, 3, 4)
'j'ai néanmoins ordonné aussi à Dexippe de revenir aussitôt en hâte, [. . .]'

5 Voir à ce propos aussi Lavency (2004 : 91) : « La limite qui sépare circonstant et actant, actant éloigné et actant immédiat [. . .] se réduit aisément selon le sémantisme du verbe recteur. »

6 Comme c'est le tout début de la *Correspondance à Lucilius*, *ita* ne fonctionne pas comme anaphorique transphrastique.

(12c) [. . .] *nuntiavit Pompeium oppidanos Ucubenses convocasse eisque* ***ita imperavisse, ut*** [. . .] *perquirerent qui essent suarum partium* [. . .] (BELL. Hisp. 20, 2)
'[. . .] il annonça que Pompée avait convoqué les habitants d'Ucubis et leur avait ordonné de rechercher [. . .] quels hommes étaient ses partisans [. . .]'

Un exemple qui pourrait aussi induire à interpréter *sic* comme cataphorisant une complétive est attesté chez Varron :

(13) [. . .], *praeconi* ***sic imperato ut*** *viros vocet : Quod bonum fortunatum felix salutareque siet populo Romano Quiritibus* [. . .], *omnes Quirites* [. . .], *voca inlicium huc ad me.* (VARRO ling. 6, 86)
'[. . .], qu'il (sc. le censeur) commande ainsi au héraut de convoquer les hommes : « Que cela soit bon, favorable, heureux et salutaire au peuple romain et aux Quirites [. . .], convoque à une invitation ici, devant moi, tous les Quirites, [. . .]. »' (trad. P. Flobert)

De fait, *sic* embraie, au-delà de la complétive en *ut*, dont il est extraposé, sur la teneur de l'injonction que le censeur doit adresser au héraut et qui, figurant au style direct, comporte l'impératif *voca.*

Plus courant et moins déroutant du point de vue syntaxique est l'embrayage immédiat, sans complétive interposée, de *ita/sic impero* sur un discours direct de modalité prescriptive :

(14) *illi autem qui in auspicium adhibetur, cum* ***ita imperavit*** *is, qui auspicatur : 'Dicito, silentium esse videbitur',* [. . .] (CIC. div. 2, 72)
'or lorsque celui qui prend les auspices a en ces termes enjoint à celui qui l'assiste dans la prise d'auspices : « Dis s'il te paraît qu'il y ait silence », [. . .]'

Que *ita/sic* puisse y être concurrencé par une forme pronominale est prouvé par (15), où *hoc imperat* est employé en incise dans un discours direct :

(15) « *Ite citi (famulis* ***hoc imperat****), ite ducemque / Attrahite huc vinctum* [. . .] ». (OV. met. 3, 562–563)
'« Allez sans tarder (il adresse cet ordre à ses serviteurs), allez, traînez ici le chef, chargé de chaînes, [. . .] ! »'

ainsi que par (16), où *hoc* renvoie en anaphore transphrastique au contenu de l'énoncé qui précède :[7]

(16) [. . .] *iste imperat lictoribus ut Sopatrum de porticu* [. . .] *praecipitem in forum deiciant nudumque constituant. Vix* ***erat hoc*** *plane* ***imperatum***, [. . .] (Cic. Verr. II 4, 86)
'[. . .] Verrès commanda aux licteurs de jeter Sopater du haut de la galerie [. . .] à bas sur le forum et de le mettre à nu. À peine cet ordre avait-il été nettement donné que [. . .].'

Avec le second des verbes de commandement, à savoir *iubeo*, la construction conjonctive est en revanche minoritaire par rapport à la construction infinitive. D'après Kühner et Stegmann (1914 : II, 1, 717–718), *ut p* intervient à l'époque classique surtout si *iubeo* prend, par rapport à des décrets du peuple, le sens de « décider ». En dehors de l'usage classique, *ut p* intervient certes aussi dans de simples ordres, mais la rareté de son emploi explique qu'on ne relève dans PHI qu'un seul exemple de *ita* cataphorisant une complétive en *ut* :

(17) *Excepit P. Scipio Nasica Cn. Filius,* [. . .], *vir optimus a senatu iudicatus, adulescens nondum quaestorius, quoniam* ***ita*** *responsum* ***iubebat ut*** *id numen ab optimo viro exciperetur consecrareturque.* (Liv. perioch. 29, 9)
'Elle (sc. une pierre dont les habitants disaient qu'elle était la Mère de l'Ida) fut reçue par Publius Scipion Nasica, fils de Cnaeus, [. . .] : il avait été jugé l'homme le meilleur par le sénat, alors qu'il n'était qu'un jeune homme qui n'avait pas encore l'âge requis pour être questeur, car la réponse (sc. de l'oracle) commandait que cette divinité fût reçue et consacrée par l'homme le meilleur.'

De façon occasionnelle, *ut p* y est aussi annoncé par une forme pronominale :

(18) *Di, precor,* ***hoc iubeant, ut*** *euntibus ordine fatis / Ille meos oculos comprimat, ille tuos.* (Ov. epist. 1, 101–102)
'Que les dieux commandent, je les en prie, que, les destins s'accomplissant dans l'ordre, il ferme mes yeux ainsi que les tiens.'

Mais on trouve avec *iubeo* surtout un nombre important d'exemples où *ita/sic*, de façon paratactique, annonce (19a) ou reprend (19b), parfois en concurrence avec

7 Pour *haec* reprenant le contenu de *x* énoncés précédents, voir Sen. epist. 36, 7.

un tour à déictique pronominal (19c), le contenu d'un ordre, ou est employé en incise (19d) :

(19a) *Plebes* **sic iussit** *: 'Quod senatus iuratus, maxima pars, censeat, qui adsient, id volumus iubemusque.'* (LIV. 26, 33, 14)
'La plèbe ordonna comme suit : « Ce que le sénat, sous la foi du serment, à la majorité des présents, décidera, c'est ce que nous voulons et ordonnons. »'

(19b) *Reddenda terrae est terra, tum vita omnibus / Metenda, ut fruges.* ***Sic iubet*** *Necessitas.* (CIC. Tusc. 3, 59)
'Il faut rendre à la terre ce qui est terre, il faut que l'existence de tous soit moissonnée comme un champ de céréales. Ainsi l'ordonne l'inéluctable Destin.'

(19c) « *Pone crucem servo.* [. . .] / ***Hoc volo, sic iubeo****, sit pro ratione voluntas.* » (IVV. 6, 219–223)
'« Mets cet esclave en croix ! [. . .] je le veux, je l'ordonne ainsi, que ma volonté suffise comme raison. »'

(19d) [. . .] *transgressus munimenta ad praetorem Saguntinum – et ipse* ***ita iubebat*** *– est deductus.* (LIV. 21, 12, 7)
'[. . .] il franchit les fortifications et fut conduit – c'est ainsi qu'il le commandait lui-même – devant le préteur de Sagonte.'

4 Le cas de *ita/sic rogo/interrogo/quaero*

En ce qui concerne la classe des verbes qui peuvent introduire une interrogation indirecte, le verbe simple *rogo* ne présente pas la même compatibilité avec *ita/sic* + interrogation indirecte que le composé *interrogo*.

En effet si l'on trouve avec *rogo*, employé au sens de « questionner, interroger », des interrogatives indirectes diaphorisées par un pronom neutre, comme c'est le cas en :

(20) *Quid nunc vis ? :: Sceleste, at etiam quid velim,* ***id*** *tu me* ***rogas*** *?* (PLAVT. Amph. 1025)
'Que veux-tu à présent ? :: Scélérat, mais tu me demandes encore ce que je veux ?'

on ne repère aucun exemple sûr d'une interrogation indirecte relayée par *ita/sic*. Le seul exemple qui, à première vue, pourrait suggérer une telle interprétation est :

(21) ***Sic*** *item quoniam simile est recto casu surus, lupus, lepus,* ***rogant*** *quor non dicatur pro portione item suro, lupo, lepo.* (VARRO ling. 8, 68)
'Pareillement aussi, puisque sont semblables au cas droit *surus*, *lupus* et *lepus* (piquet / loup / lièvre), ils demandent pourquoi on ne dit pas de même, en série, *suro*, *lupo* et *lepo*.' (trad. G. Bonnet)

Mais placé, comme dans d'autres contextes chez Varron, au contact de *item* en tête d'énoncé, *sic* établit plutôt un lien avec l'énoncé qui précède qu'il n'embraie, en incidence étroite à *rogant*, sur la subordonnée interrogative qui suit.

Il existe en revanche toute une série d'interrogations indépendantes, faisant partie d'un discours rapporté, qui sont précédées (22a–b), voire suivies (22c) de *ita/ sic rogo* :

(22a) [. . .], *quid ei respondeam qui me* ***sic roget*** *: « Si dei sunt **, suntne etiam Nymphae deae ? »* (CIC. nat. deor. 3, 43)
'[. . .], dis-moi ce que je répondrais à quelqu'un qui me questionnerait ainsi : « Si les deux existent, les Nymphes sont-elles aussi des déesses ? »'

(22b) *Nam cum* ***ita rogasset*** *dialectus : « Quod ego sum, id tu non es ? »* [. . .] (GELL. 18, 13, 8)
'En effet comme le dialecticien l'avait interrogé ainsi : « Ce que je suis, toi, tu ne l'es pas ? » [. . .]'

(22c) « *Quid sentis* » *inquis* « *de nostris, Marce, libellis ?* » / ***Sic*** *me sollicitus, Pontice, saepe* ***rogas***. (MART. 5, 63, 1–2)
'« Que penses-tu, dis-tu, de mes petits livres, Marcus ? » Voilà la question que tu me poses souvent, Ponticus, l'air inquiet.'

Par contre, avec le composé *interrogo*, la cataphorisation de l'interrogation indirecte par *ita/sic*, quoique peu usuelle, est au moins attestée par quelques exemples incontestables :

(23a) [. . .], *tunc Adrastus* [. . .] *iubet eos ad se perduci atque* ***ita interrogavit*** *quid ita hoc cultu in regna sua venissent.* (HYG. fab. 69, 3)
'[. . .], alors Adraste [. . .] ordonna de les lui amener et leur demanda pourquoi ils étaient venus dans son royaume dans un tel appareil.'

(23b) *Qui interrogatus, heredem se responderit, nec adjecerit ex qua parte, ex asse respondisse dicendum est : nisi forte* ***ita interrogatur*** *an ex dimidia parte heres sit,* [. . .] (IVST. dig. 11, 1, 9, 5)
'Celui qui, interrogé, répond qu'il est héritier, sans ajouter pour quelle partie, est censé avoir répondu qu'il l'est pour le tout : à moins qu'on ne lui demande s'il est héritier pour moitié, [. . .]'

Mais tout comme le verbe *rogo*, *interrogo* annonce ou reprend avec *ita/sic* beaucoup plus souvent des questions directes. À titre d'exemple :

(24) *Illud quoque magno tibi erit levamento, si saepe te* ***sic interrogaveris*** *: « Utrumne meo nomine doleo, an eius qui decessit ? »* (SEN. dial. 11, 9, 1)
'Ce sera encore un grand réconfort pour toi que de t'interroger souvent ainsi : « Est-ce pour moi que je m'afflige ou pour celui qui est décédé ? »'

Que ce soit avec interrogation directe (25a) ou indirecte (25b), *ita/sic* y est aussi souvent concurrencé par des déictiques pronominaux :

(25a) ***Illud interrogari*** *me posse ab aliquo scio : si certa futurae mortis indicia sunt, quomodo interdum deserti a medicis convalescunt ?* (CELS. 2, 6, 13)
'La question suivante peut, je le sais, m'être posée : s'il existe des symptômes certains d'une mort prochaine, comment se fait-il que parfois des patients abandonnés des médecins recouvrent la santé ?' (trad. G. Serbat)

(25b) *itemque* ***illud interrogo****, cum me, incertis auspiciis, profectum ab domo scirem, utrum mihi turbatis religionibus res publica in discrimen committenda fuerit an auspicia repetenda ne quid dubiis dis agerem ;* (LIV. 8, 32, 4–5)
' je te pose encore la question suivante : si, sachant que j'étais parti de chez moi sous des auspices douteux, je devais, dans ce trouble des pratiques religieuses, exposer l'État au péril ou alors renouveler les auspices pour ne rien faire sans être sûr de la volonté des dieux ;'

Qu'en rapport avec l'acte d'interroger, une différence nette entre manière et contenu puisse être marquée par la coprésence de *sic* et d'un déictique pronominal ou adjectival est prouvé par (26) ; comme *sic* y répond, dans une structure comparative, à *ut* de manière qui précède, il n'est pas simplement pléonastique par rapport à *eisdem de rebus*, qui renvoie au contenu de la question :

(26) *Visne igitur, ut tu me Graece soles ordine interrogare,* ***sic*** *ego te vicissim* ***eisdem de rebus*** *Latine* ***interrogem*** *?* (CIC. part. 2)
'Veux-tu donc que, tout comme toi qui as coutume de m'interroger d'une façon ordonnée en grec, moi, à mon tour, je t'interroge de la même manière sur les mêmes sujets en latin ?'

Le troisième verbe *quaerere* présente, quant à lui, une plus grande variété d'exemples, un fait qui s'explique peut-être par le double sens de « interroger » et « rechercher » qu'il peut prendre au contact d'une interrogation indirecte.

Avec *sic*, on observe plusieurs particularités d'emploi. On a souvent affaire à une suite d'interrogations indirectes dont seule la première est introduite par *sic* + *quaero*, les suivantes par *sic* sans verbe et/ou un syntagme extraposé servant de rubrique. Le verbe *quaero* figurant volontiers au passif, il en naît une impression de style scientifique, impersonnel. C'est le cas dans les *Topica* de Cicéron :

(27) *Notio* ***sic quaeritur*** *: Sitne id aequum quod ei qui plus potest utile est. Proprietas* ***sic*** *: In hominemne solum cadat an etiam in beluas aegritudo. Divisio et eodem pacto partitio* ***sic*** *: Triane genera bonorum sint. Descriptio : Qualis sit avarus, qualis [sit] adsentator ceteraque eiusdem generis, in quibus natura et vita describitur.* (Cic. top. 83)[8]
'Sur le concept, on enquête ainsi : si le juste est ce qui est utile au plus puissant. Sur le caractère propre, ainsi : si le chagrin affecte l'homme seul ou aussi les bêtes. Sur la division et, de la même manière, sur la répartition, ainsi : s'il existe trois sortes de biens. Sur la description : quel type d'homme est un avare, quel type d'homme un flatteur, et d'autres choses du même genre, selon lesquelles on décrit la nature et la vie d'un être.'

Dans l'exemple suivant des *Controverses* de Sénèque, on constate que, par rapport à une première interrogation indirecte de portée générale, c.-à-d. *an possit abdicari*, *sic* sert dans un second temps à embrayer sur les sous-modalités du questionnement :

(28) *LATRO illas quaestiones fecit : divisit in ius et aequitatem, an abdicari possit, an debeat. An possit abdicari,* ***sic quaesiit*** *: an necesse fuerit illum patrem alere et ob id abdicari non possit, quod fecit lege cogente. Hoc in has quaestiones divisit : an abdicatus non desinat filius esse ; an is desinat, qui non tantum abdicatus sed etiam ab alio adoptatus est ;* etc.[9] (Sen. contr. 1, 1, 13)
'Latron posa les questions suivantes : il distingua le droit et l'équité, s'il peut être chassé ou s'il doit l'être. Sur la question s'il peut être chassé, il enquêta ainsi : s'il était nécessaire qu'il nourrisse son père et si pour cette raison il ne pouvait pas être chassé parce qu'il obéissait aux obligations de la loi. Cette question, il la subdivisa en celles qui suivent : si un fils qu'on chasse ne cesse

8 Voir aussi par exemple Cic. top. 82.
9 Suivent encore plusieurs questions en *an* du même type.

pas d'être un fils ; si cesse d'être un fils celui qui a été non seulement chassé mais encore adopté par une autre personne ; etc.'

Mais dans un contexte d'enquêtes judiciaires, *sic quaero* introduit aussi volontiers des questions rapportées sous forme directe. Ainsi en (29), où la forme directe rehausse une question impromptue qui vient réorienter l'enquête :

(29) *Dictum enim est :* « *Quisquis non adfuerit, exheres erit.* » 55. *Cur non conamur et* ***sic quaerere*** *;* « *Num cuicumque non adfuerit ?* » (Qvint. inst. 7, 1, 54–55)
'Il est dit en effet (sc. dans la loi) : « Quiconque n'aura pas prêté assistance, sera déshérité. » Pourquoi ne tentons-nous pas aussi de poser la question ainsi : « En est-il ainsi quelle que soit la personne qu'on n'aura pas assistée ? »'

Pour ce qui est de la cataphorisation avec *ita*, les exemples sont moins nombreux et moins typés : n'ont été relevés que deux exemples sûrs d'interrogations indirectes, dont le premier en (30a) s'apparente par l'indication de la rubrique *tempus* à (27) :

(30a) *Tempus* ***ita quaeritur*** *: quid anni, qua hora, noctu an interdiu, et qua die, qua noctis hora factum esse dicatur, et cur eiusmodi temporibus.* (Rhet. Her. 2,7)
'Pour le temps, on demande ainsi : à quelle époque de l'année, à quelle heure, si c'était de nuit ou de jour, à quel moment de la journée, à quel moment de la nuit les faits se sont accomplis, d'après ce qu'on dit, et pourquoi à tel ou tel instant.'

(30b) *Nisi forte ex te* ***ita quaesitum est****, num perturbare rem publicam seditionibus velles et ob eam causam adoptari, non ut eius filius esses, sed ut tribunus plebis fieres et funditus everteres civitatem.* (Cic. dom. 35)
'Peut-être t'a-t-on seulement demandé ce qui suit, si tu voulais troubler la république par tes séditions et te faire adopter non pour être son fils (sc. le fils de Fonteius) mais pour devenir tribun de la plèbe et renverser de fond en comble l'État.'

Dans d'autres cas, l'interprétation de *ita* est moins claire. Ainsi en (31), il n'est pas sûr que *ita* embraie à chaque fois sur une proposition introduite par un terme interrogatif, en l'occurrence *quo(=)modo* (31a), *ut* (31b), et *quae et quanta* (31c). *Ita* peut dans le premier cas établir un lien logique avec l'énoncé qui précède, dans le deuxième, annoncer une consécutive en *ut*, dans laquelle *id agatur* cataphorise alors l'interrogation indirecte totale qui suit, dans le troisième, embrayer sur la comparative *quemadmodum*, à condition qu'on ne considère pas cette dernière comme parenthétique :

(31a) *Non quaero abs te qua re patrem Sex. Roscius occiderit, quaero quo modo occiderit.* ***Ita quaero*** *abs te, C. Eruci : quo modo,* [. . .]. (Cic. S. Rosc. 73)
'Je ne te demande plus pourquoi Sextus Roscius a tué son père ; je te demande comment il l'a tué. Oui, je te demande ainsi, Caius Erucius : comment, [. . .].'

(31b) [. . .] *huius de facto, iudices,* ***ita quaeri*** *ut id agatur licueritne ei facere quod fecit,* [. . .] (Cic. Balb. 10)
'[. . .], pour ce qui est de son acte, juges, enquêter sur son mode de déroulement, s'il lui a été permis de faire ce qu'il a fait, [. . .] OU : [. . .], pour ce qui est de son acte, juges, enquêter de façon à ce que soit réglée la question s'il lui a été permis de faire ce qu'il a fait, [. . .]'

(31c) [. . .], *sed* ***ita quaeram****, quemadmodum te velle intellego, quae tua opera et quanta fuerit in bello.* (Cic. Verr. II 5, 4)
'[. . .], mais je demanderai, suivant ce qui est, je le vois bien, ton désir, quels furent le caractère et l'importance de ton œuvre à la guerre.' (trad. G. Rabaud).

Cela dit, au cas où *ita/sic* annonce effectivement une interrogation indirecte, il peut avec *quaero*, aussi bien qu'avec les autres verbes étudiés, commuter avec un déictique pronominal, sauf en cas d'indication de rubrique sous forme d'un actant (au nominatif ou à l'accusatif) dans la régissante ; (27') serait ainsi agrammatical :

(27') * *Notio* ***id quaeritur*** *: Sitne id aequum* [. . .] (Cic. top. 83)

5 Conclusion

Retenons qu'en principe *ita/sic*, relayant une complétive, peut alterner avec un pronom déictique. Les deux sont même susceptibles d'être employés de façon pléonastique en incidence à un même verbe. Mais parfois une commutation est impossible. C'est le cas, comme nous venons de le voir avec *quaero*, lorsqu'une rubrique thématique figure déjà comme actant dans la régissante. D'une façon plus étonnante, on a observé la même exclusion en cas de prolepse, ce qui devrait peut-être nous inciter à remettre sur le métier la question du statut syntaxique de l'accusatif proleptique : peut-on parler, du point de vue syntaxique, d'un « pseudo-objet » si sa présence rend impossible l'emploi de *id, hoc*, etc. comme objet direct ?

S'il y a double présence d'un *ita/sic* et d'un pronom neutre ou si l'on compare des paires d'énoncés dans lesquels il y a emploi, dans un contexte analogue, de l'un ou de l'autre, on a souvent l'impression que *id, hoc*, etc. ont une incidence plus étroite et plus directe sur une proposition argumentale, *ita/sic*, une portée plus large et moins immédiate. Est-ce que cela nous induira à supposer qu'au cas où *ita* ou *sic* annoncent une complétive, ils renvoient, comme l'a envisagé H. Fugier (1983 : 43), à un objet interne qui resterait inexprimé, *ita*/*sic facit ut* impliquant *ita*/*sic facit <id quod facit> ut* ? Comme cette linguiste, nous pensons qu'il vaut mieux en rester à la structure de surface (Fugier 1983 : 55) et dire que l'adverbe y joue le rôle de « premier complément » (Fugier 1983 : 46) du verbe. Cela implique que *ita* ou *sic* peuvent représenter, en fonction du contexte, un constituant essentiel du noyau prédicatif, ou se situer, à titre de satellite, dans la périphérie d'une construction plus large. Qu'il en naisse naturellement des cas d'ambigüité, nous l'avons montré tout au long de cette étude.

Quoi qu'il en soit, il semblerait de bonne méthode de ne pas limiter la liste des complétives susceptibles d'être cataphorisées par *ita*/*sic* aux seules infinitives. Comme endophoriques incorporés dans la structure prédicative, *ita* et *sic* peuvent annoncer aussi des complétives en *ut*, voire des interrogations indirectes. Mais comme, dans ce cas, une forte concurrence est exercée par les tours paratactiques, il faut concéder que le tour ne relève pas au même titre de l'usage courant de la langue que *ita*/*sic* + A.c.I.

Bibliographie

PHI = *PHI Classical Latin Texts.* A Resource Prepared by The Packard Humanities Institute.

Amacker, R. (1998). Ordre des mots et subordination: la *traiectio* chez Varron. In B. García-Hernández (Ed.), *Estudios de Lingüística Latina* (pp. 139–154). Madrid: Ediciones Clásicas.

Bennett, C. E. (1910). *Syntax of Early Latin, I: The Verb.* Boston: Allyn and Bacon.

Bodelot, C. (2016). Retour sur les marges de la subordination complétive en latin. *Journal of Latin Linguistics, 15* (1), 1–32.

Bodelot, C. (2018). L'évolution de lat. *facere* + proposition complétive: deux voies de grammaticalisation? *Bulletin de la Société de Linguistique de Paris, 113* (1), 179–214.

Bortolussi, B. (1998). *Facite uentum ut gaudeam*. Quelques phénomènes d'ambigüité syntaxique. In B. García-Hernández (Ed.), *Estudios de Lingüística Latina* (pp. 203–216). Madrid: Ediciones Clásicas.

Bortolussi, B. (2014). La construction proleptique avec *facere (ut)*. In B. Bortolussi & P. Lecaudé (Eds.), *La causativité en latin* (pp. 113–130). Paris: Harmattan.

Christol, A. (1989). Prolepse et syntaxe indo-européenne. In G. Calboli (Ed.), *Subordination and Other Topics in Latin* (pp. 65–89). Amsterdam/Philadelphia: J. Benjamins.

Fugier, H. (1983). *Recte et uera loquere*: l'adverbe complément de verbe en latin archaïque, *Lalies*, *2*, 4–56.

Halla-aho, H. (2012). A historical perspective on Latin proleptic accusatives. *Revue de linguistique latine du Centre Alfred Ernout (De lingua Latina)*, *7*.

Hofmann, J. B. & Szantyr, A. (1972). *Lateinische Syntax und Stilistik.* München: Beck.

Kühner, R. & Stegmann, C. (1914). *Ausführliche Grammatik der lateinischen Sprache. Zweiter Teil: Satzlehre 1–2* (2nd edn.). Hannover: Hahn.

Lavency, M. (2004). *Sic/ita/id* cataphoriques de la proposition infinitive (A.c.I.). In C. Bodelot (Ed.), *Anaphore, cataphore et corrélation en latin* (pp. 81–93). Clermont-Ferrand: Presses Universitaires Blaise-Pascal.

Panchón, F. (2003). Les complétives en *ut*. In C. Bodelot (Ed.), *Grammaire fondamentale du latin. Tome X: Les propositions complétives en latin* (pp. 335–481). Louvain/Paris/Dudley, MA: Peeters.

Pinkster, H. (2015). *The Oxford Latin Syntax. Volume 1: The Simple Clause*. Oxford: Oxford University Press.

Pinkster, H. (2021). *The Oxford Latin Syntax. Volume 2: The Complex Clause and Discourse*. Oxford: Oxford University Press.

Rosén, H. (1992). Die Arten der Prolepse im Lateinischen in typologischer Sicht. In O. Panagl & Th. Krisch (Eds.), *Latein und Indogermanisch* (pp. 243–262). Innsbruck: Innsbrucker Beiträge zur Sprachwissenschaft.

Taillade, M. (2019). Réflexions sur la syntaxe de *fieri* en latin préclassique : chassé-croisé des circonstancielles et des complétives dans un nid de coucou. In M. Taillade, J. Gallego, F. Fatello & G. Gibert (Eds.), *Nemo par eloquentia. Mélanges de linguistique ancienne en hommage à Colette Bodelot* (pp. 163–186). Clermont-Ferrand: Presses universitaires Blaise-Pascal.

Sophie Van Laer

L'insertion syntaxique d'un constituant nominal dans la comparaison similative

Abstract: This article deals with similative comparatives, and more specifically with all expressions where a nominal constituent is introduced by *ut(i), sicut(i), velut(i), tamquam, quomodo* or *quasi*. It aims to show that, despite the diversity of semantic values (quality, identification, comparative of manner), the comparative constituent comes to be inserted by the same syntactic means. The standard (of comparison) syntactically reduplicates a constituent of the clause, with which it agrees in case (section 2.3). This type of syntactic integration explains why the comparative constituent is related to the verbal predicate while being linked by grammatical agreement with one of its constituents. According to this analysis, the standard marker is an adverb (section 2.4) and there is no need to assume an ellipsis of the so-called comparative clause of manner (section 2.5). When the standard occupies an argumental syntactic position which is vacant, *velut* or *quasi* (the only standard markers used) function as adverbial approximators (section 2.3.2.3). Two other types of comparatives are then studied: the comparatives with two nominal constituents, for which syntactic integration seems to be the same (section 3), and comparative clauses containing a verb and its complement (section 4). In the latter case, both the correlation between the two clauses and the *oratio obliqua* test make the subordinate status of the comparative uncertain.

Keywords: comparative, *ut*, syntactic reduplication, ellipsis

1 Introduction

On distingue traditionnellement deux types de propositions comparatives :[1]

– la comparative « de degré »[2]

(1a) *tu eruditior quam Piso* (Cɪc. *Pis.* 62)
'et toi, plus cultivé que Pison'

1 Tarriño (2011 : 373) à qui nous empruntons (1a) et (1b), et Pinkster (2021 : 3).

2 Également appelée comparative "de quantité" ou "d'intensité" (Cabrillana et Tarriño 2009 : 646).

Sophie Van Laer, Nantes Université & LAMO (UR 4276), France

https://doi.org/10.1515/9783111332956-028

– la comparative « similative »[3]
(1b) *solebat sic cenare, quomodo rex* (PETRON. 38, 15)
'sa table était servie comme celle d'un roi'

Cet article ne portera que sur la comparative « similative » ou « identifiante ».[4] Malgré la diversité des fonctions qu'elle peut occuper,[5] elle s'appuie sur une même structure syntaxique. Un constituant, que nous appellerons « comparant »,[6] introduit par *ut(i), sicut(i), velut(i), tamquam, quasi* ou *quomodo*, est mis en relation avec une proposition : en (1b), *quomodo* introduit le comparant *rex*. La comparative sera abordée sous un angle strictement syntaxique, afin d'avoir une vue d'ensemble.

L'étude s'articulera autour de la forme morpho-syntaxique du comparant, qui, elle, est variable. Nous étudierons successivement les comparants nominaux (section 2), les comparants comportant deux syntagmes nominaux (section 3) et les comparants propositionnels (section 4). L'objectif est de mieux cerner le mode d'insertion syntaxique du comparant, ce qui nous conduira à nous interroger sur le statut syntaxique du mot introducteur (le « standard marker »[7]) et sur la réalité de l'ellipse dans la comparaison similative.

Cette étude s'appuie sur un corpus d'historiens et de biographes de l'époque républicaine et de l'époque impériale[8].

2 Le comparant est un constituant nominal

Le comparant peut être un nom, un pronom, un groupe nominal ou un groupe prépositionnel.[9] C'est, dans notre corpus, la plus fréquente des trois configurations étudiées.

3 Bertocchi et al. (2017 : 122), également appelée proposition comparative « de manière » (Tarriño 2011 : 373 ; Pinkster 2021 : 3), « de qualité » (Cabrillana et Tarriño 2009 : 633), ou « d'égalité » (Revuelta-Puigdollers 2002 : 191).

4 Danon-Boileau et Morel (1995 : 10).

5 Voir Revuelta-Puigdollers (2002 : 193–207), Tarriño (2011 : 408–418) Pinkster (2021 : 271–278 et 762–765).

6 Authier-Revuz (1995 : 184). Tarriño (2011 : 402) appelle le comparant « standard » ou « second term » et le mot qui l'introduit « standard marker ».

7 Voir note 6.

8 CAES. Gall., SALL. Catil. et Iug., NEP., LIV. 1–2, TAC. Agr. et Germ., SVET. de Aug. à Nero.

9 Il peut aussi s'agir d'adverbes de temps susceptibles de commuter avec un nom, un groupe nominal ou prépositionnel. Nous n'aborderons pas le cas des éléments adjectivaux (adjectifs ou participes) qui excéderaient les limites imparties à cet article.

2.1 Données du corpus

Figurent dans les Tableaux 1 et 2 toutes les occurrences relevées, quelle que soit leur valeur sémantico-logique.

Tableau 1: forme syntaxique du comparant.

	CAES.	SALL.	NEP.	LIV.	TAC.	SVET.	total
nominatif	1	16	3	7	12	7	**46**
accusatif		2	3	9	6	34	**54**
génitif		2		2	1	5	**10**
datif		4		4	5	4	**17**
ablatif	1	5	2	3	2	7	**20**
groupe prépositionnel	4	10		11	13	19	**57**
adverbe de date[10]		2		4	1	1	**8**
total général	**6**	**41**	**8**	**40**	**40**	**77**	**212**

Tableau 2: mot introduisant le comparant.

	CAES.	SALL.	NEP.	LIV.	TAC.	SVET.	total
ut	4	8	6	20	25	31	**94**
sicut	2	12	1	2	2	6	**25**
velut		7	1	16	9	15	**48**
tamquam		2		2	2		**6**
quasi		12			1	25	**38**
quo . . . modo					1		**1**
total général	**6**	**41**	**8**	**40**	**40**	**77**	**212**

2.2 Hétérogénéité sémantico-logique

La même structure syntaxique peut prendre différentes valeurs sémantico-logiques. Nous n'envisagerons que deux valeurs, hors de la fonction prototypique de manière,[11] pour illustrer cette hétérogénéité.

10 Voir note 9.

11 Tarriño (2011 : 400), Pinkster (2021 : 270).

2.2.1 La fonction « qualité » (Dik et al. 1990 : 31)

Comme l'a remarqué Revuelta Puigdollers (2002 : 195–197), la qualité peut prendre la même forme qu'une comparative de manière avec un comparant nominal :[12] voir respectivement (2a) et (2b).

(2a) *Dissentiens in curia a Q. Haterio : « ignoscas », inquit, « rogo, si quid adversus te liberius (**sicut** senator) ø dixero ».* (SVET. Tib. 29, 2)
'Contredisant au sénat Q. Haterius, il [= Tibère] conclut: « Je vous prie de me pardonner, si comme sénateur, j'ai combattu votre opinion avec trop de liberté ».'[13]

(2b) *Sed <u>multi mortales</u> . . . vitam (**sicuti** peregrinantes) transiere.* (SALL. Catil. 2, 8)
'Or bien des mortels . . . ont traversé la vie comme des voyageurs.'

Dans certains cas d'ailleurs, les deux interprétations semblent se superposer, dans la perspective d'un dialogisme :[14]

(2c) *metuens ne, si consulum iniussu et ignaris omnibus iret, forte deprehensus a custodibus Romanis ø retraheretur (**ut** transfuga)* (LIV. 2, 12 ,4)
'Il [= Mucius] réfléchit qu'en y allant sans l'aveu du consul et à l'insu de tous, il risquait d'être arrêté par les sentinelles romaines et ramené comme déserteur'

Mucius Scaevola a l'intention de tuer le roi Porsenna, il n'est donc absolument pas un transfuge. Mais en quittant Rome secrètement, comme pourrait le faire un transfuge, il encourt le risque d'être considéré comme tel.

2.2.2 Les « constructions exemplifiantes » (Gibert 2013 : 141–142)

Le constituant nominal est, en tant qu'« exemplifiant », une sous-partie de la classe d'entités dénotée par l'« exemplifié ». Cet emploi se rencontre principalement, dans notre corpus, chez Suétone (14 occurrences), face à une seule occurrence chez Tite-Live.

---

12 D'autres formes syntaxiques sont également possibles : voir Tarriño (2011 : 416–418).

13 Les textes et les traductions sont ceux de la CUF. Le mot introducteur de la comparative (mise entre parenthèses) est en caractères gras. Le constituant de la proposition avec lequel le comparant s'accorde (voir section 2.3) est souligné ou indiqué par le signe ø s'il n'est pas exprimé.

14 Van Laer (2015 : 14–15).

(3) *ex qua summa pretiosissima deorum simulacra mercatus vicatim dedicabat (**ut** Apollinem Sandaliarium et Iovem Tragoedum aliaque).* (SVET. Aug. 57, 3)
'Avec cet argent, Auguste achetait de magnifiques statues de dieux, qu'il consacrait dans les différents quartiers, comme l'Apollon Sandaliarius, le Jupiter Tragédien, et d'autres.'

2.2.3 Conclusion

L'hétérogénéité sémantico-logique des occurrences relevées dans la section 2 paraît indéniable. Dans le cas de la fonction qualité ou de l'exemplification, le rapport établi excède le rapport de ressemblance, fondement même de l'opération cognitive de la comparaison,[15] pour tendre vers l'identification.[16]

Doit-on pour autant seulement souligner que le recours à une même forme syntaxique est source d'ambiguïté, comme on le fait souvent pour la comparative de manière et la fonction qualité ? Il semble que l'unicité de la forme syntaxique peut trouver un principe explicatif.

Même dans les deux cas étudiés, l'identité référentielle n'est pas totale. La qualité et l'exemplifié, parce qu'ils réfèrent à une classe d'entités, ont une extension plus grande. D'autre part, dans le cadre de la prédication seconde, la durée de validité de la qualité prédiquée est mise en relation avec celle du prédicat verbal et interprétable en termes de concomitance.[17] La même analyse semble aussi s'appliquer à l'exemplification. Autrement dit, la relation entre les deux référents s'établit dans le cadre du procès verbal.

Comme le remarque Tarriño (2011 : 409), à propos des « comparative clauses of Manner », « the comparison does not always express Manner ». L'auteur évoque au terme de son étude « a vague semantic relationship with the main clause » (Tarriño 2011 : 420). Cette relation sémantique vague, c'est sans doute la « simple ressemblance » exprimée par les constructions similatives, ce qui fait que « la comparaison similative n'est jamais parfaite » (Bertocchi et al. 2017 : 122).[18]

15 Voir Cabrillana et Tarriño (2009 : 633) et Bertocchi et al. (2017 : 122).

16 Revuelta-Puidollers (2002 :195), Tarriño (2011 : 417).

17 Pinkster (1983 : 208), Muller (2000 : 22).

18 C'est la raison pour laquelle nous préférons parler de comparatives « similatives » plutôt que comparatives « de manière ». À noter que Pinkster (2021) distingue les « Manner Clauses » (étudiés dans le chapitre consacré aux propositions subordonnées satellites [2021 : 270–278]) des « Comparative expressions of quality » et des « *Ut* phrases of qualification » (étudiés dans le chapitre consacré à la comparaison [2021 : 762–765]).

2.3 Insertion syntaxique du comparant

Dans les trois réalisations sémantiques étudiées (comparaison de manière, fonction qualité, exemplification), le nom ou la tête du groupe nominal comparant s'accorde en cas avec le nom avec lequel il est mis en relation : *mortales* (2b), *simulacra* (3). Lorsqu'il s'agit d'un pronom occupant la fonction sujet, il peut ne pas être exprimé (2a et 2c) mais la règle d'accord est la même.[19] Cette insertion, qui repose sur l'accord avec un nom, est très proche de celle de l'apposition nominale. [20] Elle s'en distingue par la présence d'un mot invariable (*ut, sicut, velut, tamquam, quasi, quomodo*), dont le rôle semble être de bloquer l'identité référentielle.[21]

Il est possible de pousser plus loin l'analyse. Le mécanisme de l'insertion syntaxique d'un comparant nominal peut alors être formulé en ces termes : l'insertion se fait par la duplication (ou le dédoublement) d'un des constituants (ou syntagmes) de la proposition. Le comparant se greffe, pour ainsi dire, par cette duplication, dans la proposition.

Une telle analyse conduit à infléchir un peu la description des éléments constitutifs de la comparative de manière telle qu'elle est proposée par Tarriño (2011 : 400–402). Même si la comparative similative de manière porte sur l'ensemble de la proposition, l'accord en cas montre qu'elle s'adosse plus particulièrement à un constituant de cette proposition, que nous appellerons le « comparé ».[22]

La duplication du poste syntaxique occupé par le comparé, rendue possible par l'accord en cas, permet au comparant de rester périphérique à la proposition et de fonctionner comme un circonstant (ou un satellite) de manière. Elle permet également de donner une assise à la comparaison similative en levant une possible ambiguïté quant à la façon dont il faut interpréter le circonstant de manière comparant.[23] On a souvent remarqué que le comparant similatif peut être coordonné

---

19 La non expression du pronom sujet n'empêche pas son existence sous-jacente, comme en témoigne par exemple l'accord de l'adjectif prédicatif apposé (Serbat 1996 : 59).

20 Dans le cas des « expressions comparatives de qualité » de forme nominale opérant une prédication seconde, Pinkster (2021 : 763) évoque l'accord en cas. Nous proposons d'étendre ce principe à tous les comparants nominaux.

21 Ce mot invariable ne véhicule qu'un signifié de ressemblance, susceptible de recevoir différentes interprétations (voir section 2.2.3).

22 Authier-Revuz (1995 : 184).

23 Pour les difficultés possibles de l'interprétation d'une construction similative circonstant de manière, voir Tarriño (2011 : 400–401).

avec un adverbe.[24] Mais l'adverbe ne donne pas de point d'ancrage à la manière dans la proposition.[25]

(4) *Hunc ego non (**ut** multi), sed artissime **ø** diligo* (PLIN. epist. 6, 8, 1)[26]
'Moi, je l'aime non pas comme tout le monde, mais avec une tendresse spéciale.'

Le nominatif de l'adjectif *multi* montre que la nature du sentiment dénoté par *diligit* est envisagée du point de vue de celui qui éprouve le sentiment, et non de celui qui en est l'objet.[27]

2.3.1 Duplication (ou dédoublement) d'un poste syntaxique

Les exemples de cette section relèvent tous de la comparaison similative de manière. Le comparant peut dupliquer différents postes syntaxiques : sujet au nominatif (5), contrôleur de l'infinitif dans une proposition infinitive (6), complément d'objet (7), complément d'objet second (8), circonstant, qu'il s'agisse d'un nom (9a) ou d'un groupe prépositionnel (9b), complément du nom (10) :

(5) *tanta vis avaritiae animos eorum (**veluti** tabes) invaserat.* (SALL. Iug. 32, 4)
'C'était comme une épidémie de cupidité qui avait envahi les âmes.'

(6) *Id [= aes alienum] . . . (**velut** tabem) pervenisse ad corpus.* (LIV. 2, 23, 6)
'Cette dette, grossie des intérêts, . . . comme un mal contagieux, avait gagné son corps.'

(7) *. . . matronae annum (**ut** parentem) eum luxerunt* (LIV. 2, 7, 4)
'Pendant un an, comme pour un père, les femmes portèrent le deuil.'

24 Revuelta-Puigdollers (2002 : 209), Tarriño (2011 : 410), Van Laer (2013 : 413), Pinkster (2021 : 272).
25 Voir Le Goffic (1993 : 469).
26 Exemple utilisé dans un précédent article (Van Laer 2013 : 413).
27 L'adverbe « rejaillit » (Le Goffic 1993 : 469) sur le sujet et montre à quel point Pline est un bon ami, ce qu'illustre la suite de la lettre.

(8) *At Iugurtha . . . filium et cum eo duos familiaris ad senatum legatos mittit eisque, (**uti** illis quos Hiempsale interfecto miserat), praecipit omnis mortalis pecunia adgrediantur.* (SALL. Iug. 28, 1)
'Jugurtha délègue auprès du Sénat son fils et deux de ses confidents, avec ordre, comme il l'avait fait après le meurtre de Hiempsal, d'essayer sur tout le monde la puissance de son argent.'

(9a) *Quibus oppressis inopinantibus, quod se Cevenna (ut **muro**) munitos existimabant . . .* (CAES. Gall. 7, 8, 3)
'Cette arrivée inattendue les frappe de stupeur, car ils se croyaient protégés par les Cévennes comme par un rempart.'

(9b) *gratia, voce, denique omnibus modis pro alieno scelere et flagitio (sua **quasi** pro gloria) nitebantur.* (SALL. Iug. 15, 2)[28]
'Crédit, éloquence, bref tous les moyens étaient par eux mis en œuvre pour défendre le crime et l'infâmie d'un autre, comme s'il se fût agi de leur propre gloire.'

(10) *Nunc de Suebis dicendum est, quorum non una, (**ut** Chattorum Tencterorumue), gens.* (TAC. Germ. 38, 1)
'Maintenant il faut parler des Suèves, qui ne constituent pas, comme les Chattes ou les Tenctères, une seule nation.'

2.3.2 Occupation d'un poste syntaxique vacant

Dans les exemples proposés précédemment, il y avait duplication d'un syntagme de la proposition. Mais il est une configuration remarquable. Il s'agit du cas où le comparant ne duplique aucun syntagme exprimé : il occupe une poste syntaxique vacant.

28 *Sua* est antéposé à *quasi* pour le mettre en relief (c'est un élément rhématique): des hommes qui devraient être au service de l'État ne se préoccupent que de leur intérêt personnel.

2.3.2.1 Les données du corpus

Tableau 3: forme syntaxique et fonction du comparant occupant un poste syntaxique vacant.[29]

	CAES.	SALL.	NEP.	LIV.	TAC.	SVET.	total
nominatif		**4**			**1**		**5**
sujet (*quasi*)		1					1
attribut du sujet (*quasi, velut)*		3			1		4
accusatif						**1**	**1**
complément d'objet (*quasi*)						1	1
génitif						**3**	**3**
génitif de qualité (*quasi, ut*)						2	2
génitif de définition (*velut)*						1	1
datif					**2**		**2**
circonstant (*ut*)					2		2
ablatif			**2**	**2**		**4**	**8**
circonstant (*ut, quasi, velut*)			2	2		3	7
nom support dans ablatif absolu (*velut*)						1	1
groupe prépositionnel	**2**	**6**		**8**	**12**	**16**	**44**
circonstant (*quasi, tamquam, velut, ut*)	2	6		8	12	16	44
adverbe de temps				**3**	**1**		**4**
circonstant (*ut*)				3	1		4
total général	**2**	**10**	**2**	**13**	**16**	**24**	**67**

Tableau 4: mot introduisant le comparant.

	CAES.	SALL.	NEP.	LIV.	TAC.	SVET.	total
ut	2	1	1	7	10	4	25
velut		1	1	6	4	8	20
tamquam		1			1		2
quasi		7			1	12	20
total général	**2**	**10**	**2**	**13**	**16**	**24**	**67**

Le Tableau 3 fait apparaître une dissymétrie. Lorsqu'il s'agit d'un actant (sujet, attribut du sujet, complément essentiel, nom support dans un ablatif absolu) cet emploi est exceptionnel (7 occurrences). Seuls sont employés, en ce cas, *quasi* et *velut*.

29 Les données reposent sur un relevé systématique des occurrences, quelle que soit la valeur sémantique du comparant.

Dans le cas d'un circonstant, l'emploi est plus usuel : 60 occurrences (89,5%) dont 44 pour des groupes prépositionnels. Sont employés dans notre corpus, outre *quasi* et *velut*, *ut* et *tamquam*.

2.3.2.2 Le poste syntaxique vacant est celui d'un circonstant

Un exemple permettra nous permettra de mieux en comprendre le mécanisme.

(11) . . . *nec remos in ordinem lateribus adiungunt : solutum, (**ut** in quibusdam fluminum), et mutabile, ut res poscit, hinc vel illinc remigium.* (TAC. Germ. 44, 2) 'Ils [= les Suiones] ne fixent pas les rames en rangée sur les bords ; l'appareil en est libre, comme sur certains fleuves, et susceptible d'être tourné, selon les circonstances, d'un côté ou de l'autre.'

Tacite évoque ici la flotte des Suiones, un peuple habitant l'actuelle Suède. Il vient d'indiquer leur localisation géographique : *ipso in Oceano* 'dans l'océan même' (TAC. Germ. 44, 2). Il n'est donc pas utile de préciser que la navigation se fait en mer. En revanche, la comparaison de l'appareillage de leurs rames avec quelque chose de connu (*in quibusdam fluminum* 'sur certains des fleuves' que connaissent les Romains) permet au lecteur de mieux comprendre la description.

Ce syntagme venant occuper un place syntaxique laissée vacante n'a donc pas de raison d'être exceptionnel (voir Tableau 4). La non-expression du constituant, restituable contextuellement, ne remet pas en cause la grammaticalité de la phrase.

On peut hésiter en ce cas entre une insertion syntaxique par duplication d'un circonstant non exprimé ou par l'utilisation d'une forme syntaxique permettant le rattachement au prédicat verbal. Le principe général reste le même que celui vu précédemment (section 2.3), au sens où cette insertion prend appui sur la proposition dans lequel le constituant s'insère.[30]

2.3.2.3 Le poste syntaxique vacant est celui d'un argument

Nous entendons par argument (ou actant) un nom occupant la fonction de sujet, d'attribut du sujet ou de complément essentiel.

Une question se pose : comment un nom adventice, qui vient se greffer dans une proposition supposée complète, peut-il occuper le poste syntaxique vacant de sujet grammatical (12) ou de support nominal (ou contrôleur) du participe dans l'ablatif absolu (13) ? Les occurrences montrent que nous avons affaire à un autre fonctionnement sémantico-syntaxique de la structure syntaxique étudiée.

30 Et non sur une ellipse supposée, comme nous le verrons section 2.5.

(12) *Sed ex eo medio (**quasi** collis) oriebatur . . . vestitus oleastro ac murtetis aliisque generibus arborum* (SALL. Iug. 48, 3)
'Du centre se détachait une sorte d'éperon . . . revêtu d'oliviers sauvages, de myrtes, et autres espèces.'

Selon Bertocchi et al. (2017 : 124–126), qui citent et étudient cette occurrence, *quasi* fonctionne ici comme un « approximateur ». Il peut être interprété comme un « adaptateur » paraphrasable par « une sorte de, une espèce de », avec un sens comparable à celui de l'adjectif *quidam*. *Quasi* exprime alors l'inadéquation d'une désignation, notamment s'il s'agit d'un nouveau concept qui n'a pas encore reçu de nom.

(13) *Proposita vitae eius (**velut** summa), partes singillatim neque per tempora sed per species exequar* (SVET. Aug. 9, 1)
'Ayant présenté en quelque sorte le sommaire de sa vie, je vais en examiner une à une les différentes parties, non point en suivant l'ordre chronologique mais (en groupant les faits) par catégories.'

Dans un passage clé expliquant le plan suivi pour une biographie, Suétone tente de donner un nom à la première partie.[31] *Velut*, qui porte sur *summa*, support nominal du participe dans un ablatif absolu, nous semble également fonctionner comme un approximateur.

2.3.2.4 Le cas de la « modalisation autonymique » (J. Authier-Revuz 1992 : 41)

Outre leur rôle d'approximateur *quasi* et *velut* peuvent opérer une démarcation dans l'énoncé, assez comparable aux signes typographiques des guillemets. Ce qui leur permet d'être des marqueurs de « modalisation autonymique », c'est-à-dire de l'emploi d'un mot à la fois en usage et en mention puisqu'il reflète le discours d'autrui :

(14) *Elatus inflatusque tantis (**velut** successibus) negavit « quemquam principum scisse quid sibi liceret »* (SVET. Nero 37, 5)
'Gonflé d'orgueil par de si brillants « succès », il [=Néron] déclara que « nul empereur n'avait su tout ce qui lui était permis ».'

---

31 La traduction de *summa* par 'sommaire' n'est pas nécessairement la mieux adaptée. Cette première partie, chronologique, regroupe les informations essentielles jusqu'à l'accession au pouvoir, avant de laisser place à deux parties thématiques, les *species* positives et les *species* négatives.

Les succès (*successus*) consistent faire mourir sous n'importe quel prétexte des personnes célèbres de Rome. La démarcation opérée par *velut* permet une mise à distance de l'énonciateur, qui ne prend pas à son compte le choix du mot.

La place de *velut* est à cet égard significative : il n'est pas placé devant le syntagme *tantis successibus* mais devant le seul *successibus*. Il semble qu'il faut comprendre 'ce qu'il appelait succès'.

2.4 Quel statut morpho-syntaxique pour le mot introducteur du comparant ?

Lorsque *quasi* et *velut* sont employés comme approximateurs (section 2.3.2.3) ou comme marqueurs d'un décrochage énonciatif (section 2.3.2.4), ils portent seulement sur le mot qu'ils précèdent sans opérer une mise en relation avec un constituant.[32] Ils semblent alors fonctionner comme des adverbes.[33]

Mais la question du statut se pose également lorsque le mot introducteur du comparant est suivi d'un constituant nominal. L'insertion syntaxique telle que nous l'avons définie section 2.3 plaide pour un statut adverbial[34] du mot introducteur, comme nous allons le voir section 2.5.

2.5 Doit-on supposer une ellipse dans le cas de la comparaison ?

L'intégration syntaxique d'un comparant nominal par duplication d'un des syntagmes de la proposition présuppose que ce comparant ne constitue pas une proposition au sens formel du terme. Ce qui revient à dire qu'il n'y a pas lieu de supposer une ellipse. Corollairement, le mot introducteur employé ne semble plus être une conjonction, mais un adverbe, ou une particule adverbiale.

L'absence d'ellipse semble difficilement discutable lorsque l'élément nominal inséré relève d'une prédication seconde (fonction « qualité »).[35] Dans le cas de l'ex-

32 La possibilité de supposer une ellipse « <quelque chose> comme », notamment dans le cas d'une inadéquation du nom choisi, ne peut néanmoins être totalement exclue.

33 C'est l'analyse proposée par Bertocchi et al. (2017 : 124).

34 C'est une question que se posent également Bertocchi et al. (2017 : 130) à propos de *quasi* introduisant un nom.

35 Revuelta-Puigdollers (2002 : 197).

emplification, supposer un accord en cas de l'exemplifiant avec l'exemplifié (ce qui ne nécessite pas de recourir à l'ellipse) semble la solution la plus économique. Le nom (ou le groupe nominal) introduit ne vise qu'à donner des exemples d'une classe d'entités dénotée par l'exemplifié et précisée par la proposition.

Il ne semble pas que l'on doive traiter différemment le cas où le nom (ou le groupe nominal) introduit relève de la comparaison de manière et supposer que la forme nominale du comparant résulte d'une ellipse, réputée fréquente dans la comparaison. Le recours à une même structure syntaxique pour les trois réalisations sémantiques, la fréquence d'un comparant nominal dans le cadre d'une comparaison, la diversité des fonctions syntaxiques que ce comparant peut occuper, le lien qui peut être établi entre duplication et fonctionnement sémantico-logique de la comparaison de manière nous semblent constituer des arguments en faveur de cette analyse.

Les deux autres sections ne visent qu'à apporter des éléments supplémentaires corroborant cette analyse. Le traitement en sera donc plus rapide.

3 Le comparant comporte deux syntagmes

3.1 Présentation

Dans cette configuration, la comparaison met en parallèle les deux syntagmes du comparant avec deux syntagmes de la proposition.[36]

(15) *(**ut** enim /Romae/ /consules/), **sic** /<u>Karthagine</u>/ quotannis /<u>annui bini reges</u>/ creabantur.* (NEP. Hann. 7,4)
'De la même manière en effet que Rome se donne des consuls, Carthage créait chaque année deux rois munis de pouvoirs annuels.'

Les syntagmes mis en parallèle sont ici *Romae* et *Karthagine* d'une part *consules* et *annui bini reges* de l'autre.

36 Un de ces syntagmes peut être un adverbe de temps, susceptible de commuter avec un nom ou un groupe prépositionnel. Chacun des deux syntagmes du comparant et de la proposition est mis entre des barres obliques.

3.2 Les données du corpus

Tableau 5: mot introduisant le comparant.

	Caes.	Sall.	Nep.	Liv.	Tac.	Svet.	total
ut		2	1	4		2	**9**
sicut	1					3	**4**
quo modo					1		**1**
quasi						1	**1**
total	**1**	**2**	**1**	**4**	**1**	**6**	**15**

Tableau 6: corrélation.

	Caes.	Sall.	Nep.	Liv.	Tac.	Svet.	total
. . . sic		1	1	4	1	1	**8**
. . . ita						1	**1**
total		**1**	**1**	**4**	**1**	**2**	**9**

Cette configuration, beaucoup moins fréquente, comme le montre le Tableau 5, fait souvent intervenir la corrélation (60% des occurrences si on confronte les totaux des Tableaux 5 et 6).

3.3 Doit-on supposer une ellipse ?

Il nous semble que l'insertion par duplication, sans recours à l'ellipse, peut aussi s'appliquer aux comparatives comportant deux syntagmes nominaux.

(16) *Sed fervidi animi vir, (**ut** |in publico periculo| |ante|), **sic** |tum| |in suo|, non tribunos modo, sed plebem oratione feroci refutando . . . periculum audacia discussit* (Liv. 2, 52, 7)
'Mais, non moins ardent à se défendre que naguère à défendre Rome, il [= Spurius Servilius] s'attaqua hardiment dans sa réplique non seulement aux tribuns, mais à la plèbe . . . et son audace dissipa l'accusation.'

La comparaison porte ici sur le groupe nominal initial, et plus particulièrement sur le génitif de qualité *fervidi animi.*[37] Tout le reste de la proposition ne concerne que l'accusation de Spurius Servilius à sa sortie de charge.[38]

Le même procédé d'insertion semble également être à l'œuvre pour l'exemplification, où exemplifié et exemplifiant peuvent comporter deux syntagmes.

(17) *Solebat . . . si quando quid invisitatum dignumque cognitu advectum esset, / id/ extra ordinem /quolibet loco/ publicare,* **ut** */rhinocerotem/ /apud Saepta/, / tigrim/ /in scaena/. . .* (SVET. Aug. 43, 11)
'Il avait coutume . . . s'il arrivait qu'on eût transporté à Rome quelque animal curieux et méritant d'être vu, de le présenter au peuple à titre extraordinaire, en n'importe quel lieu, par exemple un rhinocéros dans l'enceinte des élections, un tigre sur une scène . . .'

L'infinitif *publicare* se rattache à l'imparfait *solebat*, qui ne fait pas sens pour les exemplifiants. Si la pratique est récurrente, tel n'est pas le cas de chacun des animaux et des lieux pris un par un.

4 La comparaison similative s'exprime par la mise en parallèle de deux propositions

4.1 Présentation

Contrairement aux comparatives étudiées dans les deux autres sections, nous avons affaire ici à deux propositions qui pourraient chacune constituer une proposition indépendante.[39]

---

37 La comparaison de manière ne porte pas nécessairement sur toute la proposition, mais peut s'appliquer à un constituant : voir Pinkster (2021 : 276). Le groupe nominal initial peut d'ailleurs être considéré comme une apposition prédicative au sujet non exprimé : 'En homme d'un tempérament ardent aussi bien auparavant lorsque la république était en danger qu'alors lorsque c'était lui qui l'était, il . . .'.

38 On peut néanmoins considérer, du fait de l'articulation *non modo . . . sed* qu'il avait déjà coutume de s'en prendre aux tribuns lorsqu'il exerçait une fonction politique.

39 N'ont été retenues dans la section 4 que les comparaisons faisant intervenir deux constituants propositionnels, i.e. articulés chacun autour d'un procès verbal avec un complément essentiel exprimé.

(18) ***Ut** igitur paulo ante animum inter Fidenatem Romanamque rem ancipitem gessisti, **ita** iam corpus passim distrahendum dabis.* (Liv. 1, 28, 9)
'Hier c'était ton âme que tu partageais entre Fidène et Rome ; aujourd'hui, c'est le tour de ton corps d'être déchiré et mis en pièces.'

(18a) *Paulo ante animum inter Fidenatem Romanamque rem ancipitem gessisti.*
(18b) *Iam corpus passim distrahendum dabis.*

Il résulte de cette mise en parallèle deux effets de sens : l'expression d'une ressemblance[40] (18) ou d'un « contraste »[41] (19) entre les procès des deux propositions.

(19) *Atque hic tantusvuir **ut** naturam fautricem habuerat in tribuendis animi virtutibus, **sic** maleficam nactus est in corpore fingendo.* (Nep. Ages. 8, 1)
'D'ailleurs cet homme illustre, que la nature avait favorisé en le comblant des dons de l'esprit, avait au contraire peu à se louer du physique dont elle l'avait pourvu.'

4.2 Données du corpus

Nous avons relevé 24 occurrences relevant de cette configuration, telle que nous l'avons définie (voir section 4.1 et note 39), ce qui ne représente pas un effectif très important.

Tableau 7: mot introduisant le comparant.

	Caes.	Sall.	Nep.	Liv.	Tac.	Svet.	total
ut	5	1	2	2	5	1	**16**
sicut					3	1	**4**
quemadmodum			1	2			**3**
quo modo					1		**1**
total	**5**	**1**	**3**	**4**	**9**	**2**	**24**

40 Voir Bertocchi et al. (2017 : 122).
41 Expression empruntée à Pinkster (2021 : 273).

La proposition du comparant précède toujours l'autre proposition et le recours à un adverbe corrélatif[42] est systématique, comme le montre la confrontation entre les totaux des Tableaux 7 et 8.

Tableau 8: adverbe corrélatif.

	CAES.	SALL.	NEP.	LIV.	TAC.	SVET.	total
... sic	4		3	2	3		**12**
... ita	1	1		2	6	2	**12**
total	**5**	**1**	**3**	**4**	**9**	**2**	**24**

4.3 Quel statut syntaxique pour les deux propositions ?

L'analyse traditionnelle considère que la proposition introduite par *ut, sicut, quemadmodum* ou *quo . . . modo* est une proposition subordonnée, tandis que l'autre proposition, qui peut être précédée d'un adverbe corrélatif est la proposition principale.[43] Cette analyse tend à être remise en cause.

Selon Orlandini (2004 : 96) « les comparatives simples (d'identité ou de ressemblance) introduites par les adverbes marqueurs de corrélation sont des propositions coordonnées ». L'auteur s'appuie sur l'emploi de l'infinitif pour le verbe de la comparative dans l'*oratio obliqua*[44].

D'autre part, la notion même de corrélation fait difficulté. Dans une perspective synchronique, « le statut syntaxique des deux membres est loin d'être clair. Définira-t-on le rapport qui unit p1 à p2 en termes de dépendance ou d'interdépendance ? » (Bodelot 2004 : 24).

42 Pour le statut de la corrélation dans la comparaison similative, voir Tarriño (2011 : 419).

43 Voir Pinkster (2021 : 3).

44 Ce test de l'*oratio obliqua* est également utilisé par Pinkster (2021 : 718), mais à propos de la comparaison de degré.

L'étroitesse du corpus[45] ne permet pas de verser de nouveaux éléments à ce dossier. Nous n'avons relevé qu'une occurrence[46] où le verbe de la comparative est à l'infinitif dans le cadre du style indirect :

(20) *prae se ferre,* ***quem ad modum****, si non dedatur obses pro rupto foedus se habiturum,* ***sic*** *deditam intactam inviolatamque ad suos remissurum*. (LIV. 2, 13, 8)
'Il [= Porsenna] publiait hautement qu'un refus de livrer l'otage [= Clélie] équivaudrait à la rupture du traité, mais que, en revanche, si on la lui livrait, il ne lui serait fait aucun mal et on la rendrait aux siens.'

L'oratio obliqua révèle ainsi une hésitation des auteurs pour qui la comparative, lorsque la comparaison s'exprime par la mise en parallèle de deux propositions, n'est pas véritablement une subordonnée.

5 Conclusion

Dans cette étude de l'insertion syntaxique du constituant comparatif similatif, nous avons essayé de mettre en évidence un mécanisme d'insertion spécifique. Lorsque le comparant est un constituant nominal, il s'insère dans la proposition en dupliquant (ou dédoublant) un des postes syntaxiques de la proposition (section 2.3). Ce mode d'insertion éclaire le fonctionnement sémantique de la comparaison de manière, qui, en pratiquant l'accord en cas avec un constituant de la proposition, donne un point d'ancrage à la comparaison tout en portant sur le procès dénoté par cette proposition.

Ce mécanisme d'insertion, assez proche de celui de l'apposition, s'en distingue par la présence d'un mot invariable, qui ne semble pas être une conjonction de subordination mais un adverbe ou une particule adverbiale (section 2.4). Corol-

45 En vertu du critère précisé note 39, nous n'avons pas retenu dans la section 4 des propositions que l'on peut qualifier de « tronquées », au sens où le complément essentiel du verbe n'est pas exprimé. Cela conduit à exclure bon nombre des propositions présentées comme des « Manner adjunct clauses » par Pinkster (2021 : 271–272). Un sondage dans les occurrences relevées montre un emploi du subjonctif systématique dans l'*oratio obliqua*, ce qui serait à confirmer par un corpus plus large.

46 Citée par Orlandini (2004 : 96). Parmi les quatre occurrences relevées, le verbe de la comparative est au subjonctif dans deux occurrences (CAES. Gall. 1, 44, 8 et SVET. Iul. 10, 2) ; dans la troisième (CAES. Gall. 2, 1, 2) les deux propositions échappent au style indirect.

lairement, il n'est plus nécessaire de supposer une ellipse comme on le fait souvent (section 2.5).

Dans un stade ultime, l'adverbe fonctionne comme un adverbe approximateur, qui peut traduire l'inadéquation de la désignation ou relever de la modalisation autonymique (sections 2.3.2.3 et 2.3.2.4). L'ensemble formé par le constituant et l'adverbe *quasi* ou *velut* peut alors occuper un poste syntaxique argumental (ou actanciel) vacant.

Ce principe d'insertion syntaxique peut être étendu à un comparant comportant deux constituants (section 3).

D'un autre côté, nous avons envisagé la mise en parallèle de deux propositions (section 4). Les mots introducteurs sont les mêmes. Avons-nous ici affaire à une conjonction de subordination ? Le traitement possible de la comparative comme une proposition indépendante, mise sur le même plan que la proposition comparée dans l'*oratio obliqua*, et les difficultés soulevées par l'analyse syntaxique de la corrélation (section 3.3) font que la question reste ouverte.[47]

Bibliographie

Authier-Revuz, J. (1992). Repères dans le champ du discours rapporté. *L'information Grammaticale*, *55*, 38–42.

Authier-Revuz, J. (1995). Comparaison / reformulation / métaphore. *Faits de langue*, *5*, 183–192.

Bertocchi, A., Maraldi, M. & Orlandini, A. (2017). *Quasi*, du latin à l'italien. In T. Ponchon, S. Hava Bat-Zeev & A. Bertin (Eds.), *Mots de liaison et d'intégration. Prépositions, conjonctions et connecteurs* (pp. 119–133). Amsterdam/Philadelphia: John Benjamins.

Bodelot, C. (2004). Anaphore, cataphore et corrélation: approche générale de la problématique dans l'optique de la phrase complexe. In C. Bodelot (Ed.), *Anaphore, cataphore et corrélation en latin* (pp. 13–25). Clermont-Ferrand: PU Blaise Pascal.

Cabrillana, C. & Tarriño, E. (2009). Finales, consecutivas y comparativas. In J.-M. Baños Baños (Ed.), *Sintaxis del latín clásico* (pp. 633–655). Madrid: Liceus.

Danon-Boileau, L. & Morel, M.-A. (1995). Présentation générale. *Faits de langue*, *5*, 5–12.

Dik, S. C., Hengeveld K., Vester, E. & Vet, C. (1990). The Hierarchical Structure of the Clause and the Typology of Adverbial Satellites. In J. Nuyts, A. M. Bolkestein & J. P. Vet (Eds.), *Layers and Levels of Representation in Language Theory* (pp. 25–70). Amsterdam/Philadelphia: John Benjamins.

Gibert, G. (2013). *La subordination comparative en latin dans les textes de prose de Caton à Apulée*, Dissertation. Université Blaise Pascal-Clermont-Ferrand II.

Le Goffic, P. (1993). *Grammaire de la phrase française*. Paris: Hachette.

47 La question reste ouverte aussi pour les « Manner Clause » comportant un verbe mais analysables comme des propositions "tronquées" au sens où le complément essentiel n'est jamais exprimé : voir note 45.

Muller, C. (2000). Les constructions à adjectif attribut de l'objet, entre prédication seconde et complémentation verbale. *Langue française*, *127*, 21–35.

Orlandini, A. (2004). Comparatives et comparatives conditionnelles dans les structures corrélatives. In C. Bodelot (Ed.), *Anaphore, cataphore et corrélation en latin* (pp. 95–111), Clermont-Ferrand: PU Blaise Pascal.

Pinkster, H. (1983). Praedicativum (quantifying adjectives and adjectives denoting physical or mental state). In H. Pinkster (Ed.), *Latin Linguistics and Linguistic Theory. Proceedings of the 1st International Colloquium on Latin Linguistics, Amsterdam, April 1981* (pp. 199–214). Amsterdam/Philadelphia: John Benjamins.

Pinkster, H. (2021). *The Oxford Latin Syntax. Volume 2: The Complex Sentence and Discourse*. Oxford: Oxford University Press.

Revuelta Puigdollers, A. (2002). Oraciones comparativas de igualdad : niveles de integración. In E. Espinilla, P. J. Quetglas & M. E. Torrego (Eds.), *La Comparación en latín* (pp. 191–228). [Madrid/ Barcelona]: Universidad Autónoma de Madrid – Universitat de Barcelona.

Serbat, G. (1996). *Grammaire fondamentale du latin. Tome VI, L'emploi des cas en latin. Volume 1, Nominatif, vocatif, accusatif, génitif, datif*. Paris/Louvain: Peeters.

Tarriño, E. (2011). Comparative Clauses. In P. Baldi & P. Cuzzolin (Eds.), *New Perspectives on Historical Latin Syntax, Volume 4, Complex sentences, grammaticalization, typology* (pp. 373–426). Berlin/ Boston: De Gruyter Mouton.

Van Laer, S. (2013). *Ut* comparatif en latin: étude syntaxique et sémantico-logique. In C. Bodelot, H. Gruet-Skrabalova & F. Trouilleux (Eds.), *Morphologie, syntaxe et sémantique des subordonnants* (pp. 411–424). Clermont-Ferrand: PU Blaise-Pascal.

Van Laer, S. (2015). *Ut comparatif* en latin: un marqueur de dialogisme ? *De lingua Latina, 11*, 1–25. https://lettres.sorbonne-universite.fr/sites/default/files/media/2020-05/dll_11_s-van_laer.pdf

Sándor Kiss

Présentations différentes d'un contenu sémantique en latin : la synonymie syntaxique au niveau du syntagme et au niveau de la proposition

Abstract: In this paper we examine syntactic synonymy in Latin, that is the existence of parallel, quasi-equivalent expressions for the formulation of the same semantic content. These differences of "presentation" (or secondary semantic oppositions) appear on the level of the sentence and on that of the phrase; moreover, they can function in the manifestation of grammatical relations, and in the realization of communicative dynamism. As for the grammar of the sentence as a whole, a secondary semantic opposition can be discovered between active and non-active constructions; from the communicative point of view, the speaker has the choice, within certain limits, between different word orders, and thus he can indicate the pragmatic functions (topic and comment) in the discourse. On the level of the phrase, certain grammatical relations, clearly marked, are sometimes reinforced by the presence of special means. Grammatical devices can be used on different points of the phrase in view of an emphatic effect. Naturally, presentational differences have stylistic values, studied here in the letters of Cicero. The means of syntactic synonymy constitute an important layer in the transformational history of the sentence.

Keywords: Classical Latin, syntax, synonymy, communicative dynamism

1 Position du problème

1.1 Synonymie et choix

Au cours de la formulation d'un contenu sémantique, le locuteur est confronté à des choix. Sa décision, qui est prise généralement avec une grande rapidité, obéit à de multiples facteurs, tant psychologiques que pragmatiques. Les choix eux-mêmes peuvent concerner le lexique ; cependant ici, je voudrais aborder des phénomènes

Sándor Kiss, University of Debrecen, Hungary

https://doi.org/10.1515/9783111332956-029

de la syntaxe, et cela à des niveaux différents, allant du syntagme à la liaison interphrastique.[1] Un tel examen peut être intéressant dans la mesure où la langue offre elle-même des procédés caractéristiques qui aboutissent à des expressions synonymiques. Or, la synonymie est une opposition sémantique secondaire, que j'appellerais volontiers une différence de présentation.[2] Les termes de cette opposition ne peuvent pas être placés en contradiction logique, leur différence consiste dans l'approche réalisée par le locuteur. Ainsi, il ne serait pas possible de dire *largos effundit fletus, sed non flet.*[3] L'éventail des possibilités présentationnelles se modifie sans cesse au cours de l'histoire d'une langue ; et ces relations de quasi-équivalence peuvent fonctionner comme des réservoirs, comme des ressources de sauvetage, pour ainsi dire, lorsqu'une expression usuelle est menacée et doit être remplacée. C'est ce qui est arrivé lors du dépérissement du futur synthétique latin, quand le type *cantabo* a été relayé par des tournures périphrastiques, comme *cantare habeo* / *debeo* / *volo* – un remplacement dont l'aboutissement se reconnaît dans le futur roman.

1.2 Domaines de la synonymie syntaxique

Les phénomènes de la synonymie syntaxique appartiennent au fonctionnement normal des langues, et ils se retrouvent dans des systèmes linguistiques très différents ; néanmoins, dans chacun des systèmes, la distribution de ces phénomènes est différente : en effet, les cas de synonymie typiques se rattachent, de manière caractéristique, à des secteurs grammaticaux déterminés. En ce qui concerne ces secteurs, il convient de distinguer entre le niveau de la phrase et le niveau du syntagme ; et il faut distinguer aussi entre deux fonctionnements où la synonymie peut apparaître : en effet, elle peut viser le mode d'expression de certaines relations sémantiques, mais elle peut viser aussi le rôle d'une structure dans le dynamisme communicatif. Nous avons donc ici, en principe, quatre domaines, qui pourraient être illustrés par de très nombreux exemples. Je puiserai une partie de mes matériaux dans un petit corpus cohérent, qui offre une certaine unité thématique et affective, et qui permet aussi de gagner un enseignement stylistique : il s'agit du

---

1 Naturellement, la distinction entre « sens » et « référence », élaborée pour la signification lexicale (cf. Lyons 1977 : 197–198), est également utile en syntaxe, pour décrire des expressions qui se caractérisent comme des synonymes.

2 Cf. dans ce sens Fuchs (1982 : 53), à propos de la conception de la synonymie : « une relation d'équivalence sémantique, fondée sur l'existence d'un noyau sémantique commun sur lequel se greffent des différences sémantiques secondaires ».

3 Je m'inspire de VERG. Aen. 2, 271 *visus adesse mihi largosque effundere fletus* 'il [sc. Hector] m'a semblé apparaître [dans mon rêve], en versant des larmes abondantes'.

troisième livre des lettres de Cicéron adressées à Atticus. Cicéron est en exil, et il implore l'aide de son ami, avant tout sur le plan sentimental, pour obtenir de l'espoir et de la consolation. Étant donné les formulations variées que l'auteur des lettres utilise pour exprimer des contenus référentiels parfois identiques ou très proches, on est tenté d'étendre la notion de présentation au-delà des limites de la phrase, pour aborder le large domaine des relations synonymiques en discours.

2 Niveau global : choix offerts pour la construction de la phrase

2.1 Présentation et diathèse

2.1.1 Actif et non-actif

Au niveau de la phrase, la relation sémantique fondamentale qui unit le verbe à ses actants est saisie par le locuteur selon un certain jeu des présentations dans tous les cas où les règles de la diathèse permettent des transformations. Le choix entre actif et non-actif dépend d'abord de la perspective adoptée par le locuteur,[4] ce qui a pour corollaire que la présentation active ou non-active d'un contenu verbal peut aider la commodité du discours. C'est ce qui arrive dans

Tuae quidem litterae quo saepius a me leguntur, hoc spem faciunt mihi minorem (Cic. Att. 3, 16)
'En fait, ta lettre, plus souvent relue, plus elle diminue mon espoir',

où le terme *litterae* peut garder son statut de sujet et de thème jusqu'à la fin de la phrase. Pourtant, par le choix de la construction active ou de la construction non active, le locuteur décide souvent de remplir ou de ne pas remplir la place réservée à un « agent ». La phrase non-active permet de faire disparaître l'agent, mais cette opération se réalise à des degrés différents, pour ainsi dire. En effet, l'agent peut être facilement restitué grâce au contexte ici:

4 Cf. Pinkster (2015 : 250–251) : « the choice (. . .) depends on the language user's decision to present the state of affairs from the perspective of the first argument or from that of the second argument, respectively ».

ita ad me scribitur ut putem esse commodius nos eisdem in locis esse (Cic. Att. 3, 20, 1)
'd'après ce que l'on m'écrit, je pense qu'il est plus opportun pour nous de ne pas bouger de nos places',

mais, pour différentes raisons, l'agent peut rester vague et dilué en quelque sorte dans le contexte :[5]

Ego huic spei et exspectationi quae nobis proponitur maxime tamen volui praestolari apud te in Epiro (Cic. Att. 3, 20, 1)
'Cet événement prévu et tellement espéré, qui nous est promis si sûrement, j'avais pourtant voulu l'attendre chez toi, en Épire'

et le verbe passif ne comporte certainement pas d'agent définissable dans Cic. fam. 14, 3, 2 : *Nam mi ante oculos dies noctesque versatur squalor vester et maeror* 'En fait, devant mes yeux se montrent jour et nuit votre désolation et votre tristesse'. Le passif dit impersonnel est apte à éliminer l'expression des actants du verbe et à limiter la phrase à l'expression du seul contenu verbal, procédé qui aboutit à la phrase minimum du type *itur* ;[6] citons cette phrase amère de Cicéron à propos du silence du sénat (Cic. Att. 3, 12, 1) : *Itaque siletur* 'Donc on se tait'.

2.1.2 Non-actif pronominal

Pareillement à beaucoup d'autres langues, le latin a développé un emploi spécial des verbes transitifs, qui sert à écarter tout agent externe : il s'agit du « non-actif pronominal », dont l'importance ne cesse de croître du latin archaïque aux langues romanes. Un type *se mutat* / *se coniungit* perd facilement son sens réfléchi, pour

---

5 Ernout et Thomas (2002 : 206) parlent, dans ce cas, d'une « expression de l'indéfini », et citent Plavt. Cas. 121 : *dabitur tibi amphora* 'une amphore te sera donnée'. En effet, la différence des présentations signifie ici un degré de précision ou de « complétude », étant entendu que les phrases passives contenant l'expression de l'agent sont relativement rares et apparaissent ainsi comme « marquées » (cf. Hofmann et Szantyr 1965 : 287–288 ; Kiss 1982 : 19).

6 Ce type de phrase impersonnelle n'est d'ailleurs pas incompatible avec l'expression de l'agent (le degré d'imprécision sera alors moindre) : *Disputatur in consilio a Petreio atque Afranio et tempus profectionis quaeritur* 'Dans le conseil il y a une intervention de la part de Petreius et une autre de la part d'Afranius, et l'on discute pour fixer le moment du départ' (Caes. civ. 1, 67, 1) ; cf. Ernout et Thomas (2002 : 207), qui citent Caes. Gall. 5, 30, 1 : *cum a Cotta primisque ordinibus acriter resisteretur* 'puisqu'il y avait une forte résistance de la part de Cotta et de la part des centurions du plus haut grade'.

devenir un quasi-synonyme de *mutatur / coniungitur*. Le procédé est déjà certainement généralisé à la période classique, et la forme pronominale remplacera de plus en plus souvent le passif synthétique, en recul dans la langue tardive (cf. Ernout et Thomas 2002 : 214). La coexistence durable du pronominal « non-actif » et du passif ne manque pas de créer une différence de présentation, qui a été définie ainsi par Pierre Flobert (lors de la comparaison entre *se movet* et *movetur*) : « Le réfléchi (. . .) souligne que l'initiative du mouvement appartient au sujet, tandis que le passif intrinsèque (. . .) marque seulement l'implication du sujet dans un mouvement » (Flobert 1975 : 387). Néanmoins, la différence essentielle consistera dans le fait que la tournure pronominale ne permet pas l'introduction d'un agent extérieur:

Hic tu me accusas quod me adflictem, cum ita sim adflictus ut nemo umquam (Cic. Att. 3,12,1)
'Tu m'accuses de m'affliger lorsque je suis [effectivement] plus affligé que jamais personne'

(où nous relevons une synonymie partielle du pronominal marquant l'état et du passif résultatif). À l'appui de cette opposition secondaire, nous pouvons citer le verbe *ostendere* avec les deux nuances : Cic. ad Q. fr. 1, 2,16 *consules se optime ostendunt* 'les consuls se montrent très favorables [pour nous]'[7] à comparer avec Itin. Egeriae 2, 2 *qui locus usque in hodie ostenditur* 'cet endroit est montré aujourd'hui encore' (l'exemple prouve que la quasi-synonymie en question persiste en latin postclassique).[8] (Toutefois, il faut tenir compte de la disparition graduelle du passif synthétique.[9])

2.2 Présentation et ordre des termes

La variation de l'ordre des termes peut être envisagée sous l'angle de la synonymie syntaxique ; nous arrivons par là, après la diathèse, à un second grand domaine, où les différences de présentation concernent toute la phrase, mais portent cette fois sur le dynamisme de la communication. Naturellement, les différences présenta-

7 Cf. ibid. *Sed tamen se res sic habet* 'Mais les choses se présentent ainsi'.

8 Les domaines sémantiques privilégiés par ce rapprochement du pronominal et du passif ont été recensés par Bassols de Climent (1948 : 48–49) et Hofmann et Szantyr (1965 : 288–289). Pour une illustration convaincante de cette quasi-équivalence, cf. également la liste fournie par Cennamo (2001 : 54–55).

9 « In general, the use of the reflexive increases in correlation with the decrease of the passive morphology of the *infectum* stem » (Pinkster 2015 : 274).

tionnelles qui ont trait à la perspective communicative de la phrase recoupent celles qui sont réalisées par la diathèse (on a vu qu'un « patient » thématisé peut déclencher l'emploi du passif : Cic. Att. 3, 16 *litterae . . . a me leguntur*) ; nous devons cependant envisager ici un parcours de la phrase qui conduit des éléments déjà connus de l'interlocuteur aux informations nouvelles. Les recherches menées par Dirk G. J. Panhuis et Olga Spevak ont clarifié le rapport qui existe entre l'arrangement de la phrase et la visée communicative ; je me limiterai ici à quelques illustrations des procédés de thématisation et de rhématisation, pour souligner la flexibilité de l'ordre et la participation des différents types de syntagmes à l'« articulation communicative » de la phrase. Même si un verbe rhématique final est tout à fait usuel dans la prose classique latine,[10] il est parfaitement possible de placer un rhème au début de la phrase pour lui prêter une importance affective, comme dans Cic. Att. 3, 4 *Adlata est enim nobis rogatio de pernicie mea* 'En effet, on m'a fait connaître le projet de loi prévoyant ma ruine', ou tout simplement pour fixer une idée dominante du discours : Cic. Att. 1, 13, 1 *Accepi tuas tris iam epistulas* 'J'ai déjà reçu tes trois lettres'. Une thématisation forte a lieu lorsque le point de départ se détache du reste par une sorte de brisure de la phrase. Ainsi, une préposition « thématisante » peut réaliser l'extraction d'un syntagme, qui se placera en début de phrase : Cic. Att. 3, 7, 3 *de fratre ubi eum visuri essemus nesciebamus* 'pour mon frère, je ne savais pas où je pourrais le voir'. Également en fonction thématisante au début de la phrase, la conjonction *quod*, avec le sens 'quant au fait que', peut servir à résumer un problème, qui attend une réponse : Cic. fam. 14, 12 *In viam quod te des hoc tempore, nihil est* 'Quant au voyage que tu penses entreprendre, il ne peut pas en être question en ce moment'. Des tournures comme *hoc adfirmo, hoc confirmo, accessit ut, non faciam ut* servent également d'introducteurs de rhème. C'est ainsi que la soi-disant « liberté » de l'ordre des termes en latin est utilisée par les locuteurs conformément aux besoins de nature pragmatique qui apparaissent dans la communication.[11]

---

10 Cf. Panhuis (1982 : 117–118) ; Spevak (2010 : 29). Remarquons au passage que cette position finale du verbe n'est pas nécessairement une convention littéraire ; c'est plutôt une position non-marquée, par rapport à laquelle différents « écarts » peuvent être introduits dans la phrase.

11 Pour une récapitulation des « fonctions pragmatiques » en latin, cf. Pinkster (2015 : 31–32).

3 Niveau local : choix offerts à des points particuliers de la phrase

3.1 Relations sémantiques : marques renforcées

Pour passer maintenant au niveau du syntagme, nous pouvons constater que les phénomènes de synonymie syntaxique touchent très souvent au degré de condensation ou – ce qui est la même chose vue sous un autre angle – au degré d'explicitation grammaticale.[12] Le cas le plus simple consiste dans la présence d'une marque supplémentaire qui souligne de façon redondante l'existence d'une relation grammaticale. Un exemple banal pourrait être en latin l'expression du pronom personnel sujet, dont les locuteurs font l'économie en général, mais qui apparaît en cas d'opposition ou d'insistance.[13] Ainsi, dans les supplications adressées à son ami Atticus, Cicéron écrit:

Tu, ut adhuc fecisti, quam plurimis de rebus ad me velim scribas (Cic. Att. 3, 10, 3)
'Toi, comme tu l'as fait jusqu'ici, je voudrais que tu m'écrives d'autant de choses que possible'

Tu me, ut facis, opera, consilio, gratia iuva (ibid. 3, 11, 2)
'Toi, aide-moi, comme tu le fais déjà, de tes soins, de tes conseils, de ta gentillesse'

Sur un autre plan, nous savons bien que le subjonctif utilisé dans les propositions subordonnées sert souvent à insister sur la dépendance syntaxique ; cette insistance est particulièrement claire dans le cas de l'attraction modale, qui surajoute une marque de dépendance : Cic. Att. 3, 19, 1 *non quo mea interesset loci natura qui lucem omnino fugerem* 'non que la nature du lieu importe pour moi, qui ai toujours fui la lumière' (*fugerem* dans la subordonnée relative est un « rappel » du subjonctif *interesset*, nuance impossible à rendre en français). Les relations syntaxiques déjà indiquées dans la phrase peuvent être explicitées encore davantage, à l'aide de périphrases : *velim scribas* est un exemple absolument quotidien de la double expression de la « nécessité » (avec l'auxiliaire modal et le mode verbal à la fois). L'expression périphrastique du parfait (*litteras scriptas habeo* pour *litteras*

12 Concernant les rapports grammaticaux entre une expression réduite et une expression complétée (les procédés de « Reduktion » et d'« Ergänzung »), cf. Klein (1993).

13 Il faut ajouter naturellement les cas où le pronom personnel sujet est employé pour des raisons de clarté. Les aspects pragmatiques et diachroniques de la question ont été exposés par Herman (2006 [1991]). V. également Pinkster (2015 : 740).

scripsi) repose, à l'origine, sur le même mécanisme d'insistance. En ce qui concerne le subjonctif, la richesse temporelle de ce mode permettait, pendant un moment de l'évolution de la langue, de distinguer entre la possibilité envisagée comme réalisable et celle qui ne peut pas devenir réalité : il s'agit de l'opposition entre le type *faciam* « réalisable au présent » et le type *facerem* « non-réalisable au présent ». Or, les locuteurs peuvent user ou ne pas user de ce moyen de distinction. Dans

Troiaque nunc stares Priamique arx alta maneres (Verg. Aen. 2, 56)
'Troie, tu serais toujours debout, haute forteresse de Priam, tu serais là encore'

le temps verbal utilisé insiste sur une irréalité par ailleurs évidente ; en revanche, on peut dire que dans

o mihi praeteritos referat si Iuppiter annos (Verg. Aen. 8, 560)
'O si Jupiter voulait ramener mes années passées !'

le locuteur se contente de l'expression de l'hypothèse en tant que telle, en confiant l'interprétation (« irréelle ») au contexte. Ajoutons encore un domaine où le choix de la présentation a un effet stylistique immédiatement perceptible. Il s'agit de la transition interphrastique : la liaison entre phrases est-elle marquée et de quelle manière ? Dans ses lettres à Atticus, Cicéron penche à l'emploi d'un *nunc* délimitatif, pour expliciter la marche de sa pensée. Dans son compte rendu de voyage ayant une coloration légèrement populaire, Égérie accumule les particules « continuatrices », pour présenter un récit « bien ficelé », pour ainsi dire. Voici un passage caractéristique : Itin. Egeriae 8, 1 *De Arabia autem . . . Nos autem . . . Paret sane . . .* 8, 2 *Nunc autem*, etc.[14]

---

14 Remarquons sur ce point que le locuteur a souvent le choix entre hypotaxe et parataxe, cette dernière étant plus fréquente dans la langue parlée et dans les textes écrits proches de l'oralité. Une curieuse combinaison de l'*accusativus cum infinitivo* et de la construction paratactique peut être relevée dans un passage de Cic. Att. 3,9,2, où *dico* – à la différence de *puto* – n'est pas accompagné de la construction infinitive, mais d'un développement plus libre : *tantum dico quod scire te puto : nos non inimici sed invidi perdiderunt* 'je dis seulement ce que tu sais, je pense : ceux qui nous ont perdus, ce ne sont pas les ennemis, mais les envieux'. Cf. cette remarque de Pinkster (2021 : 9) : « there are (. . .) cases which seem to have a status in-between one complex sentence and two independent simple sentences ».

3.2 Procédés emphatiques

Le système linguistique prévoit des « présentations » emphatiques locales qui peuvent surgir à différents points de la phrase. Bien que nous ne connaissions pas dans son détail le système prosodique du latin, nous pouvons nous former une idée des divers procédés qui servent à créer des écarts par rapport à l'allure neutre d'un discours ordinaire. L'insistance sur un terme important fait partie de ces moyens : Cic. Att. 3, 15, 5 *Caeci, caeci inquam fuimus* 'Nous étions aveugles, je dis, aveugles'. La répétition d'un élément au lieu de sa pronominalisation est surprenante et dénote l'insistance, comme on l'observe chez Égérie pour des noms de lieux:

reversi sumus in Clesma. In Clesma autem cum venissemus (Itin. Egeriae 6, 4)
'nous sommes retournés à Clesma. Et lorsque nous sommes arrivés à Clesma . . .'

Nos autem . . . per media Ramesse transivimus ; quae Ramessen [sic] *civitas nunc campus est* (ibid. 8, 1)
'Et nous . . . nous avons traversé Ramesse ; cette ville de Ramesse est aujourd'hui un désert'.

Et naturellement, l'hyperbate fait partie de ces moyens emphatiques, avec un arrangement des termes qui accentue certaines relations, précisément par la distance inhabituelle des éléments:

monet annus et almum | quae rapit hora diem (Hor. carm. 4, 7, 7–8)
'la saison nous avertit et le temps qui ravit l'agrément des jours'

nec Lethaea valet Theseus abrumpere caro | vincula Pirithoo (ibid. 27–28)
'ni Thésée n'a la force de briser les chaînes infernales de son cher Pirithoos'.

La métrique a son rôle à jouer dans les deux exemples cités, puisque les éléments des syntagmes disjoints se trouvent à la fin de deux vers successifs.

4 Remarques sur les équivalences en discours

En guise d'appendice, je m'aventure dans le vaste empire du discours, avec des exemples simples pris dans les lettres de Cicéron, pour montrer comment une quasi-synonymie peut se réaliser au-delà des limites de la phrase. On peut placer ainsi côte à côte deux phrases prises dans des lettres très proches dans le temps et reflétant le même état psychique : Cic. Att. 3, 5 *Ego vivo miserrimus et maxime dolore conficior* 'Moi, je vis d'une vie misérable et je suis accablé par la plus grande douleur', Cic. Att. 3, 6 *Me vix misereque sustento* 'je me soutiens misérablement et à peine' ; et de façon semblable, nous voyons revenir l'auteur, à l'intérieur de la même lettre, sur la même thématique, par l'utilisation de la figure rhétorique appelée « commutando verba » : Cic. Att. 3, 10, 2 *Mitto cetera intolerabilia ; etenim fletu impedior* 'J'omets le reste, qui serait intolérable ; de toute façon, les larmes m'empêchent de continuer', et un peu plus loin : ibid. 3,10,3 *ad te minus multa scribo quod . . . maerore impedior* 'je t'écris plus brièvement, car . . . la tristesse m'empêche [d'être plus long]'. Les comparaisons de ce type pourraient conduire à une appréhension plus précise de la notion de style.

5 Conclusion

Les présentations différentes d'un contenu sémantique constituent une possibilité qui s'enracine profondément dans le système linguistique. Le choix entre ces présentations fait partie de la compétence des locuteurs, avec des implications psycholinguistiques, dont l'exploration reste toujours féconde. Comme le dit Catherine Fuchs, « maîtriser une langue, c'est être capable d'associer une (ou des) signification(s) aux expressions de la langue (c'est-à-dire les comprendre) et être capable de produire ou d'identifier des reformulations de ces significations » (Fuchs 1982 : 93). Notre approche se place dans le cadre de l'étude de cette « maîtrise », qui peut s'appeler la compétence paraphrastique ; cependant, à l'intérieur de ce cadre, nous nous sommes concentrés sur la sphère où la langue offre une possibilité de choix plus ou moins formalisée aux locuteurs qui cherchent l'expression adéquate. En effet, lors de la formulation d'un contenu sémantique, les locuteurs peuvent choisir entre des points de départ différents et peuvent élaborer les rapports internes de ce contenu suivant une gamme dont les degrés sont significatifs au cours de la transmission du message.

Bibliographie

Bassols de Climent, M. (1948). *Sintaxis histórica de la lengua latina II*. Barcelona: Escuela de Filología de Barcelona.

Cennamo, M. (2001). On the Reorganization of Voice Distinctions and Grammatical Relations in Late Latin. In C. Moussy (Ed.), *De lingua Latina nouae quaestiones* (pp. 51–65). Louvain/Paris: Peeters.

Ernout, A. & Thomas, F. (2002 [1953]). *Syntaxe latine*. Paris: Klincksieck.

Flobert, P. (1975). *Les verbes déponents latins*. Paris: Les Belles Lettres.

Fuchs, C. (1982). *La paraphrase*. Paris: Presses Universitaires de France.

Herman, J. (2006 [1991]). On the Grammatical Subject in Late Latin. In J. Herman, *Du latin aux langues romanes II* (pp. 55–64). Tübingen: Niemeyer.

Hofmann, J. & Szantyr, A. (1965). *Lateinische Syntax und Stilistik*. München: Beck.

Kiss, S. (1982). *Tendances évolutives de la syntaxe verbale en latin tardif*. Debrecen: Université de Debrecen.

Klein, W. (1993). Ellipse. In J. Jacobs, A. von Stechow, W. Sternfeld & T. Venneman (Eds.), *Syntax. Ein internationales Handbuch zeitgenössischer Forschung* (pp. 763–799). Berlin/New York: Walter de Gruyter.

Lyons, J. (1977). *Semantics*. Cambridge: Cambridge University Press.

Panhuis, D. G. J. (1982). *The Communicative Perspective in the Sentence. A Study of Latin Word Order.* Amsterdam: John Benjamins.

Pinkster, H. (2015). *The Oxford Latin Syntax. Volume 1: The Simple Clause*. Oxford: Oxford University Press.

Pinkster, H. (2021). *The Oxford Latin Syntax. Volume 2: The Complex Sentence and Discourse*. Oxford: Oxford University Press.

Spevak, O. (2010). *Constituent Order in Classical Latin Prose*. Amsterdam: John Benjamins.

Roland Hoffmann

“Valenzmisere” and Latin Syntax and Semantics

Abstract: Valency seems to be an established concept even in Latin linguistics. Nevertheless, there has been a long discussion, especially in German linguistics, about whether or not everything has been done to get real valency, that is: to have a homogeneous concept and not to define valency in different ways. The many and confusing ways to define valency were named by Jacobs in a special publication devoted to this problem (1994) “Valency Misery”, in German: “Valenzmisere”. One way out of this valency misery is now named “multi-dimensional valency concept” (MDV) by Jacobs himself (2003). In Latin linguistics we have several concepts, from Happ’s more syntax-oriented one (1976) to Pinkster’s semantic concept (1990; 2015) and to Lehmann’s typological approach (2002). In this paper I will first try to show what these three different approaches have in common. Secondly, it will be shown what exactly the MDV concept means in Latin linguistics. Thirdly, it will be demonstrated which theoretical prerequisites should be maintained for a successful use of the concept of valency in Latin syntax and semantics. This paper will also try to solve some questions concerning the distinction of obligatory and optional actants introduced by Happ and some so-called valency rules (Jacobs 2003) which can probably also be defined for Latin.

Keywords: facultative arguments, multi-dimensional valency concept, obligatory arguments, semantic valency, syntactic valency, valency misery, valency rules

1 Introduction

The idea of valency, which goes back to Lucien Tesnière, has long since become an integral part of the younger Latin syntax and can be found, for example, in the syntax of Touratier (1994)[1] and of Pinkster (2015). After Dressler was the first to

1 Touratier’s treatment of valency in his smaller School Grammar shows how a valency-grammatical analysis of a Latin sentence (*cēterī pecuniā ex hīs incommodīs sē līberāvērunt*, cf. Cɪc. Ver. 2, 5, 23) can be represented in an immediate constituent analysis system (Touratier 2012: 224, §421).

Roland Hoffmann, Mainz, Germany

https://doi.org/10.1515/9783111332956-030

apply this concept to Latin grammar in 1970, Heinz Happ published a special study in the 1970s, the *Grundfragen*, which are often cited to this day.[2]

Happ and Pinkster are the representatives of two opposing concepts. While Happ tried to develop a purely syntactic approach, Pinkster's approach was primarily semantically conceived. The two different approaches are clearly expressed in (1) and (2).

(1a) "Die Dependenzbeschreibung vom Verb aus ermöglicht – mit wenigen Ausnahmen alle Teile des Satzes zu erfassen und damit die *syntaktische Gesamtstruktur* des Satzes präzis und übersichtlich zu bestimmen." (Happ 1976: 21)

(1b) "Das gewählte *syntaktische* Vorgehen ist nicht problemlos, ist aber mit weniger Schwierigkeiten verbunden als eine *semantische* oder *logische* Methode und führt relativ sicher zu klaren Ergebnissen." (Happ 1976: 21)

(2a) "This clause [sc. *At enim illi noctu occentabunt ostium*. . ., PLAVT. Persa 569, R. H.] centres on the verb *occentabunt*. [. . .] the verb *occento* is a two-place verb; that is, it requires two words or phrases to complete its meaning. For elements of a clause that are semantically obligatory in this way, the term argument will be used." (Pinkster 2015: 20)

(2b) "The number of arguments a particular verb requires depends *upon its meaning*. The term VALENCY is used to describe this." (Pinkster 2015: 19, emphasis by R. H.)

These two approaches will be analyzed in Section 2 and the sources and authors, namely Gerhard Helbig (1971) and Simon Dik (1997), will be briefly discussed. It will be displayed, that Happ's approach does not, but needs not work entirely without semantics either, or conversely, Pinkster's recourse to Dik will outline that he already saw some problems of what Storrer (1992: 11) has more precisely referred to as valency determination (Valenzermittlung).[3]

2 There is also a study by Ernst Heilig from 1978 that evaluates a larger corpus but is not far from Happ's approach. Thomas Lambertz goes into more detail on Tesnière's approach in his dissertation (1982).

3 Christian Touratier's more structuralist approach, which he published in his *Syntaxe Latine* in 1994, cannot be dealt with here nor can Christian Lehmann's typological approach be studied here, which he presented in one of the longer presentations at the 11th ICLL in Amsterdam in 2001 (Lehmann 2002).

On the other hand, valency research has developed rapidly[4] and today has largely become a multi-dimensional model. This model will be presented in the Section 3 based on the pilot publication by Joachim Jacobs.

In the Section 4 we will try to work out the peculiarities of the Latin approaches. Two problems will arise: firstly, the question of optional actants ("fakultative Ergänzungen") and, secondly, the problem of verb variants. Basically, we will present Happ's and Pinkster's positions on these topics and then try to present a multi-dimensional valency approach. Finally, in the Section 5, consideration should be given to the question how the two works by Happ and Pinkster should be seen from the perspective of the multi-dimensional valency approach and where there are possibilities for further research.

2 Two Contrary Approaches to Valency in Latin Linguistics

Not only the time span between the two Latin approaches of about forty years, but also the different conceptual environment are the reasons for these quite different positions in Happ and Pinkster. If we examine just one factor, it is the attitude towards generative grammar that clearly distinguishes the two positions. Happ had a thoroughly positive relationship to Chomsky's grammar theory, which was still prevalent in the 1970s. For example, he presents the "phrase structure grammar as a generative rule system" and concludes by describing some transformation tests as "a very useful procedure" ("ein recht brauchbares Verfahren", p. 415).

Pinkster, on the other hand, had a rather negative relationship towards generative grammar, without explicitly stating this here. It is typical of one of the theories Pinkster uses, namely Dik's Functional Grammar, that at the beginning of this theory, the author describes Chomsky's assumption of an innate language ability as a "mystery [. . .] which can only be understood by assuming that language has been there all the time in the form of a genetically preprogrammed structure of the mind" (Dik 1997: 6). Furthermore, in the first chapter, Dik explicitly rejects the assumption of any transformations (3).

4 "Der Forschungsdiskussion, die lange Zeit nach der richtigen Valenzebene bzw. dem richtigen Abgrenzungskriterium für Ergänzungen bestimmt ist [. . .], gibt Jacobs [. . .] eine überraschende Wende [. . .]. Für ihn ist Valenz nicht länger ein einheitliches System, sondern eine Art Oberbegriff für eine Reihe von voneinander unabhängigen Valenzbindungsbeziehungen." (von der Becke 2021: 40).

(3) **"Avoid transformations"**
FG [Functional Grammar, R.H.] avoids transformations in the sense of structure-changing operations. Structure-changing operations are operations which effect changes in preestablished structures through deletion, substitution, and permutation of constituents. In general, FG is based on the assumption that once has been built up, this structure will be retained throughout the further derivation of the linguistic expression. In other words, a derivation is a matter of gradual expansion rather than a transformational mapping of one structure onto another." (Dik 1997: 19)

This premise of avoiding transformations clearly shows Dik's rejection of generative theory. Pinkster has never shown any sympathy for this theory either.

2.1 Happ's *Grundfragen*

We now come to the syntactic conception typical of Happ's valency approach. Firstly, when discussing the concept of valency (1976: 126ff.), Happ discussed the other two possibilities, a semantic (136f.) and a logical valency (137–144), in order finally to choose the syntactic valency as his own position. He defines the syntactic valency with recourse to a definition by Helbig as follows (4):

(4) "Die syntaktische Valenz meint 'die obligatorische oder fakultative Besetzung von Leerstellen in einer bestimmten, vom Verb her geforderten Zahl und Art, differenziert nach den Einzelsprachen also'." (Happ 1976: 144, cit. Helbig 1971: 280)

What is also interesting is a statement made by Happ on the relationship to semantic valency:

(5) "So unmethodisch und riskant es zum gegenwärtigen Zeitpunkt wäre, die syntaktische Valenz vom Semantischen her erfassen zu wollen, so engstirnig wäre es, die Semantik für alle Zeiten aus der Betrachtung der syntaktischen Valenz auszuklammern. Nur ist der geeignete Zeitpunkt, sie zu untersuchen, noch nicht gekommen." (Happ 1976: 154)

Apparently, the time for which Happ was waiting, has come since the semantic-pragmatic turn which seems to have taken place everywhere since the beginning seventies. It is also interesting that Happ did not completely ignore the semantics.

After discussing all three levels of valency, syntactic, semantic, and logical valency, he writes in (6).

(6) "Da es uns in den 'Grundfragen' um die Erhellung einer Einzelsprache geht, beschränken wir uns auf die für die Einzelsprache grundlegende syntaktische Valenz und erörtern die semantische Valenz (semantische Kombinierbarkeit) dann nur kurz zusätzlich." (Happ 1976: 146f.)

Besides the number and the morpho-syntactic form of the complements, Happ wants to add certain semantic information concerning the meaningful combination of the actants. He wants to avoid nonsense sentences, as he explains elsewhere in case of the verb *admonere* (7).

(7) "Es zeigt sich aber bald, daß man den Angaben über die syntaktische Valenz eines Verbs ein Minimum von semantischen Bestimmungen hinzufügen muß, wenn nicht widersinnige Sätze entstehen sollen. So genügt die Angabe der syntaktischen Valenz z.B. von *admonere* nicht, einen unsinnigen Satz wie
(147) *silva valetudinem de grammatica abmonuit*[5]
zu verhindern." (Happ 1976: 149f.)

Based on the Valency Dictionary for German Verbs by Helbig and Schenkel (1973), Happ has quoted their list of semantic features such as abstract, animate, indefinite, etc. (Happ 1976: 168f.). Nevertheless, this is superfluous for describing a corpus language where nearly no-nonsense sentence has been transmitted. So Happ can adhere to "purely asemantic methods" ("nach rein asemantischen Methoden", 1976: 168) for describing the syntactic valency. The author emphasizes that "this additional semantic information [. . .] can at best be omitted for purely syntactical questions such as sentence models [. . .] and for parts of the case theory" (1976: 150).[6]

5 Other nonsense sentences in German which Happ cites in his book are: (a) *Der traumlose Übermut erblickt den Lampenschirm* (1976: 362, [52]); (b) *Der Kroklokwafzi ist ein Nasobem* (1976: 431, [6]); (c) *Die Langeweile zeigt dem Auto den Durst* (1976: 431, [7]). In (a) and (c) there are transgressions of the semantic restrictions. In (a) and (c) an abstract noun cannot behave like an animate being and *observe* (*erblicken*) something and it cannot be a being which can have dreams or not (*traumlos*); in (c) we have also an abstract noun (*Durst*) which acts as a receiver of the state of affairs *to demonstrate* (*zeigen*). The same sentence referring to (b) consists of two nouns which are invented words and do not exist in the language. Happ uses these instances to show that his "Strukturformel(n)" are really asemantic ("asemantisch", p. 431).

6 In the original version: "Diese zusätzlichen semantischen Angaben kann man bei rein syntaktischen Fragen wie z.B. bei den Satzmodellen [. . .] und bei Teilen der Kasuslehre allenfalls noch weglassen."

2.2 Pinkster's *Oxford Latin Syntax*

In his semantic valency approach, which goes back to the theory of Functional Grammar,[7] Pinkster says in the sentence already quoted in (2a) that the number of arguments a particular verb requires depends on its meaning.[8] In the case of zero-valent verb *pluit* Pinkster says that this verb does not need an additional actant to "complete its meaning". This formulation is also an expression of Pinkster's semantic concept of valency.

Pinkster then addresses the problem that a verb can have more than one meaning, such as *dico*, which is a) 'to speak, to hold a speech', b) 'to say', c) 'to tell' and d) 'to appoint'. Each of these meanings has its own valency. For instance, in meaning (a) *dicere* is monovalent and requires only one speaker whereas in meaning (b) there are two arguments, namely a speaker and the content of the speech. Furthermore, Pinkster says that the issue of verb variants is even more complicated since a verb can have multiple valencies in the same meaning. The lexical properties of the arguments would also determine the valency. Pinkster illustrates this with the verb *incipere*, which is bivalent with a human agent (8a), but with a first argument signifying a period, for example *autumnus*, has only one argument (8b).

(8a) *Ita commeatus est, qui frumenti causa processerant, tuto ad se recipit* [sc. ***Caesar***] *et rem frumentariam expedire* ***incipit***. (Caes. civ. 1, 54, 5)
'Thus he [sc. Caesar] recovers in safety the stores and the men who had gone out on the foraging expedition, and begins to settle the difficulties of his food supply.'

(8b) *Nam desinit aestas, /* ***incipit autumnus*** *media sub Virgine utrimque.* (Manil. 2, 176–177, cited according to Pinkster 2015: 20)
'For at the middle of the Virgin summer on one side ceases and autumn on the other begins.'

According to Pinkster (2015: 20), valency is "essentially a quantitative notion", as he previously spoke quantitatively of zero- to three-place verbs. However, at the same time there is a semantic relationship (e.g. in the form of the case role as an agent)

7 As Pinkster expressly states in the preface (2015: xxxi), apart from the "Kühner Stegmann" itself and Dik's Theory of Functional Grammar also Talmy Givon's Syntax and the grammar of the English language by Randolph Quirk and others were his "main sources of inspiration".

8 "The number of arguments a particular verb requires depends *upon its meaning*. The term VALENCY is used to describe this." (Pinkster 2015: 19, emphasis by R. H.)

and a syntactic relationship (in the syntactic function as a subject), whereby the author refers to a later section for these two topics.

What can be said is that Pinkster undoubtedly has a semantic concept of valency, but that he also considers valency primarily as a quantitative parameter, emphasizing the semantic and syntactic relationships of the arguments to the verb. But there is no distinction between obligatory and optional in this concept. The first case applies, for example, to support verb constructions, where the noun can never or only in very few exceptional cases be missing. According to Pinkster, the semantic relationship is that the verb and its arguments together form a particular type of situation. However, a situation says nothing about the number of actants.

Pinkster's semantic approach corresponds to Dik's one. When it comes to valency, Dik speaks of "predicate frame", drafts the following valency formula for a ditransitive sentence such as *Paul gives the book to Mary*[9] and finally comments on it as follows (9):

(9) "*give* [V] (x_1: <anim> (x_1))$_{Ag}$ (x_2)$_{Go}$ (x_3: <anim> (x_3))$_{Rec}$
Each predicate frame specifies the form (here give), the type (here V), and the valency or argument structure of the predicate. The argument structure of the predicate give is here specified as consisting of three argument positions, indicated by x_1, x_2, x_3, carrying semantic functions of Agent (Ag), Goal (Go), and Recipient (Rec), where the first and the third argument are constrained by the selection <animate>.
Each basic predicate frame in the lexicon is associated with a number of *meaning postulates*, through which the predicate is semantically related to other predicates of the language. If these meaning postulates add up to a full specification of the meaning of the predicate, they may be termed *meaning definitions*. For derived predicates, the meaning resulting from the application of some predicate formation rule will be specified in that predicate formation rule itself." (Dik 1997: 59)

This valency formula, which contains only semantic entries such as the role designations for agent and goal for the ditransitive verb *to give*, but not the type of morpho-syntactic marking, clearly shows the semantic conception on the one hand, and on the other hand in the second sentence of the explanation, which speaks of meaning postulates from the lexicon and emphasizes the difference between simple and derived predicates.

9 In Latin, for example, *dabis nobis diem aliquem* 'you will assign us a day' (Cic. nat. deor. 3, 94).

3 A Multi-dimensional Concept of Modern Valency Research

The general research on the theory of valency was, at least in the German linguistics, determined for a long time by the question what the correct level of valency was, the syntactic, the semantic or even the logic level and how to distinguish arguments and free adjuncts adequately. It was a publication by Joachim Jacobs in 1994, already circulating in internal university papers since 1986 (1994: 2) that brought about a turning point. At first it looked like a "valency misery", namely the "dilemma [. . .] that completely different and competing concepts about the basic concept of valency came into circulation, which was reflected above all in the contrary conceptions of the valency dictionaries" (Hoffmann 1997: 21). Later, what was initially described as misery was recognized as the basis for a more differentiated concept of valency, which even went so far as to abolish the distinction between arguments and free adjuncts.

For Jacobs, valency is no longer a unified phenomenon, but "a kind of generic term" for a series of originally seven such relationships or syntagmatic relations that are independent of one another.[10] Later, in a "postscript" from 1993 (1994: 69–72), Jacobs eliminated two of them because they were not independent relationships.[11]

The following relationships which were later renamed to the syntactic and semantic area can be distinguished according to categorial-syntactic (10) and semantic valency dimensions (11) (which are in brackets) (von der Becke 2021: 44):[12]

(10) **Kategoriale (syntaktische) Valenzdimensionen (Categorial [Syntactic] Valency Dimensions):**
Realisierungsforderungen (≈ Notwendigkeit: Necessity)
Merkmalforderungen (≈ formale Spezifizität: Formal Specificity)

10 Namely: 1. Necessity ("Notwendigkeit"), 2. Involvement ("Beteiligtheit"), 3. Argumentativeness ("Argumenthaftigkeit"), 4. Exocentricity ("Exozentrizität"), 5. Formal Specificity ("Formale Spezifizität"), 6. Content Specificity ("Inhaltliche Spezifizität"), 7. Association ("Assoziiertheit").

11 These were "exocentricity" and "associatedness".

12 Explanation of the double designations: According to von der Becke, the more recent terminology used by Jacobs in (2003) enables "a stronger focus on the demands of the verb as a valency carrier on its respective companions" and seems to "reflect the fundamental independence and equivalence of the individual valency dimensions more clearly" (2021: 44). However, we choose the earlier terms here.

(11) **Semantische Valenzdimensionen (Semantic Valency Dimensions):**
Relatforderungen (≈ Argumenthaftigkeit: Argumentality)
Sortale Forderungen (≈ inhaltliche Spezifizität: Content Specificity)
Rollenforderungen (≈ Beteiligtheit/Partizipation: Involvement/Participation)

The individual valency dimensions have the following meaning. "Necessity" means the number of arguments, i. e. the "quantitative valency" (cf. Dik 1997: 79) while the "formal specificity" refers to the morphosyntactic form of the additions, the questions, which cases are present, whether an adposition appears or whether infinitive constructions or sentence-valued objects are used. Of the semantic valency dimensions, "argumentality" means the number of entities needed for a given issue (which may be different from the number of actants). "Content specificity" are the semantic properties of the supplements, such as the first actant having to be animated. In contrast, "involvement" or "participation" refers to the functions or semantic roles of the individual actors that arise in relation to the specific situation. For example, the first actant must be controllable. According to von der Becke, "involvement" is, in contrast to "content specificity", "implications that are affected by normal sentence negation" (12).

(12) "So folgt zwar aus *Er erblickt die Tür* die Situationskontrolle des Subjekts, aus *Er erblickt die Tür nicht* jedoch nicht." (von der Becke 2021: 55, emphasis by underlining by R. H.)

At the end of each discussion of the two groups of valency dimensions in (13) and (14), von der Becke drafts a formula to render a sentence like *He opens the door*.

(13) "(51) SynVal: /nom^{y}/akk^{x}
In dieser Repräsentation enthalten sind zunächst – durch Schrägstrich markiert – Informationen über die Anzahl der syntaktischen Begleiter, die ein Verb fordert, für verstecken zwei. Darüber hinaus enthält die Notation die mit den syntaktischen Valenzstellen verbundenen formalem Merkmale – bei dem Verb verstecken die Kasus Nominativ und Akkusativ." (von der Becke 2021: 49)

(14) "(62) SemVal: λxλyλs [VERSTECKEN] [s] ($_{+\text{konkret}}$X) $_{(+\text{belebt},\ +\ \text{Kontrolle}}$Y]
Die semantische Valenz des Satzes (Er versteckt den Schlüssel) wird durch die präfigierten Lambda- Varianten-Paare zum Ausdruck gebracht (vgl. Jacobs 1994: 289). Sie geben an, dass die Bedeutung von verstecken ein dreistelliges Prädikat ist. Die Variablen in den Klammerpaaren markieren dabei die Relate der durch das Prädikat denotierten Beziehung, wobei x

und y für Individuen oder Objekte stehen und s für eine Situation. Während dem Situationsrelat keine kategoriale Valenzstelle entspricht, repräsentiert die erste Individuenrelatposition der semantischen Valenz von *verstecken* die Stelle ‚/akk' in der kategorialen Valenz ‚/nom/akk' des Valenzträgers, die zweite Individuenposition die Stelle ‚/nom'.' Diese Korrespondenzen werden durch Individuierungen in der kategorialen Valenz [. . .] sichtbar gemacht." (von der Becke 2021: 56)

Why is this a *multi*-dimensional valency concept? In (15) Jacobs explains that these individual dimensions are independent of one another.

(15) "Die theoretische Brisanz der Zerlegung der Valenz in verschiedene Dimensionen liegt darin, dass diese Dimensionen unabhängig voneinander sind. Es handelt sich also nicht um verschiedene Aspekte ein und desselben Phänomens, die immer zusammen vorliegen müssen, sondern um verschiedene Phänomene, die zusammen vorliegen können, aber nicht müssen." (Jacobs 2003: 390)

Jacobs substantiates this thesis, which can only be asserted here, in a detailed section of an encyclopedia article (2003: 390–394). One consequence that results from this independence is that today's valency analyses should consider all five valency dimensions, since these are all independent parameters.

Apart from the demand that all five valency dimensions should be analysed is the formulation of so-called valency rules ("Valenzgesetze") which are according to Jacobs (2003: 395–398):

(16) "[Als Valenzgesetze bezeichne ich] alle Generalisierungen über natürliche Sprachen, die wesentlichen Gebrauch von Begriffen der Valenztheorie machen. Da diese Begriffe [. . .] zwischen den Dimensionen der Valenz differenzieren, tun dies auch die mit ihnen formulierten Gesetze."

4 Problems of Describing Valency

4.1 The Question of Optional Actants

A basic feature of Happ's book is known to be the distinction between obligatory and optional actants and the term of a "fakultative Ergänzung" (1976: 226–238). The missing actant in (17a) in comparison to (17b), an indication of direction, cannot be added from the context nor can it be supplied by contextually determined omissions, nor explained with a list of contextual peculiarities (1976: 241–258; similarly Heilig 1978: 145–149).[13]

(17a) *Vercingetorix ubi de Caesaris adventu cognovit,* [. . .] *obviam Caesari proficiscitur.* (Caes. Gall. 7, 12, 1)
'As soon as he heard of Caesar's approach Vercingetorix [. . .] started to meet him.'

(17b) *His rebus confectis in Haeduos proficiscitur.* (Caes. Gall. 7, 90, 1)
'When these affairs were settled, he started for the country of the Aedui.'

We will revisit this distinction here from the perspective of the multi-dimensional concept of valency. Pinkster explicitly addresses the omission of actants and cites Happ's distinction but refrains from further comment (Pinkster 2015: 80 and n. 15).

As is well known, Happ went back to Helbig when accepting optional actants, above all to explanations, published in an essay (Helbig 1971). The citation found in Helbig in (18) is interesting for the understanding and the origin of the category of optional supplements.

(18) „In der Kategorie der engen Verbergänzungen fallen somit die obligatorischen und fakultativen Aktanten zusammen: In der Tiefenstruktur gibt es keinen Unterschied zwischen beiden, da sie beide unter dem Knoten der Verbalphrase stehen und beide in den Bereich der Subkategorisierung des Verbs fallen. In der Tiefenstruktur gibt es somit keine fakultative Valenz: Eine solche fakultative Valenz entsteht erst in der Oberflächenstruktur auf Grund bestimmter kontextueller Merkmale (Vorerwähntheit, Kontrastivität, Situationskontext usw.). Eine fakultative Valenz setzt aber immer voraus, daß es sich in der Tiefenstruktur um eine enge Verbergänzung (EV) handelt; diese Tatsache unterscheidet die fakultative Valenz grundsätzlich von der freien Angabe (= FV).

13 Substantial criticism of this type of ellipse filter has already been expressed by Heberlein (1986): "Zusammenfassend läßt sich über Happs Katalog von 'Kontextbedingungen' sagen, daß er ziemlich wertlos ist, da zwei von drei Gruppen (Rubriken I–VI, 'Verbalform' und 'Satzeinleitung') nicht geeignet sind, das Phänomen der Weglassung von Aktanten adäquat in den Griff zu bekommen. Da der 'Filter' nicht alle anaphorischen Ellipsen erfassen kann, ergibt sich als Konsequenz, daß unter den Einträgen 'fakultativer Ergänzungen' in der Valenzliste (Happ 1976: 491ff.) auch anaphorische Ellipsen auftauchen. Andererseits werden, wie gezeigt, auch 'echte' Aktanten ausgefiltert, sobald sie von Rubrik I–VI erfaßt werden." (Heberlein 1986: 49f.)

Dabei ist die zuerst genannte primäre Unterscheidung unabhängig vom Kontext in der Tiefenstruktur angelegt, die zuletzt genannte sekundäre Unterscheidung ist vom Kontext abhängig und eine Oberflächenerscheinung. Wir haben somit eine doppelte Differenzierung:
1. eine primäre Unterscheidung zwischen notwendigen (=valenzgebundenen) und nichtnotwendigen (= freien) Gliedern, von denen nur die ersten durch Valenz an das Verb gebunden sind [. . .].
2. eine sekundäre Unterscheidung zwischen obligatorischen und fakultativen Aktanten andererseits, die beide im Stellenplan des Verbs verankert, nach Zahl und Art bestimmt und beschränkt sind." (Helbig 1971: 272)

At this point, a graphic tree can be easily inserted, which Helbig presents as an example (19) and which is apparently intended to depict something like a deep structure (EV = narrow complement; FV = free adjunct).

(19) Deep structure of a verb with a facultative actant according to Gerhard Helbig (1971: 272):

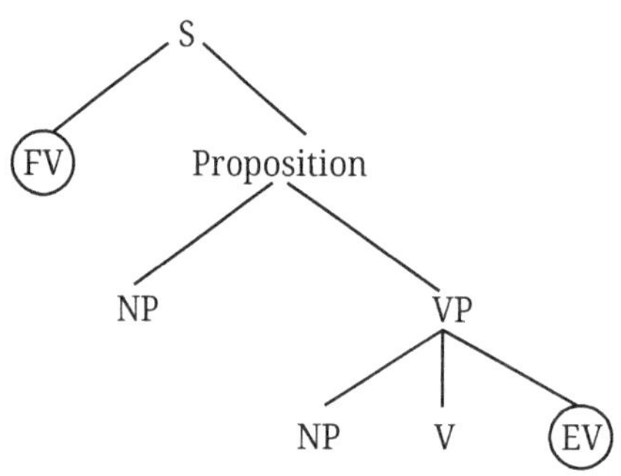

Helbig thus refers here to the two-level model of a surface and a deep structure of Generative Grammar in the 1965 version of "Aspects" and says that the "optional valency [. . .] only arises in the surface structure due to certain contextual features."

Anyone who does not share the assumption of this two-level model will have theoretical difficulties with this concept of optional actants. Accordingly, Jacobs who tries to show this contradictory sentence analysis by an own tree expresses skepticism about this assumption (20).

(20) Double tree of the sentence "dass er [den Vertrag] unterschreibt" with (20a) and without (20b) a second actant according to Jacobs (2003: 393):

a.

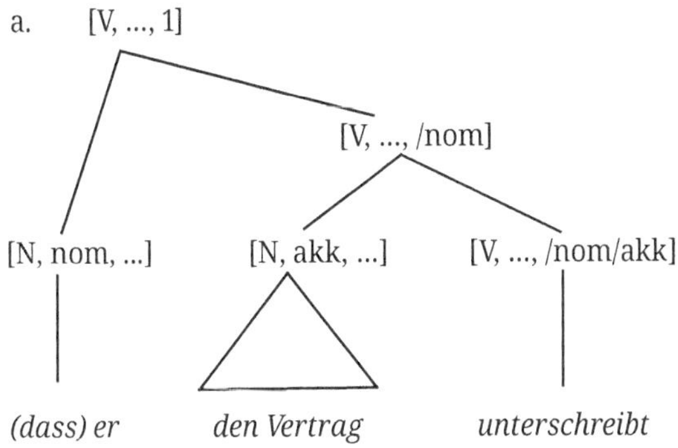

b.

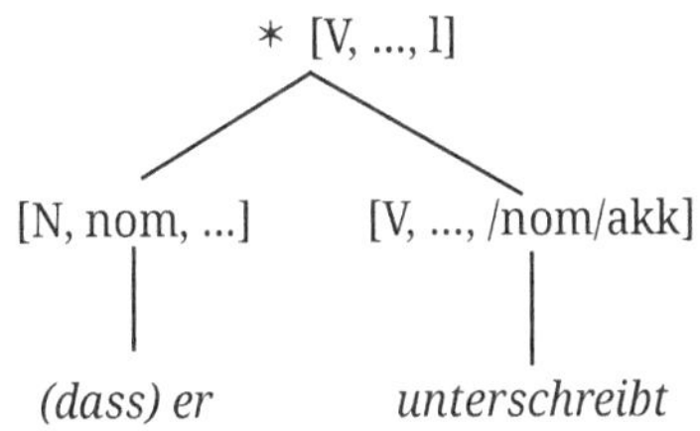

Jacobs explains this contradictory tree as follows:

(21) “[. . .] [sc. Graph] 20b verletzt für /akk das Prinzip, dass KR-Valenzstellen[14] gesättigt oder nach oben transferiert werden müssen. Und tatsächlich wäre es unlogisch anzunehmen, eine Merkmalsforderung könne ohne Realisierung einer Konstituente, die das Merkmal hat, erfüllt werden.” (Jacobs 2003: 393)

In short: Happ’s concept of an optional valency, which goes back to Helbig, should be abandoned, as it presupposes a grammar model that is no longer adequate and is sometimes vehemently criticized today. Instead, the phenomenon behind facultative valency is a phenomenon that can be better explained by the lexicon.

4.2 The Problem of Valency Variants

The second question that can be considered from the point of view of a multidimensional valency concept is the question of the valency variants. We choose an

14 KR is short for “kategoriale Repräsentation (categorical representation)” (Jacobs 2003: 379), i.e. the syntactic representation of valency. Jacobs distinguishes the KR, the “phonological representation”, i.e. “the relevant aspects of the phonetic form, e.g. the sequence of segments” and the “semantic representation that characterizes the grammatically determined meaning of the word”.

example from the documents described by Happ, namely *providere*, which, as is well known, has two distinct valencies (1976: 453) depending on the case of the actant which is either accusative (22a) or dative (22b).

(22a) *His enim in naturis nihil inest quod vim memoriae, mentis, cogitationis habeat, quod et praeterita teneat et* ***futura provideat*** *et complecti possit praesentia.* (Cic. Tusc. 1, 66)
'For in these elements there is nothing to possess the power of memory, thought, reflection, nothing capable of retaining the past, or **foreseeing** the future and grasping the present.'

(22b) *Sunt autem alii philosophi* [. . .] *qui deorum mente atque ratione omnem mundum administrari et regi censeant, neque vero id solum, sed etiam ad isdem* ***hominum vitae*** *consuli et* ***provideri.*** (Cic. nat. deor. 1, 4)
'There are however other philosophers [. . .] who believe that the whole world is ruled and governed by divine intelligence and reason; and not this only, but also that the gods' providence **watches over** the life of men.'[15]

Here, too, this newer conception of valency has enabled a more differentiated view of valency, which must also be reflected in the lexicon in the case of different valencies to be applied. In the case of homonymy and polysemy, i. e. in the case of two different but coincidentally identical lexemes with different meanings,[16] homonymy, and in the case of two lexemes of common linguistic origin, polysemy[17] (*incipere*, *accipere*), different entries in the lexicon are to be assumed.

Both authors, Happ and Pinkster, start from valency variants. In Happ, who brings an "Alphabetical verb list" (1976: 556–565) following a typology of sentence models (1976: 462ff.), there are mostly (32x) only two variants available. But there are also five verbs with three variants (*ducere* [450], *fieri* [450], *iudicare* [451], *mittere* [451], *vocare* [452]), three verbs with four variants (*postulare* [563], *relinquere* [564] and *venire* [565]), one verb each with five (*facere* [560]) and six variants (*esse* [560]). Happ distinguishes five cases that lead to variants (23):

---

15 The better translation of *provideri* is the following German one by O. Gigon and L. Straume-Zimmermann: "Es gibt jedoch andere Philosophen, [. . .], welche glauben [. . .], daß diese selben Götter sich auch um das Leben der Menschen kümmern und *für es sorgen.*" (Italics by R. H.)

16 Rarely, but certainly present in Latin with certain compounds: e.g. *crēvī* to *cernere* and *crēscere*; *dēcrēvī* to *dēcernere* (Cic. off. 3, 113: *Itaque decrevit senatus, ut ille veterator et callidus, vinctus ad Hannibalem duceretur*) and to *dēcrēscere* (Plin. epist. 2, 17, 18: *ut dies crevit decrevitque*); *efflorui*: *efflorēre* and *efflorēscere* (only documented in future tense in Late Latin: Vvlg. psalm. 102, 15; 131, 18; and in present subjunctive Ambr. epist. 2, 8).

17 As can be seen in Pinkster (2015: 197, n. 130), this has been criticized by Serbat (1983), who would reduce these six variants to two.

(23) The different types of valency variants according to Happ (1976: 447–453):
1) Changing the number of actants
2) Change of the category of "obligatory" and "facultative"
3) Change of the obligatory actants
4) Changing the grammatical forms of the obligatory fillings
5) Modification of the semantic characteristics of the supplementary fillings

An example of the first category is *dare*, which is only transitive in one valency, while being ditransitive in the other valency and then also indicates the recipient. The second category is superfluous after the previous Section 4.1. The third and fourth categories can be combined because they are similar. A well-known example is the already quoted *providere*, which appears with acc. or dat. Finally, the fifth and last category deals with the semantics of the second filling, which in the case of *petere* is either with the accusative of the person or of the thing, which is here an office. In all these cases, in my opinion, a separate valency must be applied. However, another observation is important. In almost all categories except the first one, where this is only partially the case,[18] the verb has a different meaning. This finding suggests that the meaning of a verb plays a significant role in the different valencies.

This conclusion seems to have been drawn by Pinkster, who also assumes different valencies, but accepts the importance of the verbal valency as a *conditio sine qua non*, even if, as he himself admits, this is sometimes not easy to determine (24).

(24) "Determining whether the meaning is the same to some extend depends on intuition, but corroboration can be found by studying the constituents with which the verb is used, an attempt is made to describe under which conditions they are used." (Pinkster 2015: 78)[19]

In the case of the same meaning, Pinkster is even willing to assume only one valency in the case of morpho-syntactic differences such as intransitive *somniare* without a second actant and transitive *somnium somniare* with a stem-related object (25).

(25) "In this Syntax one frame will be assigned if a verb is used in multiple combinations, but with the same meaning." (Pinkster 2015: 78)

18 E.g. *accipere* 'to hear' or 'to receive'; *ducere* 'to believe', 'to lead', 'to take for sth.'; *esse* 'to be', 'to be present', 'to be a matter of', 'to have', 'to stay', 'to reach'; *fieri* 'to happen', 'to arise', 'to be made'. But not e.g. *cogitare* 'to think', *contendere* 'to fight' or *mittere* 'to send'.

19 Happ (1976: 447) already speaks of "subjektive(n) Ermessen [. . .] schon beim Festlegen von Bedeutungsunterschieden".

However, the author seems to contradict himself when he assumes two different valencies for *incipere*, which has the same meaning [. . .], and clearly speaks of different verb frames (26).

(26) "Even with one and the same meaning, a verb may have multiple frames. The lexical properties of the argument(s) play a role as well. Thus with a human argument the verb *incipio* 'begin' is usually bivalent ('a person begins something') but with another type of first argument, inanimate *autumnus* 'autumn' for example, *incipio* is monovalent [. . .]." (Pinkster 2015: 20)

This contradiction seems to come from the fact that the author followed the semantic valency dimensions too one-sided in (25), although he otherwise has the categorial-syntactic dimensions in mind and analyses them in detail in Chapter 7, for example. Happ, on the other hand, focuses too much on the categorial-syntactic dimensions and therefore seems to overlook the change in meaning of most valency variants.

5 Conclusions

The previous considerations have shown that the multi-dimensional valency of today's research not only contributes to a more differentiated understanding of the phenomenon of valency, but also allows a better understanding of the two dominant descriptions of valency in Latin linguistics by Happ and Pinkster. On the one hand, the two categorial-syntactic valency dimensions and on the other hand, the three semantic valency relationships are to be used. These relationships are all independent of one another. The assumption of optional actants in functional models that describe natural languages such as Latin without a deep structure is a contradiction *in se ipso* and can be explained by Helbig's adoption of a long outdated generative model.

Instead, verb variants are to be assumed in the lexicon. However, a variant should also be used in which either the syntactic valency or the semantic valency dimensions show significant differences, be it that an actant occurs less or more without being able to provide it out of context or that the actants are structured differently. Since, as we have seen, there are mainly differences in meaning in the verb variants, Pinkster's semantic valency approach is the more appropriate one. In some cases, such as *incipere*, the semantic form of the valency-dependent actants plays a not unsignificant role. Such evidence, in which the importance of the valency carrier is influenced, should be further investigated to determine the semantic part of valency more clearly.

Bibliography

Becke, T. von der (2021). *Semantische Spezialisierung vs. Polysemie. Interpretationsbesonderheiten bei Komplementreduktionen lexikalischer Einheiten*. Berlin/Boston: De Gruyter.

Dik, S.C. & Hengeveld, K. (1997). *The theory of functional grammar, Part 1: The structure of the clause* (2nd rev. edn.). Berlin/New York: De Gruyter.

Happ, H. (1976). *Grundfragen einer Dependenz-Grammatik des Lateinischen*. Göttingen: Vandenhoeck & Ruprecht.

Heberlein, F. (1986). Über "Weglaßbarkeit" und "Notwendigkeit" in einer lateinischen Valenzgrammatik. In P. Krafft & H. J. Tschiedel (Eds.), *Concentus Hexachordus* (pp. 33–77). Regensburg: Pustet.

Heilig, E. (1978). *Untersuchungen zur Valenz und Distribution lateinischer und deutscher Verben an Hand von Ciceros philosophischen Schriften und den literaturtheoretischen Schriften von Thomas Mann*. Diss. Tübingen.

Helbig, G. (1971). Zu einigen Spezialproblemen der Valenz-Theorie. *Deutsch als Fremdsprache*, *5*, 269–282.

Helbig, G. & Schenkel, W. (1973). *Wörterbuch zur Valenz und Distribution deutscher Verben* (2nd edn.). Leipzig.

Hoffmann, R. (1997). *Lateinische Verbalperiphrasen vom Typ* amans sum *und* amatus fui*: Valenz und Grammatikalisierung*. Frankfurt a. M.: Verlag Peter Lang.

Jacobs, J. (1994). *Kontra Valenz*. Trier: Wissenschaftlicher Verlag Trier.

Jacobs, J. (2003). Die Problematik der Valenzebenen. In V. Ágel, L. M. Eichinger, H.-W. Eroms, P. Hellwig, H. J. Heringer & H. Lobin (Eds.), *Dependency and Valency: An International Handbook of Current Research. Vol. 1* (pp. 378–399). Berlin/New York: De Gruyter.

Lehmann, C. (2002). Latin valency in a typological perspective. In A. M. Bolkestein, C. Kroon, H. Pinkster, H. W. Remmelinck & R. Risselada (Eds.), *Theory and Description in Latin Linguistics* (pp. 183–203). Amsterdam: Gieben.

Pinkster, H. (2015). *The Oxford Latin Syntax. Volume 1: The Simple Clause*. Oxford: Oxford University Press.

Serbat, G. (1983). Le verbe sum: syntaxe et sémantique. *Vita latina*, *90*, 8–12.

Storrer, A. (1992). *Verbvalenz. Theoretische und methodische Vorschläge ihrer Beschreibung in Grammatikographie und Lexikographie*. Tübingen: Niemeyer.

Touratier, C. (1994). *Syntaxe latine*. Louvain-la-Neuve: Peeters.

Touratier, C. (2012). *Lateinische Grammatik*. Deutsch von Bianca Liebermann (Originalausgabe 2008). Darmstadt: Wissenschaftliche Buchgesellschaft.

Wim Berkelmans and Dominique Longrée

LASLA-SynthIA, a New Tool to Study Latin Word Order: the Case-Study of the Left- and Right-Dislocations in the *Pro Roscio Amerino*

Abstract: This paper uses a new NLP tool, LASLA-SynthIA, parser to address the question of left- and right-dislocations through an analysis of Cicero's *Pro Roscio Amerino*. We begin by reviewing the first attempts by LASLA, more than ten years ago, to study dislocations in LASLA's annotated dataset using the software LatSynt. We explain the methods on which the new parser LASLA-SynthIA relies, how it can produce a Universal Dependency Treebank of a text and the accuracy of its results. We then detail its contribution to the study of the right- and left-dislocations in the *Pro Roscio* and compare the data it has produced with the data collected with LatSynt. To conclude, we pinpoint the advantages that building syntactic treebanks have for the study of word order.

Keywords: NLP, word order, dislocations, syntax, treebank

In his doctoral dissertation (1977: 404) and in a paper presented at the 3rd International Colloquium of Latin Linguistics (1985: 518), Fr. Charpin claimed that Latin subordinate clauses (with the exception of the infinitive clause) are "frozen structures": "la phrase dépendante apparaît comme une structure figée où, à quelques variantes près, les éléments sont rangés selon un ordre identique et facilement repérable". More than ten years ago, with the project LatSynt, the LASLA (Laboratoire d'Analyse Statistique de l'Université de Liège) had already tried to challenge this affirmation by developing automatic ways to study word order, but the methods used at this time were limited and only allowed for the partial verification of the "frozen" nature of subordinate clauses. That research focused mainly on left and right dislocation. A new research project, LASLA-SynthIA, begun in 2022, intends to advance this research and to expand the study corpus. In this paper, we will first recall the contribution of the LASLA to research on syntax and word order. Then we will present the methods used in the framework of the LASLA-SynthIA project. To

Note: We would like to warmly thank Bret Mulligan (Haverford College) for his careful reading of this paper.

Wim Berkelmans and Dominique Longrée, LASLA, UR Mondes Anciens, University of Liège, Belgium

https://doi.org/10.1515/9783111332956-031

conclude, we will compare the results on left-and right dislocations that we obtained with the LASLA-SynthIA software to those produced by the LatSynt software.

1 LASLA and the Study of Syntax and Word Order: A Long Story

When they founded the LASLA in 1961, the philologists of the University of Liège had as their main objective the publication of indexes of classical Greek and Latin literary works. They therefore created tools in order to lemmatize Greek and Latin texts. For Greek texts, they specified only one morphosyntactic information: the part of speech. For Latin texts, however, they imagined a software able to produce a complete morphosyntactic analysis for all possible lemmas. An expert philologist then selected the correct analysis. This philologist also added a syntactic tag to all the verbs functioning as predicates of a main or of a subordinate clause, indicating the type of clause corresponding to this predicate. When a subordinate clause was introduced by a subordinator, a tag was also added to this subordinator in order to establish a link between the subordinator and the predicate it introduces (the first, if the subordinator introduces more than one predicate). LASLA is still using this method today to produce the data it makes publicly available to all researchers.

The young researcher who conceived the whole process in the early sixties was Étienne Évrard. He had probably already foreseen the potential of such syntactic annotation, but at the time, the lack of sufficient computational devices delayed the proposal of this system until the late eighties. In 1989, during the international colloquium on Latin Linguistics, É. Évrard (1989) pointed out not only the interest of exploiting those annotations, but also the necessity of adding syntactic labels to all word forms in the LASLA files and he designed an annotation system. Unfortunately, LASLA never found the resources to implement this system. In the meantime, Fr. Charpin (1977 and 1985) had developed a system, partially based on L. Tesnière's dependency theory, in order to implement syntactic tags in files he borrowed from LASLA, but he limited the tagging only to a few texts. The files were unfortunately never made public and had been lost after the premature death of Fr. Charpin.

Those files intended to provide F. Charpin a foundation for research on word order in subordinate clauses and the analysis of the Latin subordinate clauses as "frozen structure", apart from "some few alternatives". The LASLA LatSynt project (Longrée at al. 2010a, 2010b, 2012) was a first attempt to assess these claims and specify the frequency and nature of "the few alternatives" that F. Charpin reported. The research with LatSynt focused especially on the phenomena of prolepsis and appendage. This research was based on the annotations of the lemmatized Latin texts in the LASLA database, in particular, the syntactical tags, which allow for the easy location of all subordinating words and the predicates they introduce. This method could be qualified of a chunking-chinking type, the first step being to insert the text theoretical boundaries of subordinate clauses corresponding to the subordinators and their related predicates. In the following figure (Figure 1), the chain of tags correspond to tags associated to the subordinator (tags with +) and the introduced predicate (tags with -). The letters correspond to the type of subordinate clause (LN = relative clause introduced by *qui, quae quod*; GK = subordinate clause introduced by the adverb *quam*) and the number indicates the mode and the tense (14 = indicative perfect; 12 = indicative imperfect; 32 = subjunctive imperfect). The sign & corresponds to a main clause. The brackets indicate the level of embedding.

TAC. ann. 13, 11, 2 / P2849 /
<&0014>[+LN14-LN14]{+LN12[+GK32-GK32]-LN12}
<&secuta (est)> que lenitas in Plautium Lateranum [+quem ob adulterium Messalinae ordine demotum -reddidit] senatui clementiam suam obstringens crebris orationibus {+quas Seneca testificando [+quam honesta -praeciperet] vel iactandi ingenii voce principis -vulgabat}

Figure 1: Raw analysis by the program LatSynt.

The next step was a manual survey to detect elements of the subordinate clause outside its theoretical boundaries. As the next figure illustrates (Figure 2), a philologist has had to mark manually (in bold) the left dislocation of *reliquae* before *cum* and the elements postponed to *essent* (in fact we could debate whether the tag "predicate" should not instead be put on *inutiles* but the subordination/predicate tag is always placed on a verb in the LASLA annotation scheme).

CAES. Gall. 4, 29, 3 P0747 2
[+BN32-BN32][+LN12-LN12]<&0014>
compluribus navibus fractis, **reliquae** [+**cum** -essent] **funibus ancoris reliquis que armamentis amissis ad navigandum inutiles**, magna, id [+quod necesse -erat] accidere, totius exercitus perturbatio <&facta> est

Figure 2: Raw analysis by the LatSynt program modified by a philologist.

This method was time-consuming, the corpus was limited mostly to historians and the results were not compatible with other treebanks. Nevertheless, the research allowed us to pinpoint some linguistic features of both left- and right-dislocations. As far as left-dislocations were concerned, the research revealed that the phenomenon is quite limited in the treated corpus (Longrée et al. 2012, 2013). It also allowed us to propose a typology of left-dislocated elements and contributed to the detection of affinities between the phenomenon and various linguistics features, such as the morphosyntactic nature of the left-dislocated element, the nature of the subordinator (*cum* and *ubi* being the most frequent), the function of the subordinate clauses or the position of the clause in the sentence. It also identified variations according to each author's idiolect. The functioning of right-dislocation appeared to be quite different (Longrée 2012; Longrée et al. 2019): in the same corpus, right-dislocations are mainly dislocations of the subject, often directly after the predicate and at the end of the clause (if we except relative clauses functioning as appendages). We noticed affinities between right-dislocations and comparative clauses in *ut* or causal clauses in *quia* or *quod*. Some particular adverbs can also be related to some particular types of right dislocations, as for instance an adverb in the comparative form followed by *quam* opening an appendage.

The LatSynt project also allowed us to propose a typology of the instances where subjects and predicates are not the boundaries of the *ablativus absolutus* (Longrée et al. 2011). Furthermore, it has showed that the distances between subordinators and predicates can be used in order to characterize authors' idiolects (Longrée and Purnelle 2015). Despite these interesting results, the program had two main limitations: first, the A.c.I. and paratactical subjunctive clauses were not taken into account in the framework of the analysis; second, the results can only be considered as valid for idiolects because of the limited corpus. The only solution to extend the investigations was to tag the LASLA files with syntactic codes. An opportunity to do so presented itself with the SynthIA project.

2 The LASLA-SynthIA Project

Since 2016, under the auspices of the Classics department of the University of Amsterdam, W. Berkelmans has developed a new tagger and syntactic parser for Latin, the SynthIA tagger and parser ("Latin syntax through Artificial Intelligence"). This tagger analyzed the words by using a Bi-LSTM ("bi-directional Long Short-Term Memory") neural network. The parser consists of a rule-based component and a Bi-LSTM neural network. The rule-based component predicted, for each sentence in the corpus, based on grammatical rules, syntactic relationships (dependencies) between the words. The neural network did the same, being trained with manually annotated treebanks (PROIEL and Index Thomisticus Treebank), according to the guidelines of Universal Dependency (UD).

Since 2022, SynthIA and LASLA have joined forces to use the LASLA files as the morphosyntactic foundations of the Treebanks produced by the SynthIA parser.

The advantage of this method is to feed the parser with morphological information systematically verified by a trained philologist. The accuracy of the new produced syntactic data is therefore higher than it was before with the first version of SynthIA. A first treebank produced by the new LASLA-SynthIA is a UD Treebank of the *Pro Roscio Amerino*. In the LASLA-SynthIA files, all the information of the LASLA-files – word forms, lemmas, full morphologic analysis and tags for the predicates – are preserved, but the files receive a new layer of syntactic annotations. Those syntactic annotations can be represented in the form of a syntactic tree, as in Figure 3.

Figure 3: Example of a tree produced by the software LASLA-SynthIA.

On this figure, the tags indicating the Part of Speech come from the original LASLA files while the syntactic relations between words are produced by LASLA-SynthIA, as well as the tags characterizing these relations (adhering to UD Guidelines to the extent possible for Latin).

The accuracy of LASLA-SynthIA can be compared to that of other parsers. In Figure 4, the accuracy is expressed by percentages of accurate analysis. The 3 columns give information on: 1. the unlabeled accuracy score (UAS), which only concerns the accuracy of the links between words independent of the kind of the relationship; for each word, the UAS checks whether the head (parent) of that word is correct; 2. "Label" only concerns the syntactic labels associated with a word, for instance the label "Case" associated to *praeter* in Figure 3, but it doesn't check whether the syntactic head is correct; 3. the labelled accuracy score (LAS) verified if both the head and the label of the word are correct (thus, the LAS is always lower than the UAS). The parsers compared are the Rule Base Parser (RBP) of LASLA-SynthIA, the Neural Network (NN) of LASLA-SynthIA alone, the combination of both, and 4 other UD parsers (UDpipe ITTB, UDPipe PROIEL, UDpipe Perseus, UDPipe UDante). Figure 4 shows that the results of LASLA-SynthIA are always superior to those obtained with the other parsers. Some aspects of these results could seem counterintuitive, as RBP alone seems to have a higher accuracy than the combination of RBP and NN. In fact, RBP only annotates parts of the sentence, not the complete sentence: the general tree of the sentence is constructed by the NN. The accuracy of the RBP is calculated by taking into account the relationships and the labels of the words treated by the RBP. These words are then members of the parts of sentences annotated according to basic syntactic rules. In most cases, these rules result in the correct annotations, while difficult parts of the sentence and connections between annotated parts do not receive a syntactic annotation and are left to the NN parser. The accuracy of this NN parser is calculated on the results obtained for the annotation on the entire sentences. The accuracy NN + RBP is the accuracy of the combination of both parsers when we takes into account the entire sentences and the data obtained by the RBP integrated into the tree.

CICDAMER	**UAS**	**label**	**LAS**
SynthIA RBP	86.54	91.59	83.57
SynthIA NN	71.40	73.69	61.07
NN + RBP	82.64	86.46	77.41
UDpipe ITTB	65.93	65.34	51.97
UDpipe PROIEL	68.23	71.63	56.47
UDpipe Perseus	67.81	67.45	52.66
UDpipe UDante	71.30	71.85	60.19

(UAS = unlabeled accuracy score; LAS = labeled accuracy score; RBP = rule-based parser; NN = neural network; UDpipe = Universal Dependency parser; ITTB, PROIEL, Perseus, UDante = UD treebanks)

Figure 4: Comparison of LASLA SynthIA and 4 other parsers.

In order to obtain treebanks accurate enough to be used for training the SynthIA-NN, the treebanks produced by LASLA-SynthIA will be corrected manually, as it has been the case for the Treebank of the *Pro Roscio Amerino*.

If applied to a large corpus, the tags produced by the parser allow various queries. For instance, the first version of SynthIA has been applied to the corpus of the Packard Humanities Institute-PHI 5, allowing the comparison of, in this corpus, e.g. the object complements found with the near-synonym verbs *metuo* and *timeo*. The data displayed in Figure 5 have been produced without manual verification. Nevertheless, there is no need to resort to statistics to notice that the common expression is *mortem timeo* and that *mortem metuo* is exceptional, while *mortis* regularly appears as complement of the noun *metus* (54 occ.) and more seldom with *timor* (14 occ.).

Complement	***metuo* (1157 occ.)**	***timeo* (2325 occ.)**
nihil	18	42
mors	1	30
hostis	4	7
res	4	3
bellum	5	13
malum	8	5
deus	5	11
pater	2	3
uir	1	4
arma	3	10

Figure 5: Number of occurrences of direct complements of *metuo* and *timeo* according to the corresponding lemma.

3 Word Order in the *Pro Roscio Amerino*: Dislocations and Clause-types

After having processed the *Pro Roscio Amerino* with LASLA-SynthIA, we returned to the study of the left- and right-dislocations with another tool and a quite different corpus. Relying on LatSynt and on a corpus composed of Caesar and Tacitus, we noticed that, in this corpus, the left-dislocations are mainly related to *cum*- and *ubi*-clauses. In the *Pro Roscio Amerino*, we identified 1206 subordinate clauses with a subordinator word and 110 left-dislocations. As showed by Figure 6, in the case of the *Pro Roscio Amerino*, if we take into account only the cases with more than

5 occurrences of a left-dislocation, the dislocations seem to be mainly related to subordinate clauses introduced by the interrogative pronoun *quis/quid* and by the conjunctions *quod*, *si* and *cum* (by decreasing order of the relative frequency: *quis/quid* 25%, *quod* 16%, *si* 15% and *cum* 11%).

Clause-type	Total number of occurrences	Left-Dislocations
si conj. sub.	126	19
ut conj. sub.	181	16
quis, quid	57	14
cum	100	11
qui rel.	432	11
quod conj. sub.	55	9
ne conj. sub.	28	4
nisi	22	4
quare int.	4	3
quemadmodum int.	3	2
simulac, simulatque	3	2
quia	11	2
quoniam	16	2
quam int.	5	2
quomodo int.	4	2

Figure 6: Number of subordinate clauses and left-dislocations in the *Pro Roscio Amerino*.

If we compare left- and right-dislocations, the amount of subordinate clause elements postponed to the predicate of the clause (see Figure 7) are most of the time largely superior to the number of the same clauses with a left-dislocation: the lowest percentages of right-dislocations are 15% for *quis/quid* and 23% for *qui* relative. In the works by Caesar and Tacitus, the right-dislocation appears mainly in comparative clause in *ut* and causal clauses in *quia* or *quod*.

When we come to subordinate clauses with fewer occurrences, the lists also differ between left- and right-dislocations: we found causal clauses in left-dislocations, comparative clauses in right-dislocations. If we look at the nature of the postponed element, we detect differences between this discourse and the historical texts: in works by Caesar and Tacitus, the postponed elements were mainly subjects appearing alone after the predicate. In the *Pro Roscio Amerino*, amongst the 338 postponed elements in subordinate clauses, there are only 32 subjects (28 as the final element of the subordinate clause, 16 times as a substantive alone).

Clause-type	Total Number	Right-dislocations
qui rel.	432	102
ut conj. sub.	181	71
si conj. sub.	126	44
cum	100	38
quod conj. sub.	55	21
quis, quid	57	9
ne conj. sub.	28	8
nisi	22	8
sin	15	7
quoniam	16	6
postquam	9	5
quasi conj. sub.	5	5
ut adv. rel.	17	4
quantus/um int.	4	4
quin conj. Sub.	4	3
quam int.	5	3

Figure 7: Number of subordinate clauses and right-dislocations in the *Pro Roscio Amerino.*

An important benefit of LASLA-SynthIA compared to LatSynt is the possibility to study the word order in the A.c.I. and the *ablativus absolutus*. In the *Pro Roscio Amerino*, out of 320 A.c.I., 82 present a component outside the range subject-predicate, and in all cases they appear to be left-dislocations, but out of the 32 instances of the *ablativus absolutus*, only one shows a component outside the range subject-predicate.

4 Some Results, but Still a Long Way to Go . . .

By applying LASLA-SynthIA to the *Pro Roscio Amerino*, we have been able to confirm differences between left- and right-dislocations. The left-dislocation seems to be more sensitive to the type of the subordinate clause and to be conditioned by the nature of the left-dislocated element and by the literary genre. The right-dislocation appears more indifferent to the nature of the subordinator, being subject to few constraints and presenting few differences between Cicero and the historians. The study, however, is far from complete: even for the *Pro Roscio Amerino*, there remain a lot of data to analyze, for example, the analysis of the internal word order of the subordinate clauses. And the *Pro Roscio Amerino* is only one of the many speeches by Cicero. One of our main aims will be to expand as much as possible the corpus treated by LASLA-SynthIA, our final goal being to offer a global Treebank for all the LASLA files.

Bibliography

Charpin, F. (1977). *L'idée de phrase grammaticale et son expression en latin*, Lille/Paris.

Charpin, F. (1989). Étude de syntaxe énonciative : l'ordre des mots et la phrase. In G. Calboli (Ed.), *Subordination and other topics in Latin, Proceedings of the third Colloquium on Latin linguistics, Bologna, 1–5 April 1985* [*Studies in Language Companion Series, 17*] (pp. 503–520). Amsterdam/ Philadelphia: Benjamins.

Évrard É. (1989). Une informatisation de la syntaxe de dépendance en latin. In M. Lavency & D. Longrée (Eds.), *Actes du cinquième Colloque de Linguistique Latine. Louvain-la-Neuve/Borzée, 31 mars–4 avril 1989 [= Cahiers de l'Institut de Linguistique de Louvain, 15]* (pp. 115–126). Louvain-la-Neuve.

Longrée, D. (2012). Catégories adverbiales, fonctions et ordre des syntagmes chez les historiens latins. In M. Fruyt, J.-P. Brachet. & P. Lecaudé (Eds.), *Les adverbes latins, Syntaxe et sémantique* (pp. 195–210). Paris: Harmattan.

Longrée, D. & Purnelle, G. (2015). Le programme "Latsynt", un instrument pour mesurer les distances entre les prosateurs latins classiques ? *Études Classiques, 82* (1), 47–63.

Longrée, D., Philippart de Foy, C., & Purnelle, G. (2010a). Structures phrastiques et analyse automatique des données morphosyntaxiques : le projet LatSynt. In S. Bolasco, I. Chiari & L. Giuliano (Eds.), *Statistical Analysis of Textual Data, Proceedings of 10th International Conference Journées d'Analyse statistique des Données Textuelles, 9–11 June 2010, Sapienza University of Rome* (pp. 433–442). Rome: LED.

Longrée, D., Philippart de Foy, C., & Purnelle, G. (2010b). Subordinate clause boundaries and word order in Latin: the contribution of the L.A.S.L.A. syntactic parser project LatSynt. In P. Anreiter & M. Kienpointner (Eds.), *Proceedings of the 15th International Colloquium on Latin Linguistics (Innsbrucker Beiträge zur Sprachwissenschaft)* (pp. 673–681). Innsbruck.

Longrée, D., Philippart de Foy, C., & Purnelle, G. (2011). His cognitis *vs.* His cognitis rebus : *ordre des constituants et bornage de l'Ablatif absolu*. Unpublished paper presented at 16th International Colloquium on Latin Linguistics.

Longrée, D., Philippart de Foy, C., & Purnelle, G. (2012). Conditionnements linguistiques des prolepses chez César et Tacite : l'apport du projet LatSynt. *De Lingua latina, 7*. https://lettres.sorbonne-universite.fr/numero-7-etudes-sur-la-prolepse

Longrée, D., Philippart de Foy, C., & Purnelle, G. (2013). Dislocations à gauche et nature des subordonnants en Latin classique. In C. Bodelot, H. Gruet-Skrabalova & F. Trouilleux (Eds.), *Morphologie, syntaxe et sémantique des subordonnants* (pp. 445–461). Clermont-Ferrand: P.U. Blaise-Pascal.

Longrée, D., Philippart de Foy, C., & Purnelle, G. (2019). Nature et fonctionnement des syntagmes postposés dans les subordonnées latines : étude d'un corpus d'historiens classiques. In M. Taillade, F. Fatello, J. Gallego & G. Gibert (Eds.), *Nemo par eloquentia, Mélanges de linguistique ancienne en hommage à Colette Bodelot* (pp. 241–253). Clermont-Ferrand: P.U. Blaise-Pascal.

Agnes Vendel

"Long-Distance Hyperbaton": A Case Study based on Cicero's Orations

Abstract: This paper examines cases of hyperbaton where two or more constituents separate the discontinuous noun phrase. It problematises previous accounts of the phenomenon, and argues that there is no simple model for "long-distance hyperbaton". Instead, a number of factors need to be considered, including syntactic and semantic categories of the modifiers, the type of the intervening words, and the information structure in relation to the surrounding clauses. "Long-distance hyperbaton" in fact appears as the result of a combination of aspects that also feature in shorter separations.

Keywords: word order, hyperbaton, discontinuous noun phrase, Cicero

Hyperbaton, or the discontinuity of noun phrases,[1] is a common phenomenon in Latin prose as well as verse. The two parts of the split noun phrase can be separated by a single word or by several: in this article, I focus on the latter case.

I have taken as my point of departure two previous accounts of hyperbaton with multiple words placed between the two parts of the split noun phrase (henceforth "intervener"): Powell (2010), who uses the term "long-range hyperbaton", and Pinkster (2021), who instead calls it "long-distance hyperbaton". The definitions of the phenomenon are also quite different between the two scholars.

Powell tentatively lists the following rules for "long-range hyperbaton" (2010: 174–175):

- The modifier belongs to the categories of determiners and quantifiers.
- No other word precedes the modifier, with the exception of a conjunction or another word belonging to the categories just mentioned.
- The second part of the hyperbaton is usually the last "stressed" word of the clause.[2]
- The verb, often an auxiliary, is unfocused and directly follows the main focus of the sentence.

1 The term hyperbaton may also be used to describe discontinuity of other kinds of phrases, or indeed any unconventional word order; this article is only concerned with the discontinuity of noun phrases.

2 Powell does not give any examples of what unstressed words might be.

Agnes Vendel, University of Cambridge, Great Britain

https://doi.org/10.1515/9783111332956-032

An example, cited by Powell, and also present in my corpus, is given in (1). Powell notes that this is an extreme case due to the length of the separation, which however is mainly caused by the length of the interposed constituents.

(1) ***magna*** *dis immortalibus habenda est atque huic ipsi Iovi Statori, antiquissimo custodi huius urbis,* ***gratia****...* (Cic. Catil. 1, 11)
'We owe a heavy debt of gratitude to the immortal gods and not least to Jupiter Stator, the most venerable guardian of this city, in whose temple we are today...'[3]

Powell distinguishes three types of hyperbaton: "long-range", as described above, "short-range", where a single (unfocused) word intervenes, and "double focus", where both preposed modifier and intervener are focused. He argues that the third type is rare, and does not comment much further on it. Powell, furthermore, suggests that "short-range" hyperbaton is used as a focusing device and that "long-range" hyperbaton is generally not, although he does not propose how it should be interpreted.

Pinkster, on the other hand, uses the term "long-distance hyperbaton" for which he gives a much simpler definition, namely that the noun phrase must be split by more than one interposed constituent, as in (2), where the (comparatively short) separation is caused by two pronominal constituents.

(2) *... qui, cum in senatu privati, ut de me sententias dicerent, flagitabant,* ***legem*** *illi se* ***Clodiam*** *timere dicebant...* (Cic. Sest. 69)
'[The consuls...] in answer to some private members in the Senate who asked leave to speak on my case, declared that they were afraid of the Clodian Law.'

It can also be caused by the intervention of an entire clause (3), even though these function as single constituents in the superordinate clause (and could often be analysed either as noun phrase-internal, or as disjuncts).

(3) *Nam etsi [ut] tu melius existumare videris de* ***ea****, si quam nunc habemus,* ***facultate****, tamen...* (Cic. Brut. 298) (example from Pinkster 2021: 1106)
'For though you appear to have a better opinion of such skill as I now possess, yet...'

Pinkster's general classification of hyperbata is based on the type of intervening word, wherefore his "long-distance" category, as the last of the list, appears as a "miscellaneous" label.

3 Translations were taken from the LOEB online editions.

The two terms "long-range" and "long-distance" hyperbaton are thus rather different and not always compatible definitions of what we might understand by a "long" separation in hyperbaton. In this article, I will use the term "long-distance hyperbaton", although with some slight variations from Pinkster's use of it: I consider only cases where (at least) two separate, external constituents occur between the parts of the discontinuous noun phrase. This means that I did not include instances of subordinate clauses functioning as interveners, unless they occur in combination with a second intervener, since I have regarded them as single constituents.[4] Neither have I considered composite verbs (e.g. auxiliary + main verb, copula + predicative) as two constituents, and I have treated two conjuncts with the same function, for instance two mandatory complements (4), as single constituents as well.[5]

(4) *Hic si mentis esset suae, nisi* ***poenas*** *patriae disque immortalibus* ***eas****, quae gravissimae sunt, furore atque insania penderet...* (Cic. Pis. 50)
'If he had been in his senses, if he had not already, by his infatuation and madness, been paying the direst of all penalties to his country and to the immortal gods...'

Furthermore, I did not include instances where two personal or demonstrative pronouns intervene, as exemplified by (2) above, in the discussion below. While the pronouns do form separate constituents, they are regularly placed in the second position in the clause, as discussed for instance by Adams (1994a). I also decided to exclude instances where two adjunct interveners co-occur, whether in the shape of adverbs, ablative noun phrases, or prepositional phrases, as exemplified by (5). This decision was made mainly for reasons of space, but since these interveners often have a semantic or logical connection to the noun phrases within which they appear, I believe that they are better discussed apart. This means that I only included cases where at least one of the interveners is a mandatory constituent of the clause, most often the verb.

(5) *...* ***nullae*** *<u>ad senatum</u> <u>e provincia</u>* ***litterae****, nulla ex trinis aestivis gratulatio, nulla triumphi mentio: non modo quid gesseris, sed ne quibus in locis quidem fueris dicere audes.* (Cic. Pis. 97)

4 But see the discussion in 4.2 below, in which case we should perhaps regard subordinate clauses (and indeed any long constituents, cf. example (1)), as causing long-distance hyperbaton.

5 This is supported by the definition of "coordination" given by Dik (1997: 189): "A coordination is a construction consisting of two or more members which are functionally equivalent, bound together at the same level of structure by means of a linking device."

'... the absence of any dispatch to the senate from your province, and of any congratulatory message after three years of campaigning, and your silence as regards a triumph; you cannot bring yourself to tell us not only what you did, but even where you were.'

In this article, I investigate how long-distance hyperbaton actually presents itself in the selected texts, whether Powell's and/or Pinkster's definitions are effective tools for analysis, or whether other distinctions are more useful for understanding the phenomenon of long separations of Latin noun phrases.

The data for the study were collected from twenty-one of Cicero's orations.[6] The author and genre allowed me to include texts aimed at different audiences and produced over a few decades, without having to account for differences that might be due to individual preferences in style. I excerpted all instances of hyperbaton[7] from these texts, approximately 2550 items, and organised them in a database where each instance was tagged for syntactic and semantic features, allowing comparison of specific parameters that may influence the occurrence of hyperbaton.

Applied to this material, Powell's and Pinkster's definitions of "long-range" and "long-distance hyperbaton" gave very different results. Powell's definition corresponded to a mere 47 instances in the data, which represents fewer than 2% of all cases of hyperbaton. Admittedly, Powell uses a more restrictive definition of hyperbaton than most scholars, and excludes a number of constructions for different reasons that cannot be enumerated here. Therefore, the percentage would be slightly higher if those cases were excluded, although still only a few percent. Pinkster's term is less clearly defined than Powell's, wherefore I used his supplement of examples to evaluate how many instances in my data would fit his term. The (provisional) result was 357 instances, which represents 14% of all cases of hyperbaton in my data. According to my own criteria outlined above, I classified 225 instances (9%) as long-distance hyperbaton. These figures give an indication of the extent of the phenomenon in relation to hyperbaton in general, but do not tell us anything about the more precise features of it.

6 Leg. agr. 1–2, Caecin., Cael., Catil. 1–2, Deiot., div. in Caec., Manil., Marcell., Mil., Mur., Phil. 2–4, Pis., prov., Quinct., S. Rosc., Sest., Verr. 1. I used the online LOEB editions.

7 The definition of hyperbaton differs between scholars, although there is no room here to go into this question in detail. I have not considered connectors, such as *enim* and *autem*, to cause hyperbaton. Consequently, I have not considered the combination of a connector with another intervener as a case of "multiple interveners". Apart from this, I have considered all words external to the noun phrase as interveners, including prepositions, but excluding genitive complements and adnominal prepositional phrases, since these are part of the noun phrase. (Cf. Spevak's 2010: 272 "internal hyperbaton".)

In the sections below, I first evaluate the two existing concepts of long-distance hyperbaton in relation to the data in my corpus, discussing their advantages and limitations. I then examine the instances that I have classified as "long-distance hyperbaton", and use the parameters tagged in my database to identify potential patterns. In Section 2, I look at the elements that occur as interveners, before examining the words that constitute the discontinuous noun phrase itself in Section 3. In the last section, I treat some other aspects that might cause long-distance hyperbaton.

1 Existing Concepts Applied to Cicero's Orations

In this section, I discuss some aspects of Powell's and Pinkster's definitions of long separations and some questions that appear when they are applied to the data.

1.1 Noun Phrases at the Edges of the Clause

Looking closer at Powell's definition of "long-range hyperbaton", what he describes it in fact not necessarily a long (or even multiple-word) separation, but simply one where the discontinuous noun phrase occupies the edges (or almost) of the clause. In very short clauses, it is therefore possible that cases where only the verb intervenes fulfil all Powell's criteria (6).

(6) *Omitto nihil istum versum pertinuisse ad illum; non fuisse meum, quem quantum potuissem multis saepe orationibus scriptisque decorassem, hunc **uno** violare **versu**.* (Cic. Pis. 75)
'I say nothing of the fact that the line had no reference to him at all; and that it was not my way to assail with one single line the man whom I had done my best to honour in many speeches and writings.'

Powell's definition admits that some types of elements may precede the modifier, namely words that are placed in the first position for syntactic reasons or discourse coherence (e.g. *hunc* in (6)). However, setting constituents are also usually placed first or early in the clause, as exemplified in (7) by the prepositional phrase *in magna varietate sententiarum*.

(7) *Et quoniam facta mentio est ludorum, ne illud quidem praetermittam, in magna varietate sententiarum* ***numquam ullum*** *fuisse* ***locum***... (Cic. Sest. 118)
'And since I have mentioned theatrical performances, I will not omit to say that, among many and varied reflections in the comedy, there was never a passage...'

Pinkster's concept of "long-distance hyperbaton" is also sensitive to the complexity of the sentence, since in some instances, the difference between an instance of "verbal hyperbaton" (where a verb intervenes) and "long-distance hyperbaton" in his typology may simply be that in the latter case, the clause contains more constituents, for instance a personal pronoun (8).

(8) *Si quis, quod spopondit, qua in re* ***verbo*** *se obligavit* ***uno***, *id non facit, maturo iudicio, sine ulla religione iudicis condemnatur*... (Cic. Caecin. 7)
'In a case of solemn contract, he who does not perform an obligation which he has taken upon himself by pronouncing a single word, is promptly condemned without any scruple on the part of the judge.'

In fact, of the 225 instances that I have classified as "long-distance hyperbaton" nearly 150 occupy the edges of the clause, with varying degrees of complexity in the interveners.

1.2 Categories of Modifiers

Powell's criteria also predict that certain classes of modifiers appear more frequently in long-range than in short-range hyperbaton, which can appear with practically any modifier (2010: 175–176). The modifiers that occur in long-range hyperbaton belong to the categories of "preferential words" as described by Dover (1960), who uses it merely as a descriptive term for words that tend to be placed first in the clause. Powell provides no statistics for his claim, but in Tables 1 and 2, I offer some statistics based on my data for preposed modifiers in "verbal hyperbaton" (where the verb alone intervenes) and "long-distance hyperbaton".[8]

8 I have followed, in so far as possible, Pinkster's (2015 and 2021) classification of modifiers, except that I have regarded *totus* as a quantifier (Pinkster suggests an individual category, "totality expression", for this item). I also chose to list modifiers used as secondary predicates separately, although the distinction admittedly is not always unambiguous.

Table 1: "Verbal hyperbaton".

Type of modifier	Preposed	%
Interrogative	41	13,4
Relative	10	3,3
Demonstrative	36	11,7
Indefinite	11	3,6
Identifier	8	2,6
Ipse	3	1,0
Possessive	11	3,6
Quantifier	57	16,8
Partitive/quantity	0	0
Adjective of size	30	9,8
Other adjective	26	8,5
Participle	1	0,3
Gerundive	0	0
Genitive	56	18,2
Adnominal PP	5	1,6
Apposition	0	0
Secondary pred.	12	3,9
Total	**307**	**100**

Table 2: "Long-distance hyperbaton".

Type of modifier	Preposed	%
Interrogative	17	13,7
Relative	7	5,6
Demonstrative	14	11,3
Indefinite	6	4,8
Identifier	2	1,6
Ipse	0	0
Possessive	5	4,0
Quantifier	31	21,8
Partitive/quantity	0	0
Adjective of size	12	8,5
Other adjective	8	5,6
Participle	1	0,8
Gerundive	0	0
Genitive	15	12,1
Adnominal PP	2	1,6
Apposition	0	0
Secondary pred.	5	4,0
Total	**124**	**100**

A comparison of the figures in tables shows that the rates are not significantly different between verbal and long-distance hyperbaton (the categories that Powell claims to be more frequent in long-distance hyperbaton are highlighted). Thus, the length of the separation may not depend as much on the category of modifier as on other factors.

It may be argued that two separate constituents do not necessarily correspond to what Powell thought of as a long separation, wherefore I also took a closer look at the more restricted dataset of forty-seven instances that fulfil all of Powell's criteria. This dataset is too small to draw statistically reliable conclusions. However, quantifiers are present in eighteen of those instances (40%), and interrogatives in twelve (27%). The other categories mentioned by Powell (such as demonstratives and adjectives of size) also occur, but only in a few instances each – too few to provide reliable statistics.

1.3 The Place of the Verb

Furthermore, Powell's criteria state that the verb should be unfocused and follow the main focus of the clause. This suggestion, too, needs to be evaluated. In many of the examples in my data, the verb is the last of the intervening words, and therefore does not immediately follow the preposed modifier as predicted (9–10).

(9) ***Illud*** *quoque nobis accedit* ***incommodum****, quod. . .* (Cic. Quinct. 3)
'An additional disadvantage for us is that. . .'

(10) *. . . tum vero non strepitu, sed maximo clamore,* ***suam*** *populus Romanus significavit* ***voluntatem****.* (Cic. Verr. 1, 45)
'. . . then it was with no mere murmur, but with a mighty roar, that the people of Rome showed their satisfaction.'

Powell also claims that the verb is usually an auxiliary, but this is not always the case, as the examples above show. In fact, the verbs appear as the first intervening word in only about a third of the instances, and it is an auxiliary in less than half of these. There are, however, some constellations for which Powell's observation seems to be right, in particular when forms of *sum* (whether functioning as an auxiliary, a copula, or a full verb) follow an interrogative or quantifier (especially *nullus*) (11), although there are exceptions (12).

(11) *Quid tum?* ***quae*** *erit in istos agros* ***deductio****, quae totius rei ratio atque descriptio?* (CIC. leg. agr. 1, 16)
'What then? what kind of settlement will be made in those lands? what will be the method and arrangement of the whole affair?'

(12) *Age vero, ceteris in rebus* ***qua*** *ille sit* ***temperantia****, considerate.* (CIC. Manil. 40)
'And further, consider the moderation which he displays in other ways as well.'

On the whole, Powell's definition cannot be consistently applied to most instances of long-distance hyperbaton in my data.

Lastly, it is justified to question what purpose the definition of different types of hyperbaton serves. Powell identifies only three different "types" of hyperbaton: "short-range", "long-range" and "double focus", which he does not discuss at any length but argues is "rare". Given that in my corpus the "long-range" category is shown also to be rare, most instances of hyperbaton would fall into his "short-range" category, if any. Pinkster's class of "long-distance hyperbaton", on the other hand, covers a reasonable portion of the data, but does not offer any particulars that can be used as a basis for analysis.

In the following two sections, I discuss some recurring features in my corpus of long-distance hyperbaton, examining first the intervening words, and then the components that constitute the discontinuous noun phrase.

2 Patterns of Interveners

In this section, I examine the words that appear between the two parts of the discontinuous noun phrase.

2.1 Some Common Patterns

As briefly sketched in the Introduction and in Section 1.2 above, some fairly regular patterns in the intervening words seem to reflect general principles for placement of constituents in the Latin clause. For instance, personal (and some demonstrative) pronouns are regularly placed in the second position (13). In thirty-five instances, a personal pronoun and a verb intervene, in that order.

(13) *Tam autem eras excors ut tota in oratione tua tecum ipse pugnares, non modo non cohaerentia inter se diceres sed maxime diiuncta atque contraria, ut non tanta mecum* ***quanta*** *tibi tecum esset* ***contentio.*** (Cic. Phil. 2, 18)
'But in your witlessness you were fighting against yourself all through your speech. Not only did what you said lack coherence, but it was also downright out of joint and self-contradictory so that you were more in conflict with yourself than with me.'

Also frequent (eighteen instances) as interveners are adverbs in combination with verbs (14). The adverb may modify the verb (and thus the clause as a whole), but may also display a semantic or logical connection to the word that it follows, as in the example below.

(14) *An vero* ***ullam*** *usquam esse* ***oram*** *tam desertam putatis, quo non illius diei fama pervaserit...* (Cic. Manil. 44)
'Think you indeed that there was anywhere a coast so desolate that no tidings reached it of that great day...'

Adams (1994b: 89) noted that forms of the verb *sum* tend to be placed after the most heavily stressed word in the clause, which may explain its position in (14). I discuss combinations of words like *ullus/nullus* and *usquam/umquam* in a forthcoming publication (Vendel, forthc., Chapter 3).

Similar examples are found with other kinds of adverbial constituents (twenty-one instances), such as the prepositional phrase *in scelere* in (15).

(15) *Versatus in bello est; saturavit se sanguine dissimillimorum sui civium: felix fuit, si potest* ***ulla*** *in scelere esse* ***felicitas.*** (Cic. Phil. 2, 59)
'He took part in the war. He saturated himself with the blood of fellow countrymen who resembled him not at all. He was fortunate, if there can be good fortune in any crime.'

This combination also occurs when the noun precedes the intervener, here with a "heavy" postposed modifier (16).

(16) *Tum illa, ut* ***mos*** *in Sicilia est* ***omnium Veneriorum et eorum qui a Venere se liberaverunt,*** *ut...* (Cic. div. in Caec. 55)
'She thereupon followed the regular practice of those Sicilians who belong to Venus, or who having belonged to her have since become free...'

A final common combination (twenty-two instances) consists of a verb and one of its mandatory complements (17).

(17) . . . *ut intellegatis,* ***quantam*** *locus ipse adferat* ***superbiam****, quae paucis diebus, quibus illo colonia deducta est, perspici atque intellegi potuit.* (Cic. leg. agr. 2, 92)
'. . .so that you may understand what pride the very place inspires, as could be clearly seen and understood within a few days of the colony being established.'

These four constellations together cover about one hundred of the examples, with pronoun + verb being the most frequent. As already noted in Section 1.3 above, the favoured order with these combinations is that the verb follows the other intervener, except with forms of *sum* and some categories of modifiers.[9]

2.2 Expanded Patterns

Longer combinations of the elements mentioned above also occur. In (18), an adverb, an adjunct, and a verb intervene; in (19), a personal pronoun, a prepositional phrase and a verb; and in (20), an adverb, a disjunct, two prepositional phrases, and a verb.

(18) *Num vos existimatis Gracchos aut Saturninum aut quemquam illorum veterum, qui populares habebantur,* ***ullum*** *umquam in contione habuisse* ***conductum****?* (Cic. Sest. 105)
'Do you suppose that the Gracchi, or Saturninus, or any of those men of former times who were regarded as "Friends of the People", ever had any hired supporter at a meeting?'

(19) . . . *tamen mihi videmini magno consilio atque optima mente* ***potestatem*** *nobis de tota re publica fecisse* ***dicendi****.* (Cic. Phil. 3, 13)
'. . . I think you have shown great judgment and excellent intentions in thus giving us an opportunity to speak on public affairs in general.'

(20) ***Quae*** *enim* ***res*** *umquam, pro sancte Iuppiter, non modo in hac urbe sed in omnibus terris est gesta* ***maior****, quae gloriosior, quae commendatior hominum memoriae sempiternae?* (Cic. Phil. 2, 32)
'For never, holy Jupiter, was a greater deed done in Rome or anywhere else in the world; none more glorious, none more sure to live forever in the memory of mankind.'

9 Although the instances are actually comparatively few, only fourteen.

In several cases, the number of interveners simply seem to be a consequence of the number of constituents in the clause.

2.3 Not Verb-final

Finally, I would like to cite some examples where the verb is placed in an initial or at least early position among the interveners. Nearly a third of these instances can be described as the combination of interrogative or *(n)ullus* followed by a form of *sum*, as described in 1.3. *Sum* also occurs as an intervener following other classes of modifiers, such as the indefinite in (21), but not as regularly. In many cases where there are only two interveners, we simply find the opposite orders to those discussed under 2.2 above. For instance, in (22), the interveners are a verb and a personal pronoun.[10] Sometimes two verb forms, such as a matrix verb and an infinitive, are both present as interveners within the same noun phrase, which then usually occupies the edges of the clause (23).

(21) . . . *Catoni, fortissimo viro, iudicium minitanti ac denuntianti respondisset,* ***si quod*** *esset in suas fortunas* ***incendium*** *excitatum, id se non aqua sed ruina restincturum.* (Cic. Mur. 51)
'. . . told the gallant Cato who was threatening to bring him to court that he would put out any fire set to his property not with water but by destroying everything.'

(22) . . . *quam qui profitetur,* ***gravissimam*** *sustinere mihi* ***personam*** *videtur.* (Cic. Pis. 77)
'. . . and the man who professes that seems to me to have taken upon himself the most responsible of functions.'

(23) . . . ***hanc*** *puto me habere* ***actionem*** *ut per interdictum meum ius teneam atque iniuriam tuam persequar.* (Cic. Caecin. 32)
'I consider that there is a legal process which enables me to maintain my rights and to deal with the injury you have done me by means of an injunction.'

While a fair portion of the interveners that occur alongside the verb can be explained through the principles of placement of these words in the clause, it is

10 I note that this example seems incompatible with Adams' (1994a) analysis of the placement of personal pronouns.

also clear from many of the examples that the types and functions of the head and modifier of the discontinuous noun phrase play a certain role. I now turn to this question.

3 Heads and Modifiers

In this section, I present some tendencies that I observe regarding the position of the nominal heads and the modifiers. Since long-distance hyperbaton is a complex construction, it should not be assumed that these characteristics alone are sufficient to produce the phenomenon, but simply one of several factors at play. Indeed, some of the tendencies described below often co-occur, which likely contributes to the length of the separation.[11]

3.1 Clause-initial Nouns

A first observation concerns clause-initial nouns, a phenomenon that is often analysed as "topicalization" in the literature (e.g. by Devine and Stephens 2006). It seems, however, that different analyses may be necessary in different examples. In (24), there are two instances of hyperbaton, of which the second is "long", with several parallel contrasted elements.[12] Both discontinuous noun phrases have a clause-initial noun and an adjective of quantity/size occurring later in the clause.

(24) **Misericordiam** *spoliatio consulatus* ***magnam*** *habere debet, iudices; una enim eripiuntur cum consulatu omnia;* **invidiam** *vero his temporibus habere consulatus ipse* ***nullam*** *potest. . .* (Cic. Mur. 87)
'We should feel deep compassion, gentlemen, for loss of the consulship, for with the consulship all else is lost. At a time like this, however, you cannot envy the office itself. . .'

In (25), the clause-initial noun *lux* has two contrasted complements in *solis* and *lychnorum*, placed at the end of the clause.

11 Cf. Devine and Stephens' (2006: 548) proposal that "premodifier hyperbaton" is the consequence of differences in discourse functions.

12 The first hyperbaton, *misericordiam . . . magnam* does not constitute a case of long-distance hyperbaton since the intervening words, *spoliatio consulatus*, form a single constituent, *consulatus* being a genitive complement to *spoliatio* (cf. fn. 7 above).

(25) . . . *non idem iudicum comissatorumque conspectus;* ***lux*** *denique longe* <u>*alia*</u> *est* **solis**, <u>*alia*</u> **lychnorum**. (Cic. Cael. 67)
'. . .to face judges and fellow-revellers is not the same thing; in short, the light of the sun is far different from the light of lamps.'

In (26) lastly, the noun *os* precedes the conjunction of the subordinate clause to which it belongs, which suggests left-dislocation.

(26) *[reditus Gabinii] . . . quem etsi sibi ipse praecidit, ego tamen* ***os*** *ut videam* ***hominis*** *exspecto.* (Cic. Pis. 51)
'. . .for though he himself has broken it off halfway, yet I still look forward to seeing the fellow's impudent face.'

Genitive complements are present in two of the three examples above: this is not a coincidence, but they are in fact one of the most frequent categories of modifiers when the noun is clause-initial, together with adjectives of quantity and size. This challenges Powell's (2010: 172) suggestion that the noun and modifier logically belong to different syntactic components in head-initial hyperbaton, since the genitive complements are usually obligatory.

3.2 Clause-final Modifiers

A clause-initial head is often combined with a clause-final modifier. Many of these belong to certain categories that are more loosely attached to the noun that the modify, and may function as secondary predicates (cf. Pinkster 2021: 777–779), for instance participles, gerundives and adjectives indicating state (27).

(27) . . . *eorum autem castrorum imperatorem* ***ducemque hostium*** intra moenia atque adeo in senatu *videtis* ***intestinam aliquam cotidie perniciem rei publicae molientem***. (Cic. Catil. 1, 5)
'The commander of that camp and the leader of those enemies you see within the walls and even, indeed, in the Senate, plotting daily in our midst the destruction of the Republic.'

A second frequent category of postposed modifiers are adjectives of quantity and size, sometimes referred to as "floating" quantifiers (28) (e.g. by Pinkster 2021: 819–820).

(28) *Venio ad comitia, sive magistratuum placet sive legum. **Leges** videmus saepe ferri **multas**.* (Cic. Sest. 109)
'I now come to the Assemblies, whatever their purpose, whether for the election of magistrates or the passing of laws. We are aware that many laws are often passed.

In a few instances, other categories of adjectives occur, as well as genitive complements, appositions, possessives, and *ipse* (29–30).

(29) *Nemo enim illorum **inimicus** mihi fuit **voluntarius**, omnes a me rei publicae causa lacessiti.* (Cic. Phil. 2, 1)
'. . . for none of those people became my enemy by choice; they were all challenged by me for the sake of the Republic.'

(30) *Hanc sextulam illa **mercedem** isti esse voluit **assiduitatis et molestiae**, si quam ceperat.* (Cic. Caecin. 17)
'This seventy-second part she intended as an acknowledgement of his devotion to her affairs and of any trouble they might have caused him.'

3.3 Clause-initial Modifiers

I now turn to the instances where the modifier precedes the noun. Determiners are regularly found in the clause-initial position, particularly interrogatives and relatives, but also some demonstratives and indefinites. Interrogatives are by far the most common class of clause-initial modifiers (31, repeated from 17). Relative modifiers in this position are with only one exception genitive forms (32), whereas the demonstratives are either forms of anaphoric *hic* (33), or cataphoric demonstrative determiners functioning as antecedents of a subordinate clause (34).

(31) *. . . ut intellegatis, **quantam** locus ipse adferat **superbiam**, quae paucis diebus, quibus illo colonia deducta est, perspici atque intellegi potuit.* (Cic. leg. agr. 2, 92)
'. . . so that you may understand what pride the very place inspires, as could be clearly seen and understood within a few days of the colony being established.'

(32) *. . . Q. Catulo, **cuius** semper in hac re publica vivet **auctoritas**.* (Cic. Phil. 2, 12)
'. . . Quintus Catulus, a name that will ever live respected in this Republic.'

(33) *C. Antonius Macedoniam. Hunc quoque felicem! **Hanc** enim habebat semper in ore **provinciam**.* (Cic. Phil. 3, 26)

'Gaius Antonius draws Macedonia. Another lucky man! For he always had his eye on that province.'

(34) *At* ***eam*** *tibi C. Verres fecit* ***iniuriam*** *quae ceterorum quoque animos posset alieno incommodo commovere.* (Cic. div. in Caec. 55)
'You may object that the wrong Verres has done you is serious enough to stir deeply the feelings of all others, even though it does not touch them directly.'

Apart from those modifiers that occur in the clause-initial position for syntactic reasons, other categories are also found, quantifiers being the most frequent (35). Other categories of adjectives occur as well, especially adjectives of size and degree (36).

(35) *Quae si non probaret, si tibi ita penitus inhaesisset ista suspicio,* ***nullo*** *ut evelli* ***modo*** *posset. . .* (Cic. Mil. 68)
'Should he appear to fail in making good this claim; should your suspicions prove to be so deeply engrained in your mind as to be ineradicable. . .'

(36) *Ego etiam quae tu sine Verre commisisti Verri crimini daturus sum, quod te non prohibuerit cum* ***summam*** *ipse haberet* ***potestatem****.* (Cic. div. in Caec. 35)
'I shall lay to Verres' account even the wrong things you have done without his help, on the ground that he was in supreme command and yet did not stop your doing them.'

Other common categories of modifiers include genitives (37) and possessives (38). The modifier can be contrasted, either explicitly through the use of particles, or more subtly.

(37) **Mimi** *ergo est iam* ***exitus****, non* fabulae. . . (Cic. Cael. 65)
'So, then, we have the finale of a mime, not of a proper play. . .'

(38) *Quod reliquum est, iam non possum oblivisci* **meam** *hanc esse* ***patriam****,* me *horum esse consulem,* mihi *aut cum his vivendum aut pro his esse moriendum.* (Cic. Catil. 2, 27)
'For the future, no longer can I forget that this is my fatherland, that I am consul of these men, and that I must either live with them or die for them.'

3.4 Clause-final Nouns

Clause-initial determiners and other modifiers are often combined with a clause-final noun, although another word may also follow, in particular part of composite verbs (see, for instance, (35) above). Some tendencies regarding these nouns can be observed: they may be explicitly contrasted and/or part of a double (conjoined) constituent (37). They may also function as antecedents of a following relative clause (34), or be heavy constituents. Lastly, the noun may be deducible from the preceding sentence(s), as is the case in (33), where it should be possible for the audience to predict the noun *provinciam*. In other cases (e.g. 31–32), it is more difficult to explain the clause-final position of the noun. In both these instances, the postposed noun both contain new information, and they may be best interpreted as clause-final foci.

4 Other Potential Factors

4.1 Prose Rhythm

Prose rhythm and the search for suitable clausulae is sometimes adduced as a motivation for hyperbaton. It has long been known that many clause-endings in Cicero's texts end in specific clausulae (Zieliński 1904). Keeline and Kirby (2019) provide an inventory of preferred and disfavoured prose clausulae, including allowed resolutions.

I examined this factor in instances of long-distance hyperbaton that occur at the end of a sentence, and compared these instances with Keeline and Kirby's inventory. Many of the sentences did indeed end in preferred clausulae, most often cretic-trochaic or double cretic (including resolutions). However, this is perhaps unsurprising, given that the accepted combinations of syllables listed by Keeline and Kirby are very many, and that there are only two disfavoured clausulae (heroic and spondaic). In fact, in many cases, a verb-final order would also have resulted in a favoured clausula, and I therefore concluded that prose rhythm alone is generally not sufficient to explain the choice of word order. At most, it may be a minor factor, for instance in (39) below, where the adverb *diligenter* is placed last, resulting in a double trochee clausula where there would otherwise have been no clausula at all.

(39) . . . ***quorum*** *vobis pro vestra sapientia, Quirites, habenda est* ***ratio*** *diligenter.* (Cic. Manil. 17)
'. . .and wise men like yourselves know that their interests demand your careful consideration.'

4.2 Playing with Expectations

Several of the categories that regularly appear as interveners have preferred positions in the clause (e.g. personal pronouns) or in relation to other words, which may influence the number of interveners. There is, however, a different potential perspective. In the second volume to his *L'ordre des mots dans la phrase latine*, Marouzeau (1938: 86) suggests that hyperbaton (in particular when the verb is among the interposed words) is a means of managing the audience's expectations.

A consequence of this idea would be that it is not the number of constituents that matters, but their actual length, and perhaps also their semantic contents. If the separation is fairly short, for instance a personal pronoun plus verb, this would give little opportunity for the audience to guess the second part of the interrupted noun phrase. In an example like (40, repeated from 1), on the other hand, the noun *gratia* could likely have been identified from the (feminine, singular) adjective of size, the dative constituent, and the verb *habeo*.

(40) ***magna*** *dis immortalibus habenda est atque huic ipsi Iovi Statori, antiquissimo custodi huius urbis,* ***gratia***. . . (Cic. Catil. 1, 11)

5 Conclusions

Long-distance hyperbaton is fairly common in Latin, present (depending on how you define it) in just under 10% of all instances of hyperbaton in Cicero's orations. Unlike what some previous accounts seem to suggest, these longer separations constitute a highly heterogenic phenomenon. Because of the many variables at play, it is difficult to identify distinctive patterns with regards to the parameters involved. However, based on my dataset of 225 instances, I identified some tendencies where certain features are combined with some frequency. For instance, clause-initial interrogatives and negative quantifiers are frequently followed by the verb *sum*, which is also consistent with some of Powell's criteria for "long-range hyperbaton". These tendencies, however, offer only a partial explanation of the phenomena, and do not allow to draw any conclusions regarding the function of the constructions.

Instead, I would suggest that these longer separations of the two components of a noun phrase are due to a combination of different factors that influence Latin word order, of which many can individually cause hyperbaton. As such, the use of long-distance hyperbaton likely cannot be connected with specific communicative intentions. It might indeed be best examined in relation to other phenomena of noun phrase discontinuity in Latin, and of Latin word order at large.

Bibliography

Adams, J. N. (1994a). Wackernagel’s Law and the position of unstressed personal pronouns in Classical Latin. *Transactions of the Philological Society*, *92*, 103–178.
Adams, J. N. (1994b). *Wackernagel’s Law and the Placement of the Copula esse in Classical Latin*. Cambridge: Cambridge Philological Society (Suppl. Vol. 18).
Devine, A. & Stephens, L. (2006). *Latin word order. Structured meaning and information*. Oxford: Oxford University Press.
Dik, S. (1997). *The Theory of Functional Grammar. Part 2: Complex and Derived Constructions*. Berlin: Mouton de Gruyter.
Dover, K. J. (1960). *Greek Word Order*. Cambridge: Cambridge University Press.
Keeline, T. & Kirby, T. (2019). *Auceps syllabarum*: A Digital Analysis of Latin Prose Rhythm. *Journal of Roman Studies*, *109*, 161–204.
Marouzeau, J. (1938). *L’ordre des mots dans la phrase latine. Volume 2: Le verbe*. Paris: Champion.
Pinkster, H. (2015). *The Oxford Latin Syntax. Volume 1: The Simple Clause*. Oxford: Oxford University Press.
Pinkster, H. (2021). *The Oxford Latin Syntax. Volume 2: The Complex Sentence and Discourse*. Oxford: Oxford University Press.
Powell, J. G. F. (2010). Hyperbaton and register in Cicero. In E. Dickey & A. Chahoud (Eds.), *Colloquial and Literary Latin* (pp. 163–185). Cambridge: Cambridge University Press.
Spevak, O. (2010). *Constituent Order in Classical Latin Prose*. Amsterdam: John Benjamins.
Vendel, A. (forthcoming). Nulla umquam obmutescet vetustas. *Hyperbaton in Cicero’s oratory*. Doctoral dissertation. University of Cambridge.
Zieliński, T. (1904). *Das Clauselgesetz in Ciceros Reden: Grundzüge einer oratorischen Rhythmik*. Leipzig: Dieterich’sche Verlags-Buchhandlung.

Section 4: **Text Structure and Pragmatics**

Giulia Beghini

Nunc age . . . expediam: A Didactic Introductory Construction in Virgil's Poetry

Abstract: The present paper analyses a didactic three-part construction (henceforth D3C), composed of *nunc*, *age* and a first person singular commissive and metacommunicative *verbum dicendi*. The D3C is present three times in Virgil's poetry: once in the *Georgics* and twice in the *Aeneid*. This study aims to consider each element from a linguistic, sociolinguistic, and pragmatic point of view, paying special attention to context and genre. Moreover, the D3C and its variants are studied in a comparative perspective along the literary and non-literary *testimonia* both *latina* and *graeca* of Antiquity, in order to identify possible literary models.

Keywords: topic introduction marker, *nunc*, *age*, commissive and metacommunicative *verba dicendi*, Virgil

1 Introduction

The co-occurrence of *nunc*, *age* and *expediam* is present only three times in Virgil's poetry but at marked occasions (Section 2). Firstly, I describe the linguistic and functional features of each element, as well as the context, literary genre, pragmatic aspects, and prosody of each excerpt. Particular attention is paid to *age*, which presents an unusual syntagmatic combination, as it is not inserted in a directive speech act, but rather a commissive one. *Age* works in synergy with *nunc* as topic introduction marker or topic elaboration marker. However, in my opinion, it is possible to identify the specific contribution of each element (Section 3). Secondly, the data suggest that the co-occurrence of *nunc*, *age* and *expediam* could be a specific construction, which I name "didactic three-part construction" (henceforth D3C). Therefore, I expand my corpus in a comparative perspective: I consider the D3C and its variants from literary and non-literary *testimonia latina* et *graeca* of Antiquity. This passage allows us not only to confirm the label of "D3C", but also to

Note: I am sincerely grateful to Rodie Risselada, Luis Unceta Gómez and Chiara Fedriani for their insightful comments to a previous version of this paper.

Giulia Beghini, Università degli Studi di Verona, Italy

https://doi.org/10.1515/9783111332956-033

look for possible literary models (Section 4). Finally, I compare the D3C with other types of introductions of a new (sub)topic within Virgil's poetry, in order to highlight differences and specificities (Section 5).

2 The D3C in Virgil's Poetry

There are three Virgilian texts and contexts in which the D3C appears. The first passage is found in *Georgics*:

(1) *Verum haec ipse equidem spatiis exclusus iniquis*
praetereo atque aliis post me memoranda relinquo.
***Nunc age**, naturas apibus quas Iuppiter ipse*
*addidit **expediam**, pro qua mercede canoros*
Curetum sonitus crepitantiaque aera secutae
Dictaeo caeli regem pavere sub antro.[1] (Verg. georg. 4, 147–152)

After explaining some features of bees (8–115) and presenting an *excursus* on the *senex Corycius* (116–148), the poet introduces the main topic at line 149: the nature and life-style of bees. *Nunc age* introduces not a different topic, but a new and more important section on bees, i.e., "the core"[2] of the poet's account. This shift is marked not only by *nunc* (here in synergy with *age*) but also by metacomments that prepare the addressee, as Risselada (1996) has found in other texts. The metacomments consist of the *praeteritio* at lines 147–148 and the commissive and metacommunicative verb *expediam* at line 150.

The second passage consists in the median *proemium*[3] at Aen. 7, 37. We will consider lines 35–45 to better analyse this change in topic:

(2) *Flectere iter sociis terraeque advertere proras*
imperat et laetus fluvio succedit opaco.
***Nunc age**, qui reges, Erato,*[4] *quae tempora rerum,*

1 The *editio critica* is by Conte (Ottaviano and Conte 2013). For the list of consulted commentaries on Virgil's poetry, see Beghini (2020: 323–357), with the addition of Barchiesi (1980) and Biotti (1994). I will quote only the strictly pertinent contributions in the present paper.

2 Thomas (1988: 175).

3 For more on the median proems and their programmatic function in Alexandrian taste, see Conte (1984: 121–133).

4 The vocative *Erato* is due to the influence of Εἰ δ' ἄγε νῦν Ἐρατώ, παρ' ἔμ' ἵστασο καί μοι ἔνισπε (Apoll. 3, 1), but it is clear that Erato does not represent the addressee: the invocation to the Muse

quis Latio antiquo fuerit status, advena classem
cum primum Ausoniis exercitus appulit oris,
***expediam** et primae revocabo exordia pugnae.*
Tu vatem, tu, diva, mone. Dicam horrida bella,
dicam acies actosque animis in funera reges,
Tyrrhenamque manum totamque sub arma coactam
Hesperiam. Maior rerum mihi nascitur ordo,
maius opus moveo.[5] (VERG. Aen. 7, 35–45)

The narration of the *gestae* of Aeneas and his men who have already arrived at the mouth of the Tiber, i.e., the "Event Time" coined by Schriffin (1987: 261–266),[6] stops abruptly at line 36. At the beginning of line 37, the poet introduces the "Iliadic" part[7] of the *Aeneid* with *nunc age* and starts the "Discourse Time" (Schriffin 1987: 261–266). Virgil invokes the Muse Erato and draws the addressee's attention to the following and much more important section, i.e., the *horrida bella. Nunc* (in synergy with *age*) in first position announces the shift from Event Time to Discourse Time and situates the metacomments consisting in the commissive verbs *expediam, revocabo, dicam* (two times) and *moveo* in Discourse Time. These verbs constitute a kind of declaration of intents and a promise to the addressee. The importance of this new section of the *Aeneid* is also underlined by metaliterary comments such as ***maior** rerum mihi nascitur **ordo, maius opus** moveo* and by the fact that this is the only instance in which Virgil solemnly refers to himself as *vates*.

The third and last Virgilian excerpt is Aen. 6, 756–759, when Anchises announces the *futura gloria Romana* in the Underworld:

(3) ***Nunc age**, Dardaniam prolem quae deinde sequatur*
gloria, qui maneant Itala de gente nepotes,
inlustris animas nostrumque in nomen ituras,
***expediam** dictis et te tua fata docebo*. (VERG. Aen. 6, 756–759)

---

is at line 41. Virgil changes the structure of the epic model of the invocation of the Muses at lines 37–40, by introducing a didactic introductory formula and meanwhile leaving the literary model identifiable. For more on the choice of Erato, see Horsfall (2000: 67–76).

5 The *editio critica* is by Conte (2009).

6 *Nunc* is in "Event Time" when it situates a state of affairs in the time of the narrated world (not in an extralinguistic world, i.e., "Reference time"). *Nunc* is in "Discourse Time" when it relates the discourse units in the ongoing discourse, without any references to extralinguistic world.

7 For a precise commentary on these lines, with particular focus on literary models, see Horsfall (2000: 67–76).

This is the only case in which the speaker is a character, but the didactic tone and the fact that Anchises' voice and the poet's voice overlap in some points here are quite clear. The moment is certainly important, as it has been skillfully constructed from a narrative point of view. Aeneas asks about the destiny of the souls that are crowded near the river Lethe (719–721), and Anchises explains the Orphic doctrine of metempsychosis (722–751). Then there is a pause: four narrative lines create expectation by explaining the characters' change in place and position (752–755). Anchises takes his son and the Sibyl to a mound from which they can learn the faces of those who advanced. At this moment, Anchises, by the means of the introductory formula *nunc age*, calls the addressee's attention and presents the so-called "Parade of Heroes", i.e., the future Roman conquerors whose *fata* are connected to Aeneas. Metacomments consist in the commissive verbs *expediam* and *docebo*, like in (1) and (2).

These three passages present differences in terms of genre, context, narrative and function. The *Georgics* belong to didactic poem and *nunc age* functions as a topic elaboration marker that signals the introduction of the core of the poet's account on bees. Aen. 6 and 7 belong to the epic poem but in Aen. 7 the *vates* poet solemnly performs a second *proemium*, whereas in Aen. 6 a character shows his son (and the reader/listener) the *futura gloria Romana*. In both Aeneadic excerpts *nunc age* functions as a topic introduction marker. Nevertheless, these three passages present similarities: they all are characterized by an epexegetic tone in a crucial context and there is a formularity, from a linguistic and prosodic point of view, consisting in the D3C.

3 The Constituent Elements of the D3C in Virgil: *nunc*, *age*, and *expediam*

Nunc age functions as a complex marker that introduces a new topic or a new section in a sequence, warns the addressee of the importance of what is about to be said and calls his/her attention. *Nunc age* works at a metacommunicative level, acting simultaneously at discourse organisational level, mainly by the means of *nunc*, and the interactional one, mainly by the means of *age*. In fact, *nunc age* plays the roles of both discourse and pragmatic marker with different degrees: it communicates information about the structure of the poetic discourse and instructions on how the addressee should behave. Through it the poet organizes his discourse into sections and warns the addressee that a new and extremely important part is coming, and meanwhile involves the addressee pushing him/her to play an active role (to listen carefully and learn).

Nunc and *age* work in synergy, but it is maybe possible to distinguish their own main functions.

3.1 *Nunc*

Regarding *nunc*, I refer to Risselada (1996: 105–125). The scholar identifies the use of *nunc* as Discourse-internal adjunct in Latin prose and poetry (1996: 117–118), i.e., when "*nunc* functions as a 'discourse temporal' adjunct in utterances which as a whole announce a (minor or major) shift".[8] In my opinion, *nunc* is a Discourse-internal adjunct in the D3C, as it announces a shift to a more important topic within a larger unity of coherence. *Nunc* serves to situate metacomments in Discourse Time and to signal the importance of what is going to be said. All the examples in Risselada (1996) present *nunc* without *age*.

3.2 *Age*

Regarding *age*, the Romans were already aware of its exhortative value:

(4) *heia age hoc loco per αὔξησιν figuram adhortationem implevit: nam eandem rem secundo dixit "heia age", cum "heia" saepe "age" significet.* (Serv. auct. Aen. 4, 569)

(5) *hortativa "heia, age"* (Prisc. gramm. III 86, 17–19)

Recent studies consider *age* as functional marker, which can be strategically used by speakers in communicative exchanges.[9] Its process of pragmaticalization is described by Fedriani (2019: 78):[10] "The dynamic causative feature may have rendered these verbs [Latin *ago* and Greek *ágō*] privileged candidates to be reanalyzed in directive contexts, in which they were frequently coordinated (or juxtaposed) with imperatives. The original fully lexicalized request to 'move on', 'go', 'set in

8 Risselada (1996: 117).
9 Ghezzi and Molinelli (2014); Fedriani and Ghezzi (2014); Fedriani (2019). Traditional grammar considers *age* as a secondary interjection, see Hofmann and Ricottilli (2003^3: 134–151). For further references on classifications of interjections and Latin interjections, see Beghini (2024: 588, note 4).
10 See also Fedriani and Ghezzi (2014: 121–122).

motion' to accomplish an order was therefore gradually reanalyzed as an exhortative, directive pragmatic marker to drive the interlocutor into action."

To my knowledge, studies on *age*/*agite* identify the following functions:

- *age* as an exhortative directive pragmatic marker: Hand (1829: I, 204–206); Barbini (1966); Lepre (1985); Hofmann and Ricottilli (2003^3: 149); Unceta Gómez (2016 and 2024); Fedriani and Ghezzi (2014); Fedriani (2019: 82),
- *age* as a discourse marker before questions: encouragement to proceed with a communicative move or to take the floor: Hand (1829: III, 206–208); Hofmann and Ricottilli (2003^3: 149); Fedriani and Ghezzi (2014: 126–127); Fedriani (2019: 81–82); TLL (s.v. *ago* col. 1404, lin. 64): *quasi "pro age dic"*,
- *age* as a (dis)agreement pragmatic marker: an in-depth study is by Unceta Gómez (2024), see also Hofmann and Ricottilli (2003^3: 149); Fedriani (2019).

It is worth noting that the corpora of these studies mainly consist of Roman comedy. As we will see later, the literary genre and type of context should not be underestimated.

As previously said, *age* works in synergy with *nunc* in warning of the importance of the coming section of the discourse and underlining its internal structure. However, in my opinion, its specific contribution in the introductory complex marker is at the interactional level. *Age* would involve the addressee pushing him/her to an active role, in line with its exhortative nature.

In the three Virgilian excerpt *age* does not accompany a directive verb, as usual,[11] but rather the commissive *expediam*. *Expediam* is, indeed, a future indicative first person singular and not a present subjunctive, as may be clearly seen not only by the context, but also by the other syntagmatic elements: *expediam* is coordinated with other future indicative verbs, such as *revocabo* and *docebo* in Verg. Aen. 7, 40 and 6, 759. Therefore, *age* does not reinforce the illocutionary force of a self-exhortation.[12] *Age* is inserted in a primarily commissive speech act that functions also as a metacomment: the poet declares his intents and, in doing so, makes a promise to the addressee on one hand, and communicates to the addressee what he is going to tell him/her on the other hand. This communication on the poetic discourse is a metacomment which gives a clear idea of the structure of the discourse and implicitly gives instructions to the addressee on how he/she should behave. In my opinion, *age* emphasises, at a metacommunicative level, that the addressee

11 These are the only three cases out of 32 in which *age*/*agite* does not accompany a directive verb in Virgil. For more on this, see Beghini (2024: 589–594).

12 *Sic*, instead, in Barbini (1966: 360–361).

should pay attention and listen to the new (sub)topic introduced by *nunc*. In other words, *age* reinforces the illocutionary force of a directive verb, or rather a metadirective[13] one, which is implicit and which the addressee could easily infer owing to the context. The epexegetic contexts that we have found in Virgil's passages are, indeed, characterised by a fixed and clear-cut division of roles between the speaker and the addressee: the speaker is the *docens* who tries to explain the matter and to involve the addressee, whereas the addressee is the *discens*. In my opinion, the specific context allows a pragmatic inference: the addressee can easily identify the implied metadirective verb that *age* is reinforcing.

As previously said, all the example in Risselada (1996) present *nunc* introducing a new (sub)topic without *age*. Another confirmation of the fact that *nunc* functions mainly at discourse organizational level and that *age* mainly at the interactional one come from the comparison with other types of introductions of a new section with a commissive and metacommunicative first person singular *verbum dicendi*. These introductions may be in the affirmative or interrogative[14] form and may include *nunc* or other particles/expressions of discourse organisation[15] without *age*, but do not include *age* without *nunc*.

3.3 *Expediam*

Regarding *expediam*, I shall just recall that it is a commissive and metacommunicative future indicative first person singular *verbum dicendi* (Section 3.2), accompanied by *revocabo* or *docebo* in the Aeneadic passages.

The formularity[16] of the D3C clearly appears also from a prosodic point of view: *nunc age* starts a new hexameter that coincides with a new sentence in all the three occurrences. *Nunc age* always makes up the first dactyl of the hexameter and creates the diaeresis of the first foot. In the three Virgilian hexameters the metric design is highly stylized: this diaeresis is always followed by the penthemimeral and hephthemimeral caesuras and the bucolic diaeresis which is always preceded

13 Metadirectives are a subgroup of directives that mention the perlocutionary effect of the speech act and direct the addressee to realise this effect. For more on this, see Risselada (1993: 242–246, 258–278).

14 E.g., VERG. georg. 1, 311–315.

15 E.g., without *age*: *nunc* (e.g., LVCR. 4, 633–635, also with an explicit reference to the addressee, e.g., LVCR. 3, 177–178), *priusquam* (e.g., LVCR. 5, 110–115), *quod quoniam docui* (e.g., LVCR. 2, 478–480), *praeterea* (e.g., LVCR. 5, 76–79), *sed* at a presentational level (Kroon 1995: 210–217, 279) (e.g., LVCR. 4, 929–931).

16 Moscalew (1982: 220–221) listed *nunc age* in the shorter repetitions.

by the interrogative adjective *qui, quae, quod*. The diaeresis of the first foot is "significant" as it comes "after a group of words that make sense by themselves",[17] i.e., the (sub)topic introduction marker *nunc age*, and seems to reproduce a light pause[18] before the new section. This pause allows the addressee to grasp the importance of the moment: the prosody supports the semantics of the text. *Expediam* is post-positioned in all the three excerpts: it comes after its object (in the form of indirect interrogatives), and in epic poetry it always occupies the first position in the hexameter.

4 The Corpora and the Results

In order to verify my hypothesis, I searched and studied the D3C, including eventual variants, in Latin and ancient Greek. My corpora consisted of the Library of Latin Texts of antiquity, *Musisque Deoque* for poetry after the II century A.D., and the *Thesaurus linguae Graecae*. I also searched for the construction in the non-literary and unofficial[19] *testimonia* of the Latin language, such as non-literary letters, ostraca, curse tablets, graffiti and unofficial epigraphs, but found no evidence. This is unsurprising, as functional markers are preferentially used in oral language, which provides the conditions for the contemporaneous presence of the message and its context of production.

Special attention was paid to texts that preceded and were contemporaneous to Virgil in order to look for possible influences.

4.1 The D3C in Ancient Greek before Virgil

The searched items in the TLG were νῦν δ' ἄγε, νῦν ἄγε, νῦν δ' ἄγεθ', νῦν ἄγεθ', νῦν δ' ἄγετε, and νῦν δ' ἄγετε. The data show that in Greek literature[20] the D3C appears twice in the didascalic poem Θηριακά by Nicander, as we may read in:

17 Huxley (1987: 23).

18 On "light pause" and the uses of the diaeresis after the first foot, see respectively Winbolt (1903: 5–7, 7–21, 59–69). Winbolt (1903: 7): "Diaeresis has the effect of producing a more abrupt and more striking pause than the more common pauses in caesura."

19 For the list of the consulted bibliography of non-literary, and unofficial *testimonia*, see Beghini (2020: 38–39).

20 Obviously, I am aware that in Greek epic there are collocations like νῦν δ' ἄγε, νῦν δ' ἄγεθ', ἀλλ' ἄγε νῦν and εἰ δ' ἄγε νῦν, quite always positioned at the beginning of the hexameter, but their

(6) Νῦν δ' ἄγε τοι ἐπίμικτα νόσων ἀλκτήρια λέξω.[21] (Nic. *Ther.* 528)

(7) Νῦν δ' ἄγε τοι ῥίζας ἐρέω ὀφίεσσιν ἀρωγούς. (Nic. *Ther.* 636)

Like in Virgil, the collocation νῦν δ' ἄγε is always positioned at the beginning of the hexameter and of a new sentence. It introduces a new topic, which is connected to the previous one and quite extensive as well as important. Like in Virgil, νῦν δ' ἄγε accompanies a commissive and metacommunicative *verbum dicendi* in the future indicative first person singular form (λέξω and ἐρέω) which functions at a metacommunicative level in declaring the poet's intention.

In the Θηριακά there is a variant of the D3C: the introductory formula νῦν δ' ἄγε accompanies not a commissive and metacommunicative *verbum dicendi*, but rather a metadirective verb, that makes explicit the requested active role of the addressee in (8).

(8) Νῦν δ' ἄγε χερσύδροιο καὶ ἀσπίδος εἴρεο μορφὰς
ἰσαίας (Nic. *Ther.* 359–360)

The *docens* speaker explicates how the addressee should behave and ἄγε reinforces the directive force of the imperative εἴρεο.[22] This could be a first confirmation to my hypothesis that in the D3C *age* is an appeal to the addressee but without the explicit mention of what she/he should do. I hypothesised that the epexegetic context and the fixed relationship between the *docens* speaker and the *discens* addressee could allow an inference and these first data seem to confirm it.

To our knowledge, the most ancient example of the variant of the D3C seen in (8) is found in another didactic poem, Empedocles' fr. 90 (Gemelli Marciano 2009 = DK 31 B 62):

(9) Νῦν δ' ἄγ', ὅπως ἀνδρῶν τε πολυκλαύτων τε γυναικῶν
ἐννυχίους ὅρπηκας ἀνήγαγε κρινόμενον πῦρ,
τῶνδε κλύ'· οὐ γὰρ μῦθος ἀπόσκοπος οὐδ' ἀδαήμων· (Emp. *Simpl. In Ph.* 381, 29)

Empedocles, before talking of the assembling of male and female bodies, explains how the fire raised up the shoots of men and women full of lamentation. The

features and functions are different from the D3C. For the influence of Apoll. 3, 1 on Verg. Aen. 7, 37, see above note 4 with references.

21 The *editio critica* is by Jacques (2002).

22 For an overview of the meanings and translations of this verb, see Overduin (2015: 324).

importance of the passage is underlined by the introductory formula νῦν δ' ἄγ', the explicit metadirective verb κλῦ' that invites the addressee to listen carefully, and the certainty of the truthfulness of the account. Finally, the word order and the post-positioning of the metadirective verb could have influenced the order in Lucretius and Virgil.

The contexts of the D3C in examples 6 and 7 (as well as of a variant of it in examples 8 and 9) are clearly epexegetic, and the genre is the didactic poem.[23] Finally, it is worth noticing that Nicander's poetry played a significant role in Virgil's didactic production.

4.2 The D3C in Latin before Virgil

There is more evidence of the D3C in Latin literature. The clearest examples may be found in Lucretius' didactic poem *De rerum natura*, that influenced substantially Virgil's poetry.

Nunc age is always positioned at the beginning of a new hexameter and a new sentence. In six cases *nunc age* accompanies a commissive and metacommunicative *verbum dicendi* in the poet's declaration of intents, as we can see in (10):

(10) *Nunc age, Averna tibi quae sint loca cumque lacusque*
expediam, quali natura praedita constent. (LVCR. 6, 738–739)

The commissive verbs include *expediam* (three times), *agam*, *pergam*, *edam* (each once). In my opinion, Lucretius' preference for *expediam* could have influenced Virgil's choice of *expediam* as the main commissive verb in the D3C. Moreover, there is another coincidence between Lucretius and Virgil from a prosodic point of view: two occurrences of *expediam* in Lucretius constitute the first foot, as do the two in the *Aeneid*, and one occurrence of *expediam* in Lucretius is collocated immediately after the first foot, just as in the *Georgics*.

Like in Empedocles (9) and in Nicander (8), in Lucretius *nunc age* accompanies a metadirective verb of listening, understanding or learning which requires the addressee's attention in 8 cases.[24] The imperatives include *percipe* (six times),

23 Overduin (2015: 36–37, 61–63, 323, 383) talks of the section marker νῦν δ' ἄγε and then λέξω as examples of fictionalized speech in didactic poetry, as they reproduce an illusion of live epexegetic speech respectively by the means of the reference to the here and now (νῦν), the vivid address to the addressee (ἄγε), and the use of the performative future (λέξω).

24 Before Virgil and simultaneously with him, there are cases of *nunc age* which introduces a new section of the discourse with metadirective verbs of listening/ understanding/ thinking in Cicero,

accipe (two times), *cognosce* and *audi* (each once). An example of this use may be found in (11):

(11) *Nunc age quam tenui natura constet imago*
percipe.[25] (LVCR. 4, 110–111)

Moreover, the data from Lucretius provide an even more interesting case:

(12) ***Nunc age**, quo motu genitalia materiai*
corpora res varias gignant genitasque resolvant
et qua vi facere id cogantur quaeque sit ollis
reddita mobilitas magnum per inane meandi
***expediam**: tu te dictis praebere memento*. (LVCR. 2, 62–66)

This passage is remarkable for two reasons: firstly, it constitutes the model of the Aeneadic D3C in relation to the choice of the verb *expediam* and its first position in the hexameter. Secondly, the division of the roles between the *docens* poet and the *discens* addressee is explicitly indicated at line 66. The D3C and its declaration of intents are immediately followed by an emphasized[26] invitation to the addressee to pay attention. In other words, there is an explicit orientation to both the speaker and the addressee, each endowed with their own sphere of competence. Such a construction can constitute an intermediate position between a speaker-oriented (primarily commissive) speech act, which we have seen in the D3C (examples 1, 2, 3, 6, 7, 10), and an addressee-oriented (primarily directive) speech act, which we have seen in a variant of it (examples 8, 9, 11).

These examples may confirm the hypothesis that in the D3C *age* reinforces the illocutionary force of an implied metadirective verb involving the addressee and pushing him/her to an active role. As we have seen, these metadirective verbs are always verbs of listening or cognition and are inserted in an epexegetic context featuring a fixed division of roles between the *docens* speaker and *discens* addressee. These features may allow an inference of these metadirectives verbs in the D3C.

---

and Horace, but no evidence of the D3C. It is thoughtful Cucchiarelli's comment (2019: 416) on HOR. epist. 1, 14, 31. As far as the word order between *age* and *nunc* is concerned, I have already argued (Beghini 2024: 596–598) that it is regularly *age nunc* in prose and in Roman Comedy, whereas it is always *nunc age* in hexametric poetry, for metrical reasons.

25 The *editio critica* is by Bailey (1967^2).

26 The command is emphasised by the explicit personal pronoun *tu*, which is even more marked by the polyptoton *tu te*.

Finally, a further variant of the D3C with the "soziative pluralis"[27] may be seen in Lucretius.[28]

5 Other Types of (Sub)Topic Introductions in Virgil's Poetry

A further confirmation to my hypothesis come from Virgil's poetry. We will start by comparing the D3C with other types of (sub)topic introductions characterised by explicit metacomments. The appeal to the addressee is performed by *age* in the D3C, and by the parenthetical metadirective verbs *adverte / animos adhibete* in the other introductions (examples 13, 14, 15).

After reassuring Venus that she will obtain Jupiter's consent, Juno explains how the marriage of Aeneas and Dido will take place:

(13) *Mecum erit iste labor. Nunc qua ratione quod instat*
confieri possit, paucis ***(adverte)*** *docebo*. (VERG. Aen. 4, 115–116)

After reassuring Aeneas that the vision is true and foreseeing the foundation of Alba, the god Tiberinus prophesies how he will face the present situation as *victor*:

(14) *Haud incerta cano. Nunc qua ratione quod instat*
expedias[29] *victor, paucis* ***(adverte)*** *docebo*. (VERG. Aen. 8, 50–51)

Finally, after having convened the *concilium* and explained the present situation, Latinus *rex* introduces his decision:

27 Kühner and Stegmann (1962⁴: 1, 87–88); Hofmann and Szantyr (1972²: 19–20); Pinkster (2015: 1119–1120).

28 LVCR. 1, 953–954 *Nunc age, summai quaedam sit finis eorum / necne sit, evolvamus*. *Evolvamus* allows a greater closeness between the speaker and the addressee but means *evolvam* (the poet does not include the addressee in his action to explain). The verb is of a commissive nature without directive force, see Risselada (1993: 161–162). In Cicero and in Ps. Quintilian's *Declamationes maiores, nunc age* accompanies first person plural subjunctives, that seem different from the "soziative pluralis", as they seem to express a joined action which the speaker and the addressee are invited to do together.

29 All editions accept *expedias*, which is the *lectio* of the most authoritative manuscripts. The variant *expediam*, due to the influence of Aen. 6, 759 and 11, 316, does not explain the presence of *victor* (a key-word of book VIII, see Gransden 1976: 86) or the active role of Aeneas.

(15) <u>*Nunc adeo*</u>[30] *quae sit dubiae sententia menti,*
<u>*expediam*</u> *et paucis* ***(animos adhibete)*** <u>*docebo*</u>. (VERG. Aen. 11, 315–316)

The attitude of Juno, Tiberinus and Latinus is similar to that of the poet and Anchises in the D3C. They all introduce a new (sub)topic and warn the addressee of the importance of what is going to be said through metacomments. The linguistic micro-context is similar, too: there are *nunc* as Discourse-internal adjunct, and commissive and metacommunicative verbs such as *expediam* and *docebo*. The appeal to the addressee is performed by *age* without an explicit metadirective verb in the D3C (examples 1, 2, 3), whereas is performed by the present imperative *adverte* and *animos adhibete* in the other introductions (examples 13, 14, 15). These imperatives are parenthetical[31] and allow to explicit metapragmatic instructions in a primarily speaker-oriented speech act. The parenthetical form ensures speed and a colloquial touch. From a functional point of view, *age* in the D3C is similiar to *adverte / animos adhibete*. In other words, in these Virgilian examples the metacommunicative consequence (i.e., paying attention and listening), which is implicit in the D3C, is made parenthetically explicit.

From a stylistic point of view, the construction with *nunc age . . . expediam* is different from the construction *nunc . . . (adverte / animos adhibete) docebo*. In the D3C, *nunc age*, which is always positioned in the first foot of the hexameter, immediately calls the addressee's attention. Then the poet presents the new topic by the means of elegant, refined and more or less long indirect interrogatives (18 and 19 words in the *Aeneid*). After these, the quadrisyllable *expediam* closes the sentence and underlines the proud and selfconscious *poetae vox* (as previously observed, Anchises' voice overlaps the poet's voice in Aen. 6). There is a prevalent orientation to the speaker, his declaration of intent and his role of *docens* and, sometimes, *vates*. The D3C is composed of elements belonging to register-neutral and colloquial language, but the context in which it is inserted is serious and extremely important. *Nunc* is, indeed, a register-neutral[32] high-frequency word, *age* is preferentially used in colloquial and spoken language, and *expediam* is didactic in tone, but not exclusive of high poetry or elevated prose. The use of the D3C in Virgil's poetry is limited to few and extremely central moments. Conversely, the introductory construction composed by *nunc . . . (adverte / animos adhibete) docebo* is less solemn:

30 For *nunc adeo* as 'right now' see Horsfall (2003: 206).

31 On colloquial parentheses, see Hofmann and Szantyr (1972²: 728–729); Hofmann and Ricottilli (2003: 262–268). For more on the use of parentheses in Virgil, see Beghini (2020: 144–160, 181–215); and in general, see Risselada (1989); Bolkestein (1998); Mencacci (2022).

32 Dickey (2010: 4) defines "register-neutral" words and usages as "usable in any variety of language". For more on this, see Dickey (2010).

it features plain syntax, it is brief (the presentation of the new topic is expressed in 5–6 words) and refers to colloquial language and the vividness of a face-to-face conversation. Such an explicit request for attention in the form of the imperative of *animum adve(o)rto* is found 42 times in Plautus. Moreover, this type of parenthesis is clearly of oral origin and creates a realistic effect, as Horsfall (2003: 206) has already pointed out. The Aeneadic passages with *adverte* not coincidentally belong to direct speeches among characters and the literary contexts are less important than those in which the D3C appears.

6 Conclusions

Virgil uses the D3C when introducing a new and extremely important (sub)topic. Among the possible ways to introduce a new section of the discourse, the D3C performs a high degree of formularity, and a complementarity between the discourse organisational level, mainly by the means of *nunc*, and the pragmatic one, mainly by the means of *age*.

The study of the D3C in a comparative perspective allowed us not only to consider the co-occurrence of *nunc*, *age* and a first person singular commissive and metacommunicative *verbum dicendi* as a specific construction, but also to identify the literary models, the type of context and the genre. The D3C does not belong to epic but rather to the Hellenistic didactic poetry (Nicander and Lucretius) and appears in epexegetic contexts. To our knowledge, Virgil was the first to insert this phenomenon in epic, always in epexegetic and metacommunicative contexts. The occurrences of the D3C after Virgil still display almost the same distribution.[33]

Moreover, the analysis of the D3C in Latin and ancient Greek *testimonia* allowed us to confirm that the specific contribution of *age* in the (sub)topic introduction marker *nunc age* is at an interactional level. *Age*, in fact, reinforces the illocutionary force of a metadirective verb of listening or cognition, which is implied in the D3C, but explicit in a variant of it (examples 8, 9, 11), and in other types of introductions in Virgil's poetry.

From a stylistic point of view, the D3C is composed of elements belonging to register-neutral and colloquial language, but it is inserted in serious and crucial contexts in Virgil's poetry. This is a case of artistic re-elaboration of elements of colloquial language: by the means of it the poet can be more effective and draw the

33 PRISC. periheg. 1035–1036, SIL. 11, 1–3, and QVINT. decl. 252, 12, 3. After Virgil, there are also cases, different from the D3C, of *nunc age* accompanying imperatives and plural subjunctives both in poetry and in prose.

utmost addressee's attention on what he is going to say. It would be interesting to study other constructions of *nunc age*, not only in Discourse Time, but also in Reference and Event Time, in order to see possible correlations.

Abbreviation

D3C didactic three-part construction

Bibliography

Bailey, C. (1967[2]). *Lucreti de rerum natura libri sex. Edited with Prolegomena, Critical Apparatus, Translation and Commentary by C. Bailey*. Oxford: Oxford University Press.

Barbini, M. A. (1966). Interferenze fra imperativi e interiezioni. *Giornale Italiano di Filologia, 19* (4), 357–363.

Barchiesi, A. (1980). *Virgilio. Georgiche. Introduzione di G. B. Conte. Testo, traduzione e note di A. Barchiesi.* Milano: Mondadori.

Beghini, G. (2020). *Il latino colloquiale nell'*Eneide. *Approfondimenti sull'arte poetica di Virgilio*. Bologna: Pàtron.

Beghini, G. (2024). *Age/agite*: the artistic re-elaboration of a polyfunctional interjection in Virgil's works. In C. Cabrillana (Ed.), *Recent Trends and Findings in Latin Linguistics. Vol. II: Semantics and Lexicography. Discourse and Dialogue* (pp. 587–602). Berlin/Boston: De Gruyter.

Biotti, A. (1994). *Virgilio, Georgiche libro IV. Commento a cura di A. Biotti. Introduzione di N. Horsfall.* Bologna: Pàtron.

Bolkestein, A. M. (1998). Between brackets: (some properties of) parenthetical clauses in Latin. An investigation of the language of Cicero's letters. In R. Risselada (Ed.), *Latin in Use. Amsterdam Studies in the Pragmatics of Latin* (pp. 1–17). Amsterdam: Gieben.

Conte, G. B. (1984). *Virgilio. Il genere e i suoi confini.* Milano: Garzanti.

Conte, G. B. (2009). *P. Vergilius Maro. Aeneis, recensuit atque apparatu critico instruxit Gian Biagio Conte.* Berlin/New York: de Gruyter.

Cucchiarelli, A. (2019). *Orazio. Epistole I. Introduzione, traduzione e commento di Andrea Cucchiarelli.* Pisa: Edizioni della Normale.

Dickey, E. (2010). Introduction. In E. Dickey & A. Chahoud (Eds.), *Colloquial and Literary Latin* (pp. 3–6). Cambridge: Cambridge University Press.

Fedriani, C. (2019). The embodied basis of discourse and pragmatic markers in Greek and Latin. In E. Mocciaro & W. M. Short (Eds.), *Toward a Cognitive Classical Linguistics. The Embodied Basis of Constructions in Greek and Latin* (pp. 69–92). Warsaw/Berlin: de Gruyter Poland.

Fedriani, C. & Ghezzi, C. (2014). The pragmaticalization of verbs of movement and exchange in Latin and Italian: paths of development from lexicon to pragmatics. In I. Bădescu & M. Popescu (Eds.), *Studia linguistica et philologica in honorem Prof. Univ. Dr. Michaela Livescu* (pp. 116–139). Craiova: Editura Universitaria.

Gemelli Marciano, M. L. (2009). *Die Vorsokratiker 2: Parmenis, Zenon, Empedocles. Griechisch-lateinisch-deutsch. Auswahl der Fragmente und Zeugnisse, Übersetzung und Erläuterungen von M. Laura Gemelli Marciano*. Düsseldorf: Artemis & Winkler.

Ghezzi, C. & Molinelli, P. (Eds.) (2014). *Discourse and Pragmatic Markers from Latin to the Romance Languages*. Oxford: Oxford University Press.

Gransden, K. W. (1976). *Virgil. Aeneid book VIII.* Cambridge: Cambridge University Press.

Hand, F. (1829). *Tursellinus seu de particulis latinis commentarii, I vol.* Lipsiae: Weidmann.

Hofmann, J. B. and Ricottilli, L. (2003³). *La lingua d'uso latina*. Bologna: Pàtron.

Hofmann, J. B. and Szantyr, A. (1972²). *Lateinische Syntax und Stilistik*. München: C. H. Beck.

Horsfall, N. (2000). *Virgil, Aeneid 7: A Commentary*. Leiden/Boston/Köln: Brill.

Horsfall, N. (2003). *Virgil, Aeneid 11: A Commentary*. Leiden/Boston: Brill.

Huxley, H. H. (1987). Significant Diaeresis in Virgil and Other Hexameter Poets. *Vergilius*, *33* (1), 23–28.

Jacques, J.-M. (2002). *Nicandre. Œuvres. Tome II: Les Thériques, texte ètabli et traduit par Jean-Marie Jacques*. Paris: Les Belles Lettres.

Kroon, C. (1995). *Discourse Particles in Latin; a Study of* nam, enim, autem, vero *and* at. Amsterdam: Gieben.

Kühner, R. and Stegmann, C. (1962⁴). *Ausführliche Grammatik der lateinischen Sprache. II Teil: Satzlehre*. Hannover: Hahn.

Lepre, M. Z. (1985). Interiezioni. In F. Della Corte (Ed.), *Enciclopedia virgiliana* (pp. 993–996). Roma: Istituto della Enciclopedia Italiana.

Mencacci, F. (2022). Text as Interaction. *Vt Mihi (Quidem) Videtur* as a Hedging Device in Latin Literary Texts. In L. Unceta Gòmez & L. Berger (Eds.), *Politeness in Ancient Greek and Latin* (pp. 103–126). Cambridge: Cambridge University Press.

Moskalew, W. (1982). *Formular Language and Poetic Design in the Aeneid*. Leiden: Brill.

Overduin, F. (2015). *Nicander of Colophon's* Theriaca. *A Literary Commentary*. Leiden/Boston: Brill.

Ottaviano, S. and Conte, G. B. (2013). *P. Vergilius Maro Bucolica, Georgica. Bucolica edidit et apparatu critico instruxit S. Ottaviano, Georgica edidit et apparatu critico instruxit G. B. Conte*. Berlin/Boston: de Gruyter.

Pinkster, H. (2015). *The Oxford Latin Syntax. Volume 1: The Simple Clause*. Oxford: Oxford University Press.

Risselada, R. (1989). Latin Illocutionary Parentheticals. In M. Lavency & D. Longree (Eds.), *Actes du 5° Colloque de linguistique latine* (pp. 367–378). Louvain-la-Neuve: Peeters.

Risselada, R. (1993). *Imperatives and Other Directive Expressions in Latin. A Study in the Pragmatics of a Dead Language*. Amsterdam: Gieben.

Risselada, R. (1996). And now for something completely different? Temporal discourse markers: Latin *nunc* and English now. In R. Risselada, J. De Jong & A. Machtelt Bolkestein (Eds.), *On Latin. Studies in Honour of Harm Pinkster* (pp. 105–125). Amsterdam: Gieben.

Schriffin, D. (1987). *Discourse Markers*. Cambridge: Cambridge University Press.

Thomas, R. F. (1988). *Virgil. Georgics. Volume II: books III-IV edited by Richard F. Thomas*. Cambridge: Cambridge University Press.

Unceta Gómez, L. (2016). Cuando los sentimientos irrumpen: análisis de las interjecciones secundarias en las comedias de Plauto. In A. Penas Ibáñez & B. García-Hernández (Eds.), *Semántica latina y románica. Unidades de significado conceptual y procedimental* (pp. 213–241). Berna: Peter Lang.

Unceta Gómez, L. (2024). The Pragmatic Marker *age*: its Pragmatic Functions in Comedy and its Contribution to the Expression of Im/Politeness. In C. Cabrillana (Ed.), *Recent Trends and Findings in Latin Linguistics. Vol. II: Semantics and Lexicography. Discourse and Dialogue* (pp. 685–702). Berlin/Boston: De Gruyter.

Winbolt, S. E. (1903). *Latin Hexameter Verse. An Aid to Composition*. London: Methuen & Co.

Elisabetta Magni and Ottavia Cepraga

Per exempla: The Forms and Uses of Example Markers in Latin

Abstract: The ways in which exemplification is performed in Latin deserve close investigation for several reasons. First, this complex discourse operation features in almost every argued text but is essentially neglected in Latin syntax handbooks. Second, Latin authors employed a variety of example markers, but only sparse comments on individual forms can be found in the lexica and literature. Moreover, most European languages use adverbials containing epigones of the noun *exemplum* to introduce examples, but expressions like Eng. *for example* or It. *per esempio* have no direct Latin antecedents. To address these understudied issues, the present paper provides a corpus-based analysis of the different words (e.g., *ut, velut, sicut*), phrases (e.g., *exempli gratia, verbi causa*), and constructions (e.g., *ut puta, si dicas*) exploited to mark the exemplifying sequence. The discussion will cover the classification, emergence, and multiple roles of these functional signals in different textual genres, with special attention to grammatical treatises, where examples are fundamental for the description and explanation of linguistic phenomena. The results will be relevant not only for Latin but also for understanding the evolution of example markers in general.

Keywords: Latin, exemplification, example markers, ancient grammarians, pragmatics

1 Research Objectives and Methodology

Most European languages signal the linguistic operation of exemplification with expressions of Latin origin but, leaving aside archaic or formal locutions, such as Sp.

Note: This research was carried out as part of the project PRIN20 *METALINGuistic texts as a privileged data source for the knowledge of ancient languages*, funded by the Italian Ministry of University and Research (MUR). Even though this paper is the outcome of joint work by the authors, for academic purposes, the final editing is to be attributed to Elisabetta Magni for sections 1, 2, and 3, to Ottavia Cepraga for sections 4 and 5.

Elisabetta Magni, Università di Bologna, Italy
Ottavia Cepraga, Università per Stranieri di Siena, Italy

https://doi.org/10.1515/9783111332956-034

verbigracia, It. *verbigrazia*, *verbicausa*, *esemp(l)igratia*, or Eng. *e.g.*, more common adverbials containing epigones of the noun *exemplum*, such as It. *per esempio*, Fr. *par exemple*, Sp. *por ejemplo*, Rom. *de exemplu*, Eng. *for example*, do not find a direct Latin antecedent and develop their full metatextual uses only at later stages.[1]

The noun *exemplum*, which literally means 'what is taken out as a sample', is related to the verb *ex-ĭmo* 'to take out, take away, remove', a derivative from *ĕmo* 'to take, buy, purchase', and develops from the form **ex-em-lom* by adding an epenthetic *p* (Leumann et al. 1979: 165, see also Kornhardt 1936). The TLL lemma organizes the multiple meanings of the word into four major categories with several subtypes, while the OLD (s.v. *exemplum*) provides nine separate definitions.

The phrase *per exempla* in the title of our paper occurs only twice in Classical Latin, and immediately reveals two meanings relevant to exemplification. In (1) Seneca employs *per exempla* to represent a mode of learning: Lucilius' path to wisdom will be facilitated by personal observation of models for moral instruction, while in (2) Pliny summarizes a chapter on celestial portents, which will be illustrated by various facts and events:

(1) *Longum iter est per praecepta, breve et efficax* ***per exempla***. (Sen. epist. 6, 1, 1)
'Long is the way through precepts, but short and helpful if one follows patterns.'

(2) *De caelestibus prodigiis* ***per exempla*** *historica: lampades, bolides, trabes caelestes, chasma caeli.* (Plin. nat. 1, 2a)
'Sky portents through recorded instances: torches, shafts, sky-beams, sky-yawning.'

In rhetorical, philosophical, and legal writings, the *exemplum* is what we might call a "good example", that is, an exemplary anecdote or fact from history, literature, law, etc. that serves an edifying or demonstrative function.[2] In scientific, technical, or grammatical treatises, on the other hand, "proper examples" are representative cases or members of the observed phenomenon or category.

In this paper we will not discuss the abundant literature on the rhetorical *exemplum*, but rather focus on the "canonical" example, which typically entails an asymmetrical relation between two formal and logical units: an exemplified unit (the *illustrandum*) with a generic referent and an exemplifying unit (the *illustrans*) consisting of one or more elements that illustrate the first unit. In Latin, as in other

1 It. *per essemplo* is first used as an example marker in 1484 (LEI), Fr. *pour exemple* in 1580 (TLFi), Eng. *as for exempill* in 1584 (OED).

2 On the rhetorical *exemplum* see, e.g., Price (1975), Gazich (1990), Demoen (1997), Urban (2011).

languages, this relation is signaled by various example markers, i.e., different words (e.g., *ut, velut, sicut, tamquam*), phrases (e.g., *exempli gratia, exempli causa, verbi gratia, verbi causa*), and constructions (e.g., *ut puta, si dicas*, etc.), which usually precede the exemplifying sequence, as shown in (3):[3]

(3) *Quaedam*, [. . .] [*prima bona sunt*]$_{\mathrm{E}}$, [***tamquam***]$_{\mathrm{ExM}}$ [*gaudium*]$_{\mathrm{e}}$, [*pax*]$_{\mathrm{e}}$, [*salus patriae*]$_{\mathrm{e}}$ (SEN. epist. 66, 5)
'Some of them [. . .] are primary goods, such as joy, peace, and the welfare of one's country.'

In handbooks of Latin syntax, exemplification is essentially neglected, and only sparse remarks on individual expressions are found in the literature. To provide an inventory of the different example markers and to investigate their forms and uses in different contexts and literary genres, we carried out a qualitative and partially quantitative analysis of the data collected through the Library of Latin Texts and PHI Latin Texts corpora.[4]

The paper is structured as follows: Section 2 discusses the pragmatic aspects of exemplification, presents a classification of the various exemplification signals, and puts forward a hypothesis about their emergence. The following sections illustrate the ways in which exemplification is carried out in Latin, focusing first on meta-exemplification and the development of *exempli gratia* and *verbi gratia* in Section 3, and addressing para-exemplification and the uses of *ut puta* in Section 4.

2 Pragmatic Aspects of Exemplification

Exemplifying structures can be construed as non-prototypical appositions (Quirk et al. 1985, Meyer 1992, Rodríguez-Abruñeiras 2019) or concatenations (Fernández-Bernárdez 1994–1995, Manzotti 1995), in which the two juxtaposed units can have an implicit or explicitly marked linkage. While "underdetermined exemplification" employs paralinguistic signals (i.e., pauses, interjections, gestures) or

3 The capital letter *E* signifies the superior hierarchical importance and autonomous existence of the exemplified unit, while the small letter *e* marks the subordinate character and subsidiary role of the exemplifying element(s); *ExM* stands for example marker.

4 In Library of Latin Texts (ca. 153 million words spread over 11,614 works), we searched the period *Antiquitas* (< ca. 200 A.D.) and both sections *Aetas Patrum* (ca. 200–735 A.D.); PHI Latin Texts allows searching all Latin literary texts written before 200 A.D. The translations of the Latin examples follow those in the Loeb Classical Library editions, with slight modifications where necessary.

graphic means (e.g., brackets, dashes, colons), "linguistically determined exemplification" is indicated by various means.

From a functional-pragmatic perspective (Ghezzi 2014: 15), this kind of linguistic signals serve primarily as discourse markers that index the structure of the discourse, by providing textual cohesion and specifying how the message and its content are to be interpreted. In addition, they serve as pragmatic markers that index the framework of the interaction, by expressing the speakers/writers' subjective stance in relation to the content of their utterance, or by negotiating prior assertions and viewpoints at the intersubjective level.

As for exemplification, we set out to classify the strategies that guide the hearer/reader's interpretive tasks into three main types: (i) meta-exemplifiers, i.e. meta-discursive speech acts or utterances that denote the pragmatic awareness of the speaker/writer (e.g. *I will give an example*, or *an example is the following*); (ii) canonical example markers, i.e. dedicated adverbials and locutions that mark an element or segment of discourse as an example (e.g. *for example* or *for instance*); (iii) para-exemplifiers, i.e. linguistic items that originally and/or primarily have other functions, such as comparison and equation (e.g. Eng. *like*, Fr. *comme*, It. *come*), focalization and particularization (e.g. Eng. *in particular, including*, Fr. *notamment*, It. *in particolare, incluso*), reformulation and hedging (e.g. Eng. *say, let's say*, Fr. *disons, genre*, It. *diciamo, metti, tipo*), consecution and conclusion (e.g. Fr. *ainsi*, It. *così*).

As we will see in the next sections, the development of Latin example markers proceeds both from strategies of meta-exemplification and from expressions performing para-exemplification. In Manzotti (1995, 1998), the term "paraesemplificazione" applies to forms that serve operations similar or close to exemplification and that, as in metaphor and metonymy, obtain a "figurative" exemplification based on contiguity which combines the properties of the two operations involved (Manzotti 1998: 114). Not surprisingly, in the synchrony of many languages, the boundaries between para-exemplifiers and canonical example markers are often blurred, because functional markers typically have limited or no effect on propositional meaning but serve multiple procedural functions at both the paradigmatic and syntagmatic levels. Moreover, they also tend to cumulate as in *like for example* or *comme par exemple* (Rodríguez-Abruñeiras 2017).

The basic function of example markers is to guide the interlocutor in recognizing the role of the utterance in which they occur and to signal an element or segment of discourse as an example. As such, they typically have metatextual functions (Bazzanella 1995) but can acquire further discourse values and pragmatic nuances depending on the context and the intentions of the speaker/writer. This explains why these markers can also perform reformulation, focalization, or quotation at the metatextual level (Fuchs 1982, Gülich and Kotschi 1983, Rossari and Jayez 1999), convey epistemic hedging, politeness, or shared knowledge at the interactional level (Barotto 2018, Lo Baido 2018, Barotto and Mauri 2018), or even denote approximation at the propositional level (Mihatsch 2010).

As a result, categorizing exemplification signals according to their pragmatic functions is a difficult task, but alternative taxonomies based on structural or semantic parameters are no less problematic (cf. Eggs and McElholm 2013, Rodríguez-Abruñeiras 2017). In the following, we will therefore present the strategies for exemplification in Latin by referring to the notions of meta-exemplification, canonical exemplification, and para-exemplification mentioned above. This simple and inherently dynamic classification will allow us to discuss the data from both a synchronic and diachronic perspective.

3 Meta-exemplification in Latin

Meta-exemplifiers are non-formulaic expressions that contain verbs or nouns that refer to the communicative process (like *say*, *explain*, *example*, *term*, etc.) and announce an exemplification. These metacommunicative devices contribute to integrate the example into the syntax and the flow of discourse. For instance, "Quintilian likes to form the sentence with verbs such as *dicere* or *legere* in order to include the example in its syntactic environment" (Vainio 2000: 33). This is shown in (4), where materials for metalinguistic reflection are presented as fragments of spoken language:

(4) *Nam cum* ***dico*** *"hasta percussi", non utor ablativi natura, nec si idem Graece dicam, dativi.* (QVINT. inst. 1, 4, 26)
'When I say *hasta percussi*, I do not use the natural sense of the ablative; nor, if I say the same in Greek, do I use the natural sense of the dative.'

The use of the verb *dico* also shows the proximity between exemplification and quotation: just as the rhetorical *exemplum* may cite the words of an authoritative source, the grammatical example may quote words and structures of real speech.

Often combined with *pono* (and similar verbs), the noun *exemplum* performs meta-exemplification even before the intervention of co-text and context, because it embeds the operation in the propositional semantics of the sentence. In (5) Quintilian says that he will offer some examples taken from Cicero:

(5) *Singula igitur horum generum ex Cicerone (nam unde potius?)* ***exempla ponamus***. (QVINT. inst. 5, 11, 11)
'Let us set out some individual examples of these kinds from Cicero (where could we find better?).'

3.1 *Exempli gratia* and *exempli causa*

In dictionaries, the phrases *exempli gratia*, *exempli causa*, and *exempli loco* are often mentioned as equivalents of 'for example, by way of an example', but their predominant use is as meta-exemplifiers. Nevertheless, while *exempli loco* remains very rare, structures with *exempli gratia* and *exempli causa* seem to outline clearer paths towards the emergence of markers devoted to exemplification.

Table 1: *Exempli gratia* and *exempli causa* in *Antiquitas*.

	exempli gratia	*exempli causa*
Adjunct	1	11
Meta-exemplifier	6	9
Example marker	3	2
Total	10	22

As shown in Table 1, *exempli gratia*, which is the first expression that comes to mind when we think about exemplification in Latin, appears only 10 times in the *Antiquitas* section of the LLT database, and 6 cases are metacommunicative locutions. Likewise, *exempli causa* contributes to meta-exemplification 9 times within syntactically variable structures, where it usually precedes both object and verb, as in (6):

(6) *Sunt autem quaedam emplastra* [. . .] ***Exempli causa*** *<u>duo</u> <u>proponam</u>.* [. . .] (CELS. 5, 19, 11a)
'Now there are certain plasters [. . .]. I will mention two as examples. [. . .]'

In this function, *exempli gratia* is more often embedded within the verb phrase, as shown in (7):

(7) *Nam brevior illa, ut ait Cicero, a re digressio plurimis fit modis. Sed <u>haec</u>* ***exempli gratia*** *<u>sufficient</u>* [. . .] (QVINT. inst. 9, 2, 56)
'What Cicero calls the "shorter" form of Digression can be effected in many ways. The following examples will suffice [. . .]'

The only exception is the ambiguous passage in (8), where Pliny moves *exempli gratia* after the verb *pono*, and immediately before the *illustrantia*, five Greek scholars with differing opinions about the morning setting of the Pleiades:

(8) *Eorum qui in eadem regione dissedere* <u>*unam discordiam ponemus*</u> ***exempli gratia****: occasum matutinum vergiliarum Hesiodus* [. . .] *tradidit fieri cum aequinoctium autumni conficeretur, Thales xxv die ab aequinoctio, Anaximander xxx, Euctemon xliv, Eudoxus xlviii.* (PLIN. nat. 18, 213)
'As for those who had differing views in the same country, we will give one case of disagreement as an example: Hesiod gives the morning setting of the Pleiades [. . .] as taking place at the close of the autumnal equinox, whereas Thales puts it on the 25th day after the equinox, Anaximander on the 30th, Euctemon on the 44th, and Eudoxus on the 48th.'

Although evidence is scarce, similar structures could be seen as bridging contexts that lead to processes of reanalysis and rebracketing, in which postverbal phrases become parenthetical segments. Once dislocated in peripheral position, *exempli gratia* is thus detached from the syntax of the sentence and coopted (Heine 2013: 1224) as a marker introducing the exemplifying sequence, as clarified in (9):

(9) [*unam* ***discordiam*** *ponemus*]$_{E}$ [***exempli gratia***]$_{ExM}$ [*occasum matutinum vergiliarum* ***Hesiodus*** *tradidit fieri.* . .]$_{e}$ [***Thales***. . .]$_{e}$ [***Anaximander***. . .]$_{e}$ [***Euctemon***. . .]$_{e}$ [***Eudoxus***. . .]$_{e}$
'we will give one case of disagreement: <u>for example</u>, Hesiod gives the morning setting of the Pleiades. . ., Thales. . ., Anaximander. . ., Euctemon. . ., Eudoxus. . .'

This interpretation supports the hypothesis that markers devoted to exemplification can develop from strategies of meta-exemplification through syntactic shifts, bridging contexts, and parentheticalization. Moreover, it is in Pliny that we find two of the three attestations of *exempli gratia* as a true example marker:

(10) *In his quidam mille sexcentas adnotavere stellas, insignes scilicet effectu visuve,* ***exempli gratia*** *in cauda tauri septem quas appellavere Vergilias, in fronte suculas, Booten quae sequitur Septem Triones.* (PLIN. nat. 2, 110)
'In them [sc. constellations] they have indeed noted 1600 stars as being especially remarkable for their influence or their appearance, <u>for instance</u> the seven which they have named the Pleiades in the tail of the Bull and the Little Pigs in his forehead, and Bootes that follows the Seven Plough-oxen.'

(11) *Multa promi amplius circa haec possunt secreta naturae legesque quibus ipsa serviat,* ***exempli gratia*** *in Martis sidere (cuius est maxime inobservabilis cursus) numquam id stationem facere Iovis sidere triquetro, raro admodum sexaginta partibus discrete* [. . .] (PLIN. nat. 2, 77)

> 'Many more facts can be produced about these mysteries of nature and the laws that she obeys – for example, in the case of the planet Mars (whose course it is very difficult to observe) that it never makes its station with Jupiter at an angle of 120°, and very seldom with Jupiter separated 60° [. . .]'

Technical prose is the genre in which canonical examples abound, since complex categories – as remarkable stars in (10) – need to be illustrated by representative items, and general statements – as the existence of mysterious natural laws in (11) – need to be proven by detailed facts. As canonical exemplification develops its own markers, the *illustrans* is often multiplied into open lists of *illustrantia*, which are selected as parts or proofs of the *illustrandum*, and the word *exemplum* shifts from the sense of 'exemplary model, precedent' to that of 'typical instance, illustration'. In other words, while the rhetorical exemplum persuades or argues as a model or a precedent, showing similarities or analogies through comparison, the canonical example illustrates as a sample or demonstrates as a proof, highlighting details or properties through selection.

Although still widely used for meta-exemplification in *Aetas Patrum* (109x), *exempli gratia* is undoubtedly more fortunate than *exempli causa*, which in *Antiquitas* serves as an example marker only twice and increases less in frequency over time (68x).

3.2 *Verbi gratia* and *verbi causa*

Beside the phrases with *exemplum*, also those with *verbum* can contribute to exemplification, as this noun too refers to the communicative process. In the period *Antiquitas*, *verbi gratia* and *verbi causa* behave as example markers in 26 out of 27 occurrences and 10 out of 12, respectively. As shown in Table 2, the frequency of both *verbi gratia* and *verbi causa* significantly increases in Late Latin:

Table 2: Frequency of *verbi gratia* and *verbi causa*.

	Frequency in *Antiquitas*		**Frequency in *Aetas Patrum***	
	Absolute	**Per million words**	**Absolute**	**Per million words**
verbi gratia	27	4,674381	932	42,22261
verbi causa	12	2,077503	270	12,23187

Literally meaning 'for the sake of a word', these phrases act as metacommunicative devices commenting on the choice of an expression, sometimes a "loose" example without an explicit *illustrandum*, which is presented as an alternative within a set of equally illustrative items. The focus on a single term and the nuance of apparent randomness are evident in (12), where *verbi gratia* interrupts the phrase *populum Centuripinum*, which is just one of the rich communities in Sicily:

(12) *Etenim, si C. Verres HS c milia populum* ***verbi gratia*** *Centuripinum poposcisset eamque ab iis pecuniam abstulisset,* [. . .] (Cic. Verr. 2, 143)
'For surely, if Verres had simply demanded the sum of a thousand pounds from, shall we say, the people of Centuripe, and taken that sum away from them, [. . .]

However, due to their syntactic independence, these example markers can focus on discourse units of any size, and even remain ambiguous between phrasal and clausal scope, as in (13):

(13) *Age vero, quae erat aut qualis quaestio? "Heus tu, Rufio,"* ***verbi causa***, *"cave sis mentiaris:* [. . .]" (Cic. Mil. 60)
'Well now, what was the manner of examination, and how did it proceed? "Look here, Rufio", let's say, "mind you don't tell lies! [. . .]"'

Moreover, the examples introduced by *verbi gratia* or *verbi causa* are often surprising facts or improbable eventualities, whose acceptance must be negotiated. In (14), Pliny describes stones with wonderful pareidolic figures, and in (15) Cicero illustrates nonsense astrological predictions:

(14) *hi sunt fluctuosi ac rerum imagines complexi, papaverum* ***verbi gratia*** *aut avium catulorumque vel pinnarum* (Plin. nat. 37, 71)
'these stones have undulating bands and contain inclusions resembling various objects, poppies, let's say, birds, puppies, or feathers'

(15) *Sunt igitur astrologorum percepta huiusmodi: "Si quis* ***(verbi causa)*** *oriente Canicula natus est, is in mari non morietur."* (Cic. fat. 12)
'Well then, here is a specimen of the observations of the astrologers: "If (for instance) a man was born at the rising of the dogstar, he will not die at sea."'

In similar cases, the parenthetical expression performs pragmatic hedging as a shield, modulating the writer's subjective stance towards the plausibility of a reported and controversial *illustrans*, while in (16), *verbi gratia* performs semantic hedging as an approximator, rounding off quantities in conjunction with numerals:[5]

(16) *per huius mediam longitudinem duci sarculo sulcum vel cinere liniam* ***verbi gratia*** *pedum xx conveniet* (Plin. nat. 18, 327)
'through the middle of the length of this shadow you will have to draw a furrow with a hoe or a line with ashes let's say 20 ft. long'

The increasing use of *verbi gratia* in technical prose is proven by the 19 occurrences in Gaius' *Institutiones*, where it is mostly used in hypothetical contexts illustrating private law cases, since it is very common to exemplify an abstract concept or rule by proposing an imaginary situation:

(17) *Igitur, si* ***verbi gratia*** *in rem tecum agam, satis mihi dare debes.* (Gaivs inst. 4, 89)
'If then, for example, I bring an action *in rem* against you, you are bound to give me security.'

With more than 900 attestations in *Aetas Patrum*, *verbi gratia* seems to be the most fortunate of the expressions devoted to exemplification, but some para-exemplifiers are definitely more frequent.

4 Para-exemplification in Latin

As in English and Romance languages, Latin para-exemplifiers derive from various sources; in particular, the markers of similative and equative constructions *ut*, *velut*, *sicut*, *tamquam*, and the adjective *qualis* perform analogical exemplification, the parenthetical imperative *puta* serves cooperative exemplification, particularly in combination with *ut*, while the conclusive connectors *igitur* and *itaque*, and the explicative connectors *nam(que)* and *enim* are occasionally recruited for demonstrative exemplification (as in Tac. ann. 6, 7–8). On the other hand, the dubitative adverbs *forsan* and *forsitan* begin to perform mitigating exemplification in Late Latin, while the adverbs *praesertim*, *praecipue*, *speciatim* are never used for particularizing exemplification. In what follows we will focus on analogical and cooperative exemplification, with special attention to the marker *ut puta*, a combination of both types.

5 On the notions of "shield", "approximator", and "rounder" see Prince et al. (1982: 93).

4.1 Analogical Exemplification

In Latin the domain of comparison is strictly related with exemplification, firstly because the narrative and instructive rhetorical *exemplum* "is in actuality simply a special case of the broader *similitudo*" (Lausberg 1998 [1960]: 196) and, therefore, "[a]t its source exemplary thought functions by the process of comparison" (Urban 2011: 32).[6] Secondly because, even in canonical examples, the *illustrantia* always share a common property with the *illustrandum*, with which they can have a part/whole or hyponymy/hyperonymy relation.

As a result, it is hardly surprising that the most common way to introduce an example in Latin is by means of the comparative connectors *ut*, *velut*, and occasionally *sicut*, as already noted by Menge (2009 [1873]: 233).

Interestingly, the first meaning of *velut* on the OLD is 'for example, for instance'. The connector is already used with this meaning in Plautus, where it usually links two sentences at the beginning of a monologue: the first one is a general truth or common-sense statement, while the second presents the circumstance at hand. In (18), the fact that gods send strange dreams to men is illustrated by Daemon's bizarre dream about a talking monkey:[7]

(18) *miris modis di ludos faciunt hominibus, / mirisque exemplis somnia in somnis danunt: / ne dormientis quidem sinunt quiescere. /* ***Velut*** *ego hac nocte quae processit proxuma / mirum atque inscitum somniavi somnium.* (PLAVT. Rud. 596)
'The gods mystify men in a strange fashion and give them dreams in their sleep in strange ways: they don't even allow those who are sleeping to rest. For instance, I dreamed a strange and uncanny dream last night.'

In any case, *velut* is also employed in canonical exemplification to connect a superordinate unit to its hyponyms, as in (19):[8]

(19) *Est etiam admiratio non nulla in bestiis aquatilibus iis quae gignuntur in terra:* ***veluti*** *crocodili fluviatilesque testudines quaedamque serpentes ortae extra aquam simul ac primum niti possunt aquam persequuntur.* (CIC. nat. deor. 2, 124)

6 Cf. also Gazich (1990: 107) on QVINT. inst. 5, 11, 1–2.

7 See Fraenkel (2007 [1922]) on comparative openings in Plautus' speeches.

8 If *vel* derives from **welsi*, a second person of the verb *volō* (cf. Ernout and Meillet 2001 [1932], s.v. *vel*; de Vaan 2008, s.v. *volō, velle*), it can be argued that *velut* (< *vel* + *ut*) and *ut puta* (see § 4.2) have similar structures.

'Our wonder is also considerably excited by those aquatic animals which are born on land – crocodiles, <u>for instance</u>, and water-tortoises and certain snakes, which are born on dry land but as soon as they can first crawl make for the water.'

Besides *velut*, other analogical exemplifiers that convey canonical exemplification are *sicut* (cf. QVINT. inst. 9, 3, 91), *tamquam* (cf. SEN. nat. 2, 40, 6) and the adjective *qualis* (cf. CIC. div. 2, 135).

However, the most common way to introduce both rhetorical *exempla* and canonical examples is the comparative connector *ut*, which can precede simple phrases, as in (20), where Cicero illustrates moral diseases resembling avarice, or connect whole sentences, as in (21), where the distinction between canonical exemplification and rhetorical narrative *exemplum* is blurred:

(20) *eique morbo nomen est avaritia; similiterque ceteri morbi,* ***ut*** *gloriae cupiditas,* ***ut*** *mulierositas, ut ita appellem eam, quae Graece* φιλογυνία *dicitur*, [. . .] (CIC. Tusc. 4, 25)
'and for such a disease the name is avarice. And similarly, the other diseases <u>like</u> thirst for fame, <u>like</u> love of women, to give this term to what the Greeks call φιλογυνία, [. . .]'

(21) *Non enim neque tu possis, quamvis excellas, omnis tuos ad honores amplissimos perducere,* ***ut*** *Scipio P. Rupilium potuit consulem efficere, fratrem eius Lucium non potuit.* (CIC. Lael. 73)
'For however eminent you may be, you cannot lead all your friends through the various grades to the highest official rank, <u>as</u> Scipio was able to do when he made Publius Rutilius consul, though he could not accomplish this result in the case of his brother, Lucius Rutilius.'

In technical and scientific prose *ut* establishes a relation of similarity and inclusion between a theoretical statement and its concrete instances, especially to present examples of grammatical phenomena, as in (22):

(22) *mutationes, quas adferunt declinatio aut praepositio,* ***ut*** *"secat secuit", "cadit excidit", "caedit excidit", "calcat exculcat"* (QVINT. inst. 1, 4, 13)
'the changes due to inflexion and composition, <u>like</u> *secat secuit, cadit excidit, caedit excīdit, calcat exculcat*'

In the evolution from Latin to Romance languages, *ut* – being multifunctional and phonetically weak – is replaced by other markers (such as *sicut* and *quomodo*) in its comparative function. This process was already underway in Late Latin prose but, as Biville (2014: 705–706) notes, in Priscian *ut* remains quite frequent in exemplifying contexts, either alone or with other particles and reduced clauses (*ut etiam, ut est, ut puta, ut si dicam, ut si velimus dicere*). However, even in earlier texts, expressions calling for the hearers' attention and directly involving them in the co-construction of the example could cumulate with signals of analogical exemplification, as in *ut puta*, or be used by themselves, performing cooperative exemplification.

4.2 From Analogical to Cooperative Exemplification: (*ut*) *puta*

The verb *puto* normally takes the double accusative or the *accusativus cum infinitivo*, like the first *puta* in (23). Instead, the second and third are external to clausal syntax. Despite the syntactical differences, all three forms introduce examples in which the lese-majesty offense does not apply:

(23) ***Puta** aliquem dum magistratus est patrem suum occidere, veneno uxorem suam necare* [. . .]. ***Puta**, amicam habet proconsul: ideo maiestatis damnabitur? Quod amplius est dico:* ***puta**, matronam corrumpit dum proconsul est* [. . .] (Sen. contr. 9, 2, 13)
'Suppose someone kills his father or poisons his wife during his term of office [. . .]. Suppose that a proconsul has a girlfriend: will he then be condemned for lèse-majesté? Suppose, further, that he seduces a married woman during his proconsulship. He will plead on a charge of adultery, not of lèse-majesté.'

In most exemplifying contexts, *puta* is indeed a reduced parenthetical clause (Schneider 2007), and as such it has not only an intersubjective and textual value, creating a joint focus of attention between interlocutors, but it can also act as a metadirective (Risselada 1993), explicitly stating what the speakers expect from the hearers, namely that they cooperate with their imagination in the exemplification process.[9]

Puta is used parenthetically only 39 times in the *Antiquitas* section (17 times alone and 22 preceded by *ut*), always with an exemplifying value. Its inherently interactive and cooperative meaning suits well the vivid style of satiric poetry, as in (24) where *puta* has phrasal scope:[10]

9 Imperatives of cognitive verbs (such as *opinor, credo, censeo*, etc.) are a common source for parentheticals in Latin (Pinkster 2021: 909–919).

10 Interestingly, in Pers. 4, 9 parenthetical *puta* appears in a similar context, where it also introduces a fictive and illustrative dialogical example, but its scope is clausal.

(24) *"Quinte"* ***puta*** *aut "Publi" – gaudent praenomine molles / auriculae – "tibi me virtus tua fecit amicum."* (HOR. sat. 2, 5, 32)
'Say: "Quintus" it may be, or "Publius" (sensitive ears delight in the personal name), "your worth has made me your friend.'

Combined with *ut, puta* strengthens and clarifies its illustrative function in canonical examples, as in (25):

(25) *Saepe etiam causas apparere,* ***ut puta*** *lippitudinis, vulneris, neque ex his patere medicinam.* (CELS. 1, pr. 30)
'Often, too, the causes are apparent, as, for example, of ophthalmia, or of wounds, yet such causes do not disclose the treatment.'

Moreover, when used with numerals *ut puta* expresses approximation, behaving as a rounder (Mihatsch 2010: 108–109), as in (26) and (27):

(26) *Emi seu puerum togamve pexam seu tres,* ***ut puta****, quattuorve libras,* [. . .] (MART. 2, 44)
'If I buy a boy or a woolly gown or three, say, or four pounds of plate, [. . .]'

(27) *Laser in spatiosum doliolum vitreum mittis et nucleos pineos* ***ut puta*** *viginti,* [. . .] (APIC. 1, 13, 1)
'Put the asafoetida in a large glass jar with about twenty pine nuts, [. . .]'

Roman grammarians exploit the liveliness of the analogical/cooperative exemplifier *ut puta* to introduce both literary and fictive examples of grammatical phenomena (Pontani 2007).[11] The occurrences in Servius are 30 and as many as 50 in the *Ars* attributed to Palaemon. However, as its frequency increases, the vivid interactive meaning of *ut puta* bleaches out and it thus combines with other exemplifying markers or reduced clauses (as in *ut puta si dicam*, etc.). This tendency supports the idea that markers devoted to exemplification can develop from strategies of para-exemplification through semantic shifts, syntagmatic chains, and conventionalization. In Late and Medieval Latin *ut puta* is a well-established lexicalized marker of exemplification, even in the univerbated form *utputa*.[12]

11 On the use of *exempla ficta* by ancient grammarians, see also Benedetti (2022).
12 In the *Aetas Patrum*, the cooperative para-exemplifier appears 1509 times as *ut puta* and 142 as *utputa*, while in the *Medii Aevi scriptores* section of the Brepols corpus, the two forms occur 1724 and 622 times, respectively.

5 Final Remarks

Our investigation of Latin exemplifiers has taken as its starting point an inherently dynamic and cross-linguistically applicable classification. The discussion has shown that in Classical Latin exemplification is still in the process of developing dedicated markers from meta-exemplifiers and, while those with the noun *exemplum* are yet incipient and not fully lexicalized, the forms *verbi gratia* and *verbi causa* seem more versatile and, in contexts without an explicit *illustrandum*, they can also modulate the plausibility of "loose", out-of-the-blue examples. On the other hand, the class of para-exemplifiers had already provided Early and Classical Latin writers with a variegated and long-lasting inventory of example connectors, as proven by the diffusion of *ut* (*puta*) in Late Latin.

This peculiar situation can be related to the different needs of the nascent textual genres, where exemplification seeks its own strategies and structures, balanced between narration and enumeration, and between persuasion and illustration.

Bibliography

LEI = Pfister, M. & Schweickard, W. (Eds.) (1979–). *Lessico Etimologico Italiano*. Wiesbaden: Reichert Verlag.

OED = *Oxford English Dictionary*. https://www.oed.com

OLD = Glare, P. G. W. (Ed.) (2016). *Oxford Latin Dictionary*. Oxford: Oxford University Press.

TLL = *Thesaurus Linguae Latinae*. https://thesaurus.badw.de

TLFi = *Trésor de la langue Française informatisé*. http://www.atilf.fr/tlfi

Barotto, A. (2018). The hedging function of exemplification: Evidence from Japanese. *Journal of Pragmatics*, *123*, 24–37.

Barotto, A. & Mauri, C. (2018). Constructing lists to construct categories. *Italian Journal of Linguistics*, *30* (1), 95–134.

Bazzanella, C. (1995). I segnali discorsivi. In L. Renzi, G. Salvi & A. Cardinaletti (Eds.), *Grande grammatica italiana di consultazione. Vol. 3. Tipi di frase, deissi, formazione delle parole* (pp. 225–257). Bologna: Il Mulino.

Benedetti, M. (2022). Ἀπολλώνιος γράφω, *Priscianus scribo:* sugli *exempla ficta* nel discorso grammaticale. In L. Biondi, F. Dedè & A. Scala (Eds.), *Ubi homo, ibi lingua. Studi in onore di Maria Patrizia Bologna, vol. 1* (pp. 65–78). Alessandria: Edizioni dell'Orso.

Biville, F. (2014). Description du latin et métalangue au VIe siècle. Priscien, Martyrius, Cassiodore. In P. Molinelli, P. Cuzzolin & C. Fedriani (Eds.), *Latin vulgaire – latin tardif X. Actes du Xe colloque international sur le latin vulgaire et tardif, vol. 2* (pp. 679–712). Bergamo: Sestante Edizioni.

Demoen, K. (1997). A paradigm for the analysis of paradigms: the rhetorical exemplum in Ancient and Imperial Greek theory, *Rhetorica*, *15*, 125–158.

Eggs, E. & McElholm, D. (2013). *Exemplifications, selections and argumentation: The use of example markers in English and German*. Frankfurt am Main: Peter Lang.

Ernout, A. & Meillet, A. (2001 [1932]). *Dictionnaire étymologique de la langue latine. Histoire des mots* (retirage de la 4ème édition). Paris: Klincksieck.

Fernández-Bernárdez, C. (1994–1995). Marcadores textuales de 'ejemplificación' textual. *Estudios de Lingüística*, *10*, 103–144.

Fraenkel, E. (2007 [1922]). *Plautine elements in Plautus* (*Plautinisches bei Plautus*, Berlin, transl. by T. Drevikovsky & F. Muecke). Oxford: Oxford University Press.

Fuchs, C. (1982). *La paraphrase*. Paris: PUF.

Gazich, R. (1990). Teoria e pratica dell'*exemplum* in Quintiliano. In P. V. Cova, R. Gazich, G. E. Manzoni & G. Melzani (Eds.), *Aspetti della 'paideia' di Quintiliano* (pp. 61–141). Milano: Vita e Pensiero.

Ghezzi, C. (2014). The development of discourse and pragmatic markers. In C. Ghezzi & P. Molinelli (Eds.), *Discourse and pragmatic markers from Latin to the Romance Languages* (pp. 10–26). Oxford: Oxford University Press.

Gülich, E. & Kotschi, T. (1983). Les marqueurs de la reformulation paraphrastique. *Cahiers de Linguistique Française*, *5*, 305–351.

Heine, B. (2013). On discourse markers: grammaticalization, pragmaticalization or something else? *Linguistics*, *51*, 1205–1247.

Kornhardt, H. (1936). Exemplum: *Eine bedeutungsgeschichtliche Studie*. Doctoral dissertation, University of Göttingen.

Lausberg, H. (1998 [1960]), *Handbook of literary rhetoric. A foundation for literary study* (*Handbuch der literarischen Rhetorik*, Munich, transl. by M. T. Bliss, A. Jansen & D. E. Orton). Leiden: Brill.

Leumann, M., Hofmann, J. B. & Szantyr, A. (1979). *Lateinische Grammatik. Band 1. Lateinische Laut- und Formenlehre*. München: Verlag C. H. Beck.

Lo Baido, C. (2018). Categorization *via* exemplification: evidence from Italian. *Folia Linguistica Historica*, *52* (1), 69–95.

Manzotti, E. (1995). Aspetti linguistici della esemplificazione. In C. Caffi & K. Hölker (Eds.), *Examples*, special issue of *Versus*, *70–71*, 49–114.

Manzotti, E. (1998). L'esempio. Natura, definizioni, problemi. *Cuadernos de Filología Italiana*, *5*, 99–123.

Menge, H. (2009 [1873]), *Lehrbuch der lateinischen Syntax und Semantik*. Darmstadt: Wissenschaftliche Buchgesellschaft.

Meyer, C. F. (1992). *Apposition in contemporary English*. Cambridge: Cambridge University Press.

Mihatsch, W. (2010). The diachrony of rounders and adaptors: approximation and unidirectional change. In G. Kaltenböck, W. Mihatsch & S. Schneider (Eds.), *New approaches to hedging* (pp. 93–122). Bingley: Emerald.

Pinkster, H. (2015). *The Oxford Latin Syntax. Volume 2: The Complex Sentence and Discourse.* Oxford: Oxford University Press.

Pontani, P. (2007). *Ut puta si dicam*. Grammatici latini e oralità. *Aevum*, *81* (1), 201–212.

Price, B. J. (1975). Paradeigma *and* exemplum *in ancient rhetorical theory*. PhD dissertation, University of California, Berkeley.

Prince, E., J. Frader & C. Bosk (1982). On hedging in physician-physician discourse. In R. J. Di Pietro (Ed.), *Linguistics and the professions. Proceedings of the second annual Delaware symposium on language studies* (pp. 83–97). Norwood: Ablex.

Quirk, R., Greenbaum, S., Leech, G. & Svartvik, J. (1985). *A comprehensive grammar of the English language*. London: Longman.

Risselada, R. (1993). *Imperatives and other directive expressions in Latin. A study in the pragmatics of a dead language*. Amsterdam: Gieben.
Rodríguez-Abruñeiras, P. (2017). Exemplification then and now: A historical overview of English exemplifying markers. *Miscelánea. A Journal of English and American Studies*, *55* (2), 87–107.
Rodríguez-Abruñeiras, P. (2019). *When apposition meets exemplification: A semantic and syntactic description of two related categories*. Palma: Edicions UIB.
Rossari, C. & Jayez, J. (1999). Par exemple: une procédure d'exemplification par la preuve. In B. Combettes, C. Schnedecker & A. Thiessen (Eds.), *Ordre et distinction dans la langue et le discours* (pp. 461–478). Paris: Champion.
Schneider, S. (2007). *Reduced parenthetical clauses as mitigators: A corpus study of spoken French, Italian and Spanish*. Amsterdam/Philadelphia: Benjamins.
Urban, D. C. (2011). *The use of exempla from Cicero to Pliny the Younger*. PhD dissertation, University of Pennsylvania, publicly accessible Penn Dissertations, 591.
de Vaan, M. (2008). *Etymological dictionary of Latin and the other Italic languages*. Leiden: Brill.
Vainio, R. (2000). Use and function of grammatical examples in Roman grammarians. *Mnemosyne*, *53* (1), 30–48.

Francesca Mencacci

Apte dicere. Epistemic Phrases and Facework in Cicero's Oratorical Works

Abstract: My aim, in this contribution, is to present a survey of the use of epistemic expressions in Cicero's oratorical production (*ut opinor, ut arbitror, credo, ut mea opinio fert, ut mihi videtur, mea sententia*, etc.), as a means of persuasion through style (*apte dicere*). As is well known, the use of such linguistic resources can respond to multiple needs, including, of course, the more properly epistemic-evidential ones of highlighting the subjective dimension of assertions and the degree of certainty that the speaker assigns to them; but equally important are other effects, which are pragmatic in nature. Epistemic modalization may in fact modify the illocutionary force of the utterance or a part of it, in the direction of limiting the statement, or of emphasizing it, with effects on the image of the participants in the interaction. Typically dialogic, resources of this kind have indeed a considerable relevance in the *oratio*, where they can be exploited to construct the speaker's image (or *persona*), gaining the approval of his audience, and making his arguments more effective. The examination of the wide repertoire of expressions found in Cicero's speeches shows the peculiar use he makes of this class of expressions and of their effects, varying between attenuation and boosting, for the sake of self-presentation.

Keywords: Cicero's speeches, epistemic phrases, pragmatic functions

1 Introduction

The object of my contribution is the use of a group of expressions of an epistemic nature in Cicero's oratory production. These are the so-called opinion verbs (*opinor, credo, arbitror, sentio, puto, censeo*, etc.) in the first-person singular form, used in an isolated position as parentheticals[1] or in a subordinate clause introduced by

1 As well known, for this use of opinion verbs definitions vary (for a survey, see Schneider 2007: 19–63). Here I use "parenthetical" only for independent structures inserted in the main clause and syntactically not linked in any way to it (as in Pinkster 2021: 9, 917 and 2015: 926).

Francesca Mencacci, Università degli Studi di Siena, Italy

https://doi.org/10.1515/9783111332956-035

ut, and some other phrases (*ut mihi videtur, ut opinio mea fert, mea sententia, meo iudicio*), equally functioning as epistemic lexical modalizers.[2]

As we know, the use of such linguistic resources can respond to multiple needs, including, of course, the more properly epistemic-evidential ones, that is, highlighting the subjective dimension of assertions and the degree of certainty that the speaker assigns to them; equally important, however, are other effects, pragmatic in nature. Epistemic modalization may in fact be accompanied by a modification of the illocutionary force of the utterance or of a part of it, in the direction of limiting the statement, or of emphasizing it – with different effects, but almost always associated with the image of the participants in the interaction, and the management of their relationship.[3]

Typical of in-presence interaction, resources of this kind are characteristic of the style adopted by Cicero in the works that most closely reproduce the tone of oral exposition: first and foremost, the letters – which count as a *colloquium* at a distance[4] – and the dialogues, especially where a lively exchange of opinions between various characters is staged. But similar expressions also appear in the speeches, where they do not simply reflect the orality (true or mimicked) of oratorical performance, but are an important resource in themselves, in more ways than one.[5]

Now, as regards Cicero's speeches, the presence of epistemic-evidential locutions such as *credo, opinor, existimo, arbitror*, etc. is in a way expected, and almost required by the very nature of the communicative action (or, if you like, of the genre). In most cases it is a matter of presenting the audience with a version of the facts largely based on the ability to reconstruct through suppositions not only events or actions, but also the motives and intentions of the protagonists in the legal case: sometimes through evidence (*signa*), but mostly through conjecture. Conjecture, in fact, occupies an important part of the *oratio*; it can be said that the use of

---

2 These different expressions are considered here together for their pragmatic functions, despite their lexical and syntactical differences.

3 The study of epistemic modalizers and of their functions as hedging or reinforcement devices has long been the focus of linguists' attention, at least since the works of Lakoff (1972), Fraser (1980, 2010), Holmes (1984, 1990). Since Urmson (1952) this kind of expression in modern languages has been thoroughly investigated: for verb forms see, among others, Schneider (2007), Dehé and Kavalova (2007), Kaltenböck et al. (2010), Schneider et al. (2015); for nominal syntagms and adverbial constructions see Borillo (2004).

4 Letters are for Cicero *amicorum colloquia absentium* (Phil. 2, 7); but see also the definition of the rhetor Pseudo-Demetrius of a letter as a half-conversation (eloc. 223).

5 On these expressions in Latin, already listed under the forms reproducing orality by Hofmann (1951: 106, 151), see Pinkster (1988: 84, 308–309), Bolkestein (1998a, especially on Cicero's letters, and 1998b). More generally on the use of parentheticals in Cicero's oratory see Unceta Gómez (2009).

opinion verbs, with which the speaker offers the audience a point of view, his own, whose truth value is not absolute, constructs the very framework of the speech in its different sections, from the *exordium* to the *peroratio*.[6] But it is not just this.

Because of their capacity to perform pragmatic functions, epistemic modalizers of this kind represent a special asset for the speaker. A set of well-established rhetorical precepts makes it clear that to win consensus and be persuasive the orator has to work carefully on his own image: in addition to and even before offering convincing arguments, it is the speaker himself who has to appear trustworthy and authoritative. His credit may have been acquired previously, thanks to his character, personal history, and merits; but it always has to be renegotiated in the oratorical performance itself, by the way the speaker now presents himself to his audience. Persuasion, which is the goal of the *oratio*, is in fact largely constructed on the *persona* (or *ethos*) the orator can convey in the communicative performance.[7]

In many cases, to present oneself as trustworthy, or as *vir bonus*, is a matter of behaving respectfully and modestly, showing that he cares at one and the same time for the other participants' public image and his own. A task that can be all but easy to perform in the context of the judicial or political arena, where assertiveness and self-confidence are often required. The best way to succeed is to keep a balance between two contrasting needs: on the one hand, it is essential for the speaker to show himself able to highlight the points he considers decisive and to assert his view with conviction, sometimes even to the point – as Cicero himself put it – of *liberius quid audere* (orat. 138); on the other hand, he must take care not to appear overconfident, an attitude that may be irritating and interpreted as a lack of respect towards judges, colleagues, or the audience.[8] In short, a good part of the speaker's ability to persuade depends on his ability to do facework: making his own point of view prevail without imposing it and guiding the audience's judgement without giving the impression of manipulating it. That is, to convince his hearers without jeopardizing his own image, but rather because of it, by making the credit he deserves implicitly clear to his listeners.

6 On conjecture cf. Cic. orat. 126. For a recent assessment of this class of verbs, especially of *sentio*, *opinor*, *censeo* as different predicates of evidentiality and sincerity see Riesco Garcia (2022).

7 For the role Cicero assigns to the speaker's *ethos* in persuasion and its connection to style see May (1988), Wisse (1989: 222–249), Calboli Montefusco (1992). On the notion of *persona* in Cicero see the extensive research by Guérin (2011); recently, Kenty (2020) has explored Cicero's different *personae* in his late oratorical production as a means to making his arguments persuasive.

8 Cf. e.g. Cic. orat. 73. For the counterproductive effect of self-confidence see Qvint. inst. 4, 1, 33: *fiducia ipsa solet opinione adrogantiae laborare*; 4, 1, 55: *odit enim iudex fere litigantis securitatem, cumque ius suum intellegat tacitus reverentiam postulat.*

This goal can best be achieved with the use of an appropriate interactional style: as for voice, gestures and words, his whole performance must be carefully calibrated and adjusted in order to project the right image, or *persona*.[9] Different linguistic resources, depending on the context, can be of help: among these, epistemic phrases with a modalizing valence seem to play a not secondary role. In fact, by modulating the degree of assertiveness of a statement, expressions such as *credo, ut opinor, ut arbitror, mea sententia* and similar ones can produce useful illocutionary effects, both in the attenuative direction, as mitigating hedges, and in the reinforcing one.[10]

2 Forms and Frequency

Cicero takes full advantage of this opportunity. In fact, he can draw on an extensive and well-established repertoire of epistemic phrases. Plautus and Terence had already used almost all the verbs of opinion like *opinor, credo, arbitror, conicio, intellego*, introduced or not by conjunctions such as *ut* or *quantum*, which are often found in comedy as comment clauses with a pragmatic function. In addition to this group, other expressions, consisting of a noun of epistemic meaning in the ablative form and the possessive adjective, could equally imply a delimitation of the truth value of the statement (*mea sententia, meo animo*, etc.) and were therefore also used as epistemic modalizers. Most of them could also be accompanied by particles emphasizing subjectivity, like *equidem* or *quidem*, or the personal pronoun *ego*.[11]

Table 1, based on the database of Brepols (Library of Latin Texts series A, *Aetas antiqua*) presents an overview of the use Cicero makes of this repertoire:[12]

9 A convincing interpretation of Latin *persona* as an emic localization of the concept of "face" is now proposed by Unceta Gómez (forthcoming).

10 For the different forms of mitigation and its pragmatic functions see Caffi (2007).

11 For Terence see Müller (1997: 178–182); on comedy Barrios-Lech (2016: 142–154) with specific attention to the pragmatic functions.

12 The first column contains the different items, the second and third the number of occurrences respectively in Cicero's speeches and in the other works. A certain degree of approximation was unavoidable, given that the interpretation of the single expressions as comment disjuncts, especially in the case of the verb forms not introduced by *ut*, is not always easy to ascertain. This applies to many tokens of simple *credo* not governing a sentential complement in AcI, for which, lacking prosody and intonation, it can be difficult to decide between parenthetic usage and other kinds of constructs.

Table 1: Frequency of use of epistemic phrases and nominal forms as epistemic modalizers in Cicero's works.

Forms	Cicero' speeches	Cicero's other works
ut (ego) / arbitror	11	35
ut censeo / censeo	–	1
ut / quantum / credo	80	88
ut (ego) conicio / conicio	–	2
ut / quantum / (ego) (equidem) existimo / existimare possum	1	2
ut / quantum / (ego) (quidem) intellego	3	6
ut / quantum (ego) puto / puto	–	13
ut / quantum / (quidem) (ego) sentio	3	5
ut (ego) opinor / opinor	79	99
ut opinio mea / nostra fert / est	3	9
ut mihi / nobis (quidem) videtur	5	33
mea (quidem) sententia	8	25
meo (quidem) iudicio / quantum ego iudicare possum	2	22
meo (quidem) animo	1	1

As can be seen, the range of forms Cicero employs in the speeches is rather varied, and in a certain extent characteristic, as is the use he generally makes of these devices.[13] To many of the expressions already attested in comedy, Cicero adds some other formulas, such as the clause *ut mihi (quidem) videtur* and *ut mea (quidem) opinio est*, or the expression *meo (quidem) iudicio*. In contrast, some common opinion verbs, otherwise commonly used in Cicero's speeches as full verbs, do not enter at all in the set of the comment clauses, or figure only very sparingly among them. A verb like *existimo*, which Cicero frequently uses as a full verb governing an AcI construction, often also with reinforcing *equidem*, appears only once used in parenthetic form. Something similar applies to *sentio* and *intellego*, very seldom used in comment clauses with *ut*, and to (*ut*) *puto*, (*ut*) *censeo* and *conicio*, never employed in an isolated position in the speeches, although currently used as full verbs. The verbs Cicero preferentially employs in this sort of comment expressions are (*ut*) *opinor*, *credo* and, to a lesser extent, *ut arbitror*; nominal phrases appear too: *mea (quidem) sententia* more often than *meo iudicio* and *meo animo*. Regarding modifiers, Cicero resorts mainly to *quidem* and *ego*, to emphasize the subjectivity of the expression.

13 I do not deal here with the syntactic aspects that may differentiate them, already investigated by Bolkestein (1998a and 1998b); for the position of the parenthetical verb forms in the host clause (initial, medial or final, which in most cases correlates with the scope of the parenthetical, on the whole host clause or on a single unit of it) see also Pinkster (2021: 918–919).

3 Pragmatic Functions

A close examination of the occurrences suggests some further considerations.

On the one hand, not all of these expressions are used to fulfil an interpersonal function. If we compare the use of *ut opinor* with that of the parenthetical *credo*, for example, we note that, in addition to some already known syntactic and semantic particularities,[14] a difference in the function is often also present. In fact, both verbs draw attention to the subjectivity of the statement, but Cicero uses them with different intentions. *Credo* refers to a plausible but indemonstrable belief (usually about intentions, motives, or states of mind, roughly equivalent to our "I imagine", where the speaker puts himself in someone else's shoes and proposes the hypothesis he finds more likely), functioning therefore as an addition which clarifies the epistemic status of the statement, as in the following examples:

(1) *sed refugit statim nec de pudicitia plura dixit veritus,* ***credo****, ne quem inridendi nobis daret et iocandi locum* (Cic. Scaur. 6)
'but he straightway abandoned the subject, and said no more on the theme of chastity, fearing, I believe, to provide us with a handle for jest and mockery'[15]

(2) *aequum,* ***credo****, putavit vitam quam populi Romani votis retinuisset pro libertate populi Romani in discrimen adducere* (Cic. Phil. 7, 12)
'I imagine, he thought it only fair to risk on behalf of the freedom of the Roman people a life saved by the Roman people's prayers'

(*Ut*) *opinor*, on the other hand, seems to lend itself better to accompanying conjectures that have the character of obviousness, or at least rest on a good logical and inferential basis. In fact, the use of this verb is often followed by a motivation, usually introduced by a causal expression that justifies the statement (*qua re* / *quoniam* / *nam* / *enim* / *etenim* / *cum* / *hoc fuit causae* / *ex hoc* / *nimirum*), as in:

(3) *Qui sunt igitur repulsi? Non,* ***ut opinor****, ii qui aliquando honorem vitio civitatis, non suo, non sunt adsecuti;* <u>*nam*</u> *id quidem multis saepe optimis civibus atque honestissimis viris accidit.* (Cic. har. resp. 56)
'Who then, are the rejected candidates? Not, I imagine, they who some time or other have failed to attain some honour more by the fault of the city than

14 The two verbs appear in different syntactic constructions and have different epistemic statuses, implying different degrees of commitment (Bolkestein 1998a and 1998b).
15 Translations of Cicero's texts are quoted from the Loeb Classical Library collection, with slight modifications.

by their own. For that is a thing which has frequently happened to many most excellent citizens and most honourable men.'

In these cases, the emphasis on subjectivity seems to be more of a form of understatement, intended to present unimposingly an interpretation that almost has the character of necessity and which in the end one cannot but agree with. In the terms of the Brown and Levinson's politeness model, the presence of *ut opinor* can be seen as a form of negative politeness, which leaves the hearers free to judge for themselves, while helping at the same time to shape the *persona* of the orator as someone respectful of his audience and not so self-confident as to consider his arguments incontrovertible.[16]

In other instances, (*ut*) *opinor* joins statements about literary, legal or other kinds of erudite knowledge, again with an understatement function: with the addition of this comment clause Cicero aims now not to irritate his audience with an overly blatant display of culture, especially when it comes to knowledge relating to Greek literature, art or philosophy:[17]

(4) *Namque, **ut opinor**, Asia vestra constat ex Phrygia Mysia Caria Lydia.* (Cic. Flacc. 65)
'Asia, if I am not mistaken, consists of Phrygia, Mysia, Caria and Lydia.'

(5) *Ecquid tandem tibi videtur, ut ad fabulas veniamus, senex ille Caecilianus minoris facere Eutychum filium rusticum quam illum alterum Chaerestratum – nam, **ut opinor**, hoc nomine est – alterum in urbe secum honoris causa habere, alterum rus supplicii causa relegasse?* (Cic. S. Rosc. 46)
'To take an example from the stage, do you really think that the old man in the play of Caecilius thinks less of Eutychus, who lives in the country, than of the other, Chaerestratus (I think that was his name) that he keeps the one with him in the city as a token of esteem, while he has sent the other to the country as a punishment?'

When a pragmatic function is present, not only the frequency of use but also the specific direction in which the illocutionary force of the assertion is modified can vary. It is the case of *arbitror*: always introduced with *ut*, it underlines the nature of personal supposition of the statement, sometimes to reduce it, but more often to reinforce it. This boosting function is always present when the verb is preceded by

16 For this kind of strategy see Brown and Levinson (1987: 162–164).
17 Kaster (2006: *ad loc.*); Berry (2004: 302–303).

the personal pronoun *ego*, which adds even more stress to the speaker's personal endorsement:

(6) *non apud indoctos sed,* ***ut ego arbitror,*** *in hominum eruditissomorum at humanissimorum coetu loquor* (Cic. Pis. 68)
'I am speaking not to an ignorant audience, but, as I think, in an assembly of learned and accomplished gentlemen'

The effect of this strengthening intention here seems to be the intensification of the compliment,[18] but it has to be noted that the same clause can also be used to reinforce negative ideas, in order to enhance the credibility of the argument.[19]

Less frequently, *ut arbitror* seems to have the opposite function, that of a mitigating addition aiming at presenting the idea in a less imposing way; like in the following example, where *ut arbitror* functions as a hedging device which adds to the negative formulation (*nec . . . nec . . . nec*) in the host, signalling the will to limit, respectfully, the speaker's confidence about the significance of what he is going to say:

(7) *De qua pauca, iudices, dicam et,* ***ut arbitror***, *nec ab utilitate eorum qui audient, nec ab officio vestro, nec ab ispa causa P. Sesti abhorebit oratio mea* (Cic. Sest. 96)
'I will say a few words about it, gentlemen, nor, I think, will what I say be irrelevant, either to the advantage of those who hear me, or to the discharge of your duties, or to the case itself of Publius Sestius'

Sometimes different interpersonal functions can be attributed to slightly varied formulations. It is the case of the use of *ut opinio mea fert / est*, at first sight equivalent to *ut opinor*, but in fact employed with the opposite purpose:

(8) *Exstat oratio hominis,* ***ut opinio mea fert****, nostrorum hominum longe ingeniosissimi atque eloquentissimi, C. Gracchi; qua in oratione permulta in L. Pisonem turpia ac flagitiosa dicuntur.* (Cic. Font. 39)
'There is extant a speech delivered by one who was, I believe, by far the ablest and most eloquent of our fellow-countrymen, Gaius Gracchus; and in this speech he insinuates many base and scandalous actions against Lucius Piso.'

18 Cf. also Cic. har. resp. 48; Cic. Sest. 16 and 71.
19 Cf. Cic. prov. 58; Cic. div. in Caec. 44.

(9) *Pro hisce rebus vacatio data est ab isto sumptus, laboris, militiae, rerum denique omnium; per triennium soli non modo in Sicilia verum,* ***ut opinio mea fert****, his quidem temporibus in omni orbe terrarium vacui, expertes, soluti ac liberi fuerunt ab omni sumptu, molestia, munere.* (Cic. Verr. II 4, 23)
'In return for these services, he gave them immunity from all expense, all labour, all military service, in short, from everything. For three years they were the only people, not only in Sicily, but, I believe, in the whole world at such a time, who enjoyed exemption, relief, freedom, and immunity from every sort of expense, and trouble, and office.'

In the first case the presence of maximizers seems to indicate the possibility that, instead of having a down-toning function, the *ut* clause is intended to underscore the authoritativeness of the speaker's words and then acts like a boosting hedge, to give even more strength to the opinion expressed. In the second passage the formula has its scope on a conjecture, whose content is amplified again in various ways (*in omni orbe terrarum*, the use of the rhetorical figure of *accumulatio*); moreover, it seems unlikely that Cicero could intend to mitigate his attack against the responsibilities of Verres, who is the target of a harsh criticism in the whole sequence. Co-text and context suggest taking the underlining of subjectivity as a way to express commitment. In this case too, the presence of a deictic element (*mea*), blatantly insisting on the personal engagement of the speaker, accompanies the use of the formula as a reinforcement, adding to what is no more than a conjecture the weight of Cicero's personal firm belief.

The same possibility of achieving opposite pragmatic effects of this kind appears clearly in the case of two different formulations: the comment clause *ut mihi videtur* and the noun phrase *mea sententia*. The former is typical of Cicero's use: before him it was practically never employed, after him it appears rarely, mostly as a reprise of a Ciceronian stylistic mark.[20] Cicero always employs it with a specific intent, that of toning down the force of the statement, usually for reasons of polite (or self-polite) understatement. In the speeches he makes use of it when introducing especially far-fetched images or judgments, bordering on verisimilitude:

(10) *parietes, me dius fidius,* ***ut mihi videtur****, huius curiae tibi gratias agere gestiunt, quod brevi tempore futura sit illa auctoritas in his maiorum suorum et suis sedibus* (Cic. Marcell. 10)

20 Mencacci (2022).

'I swear that the very walls of this senate-house, as it seems to me, are eager to thank you; since Marcellus' honoured presence will shortly grace this place, which has been a home to his ancestors as to himself'

In the passage the personification of the walls of the *curia*, called upon as witnesses to the events, is a form of *amplificatio* evidently intended to increase the pathos of the passage. In fact, this is a particularly bold rhetorical resource, which Cicero himself recommends using with *mensura*.[21] What is more, in this context it can carry specific risks: the special prominence it gives to the *curia*, that is the symbol of senatorial power, could be counterproductive in a speech intended to celebrate Caesar's *clementia*. The insertion of *ut mihi videtur* seems a way to dilute the boldness of the idea.

But perhaps the clearest example of the mitigating effect produced by the use of *ut mihi videtur* is found in a passage from the speech *Pro Murena*, when Cicero replies to his opponent Cato, attacking his stubborn inflexibility:

(11) *accessit istuc doctrina non moderata nec mitis sed,* ***ut mihi videtur***, <u>*paulo asperior et durius*</u> *quam aut veritas aut natura patitur* (Cic. Mur. 60–61)
'to these virtues there has been added a stern and uncompromising set of beliefs and one in my view that is a little too hard and harsh for reality or human nature to endure'

Here the comment clause *ut mihi videtur*, along with the addition of *paulo* directly reducing the force of the two comparatives, contributes to blunting the harshness of the judgement and allows Cicero to exercise his criticism without appearing exaggeratedly hostile.[22] In this case we can be sure of this pragmatic interpretation of the use, because Quintilian reads it in exactly the same terms. Offering us a precious emic insight on the text, the rhetor reports the passage as a masterful example of *apte dicere* for effectiveness and elegance and comments on the skill with which Cicero manages to belittle an opponent of this calibre – one of those that one must fear to offend – without compromising his public image (*quam molli autem articulo tractavit Catonem!*) and to exercise criticism, while also maintaining due respect and esteem (*aliquid detrahere . . . salva gratia*: 11, 1, 69–72).

An opposite pragmatic function seems to be that of the ablative noun phrase *mea sententia*, which Cicero employs in the speeches, whether accompanied by the intensifier *quidem* or not, with a reinforcing role, possibly connected to the

21 Cic. orat. 81; Qvint. inst. 8, 6, 74; 8, 6, 87.
22 See also 61: *audacius paulo (. . .) disputabo.*

value of the noun (*sententia*), which, as the proper expression of official statements in the political and legal sphere, is probably itself loaded with assertive force.[23] *Mea sententia* usually appears in emphatic utterances, marked by various forms of intensification (superlatives, adverbs, the emphatic use of *ego*). Its presence in these cases seems intended to emphasise Cicero's commitment to the judgement he is uttering: the formula underlines the speaker's personal full subscription to the idea, increasing in this way its credibility. This is the case in the following passage, where *mea sententia* appears in the final part of a long sentence. After having presented a series of opposing possibilities in a kind of ascending climax, Cicero now confronts his audience with the last dilemma:[24]

(12) *Restat, iudices, ut hoc dubitemus, uter potius Sex. Roscium occiderit, is ad quem morte eius divitiae venerint, an is ad quem mendicitas, is qui antea tenuis fuerit, an is qui postea factus sit egentissimus, is qui ardens avaritia feratur infestus in suos, an is qui semper ita vixerit ut quaestum nosset nullum, fructum autem eum solum quem labore peperisset, is qui omnium sectorum audacissimus sit, an is qui propter fori iudiciorumque insolentiam non modo subsellia, verum etiam urbem ipsam reformidet, postremo, iudices, id quod ad rem* **mea sententia** *maxime pertinet, utrum inimicus potius an filius.* (Cic. S. Rosc. 88)
'The only thing that remains, gentlemen, is to consider which of the two is more likely to be the murderer of Sextus Roscius, he to whom this murder has brought wealth, or he whom it has reduced to poverty; he who before it was poor, or he who after it was reduced to beggary; he who, inflamed by avarice, rushes to attack his own relatives, or he who has always lived such a life that he knew nothing about filthy lucre but only about the fruit of his own toil; he who is the most audacious of all the brokers, or he who, owing to his inexperience of the forum and legal trials, dreads not only the sight of these benches, but even the city itself; lastly, gentlemen – and this I consider is of the greatest importance in the matter – one who was the enemy or one who was the son of Roscius.'

23 *Sententia* is also used for the expression of a universal pronouncement (Quint. inst. 8, 5, 3 *vox universalis*). According to Quintilian this *lumen* (rhetorical device) is so called because of its similarity with *consilia aut decreta.* See also the definition given in 8, 5, 1 (*sententiam veteres quod animo sensissent vocaverunt*), with the observation that the term enters in the formula of the swearing, committing the utterer to its sincerity. The same function, however, seems to be attached also to the instances of *meo iudicio.*
24 Cf. Dyck (2010: *ad loc.*).

Something similar can also be said of the next instance:

(13) *Ego, si quis, iudices, hoc robore animi atque hac indole virtutis atque continentiae fuit, ut respueret omnes voluptates omnemque vitae suae cursum in labore corporis atque in animi contentione conficeret, quem non quies, non remissio, non aequalium studia, non ludi, non convivia delectarent, nihil in vita expetendum putaret, nisi quod esset cum laude et cum dignitate coniunctum, hunc* ***mea sententia*** *divinis quibusdam bonis instructum atque ornatum puto.* (Cic. Cael. 39)
'For myself, gentlemen, if there ever was a man of mind strong enough, of character so virtuous and self-controlled, to despise all pleasures and spend the whole course of his life in bodily labour and mental exertion; to be insensible to the attractions of rest, of relaxation, of the pursuits of his friends, of love affairs and festivities; to think that nothing in life was worth striving for unless it was united with glory and honour – such a man, in my judgement, I hold to have been endowed and blessed with virtues greater than human.'

Here, in order to defend his client, Cicero depicts it as totally unrealistic to have high expectations about the restraint capacities of young people. In the passage, *ego* in the initial position implicitly contrasts Cicero's view with other old-fashioned ones, while *puto* at the end of the sentence refers to the epistemic status of the statement, presented as a personal opinion. Among them, *mea sententia* joining an especially emphatic formulation (*divinis . . . ornatus*) strongly stresses Cicero's personal commitment to this stance.[25]

4 Conclusions

The wide repertoire of epistemic expressions which dots Cicero's *orationes* certainly deserves a systematic study, much broader than that presented here. However, some preliminary conclusions can be advanced.

First, it seems possible to observe a distinctive use Cicero makes of the class of epistemic modalizers, between those preferentially aimed at expliciting the epistemic-evidential status of statements and those that have significant if not prominent pragmatic functions. To the latter Cicero often entrusts a specific interpersonal goal, finalized at communicating a certain image of himself. In other words,

25 Dyck (2013: *ad loc.*).

they serve in the first place as a strategy of self-presentation, and not – or only secondarily – to clarify the degree of truth of what is said.

The pragmatic effects Cicero intends to produce can be different, varying between mitigation and enhancement. Of course, the lack of some essential clues, such as intonation and prosody, does not always allow us to grasp exactly the function of the single expression: however, in some cases it is possible to observe a sort of pattern, which links the use of specific forms to specific effects – as is the case of *ut mihi videtur* (always mitigating) vs. *mea sententia* (strengthening).

The impression that this partial survey leaves is then that of a skilful and sophisticated exploitation of the possibilities offered by this kind of linguistic resources. Cicero seems to be well aware of the role they can play in shaping the right style of speaking, that *apte dicere* which marks the excellence of the oratorical performance, gaining the speaker approval from his audience and in this way increasing the persuasive force of his arguments.

Bibliography

Barrios-Lech, P. (2016). *Linguistic Interaction in Roman Comedy.* Cambridge: Cambridge University Press.
Berry, D. H. (2004). Literature and Persuasion in Cicero's Pro Archia. In J. G. F. Powell & J. J. Paterson (Eds.), *Cicero the Advocate* (pp. 291–311). Oxford: Oxford University Press.
Bolkestein, A. M. (1998a). Between brackets: (some properties of) parenthetical clauses in Latin. An investigation of the language in Cicero's letters. In R. Risselada (Ed.), *Latin in Use* (pp. 1–17). Amsterdam: Gieben.
Bolkestein, A. M. (1998b). Modalizing one's message in Latin: 'parenthetical' *verba sentiendi*. In Ch. M. Ternes & D. Longrée (Eds.), *Oratio soluta – oratio numerosa* (pp. 22–33). Luxembourg: Centre Alexandre Wiltheim.
Borillo, A. (2004). Les « Adverbes d'opinion forte » selon moi, à mes yeux, à mon avis,. . . : point de vue subjectif et effet d'atténuation. *Langue Française*, *142* (2), 31–40.
Brown, P. & Levinson, S. C. (1987). *Politeness. Some Universals in Language Usage.* Cambridge: Cambridge University Press.
Caffi, C. (2007). *Mitigation*. Amsterdam/Tokio: Elsevier.
Calboli Montefusco L. (1992). Cicerone, De Oratore: la doppia funzione dell'ethos dell'oratore. *Rhetorica: A Journal of the History of Rhetoric*, *10* (3), 245–259.
Dehé, N. & Kavalova, J. (2007). *Parentheticals*. Amsterdam/Philadelphia: John Benjamins.
Dyck, A. R. (2010). *Cicero. Pro Sexto Roscio*. Cambridge: Cambridge University Press.
Dyck, A. R. (2013). *Cicero. Pro M. Caelio*. Cambridge: Cambridge University Press.
Fraser, B. (1980). Conversational mitigation. *Journal of Pragmatics*, *4*, 341–350.
Fraser, B. (2010). Pragmatic Competence: The Case of Hedging. In G. Kaltenböck, W. Mihatsch & S. Schneider (Eds.), *New Approaches to Hedging* (pp. 15–34). Bingley: Emerald.
Guérin, Ch. (2015). Persona. *L'élaboration d'une notion rhétorique au Ier siècle av. J. - C.*, vol. II, *Théorisation cicéronienne de la persona oratoire*. Paris: Éditions Vrin.
Hofmann, J. B. (1951[3]). *Lateinische Umgangssprache*. München: Beck.

Holmes, J. (1984). Modifying illocutionary force. *Journal of Pragmatics*, *8* (3), 345–365.
Holmes, J. (1990). Hedges and boosters in women's and men's speech. *Language and Communication*, *10* (3), 185–205.
Kaltenböck, G., Mihatsch, W. & Schneider, S. (Eds.) (2010). *New Approaches to Hedging*. Bingley: Emerald.
Kaster, R. A. (2006). *Marcus Tullius Cicero: Speech on Behalf of Publius Sestius*. Oxford: Oxford University Press.
Kenty, J. (2020). *Cicero's Political Personae*. Cambridge: Cambridge University Press.
Lakoff, G. (1972). Hedges: A Study in Meaning Criteria and the Logic of Fuzzy Concepts. *Chicago Linguistic Society Papers*, *8*, 183–228.
May, J. M. (1988). *Trials of Character: the Eloquence of Ciceronian Ethos*. Chapel Hill and London: North Carolina Press.
Mencacci, F. (2022). Text as Interaction. *Ut mihi (quidem) videtur* as a hedging device in Latin literary texts. In L. Unceta Gómez & L. Berger (Eds.), *Politeness in ancient Greek and Latin* (pp. 103–126). Cambridge: Cambridge University Press.
Müller, R. (1997). *Sprechen und Sprache. Dialoglinguistische Studien zu Terenz*. Heidelberg: Winter.
Pinkster, H. (1988). *Lateinische Syntax Und Semantik*. Tübingen: Francke.
Pinkster, H. (2015). *The Oxford Latin Syntax. Volume 1: The Simple Clause*. Oxford: Oxford University Press.
Pinkster, H. (2021). *The Oxford Latin Syntax. Volume 2: The Complex Sentence and Discourse*. Oxford: Oxford University Press.
Riesco García, P. (2022). Un análisis pragmático de tres verbos psicológicos latinos. A propósito de *minus malum opinor quam esse censebam. . . tecum sentio* (cf. Plaut. *Pseud*. 956–958). *Revista Española de Lingüística*, *52* (2), 195–212.
Schneider, S. (2007). *Reduced Parenthetical Clauses as Mitigators. A corpus study of spoken French, Italian and Spanish*. Amsterdam/Philadelphia: John Benjamins.
Schneider, S., Glikman, J. & Avanzi, M. (Eds.) (2015). *Parenthetical Verbs*. Berlin, München, Boston: De Gruyter.
Unceta Gómez, L. (2009). Elementos parentéticos en la organización discursiva de la oratoria de Cicerón. In T. Arcos Pereira, J. Fernández López & F. Moya del Baño (Eds.), *Pectora mulcet. Estudios de Retórica y Oratoria latinas, vol. I* (pp. 247–258). Logroño: Instituto de Estudios Riojanos.
Unceta Gómez, L. (forthcoming). Roman Notions of "face": An Analysis of Latin Persona. In: G. Held (Ed.), *Face: (New) Facets of a Sociopragmatic Concept*. Leiden/Boston: Brill.
Urmson, J. O. (1952). Parenthetical verbs. *Mind*, *61*, 480–496.
Wisse, J. (1989). *Ethos and Pathos from Aristotle to Cicero*. Amsterdam: Hakkert.

Jana Mikulová

¿Cómo pedir humildemente? La perífrasis *dignari* + infinitivo

Abstract: The chapter focuses on the origin and evolution of the formula *rogo (ut) digneris* until the end of the 5th century, as can be deduced from *Brepolis* databases. In the texts of literary authors, the formula appears for the first time in Pliny's letters addressed to the emperor Trajan. Its formation was facilitated by the extension of the meaning of the verb *dignor* which, combined with the infinitive, began to express 'I consider myself worthy of doing something, I deign to do something'. Moreover, the verb *dignor* seems to have been appropriated because of its affinity to the concept of *dignitas*, which is important in Latin politeness. Among the precursors of the formula, three examples of the imperative *dignare* + infinitive seem to be important. The frequency of the formula started to increase in the 4th century. Late authors used more verbs with the meaning 'to ask' than Pliny, who employed only *rogo*. They used the formula to ask for various things (answer, prayer, favours, etc.) and sometimes reinforced it with "honorific" treatments such as *beatitudo tua* 'your beatitude'. In the same century, the frequency of *dignare* + infinitive also increased. Depending on the context, constructions with *dignari* can express impatience, urgency, irritation, and reproaches and thus cross the boundary between polite and impolite.

Keywords: *digneris*, politeness, Late Latin, *dignari*

1 Introducción

Este artículo aborda la fórmula cortés *rogo (ut) digneris* + *infinitivo* 'te pido que te digneshacer algo'. En los textos literarios se documenta por primera vez en las cartas de Plinio al emperador Trajano. Su uso ha sido comentado por varios especialistas (p. ej. Coleman 2012: 200–201; Dickey 2015: 23–26; Ferri 2022: 133), que han tenido en cuenta todo el epistolario de Plinio y las convenciones de la comunicación entre personas de distintos grupos sociales. Apoyándose en esos resultados previos, este artículo se centrará en los orígenes de esta construcción, su extensión

Note: Me gustaría hacer constar mi agradecimiento a Luis Unceta Gómez y a los revisores anónimos por todos sus comentarios y sugerencias. La responsabilidad de cualquier error es, por supuesto, mía.

Jana Mikulová, Masaryk University Brno, Czech Republic

https://doi.org/10.1515/9783111332956-036

y sus modificaciones entre los siglos II y V de nuestra era, utilizando como corpus los textos publicados en la base de datos *Brepolis*.

2 Marco teórico y primeras ocurrencias

La expresión de la cortesía en latín ha sido estudiada por muchos lingüistas, entre los que cabe mencionar a Halla-aho (2008, 2010), Hall (2009), Unceta Gómez (2009a, 2009b, 2019, 2022), Molinelli (2010), Dickey (2012, 2015, 2016), Ghezzi y Molinelli (2016), Fedriani (2017), Berger (2021), Barrios-Lech (2022), Ferri (2022), Unceta Gómez y Berger (2022), entre otros. Para ello, se han utilizado diferentes marcos teóricos cuya utilidad para analizar la cortesía en el griego antiguo y el latín es variable (un resumen puede verse en Unceta Gómez y Berger 2022: 3–37). Una de las teorías más utilizadas es la desarrollada por Brown y Levinson (1987), que se basa en la idea de que los hablantes protegen en sus enunciados las posibles amenazas a la imagen (en inglés "face") del destinatario que sus mensajes pueden contener. Según estos autores, la imagen tiene dos facetas: la imagen positiva (el deseo de ser aceptado y apreciado socialmente) y la imagen negativa (el deseo de poder decidir sobre las propias acciones). Esta teoría, sin embargo, ha recibido numerosas críticas, entre ellas la de simplificar el fenómeno, reducirlo a una dicotomía que no refleja la realidad y no considerar suficientemente los factores contextuales y culturales (véase, p. ej., Dickey 2016: 199–202; Unceta Gómez y Berger 2022: 12–15).

También se ha señalado (Unceta Gómez y Berger 2022: 25–26) que el análisis del latín tiene sus peculiaridades en comparación con las lenguas modernas. Entre otros factores, la sociedad romana era patriarcal, mucho más jerárquica que la sociedad occidental contemporánea y las relaciones entre sus miembros se basaban en un sistema de obligaciones, favores y beneficios mutuos (véase, p. ej., Dickey 2016: 210). Este entorno social se caracterizaba también por la consideración de la *verecundia* (el respeto por parte de los subordinados hacia los superiores, véase Unceta Gómez [2019: 299, 307]), la *dignitas* (la dignidad, la estima que correspondía a la posición de cada uno, equivalente funcional del concepto de la imagen[1]), la *existimatio* (la reputación) y la *auctoritas*, que se derivaba de los méritos, contactos sociales y cargos políticos desempeñados en el pasado por una persona (véase Hall 2009: 12; Barrios-Lech 2022: 62; Unceta Gómez 2019: 293–307). Basándose en la importancia de la *verecundia* y la llamada "cortesía de discernimiento"[2], Hall (2009: 8) propuso para el latín una clasificación de tipos de cortesía que modificaba las

1 Unceta Gómez (2019: 305) acepta la equivalencia entre estos términos propuesta por Hall (2005).
2 "Discernment politeness"; véase Unceta Gómez y Berger (2022: 33).

categorías de Brown y Levinson, añadiéndole la cortesía de respeto como tercera categoría. Pertenecen a ella las expresiones de cortesía que son consideradas como una norma establecida en cierto entorno social y se deducen del conocimiento de la posición social que uno tiene. Por tratarse de automatismos y frases convencionalizadas, pueden utilizarse de manera estratégica e incluso insincera (Hall 2009: 11). Una última clasificación ha propuesto Unceta Gómez (2019: 307), quien distingue cuatro categorías basadas, por un lado, en los parámetros de conexión y separación, y, por otro, en el comportamiento "político" o *decorum* (el comportamiento considerado una norma social) y el comportamiento cortés u *honorificentia* (la cortesía propiamente dicha). En todo caso, Dickey (2016) y Unceta Gómez y Berger (2022: 20) concluyen que el procedimiento metodológicamente más prometedor es la combinación de diferentes teorías y puntos de vista.

Como el presente artículo se centra en la estructura que establece la forma *digneris* con verbos de petición, a continuación se mencionarán los verbos más importantes para expresar esta noción. Estos lexemas han sido analizados en detalle por Unceta Gómez (2009a) y, limitándose al género epistolar, por Dickey (2012, 2015, 2016), Hall (2009) y Coleman (2012). En las cartas de Cicerón, los verbos *velim*, *quaeso*, *rogo* y *peto* son los más utilizados.[3] Según Dickey (2012: 733; 2016: 208), el recurso a cada uno de estos verbos varía en función de la importancia y dificultad de las peticiones que introducen. *Velim* es el verbo reservado para las peticiones menores, mientras que *quaeso*, *rogo* y *peto* se utilizan para los ruegos más difíciles de cumplir. El verbo *rogo*, utilizado por Plinio en la fórmula con *digneris*, aparece más bien en registros informales y caracteriza las relaciones de igualdad social (Unceta Gómez 2009a: 149). En el latín de Plauto significa únicamente 'preguntar', pero en las obras de Cicerón ya había adquirido la acepción de 'pedir' (Unceta Gómez 2009a: 148–150; Halla-aho 2010: 233). Con el paso del tiempo, el verbo *rogo* se hizo más frecuente[4] y se extendió a expensas de *quaeso*, que es típico del registro medio en la comedia romana (Unceta Gómez 2009b: 251, 254–255) o elevado en la obra de Cicerón (Dickey 2016: 208). La expansión de *rogo* se manifiesta también en las cartas de Plinio (véase Coleman 2012: 199–200). Por su carácter genérico y neutro, *rogo* es un verbo apropiado para el lenguaje burocrático documentado en las comedias plautinas (Unceta Gómez 2009a: 150–151), pero aparece frecuentemente también en las cartas no literarias de Vindolanda, que datan de finales del primer siglo y principios del segundo (Halla-aho 2008: 57).

---

3 Dickey (2012 y 2016) se centra en los diversos recursos verbales para expresar una petición, y no solamente en los verbos de 'pedir'. Por lo tanto, incluye también el subjuntivo volitivo *velim* 'quiera' del verbo *volo* 'quiero'.

4 Para más detalles, véase Unceta Gómez (2008).

Rogo es también el único verbo que está acompañado de *(ut) digneris* + infinitivo en las cartas dirigidas por Plinio al emperador Trajano, concretamente en seis de ellas.[5] Cuatro veces le pide a Trajano un consejo, una vez el cargo de pretor para su amigo Accius Sura y una vez un cargo religioso para sí mismo (1). Las peticiones de un favor contienen más "adornos" corteses y halagos que los demás casos. En el ruego por sí mismo, Plinio incluso ofrece un favor a cambio, en concreto una plegaria pública por el emperador.

(1) *. . . rogo dignitati, ad quam me provexit indulgentia tua, vel auguratum vel septemviratum, quia vacant, adicere* ***digneris****, ut iure sacerdotii precari deos pro te publice possim, quos nunc precor pietate privata.* (Plin. epist. 10, 13)
'. . .te ruego te dignes añadir a la dignidad a la que me elevó tu indulgencia la condición de augur o septénviro, porque están vacantes, para que pueda suplicar a los dioses por ti en nombre del Estado en mi condición de sacerdote, a los que ahora suplico a título privado.' (Trad. de González Fernández 2005: 487)

Según Ferri (2022: 134), el verbo *dignari* expresa el respeto hacia los superiores e intenta prevenir que una petición los ofenda por ser demasiado insignificante para su estatus social.

Aunque la distancia social entre el emperador y un funcionario pueda indicar que el verbo *dignari* u otra fórmula cortés especial es indispensable, las cartas de Plinio dan testimonio de lo contrario, porque Plinio se dirige al emperador utilizando fórmulas corteses "corrientes" en la mayoría de los casos.

Cabe preguntar, entonces, cuál es la aportación del verbo *dignari* a esta solicitud respetuosa. Por un lado, el verbo *dignari* podía destacar la protección de la imagen negativa, al hacer énfasis en que era el interlocutor quien decidía si consideraba digno de él cumplir la petición o no. Por otro lado, puede pensarse también que *dignari* tiene además un impacto sobre la imagen positiva del destinatario, porque destaca su *dignitas*. Esta imagen positiva de una persona de alto rango podía reforzar, a su vez, su superioridad, porque se destacaba que la decisión de otorgar amablemente un beneficio dependía completamente de él. La combinación de la cortesía negativa y positiva no sería nada excepcional e imprevisto, porque lo mismo ocurre también en las lenguas modernas, como muestra Dickey (2016: 201) en un ejemplo tomado del inglés: "Darling, could you lend me that book?".[6]

5 Plin. epist. 10, 12; 10, 13; 10, 43, 4; 10, 47, 3; 10, 81, 8; 10, 118, 3.
6 '¿Cariño, podrías prestarme este libro?'

3 Origen y precursores de la fórmula

La fórmula con *digneris* se forjó, según Ferri (2022: 132), probablemente en la cancillería del primer siglo, porque está ausente en las cartas de Cicerón y otros epistológrafos. Coleman (2012: 200–201) señala que la fórmula aparece también en las tablillas de Vindolanda, que datan del tiempo de Plinio, y en los papiros, y deduce que fue "the regular bureaucratic formula for seeking advice or confirmation."[7] Sin embargo, el acceso limitado a la producción administrativa no permite rastrear los primeros usos de esta fórmula ni su frecuencia.

Además de la datación, cabe también preguntar por qué el verbo *dignari* fue elegido para formar parte de una fórmula cortés y si se pueden observar precursores en los textos arcaicos y clásicos. Me parece que la elección estuvo motivada por su relación semántica, etimológica o morfológica con el concepto de *dignitas*, tan importante en las relaciones sociales en Roma. Según Forcellini (s.v. *dignor*), el verbo *dignari* significa 'considerar digno' y puede combinarse tanto con nombres o sintagmas nominales (p. ej., *dignor aliquem aliqua re* 'considero a una persona digna de una cosa') como con el infinitivo. El significado de la segunda posibilidad, *dignor* + infinitivo, se extendió con el tiempo hacia 'considero digno de mí hacer algo'.

La búsqueda de la construcción *rogo (ut) digneris* + infinitivo con este significado extendido no ha ofrecido resultados ni en las obras contemporáneas de Plinio ni en las anteriores; además, la mayoría de los ejemplos de otras formas de *dignari* se encuentra en poesía. En algunos de ellos, el contexto lleva a la interpretación de *dignari* como 'dignarse hacer algo desde una posición superior, importante o privilegiada o como una persona de prestigio e importancia'. En el marco teórico de la gramaticalización, Heine (2002: 84) denomina este tipo de contexto *bridging context* ('contexto puente'), porque favorece la gramaticalización de una determinada estructura. En el caso de la extensión del significado del verbo en esta fórmula, podríamos encontrar el contexto puente en aquellos casos donde *dignari*:

- tiene sujetos "de prestigio", como Júpiter en (2), los dioses (Catvl. 64, 407), *suboles Romae* 'la progenie de Roma' (Hor. carm. 4, 3, 14), o la reina Dido en (3);
- y/o aparece en contextos "solemnes" y/o con cierta carga emocional, como cuando Ovidio (Ov. Ib. 151) habla de su futuro esfuerzo de escapar del tártaro.

(2) *Nulla tamen alite verti / **dignatur**, nisi quae posset sua fulmina ferre.* (Ov. met. 10, 155–158)
'En ninguna ave, aun así, convertirse / se digna, sino la que pudiera soportar sus rayos.' (Trad. de Pérez Vega 2002)

7 'La fórmula burocrática común para buscar un consejo o una confirmación.'

(3) . . . *pariter facta atque infecta canebat: / venisse Aenean Troiano sanguine cretum, / cui se pulchra viro* ***dignetur*** *iungere Dido*. . . (VERG. Aen. 4, 189–192)
'. . .divulgaba a la par nuevas ciertas y falsas: que ha arribado / Eneas, descendiente del linaje troyano; que se ha dignado unirse con él / la hermosa Dido. . .' (Trad. de De Echave-Sustaeta 1992: 245)

Aún más cercanos a nuestra fórmula son tres casos del imperativo *dignare* + infinitivo. En el primer caso, la petición va dirigida a Pisón,[8] en el segundo, a Apolo;[9] en el tercer caso, del *Satiricón* de Petronio, una dama de la clase superior pide besos a Encolpio, quien finge ser esclavo (4). A pesar de eso, el uso de *dignari* está relacionado con el estatus social superior también en este caso, porque Encolpio se presenta aquí como un objeto de amor inalcanzable y la mujer se humilla voluntariamente ante él para conseguir su amor. En el mismo ejemplo, además, la petición expresada por *dignare* está acompañada de otra expresión cortés *cum libuerit* 'cuando te venga bien', todo esto en su esfuerzo por convencer al interlocutor.

(4) *Tu tantum* ***dignare*** *et meum osculum, cum libuerit, agnoscere*. (PETRON. 127, 2)
'Dígnate tan sólo probar, cuando te venga bien, el sabor de mis besos.' (Trad. de Rubio Fernández 1978: 183)

Un efecto parecido puede observarse en el uso de expresiones similares a 'por favor' para expresar reproches, desconfianza (Risselada 1989: 373), irritación y sorpresa (Fedriani 2017: 84, 91–101).

4 Evolución después de Plinio hasta el final del siglo V

Los primeros ejemplos de la fórmula tras el tiempo de Plinio aparecen en el siglo III, en concreto en las cartas de Cipriano, que contienen también cartas dirigidas al mismo Cipriano por otras personas.[10] La frecuencia de la fórmula aumenta considerablemente en el siglo IV y casi el mismo número de ejemplos proviene también del siglo V. La mayoría de los ejemplos de los siglos III, IV y V (79 de un total de 108) se

8 LAVS Pis. 216. Se trata de un panegírico a un miembro de la familia de los Pisones, supuestamente a Calpurnio Pisón, quien organizó una conspiración contra Nerón.
9 STAT. Theb. 10, 341.
10 CELERIN. Cypr. epist. 21, 4, 2.

encuentra en cartas. Los demás pertenecen a otros géneros, por ejemplo, tratados, polémicas, actas de concilios, sermones e historiografía.

4.1 Verbos en la fórmula con *digneris*

La fórmula no se fijó en esta época en la forma empleada por Plinio. Primero, el verbo *dignari* aparece en el singular *digneris* (en 77 ejemplos) y en el plural *dignemini* (en 31 ejemplos).[11] Algunos ejemplos de *dignemini* parecen referirse a una sola persona en singular.[12] Segundo, el verbo 'pedir' no se limita a *rogo*, sino que aparecen muchos más verbos. El resumen de los verbos en autores y siglos se encuentra en la Tabla 1, que contiene solamente casos en los que el verbo 'pedir' aparece en forma realizativa (primera persona del singular o plural). Los números diferentes en las columnas *Oraciones* y *Verbos* se explican porque en la oración principal coocurren varios verbos de 'pedir'.

El verbo más frecuente es *peto,* con 38 ejemplos, 18 de ellos en las obras de Agustín. El segundo lugar lo ocupa, con 24 casos, *quaeso,* predominantemente empleado por Símaco (14 veces). El tercero es *rogo*, en 20 ejemplos, de los cuales siete pertenecen a las obras de Agustín. Dado que la suma de los ejemplos de Agustín y Símaco representa el 46% de todos los casos, desde Plinio hasta el final del siglo V, las preferencias de Agustín y Símaco influyen considerablemente en la imagen general del uso de la fórmula con *digneris.* Esto es evidente en el caso de *quaeso,* que, dejando aparte a Símaco, aparece cuatro veces en la obra de Agustín y solamente una vez en un total de seis obras de otros autores. La preferencia de *quaeso* por parte de Símaco se debe probablemente a su afán por imitar los modelos clásicos y postclásicos, en concreto a Cicerón y Plinio (véase Haverling 1988: 14 y 229). A pesar de ello, Símaco es un "hijo de su época" y su lenguaje difiere del (post)clásico en ciertos aspectos. Al fin y al cabo, imitar el estilo clásico hasta el último detalle nunca fue su intención, como afirma Haverling (1988: 258).

11 De aquí en adelante, por brevedad, "(la fórmula con) *digneris*" se empleará para referirse tanto a la frase con *digneris* como con *dignemini.*

12 Por ejemplo: AMBR. epist. extra coll. 5, 4 y 6, 7; hex. 2, 1, 3. El estudio detallado de estos casos está fuera de los objetivos de este artículo.

Table 1: Verbos en autores y obras.

Autor	Obra	Siglo	Oraciones	*Rogo*	*Peto*	*Precor, deprecor*	*Quaeso*	*Oro*	*Posco, deposco*	*Obsecro*	Otro verbo	Total (verbos)
AMBR.	epist. extra coll.	IV	2	1	2							3
AMBR.	hex.	IV	1				1					1
ARNOB. IVN.	ad Greg.	V	1	1								1
ARNOB. IVN.	confl.	V	1			1						1
AVELL. 2		V	2			1	1					2
AVG.	anim.	V	1		1							1
AVG.	c. Fort.	IV	1				1					1
AVG.	coll. c. Maximin.	V	1	1								1
AVG.	epist.	IV/V	25	4	14		2		1	2	4	27
AVG.	epist. Divj.	V	3	1	2							3
AVG.	serm.	V	1							1		1
AVREL.	epist. conc. Cart.	V	1							1		1
CELERIN.	Cypr. epist.	III	1		1							1
	CONC. Carth. a. 411	V	5		2	2	1					5
	CONC. Carth. a. 419	V	1		1							1
CONSENT.	Aug. epist.	V	1			1						1
DAR.	Aug. epist.	V	1		1							1
DIOSC.	Aug. epist.	V	1	1	1							2
ENNOD.	epist.	V	4	2		2						4
EPISC. Gall.	Leo M. epist.	V	4	2			1	1				4
EPIST. pontif.	Lucif. epist.	IV	1							1		1
EVGEN.	Vict. Vit.	V	1		1							1
EU'VSEB. VERC.	epist.	V	1		1							1
EVOD.	Aug. epist.	V	1	1								1
FAVST. REI.	epist. ad Rur.	V	1	1					1			2

	FRG. Vat.	IV	1	1								1
HIL.	Aug. epist.	V	2	2								2
	INTERPR. Gai	IV?	1		1							1
LONGIN.	Aug. epist.	V	1				1					1
LVCIF.	non parc.	IV	1								1	1
LVCIF.	reg. apost.	IV	2			1					1	2
PAVL. MED.	vita Ambr.	V	1			1						1
PAVL. NOL.	epist.	IV/V	2		2							2
PAMMACH.	Hier. epist.	IV	1				1					1
PS. ATHAN.	Lucif. epist.	IV	2	1	1							2
PS. MVSA	herb. Vett.	V	1		1							1
PS. ORIG.	tract.	V	1	1	1							2
QVODV.	Aug. epist.	V	1			1						1
QVODV.	c. Iud. pag. Ar.	V	1		1							1
	REG. eccl. Carth. I.	V	2		2							2
SECVNDIN.	epist.	V	1			1		1		1		3
SIDON.	epist.	V	1							1		1
SYMM.	epist.	IV	19		1	1	14	1			2	19
VALENT.	Aug. epist.	V	2		1	1						2
VICT. VIT.		V	1							1		1
VIGIL. THAPS.	c. Arian.	V	1				1					1
Total			108	20	38	13	24	3	2	8	8	116

4.2 Estructura sintáctica

Como muestra la Tabla 2, la estructura sintáctica preferida es la frase con *ut*, seguida por el subjuntivo sin *ut*. Dado que *digneris* es una forma de subjuntivo, es a veces difícil determinar si se trata de la subordinada sin conjunción o *digneris* acompañado del verbo 'pedir' parentético. Por lo tanto, la última columna recoge ejemplos que son o puedan ser considerados parentéticos, porque, por ejemplo, el verbo 'pedir' sigue a *digneris* y un vocativo (5).

(5) . . .*pro regula monasterii* ***digneris****, pater,* ***petimus****, libenter accipere et per omnia nos infirmos instruere.* (VALENT. Aug. epist. 216, 57, 6)
'. . .te pedimos, padre, que te dignes aceptarlo con gusto como la regla del monasterio y enseñarnos a nosotros, débiles, en todo.'[13]

Tabla 2: Las estructuras sintácticas.

Verbo	*Ut*	Subjuntivo sin *ut*	'Pedir' parentético
peto	23	13	2
quaeso	19	2	3
rogo	18	2	
precor, deprecor	12	1	
obsecro	6	2	
oro	2	1	
posco, deposco	2		
otro verbo	8		
Total	90	21	5

Digneris sin *ut* puede seguir inmediatamente después de un verbo de 'pedir' o estar separado por pocas palabras (lo más frecuente es de una a tres). No faltan, sin embargo, ejemplos de *digneris* sin *ut* tras una estructura amplia (6). Por lo tanto, estoy de acuerdo con Coleman (2012: 200) en que la adyacencia o poca distancia entre un verbo 'pedir' y *digneris* no es un criterio decisivo para justificar la omisión *ut*. Puede deberse a que después de una estructura intercalada larga se relaja el vínculo entre el verbo de pedir y la petición misma, por lo que *digneris* funciona en cierta medida como una frase independiente. No sería sorprendente, porque, como se comentará más abajo, hay ejemplos de *digneris* en la oración principal.

13 Si no aparece el nombre del traductor, la traducción es mía.

(6) ***Rogo*** *itaque benignitatem tuam, quoniam difficile et incredibile est, ut non iam vel noveris vel nosse possis, in qua causa detentus sit, hoc interim apud apparitorem, qui eum tenet, petitionem meam adiuvare* ***digneris*** *ut faciat, quod imperatoris lege praecipitur...* (AVG. epist. 113)
'Y, puesto que es increíble y casi imposible que no sepas ya por qué ha sido detenido Favencio, ruego a tu dignidad que, entretanto, te dignes apoyar mi petición ante el alguacil que le detuvo, para que se atenga a lo que ordena la ley imperial...' (Trad. de Cilleruelo 1986: 836–837)

En la mayoría de los casos, *(ut) digneris* sigue a un verbo de 'pedir' (7), (8), pero cinco veces lo precede (9)

(7) *Ad istas ergo quaestiones* ***peto*** *breviter respondere* ***digneris****...* (AVG. epist. 98, 7)
'Te pido que te dignes contestar brevemente a estas cuestiones.'

(8) ***Deprecamur*** *te, Constanti,* ***ne*** *adhuc in his tuis malis* ***digneris*** *demorari...* (LVCIF. reg. apost. 4)
'Te pedimos, Constancio, que no te dignes seguir con tus vicios...'

(9) *Venerius episcopus te dominum in Christo meum reverentissime saluto et* ***ut digneris*** *pro me orare* ***supplex rogo****.* (EPISC. Gall. Leo M. epist. 99)
'Yo, el obispo Venerius, te saludo a ti, mi reverendísimo señor en Cristo, y te pido humildemente que te dignes rezar por mí.'

El acusativo que indica el destinatario de la petición acompaña los verbos de 'pedir' en 25 ejemplos, que documentan los verbos *peto, rogo, quaeso, obsecro, precor, deprecor, hortor*. Además de los pronombres *te* y *vos*, se emplean también los tratamientos "honoríficos" como *beatitudo tua* 'tu beatitud' (AVG. epist. 59, 2), *sanctitas tua* 'tu santidad' (AVG. epist. 115), *caritas vestra* 'tu caridad' (QVODV. serm. 4, 1), *sincerissima caritas tua* 'tu más sincera caridad' (AVG. epist. Divj. 24, 1). La ocurrencia de estos tratamientos confirma su amplio desarrollo en latín tardío, descrito por Coleman (2012: 195).

Algunas estructuras aparecen repetidamente, como por ejemplo *quaeso igitur (ut)* en el comienzo de ocho frases[14] en la obra de Símaco, y sus variantes *quare quaeso ut*[15] *y atque ideo quaeso ut*[16]. Parece que Símaco prefiere la estrategia de

14 SYMM. epist. 2, 81; 4, 9; 6, 9; 6, 29; 7, 82; 7, 96; 9, 18; 34.
15 SYMM. epist. 9, 6.
16 SYMM. epist. 6, 5.

presentar primero una situación o hechos y después pedir una ayuda o un favor. Nótese que *igitur* acompaña al verbo 'pedir' solamente en 7 casos más del total de 108 ejemplos.

4.3 ¿Qué se pide y a quién?

Ningún verbo 'pedir' se une exclusivamente a una petición de una cosa determinada. Las peticiones expresadas con la fórmula son diversas: se pide una respuesta (7), una oración (9), el perdón y la indulgencia, una información o la entrega de una información a una persona, la aceptación de una persona, la entrega de un recado, varios favores, que el corresponsal recuerde al autor de la carta, que preste atención a sus palabras y algunas cosas más.

La fórmula con *digneris* se utiliza para dirigir una petición cortés a las autoridades, o a una persona con un estatus social superior, pero también a una persona con reconocimiento y prestigio social en general, aunque el remitente y el destinatario pertenezcan al mismo grupo social – por ejemplo, cuando un obispo escribe al otro obispo, como en (9). Además de mediante los títulos "honoríficos", la deferencia de estas peticiones puede estar reforzada por vocativos como *domine dilectissime et venerabilis frater* 'señor dilectísimo y venerable hermano' (10) y expresiones que indican humildad como *supplex* 'suplicante' en (9).

(10) *. . .**peto sanctitatem tuam, domine dilectissime et venerabilis frater**, ut honorabili nobisque carissimo consulari **digneris** tradere litteras meas tradere litteras meas et has ei legere. . .* (Avg. epist. 115)
'Para ello pido a tu santidad, señor dilectísimo y venerable hermano, que te dignes entregarle esta carta para él y leerle ésta para ti al honorable y para mí carísimo gobernador. . .' (Trad. de Cilleruelo 1986: 840)

Por otra parte, la fórmula con *digneris* aparece también en pasajes polémicos en los que sirve para presionar al oponente y sonsacar su respuesta en el afán de convencerlo. Un ejemplo puede verse en (11), donde Agustín pide a Fortunato que le explique su opinión. En este caso, la presión al interlocutor está reforzada por *et tu* 'también tú'.

(11) *. . .quoniam iam respondi obiectis tuis, **quaeso, ut et tu mihi dicere digneris**. . .* (Avg. c. Fort. 21)
'Puesto que yo ya te he respondido a tus objeciones, te ruego que también tú te dignes contestar a las mías.' (Trad. de De Luis 1986: 255)

5 Estructuras similares

La fórmula con *digneris* tiene sus estructuras alternativas, que sirven también para expresar una petición cortés: *(ne) digneris* o el imperativo *dignare* + infinitivo en la frase principal.

5.1 *Dignare* + infinitivo

La frecuencia de *dignare* + infinitivo también crece en los siglos IV y V y el número de ejemplos de ambas construcciones es similar (*dignare* concurre en 111 casos y la fórmula en 108). Aparece en géneros, contextos y construcciones similares a la fórmula con *digneris*. Por ejemplo, Símaco utiliza no solamente *quaeso igitur ut digneris* + inf., sino también *igitur dignare* + inf. 'por eso, dígnate a hacer algo'. Igual que la fórmula, sirve para pedir respuesta, atención del público, favores o el recuerdo por parte del corresponsal. Esta última petición se convirtió en una formula cortés de despedida en las cartas de Sidonio Apolinar (12) donde fue usada en todas las 36 cartas dirigidas al papa (lo cual supone el 24% del total de 146 cartas). En este contexto, la petición del recuerdo puede equivaler a la petición de la oración, porque puede entenderse como 'Dígnate recordarnos en tus oraciones'.

(12) *Memor nostri esse dignare, domine papa.* (SIDON. epist. 6, 1)
'Seas tan amable de recordarnos (lit. Dígnate recordarnos), señor papa.'

Sin embargo, hay también diferencias. Por ejemplo, *dignare* + inf. no se emplea para pedir perdón o indulgencia. Por otro lado, *dignare* + inf. es la estructura preferida por Agustín[17] en el diálogo polémico con Fortunato para pedir una respuesta, explicación u opinión del interlocutor (13).

(13) *Augustinus dixit:* ***immo tu dignare respondere*** *id, quod interrogaris, has animas quae causa morti dederit.*
Fortunatus dixit: ***immo tu dignare dicere****, utrum aliquid sit praeter deum, an omnia in deo sunt.* (AVG. c. Fort. 5)
'Agustín: Más bien, dígnate tú responder a lo que se te pregunta: ¿qué ha entregado esas almas a la muerte?
Fortunato: Mejor, dígnate tú decir si hay algo fuera de Dios, o si todo está en Dios.' (Trad. de De Luis 1986: 237)

17 AVG. c. Fort. 4, 5, 5, 17, 20, 22, 23.

En estos casos, la forma cortés contrasta con el tono emocionado o incluso irritado y con reproches. En tal contexto, *dignare* funciona como un "intensificador" de estas emociones o incluso traspasa la frontera entre lo cortés y lo descortés. Esto es todavía más evidente en el ejemplo (14), donde *dignare* aparece en una frase exclamativa que expresa enfado y reproche. En las polémicas, como en el ejemplo (13), *dignare* podría conllevar también un matiz de ironía.

(14) ***Iam aliquando** nos de hoc negotio amputatis omnibus morulis adiuvante deo liberare **dignare**!* (CONC. Carth. a. 411, 3, 41)
'¡Dígnate ya de una vez, con la ayuda de Dios, librarnos de esto sin más demoras!'

En resumen, los efectos comunicativos del verbo *dignari* y *dignare* + infinitivo que se acaban de describir siguen y desarrollan el uso presente ya en el latín clásico y postclásico; véase (4) y el comentario correspondiente.

5.2 *(Ne) digneris*

(Ne) digneris + inf. en la frase principal es mucho menos frecuente – aparece solamente en 11 casos,[18] tres de los cuales son usos negativos. Los usos afirmativos son oraciones dirigidas a Dios, mientras que los negados se refieren a los hombres. *Ne digneris* atenúa la exhortación o prohibición de hacer algo y, en función del contexto, parece equivaler a 'mejor no lo hagas', 'no te dignes hacer algo' (15).

(15) *Ne itaque iam **digneris** iniuste tibi **blandiri**, imperator, ...* (LVCIF. reg. apost.11)
'Por eso, no te dignes ya ser halagado injustamente, emperador...'

6 Conclusiones

La fórmula deferente *rogo (ut) digneris* aparece en las cartas de Plinio dirigidas al emperador Trajano. Sus orígenes pueden buscarse en la construcción del verbo *dignari* con infinitivo, que no significa 'considerar a alguien digno de hacer algo', sino 'dignarse hacer algo', tiene entidades de prestigio como sujetos y/o se usa en situaciones solemnes y con cierta carga emocional. De las estructuras previas a

18 AMBR. paenit. 2, 8; exhort. virg. 14; PS. CYPR. or. 1, 1 (2x), 2, 6 (2x); PRAEF. bibl. psalm. 83 y 84; LVCIF. reg. apost. 11; moriend. 13; AVG. serm. 126A, 12.

Plinio, las más cercanas a la fórmula examinada son tres casos del imperativo *dignare* con infinitivo que podrían parafrasearse como 'sé tan amable de considerarte digno de hacer esta cosa'. La elección del verbo *dignari* para crear una fórmula cortés podría haber sido fomentada por el concepto de *dignitas*, crucial en las relaciones entre los individuos de la élite romana. El resultado de la evolución es una fórmula que puede unir la cortesía negativa y positiva, porque el hablante no solamente intenta proteger la imagen negativa del interlocutor, sino que también expresa respeto hacia su dignidad y refuerza así la imagen positiva del destinatario.

La frecuencia de la fórmula empieza a crecer en el siglo IV y, desde ese momento, se usa en los textos literarios como una forma convencionalizada para la expresión de la deferencia. A diferencia de Plinio, los autores tardíos utilizaban no solamente *rogo*, sino también otros verbos de 'pedir', entre los que destacan *peto* y *quaeso*, seguidos por lexemas menos frecuentes, como *(de)precor*, *obsecro*, *oro*, *(de)posco*. Se observan preferencias por determinados verbos en función de los autores. El caso más obvio es *quaeso* en las cartas de Símaco. La frase negada *(rogo ne digneris)* aparece solo una vez en los textos examinados. En ocasiones, la fórmula se combina con "títulos honoríficos", como *beatitudo tua* 'tu beatitud', que se multiplicaron en el latín tardío. El género donde más se documenta es la epistolografía. La fórmula se empleaba para solicitar cosas diversas, por ejemplo, la respuesta del interlocutor, indulgencia, el rezo, un favor. Paralelamente con la fórmula, se utilizaban también las construcciones *(ne) digneris* + infinitivo y sobre todo *dignare* + infinitivo, cuya frecuencia fue en aumento. Parece que su uso no era completamente idéntico al de la fórmula con *digneris*. Por ejemplo, no hay casos de petición del rezo. Además, en ciertos contextos expresaban más bien irritación, ironía, impaciencia o insistencia y se traspasa el límite entre la cortesía y la descortesía. Así, continúan el uso ya documentado en la obra de Petronio. La misma interpretación puede vislumbrarse en algunos casos de *rogo ut digneris* también, pero es menos evidente. La expansión de estas estructuras pertenece a los rasgos típicos del lenguaje tardío y merece más investigaciones en el futuro.

Bibliografía

Barrios-Lech, P. (2022). Towards a comparison of Greek and Roman politeness systems. In L. Unceta Gómez & Ł. Berger (Eds.), *Politeness in ancient Greek and Latin* (pp. 45–76). Cambridge: Cambridge University Press.

Berger, Ł. (2021). Time, timing and (im)politeness in Roman comedy. *Studi Italiani di Linguistica Teorica e Applicata*, *50* (3), 543–560.

Brown, P. & Levinson, S. C. (1987). *Politeness: some universals in language usage.* Cambridge: Cambridge University Press.

Coleman, K. M. (2012). Bureaucratic language in the correspondence between Pliny and Trajan. *Transactions of the American Philological Association*, *142* (2), 189–238.
Dickey, E. (2012). How to say 'please' in Classical Latin. *The Classical Quarterly*, *62* (2), 731–748.
Dickey, E. (2015). How to say 'please' in post-Classical Latin: Fronto and the importance of archaism. *Journal of Latin Linguistics*, *14* (1), 17–31.
Dickey, E. (2016). Politeness in ancient Rome: Can it help us evaluate modern politeness theories? *Journal of Politeness Research*, *12* (2), 197–220.
Fedriani, Ch. (2017). *Quapropter, quaeso?* Questions and the pragmatic functions of *quaeso*, *obsecro*, and *amabo* in Plautus. In O. Spevak & C. Denizot (Eds.), *Pragmatic approaches to Latin and ancient Greek* (pp. 83–109). Amsterdam: John Benjamins.
Ferri, R. (2022). Politeness formulae in Roman non-literary sources. The case of juridical texts. In L. Unceta Gómez & Ł. Berger (Eds.), *Politeness in ancient Greek and Latin* (pp. 127–144). Cambridge: Cambridge University Press.
Ghezzi, Ch. & Molinelli, P. (2016). Politeness markers from Latin to Italian: Periphery, discourse structure and cyclicity. *Journal of Historical Pragmatics*, *17* (2), 307–337.
Hall, J. (2005). Politeness and Formality in Cicero's Letter to Matius (*Fam.* 11.27). *Museum Helveticum*, *62*, 193–213.
Hall, J. (2009). *Politeness and politics in Cicero's letters.* Oxford: Oxford University Press.
Halla-aho, H. (2008). *The non-literary Latin letters. A study of their syntax and pragmatics.* Helsinki: Helsinki University Print.
Halla-aho, H. (2010). Requesting in a letter: context, syntax and the choice between complements in the letters of Cicero and Pliny the Younger. *Transactions of the Philological Society*, *108* (3), 232–247.
Haverling, G. (1988). *Studies on Symmachus' language and style.* Göteborg: Acta universitatis Gothoburgensis.
Heine, B. (2002). On the role of context in grammaticalization. In I. Wischer & G. Diewald (Eds.), *New reflections on grammaticalization* (pp. 83–101). Amsterdam: John Benjamins.
Molinelli, P. (2010). From verbs to interactional discourse markers: the pragmaticalization of Latin *rogo*, *quaeso*. In G. Calboli & P. Cuzzolin (Eds.), *Papers on Grammar XI* (pp. 181–192). Roma: Herder.
Risselada, R. (1989). Latin illocutionary parentheticals. In M. Lavency & D. Longrée (Eds.), *Actes du cinquième Colloque de Linguistique Latine. Louvain-la-Neuve/Borzée, 31 mars – 4 avril 1989. [= Cahiers de l'Institut de Linguistique de Louvain 15]* (pp. 367–378). Louvain-la-Neuve.
Unceta Gómez, L. (2009a). *La petición verbal en latín: Estudio léxico, semántico y pragmático.* Madrid: Ediciones Clásicas.
Unceta Gómez, L. (2009b). Elementos parentéticos en la organización discursiva de la oratoria de Cicerón. In T. Arcos Pereira, J. Fernández López & F. Moya del Baño (Eds.), *'Pectora mulcet': Estudios de retórica y oratoria latinas* (pp. 247–258). Logroño: Instituto de Estudios Riojanos.
Unceta Gómez, L. (2019). Conceptualizations of linguistic politeness in Latin. The emic perspective. *Journal of Historical Pragmatics*, *20* (2), 286–312.
Unceta Gómez, L. & Berger, Ł. (2022). Im/politeness research in ancient Greek and Latin. Concepts, methods, data. In L. Unceta Gómez & Ł. Berger (Eds.), *Politeness in Ancient Greek and Latin* (pp. 3–41). Cambridge: Cambridge University Press.

Traducciones

Agustín (1986). *Obras completas de San Agustín VIII. Cartas I, 1–123.* L. Cilleruelo (Trad.). Madrid: Biblioteca de Autores Cristianos.

Agustín (1986). *Obras completas de San Agustín. XXX. Escritos antimaniqueos 1.* P. de Luis (Trad. y notas). Madrid: Biblioteca de Autores Cristianos.

Ovidio (2002). *Metamorfosis*. A. Pérez Vega (Trad.). Alicante: Biblioteca Virtual Miguel de Cervantes. https://www.cervantesvirtual.com/nd/ark:/59851/bmccz361 [Consulta: 10-4-2023]

Petronio (1978). *El Satiricón* de L. Rubio Fernández. (Introd., trad. y notas). Madrid: Gredos.

Plinio el Joven (2005). *Cartas*. J. González Fernández (Trad.). Madrid: Gredos.

Virgilio (1992). *Eneida*. Vicente Cristóbal (Introd.) & J. de Echave-Sustaeta (Trad. y notas). Madrid: Gredos.

Pascal Tonnaer

The Sequence [subject + verb *sum* + *aliquid/nihil* subject complement]: A Comparative Study while Analysing an Ovidian Textual Motif

Abstract: The sequence [subject + verb *sum* + *aliquid* subject complement] is found repeatedly in Ovid. It signifies the importance the speaker attributes to the subject of the sentence. We wanted to know if it was typically Ovidian and to compare it with the semantically opposite sequence [subject + verb *sum* + *nihil* subject complement]. First, we listed all the occurrences of the PHI corpus and compared them from different points of view: form (prose/verse), syntax (word order; complement of *nihil/aliquid*), grammar (subject category; verb tense/mode). We then divided the passages into five semantic categories: occurrences with complement of *nihil/aliquid* aiming at a determinative definition or at a qualifying definition, occurrences without complement of *nihil/aliquid* aiming either to signify the (non) existence of the subject or to depart two subjects or to express the speaker's evaluation of something. In conclusion, the main similarities between the two sequences are syntactical (mostly contiguous elements; preference for the form *est*). The differences are syntactical (different tendencies in word order: verb *sum* + *aliquid* >< *nihil* + verb *sum*) and frequential (wider representation of *nihil* in the corpus and over time). In poetry, 12 occurrences in which the form [*est aliquid*] enhances the subject regarding its advantage constitute an Ovidian Textual Motif of which we give a formal, semantic and functional definition.

Keywords: Textual Motif, *aliquid*, *nihil*, Ovid

1 Introduction

This paper addresses a sequence of words whose recurrence in the Ovidian corpus was first noticed by S. Green[1] and then by R. J. Littlewood,[2] the group of words [*est*

1 Green (2004: 224).
2 Littlewood (2006: 15).

Pascal Tonnaer, University of Liège, Belgium

https://doi.org/10.1515/9783111332956-037

aliquid] in which *aliquid* functions as subject complement,[3] which we can translate as *this is quite something*:

> ***Est aliquid*** *nupsisse Iovi, Iovis esse sororem* (Ov. fast. 6, 27)
> 'It is quite something to be the wife and sister of Jupiter.'[4]

The semantic function of the sequence is to express the importance attributed by the speaker to the subject group. Moreover, the elliptical character of the formulation leads the reader to deduce the semantic value of the indefinite pronoun *aliquid* by referring to its narrative context.

Given the recurrence of this formulation in Ovid, we asked ourselves the following questions: is this sequence typically Ovidian? Did other poets or prose writers use it before or after Ovid? Does it belong to one literary genre rather than another? Has its use changed over time? Can the sequence present morphosyntactic or semantic variants? Would it not be interesting to compare the use of [*est* + *aliquid* subject complement] with that of the sequence which constitutes a priori the semantic opposite, namely [*est* + *nihil* subject complement]?

2 Purpose and Methodology

Our purpose is twofold: on the one hand to know how original Ovid is or is not when he resorts to this formulation, on the other hand to carry out a comparative study of the two following sequences [subject + verb *sum* + *aliquid* subject complement] and [subject + verb *sum* + *nihil* subject complement].[5] To ensure a sufficiently varied sample of texts from the diachronic and generic points of view, we have circumscribed our research to the corpus available on the site of the Packard Humanities Institute (PHI) which includes the entire Latin literary corpus from the oldest attested texts up to the year 200 AD.

First of all, we made a systematic statement of all the occurrences in which the form *aliquid* or one of the following forms of *nihil* (*nihil*, *nil*, *nihilum*, *nihili*) grammatically functions as subject complement of the (non-auxiliary) verb *sum*. In the case of *nihil* (but sometimes also of *aliquid*), it happens that *sum* is missing,

3 We follow Pinkster (2015: 30) by using the term "subject complement" rather than "predicate".
4 All verse numbers are taken from the Classical Latin Texts database of the Packard Humanities Institute, https://latin.packhum.org/. All translations are ours.
5 To simplify reading, we now name the sequence [*sum nihil*] and [*sum aliquid*], where *sum* means any form of the verb.

so it was not possible to rely on lemmatised bases such as the LASLA[6] database nor on mining and textometric software such as Hyperbase (University Côte d'Azur, France). We therefore had to content ourselves with a search by form in the PHI by analysing each narrative context in order to rule out any occurrence where *nihil* or *aliquid* would be subject and not subject complement. We hope to have been as exhaustive as possible.

We classified all the occurrences in chronological order of the (sometimes presumed) dates of birth of the authors and according to five different criteria: the literary form (prose/verse); the mode and tense of *sum*; the word order and the degree of contiguity between *sum* and *aliquid/nihil*; the grammatical category of the subject; the absence or presence of complements of *aliquid/nihil*.

Finally, we drew up a typology of the different semantic functions performed by the sequence.

3 Results and Analyses

Among the entire PHI corpus, we found 209 occurrences of the sequence [*sum nihil*] and 55 occurrences of the sequence [*sum aliquid*].

Some passages contain the sequence twice: in this case, it happens that the verb or the subject complement is mentioned only once. For practical reasons, we then decided to count each (half) mention in these passages as one occurrence. Thus the 209 occurrences with *nihil* concern 204 passages and the 55 occurrences with *aliquid* concern 51 passages.

3.1 Literary Form (Prose/Verse)

3.1.1 *Nihil*

Concerning the occurrences with *nihil* (cf. Table 1), we can note that the sequence is well represented at all times (from Plautus to Apuleius), by many authors (34 in all) and in various genres (in prose: history, letters, treatises, novels, speeches; in verse: comedy, tragedy, epics, didactic poetry, erotic elegy, epigrams). Three authors are more represented than the others: Cicero and Seneca the Philosopher in the prose corpus, Plautus in the verse literary. However, it would be rash to draw statistical conclusions concerning the degree of originality of these three authors, first

6 Laboratory of Statistical Analysis of Ancient Languages, University of Liège, Belgium.

because the hazards of texts transmission do not allow us to have an exhaustive view of the ancient Latin corpus, then because many authors have not been as prolific as, for example, Cicero: it would be vain to compare statistically the immense Ciceronian corpus with the few Persius' satires. We must also be careful about the prose/verse distribution. There are more occurrences in prose (130) than in verse (79), but we do not know whether these proportions reflect reality in terms of statistics: we would need to know what the total number of words in the prose corpus and similarly in the verse corpus is, information that we personally do not have.

Table 1: Literary form.

	NIHIL				
	Authors	**Occ.**		**Authors**	**Occ.**
Prose	Varro	1	**Verse**	Plautus	29
	Cicero	57		Terentius	8
	Caesar	2		Lucillius	3
	Sallustius	1		Accius	1
	Livius	8		Varro	1
	Seneca R.	5		Lucretius	7
	Val. Max.	2		Horace	3
	Seneca P.	16		Tibullus	1
	Celsius	5		Propertius	3
	Pliny Eld.	5		Ovid	3
	Petronius	7		Phaedrus	1
	Curtius	3		Manilius	1
	Quintilian	2		Seneca P.	1
	Ps.-Quint.	9		Persius	2
	Suetonius	2		Lucan	2
	Fronto	1		Statius	1
	Aul. Gell.	1		Martial	10
	Apuleius	3		Juvenal	2
		130			79
		TOTAL : 209			

Table 1 (continued)

	ALIQUID				
	Authors	**Occ.**		**Authors**	**Occ.**
Prose	Cicero	11	**Verse**	Lucretius	2
	Seneca P.	8		Catullus	1
	Quintilian	1		Propertius	1
	Ps.-Quint.	7		Ovid	17
	Pliny Young	1		Juvenal	2
	Fronto	1		*Bucolica*	1
	Ulpian (just. code)	2		*Einsiedlensia*	
		31			24
		TOTAL : 55			

3.1.2 *Aliquid*

Concerning the occurrences including *aliquid*, the sequence is less well represented in time (from Cicero and up to Juvenal only) and fewer authors are involved (13 in total), so the variety of literary genres concerned is more limited (history and theatrical works especially are not represented). In prose, three authors are more represented: Cicero and Seneca the Philosopher again, but also the Pseudo-Quintilian; in verse, Ovid totals 17 occurrences out of 24. It should be noted that the distribution between prose and verse is quite different here than for the sequence with *nihil*. Indeed, the gap here is smaller: 31 occurrences in prose, 24 occurrences in verse. At this point, it would be rash to draw statistical conclusions from the point of view of the literary genre given the over-representation of Ovid within the poetic corpus. At first sight, it seems that an author's particularity here comes into play rather than a trait specific to a literary genre.

3.2 Mode and Tense of the Verb *sum*

For this criterion, we leave it to the reader to analyse the results in detail (cf. Table 2). We content ourselves with underlining the overwhelming majority of indicative present forms for both *nihil* and *aliquid*, in prose as well as in verse. As we will see below, when we discuss semantic functions, the sequence [*sum nihil*/*aliquid*] is most often used to give a definition or express an opinion. The sequence therefore most often constitutes assertions appearing in direct speech, which explains the massive use of the present indicative.

Table 2: Mode and tense of the verb *sum*.

				NIHIL			
Mode	**Occ.**	**Pr.**	**Ve.**				
Indic.	130	70	60		**Occ.**	**Pr.**	**Ve.**
				present	115	58	57
				imperf.	3	3	0
				future	4	1	3
				perfect	8	8	0
Subj.	25	17	8		**Occ.**	**Pr.**	**Ve.**
				present	17	11	6
				imperf.	3	3	0
				perfect	3	2	1
				pluperf.	2	1	1
Infinit.	54	43	11		**Occ.**	**Pr.**	**Ve.**
				present	50	39	11
				future	3	3	0
				perfect	1	1	0

				ALIQUID			
Mode	**Occ.**	**Pr.**	**Ve.**				
Indic.	35	15	20		**Occ.**	**Pr.**	**Ve.**
				present	33	13	20
				future	1	1	0
				perfect	1	1	0
Subj.	6	6	0		**Occ.**	**Pr.**	**Ve.**
				present	5	5	0
				imperf.	1	1	0
Infinit.	14	10	4		**Occ.**	**Pr.**	**Ve.**
				present	13	9	4
				future	1	1	0

3.3 Word Order and Degree of Contiguity in the Sentence

We leave it again to the reader to analyse the results in detail (cf. Table 3). Whether in prose or in verse, whether with *nihil* or *aliquid*, the contiguity between verb and subject complement is by far the most used option (*nihil*: 110/209 occurrences; *aliquid*: 41/55). When there is no contiguity, preference is given to the smallest spacing, a single intercalated word (43/209 for *nihil*). It therefore seems that this sequence constitutes a semi-frozen segment as its core presents a certain stability of vocabulary combined with a tendency towards contiguity and as it is flexible enough to adapt to different contexts by using different verb tenses and moods and sometimes dissociating its basic elements.

Table 3: Word order and contiguity.

NIHIL					
Word order	**Occ.**	**Pr.**	**Ve.**		
SVM + nihil	18	9	9	**Spacing**	**Occ.**
				SVM nihil	9
				SVM 1 nihil	2
				SVM 2 nihil	7
nihil + SVM	169	110	59		
				nihil SVM	101
				nihil 1 SVM	41
				nihil 2 SVM	12
				nihil 3 SVM	5
				nihil 4 SVM	4
				nihil 5 SVM	3
				nihil 6 SVM	1
				nihil 7 SVM	2
(SVM) + nihil + (SVM)	22	11	11		

ALIQUID					
Word order	**Occ.**	**Pr.**	**Ve.**		
SVM + aliquid	41	18	23	**Spacing**	**Occ.**
				SVM aliquid	34
				SVM 1 aliquid	4
				SVM 2 aliquid	2
				SVM 3 aliquid	1

Table 3 (continued)

	ALIQUID				
Word order	**Occ.**	**Pr.**	**Ve.**		
aliquid + SVM	11	10	1		
				aliquid SVM	7
				aliquid 1 SVM	3
				aliquid 2 SVM	1
				aliquid 3 SVM	1
(SVM) + aliquid + (SVM)	3	3	0		

However, there is an important difference between [*sum nihil*] and [*sum aliquid*]: 169 occurrences out of 209 have *nihil* before the verb, while 41 occurrences out of 55 have *aliquid* after the verb. This difference does not seem to arise from linguistic criteria, rather from metrical constraints inherent in verse writing. Indeed, let us recall that out of 55 occurrences with *aliquid*, 24 occurrences relate to poetry, of which 17 occurrences are found in Ovid. *Aliquid* is a tribrach, that is to say a word composed of three short syllables. Tribrach is forbidden in classical Latin hexameter and pentameter, yet these are the only two meters that Ovid uses. For *aliquid* to fit into an Ovidian verse, one of its syllables must become long by position. Insofar as the use of the present indicative of the 3rd person singular (*est*) is predominant (15 out of 17 occurrences in Ovid) and insofar as, for whatever reason, contiguity takes precedence (and this is the case in 16 Ovidian passages), the poet had no choice but to place *est* before *aliquid.* This inclination to place *aliquid* after the verb cannot therefore be seriously compared to the placement of *nihil* in the sentence, which itself consists of only two short syllables and adapts all the better to the multiple metrical requirements that it can become a long monosyllabic by contraction (*nīl*).

3.4 Grammatical Category of the Subject

3.4.1 *Nihil*

The grammatical categories of the subject are varied (cf. Table 4). In the case of *nihil*, substantives are the most numerous (68/209). Next come the pronouns (58/209) then the "non lexical subjects" by this term we mean the occurrences in which the subject is indicated by the verb ending (45/209). Infinitive groups come in penultimate place (20/209) followed by conjugated subordinate clauses (18/209).

Table 4: Grammatical category of the subject.

NIHIL					
Subject	**Occ.**	**Pr.**	**Ve.**		
Substantive (gr.)	68	52	16		
Pronoun	58	33	25	**Type**	**Occ.**
				Demonstr.	31
				Pers./Refl.	15
				Relative	12
Non-lexicalised	45	19	26		
Infinitive (gr.)	20	16	4		
Conjugated subordinate cl.	18	10	8		

ALIQUID					
Subject	**Occ.**	**Pr.**	**Ve.**		
Infinitive (gr.)	19	4	15		
Substantive (gr.)	16	12	4		
Pronoun	11	9	2	**Type**	**Occ.**
				Demonstr.	5
				Pers./Refl.	5
				Relative	1
Non-lexicalised	7	5	2		
Conjugated subordinate cl.	2	1	1		

3.4.2 *Aliquid*

For *aliquid*, the results are quite different: the infinitive groups are prominent in number (19/55) and in competition with nouns (16/55), less with pronouns (11/55). However, of these 19 occurrences of infinitive, 15 are found in poetry and only 4 in prose. Here again, we must keep in mind that Ovid himself represents 17 out of 24 occurrences in verse and that 14 of these 17 occurrences have precisely infinitive groups for subject. This prominence of infinitive groups subjects is more a specificity of the author than of language or literary genre.

3.5 Complement of *nihil*/*aliquid*

3.5.1 *Nihil*

At first sight, the occurrences with complement of *nihil* (105) and those with no complement (104) are evenly distributed (cf. Table 5). However, most occurrences with no complement are found in verse literature: 64 occurrences in verse against 40 in prose. This result is surprising because verse literature is minority represented in the set of all occurrences. As a result, the overwhelming majority of occurrences with complement of *nihil* are found in prose: 90 occurrences against only 15 in verse. In this majority, the complement of *nihil* is 73 times a determinative one and 32 times a qualifying one. These two functions contribute to definitions, which are found above all in philosophical dialogues, treatises, letters and speeches, all genres usually relating to prose. This is the reason why it is therefore little valued in verse.

Table 5: Complement of *aliquid*/*nihil* and semantic function.

			NIHIL				
	Occ.	**Semantic function**	**Occ.**	**Pr.**	**Ve.**		
with complement	105	determinative definition	73	63	10		**Occ.**
						(aliud) quam	37
						(aliud) nisi	30
						aliud	1
						praeter	1
						partitive pronoun	4
		qualifying definition	32	27	5		**Occ.**
						Acc. qual./quant.	4
						negotii	12
						tanti	4
						other Gen. qual.	12

Table 5 (continued)

NIHIL							
	Occ.	**Semantic function**	**Occ.**	**Pr.**	**Ve.**		
no complement	104	non-existence	15	8	7		
		devaluate estimation	89	32	57		
						moral condemnation	18
						disesteem	8
						devaluation result	6
						devaluation advantage	4
						devaluation consequences	21
						devaluation capacity	5
						measurable quantification	2
						non-measurable quantific.	7
						absence of implication	4
						lack of relevance	8
						aporia or unavailability	1
						unavailability	2
dubious interpret.	3						

ALIQUID							
	Occ.	**Semantic function**	**Occ.**	**Pr.**	**Ve.**		
with complement	9	determinative definition	1	1	0		**Occ.**
						plus quam	1
		qualifying definition	8	5	3		**Occ.**
						Acc. qual.	6
						Gen. qual.	1
						prepos. group	1
no complement	46	existence	4	2	2		
		to depart two subjects	5	5	0		
		valuate estimation	37	18	19		
						moral praise	1
						esteem	9
						enhancement advantage	23
						enhancement capacity	4

3.5.2 *Aliquid*

We found 46 occurrences of *aliquid* without complement. Of the remaining 9 occurrences with complement, determinative function is found only once. We think there are two reasons for this. First, we saw in the previous paragraph that the determinative and qualifying complements, so frequent with *nihil*, mainly belong to the domain of prose. Precisely, the formulation with *aliquid* is more represented in poetry than in prose. Secondly, the term *aliquid* is by nature more allusive than *nihil*: while *nihil* quantifies a zero quantity, *aliquid* quantifies approximately something particular.[7] In consequence *aliquid* is less able to express (determinative or qualifying) definitions.

3.6 Typology of Semantic Functions: Five Possibilities

The presence or absence of a complement of *nihil*/*aliquid* is closely linked to the semantic function of the sequence. We distinguish five categories of semantic functions for the sequence [*sum nihil*/*aliquid*] (cf. Table 5 for figures; cf. Table 6 for references): two of them with complement of *nihil*/*aliquid* and three with no complement.

Table 6: References.

	NIHIL
Determinative definition	*nihil (aliud) quam*: Cels. 3, 19, 1; 4, 3, 1; Cic. de orat. 1, 204; epist. frg. 6, 3; Cvrt. 5, 1, 6; 7, 1, 16; 8, 12, 18; Liv. 2, 49, 9; 2, 54, 4; 5, 17, 2; 22, 22, 7; 30, 12, 15; Petron. 42, 5; Plin. nat. 11, 192; 16, 39; 16, 61; 33, 86; 37, 164; Qvint. inst. 3, 8, 34; Ps. Qvint. decl. ma. 5, 13; 6, 13; 17, 2; decl. mi. 263, 6; 269, 4; Sen. contr. 10, 1, 7 (2x); Sen. benef. 4, 7, 2; clem. 2, 4, 1; dial. 3, 10, 4; 11, 11, 2; epist. 66, 12; 83, 18; 87, 32; 102, 14; 113, 2; Svet. Claud. 35, 1; Val. Max. 5, 6, 7.
	nihil (aliud) nisi: Cels. 3, 18, 6; 6, 5, 1; 8, 1, 15; Cic. de orat. 2, 52; fam. 9, 22, 3; fin. 1, 54; 4, 27; 4, 46; inv. 2, 130; Lael. 20; 100; leg. 1, 25; nat. deor. 1, 28; 3, 36; parad. 1, 15; part. 79; Phil. 11, 28; p. red. in sen. 30; orat. 101; 227; Tusc. 1, 57; 1, 59; Ivv. 8, 52–53; Lvcr. 1, 516–517; 4, 368; Manil. 2, 37; Ov. met. 9, 493–494; Pont. 3, 1, 148; Petron. 14, 2; Ter. Ad. 394.
	nihil aliud: Sen. suas. 2, 19.
	nihil praeter: Cic. fin. 4, 28.
	nihil + partitive pronoun: Mart. 2, 28, 5; 3, 72, 7; 9, 22, 15; Ps. Qvint. decl. mi. 377, 7.

7 See Touratier (1994: 55–56, 62–63).

Table 6 (continued)

	NIHIL		
Qualifying definition	*nihil* + Acc. quant./qual.: CIC. leg. agr. 2, 37; PETRON. 4, 3; PLAVT. Truc. 305; SEN. suas. 1, 2.		
	nihil negoti: CAES. civ. 1, 66, 4; Gall. 5, 38, 4; CIC. Att. 6, 1, 10; 10, 13, 3; 12, 14, 1; 12, 21, 2; de orat. 2, 100; fam. 12, 2, 1; fin. 2, 54; Mil. 45; Tusc. 1, 16 (2x).		
	nihil tanti: HOR. ars 303–304; Ps. QVINT. decl. mi. 355, 5; SEN. contr. 7, 3, 10; SEN. benef. 2, 5, 2.		
	nihil + various G.: CIC. Att. 6, 9, 1; S. Rosc. 90, 8; Tusc. 3, 77; LIV. 4, 17, 7; 7, 26, 15; 10, 13, 9; FRONTO de *or.* 1, 3; LVCIL. 765; 489; PETRON.76, 5; SEN. benef. 6, 31, 2; TER. Andr. 350.		
To postulate non-existence	CIC. Tusc. 1, 21; 1, 24; ac. 2, 36; LVCAN. 3, 39–40; LVCR. 3, 926–927; MART. 12, 48, 5–6; OV. met. 7, 830; PETRON. 41, 10; 48, 6; PROP. 2, 34, 19; SEN. dial. 6, 19, 5; epist. 117, 28; Tro. 397; SVET. Iul. 77, 1; TER. Andr. 314.		
Devaluate estimation	Value judgement	Moral condemnation	CIC. Deiot. 21; ad Q. fr. 1, 2, 14; GELL. 2, 14, 3; HOR. sat. 2, 7, 102; PLAVT. Asin. 858–859; Bacch. 91; 1157; 1162; 1207; Cas. 119; Cist. 238 (2x); Men. 972; Most. 156; Pseud. 239; 1104; Rud. 920; Truc. 553.
		Disesteem	CIC. Sest. 114; Tusc. 4, 74; LVCAN. 9, 568; MART. 14, 193, 2; PERS. 1, 27; PROP. 3, 3, 41–42; STAT. Theb. 11, 467; TIB. 1, 5, 30.
	Pragmatic devaluation	Result	CIC. Att. 3, 18, 1; Verr. II 1, 88; PLAVT. Capt. 344; Cas. 286; Poen. 914; PROP. 4, 1b, 141–142.
		Advantage	CIC. div. 2, 24; IVV. 3, 84–85; MART. 4, 5, 9–10; PLAVT. Truc. 769.
		Consequences	ACC. trag. 371; CIC. Att. 6, 3, 9; 13, 20, 4; fam. 3, 8, 2 (2x); LVCIL. 844; MART. 9, 41, 3; 13, 2, 9–10; 13, 2, 7–8; PERS. 3, 94; PHAEDR. 3, 7, 17; PLAVT. Bacch. 92; Merc. 542; Stich. 294; SEN. dial. 2, 16, 2; epist. 78, 13; TER. Andr. 340; Eun. 638; Haut. 900; Phorm. 994–995; VAL. MAX. 4, 7, 2.
		Capacity	CIC. div. in Caec. 47 (2x); fam. 7, 27, 2; 7, 33, 1; PLAVT. Epid. 95.
	Quantity estimation	Measurable quantification	HOR. sat. 2, 3, 115–117; PLAVT. Most. 981–982.
		Non-measurable quantification	LVCR. 6, 677–679; MART. 3, 61, 1; PETRON. 34, 10; PLAVT. Mil. 19 (2x); Truc. 850–851; SEN. epist. 101, 1.
	Non-validity	Absence of implication	LVCR. 3, 830; 3, 843–846; 3, 972–973; SALL. Iug. 24, 6.
		Lack of relevance	APVL. apol. 23; 67; 42; CIC. Caecin. 96; Phil. 2, 84; PLAVT. Curc. 634; Ps. QVINT. decl. mi. 276, 3; TER. Phorm. 1000.
		Aporia (or unavailibility)	VARRO ling. 8, fr. 1.
		Unavailibility	Ps. QVINT. decl. ma. 9, 15; QVINT. inst. 2, 19, 3.

Table 6 (continued)

NIHIL			
Passages non retained	Dubious interpretation: fragmentary text/restitution		CIC. Att. 2, 1, 5; PLAVT. Asin. 203; VARRO Men. 201.
	Others	*nihil* alone = answer to the question *Quid est?*	TER. Ad. 652–653; Andr. 449.
		non/haud nihil est = est aliquid	MART. 7, 88, 9–10; 12, 74, 9–10; QVINT. inst. 9, 4, 97; TER. Eun. 640–641.
		minus nihilo	PLAVT. Pseud. 937.
		plus quam nihil = est aliquid	OV. epist. 19, 170.

ALIQUID			
Determinative definition			PS. QVINT. decl. ma. 10, 2.
Qualifying definition			BVC. Eins. 2, 7; CIC. Mur. 23; LVCR. 6, 710; OV. met. 7, 12–13; PS. QVINT. decl. mi. 305, 10 (2x); 315, 6; SEN. epist. 26, 4.
To postulate existence			LVCR. 1, 433; CIC. fin. 2, 86; PROP. 4, 7, 1; SEN. dial. 6, 19, 5.
To depart two subjects			SEN. epist. 58, 8 (2x); 92, 21; VLP. in COD. Iust. 32, 55 pr. 1 (2x).
Valuate estimation	Value judgement	Moral praise	CIC. Tusc. 5, 104.
		Esteem	CATVLL. 1, 3–4; CIC. div. in Caec. 48; 49; fam. 6, 18, 4; FRONTO ad M. Caes. et inv. 3, 18, 2; IVV. 1, 73–74; OV. met. 13, 241–242; PLIN. 1, 23, 2; QVINT. inst. 1 prooem. 20.
	Pragmatic evaluation	Enhancement advantage	Absolute: CIC. orat. 2, 59–60; IVV. 3, 230–231; OV. epist. 3, 131–132; 4, 29–31; 11, 11; fast. 1, 484; 6, 27; met. 12, 93–94; Pont. 2, 7, 65; 2, 8, 9–10; 2, 10, 39–42; 3, 4, 18; rem. 479–480; trist. 1, 2, 53–56; 5, 1, 59; PS. QVINT. decl. mi. 336, 14 (2x); SEN. epist. 22, 4. Relative: CIC. Att. 3, 15, 5; div. in Caec. 47; Cato 8; SEN. benef. 2, 32, 1; 4, 36, 2.
		Enhancement capacity	CIC. Att. 4, 2, 2; OV. am. 1, 12, 3–4; met. 6, 1, 542–543; PS. QVINT. decl. ma. 348, 6.

3.6.1 Determinative Definition

First of all, the sequence can be a determinative definition requiring a complement of *nihil/aliquid*. In this case, the sequence consists of an identity statement. Formulations with *nihil* and *aliquid* are not semantically opposed:

> *Ita **nihil est** aliud discere nisi recordari.* (CIC. Tusc. 1, 59)
> 'So learning is nothing but memorising.'

> *Infelicissima omnium mater plus **aliquid esse** quam umbram filium putat, postquam potuit includi.* (PS. QVINT. decl. 10, 2)
> 'The unhappiest of mothers believes that her son, once buried, is more than a shadow.'

This case represents 73 of the 209 occurrences with *nihil*: it is a high score. The definition is somewhat exclusive, and the complement of *nihil* is most often [(*aliud*) *quam/nisi*]. On the contrary, only one occurrence containing *aliquid* falls under this use: in this case the definition is not exclusive but very allusive.

3.6.2 Qualifying Definition

The second semantic function consists of a definition of the subject from a qualitative point of view. In this case too, *nihil/aliquid* needs to be completed with a complement. Here too, the formulations with *nihil* and *aliquid* are not semantically opposed:

> ***Nihil est** negoti eius modi causam cognoscere.* (CIC. de orat. 2, 100)
> 'It is not a great deal to study this type of affair.'

> *. . . non quia **aliquid** mali ictus **est**.* (SEN. epist. 26, 4)
> '. . . not that a hit can be anything wrong.'

From a statistical point of view, *nihil* and *aliquid* are similar: each of them represents approximately 15% of the total of occurrences. Note however that there is a difference between them: the qualifying function is less well represented than the determinative one in the corpus with *nihil* whereas it is quite the opposite in the corpus with *aliquid*.

3.6.3 To Postulate Existence or Non-existence

The third semantic function does not require any complement of *nihil/aliquid*. *Nihil est* means the absolute non-existence of something while *est aliquid* means that a thing exists, that it consists of at least something, whatever it may be. In this case, the two sequences are semantically opposed:[8]

> *Quomodo, oro te, quod adhuc* ***nihil est****, iam bonum est?* (SEN. epist. 117, 28)
> 'I ask you, how can what does not yet exist already be good?'

> *Nam quodcumque erit,* ***esse aliquid*** *debebit id ipsum.* (LVCR. 1, 433)
> 'In fact, whatever it is, it will have to be something.'

This semantic function is statistically not well represented with *aliquid* (4/55 occurrences) nor with *nihil* (15/209 occurrences).

3.6.4 To Depart Two Subjects

The fourth semantic function does not require any complement of *nihil/aliquid*. It is only represented by the sequence with *aliquid* and consists of distinguishing two things one from each other:

> *Omnes tibi exponam si ante indicavero* ***esse aliquid*** *genus,* ***esse*** *et speciem.* (SEN. epist. 58, 8)
> 'I will explain them all to you first if I show you that genus is one thing and species is another.'

This function is very little represented in the corpus: there are only three passages. Due to the presence of two subjects, the repetition of either the predicate or the verb is necessary. As said previously (see introduction to Section 3), we decided to count as one occurrence each mention of *aliquid* or of *sum*. So, we count the previous example as two occurrences of the sequence, each of which contributes solidarily to this semantic function. This type of duplication is very rare in the corpus.

8 We link this opposition to that made by Orlandini (2001: 39–40) even if the context analysed by the author refers to virtual sentences which is never the case here: "[. . .] *aliquid*, toujours souligné par un effet d'emphase, peut aussi être opposé à l'autre pôle de l'échelle, le pôle négatif: *nihil* ('le néant'); *aliquis, aliquid* exprime ainsi l'interprétation argumentative: 'au moins un/une chose', opposée à 'personne'/'rien du tout'."

3.6.5 To Give a (De)valuate Estimation

The last possibility results in giving an estimation of the subject. Either the estimation is rewarding (with *aliquid*), or devaluing (with *nihil*). This semantic function does not require any complement of *nihil/aliquid*. The two sequences are here again semantically opposed:

> ***Nil*** *tibi* ***sit*** *rauco praeconia classica cornu / flare.* (PROP. 3, 3, 41–42)
> 'May the resounding calls of the harsh trumpets of war be nothing to you.'

> ***Est aliquid*** *nupsisse Iovi, Iovis esse sororem.* (OV. fast. 6, 27)
> 'It is quite something to be the wife and sister of Jupiter.'

This kind of situation represents 89 of the 209 occurrences with *nihil* and 37 of the 55 occurrences with *aliquid*.

In conclusion for this point, we can see that most of the occurrences with *nihil* (162/209) are distributed between determinative definition and valuing estimation; for *aliquid*, only the valuing estimation is statistically prominent (37/55 occurrences).

3.7 Sub-categories of (De)valuation

We now will explore more precisely the last of the five semantic functions defined above (to give a (de)valuate estimation), first because it is the only one we can subdivide into different sub-categories according to the contexts of elocution, so making its use more varied, then because most of the Ovidian passages (16 out of 17) come under this category. We thus distinguish 11 semantic sub-functions of (de) valuate estimation which all work with *nihil* but of which only 4 work with *aliquid*. In these cases, *aliquid* as opposed to *nihil* underlines the importance of the subject, whatever small this importance may be.

3.7.1 Value Judgement

Firstly, the speaker may express, without any pragmatic aim, a value judgement from the angle of either morality or esteem.

(a) **Moral condemnation:** the speaker claims to find someone or something vile, bad, low or boorish. This situation works very often with the form *nihili* relating to a subject–human being and it constitutes 14 of the 29 occurrences in Plautus:

> ***Nihilist** autem suom qui officium facere immemor est.* (PLAVT. Pseud. 1104)
> 'He who forgets to do his duty is a good-for-nothing.'

Moral praise: on the contrary, the speaker finds someone good or virtuous. A single example is found, in Cicero:

> *An quicquam stultius quam quos singulos sicut operarios barbarosque contemnas, eos **aliquid** putare **esse** universos ?* (CIC. Tusc. 5, 104)
> 'Is there anything more stupid: to believe that those we despise individually because they are rough and uneducated, can acquire some value when they are considered together?'

(b) **Disesteem:** the speaker expresses the lack of interest or prestige accorded to someone or something:

> ***Nil** tibi **sit** rauco praeconia classica cornu / flare* (PROP. 3, 3, 41–42)
> 'May the resounding calls of the harsh trumpets of war be nothing to you.'

Esteem: the speaker expresses the interest granted to someone or something:

> *Namque tu solebas / meas **esse aliquid** putare nugas.* (CATVLL. 1, 3–4)
> 'Because you always said that for you my little trifles were something.'

3.7.2 Pragmatic Evaluation

In some cases the speaker considers the subject from a pragmatic angle: what is envisaged is the absence (*nihil est*) or the presence (*est aliquid*) of potential attributed to the subject. We count four different points of view depending on whether the evaluation criterion relates to the result, the advantage, the consequences, or the capacity of the subject.

(c) **Devaluation as to the result:** it is a question of saying that an action or an intention is not sufficient to achieve its goal:

Sed ***nihil est*** *me cupere factum nisi tu factis adiuvas.* (PLAVT. Cas. 286)
'But my wish is hopeless if you do not help me.'

The opposite, namely an enhancement as to the result, does not exist with *aliquid.*

(d) **Devaluation as to an advantage:** the speaker envisages the absence of advantage to be derived from a fact or a thing. Contrary to the previous point, no notion of goal is to be inferred from the subject:

Usque adeo nihil est quod nostra infantia caelum
hausit Aventini baca nutrita Sabina? (IVV. 3, 84–85)
'Is it then so useless that our childhood was filled with the Aventine sky and fed on Sabine olives?'

In this passage Juvenal complains that foreigners are better off than him.

Enhancement of an advantage:

Est aliquid *nupsisse Iovi, Iovis esse sororem.* (OV. fast. 6, 27)
'It is quite something to be the wife and sister of Jupiter.'

Juno here explains why a month is named after her.

(e) **Devaluation as to consequences:** the speaker says that there are no serious consequences to the action he is talking about, that it does not matter:

Cui Alexander, ***nihil est****, inquit, quod hoc nomine confundaris: nam et hic Alexander est.* (VAL. MAX. 4, 7, 2)
'It does not matter if you confused us by name, said Alexander, because he too is an Alexander.'

The opposite, namely an enhancement as to consequences, does not exist with *aliquid.*

(f) **Devaluation in terms of capacity:** the sequence signifies how little power someone has to influence an act, a situation:

Esto, ipse ***nihil est****, nihil potest.* (CIC. div. in Caec. 47)
'So be it, he himself is nothing, he cannot do anything.'

Enhancement in terms of capacity: it is the opposite situation:

> *Et si umquam in dicendo* ***fuimus aliquid.*** (Cic. Att. 4, 2, 2)
> 'And if ever in the art of pleading we were something.'

In this passage, Cicero suggests that he was competent in the causes he defended.

3.7.3 Quantity Estimation

The speaker evaluates the subject in terms of quantity. Only occurrences with *nihil* are attested.

(g) **Measurable quantification**: the subject can be estimated in numbers. It means then that the quantity is too small:

> *Positis intus Chii veterisque Falerni*
> *mille cadis,* ***nihil est****, tercentum milibus. . .* (Hor. sat. 2, 3, 115–116)
> 'Stored inside, a thousand jars – this is nothing – three hundred thousand jars of wine from Chios or old wine from Falerne. . .'

(h) **Non-measurable quantification:** the subject cannot be estimated in figures. In this case, the speaker wants to express, apart from any moral or pragmatic consideration, how little the subject consists of:

> ***Esse nihil*** *dicis quidquid petis, improbe Cinna.* (Mart. 3, 61, 1)
> 'Cinna, you cheeky man, you say that what you ask of me is nothing.'

In other words, Cinna pretends that what he asks will require little effort from Martial.

3.7.4 Non-validity

We group under this last category 3 semantic functions clearly different from each other but whose common denominator seems to be incongruity. This incongruity is always expressed by [*sum nihil*], never [*sum aliquid*]: it expresses either the lack of involvement of the enunciator with respect to the subject of the sentence, or the lack of relevance of the subject with regard to the situation of enunciation, or an aporia, a nonsense.

(i) **Absence of implication:** the speaker pretends that the subject in question has nothing to do with him. In the following example, Lucretius speaks of our relationship to death when we ourselves are dead:

> ***Nil*** *igitur mors* ***est*** *ad nos neque pertinet hilum.* (LVCR. 3, 830)
> 'Death is nothing to us, it does not concern us in the least.'

We found four occurrences only, of which three are in Lucretius and another one in Sallust. This formulation, which requires [*ad* + accusative], is more often competed by [*nihil pertinet ad* + acc.].

(j) **Lack of relevance:** the intention of the speaker is to point out the irrelevance, the inadequacy of a statement (argument, example given or proposition) in relation to the context to which this statement relates:

> *Scierunt et ipsi argumentum piscarium futile et* ***nihil futurum****.* (APVL. apol. 42)
> 'They themselves were understanding that the fish argument was futile and would lead nowhere.'

This example shows that the distinction can be tenuous between the semantic functions "lack of relevance" and "devaluation as to the result". In fact, sense of irrelevance comes into play about declarations and with the aim of making known the lack of legitimacy of those declarations. The formulation [*nihil est*] is then in competition with [*nihil valet*]. As for sense of no result, it occurs in the case of actions and in order to underline their insufficiency to achieve a goal.

(k) **Aporia:** the speaker underlines a nonsense, he says of a thing that it is not valid, not from the point of view of legitimacy, but of absurdity:

> Sentior *nemo dicit et id per se* ***nihil*** *est,* adsentior *tamen fere omnes dicunt.* (VARRO ling. 8, fr. 1)
> 'Nobody says *sentior* and in itself this word means nothing, while everyone says *adsentior*.'

However, we can wonder if Varro does not mean more precisely that *sentior* without a prefix is out of use. In this case, rather than nonsense, Varro underlines an insufficiency: *sentior* alone is not sufficient to mean anything and requires the prefix *ad*-. Moreover, we can relate Varro's sentence to the following passage:

> *Nec ignoro, iudices, quam male ista defensio de humano genere mereatur, si adeo nihil est per se misericordia* [. . .] (Ps. QVINT. decl. 9, 15)
> 'And I am well aware, judges, how ungrateful this defense would be to the human race, if pity in itself were so nothing at all that [. . .]'

Indeed, the adjunction of the terms *per se* to the verb possibly allows us to rather group these two passages under the notion of non-efficiency or unavailability. We can even add the following passage:

> *Nihil ars sine materia, materiae etiam sine arte pretium est.* (QVINT. inst. 2, 19, 3)
> 'Art without matter (on which to practice) is nothing, while matter itself even without art has value.'

In other words, *nihil (est) ars sine materia* could be replaced by *ars nihil (est) per se.*

4 Conclusion

As a reminder, we pursued two objectives in this study: on the one hand to establish a morphosyntactic and semantic comparison between the sequences [*sum* + *aliquid* subject complement] and [*sum* + *nihil* subject complement], on the other hand to determine if Ovid demonstrated originality in the use he made of [*sum* + *aliquid* subject complement].

4.1 Comparison Between the Two Sequences

There are convergent and divergent tendencies in the use of the two sequences. The first strong convergence is the massive use of the present indicative and even the predominance of the form *est*. The explanation is that the majority of occurrences occur within the framework of a definition to be given or an opinion to be expressed. In both cases, these are mainly peremptory assertions which are therefore more often found in the context of direct speech. One second convergence consists of a clear preference for the contiguity between the verb and the subject complement or, in the case of non-contiguity, for a close proximity of the two terms. We can assume pragmatic reasons for this: better understanding of the sequence, stylistic effect aimed at making the definition or opinion impressive, metrical constraints inherent in verse literature.

On the other hand, the word order presents two striking divergences. First, most of the cases with *nihil* have the order [subject complement + verb], while most of the cases with *aliquid* have the reverse order. In fact, for the form [*est aliquid*], very present in poetry and over-represented in Ovid, metrical constraints come into play. This choice of word order is therefore due both to the versified form and to stylistic choices.

Another striking divergence between the two sequences lies in their representation within the corpus. The sequence [*sum nihil*] is better represented in time (from Plautus until Apuleius) and in the different literary genres both in prose and in verse. The sequence [*sum aliquid*] is distributed among a minority of authors (from Cicero to Juvenal), and in a lesser variety of genres (mainly in the absence of history and plays). The explanation seems to be the following one: *aliquid* and *nihil* are said indefinite pronouns but there is a difference of degree in the quantification assumed by each other. More restrictive than *aliquid*, *nihil* expresses an absolute negation. To use *nihil* therefore proves to be a very economical way to define something by exclusion (*nihil est aliud quam*). Precisely, out of 209 occurrences of [*sum nihil*], 73 are determinative definitions whereas there is only one occurrence with [*sum aliquid*]. This fact is the first reason why [*sum nihil*] is more represented in the corpus. Furthermore, the very marked sense of exclusion implied in the term *nihil* makes the sequence [*sum nihil*] very suitable for a greater variety of narrative contexts. This is what emerges from the study of the semantic sub-functions relating to (de)valuate estimations: out of 11 possibilities of meaning, all are assumed by [*sum nihil*], while only four of them provide examples of an opposite semantic formulation with [*sum aliquid*]. Precisely 37 occurrences out of 55 with *aliquid* include these four semantic sub-functions. This smaller variety of semantic functions assumed by [*sum aliquid*] constitutes the second important factor to explain the better representation of [*sum nihil*] in the studied corpus.

4.2 Ovid's Originality

To conclude this study, we would like to show Ovid's originality in the use he makes of the sequence [*sum aliquid*]. First of all, out of 17 Ovidian occurrences, only one consists of a qualifying definition, while the 16 others consist of an enhancement of the subject of which two are pragmatic estimations as to the capacity of the subject and only one corresponds to a praise of esteem. The remaining 13 occurrences (the majority of Ovid occurrences therefore) are pragmatic estimations stressing the advantage to be drawn from the subject. Within the entire corpus studied, 23 occurrences out of 55 fall under this semantic function: Ovid therefore represents more than half of the estimations as to the advantage (Ovid 13, Cicero 4, Seneca 3, Pseudo-Quintilian 2, Juvenal 1). Moreover, a distinction must be made among these 23 occurrences between *relative* and "absolute enhancement". We mean by relative enhancement the case in which the speaker uses the sequence [*sum aliquid*] to emphasise the importance of the subject but immediately depreciating it in favour of a second subject whose importance is greater in his opinion:

> ***Est aliquid*** *in eo quod promiseris perseverare,* ***est rursus multum*** *in eo, ne indigno beneficium des.* (SEN. benef. 4, 36, 2)
> 'It is quite something to keep a promise, but more important is not to attribute some benefit to who is not worthy of it.'

We mean by absolute enhancement any situation where the subject to which *aliquid* relates is the only subject of the sentence and whose importance is not relativised in any way by the speaker:

> ***Est aliquid*** *spectare deos et adesse putare*
> *et quasi cum vero numine posse loqui.* (Ov. Pont. 2, 8, 9–10)
> 'It is quite something to contemplate gods and to think that they are present and to be able almost to talk with a real divinity.'

Out of 23 occurrences of enhancement as to the advantage, 5 of them are relative enhancements: 3 in Cicero, 2 in Seneca. This means that the sequence [*sum aliquid*] that semantically functions as an absolute enhancement of the subject relative to its advantage is found for the first time in Cicero (1 occurrence), then recurrently in Ovid (13 occurrences), himself followed once by Seneca, twice by Pseudo-Quintilian (in the same sentence), once by Juvenal. On this point, Ovid is a special case.

Last point, all semantic functions combined, in 19 of the 55 occurrences of [*sum aliquid*], the subject consists of an infinitive group. Among these 19 occurrences, there are 14 of the 17 Ovidian passages, one Ciceronian passage, three extracts from Seneca and the only passage from Juvenal. In 12 of these 14 Ovidian passages, the form [*est aliquid*] begins the verse and the infinitive group begins after the trihemimeral cut, in which fact Ovid is imitated by Juvenal. On this point too, Ovid is a special case.

In conclusion, we postulate the existence of a properly Ovidian Textual Motif, of which we give the following formal, semantic and functional definition: [*Est aliquid*-subject complement at the head of verse and sentence + trihemimeral cut (hexameter/pentameter) + subject infinitive group] whose semantic function is to say the importance of the subject group as to the advantage to be drawn from it. It also performs an emphatic rhetorical function (stressing the importance of the subject by the position of *est aliquid* at the head of verse), as well as a strong characterising function since this Textual Motif sets Ovid apart from the rest of the corpus.

For the notion of Textual Motif, we refer the reader to the works of Sylvie Mellet and Dominique Longrée[9] especially. For a detailed analysis of each occurrence of this Ovidian Textual Motif, both from the morphosyntactic, functional and stylistic points of view, please see Tonnaer (2023).

Bibliography

Green, S. (2004). *Ovid,* Fasti *1: A Commentary*. Leiden: Brill.

Littlewood, R. J. (2006). *Commentary on Ovid's* Fasti, *Livre 6*. Oxford: Oxford University Press.

Longrée, D., Luong X. & Mellet, S. (2008). Les motifs: un outil pour la caractérisation topologique des textes. In S. Heiden & B. Pincemin (Eds.), *JADT 2008, Actes des 9e Journées internationales d'Analyse statistique des Données Textuelles* (pp. 733–744). Lyon: Presses Universitaires de Lyon.

Mellet, S. & Longrée, D. (2012). Légitimité d'une unité textométrique: le motif. In A. Dister, D. Longrée & G. Purnelle (Eds.), *JADT 2012, Actes des 11e Journées internationales d'Analyse statistique des Données Textuelles* (pp. 716–728). Liège: Université de Liège.

Orlandini, A. (2001). *Grammaire fondamentale du Latin, Tome VIII: Négation et argumentation en Latin.* Peeters: Louvain-la-Neuve.

Pinkster, H. (2015). *The Oxford Latin Syntax. Volume 1: The Simple Clause*. Oxford: Oxford University Press.

Tonnaer, P. (2023). [*Est aliquid* + groupe infinitif sujet]: un Motif Textuel proprement ovidien. *Les Études Classiques, 91*, 227–252.

Touratier, C. (1994). *Syntaxe latine*. Peeters: Louvain-la-Neuve.

9 Longrée et al. (2008); Mellet and Longrée (2012).

Anna Novokhatko

Translatio facta: Pomponius Porphyrio on the Comprehension and Production of Metaphors

Abstract: The paper argues that Pomponius Porphyrio, as an educated and learned grammarian, was aware of the various concepts of metaphor as a linguistic and/or conceptual phenomenon in Republican and Imperial Rome, even if in his commentary on Horace's poetic work, he confuses the terms and uses them in a practical and implicative way. The aim, therefore, is twofold: to discuss Porphyrio's concept of metaphor and his use of the terminology in relation to its use and function in Horace with his brief remarks on the use of metaphor in Horace, commenting on a particularly bold poet with a variety of innovative metaphors, but more importantly to discuss Porphyrio's place in the history of debates about the linguistic and conceptual function of metaphor in ancient and especially Roman thought.

Keywords: Porphyrio, Horace, cognitive metaphor theory, image, imagination, sensory perception

The Latin grammarian Pomponius Porphyrio from the third century CE, who possibly originated from Africa, was educated as a learned intellectual with extensive knowledge of Greek and Latin texts. He is known to us as the author of one of the earliest surviving commentaries on Horace, in which he explains Horace's grammar and diction.[1] Porphyrio was particularly interested in the unusual use of words, the deviation from everyday usage, that is, the realm of metaphor and, as I will argue, also cognitive metaphor and conceptual mapping.[2]

In the first part of my paper, I will briefly outline the main trends in contemporary theories of cognitive metaphor in language and linguistics and explain to what extent these theories might be relevant to the ancient discussions. In the second part, I will look at the tradition of Roman linguistic thought and emphasize some essential points in the discussions of metaphor as a linguistic and/or conceptual phenomenon in Republican and Imperial Rome. This tradition is particularly

1 On Porphyrio's commentary in the framework of the intellectul tradition of Imperial Rome, see Diederich (1999).

2 On the use of the term "metaphor" in Porphyrio, see Kalinina (2007: 61–76).

Anna Novokhatko, Aristotle University Thessaloniki, Greece

https://doi.org/10.1515/9783111332956-038

important because Pomponius Porphyrio, being an educated and learned grammarian, intentionally or unintentionally belonged to it, as I explain in this article. On the one hand, he reflected enduring classical ideas about metaphor; on the other, he contributed to metacognitive discourse with his brief remarks on the use of metaphor in Horace, commenting on a particularly bold poet with a variety of innovative metaphors. In the third part, I will discuss Porphyrio's approach to metaphor, his use of the terms and his way of commenting on Horace's metaphors.

I suggest that Porphyrio, as a representative of a long legacy of Roman metacognitive and linguistic thought in general and the discourse on metaphor in particular, was aware of the various concepts of metaphor that existed before him in the Roman intellectual thread, even if in his commentary on Horace's poetic work, he confuses the terms and uses them in a practical and implicative way. My aim is therefore twofold: to discuss Porphyrio's concept of metaphor and his use of the terminology in relation to its use and function in Horace, but, more importantly, to discuss Porphyrio's place in the history of debates about the linguistic and conceptual function of metaphor in ancient and especially Roman thinking.

1 Metaphor in Linguistics: Theoretical Preliminaries

The emergence of cognitive metaphor theory has highlighted unspectacular metaphors in everyday language and opened up entirely new ways of looking at metaphor not only in the context of language but, more importantly, in the context of human thought.[3] In other words, we use metaphors so often and on so many occasions that we hardly notice them. And it seems to be a natural property of language that can be applied synchronically and diachronically to different societies, although the cognitive domains and patterns differ from culture to culture, as recent studies show.[4]

Metaphors, as defined in cognitive linguistics, are conceptual mappings that link one domain of experience or knowledge to another, initially in an unexpected or creative way that later becomes the most familiar and known route, until the metaphor becomes a dead metaphor.[5] For example, the conceptual mapping TIME IS MONEY links two conceptual domains explain one concept ("what is time?") in terms

3 See especially Lakoff and Johnson (1980), Lakoff and Turner (1989). On the interaction of the conceptual metaphor theory with cognitive linguistics see Gibbs (1994) and Kövecses (2010).
4 On metaphor and the question of universality, see Kövecses (2010: 195–213).
5 Lakoff (1993), Gibbs (1994: 120–264), Steen (2011).

of the other ("time is money!"), it draws from the domain of economics (the source domain MONEY) in order to explain the domain of time, implying that time is scarce and valuable (the target domain TIME).

Research in recent decades has shown that metaphorical mappings are useful for analogy, that metaphor is a powerful tool with which we interpret the world, and that metaphor plays a crucial and vital role in our conceptual and epistemological formation. "Our ordinary conceptual system, in terms of which we both think and act, is fundamentally metaphorical in nature", as Lakoff and Johnson famously claimed.[6]

As has been the subject of much recent analysis, metaphors are categories of intentionality ("deliberateness"), signalling, and attention-drawing.[7] To understand the importance of attention-drawing strategies used in metaphorical context, it is important to re-evaluate the range of metaphors that are ubiquitous and used both consciously and unconsciously. One of the very fruitful recent approaches in cognitive linguistics therefore argues in favour of classifying metaphors as "deliberate" and "non-deliberate", with deliberate metaphors being important for interpretation purposes.[8] All metaphors are useful as information about the conceptual system of the community of speakers and can be analysed in this way. Furthermore, when analysing a literary or rhetorical text, the author's use of diction, textual strategies and narratological devices can help with interpretation.

As will be suggested below, contemporary analysis of metaphor can shed new light on Porphyrio's reading of Horace's metaphors and the way in which Porphyrio comments on them. Before turning to Porphyrio's commentary, however, I would like to briefly recall the Roman tradition of metaphor studies in order to place Porphyrio in the context of conceptual and linguistic thought.

2 Treatment of Metaphor in Latin Sources before Porphyrio

The ancient scholarly treatment of metaphor, which began primarily with Aristotle's seminal discussion of metaphor, has been heavily reconsidered in recent years.

6 Lakoff and Johnson (1980: 3).

7 On the attention-drawing strategies and the category of "deliberateness" in metaphor, see Di Biase-Dyson and Egg (2020), a very useful collection of diachronic and interdisciplinary essays, with an extensive bibliography.

8 Gerard Steen has published extensively on the subject of deliberate metaphor, including e.g. Steen (2011: 38–43).

In particular, the cognitive metaphor theory developed by Lakoff and Johnson has triggered a renewed interest in re-evaluating ancient approaches to metaphor.

As has been shown, there are already many cognitive and semiotic elements and components in Aristotle's treatment of metaphor.[9] The Aristotelian influence also remained strong in the Hellenistic and early Roman period. The anonymous author of the treatise *On Style* (second century BCE?), conventionally called Demetrius, claimed that "according to Aristotle, the best (type of) metaphor is the one referred to as the metaphor based on action" (Ἀρίστη δὲ δοκεῖ μεταφορὰ τῷ Ἀριστοτέλει ἡ κατὰ ἐνέργειαν καλουμένη, *Eloc.* 81).[10]

In Roman Republican and Imperial thought, metaphor is systematically discussed as a figure of speech in a rhetorical context. But other authors also deal with metaphor, and it is obvious that it was part of long-standing philosophical and linguistic debates, because some parts of the discussion develop and expand from one epoch to another, from one author to another. The most important – but by no means all – sources for the theoretical discussion of the meaning and functions of metaphor before Porphyrio are the *Rhetoric to Herennius* (Rhet. Her. 4, 34 and 45), Philodemus (Phil. Rhet. 1, 171 and 180 Sudhaus), Cicero (de orat. 3, 152, 155–165; orat. 81–82, 92–94; Brut. 274), Verrius Flaccus (Fest. 136, 23–138; 138, 13–23 Lindsay), Trypho (3, 191, 14 Spengel), Seneca (benef. 4, 12, 1; epist. 59, 6, 9), Plutarch (quest. conv. 747c–d), Quintilian (inst. 8, 3, 38; 6; 11, 2, 2; 12, 10, 33–34), and Fronto (ad amic. 1, 11; ad Marc. 3, 8, 1–2; ad Marc. 4, 3, 7; ad Marc. 4, 12, 2).[11]

If one attempts to create a typology of assessments and approaches to metaphor from these texts, one realises that, in addition to the traditional rhetorical and stylistic treatment of metaphor as a figure of speech, the Roman authors considered metaphor in a semantic and semiotic, experiential, cognitive and sensory context and ultimately worked with image schemata and conceptual mapping. Thus, particular attention is paid to the communication of meaning in metaphor in Quintilian (*significantius est* and *significandi gratia*, inst. 8, 6).[12] Quintilian emphasised the ability of metaphor to facilitate understanding by saying that "none of these (i.e. concepts such as *incensum ira* or *inflammatum cupiditate*) will be more appropriate in their own words (*suis verbis*) than in these imported ones" (*quam his arcessitis,*

---

9 See especially Swiggers (1984), Kirby (1997), and Laks (1994). For certain doubts and reservations, see Silk (2003) and Wood (2017). On a philosophic reading of metaphor in ancient and medieval authors, see Johnson (1981: 3–11). See also Kittay (1987: 2–11 and 14–17).

10 All translations of the Greek and Latin texts are my own.

11 On Roman theoretical treatment of metaphor, see my previous publications Novokhatko (2016, 2017, 2019, 2021, 2024). See also a (not complete) collection of passages on the discussion of metaphor in ancient authors in Guidorizzi and Beta (2000) and Lau (2006).

12 On *significare* as the verb of meaning, see Zanker (2016: 79–86).

inst. 8, 6, 7). Or elsewhere Quintilian claimed that "metaphor should either occupy an empty place, or, if it enters the others' place, it should convey a meaning more effectively that the word/phrase it banishes" (*metaphora enim aut vacantem locum occupare debet aut, si in alienum venit, plus valere eo quod expellit*, inst. 8, 6, 18).[13]

The experiential nature and the recourse to everyday routine in relation to the production of metaphors were already discussed by Cicero, and Quintilian developed the discussion further. For example, Cicero noticed that metaphor is ubiquitous and is found everywhere (*sermo omnis*, Cic. orat. 81). Cicero highlighted the use of metaphor in various linguistic and social registers from an urban to those from a rural context (*non modo urbanorum, sed etiam rusticorum*). Quintilian retains Cicero's register variation, which suggests at least two different groups of speakers, the set of peasants (*rustici*) and the set of the educated Roman élite (*nos*). Out of necessity, he says, peasants and nobles use metaphors and call a man, say, 'hard' (*durus*) or 'rough' (*asper*): *non enim proprium erat quod daremus his adfectibus nomen* 'because there was no proper designation which we could apply to these qualities' (inst. 8, 6, 6).[14]

The discussion of metaphors can also have a sensory and cognitive dimension. Quintilian's classification, which distinguishes between animate (*animalia*) and inanimate (*inanima*) relationships, was first mentioned by Philodemus in book 4 of his *Rhetoric* (*empsycha* versus *apsycha*), but is based on Aristotle's *Rhetoric*.[15] The metaphor as a whole can essentially be divided into four classes: 1) the substitution of one animate thing for another, 2) the substitution of inanimate things for other inanimate things, 3) inanimate for animate, 4) animate for inanimate. We do not know the context in which Philodemus initially set out this fourfold typology, as the corresponding papyrus fragment is difficult to reconstruct at this point, but he complains that the rhetoricians offer us no practical help in dealing with metaphor, whether we pass from the animate to the inanimate or from the inanimate to the animate, and likewise from the genus to the species or from the species to the genus.[16] This passage became a commonplace in Greek theories of metaphor. It was then completely ignored by Cicero and first appears in Latin in Quintilian.[17]

Quintilian suggests that these substitutions are not to be understood *verbum pro verbo*, but that words that function as metaphors are given a double reference,

---

13 Novokhatko (2017: 311–313), Novokhatko (2019, 387–388). On *valere* as the verb of meaning, see Zanker (2016: 65–69).

14 Novokhatko (2017: 314–315).

15 Arist. *Rh.* 1411b32–33. See Novokhatko (2016: 399–400).

16 Phld. *Rh.* 1, 171–172 Sudhaus.

17 Qvint. inst. 8, 6, 9–10. See Novokhatko (2017: 316–317), Lau (2006: 354–356).

with one concept being replaced by the other.[18] The metaphor is cognitively meaningful and the conceptual mapping in each part of the fourfold process should be recognised and interpreted by the recipient. The original sentence with its literal meaning should be identified first; the subsequent interpretations are then derived from it; thus, divergent and non-divergent elements meet, merge and coexist.

I will discuss below some further passages on sensory metaphors and image schemata that relate specifically to Porphyrio's commentary on Horace. Porphyrio seems to be well aware of the categorisation of metaphor even if he does not refer to it directly.[19] What has been said in this section should suffice as background for the following argument that Porphyrio's definitions and terminology in relation to the metaphor used by Horace are based on a solid and long-standing Greek and Roman tradition of theoretical discussion and debate on the nature and function of metaphor. Porphyrio's approach to the metaphors of Horace can only be fully understood in the context of Roman linguistic thought.

3 Porphyrio and the Concept of Metaphor

The metaphorical act is mentioned in various ways in Porphyrio's work, eight times using the Greek term *metaphora*/*metaphorikos*, sixteen times the Latin *translatio*/*translative*, and at least four times he calls the process *allegoria*/*allegorice*/*allegoricos*, and by this he means "metaphor" as will be shown.[20]

3.1 Cognitive Metaphor in Porphyrio

In his commentary to Horace' s *Ode* 2, 1, 1 Porphyrio writes:

(1) HOR. carm. 2, 1, 1: motum ex Metello consule civicum [m.] *Haec ode ad Asinium Pollionem consularem virum et triumphalem scripta est, qua hortatur eum, ut, omisso tragoediarum scribendarum studio, inchoatum historiae opus consummet, ac deinde in parecbasi [id est in translatione] bellorum civilium calamitatem refer[a]t.*

18 QVINT. inst. 8, 6, 3 and 8, 6, 8.

19 See the discussion and relevant passages in Kalinina (2007: 65).

20 See the table with statistics on the use of the term in Kalinina (2007: 63). Porphyrio's text here and below is quoted from the edition by Alfred Holder (Holder 1894).

> '*Civil wars from the consulship of Metellus onwards*: This ode is written to Asinius Pollio, a former consul and a distinguished man, in which he (Horace) encourages him to abandon the pursuit of writing tragedies and instead complete the historical work he has begun. Afterward, he narrates the disaster of civil wars in the *parecbasis* [that is, in metaphor].'

As can be seen from the transmission of the text, the whole phrase *id est in translatione* could be not Porphyrio's own text, but a later interpolation intended to explain an obscure Greek term *parecbasis*.[21] *Parecbasis* (Gr. παρέκβασις, Lat. *digressio*) is an excursus, a part of a literary text that temporarily departs from the main subject and deals with an unrelated story. Firstly, since the account of the civil wars in Horace's *Ode* 2, 1 does not seem to be a digression or an excursus, but is well integrated into the structure of the poem from the beginning, and secondly, since the *translatio* cannot be an exegetical note or an explanation of the term *parecbasis*, it seems to me reasonable to assume that either Porphyrio himself or a later interpreter of his commentary used the expression *id est in translatione* in a different sense. Let us say from the outset that the interpretation of a scholion (if the phrase in square brackets is a marginal scholion) is a temptation in itself. There are several possibilities, starting with the obvious one that the scholar made a mistake and translated the Greek term incorrectly. In this case it should definitely be ruled out, as it is highly unlikely that Porphyrio would explain *parecbasis* in this way. However, I would like to propose another reading of *id est in translatione*, as an *imago* or cognitive metaphor, to use contemporary terminology. *Translatio* here can mean the mental image of the entire narrative in the poem, whose main theme could be formulated as the consulship of Asinius Pollio against the *bellorum civilium calamitas*, "translated" into a literary work by Pollio, who was both a politician and a poet, and thus a programmatic statement by Horace himself as a civic poet whose poetry is civic poetry. This ode is indeed about writing poetry, as John Henderson, among others, has argued. "This *Ode* teaches how Horace reads and writes, sees reading and writing, lives open to others' readings, of texts, politics, people and history, and opens to his readers a sight of a life lived among others", thus Henderson.[22] That is how the metaphor of civil wars/civil discourse/poetry works in the ode, where the first word *motum* stands for movement itself.[23] That is how the concept of *translatio* was used in Roman thought, for example by Seneca.[24]

---

21 See a discussion in Kalinina (2007: 71–72, with bibliography).

22 Henderson (1996: 59).

23 Cf. Henderson (1996: 59–60).

24 For a discussion of Seneca's use of the concept "metaphor" in this and other passages, see Novokhatko (2019: 392–396).

In fact, on several occasions, Seneca uses the term *translatio* for 'metaphor' as a mental image. On one occasion, he uses a concrete and structured vocabulary from economics (source domain) when talking about the abstract and unstructured topic of "favour" (target domain). He understands "favour" as a loan and compares it to money. 'When we say "loan" we are using a mental picture and a metaphor' (*cum creditum dicimus, imagine et translatione utimur,* SEN. benef. 4, 12, 1), thus Seneca. *Translatio* and *imago* are obviously related. Metaphor functions iconically to represent similarities between two objects or situations. The iconicity of a metaphor is a creative process involving the relationship between the form and meaning of language. It is based on experience and implies similarities that are perceived according to cultural codes. As Marcel Danesi put it out, "the particular *content* of a metaphor can be said to constitute an interpretation of reality in terms of mental icons that literally allows us to *see* what is being talked about".[25]

In a similar vein, in his letter 59 Seneca puts metaphors and mental images on one level revealing his theoretical interest in metaphor. He says: "I discover metaphors (*translationes verborum*), both those that are not over the top and those that have stood up to the test. I discover mental pictures (*imagines*), – if anyone forbids us from employing them and believes that only poets are permitted them – then he does not seem to know any classical authors whose speech has not yet been dominated by the need to please good opinion" (SEN. epist. 59, 6).

Both objects *translationes* and *imagines* provide a structural analogy, considered syntactically. Seneca is the first attested author to ascribe a "constitutive" role to images and the power of the imagination, explicitly linking metaphor and image. He seems to have been very aware of this structural analogy between the cognitive and the imaginative, between *translationes* and *imagines*.

These passages seem to provide a good parallel, suggesting that either Porphyrio himself or his commentator or later scribe – whoever was the author of the interpolation *id est in translatione* – might be a bearer of the discourse on the mental images and imaginary power of metaphor that is so strong in Roman texts of the imperial period.[26] The enumeration of civil war disasters in Horace's text forms the self-referential imagery of the poem; writing about civil wars, being a politician, living civic life and writing poetry are all fused into one image, and in the first line Porphyrio comments on the whole poem. It is a mental image of the "motum" which functions as a revealing feature or sign and characterises its essence.

25 Danesi (1995: 266). Italics of the author.

26 Cf. Ps.-Long. *subl.* 15, 1; Plu. *quaest. conv.* 747c–d; QVINT. inst. 6, 2, 27–32; 8, 3, 62; 8, 6, 11. See Novokhatko (2021).

The following example seems to further confirm my suggestion about Porphyrio's use of conceptual mapping. Porphyrio comments on Horace's *Satire* 1, 5.

(2) Hor. sat. 1, 5, 65–66: donasset iamne catenam ex voto laribus, quaerebat. *Urbanissima contumelia haec dicta sunt in eum, qui servilibus esset natalibus, translatione sumpta a generosis pueris, qui bullam auream egressi pueritiae annos apud lares solent suspendere.*
'*Hadn't he dedicated that chain to the Lares, he asked.* These words of a very subtle offence were spoken against him, who was born of servile lineage, with the metaphor borrowed from noble boys, who, having received the gold locket, are accustomed to hang it at the Lares during the years of adolescence.'

The status of the freedman Sarmentus and his servile origins are mocked here with reference to the chains of servitude dedicated to the guardian deities. Modern scholars suggest that these lines are a more generalised parody of the practice of dedicating the tools of a trade to a patron deity upon retirement.[27] Porphyrio refers to the tradition of free-born boys dedicating their *bulla* ('a locket, containing an amulet, hung round the neck of children', OLD s.v.) or phallic amulet to Lares at adolescence and calls the whole implication a very subtle offence (*urbanissima contumelia*). The striking passage in Porphyrio is 'with the metaphor borrowed from noble boys' (*translatione sumpta a generosis pueris*). Because which *translatio* is borrowed exactly? What exactly is being translated? Porphyrio was well aware that *translatio* was a technical term in rhetorical and grammatical circles in his day – why does he use this word and for what? It is clearly none of single words: neither *catena* nor *laribus*, still less *donare ex voto*. Not a specific word is borrowed, but the entire act of dedicating a necklace to Lares is meant. So once again we have what we would now call a cognitive metaphor and a conceptual mapping of the behaviour of the freedman with the behaviour of "noble boys". And this kind of behaviour, a transferred imaginary scene that is not static but dynamic, conditioned by a necessary cultural common ground of shared knowledge about what exactly free-born boys tend to do, is parodied and taken as a metaphor.

And here again I suggest that Porphyrio participates, perhaps unwillingly and unintentionally, in the contemporary shared intellectual discourse on metaphor and imagery that is evident in the passages from Seneca mentioned above, and especially in Fronto's language exercises for the young Marcus Aurelius.[28] Fronto's

27 Gowers (2012: 203).
28 For a discussion of Fronto's use of metaphors and images in this and other passages, see Novokhatko (2024).

teaching method consisted of providing his students a set of conceptual metaphors getting them to develop a domain and relate it to another given domain (*imago*). Fronto explains the technique of working out mental patterns.

FRONTO ad Marc. 3, 8, 1: *Imaginem, quam te quaerere ais, meque tibi socium ad quaerendum et optionem sumis, num moleste feres, si in tuo atque in tui patris sinu id futurum quaeram?*
'As for the image you say you are seeking and in the quest for which you want me to be your partner and helper, will you mind if I seek it forthcoming in your breast and that of your father?'[29]

As we soon learn, the given *imago* was an "island" (*insula*), and Fronto creates a mapping "as the island lies in the sea, warding off the waves of the ocean, so your father bears on his shoulders the toils of the empire" (FRONTO ad Marc. 3, 8, 1).[30] In terms of the theory of conceptual metaphor, Fronto provides Marcus with source domains, i.e. the conceptual domains from which metaphorical expressions originate, such as the *insula* in this case, and asks him to find various appropriate target domains, such as the emperor and his duties here. The target domain is the quality or experience described by or identified with the source domain.

Imago is 'sought' and can be found as a forthcoming act in Marcus' own and his father's heart (*in tuo atque in tui patris sinu*). It originates both in the mind of the narrator and in the mind of the recipient and is then transferred to a corresponding domain. Marcus should continue the exercise of trying to find the source domains and apply them to the target domains ('Send me the images you searched for and found with the same method by which the matter was demonstrated', *tu quas* εἰκόνας *in eandem rem demonstrata ratione quaesiveris et inveneris, mittito mihi*, FRONTO ad Marc. 3, 8, 1).

Furthermore, the *imago* in Fronto is used to embellish, discredit, compare, devalue, reinforce, or transform a less credible thing into a credible one (εἰκόνα *ei rei adsumi ut aut ornet quid aut deturpet aut aequiperet aut deminuat aut ampliet aut ex minus credibili credibile efficiat*, FRONTO ad Marc. 3, 8, 2). These functions of *imago* are very similar to the functions of *translatio* in the earlier classical manuals. For example, the author of the *Rhetoric to Herennius* where the author emphasizes six functions of *translatio*: that of setting the matter before one's eyes (*rei ante oculos ponendae causa*), of brevity (*brevitatis causa*), of avoiding obscenity (*obscen-*

29 I follow the text of Fronto, edited by M. P. J. Van den Hout (Teubner 1988).
30 On the island metaphor here see particularly Poignault (2002) and Ronnick (1997: 240–241).

itatis vitandae causa), of expanding (*augendi causa*), of devaluing (*minuendi causa*), and of embellishment (*ornandi causa*).[31]

The experientiality of such mapping is striking.[32] The physical experience of the participants, the situational, discursive, and conceptual-cognitive context are all involved in the metaphorical process in which the images are created.[33] And this is what we observe in Porphyrio's text. Porphyrio and his readers – and, by implication, Horace and his readers – can participate in the imaginative act of transfer between the chains of the freedman Sarmentus and the amulet of the 'noble boys', since they must necessarily share the knowledge of the locket with an amulet that the freeborn boys tend to dedicate to the Lares.

When composing an *imago* for a proposed subject (*ubi rei propositae imaginem scribes*), Fronto continues, one should also consider the features of the object one is painting (*insignia animadverteres eius rei cuius imaginem pingeres*, Fronto ad Marc. 3, 8, 2) when writing, just as one would as a painter. The actual workshop of how metaphorical mapping is created is presented: such features can be taken up from various points of view (*multis modis*), such as similarities of kind (τὰ ὁμογενῆ), similarities of form (τὰ ὁμοειδῆ), the whole (τὰ ὅλα), the parts (τὰ μέρη), individual features (τὰ ἴδια), differences (τὰ διάφορα), oppositions (τὰ ἀντικείμενα), consequences and results (τὰ ἑπόμενα καὶ παρακολουθοῦντα), names (τὰ ὀνόματα), accidents (τὰ συμβεβηκότα), elements (τὰ στοιχεῖα) and generally everything from which arguments are drawn (Fronto ad Marc. 3, 8, 2).[34] Fronto actually always speaks of *imago* here and never uses the term *metaphora*/*translatio* in this context; however, it is clear that his discussion is framed by the theories of metaphor and mapping as mental and imaginative power. "Transference"/mapping is constantly present, and the coexistence of two or more mental spaces is actually assumed and presupposed in all the features listed. This passage is thus conceived entirely in the spirit of conceptual metaphor theory: the source domain, an "island", is given to find the target domain ("ruling empire") to be understood.

Fronto's aim is to be as close as possible to reality.[35] His method originally consisted in the fact that it 'grasped' (*conprehendundas*) *imagines* such as "island" from reality in order to 'transfer'/'adapt' (*adcommodandasque*) them to an imagi-

---

31 Rhet. Her. 4, 45. See Novokhatko (2016: 398–399). See also Schmitt (1934: 20–22).

32 The term "experientiality" was introduced by Monika Fludernik as a designation for the "quasi-mimetic evocation of real-life experience" through narratives and was subsequently much discussed. See especially Fludernik (2010) and Caracciolo (2012 and 2014).

33 On the context that generates metaphors, see Kövecses (2015).

34 On Fronto's possible sources here, see Van den Hout (1999: 111). See also Schmitt (1934: 23–25).

35 On a debate on the link between reality and the images of Fronto, see Portalupi (1974: 26) and Portalupi (1993 277). See also Fleury (2006: 56–58).

native domain.[36] The image that the mind forms of an object must be transferred to other things because the human mind needs this transfer in order to represent them. Here lies a profound principle of experientiality: the art of images can only propose, he says, to render the world real, *imagines quasdam rerum*. The *imago* thus materialises and embodies that which is too fleeting and difficult to analyse in the movements of the mind.

Porphyrio's metaphor *sumpta a generosis pueris*, like Fronto's *imago*, is based on the substrate of common experience, and it is meant to facilitate the understanding of Horace's passage. The *translatio* does not intend to colour the poetic text but to clarify the topic and gives the recipient support.

The last example is also a case where the "metaphor" refers to the entire imaginary scene and not to one specific word.

(3) Hor. epist. 2, 2, 114: et versentur adhuc inter penetralia Vestae. *Id est: domi. Per quam metaforan ostendit, licet in animo nostro fixa versentur, tamen excludenda esse, quod fit, etiam temere admissis hominibus. Alii[s] intellegunt: Cum adhuc populo placeant.*
'*although they will still dwell in the midst of the precincts of Vesta.* This means at home. With this metaphor, he points out that although they are firmly anchored in our minds, they must be excluded, as is the case with people who have been recklessly let in. Another interpretation: As long as they continue to please the people.'

As scholars have noted, Horace's argumentation seems to require a double meaning: He could mean words in the sense of "although they still dwell in sacred places (in the poet's mind) and resist his decisions". On the other hand, he could also mean people in the sense of "although they still dwell in sacred places and resist the censor's decisions".[37] However, there is no indication that the temple of Vesta, the virgin goddess of the hearth, the home and the family, was a place where one could claim immunity. This wording therefore remains unclear. Even in Porphyrio's time it seemed difficult and required commentary. Porphyrio tries to resolve the ambiguity by explaining the entire passage as a "metaphor" (*per quam metaforan ostendit*): he comprehends *versentur* as a predicate for "words", which may remain firmly anchored in our mind (*in animo nostro fixa*). The last remark, that other people 'understand' (*intellegunt*) the line differently, confirms that Porphyrio seeks the way to explain the whole

36 On the Stoic background of the cognitive process, which is only conceivable from a rigorously exact "grasping" of reality, see Collin (2010: 223–227).
37 Rudd (1989: 137).

thought and sees the metaphor as the key to solving the meaning. The mind is shown as the chaste place of the goddess Vesta, and poet's words are meant to be chased outwards, and this is how it works when people are carelessly let in the precincts of Vesta. The whole scene in the mind, human behaviour, and the way in which the poet produces his work is understood and explained by Porphyrio as an extended and expanded metaphor, what in today's language would be called a conceptual metaphor and by no means a mere embellishment of language.

In all three examples in which Porphyrio (or Porphyrio's commentary with later interpolations) comments on a use of metaphor in Horace, *id est in translatione* (Hor. carm. 2, 1, 1), *translatione sumpta a generosis pueris* (Hor. sat. 1, 5, 65–66) and *per quam metaforan ostendit* (Hor. epist. 2, 2, 114), it is not a specific word but a whole imaginative scene that is meant and commented on, in which the pre-existence of two conceptual domains is meant and is where the mapping is, and that's exactly what Porphyrio is interested in.

Furthermore, an understanding of the poet as a citizen and the writing of poetry as a civic act (ex. 1), a mapping of the behaviour of the freedman with that of "noble boys" (ex. 2), and an obscure sojourn in the sacred temple of Vesta as verses that linger in the poet's mind (ex. 3) reveal Porphyrio's mental organisation of information into source and target domains, which is indeed the basic phenomenon that triggers metaphorical use in language. Conceptual mapping, the presence of two imaginary scenes or two concepts simultaneously, contributes to the reader's participatory sense-making and meaning-making, and although Porphyrio does not explore the nature and function of conceptual metaphor more deeply and fully, the presence of the term *translatio* in the commentary on the passages where conceptual mapping takes place is at least noteworthy and remarkable. It is not just a rhetorical figure, it indicates that some more substantial processes were going on in the Roman understanding of language and cognition, and Porphyrio reflects the earlier tradition of understanding the phenomenon of metaphor, based, as we have seen, on texts such as those of Quintilian, Seneca and Fronto.

3.2 Metaphor and Senses in Porphyrio

Another group of metaphors in Porphyrio's commentary reveals the experiential nature of metaphor, which has been noticed in the earlier ancient scholarly tradition of metaphor discussion.

(4) Hor. carm. 1, 11, 8: carpe diem quam minimum credula postero. *Metaforicos 'primo quoque' inquit 'die fruere'. Translatio autem a pomis sumpta est, quae scilicet ideo carpimus, ut fruamur.*

'*pluck the day and rely as little as possible on the following.* He says metaphorically: "enjoy the very first day". But the metaphor is taken from the fruit that we pluck in order to enjoy it.'

Horace's metaphor is original and actually comes from the garden and horticultural life, from people's everyday experiences. The fact that the metaphor involves all the senses and functions experientially in our brain has already been explained by Cicero. In the third book of his *De oratore* Cicero claims notoriously that every metaphor that is taken with deliberation (*omnis translatio, quae quidem sumpta ratione est*) appeals immediately to our senses (*ad sensus ipsos admovetur*), and principally to the sense of sight, which is the acutest of them all. For such expressions as the odour of urbanity (*odor urbanitatis*), the softness of humanity (*mollitudo humanitatis*), the murmur of the sea (*murmur maris*), and sweetness of speech (*dulcitudo orationis*), are derived from the other senses (*ducta a ceteris sensibus*, CIC. de orat. 3, 160–161).[38] The sensory imagination and the extended association and interweaving of the metaphor with all five senses – sight, smell, touch, hearing, and taste – was therefore part of general academic knowledge and was certainly known to Porphyrio, when he describes the embodied tactile metaphor *carpe diem* as *a pomis sumpta.*

Porphyrio comments on the tactile metaphor elsewhere and goes into even more detail. In his *Satire* 2, 1 Horace creates an extended metaphor of the ears and represents himself and Octavian as two animals, himself as a donkey, Octavian as a noble steed.[39] The poet has floppy ears (*Flaccus*, v. 18), while Octavian's ears are pricked up, attentive and eager to listen (*attentam*, v. 19). Porphyrio explains here verse 20.

(5) HOR. sat. 2, 1, 20. cui male si palpere. *Metaforicos: cui si adularis, offenditur. Palpari proprie: manu mulcere.*
'*if you stroke him the wrong way.* Metaphorically: if you flatter him, he is offended. *Palpari* in its literal sense means to soothe by hand.'

Porphyrio emphasises the signification of *palpari* as a deponent verb but also the entire passage (*cui si adularis, offenditur*) in both metaphorical (*metaforicos*) and literal (*proprie*) senses, the physical, corporeal and tactile nature of *manu mulcere* being essential to the meaning.

---

38 On the discussion of this passage, see Mankin (2011: 247–248). Cf. also CIC. de orat. 3, 98–99. On the use of body and senses in Cicero's metaphors, and in particular on the tactile metaphors of touch, see Sjöblad (2009: 50–56).
39 Freudenburg (2021: 61).

There are two other cases in which Porphyrio draws attention to the corporeal metaphor and appeals to the bodily senses. The first case is quite simple: an experiential physical metaphor is otherwise attested in Latin poetry, but still deserves Porphyrio's rather lengthy explanation.

(6) Hor. carm. 3, 16, 18: maiorumque fames. *Pecuniarum maiorum scilicet. Et famem nunc pro desiderio posuit metaforicos. Dicit autem, quod re vera videmus, tanto cupidiores avarioresque fieri homines, quanto plus adquirant.*
'*and the hunger for more.* It implies for more money. And Horace placed here hunger metaphorically in the stead of desire. However, he says that, in truth, we see that people become all the more eager and avaricious as they acquire more.'

Hunger is a common metaphor for greed and avarice (cf. Verg. Aen. 3, 57: *auri sacra fames*).[40] *Fames* is a natural and physical need and desire for food and thus an obvious source for the metaphor (*famem nunc pro desiderio posuit metaforicos*).

The other example (ex. 7) is more conceptual. In his epode 12 the narrator is a youth who complains about an older woman nagging him to have sex, but he finds it difficult because he does not find her attractive. Porphyrio explains lines 11 and 12.

(7) Hor. *epod.* 12, 11–12. iamque subando tenta cubilia tectaque rumpit. *Subare proprie sues dicuntur cum libidinantur. Inde iam translatio facta in cetera animalia. Tenta autem cubilia lectum dicit restibus sive fasciolis subtentum.*
'*and now, in her animal lust, she tears apart the bonds of the bed and its canopy.* They say "subare" to refer to pigs when they are on heat. From there, the metaphor was transferred to other animals. Horace calls "tenta cubilia" a bed that is supported by ropes or straps.'

A vivid bodily and sensual image of a woman in a state of arousal is enacted as an animalistic metaphor in Horace. Porphyrio is concerned with the metaphorical use and function of the physical verb *subare* ('to be in a state of sexual excitement [of female animals]', OLD s.v.), which he perhaps connects etymologically or rather onomatopoeically with *sues* 'sows'. He picks up on this imagery and claims that this sensory metaphor was transferred from sows to other animals and further on to humans. According to neuroscientists, concepts and metaphors are anchored in the sensorimotor system "to the extent that even the inferences that these concepts

40 Woodman (2022: 256–257).

produce can be described as inferential chains taking place in the sensorimotor system".[41] Physical, bodily and sensory metaphors are understood by Porphyrio in terms of experience: the inner state of the body, charged with the emotions of desire, is put into words by figurative means and by an embodied metaphor involving the human senses.

4 Conclusions

Many other passages in Porphyrio's commentary treat metaphor in a purely grammatical tradition, but these seven are sufficient to suggest that Porphyrio (or, as in ex. 1, a later scribe or interpreter of Porphyrio) belongs to the tradition of treating metaphor from what is now called the cognitive perspective. It is also aware that our experiences are both imposed by our bodies and deeply rooted in culture and practice.

There is no evidence that Porphyrio was a philosopher of language and that he was interested in the discussion of language and cognition. What I would like to suggest is that these seven examples discussed in the paper provide some information about the circulation of intellectual discourses in Roman thought over several centuries. Porphyrio was a carrier of these discourses – how active or passive we cannot judge because too little of his work has survived.

The examples of Porphyrio's approach to metaphor discussed above show at least three perspectives of his understanding of metaphor: the body, the mind, and the cultural context. Recent studies of cognition certainly provide an interpretive key to Roman views of the metaphorical act. Cognition is necessarily embedded in a shared context. The human being interacts with other human beings, with physical objects and cultural entities, all of which creates an act of embodiment in which the body and its senses contribute to the whole process. When two imaginative scenes based on shared sensory and cultural experience overlap, a metaphorical fusion takes place, and this phenomenon, as discussed above, was already well established in Roman thought. It is therefore safe to assume that, consciously or (rather) unconsciously, Porphyrio was part of the treatment of metaphor as a cognitive linguistic agency.[42]

---

41 Cuccio (2018: 45).

42 I would like to thank the anonymous referees for the considerable improvements they have made to this text and for their fruitful suggestions.

Bibliography

Caracciolo, M. (2012). Notes for a(nother) Theory of Experientiality. *Journal of Literary Theory, 6* (1), 177–194.

Caracciolo, M. (2014). *The Experientiality of Narrative: An Enactivist Approach*. Berlin/Boston: De Gruyter.

Collin, F. (2010). L'art de la parole imagée chez Fronton: philosophie et pensée littéraire. In P. Voisin & M. de Béchillon (Eds.), *L'art du discours dans l'antiquité: de l'orateur au poète* (pp. 213–234). Paris: L'Harmattan.

Cuccio, V. (2018). *Attention to metaphor: from neurons to representations*. Amsterdam/Philadelphia: John Benjamins.

Danesi, M. (1995). The iconicity of metaphor. In M. E. Landsberg (Ed.), *Syntactic iconicity and linguistic freezes: The human dimension* (pp. 265–283). Berlin/Boston: De Gruyter.

Di Biase-Dyson, C. & Egg, M. (Eds.) (2020). *Drawing Attention to Metaphor: Case Studies Across Time Periods, Cultures and Modalities*. Amsterdam/Philadelphia: John Benjamins.

Diederich, S. (1999). *Der Horazkommentar des Porphyrio im Rahmen der kaiserzeitlichen Schul- und Bildungstradition*. De Gruyter, Berlin/New York.

Fleury, P. (2006). *Lectures de Fronton. Un rhéreur latin à l'époque de la Seconde Sophistique*. Paris: Les Belles Lettres.

Fludernik, M. (2010). Experience, Experientiality, and Historical Narrative: A View from Narratology. In T. Breyer & D. Creutz (Eds.) *Erfahrung und Geschichte: Historische Sinnbildung im Pränarrativen* (pp. 40–72). Berlin/New York: De Gruyter.

Freudenburg, K. (2021). *Horace: Satires Book II, ed. and comm.* Cambridge Greek and Latin Classics. Cambridge: Cambridge University Press.

Gibbs, Jr. R. W. (1994). *The poetics of mind*. Cambridge: Cambridge University Press.

Gowers, E. (2012). *Horace: Satires Book I, ed. and comm.* Cambridge: Cambridge University Press.

Guidorizzi, G. & Beta, S. (2000). *La metafora: testi greci e latini*. Pisa: Edizioni ETS.

Henderson, J. (1996). Polishing off the Politics: Horace's Ode to Pollio, 2, 1. *Materiali e Discussioni per l'analisi Dei Testi Classici, 37*, 59–136.

Holder, A. (1894). *Pomponi Porfyrionis Commentvm in Horativm Flaccvm Werktitel Commentarii in Q. Horatium Flaccum*. Innsbruck: Wagner.

Johnson, M. (1981). *Philosophical Perspectives on Metaphor*. Minneapolis: University of Minnesota Press.

Kalinina, A. (2007). *Der Horazkommentar des Pomponius Porphyrio. Untersuchungen zu seiner Terminologie und Textgeschichte*. Stuttgart: Steiner.

Kirby, J. T. (1997). Aristotle on Metaphor, *American Journal of Philology, 118*, 517–554.

Kittay, E. F. (1987). *Metaphor: its cognitive force and linguistic structure*. Oxford: Clarendon Press.

Kövecses, Z. (2010). *Metaphor: a practical introduction* (2nd edn.). New York/Oxford: Oxford University Press.

Kövecses, Z. (2015). *Where metaphors come from: reconsidering context in metaphor*. Oxford: Oxford University Press.

Laks, A. (1994). Substitution et connaissance: Une Interprétation Unitare (Ou Presque) de la Théorie Aristotélicienne de la Métaphore. In D. J. Furley & A. Nehamas (Eds.), *Aristotle's Rhetoric, Philosophical Essays* (pp. 283–305). Princeton: Princeton University Press.

Lakoff, G. (1993). The contemporary theory of metaphor. In A. Ortony (Ed.), *Metaphor and thought* (pp. 202–251). Cambridge: Cambridge University Press.

Lakoff, G. & Johnson, M. (1980). *Metaphors we live by*. Chicago: University of Chicago Press.

Lakoff, G. & Turner, M. (1989). *More Than Cool Reason: A Field Guide to Poetic Metaphor.* Chicago: University of Chicago Press.
Lau, D. (2006). *Metaphertheorien der Antike und ihre philosophischen Prinzipien: ein Beitrag zur Grundlagenforschung in der Literaturwissenschaft*. Frankfurt am Main: Peter Lang.
Mankin, S. (2011). *Cicero, De oratore book III, ed. and comm.* Cambridge: Cambridge University Press.
Novokhatko, A. (2016). The use of the term 'metaphor' in Latin linguistic discourse before Quintilian. In P. Poccetti (Ed.), *Latinitatis rationes. Descriptive and Historical Accounts for the Latin Language* (pp. 395–409). Berlin/Boston: De Gruyter.
Novokhatko, A. (2017). The linguistic treatment of metaphor in Quintilian, *PALLAS, 103*, 311–318.
Novokhatko, A. (2019). The typology of linguistic metaphor in 1st c. CE Roman thought. In N. Holmes, M. Ottink, J. Schrickx & M. Selig (Eds.), *Lemmata Linguistica Latina, Vol. 1: Words and Sounds* (pp. 384–398). Berlin/Boston: De Gruyter.
Novokhatko, A. (2021). Images and cognitive metaphor in 1st c. CE Roman discourse. In A. M. Martín Rodríguez (Ed.), *Linguisticae Dissertationes. Current Perspectives on Latin Grammar, Lexicon and Pragmatics* (pp. 149–160). Madrid: Ediciones clásicas.
Novokhatko, A. (2024). Fronto's Theory of Metaphor? An Enactivist and Psycholinguistic Perspective. In C. Cabrillana (Ed.), *Recent Trends and Findings in Latin Linguistics, Vol. II: Semantics and Lexicography. Discourse and Dialogue* (pp. 569–584). Berlin/Boston: De Gruyter.
Poignault, R. (2002). Deux îles, des poulets et quelques divinités : images des rapports de parenté dans la famille impériale selon la correspondance de Fronton. In *Hommages à C. Deroux, II : Prose et linguisitique, médecine* (pp. 357–371). Bruxelles: Latomus.
Portalupi F. (1974). *Nota Frontoniana*. Torino: Giappichelli.
Portalupi F. (1993). Frontone e l'eloquenza dei Cesari, *Civiltà Classica e Cristiana, 14*, 275–284.
Ronnick, M. V. (1997). Substructural Elements of Architectonic Rhetoric and Philosophical Thought in Fronto's Epistles. In W. J. Dominik (Ed.), *Roman Eloquence. Rhetoric in Society and Literature* (pp. 229–245). London/New York: Routledge.
Rudd, N. (1989). *Horace: Epistles Book II and Ars Poetica, ed. and comm.* Cambridge: Cambridge University Press.
Schmitt, A. (1934). *Das Bild als Stilmittel Frontos*. Dissertation. München.
Silk, M. (2003). Metaphor and metonymy: Aristotle, Jakobson, Ricoeur, and others. In G. R. Boys-Stones (Ed.), *Metaphor, Allegory, and the Classical Tradition: Ancient Thought and Modern Revision* (pp. 115–147). Oxford: Oxford University Press.
Sjöblad, A. (2009). *Metaphors Cicero lived by: the role of metaphor and simile in* De senectute. Lund: Lund Univ.
Steen, G. J. (2011). The contemporary theory of metaphor—now new and improved! *Review of Cognitive Linguistics, 9* (1), 26–64.
Swiggers, P. (1984). Cognitive aspects of Aristotle's theory of metaphor, *Glotta, 62*, 40–45.
Van den Hout, M. P. J. (1999). *A commentary on the Letters of M. Cornelius Fronto*. Leiden/Boston/Köln: Brill.
Wood, M. S. (2017). Aristotle's Theory of Metaphor Revisited. *Mouseion: Journal of the Classical Association of Canada, 14* (1), LVIII Series III, 63–90.
Woodman, A. J. (2022). *Horace: Odes Book III, ed. and comm.* Cambridge: Cambridge University Press.
Zanker, A. T. (2016). *Greek and Latin expressions of meaning. The classical origins of a modern metaphor*. München: Beck.

Section 5: **Conversation and Dialogue**

Łukasz Berger

The Quotative *inquit* as a Device of Speech Segmentation in the Roman Novel

Abstract: The paper explores how Roman novels (by Petronius and Apuleius) use reporting clauses to segment quotations and convey prosodic and pragmatic phenomena. The use of parenthetical *inquit* creates a concise left periphery for reported speech that can contain full segments of talk or discourse-marking devices that function as communicative pre-units. This type of segmentation helps to instigate interaction (e.g. changes of addressee, attention-managing devices) and inform the recipient about the type of action to come in the first turn-unit. When the first segment of reported speech contains syntactically dependent elements, the placement of *inquit* serves the narrator as a focalising or highlighting mechanism, which affects the representation of the message and the meaningful organisation of its content vis-à-vis the reader/listener. Finally, the article collects the most common speech-opening segments, which indicate the type of the subsequent illocution and fulfil the function of what is called here a speech-act quotative.

Keywords: direct discourse, reporting clause, *inquit*, Petronius, Apuleius, Roman novel, discourse organisation

1 Introduction

The corpus of the Roman novel is replete with depictions of spoken discourse. According to the calculations by Dalbera (2024: 506), over three-quarters of the reported speech in Petronius' *Satyricon* and Apuleius' *Metamorphoses* has the form of *oratio recta*. Despite some stylistic variation in the patterns for the reproduction of dialogue, the most frequent quoting device in both authors is *inquit* ('s/he said'), typically inserted near the left periphery of the quotation. In such cases, the reporting verb – as any parenthetical remark – creates a separate intonational phrase, which, nevertheless, does not always correspond with the boundaries of syntactic constituents. Accordingly, this paper undertakes to analyse the linguistic tokens isolated by *inquit* and their structural relation to the rest of the reported utterance. The main objective of this examination, informed by the methods of Conversation

Łukasz Berger, Adam Mickiewicz University, Poznań, Poland

https://doi.org/10.1515/9783111332956-039

Analysis, is to pinpoint the pragmatic implications of isolating different types of segments that initiate the direct discourse.

My main premise in the analysis of *oratio recta* in Petronius and Apuleius is that, in contrast to modern prose, the ancient novel was read out loud and in public, like so many other Roman texts, from epic poetry to epistolography (see Dupont 1997). When treating the differences in the original reception of the *Satyricon*, Slater (2009: 16) stresses that the members of the Roman elite would make their slaves (*lectores*) read them the text privately or during social gatherings – a practice depicted in the novel itself.[1] Konstan (2009), in turn, convincingly argues for a collective (and active) readership of the genre, noting that often the authors – through different textual strategies – invite the readers/listeners' participation.[2] The prologue of the *Metamorphoses*, for instance, contains references to writing and reading mixed with markers of oral performance.[3] Thus, I assume that the novels, if orally reproduced in front of at least one aural recipient, gain an additional interactional dimension.

2 The Quotatives in Petronius and Apuleius

The introduction of direct speech into the narration marks a shift in the communicative mode, whereby the reader gets the impression of a faithful reproduction of the character's actual words.[4] As for the strategies of representing direct discourse, the reporting clause (or verb) can precede the quotation (with or without cataphoric elements), be inserted within, or follow it, marking the return to the narrative mode. In his recent examination of reporting verbs in the Roman novel, Dalbera (2024: 507) notices a spectacular imbalance in the distribution of the quotatives (see Table 1). In the whole corpus, *inquit* (or *inquam*) covers approx. 63% of all instances of *oratio recta* introduced with a reporting clause. Other than that, there

1 Trimalchio orders his slave to read out loud the news from his estate (PETRON. 53). At some point, he also recites to his guests from a scroll (59) or reads a copy of his will (71).

2 De Jong (2001: 205) finds that the prologue of Apuleius' *Metamorphoses* implies the presence of three different figures: the narrator (Lucius), the narratee (1, 1: *at ego* ***tibi*** *. . .*) and a third person whom the narratee asks about Lucius' identity (*quis ille*?). Schmeling (1991: 375) argues that the episodic nature of the plot in Petronius suggests it was created for a group recitation.

3 This leads Fowler (2001: 225) to conclude that the *Metamorphoses* "is a work in which the 'pretended' mode of reception is at odds with the 'actual' mode", but, at the same, he opts for taking seriously both possibilities. See also Keulen (2007: 13–14), with further bibliography, and Dalbera and Fleck (this volume).

4 See Laird (1999: 88–90) and Mikulová (2022: 11–18) for a full discussion of the defining criteria of direct discourse.

is a group of only seven fairly common speech-related lexemes (20% of the corpus) which are used five or more times in either of the authors.

Table 1: The most frequently used speech-reporting verbs in Petronius and Apuleius, as compared to other quoting strategies. Based on the calculations by Dalbera (2024: 507).

quotative verbs	PETRON.	APVL. met.	total
inquit	220	182	402
ait	12	27	39
(con/ex/pro)clamat	25	11	36
dicit	12	2	14
infit	–	9	9
respondet	2	7	9
suscipit	–	7	7
incipit	–	6	6
adicit	5	1	6
other (used less than 5 times)	–	17	17
hapax quotatives	12	42	54
without a quotative (ellipsis)	13	24	37
total	301	353	**671**

As noted by Dalbera, these more habitual expressions also have the least specific semantics indicating only the mere act of speaking (*inquit*, *ait*, *dicit*) or different ways of participation in a dialogue (*respondet*, *suscipit*, *adicit*, *infit*, *incipit*). Since the whole group, if not used with some modifiers,[5] concerns exclusively the speakership management, I will refer to them as "turn-taking quotatives".

Furthermore, there is a considerable group of reporting verbs used only once within either of the novels (the hapax quotatives in Table 1) – 54 lexemes which cover 8% of all instances. These have the most specific meaning, which, apart from emotions (*congemo*) and prosody (*erumpo*), have to do – especially in Apuleius – with the pragmatic action implemented through the utterance (e.g. *adulo*, *admoneo*, *annuntio*, *argumentor*, *interpello*, *postulo*).[6] I will describe the latter group as "speech-act quotatives", given the fact that they refer to the (dominant) illocution type of the reported speech (e.g. 's/he requested'). Accordingly, these hapax forms are extreme opposites of *inquit*, which is the most routine and semantically neutral

5 E.g. APVL. met. 6, 28: *Tunc illa* ***spirans*** *altius caelumque sollicito vultu petens*: *"Vos,* ***inquit****, Superi, . . ."* ('Then she sighed deeply and turned her face anxiously toward heaven. "O gods above," she said . . .').

6 The full list of hapax quotatives is offered by Dalbera (2024: 508).

device (Fleck 2019: 55–56). One should note also the discrepancy in the preference for *inquit* between Petronius (73%) and Apuleius (54%), who seems to favour a more varied and balanced expression of direct-speech lexemes.

3 The Use of *inquit* in the Roman Novel

As in all Latin texts, the default position of *inquit* in the novels by Petronius and Apuleius is within the quotation. Accordingly, the inserted verb functions as a parenthetical, which typically separates one or two words of the reported speech.[7] Occasionally, one can also find longer segments of three up to eight items. These proportions are similar in both authors, as illustrated in Figure 1. The parenthetical use is also characteristic of another turn-taking quotative *ait* (see [2] below), where it is found in 32 of the 39 instances, but the form itself is (with these 39 instances) much less frequent than *inquit*.[8] It is worth noting that all of the hapax quotatives mentioned in the previous section prefer the ante-position (see the figures in Dalbera 2024: 511–512) – I will get back to this observation by the end of this paper.

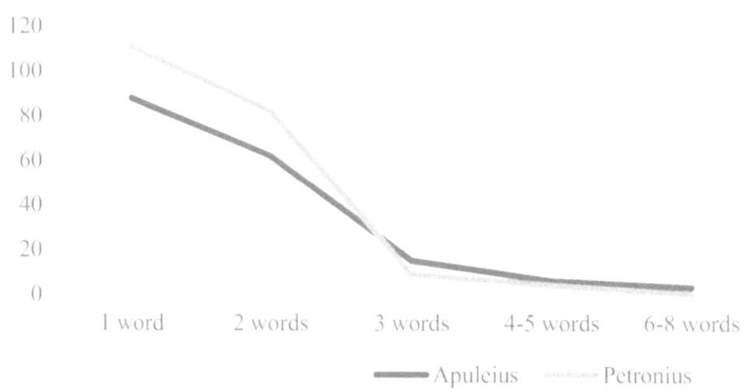

Figure 1: Length of the reported speech preceding *inquit*.

In the absence of any specific typographic conventions for distinguishing direct speech in Latin (e.g. a hyphen or quotation marks), early placement of *inquit* within

7 According to the calculations by Mikulová (2022: 44–45), the same pattern prevails in all authors and in all periods. 96% of *inquit* in her data is used in interposition, whereas one-or-two-word opening segments amount to 87% of all her cases (679 instances); even the lowest percentage (in the Classical period) is 77%.

8 Mikulová (2022: 55) shows that, except for Petronius and Apuleius, other authors prefer to use *ait* in ante-position (86% of all instances in her corpus). This irregularity in the Roman novel perhaps is the effect of the influence of the dominant *inquit*-segmentation pattern.

the reported speech may contribute to its better recognition. On the other hand, already Ricottilli (1978: 215) argued that the first words of a quotation (typically vocatives, interjections, deictic elements, 1st- and 2nd-person verbs and pronouns, etc.) already signal the transition to *oratio recta*.[9] Thus the function of *inquit*, just as often placed later in the reported speech, after two or more lexemes, has to go beyond a mere quotation mark.

Quite interestingly, *inquit* can also appear twice in the reported speech of one and the same character, where seemingly there is no need for another direct-discourse marking. In (1), the use of the second quotative can be explained by the fact that the speaker (the priest of Isis) implements a new type of action, which is here also related to the change in his (emotional) disposition towards the addressee.

(1) *At ille statim ut me conspexit, prior: "O* | ***inquit*** | *Luci, te felicem, te beatum, quem propitia voluntate numen augustum tantopere dignatur"; et "Quid* | ***inquit*** | *iam nunc stas otiosus teque ipsum demoraris?"* (APVL. met. 11, 22)
'The moment he caught sight of me, however, he anticipated me. "O | he said | Lucius, how fortunate you are, how blessed, that the hollowed deity so greatly favours you with her benevolent will. Why | he said | are you still standing around doing nothing, causing your own delay?"'[10]

First, the priest praises Lucius for receiving the goddesses' favours, but then he admonishes him for his immobility (*quid iam nunc stas . . .?*). In such cases, the second *inquit* marks its host stretch of talk as a separate unit of spoken discourse, governed by a different communicative intention.[11] The slight discursive break implies the sudden shift in dialogue, allowing for time to process the change through the narrator's intervention. In the following sections, I will argue that this peculiar repeated use of *inquit* derives from a more general role it plays in the pragmatic marking of the reported discourse.

9 Ricottilli (1978) referred to Petronius, but similar claims have been convincingly presented for Apuleius (Fleck 2019: 60–66) or the whole corpus of Roman novels (Dalbera forth.).

10 For the quotations and the translations of the novels, I use the corresponding Loeb edition of Petronius (Schmeling 2020) and Apuleius (Henderson 1989). For the sake of clarity, I will mark the *inquit*-segmentation with "|" and introduce, whenever it seems relevant, slight modifications in the English text.

11 Elsewhere in Apuleius, the second quotative (*et inquit*) regularly marks the change of the addressee (APVL. met. 6, 9; 7, 22; 9, 33). In PETRON. 116, 4–9, the repeated *inquit* appears amidst a third-person descriptive discourse when the speaker shifts the focus back to the addressees (*adibitis* | *inquit* | *oppidum*. . . 'You will enter, he said, a town. . .'). Note also that this second quotative introduces an impactful conclusion to the description of the town and its inhabitants.

4 Different Types of the *inquit*-segmentation

In general, the insertion of *inquit* can isolate almost every type of word class from the rest of the reported utterance: interjections, particles, markers of negation, personal pronouns, subordinators, verbs, nouns, adverbs, etc. On many occasions, the placement of the quotative is sensitive to the syntactical constituency, as longer segments can include full phrases, clauses or different structures displaying a constituent status, which, prototypically, also create separate prosodic segments such as phonological or intonational units. The latter is "a stretch of speech uttered under a single coherent intonation contour" (Du Bois et al. 1993: 47) and corresponds roughly to a clause or a smaller rhythmical colon. Phonological phrases "are made up of syntactically related words, typically the syntactic head and its modifiers" (Devine and Stephens 1994: 377). The remainder of this paper will survey the different patterns of speech segmentation in the corpus of Roman novels, taking into account this tension between syntactical and phonological units vis-à-vis their status within the conversational structure.

4.1 Breaks Between Full Units of Talk

For my analysis of the *oratio recta* in Petronius and Apuleius as an imitation of spoken communication, I will employ the tools of Conversation Analysis, stressing its intersections with syntax.[12] Conversation analysts describe talk as an orderly organised sequence of turns (utterances) alternating between two (or more) participants. The building blocks of each turn are different syntactic units which – in a given context – are meaningful and recognisable as particular actions. The most evident case of an independent turn-constructional unit separated by a quotative is a full clause, as in example (2). Both the following speech-opening segments produced by Encolpius and Ascyltos are vehicles of distinct pragmatic actions: a question (*quid cogitas?*) and an answer (*assentemur*).

(2) *Ego respiciens ad Ascylton: "**Quid cogitas?** | inquam | ego **enim** si videro balneum, statim expirabo." "**Assentemur** | ait ille | **et** dum illi balneum petunt, nos in turba exeamus."* (PETRON. 72, 5–7)

12 The seminal paper on turn organization is by Sacks et al. (1974). Syntax in the context of turn construction is discussed with more detail by Schegloff (1996).

'Looking over at Ascyltus, "What are you thinking? | I said | For if I even see a bath, I will die on the spot." "Let us agree to their plan | he said | and while they are making for the bath, we can slip away in the crowd."'

Apart from syntactical and pragmatic resources, speakers recognise the boundaries of a turn-constructional unit based on prosodic phenomena such as a distinct and coherent phonetic realisation (Schegloff 2007: 3–4). Since the insertion of a parenthetical always provides the preceding segment with a separate intonational contour, I will consider every non-clausal element that seems to have an independent contextual meaning as a turn-constructional unit. Accordingly, the noun phrase *saga* in the following example (3) should, in my view, be analysed as a self-contained unit, responding to the prior turn of speaking.

(3) *"Potens illa et regina caupona quid mulieris est?"* ***"Saga*** | *inquit* | ***et*** *divina, potens caelum deponere, terram suspendere. . ."* (APVL. met. 1, 8)
'"What kind of woman is this powerful and royal innkeeper?" "A witch | he replied | and one with supernatural powers, she can lower the sky. . ."'

This type of *inquit*-segmentation that exploits the natural junctures between turn-units arguably contributes to the representation of the turn-construction. In all of these examples, the speakers produce complex, multi-unit turns, adding further chunks of talk after the pause marked by the quotative. Significantly, these additional units are introduced by the connectives *et* (2), (3), which suggest discursive independence of the first segment. The same can be inferred from the use of *enim* in (2), where it signals the beginning of a new stretch of discourse after the quotative.[13]

By contrast, the few examples of *inquit* used in postposition[14] – like in (4) – concern always one turn constructional unit which contains one or two words (sometimes with lexical repetition).

(4) *"Si scires* | *inquit* | *quae mihi acciderunt." "Quid novi?"* ***inquam*** *ego.* (PETRON. 8, 1)
'"If you only knew | he said | what happened to me!" "What happened?" I said.'

13 See Kroon (1995: 203): "*enim*-units often function as common-ground arguments that support a challengeable central unit."
14 APVL. met. 1, 8; 1, 22; PETRON. 7, 1; 8, 1; 36, 6; 45, 2; 48, 5; 87, 8.

Accordingly, they have a form of a typical speech-opening segment isolated by *inquit* – albeit one where the speaker does not continue talking after the parenthetical. It may give further support for the argument that the quotative has to appear early within the reported speech to mark the change in the communicative mode.

4.2 Breaks after Turn-beginning Objects

Many of the *inquit*-segments in the Roman novel are formed by linguistic elements which are syntactically independent of the rest of the utterance. These items prefigure the ensuing turn-constructional unit, and hence, following the conversation-analytic studies, I will refer to this group as turn-initial objects or pre-units (cf. Lindstrom 2006, Heritage 2013). Their functions derive from the significance of turn beginnings, which, as argued by Schegloff (1996: 71), "are an important initial place, and an initial resource, for the projection of the turn-shape or the turn-type of the turn that is being begun". Elaborating on the functionalities of the turn-initial objects, Depperman (2013: 93) proposes four tasks speakers have to deal with when launching a new turn:

i. Achieve joint orientation to the upcoming turn by securing the recipient's attention.
ii. Display the uptake and the understanding of the prior turn.
iii. Deal with projections from the prior talk.
iv. Project properties of the upcoming turn.

I will start my short survey of the turn-beginning objects in Petronius and Apuleius with items which serve to manage the addressee's attention (i). Here we may find vocatives and attention-getters, which identify the recipient of the ensuing utterance. The form of address *amici* (5), for instance, is used several times by Trimalchio towards his guests. Various forms of attention-getters such as *heus tu* (6) and *quid dicis* (7) serve to select the next recipient or initiate a new dialogic exchange.[15]

(5) *Tum Trimalchio: "**Amici** | inquit | hodie Croesus meus barbatoriam fecit, homo praefiscini frugi et micarius."* (PETRON. 73, 6)
'Then "Friends | Trimalchio said | today my Creosus celebrated his first shave: he's an honest fellow, so help me, frugal and economical."'

15 The attention-getter *heus (tu)* appears exclusively in Apuleius (met. 1, 13; 1, 15; 2, 18; 8, 10; 9, 33). Petronius uses, in addition to *quid dicis?*, also *quid est?* (98, 6; 128, 1; 131, 3; 131, 10), and *quid tu/vos?* (26, 9; 74, 6; 82, 3; 117, 2; 127, 4; 134, 7) – for the latter, see the discussion in Ricottilli (1978).

(6) *Tunc ego in verba fidentior: "**Heus tu** | inquam | qui sermonem ieceras priorem…"* (APVL. met. 1, 3)
'At that point, I spoke more confidently: "You there | I said | the one who started the story before…"'

(7) *Respiciens deinde Habinnam: "**Quid dicis** | inquit | amice carissime? Aedificas monumentum meum quemadmodum te iussi?"* (PETRON. 71, 5–6)
'Looking over at Habinnas, "Tell me | he said | my dearest friend, are you building my tomb in the way I ordered you?"'

Mikulová (2022: 47) rightly observes that this type of segment with addressee-oriented expressions, "aimed at instigating interaction", can make the represented conversations more dynamic by signalling – I may add – the changes within the configuration of the interlocutors not always announced by the narrator. Compare the selection of the addressee within the narration in (7) with the lack thereof in (5).

Furthermore, the attention of the dialogue participants can be (re)directed towards some external objects, places or persons. Thus I include here also turn beginnings with deictic elements such as *ecce* and *en*, which – typically in Apuleius – establish a common point of reference in the extra-linguistic reality of the represented world.[16] In (8), Milo welcomes his guest Lucius by showing him – as a display of extreme stinginess – an empty table. The speaker's gesture (*monstratu*) and its verbalisation (*en*) create a joint visual focus needed for launching the rest of the utterance (*hospitium*).

(8) *Assidebat pedes uxor et mensa vacua posita, cuius monstratu: "**En** | inquit | hospitium."* (APVL. met. 1, 22)
'His wife was sitting at his feet, and there was an empty table set up, to which he pointed and "Look | he said | this is your welcome."'

On the level of the reproduction of the text, the slight discursive (and prosodic) break following the deictic seems to have been designed to raise the expectations of the recipients of the text, who are invited "to form a vivid picture" of the presented entity (Keulen 2007: 401).

16 See ***en*** | *inquit* in APVL. met. 1, 18; 1, 19; 2, 2; 7, 8; 8, 12 and *(et)* ***ecce*** | *inquit* in 2, 11; 2, 24, 6, 9; 6, 22; 6, 30. For this purpose, Petronius uses demonstratives, see PETRON. 24, 7: *Mox manum etiam demisit in sinum et pertractato vasculo tam rudi "**Haec**" inquit "belle cras in promulside libidinis nostrae militabit…"* ('Then she slipped her hand into his underwear and fondled his very inmature implement: "This," [she said], "tomorrow will serve nicely as an hors d'oeuvre to whet my appetite…"'). See also 7, 3 (*hic*).

The next group of *inquit*-segments deals with the evaluation of prior talk, showing the speaker's (ii–iii) understanding of what has been said in the preceding turn but also (iv) projecting the type of response s/he is about to give. Accordingly, this type of turn-initial objects serves to index continuity with prior (reported) talk or departures from it by conveying, respectively, discourse cohesion between two consecutive turns or pragmatic disalignment (Heritage 2013: 333). In the excerpt from Petronius (9), Encolpius hints that his companion Ascyltos should also enjoy the sexual advances of a *cinaedus*. His addressee, Quartilla, starts her response with *ita* ('you're right') showing that she understands the intention behind the prior turn and signaling that her upcoming utterance will convey compliance.

(9) *"Per fidem | inquam | vestram, Ascyltos in hoc triclinio solus ferias agit?" "**Ita** | inquit Quartilla | et Ascylto embasicoetas detur." Ab hac voce equum cinaedus mutavit. . .* (PETRON. 24, 3–4)
'"Be fair | I said | Is Ascyltus the only one in this dining room who gets to enjoy a holiday?" "Just so | Quartilla said | Ascyltus too must be given a lewd mug." After these words the catamite changed horses. . .'

The following example (10), by contrast, contains tokens of the speaker's departure from the prior talk. When Encolpius, enraged, wanders around the city with a sword in his hand, he is taken for a soldier by some passer-by member of the military. When he blatantly lies about his legion and centurion, the stranger expresses strong scepticism and disbelief in the form of a rhetorical question: what sort of a *miles* walks around in slippers?

(10) *. . . notavit me miles, sive ille planus fuit sive nocturnus grassator, et: "**Quid tu** | inquit | commilito, ex qua legione es aut cuius centuria?" Cum constantissime et centurionem et legionem essem ementitus: "**Age ergo** | inquit ille | in exercitu vestro phaecasiati milites ambulant?"* (PETRON. 82, 2–4)
'. . . Then a soldier, who might have been an imposter or a night-prowling thief, spotted me and "What are you up to there | he said | comrade? From what legion are you, and who's your centurion?" When I lied brazenly both about my centurion and the legion, "Come now | he said | in your army, do the soldiers walk round dressed in white slippers?"'

The beginning of his turn, separated by *inquit*, contains the pragmatic marker *age*, whose secondary function is to convey disagreement in reactive actions (Unceta Gómez 2024: 691). As for the particle *ergo*, it highlights that the upcoming turn relates to Encolpius' answer and that it will require some readjustments of its implications (Kroon 1995: 92–93). Thus, the pre-unit consisting of two functional words (*age ergo*) and produced as a separate intonational phrase already challenges the protagonist's lie, signaling the speaker's epistemic stance and, at the same time, indicating the relations of dialogic coherence.

It is worth noting that the attention-getter *quid tu?*, used by the passer-by to start the conversation with Encolpius (10), regularly precedes questions[17] and hence it also projects the function of the upcoming turn-unit. In other initiating utterances, I can find various turn-opening objects that specialise in foreshadowing the type of action that is about to be implemented. The most numerous groups are performative verbs and metadirectives, used parenthetically as pre-units in the first segment of the reported speech. As explained by Risselada (1993: 243), these linguistic forms specify the speech act function of the host utterance, either from the perspective of the speaker (performatives) or the addressee (metadirectives). Let (11) be an example of the latter, where Photis is introducing her request for permission with *patere* ('allow me'). The remaining excerpts contain turn-initial performatives of an encouragement (12) and a question (13).[18]

(11) *"**Patere** | inquit | oro, prius fores cubiculi diligenter obcludam, ne sermonis elapsi profana petulantia committam grande flagitium."* (APVL. met. 3, 15)
"'Allow me | she said | I beg you, first let me carefully lock the doors to the room, lest with the wanton profanity of an indiscrete tongue, I perpetrate a monstrous crime."'

(12) *Nos ut tristiores ad tam viles accessimus cibos, "**Suadeo** | inquit Trimalchio | cenemus; hoc est ius cenae."* (PETRON. 35, 7)
'Once we approached – with rather sour faces – such cheap fare, "I encourage you | said Trimalchio | Let's have dinner. This is the sauce of the dinner."'

(13) *At ille circumspiciens ut cervicem meam iunxit amplexu: "**Rogo** | inquit | domine, ubi est asturco?"* (PETRON. 86, 7)
'As he threw his arms around my neck, he looked all around and "Tell me | he said | sir, where is my stallion?"'

I have decided to analyse these expressions as turn-initial objects rather than turn-proper content because they are syntactically independent from the rest of the utterance while being vehicles of procedural meaning. Risselada (1993: 250) duly relates their use with politeness strategies, through which "the speaker wants to be

17 Ricottilli (1978).
18 The performative *rogo* can introduce both a question or a request – see the data in Table 2.

explicit about his illocutionary intentions in order to (emphatically) exclude misinterpretation by the addressee". Arguably, the same function gains relevance on the level of communication between the text and its reader/listener. Placed at the left periphery of the reported speech, the performatives and metadirectives serve the authors to give the recipients some cues regarding the upcoming speech acts, securing their straightforward understanding. This feature of the *inquit*-segment seems particularly useful for the interpretation of some pragmatically ambiguous sentence types (e.g. questions) and grammatical forms (e.g. imperative, subjunctive).

4.3 Breaks within the Turn-proper Content

If the prosodic break induced by the parenthetical falls within the content of the turn, it can coincide with the boundaries of its syntactic constituents. Here I will limit myself to offering only a few examples. The quotative *inquit* can separate the main from the subordinate clause (14), the subject from the predicate (15), or an adjunct (16) from the nucleus of the clause.

(14) *"**Dum annuntio** | inquit | hic ibidem me opperimino."* (APVL. met. 1, 22)
'"While I announce you | she said | wait for me right here."'

(15) *"**Dies** | inquit | nihil est. . ."* (PETRON. 41, 10)
'"Day | he said | is nothing. . ."'

(16) *"**Cito** | inquit | te ipsum caede, quia nugas es."* (PETRON. 52, 4)
'"Quick | he said | kill yourself right now for being so stupid."'

In such cases, the speech-opening segments constitute independent phonological phrases, which – in contrast to the turn-initial objects (Section 4.2) – convey meaning on the representational level of the discourse. However, they cannot count as self-contained utterances. Instead, they build up the tension and raise the expectations for the remaining constituents as the syntax of the clause unfolds gradually after the incision (cf. Mikulová 2022: 47). Significantly, the same units have been identified as Latin rhythmical cola and mark the places in which the speaker would pause in a curated and/or emphatic delivery.[19]

19 See the discussion in Habinek (1985: 4–8) with further bibliography. Habinek (1985: 14) states that, "[i]n ideal delivery of speech, pauses always come at constituents' boundaries and most often at the boundaries of sentence constituents", but he also points out that, whether the speaker actually makes there a prosodic break depends on the speed of delivery. For the use of rhythmical cola

On the other hand, there are instances where the quotative is used to separate words that have closer syntactical bonds, for example, the head and its modifier, as in the following examples, where the parenthetical divides the constituents of a noun (17) and a (18) verbal phrase.

(17) *. . . cum ecce iam vespera lucernam intuens Pamphile: "Quam* ***largus*** *| inquit |* ***imber*** *aderit crastino."* (APVL. met. 2, 11)
'Evening had come now, and Pamphile was staring at the lamp. "A huge | she said | rainstorm is coming tomorrow."'

(18) *At ille: "Quid* ***me*** *| inquit |* ***rogas****? Tanquam ego tibi molestus sim. Suadeo, a te impetres, ne sis nugax."* (PETRON. 52, 5)
'But "Why do you ask me | Trimalchio said | as if I were giving you trouble? I suggest rather that you ask yourself to take more care.'"'

Here, the inserted *inquit* disturbs the internal structure of syntactical units and the phonological phrases they create. This feature, as stated by Devine and Stephens (1994: 417), "can be used by the speaker as a pragmatic device to set off and therefore further highlight focused items". Indeed, the parenthetical *inquit* has been recognised to indicate the focus or emphatic constituents by Spevak (2010: 163–164), which – in 33% of the cases in her Classical Latin corpus – precede the quotative, as in (18). Bolkestein (1998: 9–10), however, noted that the focal constituents can also follow the incision – this is the case of (17). Due to the limitation of space, I cannot further pursue this issue of the information structure and the *inquit*-segmentation. Suffice it to say that, since there is a pause before and after the parenthetical, both places are potentially apt for emphatic pronunciation, which would accompany the focal element.

Finally, there remain the cases with speech-opening segments filled by interrogatives (20) or subordinators (19), which cannot possibly be focalised as it happens with the quotatives separating elements of a noun or verbal phrase (Spevak 2010: 164).

(19) *. . . Ascylton autem truci intuens vultu "****quoniam*** *| inquam | fidem scelere violasti et communem amicitiam, res tuas ocius tolle. . ."* (PETRON. 79, 11)
'. . . but I looked savagely at Ascyltos. "Since | I said | you have broken the trust and friendship between us, collect your things at once. . ."'

in Apuleius' prologue, see Nisbet (2001). Aspects of Petronian prosaic style (and rhythm) are treated in Rochette (2007).

I argue that some of these clause-initial items behave in a similar way as the turn-initial objects; namely, they are projecting information about the (communicative) nature of the upcoming syntactical structure early on within the reported speech. Accordingly, the segments like the one given in (20) functionally are equivalent to turn-initial performatives since the sequence *quin igitur* | *inquit* ('Then why not | he said') informs the recipient(s) that the reported utterance is a proposal.

(20) *Sed ille iuvenis sermone repetito: "**Quin igitur** | inquit | supplicatum Marti Comiti pergimus?. . ."* (APVL. met. 7, 10).
'In the meantime, the young man spoke again: "Why don't we then | he said | make offerings to Mars the Comrade?. . ."

Accordingly, this use of *inquit*-segmentation, which offers pragmatic marking, seems to be complementary with the speech-act quotatives used regularly in the anteposition, where they can foreshadow the communicative intention of the speaker before reporting their words (see [21]).

(21) *Interea Psychen maritus ille, quem nescit, rursum suis illis nocturnis sermonibus sic **commonet**: "Videsne quantum tibi periculum?. . ."* (APVL. met. 7, 10).
'Meanwhile Psyche was again being warned by her unknown husband in his nightly talks with her: "Do you see how much danger you are in?. . ."'

I can also find one example (22), in which the direct discourse is introduced with both reporting strategies – a speech-act quotative (*dehortabar*), and an interposed *inquit*.

(22) *. . . populi circumfluentis turbelis immisceor et, in quo solo poteram celatum auxilium bono ferre commilitoni, sic indaginis principes **dehortabar**: "O grande | **inquam** | et extremum flagitium, magnam et vere pretiosam perdimus bestiam." Nec tamen nostri **sermonis artes** infelicissimo profuerunt iuveni.* (APVL. met. 4, 20)
'. . . I mingled with the crowds of people surging around and covertly tried to help a good fellow-soldier in the only way I could, by trying to dissuade the leaders of the hunt: "What a tremendous | I said | and monstrous crime! We are destroying a large and really expensive animal." But my rhetorical skills were of no help to the poor unfortunate youth.'

In this excerpt, one of the robbers recounts how he tried to help his comrade, disguised as a bear and persecuted by an angry crowd. His attempts at dissuading the hunters take on an indirect form of a pathos-laden exclamation, in which he criticises the maltreatment of the animal. The reporting clause in the anteposition states explicitly the illocutionary force of his speech, while *inquit* clearly serves different means. I argue here that it helps to rhythmically segment the utterance after the first cues of its exclamatory force (*o grande* | *inquit*) thereby imbuing it with a distinct rhetorical flair (*artes sermonis*).

In Table 2, I collect the most recurring speech-opening segments – both syntactically isolated (Section 4.3) and integrated (Section 4.4) with the rest of the turn-unit – which are somehow indicative of the ensuing illocution. I believe that their position on the left periphery of the direct discourse, next to *inquit*, fulfils the function of the speech-act quotatives.

Table 2: Speech-opening segments in Petronius and Apuleius with the communicative intentions they convey.

Speech-opening segments	type of pragmatic action
Unde (autem) | inquit. . .? (APVL. met. 1, 15; 6, 1)	X asked (a question)
Ubi | inquit. . .? (APVL. met. 9, 39)	
Quid (ergo) | inquit. . .? (APVL. met. 1, 14; 2, 21; 5, 2; 5, 7; 6, 17; 11, 22, PETRON. 52, 5; 53, 6; 67, 10; 107, 15; 117, 4)	
(Et/at) quae | inquit. . .? (APVL. met. 1, 25; 2, 13; 2, 24; 3, 27, PETRON. 56, 1; 104, 4)	
Quare ergo | inquit. . .? (PETRON. 24, 6; 83, 9)	
Videsne | inquit. . .? (APVL. met. 1, 21, PETRON. 105, 1)	
Rogo | inquit. . . (PETRON. 7, 1; 48, 7; 55, 5; 86, 7; 90, 3; 95, 2; 126, 8)	
Vis | inquit. . .? (APVL. met. 1, 8; 9, 7)	X proposed
Quin (potius/igitur) | inquit. . .? (APVL. met. 1, 13; 2, 2; 7, 10, PETRON.102, 1)	
[imperative] | ***inquit***. . . (APVL. met. 1, 2; 2, 16; 2, 24; 8, 13; 10, 16, PETRON. 59, 1; 91, 2; 101, 2)	X requested/demanded
Rogo | inquit. . . (PETRON. 20, 1; 75, 3; 137, 4; 137, 6)	
Oro | inquit. . . (APVL. met. 1, 8; PETRON. 45, 1)	
Quaeso | inquit. . . (PETRON. 24, 1; 91, 8; 128, 2)	
Quam vellem | inquit. . . (APVL. met. 3, 12; 6, 4)	X expressed a regret
Patere | inquit. . . (APVL. met. 3, 15; 3, 22)	X asked for permission
Sinite me | inquit. . . (PETRON.115, 4)	
Caveas | inquam. . . (APVL. met. 4, 17)	X advised
Suadeo | inquit. . . (PETRON. 35, 7; 74, 15)	
Per ego te | inquit. . . (APVL. met. 4, 31)	X implored
Per fidem vestram | inquit. . . (APVL. met. 2, 27)	

The gathered data contains 64 examples (16 % of all instances of the parenthetical *inquit*), with the biggest representation of questions and various types of directive acts (requests, suggestions, etc.), whereas some illocution types appear only once, which does not mean, however, they are not easily understandable after hearing the first one-or-two items.

5 Conclusions. (Meta)pragmatic Uses of the *inquit*-segmentation

The reported discourse used by the authors of the fiction narrative, despite (admittedly) quoting the character's own words, is not able to reproduce the intricacies of their delivery. In this context, Laird (1999: 90) duly remarks that "a precise timing for enunciation, pauses in or between enunciation and the timing for those, qualities of accent, tone and voice all defy notation". While some prosodic phenomena, such as volume or emotional investment, can be mentioned – in some specific episodes – by the narrator, I have tried to show in this paper that some information about its time-sensitive delivery has been codified in the structural design of the quotation itself. It seems that the insertion of the reporting clause – the most frequent pattern used in the Roman novel – forces the reader/performer of the text to segment the quotation at least in one strategic place – right after its beginning.

By using the parenthetical *inquit*, the authors of the Roman novel create a short (one-, two- or three-word) left periphery of the reported speech, which – as indicated by the examples provided – can contain full units of talk or discourse-marking devices that function as pre-units. This type of segmentation has to do with the time-sensitive process of managing the interaction, whereby the pause created by *inquit* may suggest the speakers' efforts in construing their multi-unit turns of talk while securing recipiency and guiding their understanding. These tasks, belonging to the turn beginnings, were considered relevant both for the intratextual addressee – within the frame of the naturalistic depiction of verbal interaction – and for the extratextual recipient of the novel, especially if the text was presented orally.

Furthermore, the quotative can intervene within the content of the utterance, isolating some syntactic constituents or even interrupting the structure of syntactic (and phonological) phrases. In both cases, the placement of *inquit* serves the narrator (who works, I submit, as if in the name of the speakers themselves) as a focalising or highlighting mechanism. This type of segmentation concerns the representational level of the message and the meaningful (e.g. emphatic, tension-building, etc.) organisation of its content vis-à-vis the addressee – including, again, the reader/aural recipient of the text. Finally, I have argued that some of the clause-initial elements (e.g. interrogatives), which get isolated by *inquit*, might realise the same function as turn-beginning items. In summary, the textual relevance of *inquit* goes beyond the one of a quotative. Within a fairly complex system of reporting clauses in the novel, it becomes a rhythm- and information-managing device which partakes in (meta)pragmatic discourse marking, promoting an auditive reception of the text.

Bibliography

Bolkestein, A. M. (1998). Between brackets: (some properties of) parenthetical clauses in Latin. An investigation of the language of Cicero's letters. In R. Risselada (Ed.), *Latin in Use* (pp. 1–17). Amsterdam: Gieben.

Dalbera (forthcoming), Les marques d'ouverture du discours direct dans le roman latin (le *Satyricon* de Pétrone et les *Métamorphoses* d'Apulée). In *Latin vulgaire – latin tardif XIV*.

Dalbera, J. (2024). Verbes introducteurs et stratégies d'introduction du Discours Direct dans la narration romanesque latine (le *Satyricon* de Pétrone et les *Métamorphoses* d'Apulée). In C. Cabrillana (Ed.), *Recent Trends and Findings in Latin Linguistics* (pp. 503–520), Berlin/Boston: De Gruyter.

Deppermann, A. (2013). Turn-design at turn-beginnings: Multimodal resources to deal with tasks of turn-construction in German. *Journal of Pragmatics*, *46* (1), 91–121.

Devine, A. M., & Stephens, L. D. (1994). *The Prosody of Greek Speech*. New York: Oxford University Press.

Du Bois, J. W., Schuetze-Coburn, S., Cumming, S., & Paolino, D. (1993). Outline of discourse transcription. In J. A. Edwards & M. D. Lampert (Eds.), *Talking data: Transcription and Coding in Discourse Research* (pp. 45–89). New York/London: Psychology Press.

Dupont, F. (1997). *Recitatio* and the Reorganization of the Space of Public Discourse. In T. Habinek & A. Schiesaro (Eds.), *The Roman Cultural Revolution* (pp. 44–59). Cambridge: Cambridge University Press.

Fleck, F. (2019). Le marquage du discours rapporté chez Apulée: du discours direct au discours direct libre. In. J. Dalbera & D. Longrée (Eds.), *La Langue d'Apulée dans les Métamorphoses* (pp. 53–69). Paris: L'Harmattan.

Fowler, D. (2001). Writing with Style: The Prologue to Apuleius' *Metamorphoses* between Fingierte Mündlichkeit and Textuality. In A. Kahane & A. Laird (Eds.), *A Companion to the Prologue of Apuleius' Metamorphoses* (pp. 225–230). Oxford: Oxford University Press.

Henderson, J. (1989). *Apuleius.* Metamorphoses. Vol 1–2. Cambridge, MA/London: Harvard University Press.

Heritage, J. (2013). Turn-initial position and some of its occupants. *Journal of Pragmatics*, *57*, 331–337.

Jong, I. J. F. de (2001). The Prologue as a Pseudo-Dialogue and the Identity of its (Main) Speaker. In A. Kahane & A. Laird (Eds.), *A Companion to the Prologue of Apuleius'* Metamorphoses (pp. 201–212). Oxford: Oxford University Press.

Keulen, W. (2007) *Apuleius Madaurensis* Metamorphoses*: Book 1 – Text, introduction and commentary.* Groningen: Egbert Forsten.

Konstan, D. (2009). The active reader and the ancient novel. In M. Paschalis, G. Schmeling & S. Panayotakis (Eds.), *Readers and Writers in the Ancient Novel* (pp. 1–17). Groningen: Barkhuis.

Kroon, C. (1995) *Discourse Particles in Latin: a Study of* nam, enim, autem, vero *and* at. Amsterdam: J. C. Gieben.

Laird, A. (1999). *Powers of Expression, Expressions of Power: Speech Presentation and Latin Literature.* Oxford: Oxford University Press.

Lindstrom, J. (2006). Grammar in the service of interaction: Exploring turn organization in Swedish. *Research on Language and Social Interaction*, *39* (1), 81–117.

Mikulová, J. (2022). *Evolution of Direct Discourse Marking from Classical to Late Latin*. Amsterdam: Brill.

Nisbet, R. G. M. (2001). Cola and Clausulae in Apuleius' *Metamorphoses* I.1. In A. Kahane & A. Laird (Eds.), *A Companion to the Prologue of Apuleius' Metamorphoses* (pp. 16–26). Oxford: Oxford University Press.

Ricottilli, L. (1978). *Quid tu? quid vos?* (per il recupero di una locuzione oscurata nel Satyricon). *Materiali e discussioni per l'analisi dei testi classici*, *1*, 215–221.

Risselada, R. (1993) *Imperatives and Other Directive Expressions in Latin: A Study in the Pragmatics of a Dead Language*. Amsterdam: J. C. Gieben.

Rochette, B. (2007). Les éléments hors stucture dans la *Cena Trimalchionis*. Remarques sur la structure de la phrase de Pétrone. In C. Bodelot (Ed.), *Eléments "asyntaxiques" ou hors structure dans l'énoncé latin* (pp. 265–294). Clermont-Ferrad: Presses Universitaires Blaise Pascal.

Sacks, H., Schegloff, E. A., & Jefferson, G. (1974). A Simplest Systematics for the Organization of Turn-taking in Conversation. *Language*, *50* (4), 696–735.

Schegloff, E. A. (1996). Turn organization: one intersection of grammar and interaction. In E. Ochs, E. A. Schegloff & S. A. Thompson (Eds.), *Interaction and Grammar* (pp. 52–133). Cambridge: Cambridge University Press.

Schegloff, E. A. (2007). *Sequence Organization in Interaction*. Cambridge: Cambridge University Press.

Schmeling, G. (1991). The *Satyricon*: The Sense of an Ending. *Rheinisches Museum für Philologie*, *134* (3/4), 352–377.

Schmeling, G. (2020). *Petronius:* Satyricon*; Seneca:* Apocolocyntosis. Cambridge, MA: Harvard University Press.

Slater, N. W. (2009). Reading the *Satyrica*. In J. R. Prag & I. D. Repath (Eds.), *Petronius: A Handbook* (pp. 16–31). Oxford: John Wiley & Sons.

Spevak, O. (2010). *Constituent Order in Classical Latin Prose*. Amsterdam: John Benjamins.

Unceta Gómez, L. (2024). The Pragmatic Marker *age*: Its Pragmatic Functions in Comedy and its Contribution to the Expression of Im/Politeness. In C. Cabrillana (Ed.), *Recent Trends and Findings in Latin Linguistics* (pp. 685–701), Berlin/Boston: De Gruyter.

Joseph Dalbera and Frédérique Fleck

(Story)telling in the Latin Novel and Epigram

Abstract: The aim of this study is to analyse storytelling in Latin texts using the framework of Conversation Analysis. We focus on two literary genres: the novel and the epigram. The novels of Apuleius and Petronius offer extended examples of storytelling, with a narrative frame indicating how the telling is launched and how the recipients react to the telling, which at times also provides some hints about the bodily behaviour of the teller or recipients. Martial's epigrams, on the other hand, present a condensed form of storytelling: they begin directly with the telling and feature only very brief recipient reactions, which occur either during the telling or, in a few cases, at the end of it. This study will focus primarily on recipient responses to demonstrate how tellers shape them and how recipients respond to the storytelling both during the telling and at the end.

Keywords: Conversation Analysis, Storytelling, Latin novel, Latin epigram, Apuleius, Martial, Petronius

Applying Conversation Analysis to a language such as Latin, which is documented only in a written and mainly literary corpus, generally involves the study of drama. So far, comedies have received sustained critical attention since they most closely resemble real-life conversations. Even though they are obviously not transcriptions but rather stylised literary artefacts, these comedies are still structurally very close to the conversations analysed from recordings in modern languages and it has been demonstrated that Conversation Analysis yields similar results when applied to Latin.[1] Building on these earlier results, our aim is to study how Latin writers stylise conversations and how literary genre affects the choice or omission of certain conversational elements.

In this study, we will focus on telling. Thus far, Conversation Analysis of Latin texts has mostly focused on sequences, or larger sequential organisations (called activities), made up of adjacency pairs. These consist of a first pair part, which

1 See Letessier (2000), Roesch (2002, 2005 and 2008), Unceta Gomez (2010 and 2014), Berger (2020 and 2022), and Risselada (forthcoming).

Note: We would like to extend our whole-hearted thanks to the anonymous reviewers whose remarks enabled us to improve this paper.

Joseph Dalbera, Université de Corse, France
Frédérique Fleck, École normale supérieure de Paris, France

https://doi.org/10.1515/9783111332956-040

imposes a normative obligation to perform a type-fitted response, called a "second pair part", such as question–answer or request–compliance.[2] Our study will deal with one specific kind of activity, telling, which may include some adjacency pairs, but is fundamentally built around one central turn-at-talk on the part of the teller. That central turn is typically an extended, multi-unit turn, with the recipient allowing the teller to hold the floor until they have completed their telling. The telling can either be initiated by the teller, who often secures the floor for an extended turn-at-talk in a pre-sequence, or prompted by a prospective recipient.[3] Mid-telling responses on the recipient's part are frequent, but not normatively required. At the end of the telling, a recipient response is expected. The activity of telling could be defined as follows: it consists in reporting facts and conveying a stance towards those facts.[4] Storytelling is the kind of telling which has received the most attention, but there are also other types of telling, such as descriptive telling, which will also be addressed in this paper.

We will examine two literary genres that are very different in nature and scope, viz. the novels of Petronius and Apuleius on the one hand and the epigrams of Martial on the other. While these two genres do of course differ considerably in terms of the number, extension, and types of telling incorporated, such contrasts will shed light on the various ways in which telling can be handled. Our aim is not only to show that it is worthwhile applying Conversation Analysis to these works, but also to outline the elements of telling that each writer adopts and adapts to the norms imposed by the literary genre in question.

1 The Latin Novel: Telling Lots of Stories?

The novel is a narrative genre, just like history or the epic. However, this Latin literary genre is distinguished by the importance given to the spoken word, which is abundantly present in all its forms – monologues, conversations, dialogues, insults, prayers, accusations, etc. – as well as in a number of stories recounted orally by internal characters. Direct speech thus becomes the driving force of the novel, especially through the use of embedded stories, multiple tellers, and polyphonic narrative.

2 On sequence organisation, see Schegloff (2007) and Stivers (2013); on adjacency pairs more specifically, see Schegloff (2007: 13–27) and Stivers (2013: 192–193).

3 See Mandelbaum (2013: 495–497) and Schegloff (2007: 37–44).

4 See Stivers (2013: 200–203).

The two Latin novels (*The Satyricon* and *The Metamorphoses*) thus offer a rich source of orality (telling, storytelling, stories, narrative, etc.), making it important to specify which type we will focus on here.

We will begin with an example that seems to be representative of the type of telling that forms the focus of this study: the passage from Book 7 of *Metamorphoses* which depicts a young girl held hostage by brigands. Her fiancé comes to meet them, disguised as a thief, and tries to win the group's trust by recounting his feats as a brigand, as can be seen in (1):

(1) *Nec me putetis egenum vel abiectum neve de pannulis istis virtutes meas aestimetis. Nam* ***praefui*** *validissimae manui totamque prorsus* ***devastavi*** *Macedoniam. Ego* <u>*sum*</u> *praedo famosus Haemus ille Thracius cuius totae provinciae nomen* <u>*horrescunt*</u> [. . .]. *Sed omnem pristinam sociorum fortium multitudinem magnasque illas opes exiguo temporis* ***amisi*** *spatio. Nam procuratorem principis ducenaria perfunctum, dehinc fortuna tristiore decussum, praetereuntem Jove irato fueram adgressus* ***sed rei noscendae carpo ordinem.***

Fuit *quidam multis officiis in aula Caesaris clarus atque conspicuus, ipsi etiam probe spectatus. Hunc insimulatum quorundam astu* ***proiecit*** *extorrem saeviens invidia.* (Apvl. met. 7, 5–6)

'And do not think me destitute or an outcast; do not judge my virtues from these rags. **I was in command** of a strong and mighty band and **laid waste** the whole of Macedonia. <u>I am</u> the famous brigand, Haemus the Thracian, at whose name every province <u>trembles</u>. [. . .] But **I lost** the whole host of brave comrades and all the wealth I once commanded in one brief span of time. One of the emperor's procurators with a two hundred thousand salary had been driven from his position by a harsh turn of Fortune. To my misfortune I had attacked him as he was passing by. **But I will tell the story from start** to finish so that you will understand what happened.

There was once a man, famous and distinguished for his numerous services in Caesar's court and well regarded even by the emperor himself. Falsely accused through the duplicity of certain individuals, **he was** cast forth into exile by savage Envy.'[5]

In the first part, the young man appears: he shows the brigands that his past actions make him a potential accomplice. The perfect forms *praefui . . . devastavi . . . amisi*

5 Latin text translated by Arthur Hanson for Apuleius' *Metamorphoses* (Loeb Classical Library 44) and by Gareth Schmeling for Petronius' *Satyricon* (Loeb Classical Library 15).

. . . situate these actions in the past, yet they do not "narrate" them; the teller is merely describing himself by saying who he is. Each of these actions denoted by the verbs is understood in relation to the moment of speaking (the so-called "report mode"[6]), without a chronological link with the other two.

The present tense used here refers to a larger context that encompasses the moment of speaking, thus contrasting with the historic present: *Ego* ***sum*** *praedo famosus Haemus . . . cuius totae provinciae nomen* ***horrescunt***.

The character then goes on to state the reasons for his condition, recounting a sequence of events. He moves from report mode to "narrative mode", as he makes clear: *sed rei noscendae carpo ordinem* – '**But I will tell the story from start** to finish so that you will understand. . .'. The narrative then begins and the teller constructs his story, still using perfect indicative forms, but now breaking away from the conversational situation, because the moment of speaking is no longer a point of view about the narrated events: ***Fuit*** *. . . in aula Caesaris clarus atque conspicuus, . . . Hunc . . .* ***proiecit*** *extorrem saeviens invidia. . .*

This example shows that within the same turn-at-talk that reports past events, the teller can alter the interactional construction. It depends on the point of view within the interactional framework from which we look at the event; either from *hic et nunc* (report mode) or, alternatively, each process carrying its own point of view (narrative mode): two poles of the same *continuum*, with varying degrees, according to the importance given to the interactional framework.[7]

This example illustrates the most common type of story in the novel; narrated in a conversational context, in the first person, with "points in context", such stories tend to break away from the *hic et nunc* with astonishing rapidity, coming closer to the narrative mode.

Should we thus consider that we are still within the scope of Conversation Analysis? This is a complex question, as these stories (even monologic ones) are generally embedded in broader sequences, which often introduce an audience, thus giving the impression (or even the illusion) that the story is a conversation. This is what we need to clarify.

---

6 These expressions ("report mode" / "narrative mode") reflect the famous distinction inspired in French by Benveniste and the "linguistique de l'énonciation", between "discours" and "Histoire" (or "discours" / "récit"). This distinction is used in Dalbera (2016) to analyse the functioning and values of the Latin indicative perfect.

7 See Dalbera (2016: 69–194).

1.1 Stories Where the Reader is the Only Recipient

We will begin with what is most distinctive about the novel of Apuleius: the dialogue with the reader, set up already in the prologue, which serves to frame the entire story. *Metamorphoses* is a conversation: a *sermo milesius* presenting a continuous interplay of discourses and voices, since the book itself speaks in this prologue (1, 1),[8] addressing the reader directly, before giving Lucius, the primary, internal narrator, the floor. Lucius, in turn, hands the floor over to a number of characters – secondary narrators (Theramenes, Socrates, Telyphron, etc.).[9]

After this first occurrence in the prologue, *Lector intende laetaberis* (1, 1), the narrator addresses the reader sixteen more times in the novel. This always occurs at the metadiegetic level, whether through the use of vocatives – *lector scrupulosus* (9, 30), *lector optime* (10, 2), *studiose lector* (11, 23) – or second-person pronouns and verb forms.[10] Within this conversational framework, the narrator sets out to tell different stories: often, these take the form of short, self-contained stories which have no effect whatsoever on the rest of the narrative. Here are two examples:

(2) *devertimus ad quempiam pagum... cognoscimus lepidam de adulterio cuiusdam pauperis fabulam, quam vos etiam cognoscatis volo...* (Apvl. met. 9, 4)
'We halted at a village . . . and there we heard an amusing story about the cuckolding of a certain poor workman, which I want you to hear too...'

(3) *Fabulam denique bonam prae ceteris, suave comptam ad auris vestras adferre decrevi, et en occipio.* (Apvl. met. 9, 14)
'And so here is a story, better than all the others and delightfully elegant, which I have decided to bring to your ears. So here goes.'

Such stories would not be of interest were it not for this fictitious underlying conversation[11] which the narrator "reactivates" every time (s)he wants to fully engage the reader. In these two instances, the story had been launched without a pre-telling

---

8 See Harrison (1990) and his "Speaking book". See Dalbera (2021a).

9 Dalbera (2021b: Ch. 1).

10 See Puccini-Delbey (2004).

11 This narrator-reader pairing constructs what M. Vuillaume (1990) calls the "2nd level of fiction", where both seem to contemplate the first level (that of the characters), which they discuss together, building a kind of conversation.

sequence, imposing the telling, which is justified in the second case by affirming its "tellability":[12] *"Fabulam . . . bonam prae ceteris" . . . suave comptam ad auris vestras.*

The narrator sometimes goes further, however, and brings this conversational space to life through dialogues. The reader can be depicted as interrupting the (story)teller in the middle of his story:

(4) *Sed forsitan, lector scrupulosus reprehendens narratum meum, sic argumentaberis:* ***Unde autem astutule asine . . . quid secreto ut affirmas, mulieres gesserint scire potuisti.*** (APVL. met. 9, 30)
'But perhaps as a careful reader you will find fault with my story, reasoning as follows: "**How did it happen, you clever little ass, that . . . you were able to find out what the women were doing in secret, as you insist?**"'
Sed nequis indignationis meae reprehendat impetum secum sic reputans: "Ecce nunc patiemur philosophantem nobis asinum?", rursus, unde decessi, ***revertar ad fabulam*** (APVL. met. 10, 33)
'But I am afraid one of you may reproach me for this attack of indignation and think to himself, "So, now are we going to have to stand an ass lecturing us on philosophy?" **So I shall return to the story** at the point where I left it.'

These are interesting yet marginal cases because, most of the time, stories are told during a conversation – or at least a verbal exchange – between the characters, and many aspects therefore fall under "conversational storytelling".

1.2 The Tale of Telyphron (2, 19–2, 31): Conversational Storytelling?

There are a large number of stories (tales) embedded in the two novels. The story may appear in a simple dialogue between two characters, in larger conversations, or may even be told in front of an entire group. The latter is the case with Book 2 of *Metamorphoses*, when Byrrhena invites Telyphron to tell his story in front of a group of guests at a dinner party.

It is quite remarkable how the narrative trajectory and the conversation between characters help the story unfold so realistically and with such fluidity. Lucius goes to the town of Hypata, where he meets a woman called Byrrhena. She

12 On tellability, see Norrick (2007: 134–135).
This attitude by the audience is represented in a very similar way in Martial: see example (10), section 2.3.

recognises him as a relative and invites him over for dinner, together with some friends. There, the conversation begins. Byrrhena asks how Lucius is settling in Hypata (*quam commode versaris in nostra patria?*) before going on to praise the comforts of town life. Lucius agrees (*Vera memoras. . .*) but says that he fears witches who prey on the dead. 'They don't even spare the living', adds a guest (*nec viventibus quidem ullis parcitur*), and while the whole room bursts into unbridled laughter (*licentiosos cachinnos effunditur*), all eyes turn to a guest who stands up to leave. Byrrhena intervenes and asks him to tell a story: *Immo mi Telyphron, Byrrhena inquit . . . fabulam tuam remetire comitate . . . ut . . . Lucius lepidi sermonis tui perfruatur* (2, 20) 'Byrrhena cried: "No, no, dear Thelyphron, . . . tell us that tale of yours again, so . . . Lucius here can enjoy the charm of your delightful story-telling."' Reluctant at first, Telyphron eventually agrees: he launches into his story and recounts how, while he was watching over a dead body, a witch mutilated his face. This story continues for eight pages before provoking the laughter of the audience once again.

This is a fine example of the numerous embedded stories that appear in a conversation. Let us examine the extent to which the novel as a genre adopts the codes of conversational storytelling.

While some stories are launched spontaneously by the upcoming narrator, as the first pair part of an adjacency pair, the tale of Telyphron, like many others, begins at an invitation, as a second pair part. It is Byrrhena here who attests to the interest aroused by this story (which the whole audience knows and appreciates: *convivium totum in licentiosos cachinnos effunditur*), as well as to its tellability: *Lucius lepidi sermonis tui perfruatur comitate.* With these words, Byrrhena urges the entire audience to be silent and listen.

Therefore, Telyphron does not have to arouse the audience's interest in his story (nor does he have to justify its truthfulness);[13] nevertheless, clearly annoyed by the mockery, he first shows some signs of reluctance, perhaps to direct the reception of his story: *ferenda non est quorundam insolentia* (2, 20).

This pleasure of storytelling, like the resulting mockery, attests to the interaction between the teller and the audience, as do the gestures Telyphron makes before telling the story (*porrigit dextram et ad instar oratorum conformat articulum*). The teller plays a role in front of his audience and his performance elicits repetitive laughter: this occurs first when he simply alludes to the anecdote (*licentiosos cachinnos*; 2, 20) and again at the end of the story, among Byrrhena's guests, *rursum cachinnum integrant* (2, 31), echoing the characters of the embedded story,

13 Like other tellers, who must protest the truth of their tale, such as Niceros, Trimalchion, and Theramenes.

when a dead man reveals to the crowd that Telyphron was mutilated: *dum risus ebullit* (2, 30).

We can find some recurrent elements of conversational storytelling here, just as we can easily identify the main features of narrative structure, as the sociolinguist Labov points out in his works, which Norrick further exploits. Below is the narrative structure that can be applied to the tale of Telyphron:

The "abstract" (which answers the question "what was it about?")[14] is given by one of the guests before Telyphron starts telling the story: *Immo vero istic nec viventibus quidem ullis parcitur. Et nescio qui simile passus ore undique omnifariam deformato truncatus est* (2, 20) – 'Yes, but here they do not even spare the living. There was a man who had an experience of that kind; his face was completely mutilated and disfigured.'

The "orientation" (which answers the questions "who, what, when, where?") is essentially signaled by the teller from the very first sentence he utters: *Pupillus ego Mileto profectus ad spectaculum Olympicum . . . procerum quendam senem . . . praedicabat siquid mortuum servare vellet de pretio liceretur. . .* (2, 21) – 'When I was still a minor I set out from Miletus to see the Olympic games [. . .] a tall old man [. . .] proclaiming [. . .] that anyone willing to guard a dead man should bid for the job. . .'

As for the "complicating action" (which consists of sequentially ordered narrative clauses), the narrative is perfectly structured to follow a chronological path (having arrived in town, Telyphron agrees to guard the dead body – he goes to the home of the dead man, etc.)

There is no separate "evaluation" (which answers the question "so what?") here, despite the length of the story, and at no point does the teller go back to his *hic et nunc*, in order to evaluate. At best, we might be able to identify some subtle hints in the teller's attitude: Telyphron is hiding, wants to leave, and cannot take the mocking tone triggered by the past events he is recounting.

The "resolution" (which answers the question "what finally happened?") is present: as soon as he has heard the story of the dead man, Telyphron realises that he was mutilated by the *strigas* and tries to check: *nasum prehendo: sequitur, aures pertracto: deruunt . . . dum risus ebullit . . . evado* (2, 30) – '[I] grasped my nose: it came away; I rubbed my ears: they fell off . . . laughter broke out . . . I escaped.'

There is no real "coda" (which puts off any further questions about what happened or why it mattered), at least not in direct speech: the tale is quickly interrupted by a return to the main narrative, perhaps because the story is already known and the punchline is quite clear. There is a simple return to the narrative: *Cum primum*

14 On these various stages of Labov's narrative structure, see Norrick (2007: 129).

Telyphron hanc fabulam posuit (2, 31) – 'As soon as Thelyphron finished this story', which points to the reaction of the drunk guests: *rursum cachinnum integrant* (2, 31) – '[the banqueters] renewed their uproarious laughter', raising a toast to the God of Laughter. . .

In this example, a number of the elements of an oral story or even a conversational story appear to occur. Now we need to consider the limits of such occurrences.

1.3 Limitations of Conversational Storytelling: Telyphron vs Niceros

On the whole, we have seen that the tale of Telyphron contains far more narrative clauses (which describe an irreversible series of events) than free clauses (which can be moved or eliminated without destroying the basic narrative structure);[15] they are preliminary to the story and are expressed by the teller's own actions or by the group. Moreover, if the story is initiated within a real conversation, it quickly turns into a narrative which no longer involves any turn-at-talk, consequently involving no real interaction between the teller and the audience: herein lies the distinction made by Norrick between "genuine" conversational storytelling (which is interactive, negotiated and contextualised), and "oral storytelling" (which involves monologic, non-conversational stories).[16]

To better understand in what respect this story moves away from the conversational model, we will compare the tale of Telyphron to a story from the *Satyricon*, taken from the *Cena Trimalchionis*. The *Cena Trimalchionis* represents a unique moment in the novel, because some characters, such as the freedmen, speak in authentic spoken Latin; their language provides a far more precise description of linguistic reality than the rest of the corpus.[17] Despite this particular feature, the popular tale of Niceros (the werewolf story, Petron. 61, 6–9) seems to echo the setting of the story of Telyphron[18] with great precision. In fact, in a paper from 1995, F. Gaide compared this story of Niceros to the stories of "personal experience" examined by Labov (1972) to show how closely they match. A quick comparison with the previous story will help us understand what sets it apart from real conversational storytelling.

15 For this distinction between narrative/free clauses, see Norrick (2007: 128–129).

16 Norrick (2007: 127).

17 See Boyce (1991).

18 They are both part of the Milesian tradition, performed at the invitation of the host in an assembly and are accounts of experience (in the first person) in a context of death.

The host Trimalchio asks Niceros to tell a story. At first, Niceros is reluctant to speak before *scholasticos*, but eventually he consents (as did Telyphron). He begins with long considerations in which the orientation is far more developed than in Telyphron's case; as can be seen in the following extract,[19] we can identify the time (*Cum adhuc servirem*), place (*in vico angusto*), and characters involved (*Melissa, contuberbalis. . .*).

(5) [. . .] *talem fabulam exorsus est: "Cum adhuc servirem, habitabamus in vico angusto;* ***nunc*** *Gavillae domus* ***est****. Ibi, quomodo dii volunt, amare coepi uxorem Terentii coponis:* ***noveratis*** *Melissam Tarentinam, pulcherrimum bacciballum. Sed ego non mehercules corporaliter illam autem aut propter res venerarias curavi, sed magis quod benemoria fuit. Si quid ab illa petii, numquam mihi negatum; fecit assem semissem habui; in illius sinum demandavi, nec umquam fefellitus sum. Huius contubernalis ad villam supremum diem obiit. Itaque per scutum per ocream egi aginavi, quemadmodum ad illam pervenirem;* ***scitis autem, in angustiis amici apparent.****"* (PETRON. 61, 6–9)
'[. . .] he began this story: "When I was still a slave, we lived on a narrow alley in the house **now belonging** to Gavilla. There, as the gods arranged it, I fell in love with the wife of Terentius, the innkeeper; **you all knew Melissa** of Tarentum, a round thing of pure beauty. But I swear that I was drawn to her not for her physical beauty or because of sexual attraction, but rather because she was sweet-natured. She never refused anything I asked of her. If she made an as, I got a half: I entrusted it all to her keeping, and she never cheated me. Then her common-law partner died on the estate, and so by might and main I did everything in my power to get to her: **as you know, friends turn up in tight places**. . ."'

Unlike in the tale of Telyphron, free clauses are full of frequent references to the *hic et nunc* (*nunc Gavillae domus est*), addresses to the audience (*noveratis*), as well as "disfluencies" typical of a conversational story: the incomplete and irrelevant elements that "require special attention and delay the narrative";[20] remarks about Melissa's beauty, honesty or generosity have no effect whatsoever on the rest of the story.

In addition to being short, the narrative phase (the complicating action) is repeatedly interrupted by moments when the narrator goes back to the interac-

19 The tale is too long to be transcribed here in full.
20 ". . . *disfluencies* flourish, such as false starts with abrupt cutoffs, and restarts or self-corrections and repetitions. False starts and pausefillers. . ." (Norrick 2007: 130).
For this reading of the passage, see Martin (1999).

tional situation, and is full of declarations of honesty (*nolite me iocari putare*; *si mentior*), rendering the story unwieldy.

There is a clear reversal in the significance of free clauses and narrative clauses in the two stories. This creates an imbalance in the content of Niceros' story: delivered without suspense, the metamorphosis itself, which should be the climax in the story, is rushed through in just three words (*lupus factus est*), being delivered so quickly that nothing is actually conveyed. This has led some critics, such as R. Martin, to regard the story as "a bad narrative". However, Niceros clearly manages to captivate his audience. It is a total success, as reported in the story: *Attonitis admiratione universis* (63, 1) – 'With everyone dumbfounded', before Trimalchio articulates the collective sentiment: *Salvo, inquit, tuo sermone, Trimalchio, si qua fides est, ut mihi pili inhorruerunt* (31, 1) – 'In all respect for the truth of your story, if you'll believe me, my hair stood on end'. Fear is infectious, and the emotion is so intense that it gives rise to another story, which is its thematic counterpoint:[21] *Et ipse vobis rem horribilem narrabo* (63, 1) – 'But I too will tell you a hair-raising tale'. This is a response-story, as defined by Norrick,[22] which is given in response to the first story and seeks to establish a common experience, through the suggestion that "the same thing happened to me". Such response stories attest to attentive listenership and ratify foregoing stories, providing a form of endorsement of them.

It is clear from these elements that what distinguishes the story of Niceros is that it takes the audience into account: this is why it may be a bad narrative, but an excellent story!

On the other hand, taking the audience into account remains very superficial in Telyphron's story; especially as it shows no disfluencies. We never look at the story from the moment of speaking; his story is monologic and involves no real interaction with the audience.

Some choices are clearly dictated by the requirements of the literary genre, since it is obvious that the two novelists invest meticulous care in depicting the ways in which a teller modifies their speech according to their recipient. We find rich vocabulary and expressions that act as *didaskalia* introducing direct speech. We cannot enter into detail here but the novels contain many expressions[23] that denote the teller's act of gazing at his interlocutor: *conversus ad me* (PETRON. 98, 6); *respiciens ad Ascylton* (PETRON. 72, 5); *Et ad Venerem conlata facie* (APVL. met. 6, 23); *Eam suus dominus intuens* (APVL. met. 9, 33); *Trimalchio autem miti ad nos vultu respexit* (PETRON. 48, 1). The character's eyes also sometimes show a strong feeling

21 On the contrary, the coda for Telyphron is extremely limited, without any story in counterpoint.

22 Norrick (2007: 137).

23 Here are just a few of them. See Dalbera (2021b: Ch. 2.1.3).

of affection: *limis et morsicantibus oculis. . .* (APVL. met. 2, 10), while his emotions or intentions appear in gestures, which precede speech: *diu capite quassanti* (APVL. met. 8, 19); *perfricata fronte* (PETRON. 132, 12); *complosis manibus* (PETRON. 137, 1); *Contorta et vituperanti nare* (APVL. met. 7, 9); *adrepta manu Photidis et admota meis luminibus* (APVL. met. 3, 22), etc.

The novelists even pay attention to the tone of voice and its modulations: *voce asperrima increpans* (APVL. met. 1, 25); *lugubriter eiulantes* (APVL. met. 3, 8); *tertiata verba semihianti voce substrepens* (APVL. met. 5, 18); *lentissima voce* (PETRON. 36, 7); *cruciabilem spiritum ducens* (APVL. met. 1, 7); *nam rursus altius ingemescens* (APVL. met. 2, 30), as well as to the sighs and all the forms of laughter that accompany their words.

This rich lexical array could enrich the conversational stories in the novel, adding to the sense of realism. However, most of these expressions are, in fact, to be found in dialogues and conversations, including those inside the embedded stories, rather than in conversational sequences that introduce the story itself.

To conclude this section, we might therefore deduce that the tales of Telyphron and Niceros demonstrate different degrees of realism in the representation of a conversational story in a novel. Although much more faithful in Niceros' story, this representation is still far from accurate: his story shows no evidence of a false start, hesitations, turn-taking in dialogue, and not even a single narrative interruption. Even more striking is that the whole audience is familiar with his story, which is predictable and "performed" again (as is the case with Telyphron). Yet none of the listeners interact to construct a polyphonic narrative, as is characteristic of conversational stories. It is true that the two tellers who deliver a personal story tend to retain "storytelling rights",[24] but in reality we might have expected more interaction and a more collaborative construction.

In the way it is developed, narration in a novel clearly chooses fluidity and command of a storyline (at least for Telyphron). To avoid the pitfalls and unwieldiness of a monologic story, the novelists choose other ways of introducing polyphony: orality is largely present in their narratives with the many episodes of dialogue and conversation they contain. Orality is also conveyed through embedding: Telyphron himself brings the words of an old man, a prophet and then a dead man into his story. They all, in turn, report another aspect of the narrated event. The conversational dimension of the narrative is therefore internal: these are no longer external and simultaneous voices that construct the narrative, but internal, embedded, and successive voices that orally report past events, often with all the nuances of orality, as they take turns delivering their stories.

24 Norrick (2007: 127).

2 The Epigram: Telling in a Nutshell

2.1 The Development of Conversational Telling in Epigrams

While the novel, being full of characters telling stories, clearly features telling, the choice of the epigram to study telling may seem more surprising. Yet the epigram has, from the very beginning, been a kind of telling. A speaker, who is often a tomb or a votive object, addresses the passer-by to tell them who the deceased was and how he died, or why it was dedicated to such and such a deity. While this kind of telling is indeed part of an interaction with an addressee, it is reduced to the telling proper, with the teller simply reporting facts without any recipient response. From classical Greek times onwards, however, the function of the passer-by developed, leading to the appearance of dialogues between the passer-by and the tomb or between the passer-by and the deceased themself, for instance.[25] These dialogues are "etiological": the aim of the questions is to extract the information that the epigram is supposed to provide anyway.[26] From the point of view of Conversation Analysis, dialogical epigrams can be said to develop in two main directions.[27] Some take the form of more or less balanced dialogues, presented as a series of adjacent question–answer pairs, as below in (6):

(6) **α. Εἶπον ἀνειρομένῳ τίς καὶ τίνος ἐσσί.** β. Φίλαυλος
Εὐκρατίδεω. **α. Ποδαπὸς δ᾽ εὔχεαι** . . .
α. Ἔζησας δὲ τίνα στέργων βίον; β. Οὐ τὸν ἀρότρου,
οὐδὲ τὸν ἐκ νηῶν, τὸν δὲ σοφοῖς ἕταρον.
α. Γήραϊ δ᾽ ἢ νούσῳ βίον ἔλλιπες; β. Ἤλυθον
Ἅιδαναὐτοθελεί, Κείων γευσάμενος κυλίκων.
α. Ἠ πρέσβυς; β. Καὶ κάρτα. **α. Λάχοι νύ σε βῶλος ἐλαφρὴ
σύμφωνον πινυτῷ σχόντα λόγῳ βίοτον.** (Meleager, *A.P.* 7, 470)
'**A. "Tell him who enquires, who and whose son thou art."** B. "Philaulus son of Eucratides." **A. "And from whence dost thou say?"** B. ". . ." **A. "What livelihood didst thou choose when alive?"** B. "Not that from the plough nor that from ships, but that which is gained in the society of sages." **A. "Didst thou depart this life from old age or from sickness?"** B. "Of my own will I came to Hades, having drunk of the Cean cup." **A. "Wast thou old?"** B. "Yea, very

25 On the development of the dialogical epigram, see Tueller (2008: Ch. 1) and del Barrio Vega (1989).
26 See Tueller (2008: Ch. 13).
27 On these two types, see del Barrio Vega (1989: 192–193).

old." A. **"May the earth that rests on thee be light, for the life thou didst lead was in accordance with wisdom and reason."'**[28]

Others consist of a single question–answer pair, with the passer-by simply eliciting the telling at the beginning of the epigram with an inciting question, as below in (7):

(7) **α. Ἀρχαίης ὦ θινὸς ἐπεστηλωμένον ἄχθος,**
εἴποις ὅντιν' ἔχεις, ἢ τίνος, ἢ ποδαπόν.
β. Φίντων' Ἑρμιονῆα Βαθυκλέος, ὃν πολὺ κῦμα
ὤλεσεν, Ἀρκτούρου λαίλαπι χρησάμενον. (Leonidas of Tarentum, *A.P.* 7, 503)
'**A. "O stone standing a burden on the ancient beach, tell me whom thou holdest, whose son and whence."** B. "Phinto the son of Bathycles of Hermione, who perished in the heavy sea, encountering the blast of Arcturus."'

In this last kind of epigram, the question and answer can both occupy a distich, as in (7). Yet the epigram may also retain a structure which is more characteristic of telling, with an extended turn-at-talk of the teller, as in (8):

(8) α. Ξεῖνε, τί μὰν πεύθῃ; **β. Τίνες ἐν χθονὶ τοῖσδ' ὑπὸ τύμβοις;**
α. Οὓς γλυκεροῦ φέγγους Ζώπυρος ἐστέρισεν,
Δᾶμις, Ἀριστοτέλης, Δημήτριος, Ἀρκεσίλαος,
Σώστρατος, οἵ τ' ὀπίσω μέχρι Παραιτονίου.
Κηρύκιον γὰρ ἔχων ξύλινον, καὶ πλαστὰ πέδιλα,
ὡς Ἑρμῆς, κατάγει τοὺς θεραπευομένους. (Nicarchus, *A.P.* 11, 124)
'A. Stranger, what dost thou seek to know? **B. Who are here in earth under these tombs?** A. All those whom Zopyrus robbed of the sweet daylight, Damis, Aristoteles, Demetrius, Arcesilaus, Sostratus, and the next ones so far as Paraetonium. For with a wooden herald's staff and counterfeit sandals, like Hermes, he leads down his patients to Hell.'

The difference between these two types is not always clear-cut, however, due to the characteristic brevity of the epigrammatic genre: on the one hand, the passer-by never asks a great number of questions and, on the other, the turn-at-talk dedicated to telling proper is never much extended.

The aim of the second part of this paper is to study in which way the epigram, as a literary genre marked by the constraints of brevity, affects the representation of

---

28 The translations of the epigrams from the *Greek Anthology* are those of W. R. Paton in the Loeb collection.

conversational telling. To this end, we will examine Martial's *Epigrams*, written at the end of the first century AD, a corpus in which the dialogical epigram has greatly evolved. Using the model developed by Conversation Analysis on the basis of conversations recorded in modern languages such as English, we will try and see what kind of recipient response Martial chooses to include in his epigrammatic telling. As mentioned in the introduction, the recipient may intervene to prompt the telling (as exemplified by the tale of Telyphron, in section 1.2), but the telling is often spontaneous, that is, launched by the teller himself.[29] The study of modern language storytelling also shows that mid-telling responses are not normatively required, but are frequent. The recipient often provides acknowledgment tokens early on in the telling (English *Mm hm, Uh huh*), indicating activity alignment, that is, that he/she is listening to the telling and willing to let the teller go on with their extended multi-unit turn. When the teller's evaluative stance towards the reported facts appears more clearly, and especially when the high point of the story is near, the recipient usually provides affiliative tokens (such as the English *Wow!*), showing his own evaluative stance, so that the teller and the recipient can negotiate the extent to which their stances are matched during the telling.[30] These mid-telling responses range from passive to active, depending on the extent to which they constrain the teller to respond and/or reshape the ongoing telling.[31] At the completion of the telling, a recipient uptake is due: the recipient is supposed to react to the telling, thus showing his/her evaluative stance toward it. The preferred recipient stance is "affiliative": the teller expects the recipient to support his/her own affective stance (see the reaction of the audience to Nyceros' tale in section 1.3, for example).[32]

2.2 Mid-telling Responses in Martial's *Epigrams*

The most common type of epigram featuring a telling with recipient response in Martial's work is a well-known kind of scoptic epigram, in which the recipient asks a question near the end of the epigram; the answer provides the surprise ending expected at the closure of the epigram.[33] The main part of these epigrams consists in a telling which begins abruptly, without any preface, with the poet's *persona* acting as the teller. The telling, which is generally descriptive and uses the present general tense, describes the behaviour of the target of the epigram, reporting on his

29 Mandelbaum (2013: 495–497).

30 Stivers (2013: 201).

31 Mandelbaum (2013: 501).

32 Stivers (2013: 201–202); on the concept of "affiliation", see Lindtröm and Sorjonen (2013: 350–353).

33 See Valette and Vallat (2022).

or her actions. Unlike other scoptic epigrams, which do not involve any recipient response, the epigrams in which we are interested contain a telling that is deliberately obscure, making it impossible to understand what the teller is getting at. The recipient's question is triggered by the difficulty in understanding, and is essential to the completion of the telling, since it is only with the teller's answer that we perceive exactly what his/her affective stance towards the reported facts is. In other words, the telling is co-constructed by the teller and the recipient.[34]

An example of this can be seen in (9), an epigram in which recipient response is more important than usual, with two successive questions instead of one:

(9) — *Petit Gemellus nuptias Maronillae*
et cupit et instat et precatur et donat.
— ***Adeone pulchra est?*** — *Immo foedius nil est.*
— ***Quid ergo in illa petitur et placet?*** — *Tussit.* (MART. 1, 10)
'— Gemellus is a-wooing Maronilla. He is eager and insistent, begs her, gives her presents.
— **Is she such a beauty?**
— On the contrary, she couldn't be uglier.
— **So what is so desirable about her, so attractive?**
— Her cough.'[35]

The teller launches into the telling in line 1 by succinctly announcing his subject: Gemellus's courtship of Maronilla. This is equivalent to what Labov calls "abstract" in his analysis of the elements of narrative,[36] though we are dealing with a descriptive form of telling here.[37] In line 2, the teller describes Gemellus's insistence by indicating the character's various actions.

The question that opens line 3 shows the recipient's interest in the telling and makes it clear that he is striving to understand. This attitude aligns with the activity of telling.[38] The description of Gemellus's insistence on marrying Maronilla suggests that Gemellus is deeply in love with her. The recipient therefore assumes that the

34 On the "audience" as co-author, see Duranti (1986).
35 The translations of Martial's *Epigrams* are those of D. R. Shackleton Bailey in the Loeb collection.
36 On Labov's elements of narrative, see section 1.3 of this paper.
37 Unlike storytelling, which presents several successive events in chronological order, descriptive telling consists of a description; in the case of scoptic epigrams, this is a description of a character's behaviour.
38 "Aligned" means contributing to the smooth running of the conversational activity in progress, in this case telling. On alignment in storytelling, see Mandelbaum (2013: 500); on the distinction between alignment and affiliation, see Lindström and Sorjonene (2013: 352–353).

purpose of the telling is to praise Maronilla's qualities, namely her beauty. His question is, *de facto*, a request for confirmation: "Is she so beautiful?" This question also shows that he is willing to share what he believes to be the teller's affective stance, and to admire Maronilla's outstanding attractiveness.[39] The teller gives a negative answer, thus invalidating the recipient's assumption, but gives him no other clue. He offers no explanation for the actions he is describing, nor does he reveal his affective stance.[40] This leads the recipient to ask another question, this time more cautiously, as it is no longer a request for confirmation, but an open question. However, the verbs *petitur* and *placet* show that the recipient still assumes that Maronilla has some good qualities, which have led Gemellus to fall so much in love. The teller's answer, which ends the epigram, reveals that it is in fact Maronilla's illness that attracts Gemellus. It is only then that we understand that Maronilla is not an attractive young woman, but a wealthy woman, probably elderly and in poor health. Gemellus hopes that he will soon be widowed so that he can enjoy his inheritance freely. The aim of this descriptive telling is not to praise Maronilla's qualities, as the recipient first assumes, but to criticise Gemellus's greediness.

The introduction of a recipient response in the epigram has several advantages. Firstly, it allows the author to construct a cooperative reader, interested in the telling and trying to understand the teller's stance. Its main value, however, lies in the recipient's misinterpretation. This misinterpretation is induced by the way in which the facts are reported. The maxim of quantity is not observed: the teller provides no information about the characters he is talking about (their physical appearance or their economic and social situation), even though they are clearly not known to the recipient. Instead of providing the elements needed to shape an affiliative reaction on the recipient's part, the teller creates a discrepancy here. The recipient's misinterpretation helps emphasise the surprise ending of the epigram, as has often been noted.[41] Its most important function, however, seems to be to underline the paradoxical nature of the behaviour described. By assuming that Gemellus's courtship is motivated by his feelings, a deep love inspired by Maronilla's qualities, the recipient indicates what is expected. By not conforming to this pattern, Gemellus's actions appear deviant. The recipient response in mid-telling also allows us to sense what his response will be when the telling comes to an end, when he finally understands what is at stake. This response, which should follow the teller's final revelation, "*Tussit*", is not given in the epigram, but the previous response leaves no doubt as to its nature. The reaction will be one of surprise, but

39 On affiliation in storytelling, see Mandelbaum (2013: 500–501).

40 On the shaping of recipient response by the teller, see Mandelbaum (2013: 498–499).

41 See Laurens (2012: 346–359), Valette and Vallat (2022).

also, and above all, one of disapproval, an affiliated attitude, as the teller aims to criticise Gemellus.

This example shows how sparing the epigram is of its means. Neither the conversational context in which the telling takes place nor the recipient response to the punch line are represented. The only responses shown are those that occur mid-telling. These responses are of a very specific type: they are always questions. Insofar as they have an impact on the course of the telling, questions constitute what are known as "active" reactions on the part of the recipient, in contrast to passive or less active reactions such as acknowledgment tokens or evaluations, respectively.[42] Indeed, questions, prototypically first pair parts, require answers which may cut off or modify the telling. We can thus see that the recipient must be a true "co-author" of the telling if his or her responses are to be mentioned within the tight framework of epigram.

2.3 Recipient Response at the Completion of the Telling

The recipient response at the completion of the telling may also, albeit more seldomly, be presented in epigrams. To be worthy of inclusion, however, this uptake must be more than just the expected affiliative reaction. Epigram 1, 96, which has a fairly complex structure, features the poet's *persona* instructing his meter, the scazon, to report a telling to his friend Maternus. This telling appears here in direct speech, in lines 4–8. It is an epigram within an epigram (see the framed section in [10]).

(10) *Si non molestum est teque non piget, scazon,*
nostro rogamus pauca verba Materno
dicas in aurem sic ut audiat solus:

> *"Amator ille tristium lacernarum*
> *et baeticatus atque leucophaeatus,*
> *qui coccinatos non putat viros esse*
> *amethystinasque mulierum at vestes,*
> *nativa laudet, habeat et licet semper*
> *fuscos colores, galbinos habet mores."*

42 See Mandelbaum (2013: 501).

Rogabit unde suspicer virum mollem.
Una lavamur: aspicit nihil sursum,
sed spectat oculis devorantibus draucos
nec otiosis mentulas videt labris.
Quaeris quis hic sit? Excidit mihi nomen. (MART. 1, 96)

'If it's not too much trouble and you don't mind, please, my limping verse, say a few words in friend Maternus' ear, so that he is the only one to hear them. "That lover of sad-colored cloaks, who goes about in Baetic wool or grey, thinks people who wear scarlet unmanly, and calls violet clothes dress for women, though he praise native stuff and be always somberly attired – his morals are green." **He will ask how I come to suspect the man of effeminacy.** We bathe together. He never looks up, but watches the athletes with devouring eyes and his lips work as he gazes at their cocks. Who is it, you ask? The name has escaped me.'

The second half of line 8, *galbinos habet mores*, closes the telling by denouncing the morals of an anonymous character. This character is in the habit of wearing austere, dark clothes, and of attacking those who wear coloured clothing: he accuses them of taking on the receptive role in a homosexual relationship, a role that most Romans considered to be effeminate and unworthy of a citizen. Martial rejects this link between the colour of clothes and sexual behaviour and accuses this character of himself exhibiting the sexual behaviour he denounces in others, despite his dark clothes. The end of the telling thus clearly indicates the teller's affective stance, which is to criticise this anonymous character.

Line 9 shows the supposed reaction of the recipient, Maternus, at the end of the telling. This response is disaffiliative insofar as Maternus, instead of laughing and sharing the teller's attitude of blame, refuses to give immediate credence to what is reported to him.[43] In fact, the teller is making an accusation without any proof, and Maternus can rightly question its veracity. In response, the teller provides evidence based on autopsy: he has himself seen the man he denounces behave in a way that leaves little doubt as to his sexual inclinations. The epigram does not record Maternus's final reaction.[44] Yet Maternus's earlier response suggests that he will share the teller's attitude of blame once the teller has substantiated his claims. A further

43 This disaffiliative attitude is closely paralleled by the recipient response displayed in example (4) of section 1.1, a passage from Apuleius' *Metamorphoses* where the reader interrupts the storyteller to express his distrust.

44 The question in the last line is asked by the scazon, not by Maternus.

response from Maternus showing his affiliation can therefore be dispensed with, as it would add nothing to the epigram.

We find another disaffiliative response at the completion of the telling in epigram 1, 44. Here, we are no longer faced with a single epigram, but rather a cycle comprising epigrams 1, 6, 1, 14 and 1, 44. In 1, 6 and 1, 14, we have what we might call, using the distinction proposed by Norrick (2007: 138–139), two distinct performances: a telling and a retelling of the same event. This event took place during the circus games: it is the moment when a rabbit was spared by a lion and even entered its mouth and emerged unharmed.

(11) *Aetherias aquila puerum portante per auras*
inlaesum timidis unguibus haesit onus:
nunc sua Caesareos exorat praeda leones
tutus et ingenti ludit in ore lepus.
Quae maiora putas miracula? Summus utrisque
auctor adest: haec sunt Caesaris, illa Iovis. (MART. 1, 6)
'As the eagle bore the boy through the airs of heaven, the timid talons did not harm their clinging freight. Now Caesar's lions are won over by their prey and the hare plays safely in the massive jaws. Which do you think the greater marvel? Behind both stands the Highest. The one is Caesar's, the other Jove's.'

(12) *Delicias, Caesar, lususque iocosque leonum*
vidimus – hoc etiam praestat harena tibi –
cum prensus blando totiens a dente rediret
et per aperta vagus curreret ora lepus.
Unde potest avidus captae leo parcere praedae?
Sed tamen esse tuus dicitur: ergo potest. (MART. 1, 14)
'We have seen the pranks, the sportive gambols of the lions, Caesar (this too the arena offers you), when the hare as often as seized returned from the gentle fang and ran at large through the open jaws. How comes it that a greedy lion can spare his captive prey? Ah, but he is said to be yours. Therefore he can.'

Epigram 1, 44 comments on this retelling: *bis idem facimus* (line 3). It presents a putative response from Stella, Martial's patron:

(13) *Lascivos leporum cursus lususque leonum*
quod maior nobis charta minorque gerit
*et bis idem facimus, **nimium si, Stella, videtur***
***hoc tibi**, bis leporem tu quoque pone mihi.* (MART. 1, 44)

'Do my pages large and small contain the gamesome runs of hares and the play of lions? Do I do the same thing twice over? Well, **if this seems too much to you, Stella**, why not on your side give me hare twice over for dinner?'

Stella's supposed reaction is to question the tellability of the telling, based on the criterion of newness. Tellability is typically negotiated before the telling, often in a pre-telling sequence.[45] The teller may ask the recipients if they already know the facts he is about to report. Or one of the recipients may ask for a retelling. In the case of epigram 1, 14, the teller knowingly imposes a retelling. He justifies this at the end of epigram 1, 44: just as one never tires of a good dish, one never tires of a good telling. Retelling typically serves to convey group values.[46] The retelling here plays a role in the cohesion of the group of Roman citizens around its leader, the emperor. Its aim is to praise the Prince by applauding the games over which he has presided.

2.4 Concluding Remarks on Epigrammatic Telling

Recipient response is represented sparingly – but very effectively – in the epigrammatic genre. In Martial, telling usually begins without any invitation, announcement, or prior negotiation. It is not uncommon, however, for it to be interrupted by a question from the recipient who, by actively intervening, becomes a co-author of the telling. At the completion of the telling, the expected response demonstrating the recipient's affiliation is not directly represented; it is taken for granted. Only disaffiliative responses are of sufficient interest to sometimes be represented.

3 Conclusions

Thanks to the rich, multiple, varied examples of telling they contain, novels and epigrams are clearly a corpus to which Conversation Analysis can be fruitfully applied. Our study has enabled us to identify representations of the main phases we can expect to find in a telling: pretelling, with an invitation by the recipient or an announcement by the teller; telling itself, with its various stages; recipient mid-telling responses; and recipient response at the completion of the telling. We have also been able to identify – in both genres – the retelling of a story already

45 On this issue, see the discussion of example (3) in section 1.1.
46 See Norrick (2007: 138–139).

known to the recipient. Finally, the novel and the epigram both present examples of literary telling in which the recipient is the reader or a particular reader: as in the case of a letter as compared to a dialogue, a recipient response may be integrated but it is then simply assumed by the teller who anticipates it.

The two genres we have chosen to study display a much more marked stylisation of telling than comedies.[47] This dramatic genre, which consists exclusively of dialogue, is more suited to represent the many interactional phenomena that are characteristic of real conversation. In comedy, (story)telling generally includes numerous recipient responses, at all stages of the telling. It is clear that the literary treatment of telling is closely linked to the nature of the genre concerned. These results show how interesting it would be to apply Conversation Analysis to an even wider range of genres.

For the novel, the use of Conversation Analysis allows us to better identify the writing techniques of the two Latin novelists: although both Petronius and Apuleius produced a few tales that can be considered as imitations of genuine storytelling, it is clear that their novels present several degrees of stylisation of storytelling, depending on the degree of realism desired by the author. A careful comparison with real storytelling shows that most of the time, the storytelling is highly stylised, with no real co-construction of the story by the recipient. Latin novelists prefer to show only the exchanges that frame the story: pre-telling sequences and recipient response at the completion of the telling. They seldom represent recipient responses that interrupt the telling, in order to present a fully mastered narrative whose quality must rival that of the main story. This provides us with a better understanding, then, of why these embedded stories include many dialogues and conversations, which make up a large part of them: their function is to re-introduce *sermo cotidianus* while constructing another form of co-narration.

With its characteristic brevity, the epigram incorporates telling in a very concise way. As in the novel, recipient responses are limited in number compared to comedies. Yet the selection which the author makes of these responses is not the same. Unlike the novel, the epigram seldom presents the responses that frame the telling proper. The telling begins directly, without any prior announcement or invitation. As for recipient response at the completion of the telling, the reader must generally imagine it. When it is included, the response is disaffiliative, while the novel often includes affiliative recipient response at the completion of the telling. In epigrams, we usually find mid-telling recipient responses. Through these responses, the recipient becomes a co-constructor of the telling, something that we seldom find in the novel. Applying Conversation Analysis to the Latin epigram thus enables us to fully

47 On storytelling in Latin comedies, see Risselada (forthcoming).

appreciate the importance of the brief recipient responses included. Pre-closing questions are not merely a stylistic device employed to give greater prominence to the point; they play a full part in the construction of the telling and guide its reception by constructing a reader figure whose affective stance matches that of the epigrammatist.

Bibliography

Berger, Ł. (2020). Forms of Talk in Roman Comedy. Reading Plautus and Terence with Goffman and Conversation Analysts. *Dionysus ex machina, 11*, 137–167.
Berger, Ł. (2022). Im/Politeness of Interruptions in Roman Comedy. In L. Unceta Gómez & Ł. Berger (Eds.), *Politeness in Ancient Greek and Latin* (pp. 202–226). Cambridge/New York: Cambridge University Press.
Boyce, B. (1991). *The Langage of the Freedmen in Petronius* Cena Trimalchionis. Leiden: Brill.
Dalbera, J. (2016). *Le parfait de l'indicatif latin. Analyse linguistique à partir d'un corpus narratif romanesque*. Louvain/Namur/Paris/Bristol: Collection d'Etudes Classiques, Peeters.
Dalbera, J. (2021a). L'imbrication des voix dans les *Métamorphoses* d'Apulée. *Vita Latina, 200*, 5–24.
Dalbera, J. (2021b). *L'imbrication des voix* dans *la narration romanesque latine. Outils pragmatiques et informatiques*. Mémoire d'Habilitation à Diriger les Recherches, Université de Corse.
del Barrio Vega, M. L. (1989). Epigramas dialogados: orígenes y estructura. *Cuadernos de Filología Clásica. Estudios griegos e indoeuropeos, 23*, 189–201.
Duranti, A. (1986). The Audience as Co-Author: An Introduction. *Text, 6* (3), 239–347.
Fleck, F. (2020). Les discours directs non marqués dans les *Épigrammes* de Martial. *Lalies, 40*, 61–81.
Gaide, F. (1995). Les Histoires du Loup-garou et des Striges dans la *Cena Trimalchionis* ou la narration du 'vécu': deux joyaux du *latin vulgaire*. In L. Callebat (Ed.), *Latin vulgaire-latin tardif IV: Actes du 4e Colloque International sur le latin vulgaire et tardif, Caen, 2–5 septembre 1994* (pp. 715–723). Hildesheim: Olms.
Harrison, S. J. (1990). The Speaking Book: The Prologue to Apuleius' *Metamorphoses*. *Classical Quarterly, 40*, 507–513.
Labov, W. (1972). The Transformation of Experience in Narrative Syntax. In Labov, W. (Ed.), *Language in the Inner City* (pp. 354–396). Philadelphia: University of Pennsylvania Press.
Laurens, P. (2012) [1989]. *L'abeille dans l'ambre. Célébration de l'épigramme de l'époque alexandrine à la fin de la Renaissance*. Paris: Les Belles Lettres.
Letessier, P. (2000). La *salutatio* chez Plaute, adaptation ludique d'un rituel social. *Lalies, 20*, 151–163.
Lindström, A. & Sorjonen, M. L. (2013). Affiliation in Conversation. In J. Sidnell & T. Stivers (Eds.), *The Handbook of Conversation Analysis* (pp. 250–369). Malden (MA): Blackwell Publishing.
Martin, R. (1999). *Le Satyricon Pétrone*. Paris, Ellipses.
Mandelbaum, J. (2013). Storytelling in Conversation. In J. Sidnell & T. Stivers (Eds.), *The Handbook of Conversation Analysis* (pp. 492–511). Blackwell Publishing.
Norrick, N. R. (2007). Conversational Storytelling. In D. Herman (Ed.), *The Cambridge Companion to Narrative* (pp. 127–141). Cambridge: Cambridge University Press.
Puccini-Delbey, G. (2004). Présence-Absence de la figure du *Lector* dans les romans latins de l'époque impériale, *Cahiers de Narratologie, 11*, https://doi.org/10.4000/narratologie.15

Risselada, R. 2021. How to Anchor Reactions: Interactional common ground, preference structure and (im)politeness in Roman comedy. In A. M. Martín Rodríguez (Ed.), *Linguisticae Dissertationes. Current Perspectives on Latin Grammar, Lexicon and Pragmatics* (pp. 717–732). Madrid: Ediciones Clásicas.
Risselada, R. (forthcoming). Conversational Storytelling in Latin Comedy.
Roesch, S. (2002). Les stratégies de clôture du dialogue dans les comédies de Plaute. In M. Bolkestein, C. Kroon, H. Pinkster, Remmelink & R. Risselada (Eds.), *Theory and description in Latin linguistics* (pp. 317–332). Amsterdam: Brill.
Roesch, S. (2005). L'échec des clôtures du dialogue dans les comédies de Plaute. In G. Calboli (Ed.), *Papers on grammar, 9* (2) (pp. 921–932). Roma: Herder.
Roesch, S. (2008). Les débuts des dialogues dans la comédie et la tragédie latines. In B. Bureau & Ch. Nicolas (Eds.), *Commencer et finir : débuts et fins dans les littératures grecque, latin et néolatin* (pp. 207–222). Lyon: CERG.
Schegloff, E. A. (2007). *Sequence Organization in Interactions. A Primer in Conversation Analysis*. Cambridge: Cambridge University Press.
Stivers, T. (2013). Sequence Organization. In J. Sidnell & T. Stivers (Eds.), *The Handbook of Conversational Analysis* (pp. 191–209). Blackwell Publishing.
Tueller, M. A. (2008). *Look Who's Talking. Innovations in Voice and Identity in Hellenistic Epigram.* Leuven: Peeters.
Unceta Gómez, L. (2010). La expresión del agradecimiento en la comedia latina. In P. Anreiter & M. Kienpointner (Eds.), *Latin linguistics today. Akten des 15. internationalen Kolloquiums zur lateinischen Linguistik* (pp. 625–637). Innsbruck: Innsbrucker Beiträge zur Sprachwissenschaft.
Unceta Gómez, L. (2014). Pedir perdón en latín. El acto de habla de la disculpa en las obras de Plauto y Terencio. *Emerita, 82* (1), 69–97.
Valette, E. & Vallat, D. (2022). L'art de la question chez Martial: formes et enjeux stylistiques et pragmatiques. In D. Vallat & F. Garambois-Vasquez (Eds.), *Stylistique et poétique de l'épigramme latine. Nouvelles études* (pp. 95–137). Lyon: MOM Editions.
Vuillaume, M. (1990). *Grammaire temporelle des récits*. Paris: Minuit.

Nigel Holmes

Continuations by Others

Abstract: This article examines passages in the surviving comedies of Plautus and Terence where a second speaker uses the previous speaker's words as the basis for a continuation, adding either part of a sentence which is syntactically dependent on what the other had said, equivalent to what Shegloff (2016) calls "other-initiated increments", or a new sentence joined by a connector such as *et* or *nec*. Such continuations often take the previous speaker's words in a direction they would not have wanted, ironically commenting on them, often with the addition of *quidem* or an invocation of a god, such as *pol*. I suggest that the aptness of such continuations for sarcasm is in part due to speakers noting a deficiency in what the other had said.

Keywords: Conversation Analysis, other-initiated increments, particles

1 The Phenomenon and the Material Investigated

Sometimes in a conversation, after one speaker has completed their turn, another speaker continues it, using the first speaker's own words as the basis of their continuation. Often the continuation goes in a direction which the first speaker would not have wanted, giving an effect of wit. The second speaker uses the adversary's weapon against them, as in (1), from Quintilian's discussion of how an orator can make use of jokes.

(1) QVINT. inst. 6, 3, 81
Afer, cum . . . quidam . . . exclamasset: "praeterea tu semper in libertos Caesaris dicis", "nec mehercule" inquit "quicquam proficio".
'When someone had called out "What's more, you're always attacking Caesar's freedmen", Afer replied, "And, by god, I get nowhere with it".'

Domitius Afer is acting against a freedman of Claudius. His opponents attack his motives, saying that he always speaks against Caesar's freedmen. Instead of denying this, he diverts the attack with a joke ('and by god I get nowhere with it')

Note: I owe thanks for comments and suggestions to Łukasz Berger, Caroline Kroon, Rodie Risselada, Josine Schrickx, Luis Unceta Gómez, and the anonymous reviewers.

Nigel Holmes, Thesaurus linguae Latinae, Munich, Germany

https://doi.org/10.1515/9783111332956-041

apparently at his own expense, but very likely with an appeal to hearers who think that imperial freedmen are too powerful. All this, though, could have been done without using the connector[1] *nec*, a word which normally joins two sentences by the same speaker. What purpose do connections like this serve?

To understand this practice, I looked at all the examples I could find in Plautus and Terence where a second speaker responds with words that are either syntactically dependent on the previous speaker's words or, as here, joined to them by a connector. The texts used were the Loeb editions (de Melo 2011–13 and Barsby 2001). These are also the source of translations of examples from Plautus and Terence.

2 Continuations in the Literature of Conversation Analysis

Some of the instances that I will be discussing are very similar to what Schegloff (2016: 258–261) has described as "other-initiated increments". Before we discuss those, we will need to see what "increments" are. Increments (Schegloff 1996 and 2016) are additions by a speaker to the end of a turn-constructional-unit. A turn-constructional-unit is a unit of communication which appears complete in such a way that its end is an appropriate place for another speaker to begin their turn. Sometimes however, the first speaker adds a further turn-constructional-unit to their own turn. And sometimes they add an increment, which differs from a turn-constructional-unit in that it is not a stand-alone construction. It is grammatically fitted to the previous unit (Schegloff 2016: 240–242). The words "pretty much for sure" in (2) are such an "increment" as Schegloff defines it.

(2) Bonnie asks Marina if she will come to her party
Bon: And (3.0) okay d'you think you'd come? **pretty much for sure?**
Mar: What?
Bon: Do you think yuh c'd come pretty much for sure?
Mar: Sure.

The initial question would have made a reasonable point to end the turn, but after completing it, Bonnie recompletes it with the phrase "pretty much for sure". Both

1 Most terminology in this article follows Pinkster (2015 and 2021). A connector is a word that links and shows the relationship between two sentences (Pinkster 2015: 68).

Schegloff and Ford, Fox and Thompson warn against the temptation to understand increments as afterthoughts. Ford, Fox and Thompson (2002: 19 and 30) diagnose the use of increments as being associated with difficulties in transition to the next speaker. Self-initiated increments such as these may be impossible to study in ancient texts, as intonation, pauses and sometimes visual evidence such as eye contact are relevant.[2]

Occasionally another participant in the conversation adds an utterance to the previous speaker's words which very much resembles these increments, as in (3) (Schegloff 2016: 258–261). A doctor comments on a child: "He doesn't like to be manipulated", and the mother chimes in with the adverbial phrase "At all". These are what Schegloff calls "other-initiated increments". Like increments, in Schegloff's words (2016: 260), "they are designed to be added to the just preceding talk; they are grammatically symbiotic with it and fit to its end".

(3) At the doctor
Doc: He doesn't like to be manipulated.
Mom: **At all.**

Some of Schegloff's examples express disagreement with the previous speaker.[3] Even in the example cited here, which looks like an expression of agreement, he comments, "surely something else is involved thereby (such as a hint that the physician desist, for example)". We will come back later to the question of how significant the relationship between increments and other-initiated increments is (see Section 7).

Schegloff's increments only describe syntactically dependent continuations; but Sidnell (2012), who discusses additions to the end of a speaker's turn, either by themselves or by others, also includes sentences joined by a connector. He uses the term "other-continuations" to describe continuations by a second speaker, which are the main focus of his study.

2 Metre might provide hints to the first two characteristics.

3 Other-initiated increments also feature among the instances of "subversive completion" in Bolden et al. (2019).

3 Some Exclusions

Before we look at what kinds of continuation we find in Plautus and Terence, I want to exclude some patterns of conversation, which might belong or seem to belong here.[4]

Firstly, there are replies to questions. Normally such replies only give the requested information (what, why, who), they do not need to repeat the parts that are common to question and answer. So we quite naturally get answers that are syntactically dependent on the question. Even with "yes/no" questions there may be an answer that is syntactically dependent on the question. These occur when the second speaker implies a "yes" answer by going beyond it. We find examples with adverbs (4) and coordinators[5] (5).

(4) TER. Andr. 381–382 (the slave Davos warns his owner's son Pamphilus of danger from Pamphilus' father)
DAV *dictum factum invenerit*
aliquam causam quam ob rem eiciat oppido.
PAM *eiciat?*
DAV *cito.*
'DAV He'll find a pretext for driving her out of town, sooner said than done. PAM Driving her out? DAV And quickly.'

(5) PLAVT. Pseud. 739 (Pseudolus examines the capability of a potential accomplice)
PSEU *ecquid is homo habet aceti in pectore?*
CHAR *atque acidissumi.*
'PSEU Does he have any vinegar in his breast? CHAR Yes, and what's more, it's very biting.'

Secondly, I exclude questions that look for confirmation or information about something in the previous speaker's utterance. Here too it is unremarkable for the question to be syntactically dependent on the first speaker's words, as in (6). Bacchis tells Parmeno to say "I'm begging him to come". Parmeno just asks "To you?" relying for the rest on Bacchis' own words.

---

4 Some uses of specific vocabulary which in my view do not continue the other's words are also excluded in Section 4.2.

5 A coordinator is a word used to link clauses, phrases and words (Pinkster 2015: 68).

(6) TER. Hec. 809 (the *meretrix* Bacchis wants the slave Parmeno to find his master's son)
BAC *dic me orare ut veniat.*
PAR *ad te?*
BAC *immo, ad Philumenam.*
'BAC. Tell him, I beg him to come. PAR To you? BAC No, to Philumena.'

The same applies to sentences with *nempe*, even when they are edited as statements, as in (7). These still submit the hearer's understanding of what the other had said to confirmation or possible rejection (Schrickx 2011: 75–105).

(7) PLAVT. Cas. 235 (Lysimachus calls to his wife Cleostrata)
LYS *respice, o mi lepos.*
CLEO *nempe ita ut tu mi es.*
'LYS Look back at me, my delight. CLEO Yes, just as you're mine.'

Sidnell (2012: 321–328) discusses such "appendor questions" as a kind of other-continuation. He sees them as one end of a continuum from statements in which speakers have complete confidence, to those in which they have none.

Thirdly, I will not be considering interruptions.[6] In some respects these can be quite similar. We do find interruptions which use the same syntactic dependence on the first speaker's words to give them a different meaning, as in (8); but I will be suggesting that a continuation added after a speaker has finished their turn has a slightly different character to one where they are prevented from doing so by an interruption (see Section 7).

(8) PLAVT. Capt. 886 (Hegio curses the parasite Ergasilus)
HEG *vae aetati –*
ERG *tuae!*
'HEG Bad luck to – ERG (*interrupting*) You!'

Finally, I exclude passages where a speaker connects not to the previous speaker's words, but to their own before those. In (9) Theopropides twice uses *-que* to link back to his own words over the intervening answer from Simo.[7]

6 On interruptions in Latin comedy, see Berger (2022).
7 Further examples at TLL IX 1, 25, 37–46 (*nam*); 593, 9–21 (*neque*).

(9) PLAVT. Most. 1037–1040 (Theopropides wants help from his neighbour Simo)

SIM *quid vis?*
THEO *i mecum, opsecro, una simul.*
SIM *fiat.*
THEO *servorumque operam et lora mi cedo.*
SIM *sume.*
THEO *eademque opera hace tibi narravero*
quid med exemplis hodie eludificatus est.

'SIM What do you want? THEO Please come along with me. SIM Yes. THEO Give me your servants' help and some straps. SIM Take them. THEO At the same time I'll tell you how he fooled me today.'

4 The Types of Continuations

4.1 Syntactically Dependent Continuations

With these exceptions put aside, we can look at what kind of other-initiated continuations we find in Plautus and Terence. The syntactically dependent continuations have a variety of types. I will give just a few examples. There are various secondary clauses. In (10) a slave expresses confidence in the drawing of lots, "the lot will fall to me", and his owner adds an *ut* argument clause (cf. Pinkster 2021: 81) "to die through terrible torture". The addition reinterprets the first speaker's words, giving them a new syntax and a new meaning.

(10) PLAVT. Cas. 299–300 (at a lottery to decide whether Casina shall be alotted to the slave Chalinus or to another slave favoured by his owner Lysidamus)

CHAL *attamen*
mi optinget sors.
LYS *ut quidem pol pereas cruciatu malo.*

'CHAL. But the lot will fall to me. LYS Yes, it'll be your lot to die through terrible torture.'

We find relative clauses introduced by a relative pronoun, as in (11). Here Lysimachus and Eutychus are combining to abuse Demipho. After Lysimachus brings up the injury Demipho did to his son, Eutychus adds a relative clause with further details. Note that this continuation is not, as in most cases, a response to the previous speaker, but a genuine collaboration with him on the same action.

(11) PLAVT. Merc. 978–980 (Eutychus and father Lysimachus cooperate to abuse Lysimachus' friend Demipho)

LYS *quibus est dictis dignus oneremus ambo.*
DEM *nullus sum.*
LYS *filio suo qui innocenti fecit tantam iniuriam.*
EVT *quem quidem hercle ego, in exilium quom iret, redduxi domum.*

'LYS Let's both burden him with the words he deserves. DEM I'm dead. LYS To have done such an injustice to his innocent son! EUT A son whom I brought back when he was going into exile.'

We have a variety of adverbs and adverbial phrases, as in (12)

(12) PLAVT. Poen. 1106–1107 (trickster slave Milphio praises Carthaginian Hanno's performance of grief, unaware that it is real)

MIL *lepide hercle assimulas. Iam in principio id mi placet.*
HAN *pol magis quam vellem.*

'MIL You're pretending in a delightful way. Already in the beginning I like it. HAN Well, more than I'd wish.'

We have coordinators (see note 6) such as *et* or *atque* which introduce an addition or alternative to something in the previous speaker's sentence, rather than joining two sentences. In (13) Charinus learns that the girl he loves is not in fact marrying someone else, and thanks the slave Davos for the news: "I'm a free man". Davos adds "and nowhere" to remind him that he has still not established his own position as a suitor.

(13) TER. Andr. 370 (Charinus thanks the slave Davus for good news)

CHA *liberatus sum hodie, Dave, tua opera.*
DAV *ac nullus quidem!*

'CHA I'm a free man today, Davus, thanks to you. DAV Oh no, you're not.'

I include these parts of sentences linked by coordinators in the syntactically dependent continuations, although they are similar to the continuations by connectors, which we will discuss in Section 4.2. It can be hard to say which we are dealing with, as there is often the possibility of understanding an ellipse.

Sometimes a speaker adds a noun or pronoun as a new or different argument to the verb. In (14) one speaker says *dolet*, 'it hurts', and the other changes the meaning of that by adding a pronoun *mihi*, 'me, it hurts me'.

(14) PLAVT. Poen. 150–151 (Agorastocles promises his slave Milphio that he will not beat him)

AGO *quin si feriri video te, extemplo dolet.*
MIL *mihi quidem hercle.*
AGO *immo mihi.*

'AGO No, if I see you being beaten, it's very painful at once. MIL Yes, for me. AGO No, for me.'

This example is a rare case where the first speaker resists the continuation by asserting the meaning of his original statement.

A few constructions that did not occur may also be worth noting. I found no purpose satellite clauses (Pinkster 2021: 297–306) and no result clauses (Pinkster 2021: 308–314), the latter unsurprisingly, as these are generally prepared by something in the sentence to which they are attached. I found no reason clauses introduced by a subordinator such as *quia* (Pinkster 2021: 281–297). Among the coordinators there were no instances of *-que*[8] and probably none of the disjunctive coordinators *vel*,[9] *-ve* and *aut*.

4.2 Continuations Joined by a Connector

Turning to the connectors, we find many utterances beginning with a connector, or what might be a connector. Some connectors are commonly used in this position and their use does not make any pretence of continuing the other speaker's sentence. These are mostly adversative and conclusive connectors,[10] as shown in Table 1. In fact, both *at* and *ergo* are not just acceptable after a change of speaker, they are mostly found there and seem to be specifically intended for that purpose.[11]

8 Contrast (7) above, where it links back to the speaker's own words.

9 PLAVT. Bacch. 902 should probably be excluded (Lodge 1914–1933: II 829).

10 Some of the instances collected as conclusive connectors here may in fact be adverbs which indicate the same relation as a connector would, but do not serve to remove asyndeton. The single instance of *proinde* (TER. Phorm. 668) is also suspect, because not only is its use in a response unique, but it also has an unusual position (Holmes 1999: 106). Some see instead *proinde*'s other use as a comparative adverb.

11 On *at*, see particularly Kroon (1995: 333–370). From a search of the Library of Latin Texts, *ergo* is found in the first sentence of a response 185 times in Plautus and Terence, 16 times in other contexts.

Table 1: Connectors joining utterances of different speakers.

Adversative		Conclusive		Copulative		Explicative	
at	315	*ergo*	104	*ac/atque*	22	*nam*	5
atqui	17	*igitur*	67	*et*	21	*namque*	9
attamen	8	*proinde*	1	*nec/neque*	6		
autem	17						
ceterum	2						
enimvero	1						
sed	34						
tamen	10						
vero	9						
verum	5						
Total	418		172		49		14

Copulative connectors, as we see from the table, are much rarer. I should note that the figure of 40 times for *et* is not exact, because it is hard to distinguish the sense "also", which in Plautus and Terence is particularly associated with responses, especially in the exchange of greetings (TLL V 2, 906, 76–907, 31). Example (15) shows an instance with *atque*[12] and (16) one with *et*:[13]

(15) Ter. Andr. 349–350 (the slave Davos reassures his master's son Pamphilus and Pamphilus' friend Charinus)

DAV *id paves ne ducas tu illam, tu autem ut ducas.*
CHA *rem tenes.*
PAM *istuc ipsum.*
DAV *atque istuc ipsum nil periclist.*

'DAV You're in a panic in case you have to marry her, and (*to Charinus*) *you're* in one in case you can't. CHA You've got it. PAM Exactly. DAV But there's exactly no danger.'

12 The use of *atque* is complicated by its occasional appearance in sentences where an adversative connector might seem appropriate. Many recognise an adversative sense (Lodge 1914–1933: I 181; McGlynn 1963–1967: I 59-60; OLD s.v. 9 "(with slight adversative sense) And yet".

13 I found no instances with *-que* as a connector. Compare its absence as a coordinator (Section 4.1).

(16) PLAVT. Truc. 813 (Callicles reacts to a slave woman's report of the rape of his daughter)

ANC *vir erat, plus valebat: vicit quod petebat apstulit.*
CAL *et tibi quidem hercle idem <vir> attulit magnum malum.*
'SERVANT He was a man, he was stronger. He overpowered her and took away what he was after. CAL And to you that same man brought a great thrashing.'

The explicative connectors that we find are *nam* and *namque*.[14] My material had no instances of *enim* as a connector. It is rare for either *nam* or *namque* to connect one speaker's words to another's, as we see in the table. That is what we would expect from the nature of the words. When *nam* connects two sentences by the same speaker, it introduces a sentence which is subsidiary to the previous sentence, as Kroon has argued. Specifically, the speaker anticipates a question or complaint that the first sentence might raise in the hearer's head and answers it. A second speaker who adds their explanation to the first speaker's words is abusing the character of the connector. In (17) Thraso has just heard his rival's slave praising the modesty of his master's expectations of her to a *meretrix*. This allows him to comment disparagingly, "This is obviously the slave of a wretched poverty-stricken master". His hanger on Gnatho, who had earlier quarrelled with the slave, takes that as an opportunity to attack him, explaining Thraso's words with the reasoning "because nobody who had money to buy a different slave would put up with this one".

(17) TER. Eun. 486–488 (soldier Thraso comments on the modest demands of his rival's slave to his parasite Gnatho)

THR *apparet servom hunc esse domini pauperis*
miserique.
GNA *nam hercle nemo posset, sat scio,*
qui haberet qui pararet alium, hunc perpeti.
'THR This is obviously the slave of a wretched poverty-stricken master. GNA Yes. I'm quite sure nobody would put up with such a slave if he had the means to get himself another one.'

14 Although *enim* in classical Latin comes close to the use of *nam* as an explicative connector, I found no such instances in my material. On *enim* and *nam* Kroon (1995: 144–170); on *nam* and *namque* Schrickx (2009).

My figures for *nam* exclude the special use of *nam* in questions that we find in (18).

(18) PLAVT. Amph. 552 (Amphitruo to his slave Sosia)
AM *scelestissumum te arbitror.*
SOS *nam quam ob rem?*
'AM I think you're a hardened criminal. SOS But why?'

Here *nam* is not a connector. It characterises the question. It is typically found in questions where the answer seems hard to find, where the speaker is reacting with irritation and surprise. Caroline Kroon points out that these *nam* questions reverse the character of connective *nam*, demanding the information that a sentence introduced by connective *nam* supplies (Kroon 1995: 166). In my view this interrogative use was originally a sarcastic use of the connector. The irritation and lack of confidence in finding an answer would go back to the first speaker's failure to supply unprompted necessary information, a deficiency that the second speaker's use of *nam* emphasises (Holmes 2012).

5 Who Uses Continuations, and How?

If we leave aside the adversative and conclusive connectors, which seem to be either completely compatible with or (in the case of *at* and *ergo*) dedicated to linking utterances of different speakers (Section 4.2), we are left with 149 instances (85 syntactically dependent and 64 joined by copulative or explicative connectors). Unless otherwise indicated, these will be what I mean by continuations in what follows. Many of these show the pattern that I mentioned in Section 1: they use their dialogue partner's words for a new purpose, often to make a sarcastic comment on them. Examples (1), (10) and (14) are good illustrations. This usage, which I will call hijacking, accounts for 50 instances. There are also many uncertain cases. As with Schegloff's interpretation of (3) in Section 2, the hijacking may not be immediately apparent; and sometimes I simply could not see what the speaker's point was.

There are also many instances that should probably be excluded from discussion of continuations, since although they make use of the other speaker's words for the syntactical connection, they make no pretence to continue their sentence, and function more like the responses we ruled out in Section 3. Terence, for instance, several times allows characters to express approval of what the other is saying by adding an adverb or adverbial phrase as a subjective evaluation disjunct (Pinkster 2015: 928–930), as in (19):[15]

(19) TER. Andr. 59–61 (Simo to his freedman Sosia)

SIM *nil egregie praeter cetera*
studebat et tamen omnia haec mediocriter.
gaudebam.
SOS *haud iniuria. nam id arbitror.*
apprime in vita esse utile, ut ne quid nimis.

'SIM he didn't pursue any one of these things in particular but all of them in moderation. I was delighted. SOS And rightly so. I believe that the best principle in life is nothing in excess.'

Collaborations like (11) above are examples of genuine continuations which do not seem to be hijacking the other's words. Even there one could see an element of friendly competition. We find another example in (20). This could be seen as a collaboration. The first speaker states his desire. The second (the brother of the character to whom the previous speaker was appealing) adds a continuation by apposition, with what could be taken as support. The first speaker then adds a further argument for what he wants, by linking a new sentence with *et*.

(20) TER. Ad. 972–975 (after receiving his freedom Syrus tries to get his former owner to also free his wife)

SYR *utinam hoc perpetuom fiat gaudium,*
Phrygiam ut uxorem meam una mecum videam liberam!
DEM *optumam quidem mulierem.*
SYR *et quidem tuo nepoti huius filio*
hodie prima mammam dedit haec.

'SYR If only, so that my joy could be full, I could see my wife Phrygia freed with me! DEM An excellent woman. SYR Yes, and she was the first to breastfeed your grandson, (*indicating Aeschinus*) his son, today.'

Roman comedy often shows differences in the way language features are used according to the social position of the speaker.[16] A full investigation would need to

15 Some of these, as the reviewer warns, should perhaps instead be understood as describing an elliptical verb of speaking, so that e. g. *recte* has the meaning 'well said'.
16 See particularly Barrios-Lech (2016).

compare material outside of other-initiated continuations, which I have not done; but it seems at least that such continuations were available to all character types. We find these continuations of other's words from all kinds of speakers: men and women, young and old, slaves and owners. I tried to see if social inferiors, and within that the subgroup of subordinates (e. g. sons speaking to fathers, slaves to owners), were less likely to use continuations which hijacked the first speaker's words to their own purposes. At any rate a comparison with the frequency of less antagonistic continuations did not show any real difference (Table 2).

Table 2: Relative status of second speaker to first in continuations by type.

Status	Hijack (50)		Other (99)	
Equal or superior	35	70%	70	71%
Inferior	15	30%	29	29%
Subordinate (subset of inferior)	8	16%	17	17%

6 Markers of Pointed Continuation

You will have noticed that in the cited passages, two types of words often accompany the continuation (shown in Table 3). There are the particles *quidem* and *equidem*:[17] examples (10), (11), (13), (14), (16), (20). There are appeals to the gods like *pol* and *mehercule:*[18] examples (1), (10), (11), (14), (16), (17). Examples (10), (11) (14) and (16) have both types. These words are somehow particularly apt for those continuations where the speaker is hijacking the first speaker's utterance. Of the 50 passages in which this occurs 37 (74%) had at least one of these types of words. When the continuation is not of this type, these words are much rarer, 50 out of 100.

17 There are various opinions on the core use of *quidem*: Solodow (1978); Kroon (2004, 2005 and 2009); Danckaert (2014 and 2015); Danckaert and Gianollo (2021) The only instance of *equidem* is PLAVT. Merc. 508. The sentence is in the first person singular, as in most, but not all (Solodow 1978: 19–29), passages of Plautus where it occurs.

18 See Adams (1984: 47–54); Müller (1997: 139–149); Unceta Gómez (2016: 219–233).

Table 3: Reinforcing words in continuations with copulative or explicative connectors or syntactic dependence.

Word	in all continuations	in continuations that hijack the other's words
ecastor	1	0
edepol	14	7
hercle	20	10
pol	10	6
equidem	1	1
quidem	47	23

A puzzling exception here is that after *nam* and *namque*, even where the second speaker is offering an explanation which would sound quite reasonable if the first speaker had said it, we still often get a "by god": 13 of 14 instances of *nam* or *namque* have *hercle, pol* or *edepol*, althought only six passages seem clearly to be adding an explanation that the first speaker would not have offered. Perhaps this is because *nam* and *namque* by their nature are supposed to be a self-correction anticipating the needs of the hearer, so that when a second speaker says them, it is always a creative misuse of the word.

I am not certain what these words do for the continuations in which they are found. Probably *quidem* and appeals to the gods are doing slightly different things. The fact that both can occur in one passage suggests that; and there is also a difference in distribution between their occurrence in syntactically dependent continuations and in those linked by a connector (Table 4). Appeals to gods are more strongly associated with continuations by connectors, *quidem* with syntactically dependent continuations. In the literature on *quidem*, those interpretations that see it as indicating that the text unit in which it is found needs to be understood in relation to another unit are most interesting. Solodow (1978: 13) sees this relation as one of contrast. Kroon (2005: 577) notes that "in a considerable proportion of its occurrences, *quidem* is used with a text unit which, from a communicative point of view, constitutes an autonomous discourse act, while from a grammatical perspective it is integrated in the semantico-syntactic structure of a preceding unit". Continuations like ours form part of her evidence (Kroon 2005: 584–585). The appeals to gods need further investigation. In the case of *pol*, the only one to have been covered by the Thesaurus, it is at least strongly associated with responses in dialogue (TLL X 1, 2252, 75-2254, 28).[19]

19 Cf. Müller (1997: 141) on *hercle*.

Table 4: Continuation markers by continuation type.

	Syntactically dependent (85)		Explic. and copulative connectors (64)	
quidem	36	42%	12	19%
Appeals to gods	18	21%	28	44%

7 What Advantage Do Continuations Provide?

Some advantages of using continuations like this are obvious. Often, they are efficient, saving time by avoiding repetition. And because they demand that the second speaker immediately recognise the potential in the first speaker's words, their use is an opportunity for speakers to show how quick witted they are. The pretence of engaging in a collaborative action is also doubtless part of the joke. We find something very similar in the use of *nempe*. Speakers use *nempe* to check their understanding of what the other has just said, often by adding some detail. But a common trick is to add a detail which the other would rather not mention, and so attack the other's utterance under the guise of checking that both participants in the dialogue are on the same page (Schrickx 2011: 101–102).

But I want to end by suggesting an implication that the choice of using a continuation has, which perhaps explains its aptness for use in sarcastic comment. As with interrogative *nam* (Section 4.2), I think that the completion of another speaker's words lends itself to an implication that those words were deficient in some way, that the first speaker left out an aspect of the subject that should have been mentioned. With this idea we might come back to the question of what Schegloff's other-initiated increments have to do with increments. A speaker's addition of an increment to their own words can be due to a perceived or anticipated problem in its reception by their dialogue partner. If other-initiated increments raise the problem that the first speaker failed to deal with, the choice of expression becomes itself a comment on the first speaker's words. In the same way that interrogative *nam* (in my view) reflects the previous speaker's failure to accommodate their hearers (which they would typically do using explicative *nam*), other-initiated increments can reflect the previous speaker's failure to accommodate their dialogue partners, by taking the form of a self-initiated increment, often used for that purpose. Much the same could apply to certain types of connector used to add a further turn-constructional unit to a speaker's own turn.

There are interesting parallels in two articles (Lerner 2004; Bolden 2010) that discuss the use of connectors or words typically found at the beginning of a self-initiated increment to handle a deficiency in a previous speaker's utterance. Lerner writes that certain function words are typical initiators of an increment (Lerner 2004: 152). When one speaker's utterance is perceived as deficient, another speaker may prompt expansion by using one of these initiators alone (Lerner 2004: 162–174), as in (21).

(21) After a trip
Jack: I just returned
Kathy: from
Jack: Finland

Bolden describes the use of and-prefaced assertions to supplement another speaker's utterances by making explicit relevant information that the speaker had left unsaid, as in the final line of (22), where Beth reacts to Jen's failure to continue (a short pause) by supplying a possible completion.

(22) Second trimester
JEN: Yea:h, [I was really I had really bad morning
BET: [Ah:.
(.)
BET: o::h, gee::=
JEN: =an::d u::m: (.1 then I jus' had all sorts of a:ches. an pai::ns. an:'(0.2)
BET: An' now you're starting tuh get pas that- proble:m?

These are more specific phenomena than my topic, and I have not noticed instances of either phenomenon in Plautus or Terence. Still, they seem to show the same pattern of addressing another speaker's failure to say something by using the means that that speaker could have employed.

8 Conclusions

There are connections which are typically used by a single speaker (Section 4). When a second speaker makes use of them to continue the other's words, there are various possibilities, including genuine collaboration, but also quite frequently a hijacking of the other's words to some new purpose, often antagonistic (Section 5). These continuations are often accompanied by *quidem* or by invocations like *pol*, and these are more frequent in hijackings (Section 6). The special aptness of other-initiated continuations to sarcastic comment on the previous speaker is perhaps linked to the fact that they imitate the form of a continuation that the previous speaker could have made but did not, and so call attention to a deficiency in what they did say (Section 7).

Bibliography

OLD = Glare, P. G. W. (Ed.) (1968–1982). *Oxford Latin Dictionary.* Oxford: Oxford University Press.
TLL = *Thesaurus Linguae Latinae* (1900–). Leipzig: Teubner; Berlin/Boston: De Gruyter.

Adams, J. N. (1984). Female speech in Latin comedy. *Antichthon, 18*, 43–77.
Barsby, J. (2001). *Terence, vol. 1–2.* Cambridge, MA: Harvard University Press.
Barrios-Lech, P. (2016). *Linguistic Interaction in Roman Comedy.* Oxford: Oxford University Press.
Berger, Ł. (2022). Im/Politeness of Interruptions in Roman Comedy. In L. Unceta Gómez & Ł. Berger (Eds.), *Politeness in Ancient Greek and Latin* (pp. 202–226). Oxford: Oxford University Press.
Bolden, G. B. (2010). 'Articulating the unsaid' via *and*-prefaced formulations of others' talk. *Discourse Studies*, *12* (1), 5–32.
Bolden, G. B., Hepburn, A. & Potter, J. (2019). Subversive Completions: Turn-Taking Resources for Commandeering the Recipient's Action in Progress. *Research on Language and Social Interaction*, *52* (2), 144–158.
Danckaert, L. (2014). *Quidem* as a Marker of Emphatic Polarity. *Transactions of the Philological Society*, *112*, 97–138.
Danckaert, L. (2015). Spelling out the obvious: Latin *quidem* and the expression of presuppositional polarity. *Journal of Historical Pragmatics*, *16* (1), 109–141.
Danckaert, L. and Gianollo, C. (2021). Towards a unified account of *quidem* and *ne . . . quidem*. In A. M. Martín Rodríguez (Ed.) *Linguisticae Dissertationes. Current Perspectives on Latin Grammar, Lexicon and Pragmatics* (pp. 851–870). Madrid: Ediciones Clásicas.
De Melo, W. D. C. (2011–2013). *Plautus, vol. 1–5.* Cambridge, MA: Harvard University Press.
Ford, C. E., Fox, C. E. & Thompson, B. A. (2002). Constituency and the Grammar of Turn Increments. In C. E. Ford, C. E. Fox & B. A. Thompson (Eds.) *The Language of Turn and Sequence* (pp. 14–38). Oxford: Oxford University Press.
Holmes, N. (1999). On Plaut. *Bacch.* 739. *Museum Helveticum*, *56*, 105–106.
Holmes, N. (2012). Interrogative nam in Early Latin. *Mnemosyne*, *65* (2), 203–218.
Kroon, C. (1995). *Discourse particles in Latin, a study of* nam, enim, autem, vero *and* at. Amsterdam: Gieben.
Kroon, C. (2004). Latin *quidem* and the structure of the move. In H. Aertsen, M. Hannay & R. J. Lyall (Eds.), *Words in Their Places. A festschrift for J. Lachlan Mackenzie* (pp. 199–209). Amsterdam: Vrije Universiteit Amsterdam.
Kroon, C. (2005). The relationship between grammar and discourse. Evidence from the Latin particle *quidem*. In G. Calboli (Ed.), *Papers on Grammar 9. Latina Lingua! Proceedings of the 12th International Colloquium on Latin Linguistics* (pp. 577–590). Rome: Herder.
Kroon, C. (2009). Latin linguistics between grammar and discourse. Units of analysis, levels of analysis. In E. Rieken & P. Widmer (Eds.), *Pragmatische Kategorien. Form, Funktion und Diachronie* (pp. 143–158). Wiesbaden: Reichert.

Lerner, G. H. (2004). On the place of linguistic resources in the organization of talk-in-interaction: Grammar as action in prompting a speaker to elaborate. *Research on Language and Social Interaction*, *37* (2), 151–184.

Lodge, G. (1914–1933). *Lexicon Plautinum*. Leipzig: Teubner.

McGlynn, P. (1963–1967). *Lexicon Terentianum*. Glasgow: Blackie and Son.

Müller, R. (1997). *Sprechen und Sprache: dialoglinguistische Studien zu Terenz*. Heidelberg: Winter.

Pinkster, H. (2015). *The Oxford Latin Syntax. Volume 1: The Simple Clause* Oxford: Oxford University Press.

Pinkster, H. (2021). *The Oxford Latin Syntax. Volume 2: The Complex Sentence and Discourse* Oxford: Oxford University Press.

Schegloff, E. A. (1996). Turn organization: one intersection of grammar and interaction. In E. Ochs, E. Schegloff & S. A. Thompson (Eds.), *Interaction and Grammar* (pp. 52–133). Cambridge: Cambridge University Press.

Schegloff, E. A. (2016). Increments. In J. D. Robinson (Ed.), *Accountability in Social Interaction* (pp. 239–263). Oxford: Oxford University Press.

Schrickx, J. (2009). *Namque* als Variante von *nam? Mnemosyne*, *62* (2), 250–271.

Schrickx, J. (2011). Lateinische Modalpartikeln. *Nempe, quippe, scilicet, videlicet* und *nimirum*. Amsterdam Studies in Classical Philology 19. Leiden: Brill.

Sidnell, J. (2012). Turn Continuation by Self and by Other. *Discourse Processes*, *49*, 314–337.

Unceta Gómez, L. (2016). Cuando los sentimientos irrumpen: análisis de las interjecciones secundarias en las comedias de Plauto. In A. Penas Ibáñez & B. García-Hernández (Eds.), *Semántica latina y románica. Unidades de significado conceptual y procedimental* (pp. 213–241). Bern: Peter Lang.

Federica Iurescia and Merlijn Breunesse

Movenda iam sunt bella: Persuasion in Juno's Prologue to *Hercules Furens*

Abstract: Seneca's *Hercules Furens* opens with a monologue delivered by Juno (lines 1–124). Similar to other Senecan prologues, Juno's speech is widely considered a train of thought whose main dramatic function is to display the goddess' violent emotions. This paper, by contrast, considers the prologue's rhetorical side, exploring the idea that it is shaped as a piece of communication aimed at persuading the audience to side with Juno's negative evaluation of Hercules. Relying on an approach that combines insights from Discourse Analysis and common ground theory, we study the prologue both on a macro-level, by looking at its structure, and on a micro-level, by analyzing the linguistic elements that index the communicative function of Juno's words. Rather than uttering an erratic flow of words dictated by her anger and hunger for revenge, Juno in her prologue builds upon a specific aspect of her current circumstances to argue that her personal situation applies (or will apply) to the whole universe. This structure ultimately underlines the urgency to stop Hercules.

Keywords: Seneca, common ground (CG), Roman tragedy, communication, Discourse Analysis (DA)

1 Introduction

In the prologue to Seneca's *Hercules Furens*, Juno announces that she will punish her stepson, Hercules, during the course of the play. Interpretations of this prologue emphasize two central aspects of the speech.[1] First, Juno is depicted as exceedingly

1 Fitch (1987); Billerbeck (1999); Zanobi (2014).

Note: We would like to thank two anonymous reviewers and Matthew Payne for their helpful comments on earlier versions of this paper. Breunesse's research project is part of the Anchoring Innovation project. Anchoring Innovation is the Gravitation Grant research agenda of the Dutch National Research School in Classical Studies, OIKOS. It is financially supported by the Dutch ministry of Education, Culture and Science (NWO project number 024.003.012). For more information about the research programme and its results, see the website www.anchoringinnovation.nl.

Federica Iurescia, Università Cattolica del Sacro Cuore Milano, Italy
Merlijn Breunesse, Leiden University, Netherlands

https://doi.org/10.1515/9783111332956-042

emotional. For instance, Fitch argues that Juno's speech is aimed at creating "a portrait of violent, uncontrolled emotion, and the atmosphere of horror and suspense that naturally accompanies it".[2] Secondly, Juno does not provide information in a structured manner, but divulges it haphazardly.[3] Thus, the prologue is often interpreted as an internal monologue (or "soliloquy"), representing Juno's train of thought.[4]

In this paper, we offer an interpretation of Juno's prologue that, in addition to its emotional side, acknowledges its rhetorical side as well.[5] Such an interpretation ties in with the vast amount of literature on the influence of rhetoric, especially declamation, on Seneca's tragedies.[6] Although declamations do provide a stage for emotional appeals, they are also exercises in rhetoric, aimed at persuading the audience. In Section 2, we demonstrate, based on a Discourse Analysis approach, that Juno's prologue has a communicative structure serving her persuasive goal, which is to convince her intended addressee that her revenge on Hercules is justified.

In Section 3, we delve deeper into the notion of Juno's prologue as part of a communicative exchange by conducting a micro-level analysis. This section focuses on dialogic elements and common ground markers, both of which reflect the communicative nature of the speech.

Based on this analysis, we suggest in Section 4 that Juno's prologue contains emotional passages that (structurally and linguistically) resemble soliloquies – notably the passages in which she addresses her *ira* (lines 75–88), Hercules (lines 89–99), the Furies (lines 100–112), and herself (line 109) –, as well as argumentative passages that seem to be addressed to somebody else. This observation prompts us to contemplate the identity of the intended addressee of these argumentative passages, which ultimately leads us to propose an analysis of the prologue that combines linguistic and literary insights to unite the two types of passages into one coherent whole.

2 Juno's Prologue from a Discourse Analysis Perspective

At the beginning of the prologue to *Hercules Furens*, Juno, angry with her husband Jupiter for his frequent extramarital affairs, has abandoned heaven and come to

2 Fitch (1987: 115); see also Billerbeck (1999: 183–184); Zanobi (2014: 70).
3 Fitch (1987: 115); Billerbeck (1999: 184).
4 Fitch (1987: 115); Billerbeck (1999: 184); Zanobi (2014: 70).
5 For a similar approach to the prologues of Euripides, see De Jong (2007).
6 See, e.g., Leo (1878: 47–59); Canter (1925); Goldberg (1997); Casamento (2002).

earth (lines 1–5; see passage [3] in Section 3.2). The imminent deification of Alcmena and Hercules has triggered a violent anger, and she announces her revenge on Hercules (lines 21–29). After several digressions about Hercules' previous exploits (lines 30–63) and his potential future undertakings (lines 63–68), which guide Juno to the proper method for defeating Hercules, the goddess concludes that Hercules can only be beaten by himself (line 85). Upon this realization, she summons the Furies to drive Hercules mad (lines 100–109), a fit of rage in which he will eventually kill his own children and his wife. The prologue ends with the arrival of dawn (lines 123–124), and Juno disappears without returning to the stage again.

To study the communicative structure of Juno's prologue, we approach it from a Discourse Analysis (henceforth DA) perspective, which has been fruitfully used in the past to investigate Latin literary texts.[7] In this field of studies, discourse is conceived of as a sequence of discourse units that are hierarchically structured.[8] The smallest identifiable units are "acts"; higher rank units are called "moves":

(1) Acts can be defined as the smallest identifiable units of communicative behaviour. In contrast to the higher order units called moves they do not necessarily further the communication in terms of approaching a conversational goal. This appears for instance from the fact that acts often need other, subsidiary acts to call forth the intended reaction from the addressee. The higher-rank unit called *move* is defined as the minimal free unit of discourse that is able to enter into an exchange structure. Unlike the act, a move is defined not only in terms of communicative unity, but also in terms of thematic unity. A move usually consists of a central act (which is the most important act in view of the speaker's intentions and goals) and one or more subsidiary acts, which also cohere thematically with the central act.[9]

Each communicative exchange comprises at least an initial move and a reactive move, each of which can consist, as we will explain in more detail later, of several acts and/or subsidiary moves. For example, in the exchange shown in Figure 1 below,[10] speaker A's move, which is intended as an invitation, consists of two acts.

7 See the foundational work of Kroon (1995), which relies on the Geneva Discourse model as outlined in Roulet et al. (1985) and Roulet et al. (2001).

8 For an overview of hierarchical discourse structure, see Hannay and Kroon (2005: 91–95). These authors rely on Functional Discourse Grammar (FDG) and pay particular attention to the definition of discourse act. On FDG see, e.g., Hengeveld (2004a, 2004b).

9 Kroon (1995: 65–66; emphasis in the original).

10 Kroon (1995: 65).

The move from speaker B, with which they accept the invitation, completes the communicative exchange.

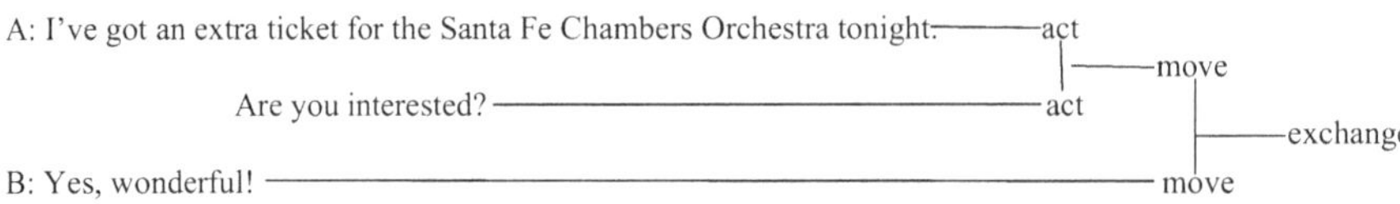

Figure 1: Hierarchical structure of discourse units.

The DA definition of communication does not only apply to exchanges between two speakers, but also to monologues,[11] such as Juno's prologue to *Hercules Furens*.[12] From a DA perspective, Juno's words constitute a move. As observed by Kroon, moves can have different degrees of complexity. In the case of longer monologues, "a move consists of a configuration of discourse units of varying sizes and hierarchical orders (e.g. acts, but also lower order, embedded moves) [...], which together constitute an extended monological stretch of text".[13] Juno's monologue has a complex structure as well, which is outlined in Figure 2. As we interpret it, her move consists of two subsidiary moves, which can theoretically enter into a communicative exchange themselves, but which here prepare for the central move, which conveys the goddess' core message:

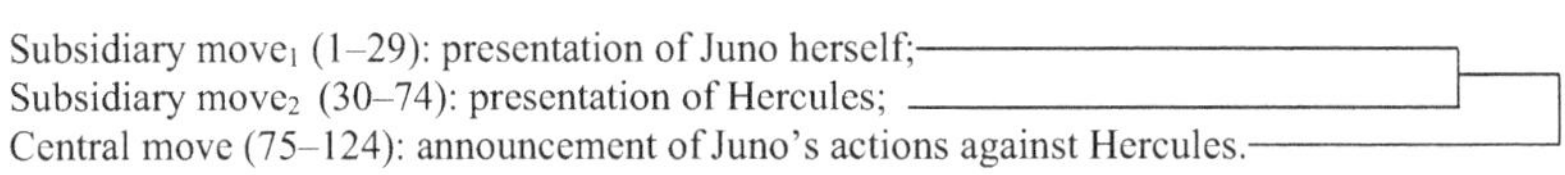

Figure 2: Hierarchical discourse structure of Juno's prologue.

The two subsidiary moves, one focusing on Juno herself and one on Hercules, reveal Juno's reasons for wanting revenge. She does not merely communicate her emotions and intentions in a train of thought, but she deliberately constructs a piece of discourse with a persuasive aim.

Juno's subsidiary moves consist of different acts (see Figures 3 and 4). Subsidiary move$_1$ is articulated as follows:

11 For a classification of discourse types based on the number of speakers involved, see Kroon (1995: 109–113) and Section 3.1 of this paper.

12 For an example of a piece of Latin discourse uttered by only one speaker, see Kroon (2009: 147).

13 Kroon (1995: 80).

Subsidiary act$_1$ (1–5): self-presentation as *soror Tonantis*;
Subsidiary act$_2$ (6–18): description of the constellations in heaven;
Central act (19–29): description of Juno's feelings.

Figure 3: Structure of subsidiary move$_1$.[14]

In this first subsidiary move, Juno depicts herself as a woman betrayed and abandoned. In the three acts which constitute her move, she explains who she is (subsidiary act$_1$), describes the divinities who have taken her place in heaven (subsidiary act$_2$, which elaborates on *paelices caelum tenent* 'whores inhabit the skies' in subsidiary act$_1$), and reveals how she feels about the situation she has to face (central act). These feelings, which are at the core of this first subsidiary move, trigger her subsequent actions, as hinted by the future tenses in the final part of the central act.[15] Note that the two subsidiary acts are thematically related: Juno explains that Jupiter's betrayal has motivated her descent from heaven (subsidiary act$_1$), where she finds evidence of Jupiter's infidelities in the constellations representing Jupiter's mistresses and their children (subsidiary act$_2$).

In her second subsidiary move Juno then singles out Alcmene and her son, Hercules:

Subsidiary act (30–62): description of Hercules' previous actions;
Central act (63–74): prediction of Hercules' future actions.

Figure 4: Structure of subsidiary move$_2$.

Juno here presents Hercules through his actions. He is depicted in a negative way (see Section 3.2): his past actions have proved him to be a threat for Juno and predict him to be a threat for the universe as a whole. This is the most important point she makes in this move: the danger posed by Hercules calls for urgent action. He needs to be stopped, and Juno will take care of this, as she subsequently outlines in her central move (see Figure 5):

Subsidiary act (75–122): planning of Juno's actions;
Central act (123–124): inception of revenge.

Figure 5: Structure of Juno's central move.

14 We use the text and translation by Fitch (2018); departures from this edition are indicated in the footnotes.

15 Sen. Herc. f. 27–29: *non sic abibunt odia: vivaces aget / violentus iras animus, et saevus dolor / aeterna bella pace sublata geret*. 'Even so, my hatred will not just evaporate. My mind will aggressively pursue undying anger, and my fierce resentment will abolish peace and wage eternal warfare.'

In her central move Juno rouses her anger to defend herself and the world against Hercules. The most promising strategy for this – Hercules must be defeated by himself – becomes explicit in line 85,[16] and in line 123 she can finally start: *movenda iam sunt bella* 'now let warfare begin'.

To conclude, violent emotions certainly play a role in Juno's prologue. However, studying the speech from a DA perspective reveals a clear internal structure that responds to a communicative purpose. Juno's first subsidiary move is concerned with her present condition and reveals her personal reason for wanting to take revenge on Hercules. Her second subsidiary move zooms out and considers the safety of the community as a whole: Hercules was arrogant in the past and will be a threat in the future. This forces the goddess to punish Hercules, and she formulates a strategy to do so in her central move. By moving from her personal motives to her concerns for the safety of the community, Juno presents her own, negative opinion of Hercules as grounded in facts. In other words, she aims to persuade her intended addressee of Hercules' danger and the justness of punishing him.

3 Diaphony and Common Ground in Juno's Prologue

Our analysis of Juno's prologue as a piece of communication with a persuasive goal is corroborated by the presence of two types of linguistic elements: dialogic elements, which will be explored in Section 3.1, and common ground markers, the focus of Section 3.2.

3.1 Dialogic Elements

Building upon the approach to discourse of the Geneva school of linguistics,[17] Kroon makes a distinction between five discourse types.[18] Monologal texts are produced by a single speaker, whereas dialogal texts involve two or more speakers engaged in a conversational exchange. Both text types can be monological, when they represent a single move, or dialogical, when they consist of alternating moves. Mon-

16 This realization is central to Juno's thought process but does not play a large role on the communicative level of her monologue.

17 See references in footnotes 7 and 8 above.

18 Kroon (1995: 109–110).

ological monologal texts and dialogical dialogal texts correspond to monologues and dialogues in the conventional sense. Dialogical monologal text segments can be observed, for example, in Cicero's letters and speeches, when he simulates discussions with conversational partners (real or fictitious). Monological dialogal text segments make occasional appearances in the works of Plautus, when characters complement each other's utterances.[19]

A fifth discourse type – the "diaphonic" discourse type – refers to monologal monological texts that make explicit references to the broader communicative context in which they are situated.[20] Although they are produced by a single speaker, monologal monological texts can serve a function within a communicative context. In such instances, they encompass two layers: a presentational layer, which corresponds to the core information being transmitted, and a communicative layer, which involves the interaction between the speaker or writer and their intended addressee or reader. Diaphonic texts are texts in which this communicative layer comes to the fore repeatedly.

In this paper we will call explicit references within a monologal monological text to its communicative context "dialogic elements". Examples of such elements are first- and second-person pronouns and verb forms, metadiscursive expressions (e.g., *I should now mention*), expressions of subjectivity, rhetorical and non-rhetorical questions, directives, and extra-clausal elements such as vocatives.[21] Additionally, Kroon posits that the Latin particles *at*, *vero*, and *enim* are associated with the diaphonic discourse type.[22] Monologal monological texts differ in the degree to which their communicative layer is apparent. Dialogic elements often appear in clusters within such a text, and it is their combined presence, rather than their individual occurrence, that serves as a reliable indicator of the diaphonic discourse type.[23]

While Juno's prologue is produced by a single speaker and thus qualifies as a monologal text, it contains a multitude of dialogic elements. One the one hand, Juno's prologue contains specific sections where individuals are directly addressed, as exemplified in the passage below. In these lines, Juno addresses the Furies, and the first-person pronouns *me* and *mea*, as well as the first-person verb form *apparo*, the vocative *sorores*, and the imperative *versate* indicate the communicative nature of the passage.

19 See Holmes (this volume: 703–720).
20 Kroon (1995: 111–115).
21 Kroon (1995: 114–115).
22 Kroon (1995: 114).
23 Kroon (1995: 115).

(2) *me me, sorores, mente deiectam mea*
versate primam, facere si quicquam apparo
dignum noverca. (SEN. Herc. f. 110–112)
'Harry me, sisters, overthrow my mind first, if I plan to take some action worthy of a stepmother.'

However, there are other sections within the prologue that lack explicit addressees, some of which will be discussed in Section 3.2. This second type of passage also contains dialogic elements.[24] Together, these passages constitute a monologal monological text with a diaphonic discourse type – i.e., an instance of a monologue that repeatedly references the communicative context in which it is situated. This observation corroborates our analysis, presented in Section 2, of the prologue as part of a communicative exchange.

3.2 Common Ground Markers

Common ground refers to the shared knowledge between a speaker or writer and their addressee(s) or reader(s). Clark distinguishes between two types of common ground: "communal" common ground, which arises from the participants' shared membership of a cultural community, encompasses cultural values, ideas, and conventions; "personal" common ground includes the participants' shared perceptual surroundings, past interactions, and private memories.[25] Recently, several studies in Latin and Ancient Greek linguistics have explored how new information is anchored to common ground in these languages.[26] The elements utilized for this anchoring are termed "common ground markers". Essentially, these markers serve a communicative function, and, like other dialogic elements, their presence in Juno's monologue indicates that the speech is part of a communicative exchange.

Juno draws on common ground – especially communal common ground – at important moments in her speech and uses common ground markers to elicit the spectators' agreement with her arguments. As observed in Section 2, in her first subsidiary move, Juno puts forth a personal reason for her desire to punish Hercules: the imminent deification of himself and his mother, Alcmena. The disgrace this casts upon Juno has ignited her thirst for revenge. The excerpt below presents

24 For example, the particle *enim*, the first-person pronoun *mihi*, and the first-person verb forms *deserui* and *dedi* in (3); see also *ecce* in (4).

25 Clark (1996: Ch. 4).

26 E.g., Allan and Van Gils (2016); Kroon (2016); Risselada (2016); Van Gils (2016); Allan (2017); Kroon (2017); Van Gils and Kroon (2019); Breunesse and Fantoli (2022).

the initial five lines of Juno's speech, which introduce this first subsidiary move. In these lines, Juno explains that she has descended to earth because Jupiter's numerous mistresses inhabit the skies.

(3) *Soror Tonantis—hoc enim solum mihi*
nomen relictum est—semper alienum Iovem
ac templa summi vidua deserui aetheris,
locumque caelo pulsa paelicibus dedi;
tellus colenda est, paelices caelum tenent. (SEN. Herc. f. 1–5)
'Sister of the Thunder God: this is the only title left me, as you know (*enim*). Wife no more, I have abandoned ever-unfaithful Jove and the precincts of high heaven; driven from the skies, I have given up my place to his whores. I must dwell on earth; whores inhabit the skies.'[27]

Juno identifies herself with the phrase *soror Tonantis*. Apparently recognizing that *soror* is an unusual and perhaps inappropriate term for someone who is not only Jupiter's sister but also his wife, Juno attempts to counter her interlocutor's possible surprise at hearing this term by promptly justifying her choice of words with the phrase *hoc enim mihi solum nomen relictum est.*[28] She explains that her husband's frequent extramarital affairs – Jupiter is *semper alienum* – compel her to merely refer to herself as *soror* rather than *uxor Tonantis*.

Kroon has shown that utterances including *enim* typically contain information belonging to the common ground of the speech participants.[29] This common ground can be personal, stemming from the speech participants' prior interactions or from their mutual experiences. However, in the excerpt above, *enim* marks communal common ground: the extramarital affairs of Jupiter and the consequent status of Juno as merely his sister are (presented as) part of culturally shared knowledge. Like other common ground markers, *enim* can be used to elicit agreement from the addressee: "By using *enim* the speaker/author appeals to common knowledge or a shared view in order to get the addressee to consent to a certain utterance".[30] Juno thus uses *enim* to elicit the agreement of her intended addressee with respect to her status as Jupiter's spurned wife. As we argued in Section 2, this constitutes

27 We have adapted Fitch's (2018) translation to illuminate the function of *enim* here.
28 The demonstrative pronoun *hoc* anchors this sentence to the previous assertion – *soror Tonantis* – and thus marks personal, discourse-based common ground. For the proximal demonstrative pronoun *hic* as a marker of common ground, see Kroon (2017).
29 Kroon (1995: 185); see also Kroon (2016).
30 Kroon (1995: 198). For a similar use of the common ground marker *quoniam* in Plautus' comedies, see Breunesse and Fantoli (2022).

her personal reason for wanting to punish Hercules and presents a first step in her argumentation. By using *enim* at such a crucial point, the goddess attempts to secure her intended addressee's agreement from the start, thereby increasing the chances of ultimately persuading them of the necessity to punish her stepson.[31]

As demonstrated in Section 2, the second subsidiary move of Juno's prologue is focused on depicting Hercules through his exploits on earth and in the underworld. Again, the persuasive force of this subsidiary move is reinforced by markers of communal common ground. Specifically, the negative portrayal of Hercules is in part achieved through the explicit negation of communal common ground. Allan and Van Gils have examined the communicative purpose of negations and their role in common ground management in Latin and Ancient Greek historiography.[32] They demonstrate that negations serve to establish two opposite poles, one of which (typically the negated pole) is regarded as good, while the other is seen as diverging from the norm. Negative expressions invite the addressee to concur with the speaker's evaluation of one pole as positive and the other as negative, because the norm is part of their common ground.

Consider, for example, the passage below. These lines occur in Juno's second subsidiary move and mark the thematic transition from Hercules' feats on earth to those within the underworld.

(4) *Nec satis terrae patent:*
effregit ecce limen inferni Iovis
et opima victi regis ad superos refert. (Sen. Herc. f. 47–49)
'Even the earth is not room enough. See, he has broken through the gates of nether Jove, and brings spoils of triumph over that conquered king back to the upper world.'

Underlying the phrase *nec satis terrae patent* is the implicit assumption that Hercules' thirst for glory has been (or should have been) quenched by his triumphs on earth. This assumption stems from communal common ground: conquering all earthly monsters represents the ultimate achievement and would fulfil any hero's ambitions. By rejecting this assumption with *nec satis terrae patent*, Juno contrasts what is considered standard and/or acceptable behavior for a hero (the positive pole) with Hercules' actions (the negative pole). Throughout her second

31 Linguistic similarities between Juno's speech in *Hercules Furens* and Seneca's models for this speech – notably Vergil's *Aeneid* (1, 37–49) and Ovid's *Metamorphoses* (3, 260–270) (see, e.g. *enim* in Ov. Met. 3, 262) – invites a comparison of these passages with a focus on their discourse structure. For the time being, however, such a comparison remains a desideratum for future research.
32 Allan and Van Gils (2016).

subsidiary move, Juno employs such negative formulations to cast Hercules as an unconventional and abnormal hero deviating from the cultural norms governing heroes' behavior (e.g., in lines 49, 66 and 71). As we argued in Section 2, this constitutes a second step in the prologue's argumentative structure. Negating positive characteristics instead of simply employing subjective (negative) terminology in her depiction of Hercules allows Juno to tap into communal common ground with her intended addressee, thereby eliciting their agreement with her assessment of the hero.[33]

4 Juno's Addressees

Analyzing Juno's prologue as part of a communicative exchange raises the question of her intended addressee. Juno occasionally addresses somebody explicitly: her *ira* in lines 75–88, Hercules in lines 89–99, the Furies in lines 100–112, and herself in line 109. However, the remainder of the speech is not explicitly directed at anyone. There are significant differences in common ground management between these two types of passages, which are closely linked to their functions within the prologue.

Juno's addresses of Hercules and herself are presented in (5) and (6) below.[34]

(5) *i nunc, superbe, caelitum sedes pete,*
humana temne! Iam Styga et manes feros
fugisse credis? Hic tibi ostendam inferos. (SEN. Herc. f. 89–91)
'Go ahead, proud man, aspire to the gods' abodes, despise humanity! You think you have now escaped the Stygian world and its merciless spirits? Here I will show you infernal powers.'

(6) *Iuno, cur nondum furis?* (SEN. Herc. f. 109)
'Juno, why are you not yet raging?'

As expected for a passage with an explicit addressee, Juno's address of Hercules in (5) contains several dialogic elements. These include the imperatives *i*, *pete* and *temne*, the vocative *superbe*, the second-person verb *credis*, and the second-person

33 In this passage, Juno also draws on "personal" common ground to strengthen her argument. Specifically, the use of *ecce* 'behold' (see OLD, *ecce* 1) evokes the physical presence of Hercules, emphasizing the threat he poses and underlining the urgency to stop him.
34 See also our discussion of dialogic elements in Juno's address of the Furies presented in (2).

pronoun *tibi*. In her self-address, presented in (6), we find a number of such elements as well: the vocative *Iuno* and the question *cur nondum furis?*, which includes the second-person verb form *furis*. Butzer's diachronic analysis of soliloquies has revealed that in ancient soliloquies, the self is often linguistically constructed as the speaker's own conversational partner.[35] The presence of dialogic elements in Juno's self-address is therefore to be expected.[36]

In passages that have an explicit addressee, such as (5) and (6), common ground is used differently than in passages without an explicit addressee, such as those discussed in Section 3.2.[37] First, although spatiotemporal common ground is evoked quite frequently in passages with an explicit addressee – especially in Juno's address of Hercules (see passage [5]), where it refers to the place and location where his destruction will take place –, references to communal common ground and discourse-based common ground are relatively rare. Moreover, references to communal common ground, such as the fire burning in the Etna in line 106 during Juno's address of the Furies (see passage [8]), are not accompanied by common ground markers.

These differences between passages with and without explicit addressees can be attributed to their functions within the prologue. As demonstrated in Section 3.2, Juno marks communal common ground at crucial points in her argumentation to invite her intended addressee to align with her reasoning. However, persuading Hercules, her own *ira*, the Furies, and even herself of this seems unnecessary. In fact, the passages addressed to these entities do not contribute to the persuasive structure of the prologue outlined in Section 2. Instead, these passages have been argued to serve a metadramatic function, which, as we will show, ties in with the entire prologue's persuasive function.

In his analysis of metatheatre in *Hercules Furens*, Frangoulidis discusses the metadramatic aspects of Juno in the play's prologue.[38] Analyzing Juno as a "hellish poet",[39] Frangoulidis notes that the goddesses' search for a new strategy to defeat Hercules reflects the novelty of the play's plot construction. After extensively discussing previous failed plans (or plots) that have inadvertently enhanced Hercules'

35 Butzer (2008: 14–21).

36 Moreover, speakers of ancient soliloquies frequently address another intradiegetic character, such as an allegoric character or an individual that is absent at the scene, as Juno does repeatedly during the prologue.

37 In this paper we focus on common ground differences between passages with and without an explicit addressee, leaving aside differences in common ground management between Juno's address of Hercules, her *ira*, the Furies, and herself.

38 Frangoulidis (2020: esp. 145–148); see also Schiesaro (2003: esp. 183–184).

39 Frangoulidis (2020: 147).

fame through his exploits on earth and in the underworld (lines 30–63), Juno calls upon her *ira* to inspire a new tactic in lines 75–76:[40]

(7) *Perge, ira, perge et magna meditantem opprime,*
congredere, manibus ipsa dilacera tuis; (SEN. Herc. f. 75–76)
'Onward, my anger, onward! Crush this overreacher! Grapple with him, tear him apart with your own hands.'

Juno then devises a new strategy (the plot of *Hercules Furens*): Hercules, driven to madness by the Furies, must be defeated by himself (lines 84–88). She subsequently addresses the hero in lines 89–91, presented in (5) above, and reveals this new plot, declaring her intention using the first-person future verb form *ostendam*.[41]

Afterwards, Juno's address of the Furies in lines 100–112, shown in part in (8) below, serves to set the plot in motion and initiate her revenge on Hercules. The imperative *incipite* 'begin!' in line 100 makes this especially clear.[42]

(8) *Incipite, famulae Ditis, ardentem incitae*
concutite pinum, et agmen horrendum anguibus
Megaera ducat atque luctifica manu
vastam rogo flagrante corripiat trabem.
Hoc agite, poenas petite vitiatae Stygis.
Concutite pectus, acrior mentem excoquat
quam qui caminis ignis Aetnaeis furit; (SEN. Herc. f. 100–106)
'Begin, handmaids of Dis, brandish the blazing pine torch violently. Let Megaera lead your troop, fearsome with snakes, and snatch a huge beam from a blazing pyre in her baleful hand. To your work: avenge the desecration of the underworld! Rouse your hearts, scorch your minds with fiercer fire than that raging in Etna's furnaces.'

Finally, Juno's self-address in line 109, presented in (6) above, serves a similar inceptive function. The self-posed question *cur nondum furis?* is aimed at propelling Juno into action. In his diachronic study of soliloquies, Butzer notes: "die Aufgabe des antiken Soliloquiums ist es nicht oder jedenfalls nicht in erster Linie, ‚dem Herzen Luft zu machen', sondern das Herz sprachlich zu bearbeiten".[43] According to

40 Schiesaro (2003: 183); cf. Frangoulidis (2020: 147).

41 The adverb *hic* in 91 can also be interpreted metadramatically as referring to the stage as a stage, viz. the location where the plot is performed.

42 Cf. Schiesaro (2003: 183); Frangoulidis (2020: 147).

43 Butzer (2008: 22).

Butzer, ancient soliloquies do not aim to merely showcase a character's thoughts and emotions; instead, they guide characters towards taking action. The question *cur nondum furis?* fulfils precisely this self-guiding function. It moves Juno into action, thereby contributing to the setting in motion of the play.

Thus, Juno's prologue can be divided into two distinct parts. The second part formulates a strategy to overcome Hercules and sets the play in motion, thereby initiating Juno's revenge. This part encompasses Juno's address to her *ira*, Hercules, the Furies and herself. It can be seen as Juno acting upon the outcome of the prologue's first part, which has a persuasive purpose: Juno explains *why* Hercules must be defeated (and a new plot devised). This initial part lacks an explicit addressee, which poses the question: Who is the intended addressee of these lines? Who needs to be convinced that Hercules must be defeated?

As the driving force behind the plot of *Hercules Furens* and effectively the "playwright" of the drama, Juno's primary concern in "putting on" the play was to secure the approval of the spectators (or, in the case of recitation, the listeners).[44] Given the audience's likely awareness of the contemporary debate concerning Hercules' ambivalent status as a (stoic) hero or anti-hero,[45] Juno needed to defend her position and the construction of her plot before the play commenced. Thus, while the whole prologue, like the rest of the tragedy, is in a sense communicated to the audience, there are parts of Juno's speech that are more explicitly formulated with the spectators (or listeners) of *Hercules Furens* in mind. It is also telling in this regard that Juno draws upon common knowledge rooted in Roman culture – her status as Jupiter's spurned wife and the expected behavior of the ideal hero – to bolster her argument.

Schiesaro's study of Seneca's *Thyestes* provides further significance to identifying the addressee of Juno's prologue as the play's audience.[46] In his examination of Seneca's treatment of time in the prologue to *Thyestes*, Schiesaro observes that the Fury describes or envisions actions that will later unfold on stage. According to Schiesaro, "one of the most significant outcomes of this dramatic technique consists in a further blurring between the responsibilities of the characters on the stage and the audience [. . .]. The audience is involved from the very beginning in the Fury's

44 Whether Senecan tragedies were intended for performance on stage or not has been debated for a long time. For the interpretation as "Rezitationsdramen", see, e.g., Zwierlein (1966) and Kugelmeier (2007). For an examination of how tragedies could be staged, see, e.g., Calder (1975), Sutton (1986), and Kragelund (2008). On the relation between tragedies and pantomime, see, e.g., Zimmermann (1990) and Zanobi (2014).

45 For an overview of the discussion concerning the role of Hercules in the Stoic tradition, see Billerbeck (2014: 428–430). One of the reviewers reminded us that Hercules is, in fact, portrayed by Seneca as a (comic) anti-hero in the *Apocolocyntosis*.

46 Schiesaro (2003: 178–183).

scheming, and subsequently treated, either willingly or *malgré soi*, to a detailed account of events already foreseen and foretold".[47]

In the prologue to *Hercules Furens*, Juno also describes events that will later be enacted on stage.[48] For instance, in lines 47–52 Juno claims that Hercules has already left the underworld, while the hero emerges from the underworld no earlier than line 520 in the play. We can therefore posit that Juno's prologue may have been aimed at a similar effect on the audience as the Fury's prologue in *Thyestes*. As a playwright, Juno is responsible for the plot and the play's progression. However, by persuading the audience that her vengeance against Hercules is justified and by disclosing early on what will happen to him, she implicates the spectators in the gruesome events that ensue.

5 Conclusion

Juno's prologue in Seneca's *Hercules Furens* has often been interpreted as a soliloquy. Displaying the goddess' violent anger, the speech is seen as conveying her interior search for a strategy to defeat Hercules. This paper complements this picture of Juno's prologue as an emotional account of her thoughts by considering its rhetorical side. Using a DA approach, we showed in Section 2 that the prologue's structure has a clear communicative function: it presents Hercules as a concrete and imminent threat for divine and human beings and advocates urgently for him to be stopped. In Section 3, we demonstrated that Juno uses markers of communal common ground to elicit her intended addressee's agreement with her arguments, aiming to persuade her addressee of the justness and necessity of punishing Hercules. We thus interpreted Juno's prologue as a communicative utterance that is structured with a persuasive aim. In Section 4, we argued that Juno's prologue is directed at the play's audience, an interpretation that explains Juno's use of *cultural* shared knowledge to persuade her intended addressee and that, moreover, ties in with the metatheatrical function that has previously been attributed to the goddess by scholars of the *Hercules Furens*.

Applying a linguistic analysis to Juno's prologue to *Hercules Furens* thus reinforces previous observations, while also providing new insight into this literary work. This illustrates the promise of linguistic insights for advancing our understanding of Seneca's tragedies, especially when it comes to their interactional nature and their strategies of audience involvement.

47 Schiesaro (2003: 182–183).

48 See also Schiesaro (2003: 185–186).

Bibliography

Allan, R. J. (2017). Ancient Greek adversative particles in contrast. In C. Denizot & O. Spevak (Eds.), *Pragmatic approaches to Latin and Ancient Greek* (pp. 273–302). Amsterdam: Benjamins.

Allan, R. J. & van Gils, L. W. (2016). *Anchoring new ideas in common ground: A linguistic approach.* https://research.vu.nl/ws/portalfiles/portal/168310810/Allan_Van_Gils_2016_Anchoring_New_Ideas_in_Common_Ground.pdf (accessed August 5, 2024)

Billerbeck, M. (1999). *Seneca: Hercules Furens. Einleitung, Text, Übersetzung und Kommentar.* Leiden: Brill.

Billerbeck, M. (2014). *Hercules furens*. In A. Heil & G. Damschen (Eds.), *Brill's Companion to Seneca* (pp. 425–433). Leiden: Brill.

Breunesse, M. & Fantoli, M. (2022). *Quia*, *quoniam*, and information management in Plautus. *Journal of Latin Linguistics, 21* (2), 163–185.

Butzer, G. (2008). Soliloquium. *Theorie und Geschichte des Selbstgesprächs in der Europäischen Literatur.* Munich: Fink.

Calder, W. M. (1975). The size of the chorus in Seneca's *Agamemnon*. *Classical Philology, 70* (1), 32–35.

Canter, H. V. (1925). *Rhetorical elements in the tragedies of Seneca.* Urbana: University of Illinois Press.

Casamento, A. (2002). Finitimus oratori poeta: *Declamazioni retoriche e tragedie senecane.* Palermo: Flaccovio.

Clark, H. H. (1996). *Using language*. Cambridge: Cambridge University Press.

De Jong, I. J. F. (2007). Sophocles *Trachiniae* 1–48, Euripidean prologues, and their audiences. In R. J. Allan & M. Buijs (Eds.), *The language of literature. Linguistic approaches to classical texts* (pp. 7–28). Leiden: Brill.

Fitch, J. G. (1987). *Seneca's Hercules Furens.* Ithaca/London: Cornell University Press.

Fitch, J. G. (2018). *Seneca. Tragedies, Volume I: Hercules. Trojan Women. Phoenician Women. Medea. Phaedra.* Cambridge, MA: Harvard University Press.

Frangoulidis, S. (2020). From victor to victim: Metadrama and movement of plot in Seneca's *Hercules Furens*. *Eugesta*, *10*, 144–162.

Goldberg, S. M. (1997). Melpomene's declamation (rhetoric and tragedy). In W. J. Dominik (Ed.), *Roman eloquence: Rhetoric in society and literature* (pp. 136–149). London/New York: Routledge.

Hannay, M. & Kroon, C. H. M. (2005). Acts and the relationship between discourse and grammar. *Functions of Language*, *12* (1), 87–124.

Hengeveld, K. (2004a). The architecture of a Functional Discourse Grammar. In J. L. Mackenzie & M. A. Gómez-González (Eds.), *A new architecture for functional grammar* (pp. 1–21). Berlin: Mouton de Gruyter.

Hengeveld, K. (2004b). Epilogue. In J. L. Mackenzie & M. A. Gómez-González (Eds.), *A new architecture for functional grammar* (pp. 365–378). Berlin: Mouton de Gruyter.

Holmes, N. (2024). Continuations by Others. In L. Pultrová & M. Vaníková (Eds.), *Exploring Latin: Structures, Functions, Meaning* (pp. 703–720). Berlin/Boston: De Gruyter.

Kragelund, P. (2008). Senecan tragedy: Back on stage? In J. G. Fitch (Ed.), *Seneca* (pp. 181–194). Oxford: Oxford University Press.

Kroon, C. H. M. (1995). *Discourse particles in Latin: A study of* nam, enim, autem, vero *and* at. Leiden: Brill.

Kroon, C. H. M. (2009). Latin linguistics between grammar and discourse. Units of analysis, levels of analysis. In E. Rieken & P. Widmer (Eds.), *Pragmatische Kategorien. Form, Funktion und Diachronie* (pp. 143–158). Wiesbaden: Reichert.

Kroon, C. H. M. (2016). 'Anchoring' as a communicative device in Roman historiography: A discourse-linguistic perspective. https://www.academia.edu/24059119/Anchoring_as_a_communicative_device_in_Roman_historiography_a_discourse_linguistic_perspective (accessed August 5, 2024)
Kroon, C. H. M. (2017). Textual deixis and the 'anchoring' use of the Latin pronoun hic. *Mnemosyne*, *70* (4), 585–612.
Kugelmeier, C. (2007). *Die innere Vergegenwärtigung des Bühnenspiels in Senecas Tragödien.* Munich: Beck.
Leo, F. (1878). *Senecae tragoediis: Observationes criticae.* Berlin: Weidmann.
Risselada, R. (2016). The pragmatics of 'at least': *saltem*, *utique*, *dumtaxat*, *certe*. *Pallas*, *102*, 191–199.
Roulet, E., Auchlin, A. & Moeschler, J. (1985). *L'articulation du discours en français contemporain.* Bern: Lang.
Roulet, E., Filliettaz, L., Grobet, A. & Burger, M. (2001). *Un modèle et un instrument d'analyse de l'organisation du discours.* Bern: Lang.
Schiesaro, A. (2003). *The passions in play: Thyestes and the dynamics of Senecan drama.* Cambridge: Cambridge University Press.
Sutton, D. F. (1986). *Seneca on the stage.* Leiden: Brill.
van Gils, L.W. (2016). Common ground in Latin discourse: Two case studies of narrative negation in Cicero and Vergil. In P. Poccetti (Ed.), *Latinitatis rationes: Descriptive and historical accounts for the Latin language* (pp. 763–779). Berlin/Boston: De Gruyter.
van Gils, L. W. & Kroon, C. H. M. (2019). Engaging the audience: An intersubjectivity approach to the historic present tense in Latin. In L. W. van Gils, C. H. Kroon & R. Risselada (Eds.), *Lemmata Linguistica Latina. Volume 2: Clause and discourse* (pp. 351–373). Berlin/Boston: De Gruyter.
Zanobi, A. (2014). *Seneca's tragedies and the aesthetics of pantomime.* London: Bloomsbury.
Zimmermann, B. (1990). Seneca und der Pantomimus. In G. Vogt-Spira (Ed.), *Strukturen der Mündlichkeit in der römischen Literatur* (pp. 161–167). Tübingen: Narr.
Zwierlein, O. (1966). *Die Rezitationsdramen Senecas. Mit einem kritisch-exegetischen Anhang.* Meisenheim am Glan: Hain.

Luis Unceta Gómez

Pro di immortales! Invocations and Oaths as Interjections

Abstract: The religious sphere is a common lexical source for interjections in many languages, and Latin offers a wide variety of examples of invocations that became interjections through a process of grammaticalization. Grounding on previous research, this paper offers an analysis of certain invocations to the gods or oaths – such as *di boni!*, *di immortales!*, *pro di immortales!* or *pro Iuppiter!* – that came to behave as interjections in Latin. Surveying a large corpus (from Plautus to Aulus Gellius), this analysis focuses on the functions of these expressions, and on their diachronic evolution.

Keywords: oaths, invocations to gods, interjections, interjectional phrases

1 Introduction: What Is an Interjection?

This paper aims at offering a pragmatic account of certain invocations to the gods or oaths – such as *di boni!*, *di immortales!*, *pro di immortales!*, *pro Iuppiter!*, among others – that came to behave as interjections in Latin and became "interjectional phrases" (Ameka 1992) or "interjectional expressions" (Hill 1992), thus contributing to the expression of emotivity. Even if interjections still remain a problematic and contested class, their typical realization, according to their traditional linguistic description, is a single word; thus, these complex interjections can help us to reassess the functional account of this category.

In recent decades, even though it has become commonplace to refer to this category as neglected in linguistic studies, we have witnessed a proliferation of publications on interjections in different languages (including classical languages). Despite the great variety of opinions and discrepancies, there is some consensus on certain features that characterise interjections, such as the following (adapted from Padilla Cruz 2010: 39):

- Commonly, they have a brief structure (mono- or disyllabic), with predominance of vowels and anomalous phonetic constitutions.[1]
- They are grammatically invariable.

1 Regarding Latin, see Biville (1996: 216–219).

Luis Unceta Gómez, Universidad Autónoma de Madrid, Spain

https://doi.org/10.1515/9783111332956-043

- They usually appear in exclamative environments.
- They are extra-predicative.
- They may function as expressive reinforcement within a larger utterance, or autonomously, as an utterance on its own.[2]
- Their meaning is not conceptual, but indexical or procedural.

Interest in the study of interjections was stimulated by the 1992 publication of a special issue of *Journal of Pragmatics*, where Felix Ameka's introduction offered a classification of primary interjections that included elements with very different characteristics and functions: (1) expressive interjections ("vocal gestures which are symptoms of the speaker's mental state"), subdivided into two groups: (1a) emotive interjections ("express the speaker's state with respect to the emotions and sensations they have at the time"), and (1b) cognitive interjections ("those that pertain to the state of knowledge and thoughts at the time of utterance"); (2) conative interjections ("which are directed at an auditor" and "are either aimed at getting someone's attention or they demand an action or response from someone of a speaker's wants"); and (3) phatic interjections ("used in the establishment and maintenance of communicative contact") (all quotations from Ameka 1992, 113–114).

Nonetheless, this approach clearly follows from the traditional conception of the interjection, which includes numerous heterogeneous elements that can be considered to belong to different functional categories. Today, some of those expressions can be better understood as discourse markers, pragmatic markers, conversational routines or appellative elements. This is especially clear in the case of grammaticalized words in such functions, but my claim is that this functional criterion should also apply to minimal units, traditionally understood as primary interjections. I return to this idea below.

Authors such as Ameka (1992), Wierzbicka (1992) and Wilkins (1992), who share a "conceptualist" approach, consider interjections as linguistic units with complex semantic structures but underestimate the contribution of pragmatic and contextual factors to their correct interpretation. In contrast, according with Wharton's (2003) relevantist proposal, interjections can be understood as units that provide with a procedural instruction; they do not modify the truth conditions of the utterance containing them, but the latter is modified by their effect as an expressive speech act (on Latin, see Unceta Gómez 2012). This restrictive definition of interjections is closely in line with that offered by the Latin grammarians, to whom we owe its identification as a different grammatical category. According to them, the

2 Poggi (2009) defines them as "holophrastic codified signals", and Nordgren (2015: 8) calls such uses "free-standing interjections".

main defining feature of this class is not the expression of a lexical content, but the evidence of an emotional state. As Palaemon (apud CHAR. gramm. I 238, 23–25), for instance, explains it, *interiectiones sunt quae* ***nihil docibile habent****; significant tamen* ***adfectum animi***.

Thus, from the functional viewpoint adopted here, the category of interjection does not include what are understood to be cognitive, conative and phatic interjections in classifications like Ameka's (1992). It is preferable to analyse the latter elements in their respective linguistic systems, regardless of whether certain minimal units are formally akin to primary interjections (Unceta Gómez 2012: 354–361).

For example, *pax* ('stop it!', from Greek πάξ), or *st!* are not words conveying proper procedural instructions but are conventionally interpreted as requests of cessation of an action. The same can be said of other units with minimal phonic substance (*heus!*, *o[h]* + vocative) which belong to the address system, in which conative and phatic functions are blended. Finally, although traditional studies on interjection in classical languages systematically dedicate a section to certain grammaticalized imperatives with allegedly interjective functions, other interpretations are preferable. For example, *age* is best interpreted as an illocutionary reinforcer of directive speech acts (see Unceta Gómez 2024). Similarly, greetings and farewell formulas, like *ave* and *vale*, are actually conversational routines (Coulmas 1981); unlike interjections, their use is predictable and socially regulated.[3]

By contrast, interjections are linguistic units that function, either primarily or derivatively, as an indicator of the speaker's emotional state. Therefore, they do not alter the propositional content of the utterance in which they are included, nor do they modify its truth conditions, but they do guide the interpretation of the speaker's attitude and affect the illocutionary force that the speaker is applying to their message.[4] Interjections, therefore, are modalizers[5] that incorporate an indication of expressive illocutionary force in their procedural meaning but lack propositional content. According to Searle (1976: 12), the illocutionary point of expressives "is to express the psychological state specified in the sincerity condition about the state of affairs specified in the propositional content".

This speaker's mental state can take on different qualities: sadness, pain, anger, fear, happiness, surprise, indignation, and so on. Although some interjections are clearly dependent on the context to be correctly interpreted, a good number are conventionally associated with particular emotions. These conventional asso-

3 Oaths can also function in this way: *di vortant bene* (*quod agas*), for instance, is a conventional expression of leave-taking (Puekert Stock 2021: 51).

4 Biville (2002) goes so far as to use the term "interjective modality", since it is more an enunciative modality than a grammatical category.

5 See Rosén (2009: 321–322) for a definition of "modalising particles".

ciations allow us to approach the analysis of interjections in classical languages and help compensate for the many lost linguistic features (tone of voice, intonational structure, vowel lengthening, gestures, etc.), especially in texts that can be described as written orality.

In order to disentangle this combination of disparate linguistic elements produced by the confusion of formal and functional criteria in the description and classification of interjections, the label "pragmatic noise" can be helpful, since it allows to account for formal and functional differences, as shown in Figure 1. Culpeper and Oliver define this category as follows:

> Pragmatic noise concerns material that lies outside the main syntax and is pregnant with pragmatic meaning. [. . .] [they] are almost always monosyllabic and sometimes phonologically unusual [. . .]. They are formed of semi-natural or instinctive noises, including not only single types like AH, HA, OH, HUM, but also reduplicative forms such as HA HA. (Culpeper and Oliver 2020: 12)

This proposal also takes into account the possibility that certain words from other categories may take on interjective functions (Norrick 2009; Ghezzi 2014: 16), as a result of a subjectification process (Traugott 1995). Thus, it is possible to identify interjectional uses in pragmatic markers such as *quaeso* and *obsecro* (Unceta Gómez 2016: 235–237; Fedriani 2017), *em* (Unceta Gómez 2017b) or *abi* (Unceta Gomez 2017c), which, in specific cases, can modalize the utterance in an expressive sense. Following a similar line of argument, it can be said that interjections essentially lack discursive functions, although they can develop them subsidiarily due to their high degree of conventionalization in certain contexts.[6]

2 Oaths as Interjections

Latin grammarians were already aware that some units were interjections in their own right, but certain other elements could perform the same functions, though they originally belonged to other categories.[7] This distinction between primary and

6 Padilla Cruz (2009a and 2009b), in response to Wharton's (2003) relevantist proposal, suggests that the repeated and intentional use of an interjection in well-defined communicative situations facilitates the encoding of a specific meaning, which Padilla Cruz interprets as the grammaticalization of that meaning. Although Wharton (2016) himself has accepted the possibility of the diachronic enrichment of some interjections, which may lead to their grammaticalization or systematic association with a certain conceptual content, it seems clear that the automatization of certain uses does not imply any expansion of semantic content.

7 See, e.g., Prisc. gramm. III 90, 23–27.

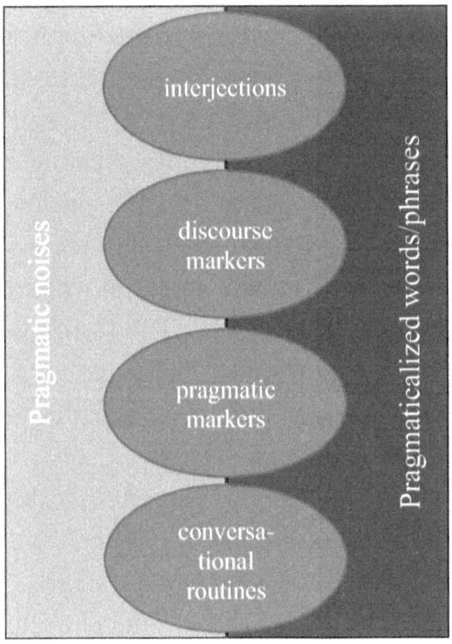

Figure 1: Formal and functional criteria for cataloguing pragmatic units.

secondary interjections continues to be operational, since it allows us to capture the phenomenon of attrition and continuous renewal within this category. The religious sphere is a very common lexical source for interjections in many world languages,[8] and Archaic Latin offers a good number of pragmaticalized items that are understood to originally have been oaths.[9] The group that most commonly appears comes from the names of Hercules, Castor and Pollux: *hercle*, *mehercle*, *ecastor*, *mecastor*, *pol* and *edepol*. All these forms were fully pragmaticalized by the 2nd century BC,[10] which hinders their etymological interpretation.[11] Regardless of their origin, these elements have traditionally been considered "expletives", and have attracted high interest due to their clearly gender-specific distribution in archaic comedy (Ullman 1943: 88). Adams (1984) considers them obsolete in the time of Terence; at the end of the Republic, they disappear almost completely, and are no longer attested in Seneca.

Despite the traditional interpretation, these elements do not function primarily as interjections, but are a mark of the commitment of the speaker to the truth of the

8 On English, for example, see Gehweiler (2008).

9 Puekert Stock (2021) refers to them as "informal/interjectional oaths".

10 In fact, the later-attested extended formulas – *hercule* (Livy, Petronius), *mehercule* (Cicero), *hercules* (Cicero, Petronius), *mehercules* (Cicero, Petronius) – may be thought to be restitutions or the result of analogical formative processes (Ashdowne 2008: 20).

11 Unceta Gómez (2016: 219) offers a review of the proposals.

propositional content conveyed in the utterance, thus they belong to the domain of epistemicity (Unceta Gómez 2016), similar to other performative expressions such as *ita me di ament* (Griffe 1989; Mesa Sanz 1998). According to Ashdowne (2008), in order to understand the discursive functions of these units, we must take into account the basic structure of the speech act of "oath", in which the speaker expresses before the interlocutor their commitment to the truthfulness of the utterance, by appealing to the divinity which acts as guarantor of that truthfulness and is interpreted as a secondary receiver of the utterance. Its most complete formulation includes, therefore, an oath-taking verb, the divine guarantor's name of, introduced by means of a prepositional syntagm, and the propositional content (in the form of an infinitive sentence or a complement clause introduced by *ut*).

Given the strong fixation of this type of formula, the lexical expression of the guarantor gradually assumes the pragmatic function made explicit by the performative verb, to the point that it can convey the same illocutionary point even without the verb. At a later stage, the intensifying function of the assertion begins to be combined with expressive petitions and entreaties, where it emphasizes the need for what is requested. In this value, we often find expressions such as *per deos*, *pro dii* or *per/pro (deum) fidem*,[12] *per genium* and *per dexteram tuam*. R. Ashdowne explains the phenomenon as follows:

> The force of the oath here is clearly a non-neutral attitude, but it is one somewhat attenuated [. . .]: the oath-taker is not swearing to the veracity of the accompanying words (i.e. those words' status in the internal / external situation) but rather the oath is emphasizing the intensity of the speaker's entreaty (i.e. their status in the metalinguistic situation) [. . .]. The development is from 'I swear that X' → 'I really am saying that X' → 'I really am asking X', i.e. 'I mean what I am saying: this is a genuine request'. (Ashdowne 2008: 18)

The next step is the transformation of these phrases into mere marks of the speaker's subjectivity, thus modalising the utterance in an expressive sense, as in (1):[13]

(1) [. . .] SOPH. *quis hic loquitur?* CHR. *Sophrona!* SOPH. *et meum nomen nominat?* CHR. *respice ad me.* SOPH. ***di obsecro vos****, estne hic Stilpo?* CHR. *non.* SOPH. *negas?* (TER. Phor. 740)
'SOPH. *(hearing him)* Who's that talking?
CHR. Sophrona!
SOPH. And calling me by name?

12 See Unceta Gómez (2009: 69, 100, 169–171), and below, examples (16) and (17).

13 All the texts and translations in this paper are those of the Loeb Classical Library: Barsby (2001a and 2001b); De Melo (2011a, 2011b), Freese (1930); Gummere (1917); Ker (1926); Sutton (1942); Thomson (1953); Windstedt (1912).

CHR. Look at me.
SOPH. *(turning round)* **In the name of the gods**, is it Stilpo?
CHR. No.
SOPH. *(going up to him)* Did you say no?'

Although I cannot go into the details here, most of the uses of *hercle*, *mehercle*, *ecastor*, *mecastor*, *pol* and *edepol* in enunciative sentences express the speaker's commitment to the truthfulness of the proposition, especially in those cases where the speaker is clearly involved, as in (2):[14]

(2) [. . .] LEO. *Ehem, optume. Quam dudum tu advenisti?*
Non **hercle** *te provideram (quaeso ne vitio vortas).* (PLAVT. Asin. 450)
'LEO. Oh, very good. How long ago did you come? I **really** hadn't noticed you before – please don't take any offense.'

But, as Cornillie states,

> From a linguistic point of view, speakers express that they are committed to the claim they make (overtly). Yet, speakers can also be committed to presuppositions and thoughts (covertly). In talk-in-interaction speakers are, in one way or another, also committed to the consistency of the flow of discourse, to the interaction with their coparticipants as well as to their well-being or to their face (face-saving strategies). The analysis of commitment to the proposition and the analysis of the sequential organization of the discourse go hand in hand, indeed. Finally, speaker commitment can also be understood as commitment to a future course of action (intentions or obligations). (Cornillie 2018: 161)

Therefore, pragmaticalized oaths such as *hercle* likewise intensify certain commissive speech acts, such as (3), and can also modify imperative sentences, thus reinforcing the directive speech act, especially in entreaties (4):

(3) SOS. *ut lubet quid tibi lubet fac, quoniam pugnis plus vales;*
verum, utut es facturus, hoc quidem **hercle** *hau reticebo tamen.* (PLAVT. Amph. 396–397)[15]
'SOS. Do what you like as you like, since you have more strength in your fists; but however you're going to treat me, still, I shan't be silent about this.'

---

14 All examples are of *hercle*, the most widely represented element, which therefore illustrates the widest functional spectrum; for the behaviour of the rest, see Unceta Gómez (2016: 219–233).
15 In this and the two following examples, *hercle* has been left unexpressed by the translator.

(4) [. . .] LIB. *Ah,*
neque hercle ego istuc dico nec dictum volo,
teque ***opsecro hercle*** *ut quae locutu's despuas.* (PLAVT. Asin. 37–39)
'LIB. *(in fear)* No, no! I'm not mentioning that, and I don't want it to be mentioned, and I implore you, spit out what you've said.'

However, its combination with the interrogative modality, which blocks its interpretation as an epistemic device, begins to show a different value, which we can consider close to the interjectional, especially in rhetorical questions that betray disagreement or reproach:

(5) [MER.] *nam mihi quidem* ***hercle*** *qui minus liceat deo minitarier*
populo, ni decedat mihi, quam servolo in comoediis? (PLAVT. Amph. 986–987)
'[MER.] Why should I, a god, not be allowed to threaten people if they don't get out of my way just as much as some paltry slave in comedies?'

Finally, and these are the least represented uses, there are other cases where certain expressiveness can be felt, especially if the unit is included in an exclamatory context or in combination with primary interjections, as *attat!* in (6), in an aside:

(6) [THER.] *Attat! Curculio* ***hercle*** *verba mihi dedit, quom cogito.* (PLAVT. Curc. 583)
'[THER.] Goodness! Curculio has **really** tricked me when I think about it.'

So already in Plautus' comedies we find a full pragmaticalization of these units, where they have shed their conceptual meaning and are gradually taking on discursive functions, whether epistemic, deontic, or, much less often and not always easily identifiable, the sudden expression of an emotion. But invocations to Hercules, Castor and Pollux are not the only oaths with potential interjectional uses. Actually, in other invocations, interjectional uses are much more easily recognizable.

3 Complex Invocations

Other forms of invocation or oaths, somewhat less represented than the former, more clearly behave as interjectional phrases. To begin, the invocation (*o*) *di boni!* appears increasingly over the centuries. From a single example in Plautus (7), and four in Terence (8),[16] (*o*) *di boni!* appears no less than twenty times in Cicero, and Seneca the Younger also uses it (but not in his theatrical works). Note that although the latter authors mainly use it as an interjectional expression (examples [10] and [11]), a few instances in Cicero, as in example (9), illustrate an epistemic meaning similar to the one conveyed by *hercle* in the examples analysed above:

(7) PHIL. ***Di boni!*** *Visitavi hunc an non antidhac?* (PLAVT. Epid. 539).
'PHIL. *(noticing Periphanes)* **Good gods!** Have I seen this man before or not?'

(8) [. . .] ***o di boni!***
Ne illius modi iam magna nobis civium
paenuriast. [. . .] (TER. Ad. 440–442).[17]
'**Heaven knows**, there's a great shortage of such citizens these days.'

(9) *At te apud eum,* **di boni**, *quanta in gratia posui! Eique legi litteras non tuas, sed librarii tui.* (CIC. Att. 6, 6, 10)
'But, **heavens**, how I have put you in his good books. I read him a letter, not in your own hand, but in that of your secretary.'

(10) *Ad hunc,* **di boni!**, *legatos mitti placet? Norunt isti homines formam rei publicae, iura belli, exempla maiorum, cogitant, quid populi Romani maiestas, quid senatus severitas postulet?* (CIC. Phil. 5, 25)
'Is it to this man, **good Heavens!**, we are pleased to send envoys? Do those friends of yours know the constitution of the State, the laws of the war, the precedents of our ancestors?'

(11) *Lectus est deinde liber Quinti Sextii patris, magni, si quid mihi credis, viri et, licet neget, Stoici. quantus in illo,* **di boni**, *vigor est, quantum animi!* (SEN. epist. 64, 3)
'We then had read to us a book by Quintus Sextius the Elder. He is a great man, if you have any confidence in my opinion, and a real Stoic, though he himself denies it. **Ye Gods**, what strength and spirit one finds in him!'

Instead of *di boni*, Plautus uses (*o*) *di immortales* (27 examples), compared to a single instance in Terence and two of *pro di immortales* (see infra). In all these

16 In Terence, according to Barsby (1999: 124), the expression conveys emotions of surprise, indignation and satisfaction.
17 See also TER. Andr. 338; Eun. 225; Haut. 254.

cases, clearly reactive – especially "in reaction to unwelcome news" (Barsby 1999: 128, n. 232) –, the combination with exclamatory sentences, indignant questions, or utterances that communicate the speaker's surprise, makes the interjectional function of the syntagm perfectly recognisable, as (12) illustrates:

(12) [. . .] MNE. ***Di immortales***, *meum sodalem hic nominat.* (PLAVT. Bacch. 414)[18]
'MNE. *(aside)* **Immortal gods**, he's naming my friend.'

Again, the frequency increases with Cicero, where the formula appears in 66 instances, generally in combination with exclamative statements (note the exclamatory accusative in [13]) expressing disagreement or displeasure:

(13) *Reliquum est, ut per servos id admiserit.* ***O di immortales***, *rem miseram et calamitosam!* (CIC. S. Rosc. 77)
'There remains the alternative that he committed the crime by the agency of slaves. **O immortal gods**, what a misfortune.'

Cicero also offers an example that probably illustrates the kind of context that originally facilitated the development of the interjective use of this syntagm:

(14) *Qui, dum hic sit, quod rapiant, quod auferant, nihil sibi defuturum arbitrantur; quibus M. Antonius (**o di immortales**, avertite et detestamini, quaeso, hoc omen!) urbem se divisurum esse promisit.* (CIC. Phil. 4, 9–10)
'Men that think nothing will fail them provided there be here some subject for rapine, for robbery; men to whom – **O ye immortal Gods**, avert, I pray, and make harmless this omen! – Marcus Antonius has promised the division of the city.'

Finally, Terence also uses the invocation (*o*) *Iuppiter!* (10 examples), again clearly interjective in all its appearances:

(15) [. . .] DEM. ***O Iuppiter***,
hancin vitam! Hoscin mores! Hanc dementiam! (TER. Ad. 757–758)[19]
'DEM. *(to himself)* **Jupiter!** What a life! What a way to behave! What madness!'

18 See also PLAVT. Capt. 891; Most. 912, among others.
19 See also TER. Ad. 731; Andr. 464, 930; Eun. 946; Haut. 256, 630, 690; Phorm. 816.

All these invocations also present variations with *pro*. According to Hofmann (2003²: 134), it is the preposition *pro* in tmesis, with the meaning 'here in front', 'here out' (cf. *proclamo*), preserved in ancient legal formulas for requesting help. This is easily noted in expressions with *fidem*, as in (16) and (17), usually with negative overtones:

(16) [. . .] CAP. ***Pro deum atque hominum fidem!***
Hocin pacto indemnatum atque intestatum me abripi?
Opsecro, Planesium, et te, Phaedrome, auxilium ut feras. (PLAVT. Curc. 694–696)[20]
'CAP. **In the name of all that's sacred on heaven and earth!** That I should be dragged off in this way without sentence and without witnesses against me! I implore you, Planesium, and you, Phaedromus, bring me help.'

(17) DEM. *Quid igitur facies?* MIC. *Domi erit.* DEM. ***Pro divom fidem!***
Meretrix et materfamilias una in domo?
MIC. *Quor non?* [. . .] (TER. Ad. 746–748)[21]
'DEM. What will you do then?
MIC. She'll be kept at home.
DEM. **Heaven help us!** A wife and a mistress under the same roof?
MIC. Why not?'

However, in combination with a vocative, *pro* is usually understood as an interjection (Ashdowne 2008: 22, n. 14).[22]

In the case of *pro di boni*, it is attested only in Lucius Anneus Seneca's *Controversiae* (3 times). By contrast, *pro di immortales* appears since Archaic times (27 examples in Plautus, 3 examples in Terence[23]), typically with negative overtones, as

20 Cf. PLAVT. Amph. 376.

21 Cf. TER. Eun. 943 (*pro deum fidem*); Andr. 246; Haut. 61; Hec. 198 (*pro deum atque hominum fidem!*). The complete formula, according to Hofmann (2003²: 134–135; or rather a comical exaggeration, as Ricottilli indicates in her note), is found in CAECIL. com. 211: *pro deum, popularium omnium, omnium adulescentium clamo postulo obsecro oro ploro atque imploro fidem*. See also PLAVT. Rud. 615: *pro, Cyrenenses populares, vostram ego imploro fidem*.

22 An obvious example of this is PLAVT. Most. 77, where the syntagm *pro dii immortales* is the recipient of a prayer. In Seneca's tragedies it behaves very similarly to the interjection *o*, since it introduces invocations, accompanying a vocative, but also appears in combination with exclamatory phrases (cf. SEN. Herc. O. 770; 1231–1232); and in one case it even seems able to modify an entire utterance in an expressive sense (Herc. O. 1803–1804). See Unceta Gómez (2017a: 141).

23 TER. Eun. 232; Phorm. 1008; the variant *pro deum immortalium* in Phorm. 351. All these are reactions to unpleasant news (Barsby 1999: 128).

in (18), where Amphitruo is trying to make Alcmena understand that it was impossible for him to be with her before his arrival back home, or in (19):

(18) ALC. *Istuc facinus quod tu insimulas nostro generi non decet.*
Tu si me impudicitiai captas, capere non potes.
AMPH. ***Pro di immortales***, *cognoscin tu me saltem, Sosia?* (PLAVT. Amph. 820–822)[24]
'ALC. The deed you're accusing me of doesn't become our family. If you're trying to catch me in immoral conduct, you won't succeed.
AMPH. **Immortal gods**, can at least you recognize me, Sosia?'

(19) HEG. ***Pro di immortales!*** *Facinus indignum, Geta!*
Quid narras? GET. *Sic est factum.* HEG. *Ex illan familia*
tan illiberale facinus esse ortum! [. . .] (TER. Ad. 447–449)
'HEG. **Ye immortal gods!** What a shocking business, Geta! What a story!
HEG. Such ungentlemanly conduct from that family!'

Examples continue to appear in Cicero's work, although less frequently than the variant without *pro* (12 instances):

(20) ***Pro di immortales!***, *quae fuit illa, quanta vis! quam inexspectata! quam repentina! cum coniectis oculis, gestu omni ei emminenti, suma gravitate et celeritate verborum "Brute, quid sedes?".* (CIC. de orat. 2, 225)
'**Ha! ye deathless gods!** what boundles vigour he displayed! and how sudden and unlooked-for it was! when, with piercing gaze, with menace in his every motion, in the severest tones, and in a torrent of words he declaimed: "Brutus, why seated?".'

Also *pro Iuppiter!* shows large representation over the centuries, although its presence is much sparser than that of *pro di immortales.* Although swearing by Zeus seems to be one of the default oaths in Greek comedy, the expression is attested only scarcely in ancient comedy (11 instances in Plautus; 5 in Terence):[25]

24 See also PLAVT. Aul. 460, 616; Bacch. 182; Capt. 697, 974; Curc. 274; Men. 1062, etc.

25 "The Greeks utilized informal oaths by Zeus most frequently of all, while Jupiter is much more sparsely called upon in Roman comedy, thus making it more effective when used" (Puekert Stock 2021: 64).

(21) [. . .] THER. *Cedo ut inspiciam.* CVR. *Sanan es,*
quae isti committas? PLA. *Sine modo.* THER. ***Pro Iuppiter!***
Hic est quem ego tibi misi natali die.
Tam facile novi quam me. Salve, mea soror. (PLAVT. Curc. 654–657)[26]
'THER. Give it to me so I can examine it. *(she hands it over)*
CUR. *(to Planesium)* Are you in your right mind, giving it to this person?
PLA. Just let him have it.
THER. **O Jupiter!** This is the one I sent you on your birthday. I know it as well as myself. Greetings, my dear sister.'

(22) [. . .] PAM. *noli fabularier.*
Pro Iuppiter! *Rumorem audivi* [. . .] (TER. Hec. 316–317)[27]
'PAM. Don't speak a word. *(changing his tone as he hears a cry from inside)* **Great Jupiter!** I heard a scream.'

In all the cases, *pro Iuppiter* is typically reactive, both to a previous intervention from the addressee or to a sudden stimulus (either linguistic or extralinguistic), and it is always connected to strong emotions (Puekert Stock 2021: 42), both positive or negative. Charisius notes that *pro Iuppiter* could indicate joy or anger depending on the context,[28] Servius interprets it as an expression of anger,[29] and Donatus considers *pro Iuppiter!* as a characteristic expression of the tragic style, and thus is usually pronounced by high-status characters in comedy.[30] The fact that it belongs to a high register is evidenced by its appearance, albeit very limited, in the epic genre (Virgil, Valerius Flaccus, Silius Italicus). In fact, it may have become the typical oath of paganism in Christian times:

26 Cf. PLAVT. Amph. 791, 1074; Aul. 241; Curc. 638; Men. 412, 957; Mil. 1133; Most. 191; Pseud. 574; Poen. 1122 (*pro supreme Iuppiter!*).

27 See also TER. Ad. 111, 366; Andr. 732; Eun. 550; Ad. 196 (*pro supreme Iuppiter!*). Barsby (1999: 260–261) underscores that in Terence, of the 15 examples of expressions including *pro*, only two are pronounced by women.

28 *Pro Iuppiter* [pro] *gaudentis: "Pro Iuppiter, ut mihi, quidquid ago, lepide omnia prospereque eveniunt"; pro Iuppiter irati Terentius in Adelphis: "pro Iuppiter, tu homo adigis me ad insaniam"* (CHAR. gramm. I 314, 28).

29 PRO IVPPITER *aut irascentis exclamatio est, ut in Terentio "pro supreme Iuppiter": aut certe testatur Iovem, quem in Aeneae invocavit adventu, ut "Iuppiter hospitibus nam te dare iura loquuntur"* (SERV. Aen. 4, 590). See, for instance, TER. Ad. 111–112.

30 PRO IVPPITER *quia pro Iuppiter tragica exclamatio est, bene tamquam ipse se reprehenderet Demea adiecit tu homo rediges me ad insaniam.* (DON. Ter. Ad. 111, 1). PRO IVPPITER ISTOCINE PACTO FIERI OPORTET *pro Iuppiter tragice adiecit aversus, istocine pacto ad ipsum Micionem respiciens dixit* (DON. Ter. Ad. 731, 2).

(23) *Dudum coquebat disserente martyre*
Asclepiades intus iram subdolam
stomachatus alto felle, dum longum silet
bilemque tectis concipit praecordiis;
tandem latentis vim furoris evomit:
*"**Pro Iuppiter!** Quid est quod ex hoc audio?"* (PRVD. perist. 391–396)
'While the martyr was discoursing, Asclepiades had long been privily nursing wrath within him, for he was fuming and his ire was deep while he kept this long silence and displeasure was rising secretly in his heart. At last he discharged the violence of the rage he had been cloaking: "**Jupiter!** What is it that I hear from this fellow?".'

As a final note, although these are the most represented and probably also the most automated expressions, there are other invocations that also seem to function as "interjectional phrases", such as *di vostram fidem* in example (24), which in Terence (10 times as interjection) is mainly used as an expression of surprise and wonder (Puekert Stock 2021: 50), *di obsecro vos* (see above example [1]), *pro divom fidem!*, or *pro deum atque hominum fidem* (see examples [16] and [17]):

(24) [. . .] PHAE. ***Di vostram fidem!*** *Incredibilia*
Parmeno modo quae narravit! [. . .] (TER. Eun. 1049–1050)[31]
'PHAE. *(to himself)* **Heaven help us!** What Parmeno has just told me is unbelievable.'

4 Conclusions

This paper has shown that the religious sphere is a fertile ground for the creation of interjectional phrases. Needless to say, not every oath or invocation can be straightforwardly interpreted as a secondary interjection,[32] that is to say, linguistic units that function, either primarily or derivatively, as an indicator of the speaker's emotional state. Elements such as *hercle, mehercle, ecastor, mecastor, pol* and *edepol*, in spite of their traditional description, cannot be considered interjections in most of their uses, since their main function is epistemic and, only rarely – in a low number

31 The same expression occurs in TER. Ad. 381; Andr. 716, 744; Eun. 418, 790, 924; Haut. 502; Phorm. 757, 808.
32 Consider, for instance, *di istaec prohibeant!* (TER. Haut. 1037) or *ita di (deaeque) faxint* (TER. Haut. 161).

of contexts which include other elements favouring this interpretation –, they can be understood as a spontaneous manifestation of the speaker's emotions.

However, in this review of interjectional phrases based on invocations to the gods or oaths, we have found a number of other expressions that do express this kind of pragmatic meaning and can therefore be considered interjectional expressions: (*o*) / *pro di boni*, (*o*) / *pro Iuppiter*, (*o*) / *pro di immortales* are, strictly speaking, secondary interjections in most of their uses. That is to say, all these "interjectional phrases" clearly behave as an externalization of the speaker's subjectivity, unlike what seems to have happened in Greek. In this language, according to Nordgren (2015: 22), oaths like *ne Día, mà (pros) tôn theôn* "regularly express affirmation; they are also frequently used to add an element of emphasis of intensification". In other words, these syntagms are closer to the *hercle*-like expressions than to those Latin complex invocations.

The quantitative distribution of the interjectional phrases, presented in Table 1, is not overly informative, as, after Plautus and Terence, most "dialogic" works, such as Horace's satires, Petronius or Apuleius or the epic dialogues, do not present significant insights (or do not offer any data at all), and the majority of the examples are covered by Cicero and Seneca the Younger.

Table 1: Occurrences of interjectional phrases based on invocations to the gods.

	(o) di boni	*(o) di immortales*	*(o) Iuppiter*	*pro di boni*	*pro di immortales*	*pro Iuppiter*
Plautus	1	23			27	11
Terence	4	1	10		2	5
Cicero	20	66			12	1
Seneca the Elder	1			3		3
Vergil						1
Ovid						2
Persius						1
Seneca the Younger	10					
Valerius Flaccus						2
Silius Italicus						2
Apuleius	2					
Aulus Gellius	1					2
TOTAL	**39**	**90**	**10**	**3**	**41**	**30**

However, the comparison of these data with the presence of the *hercle*-like expressions in comedy[33] and in Cicero (Table 2), is very telling about the fact that, even if they cover different pragmatic functions (mainly epistemic in the case of the former), the interjectional phrases analysed in this paper, and specially (*o*) *di boni* and (*o*) *di immortales*, which find much less representation in Archaic Latin, replace in the formal dimension the characteristic units of comedy as pragmaticalized oaths. And this provides us with additional evidence of the need to reassess the structural and functional account of the grammatical category of interjections.

Table 2: Occurrences of *hercle*-like expressions.

	hercle	*mehercle*	*edepol*	*pol*	*ecastor*	*mecastor*
Plautus	639	3	365	250	101	17
Terence	96	2	22	55	2	2
Cicero	11		1	2		

(Source of the data of Plautus and Terence: Nicholson [1983: 99])

Bibliography

Adams, J. N. (1984). Female speech in Latin comedy. *Antichthon, 18*, 43–77.
Ameka, F. (1992). Interjections: the universal yet neglected part of speech. *Journal of Pragmatics, 18*, 101–118.
Ashdowne, R. (2008). E-vocative invocation: on the historical morphosyntax of Latin oaths. In R. Wright (Ed.), *Latin vulgaire – Latin tardif VIII. Actes du VIIIe colloque international sur le latin vulgaire et tardif (Oxford, 6–9 septembre 2006)* (pp. 13–25). Hildesheim: Olms-Weidmann.
Barsby, J. (1999). Terence, *Eunuchus*. Cambridge: Cambridge University Press.
Barsby, J. (2001a). *Terence, The Woman of Andros, The Self-Tormentor, The Eunuchus*. Cambridge, MA: Harvard University Press.
Barsby, J. (2001b). *Terence, Phormio, The Mother-in-Law, The Brothers*. Cambridge, MA: Harvard University Press.
Biville, F. (1996). Le statut linguistique des interjections en latin. In H. Rosén (Ed.), *Aspects of Latin. Papers from the 7th International Colloquium on Latin Linguistics* (pp. 209–220). Innsbruck: Innbrucker Beiträge zur Sprachwissenschaft.
Biville, F. (2002). Les modalités interjectives (Virgile, Enéide). In M. Fruyt & C. Moussy (Eds.), *Les modalités en latin* (pp. 275–289). Paris: PUPS.
Cornillie, B. (2018). On speaker commitment and speaker involvement. Evidence from evidentials in Spanish talk-in-interaction. *Journal of Pragmatics, 128*, 161–170.
Coulmas, F. (Ed.) (1981). *Conversational Routine*. Mouton: The Hague.

33 As stated above, Adams (1984) considers these expressions obsolete in the time of Terence.

Culpeper, J. & Oliver, S. J. (2020). Pragmatic noise in Shakespeare's plays. In E. Jonsson & T. Larsson (Eds.), *Voices Past and Present – Studies of Involved, Speech-related and Spoken Texts: In honor of Merja Kytö* (pp. 11–30). Amsterdam/Philadelphia: John Benjamins.

de Melo, W. C. (2011a). Plautus, *Amphitryon, The Comedy of Asses, The Pot of Gold, The two Bacchises, The Captives*. Cambridge, MA: Harvard University Press.

de Melo, W. C. (2011b). Plautus, *Casina, The Casket Comedy, Curculio, Epidicus, The Two Menaechmuses*. Cambridge, MA: Harvard University Press.

Fedriani, Ch. (2017). *Quaepropter, quaeso?* 'Why, for pity's sake?' Questions and the pragmatic functions of *quaeso, obsecro* and *amabo* in Plautus. In C. Denizot & O. Spevak (Eds.), *Pragmatic Approaches to Latin and Ancient Greek* (pp. 83–109). Amsterdam/Philadelphia, John Benjamins.

Freese, J. H. (1930). Cicero, *Pro Publio Quinctio; Pro Sexto Roscio Amerino; Pro Quinto Roscio Comoedo; De lege agraria*. Cambridge, MA: Harvard University Press.

Ghezzi, Ch. (2014). The development of discourse and pragmatic markers. In Ch. Ghezzi & P. Molinelli (Eds.), *Discourse and pragmatic markers from Latin to the Romance languages* (pp. 10–26). Oxford: Oxford University Press.

Gehweiler, E. (2008). From proper name to primary interjection: The case of *gee! Journal of Historical Pragmatics*, *9* (1), 71–88.

Griffe, M. (1989): *Ita me di ament* (*ut. . .*). Une formule de serment en latin ancien. *Lalies*, *7*, 289–298.

Gummere, R. M. (1917). Seneca, *Ad Lucilium epistulae morales*, vol. I. Cambridge, MA: Harvard University Press.

Hill, D. (1992). Imprecatory interjectional expressions: Examples from Australian English. *Journal of Pragmatics*, *18* (2–3), 209–223.

Hofmann, J. B. (2003). *La lingua d'uso latina (Introduzione, traduzione e note a cura di Licinia Ricottilli)* (3rd edn.). Bologna: Patron.

Ker, W. C. A. (1926). Cicero, *Philipics*. Cambridge, MA: Harvard University Press.

Mesa Sanz, J. F. (1998a): *Di me perdant si. . .* análisis de los llamados optativos aseverativos. *Cuadernos de Filología Clásica (Estudios Latinos)*, *14*, 9–26.

Nicolson, F. W. (1893). The use of *hercle* (*mehercle*), *edepol* (*pol*), *ecastor* (*mecastor*) by Plautus and Terence. *Harvard Studies in Classical Philology*, *4*, 99–103.

Nordgren, L. (2015). *Greek Interjections. Syntax, Semantics and Pragmatics*. Berlin/Boston: De Gruyter.

Norrick, N. R. (2009). Interjections as pragmatic markers. *Journal of Pragmatics*, *41* (5), 866–891.

Padilla Cruz, M. (2009a). Towards an alternative relevance-theoretic approach to interjections, *International Review of Pragmatics*, *1* (1), 182–206.

Padilla Cruz, M. (2009b). Might interjections encode concepts? More questions than answers. *Lodz Papers in Pragmatics*, *5* (2), 241–270.

Padilla Cruz, M. (2010). What do interjections contribute to communication and how are they interpreted? A cognitive pragmatic account? In I. Witczak-Plisiecka (Ed.), *Pragmatic perspectives on language and linguistics. Vol. 1, Speech actions in theory and applied studies* (pp. 39–68), Newcastle upon Tyne: Cambridge Scholars Publishing.

Peukert Stock, O. (2021). "Pro Iuppiter!" *A Study of the Use of Oaths, Curses, and Prayers in Roman Comedy*. MA thesis, Lund University, https://lup.lub.lu.se/luur/download?func=downloadFile&recordOId=9057276&fileOId=9057286 (accessed 30/01/2023).

Poggi, I. (2009). The language of interjections. In A. Esposito, A. Hussain, M. Marinaro & R. Martone (Eds.), *Multimodal Signals: Cognitive and Algorithmic Issues* (pp. 170–186). Berlin/Heidelberg: Springer.

Rosén, H. (2009). Coherence, sentence modification, and sentence-part modification. The contribution of particles. In P. Baldi & P. Cuzzolini (Eds.), *New Perspectives on Historical Latin Syntax. Vol. 1, Syntax of the sentence* (pp. 317–441). Berlin/New York: Mouton de Gruyter.
Searle, J. R. (1976). A classification of illocutionary acts. *Language in Society*, *5* (1), 1–23.
Sutton, E. W. (1942). Cicero, *De oratore*. Vol. I. Books I–II. Cambridge, MA: Harvard University Press.
Thomson, H. J. (1953). Prudentius, *Against Symmachus 2. Crowns of Martyrdom. Scenes From History. Epilogue*. Cambridge, MA: Harvard University Press.
Traugott, E. C. (1995). Subjectification in grammaticalization. In D. Stein & S. Wright (Eds.), *Subjectivity and subjectivisation. Linguistic perspectives* (pp. 31–54). Cambridge: Cambridge University Press.
Ullman, B. L. (1943). By Castor and Polux. *Classical Weekly*, *37*, 87–89.
Unceta Gómez, L. (2009). *La petición verbal en latín. Estudio léxico semántico y pragmático*. Madrid: Ediciones Clásicas.
Unceta Gómez, L. (2012). Cuando los sentimientos irrumpen (1): Valores expresivos de las interjecciones primarias en las comedias de Plauto. In R. López Gregoris (Ed.), *Estudios sobre teatro romano: El mundo de los sentimientos y su expresión* (pp. 347–395). Zaragoza: Pórtico.
Unceta Gómez, L. (2016). Cuando los sentimientos irrumpen (2). Análisis de las interjecciones secundarias en las comedias de Plauto. In A. Penas Ibáñez & B. García-Hernández (Eds.), *Semántica latina y románica. Unidades de significado conceptual y procedimental* (pp. 213–241). Berne: Peter Lang.
Unceta Gómez, L. (2017a). Cuando las emociones irrumpen: análisis comparativo del empleo de las interjecciones en las comedias de Terencio y las tragedias de Séneca. *Onomázein*, *38*, 107–146.
Unceta Gómez, L. (2017b). Discoursive and Pragmatic Functions of Latin *em*: Grammaticalization, Pragmaticalization. . . Interjectionalization? In C. Denizot & O. Spevak (Eds.), *Pragmatic Approaches to Latin and Ancient Greek* (pp. 63–82). Amsterdam/Philadelphia: John Benjamins.
Unceta Gómez, L. (2017c). Pragmaticalización y lenguas clásicas: el caso de latín *abi*. *Graeco-Latina Brunensia*, *22* (1), 205–220.
Unceta Gómez, L. (2024). The Pragmatic Marker *age*: Its Pragmatic Functions in Comedy and its Contribution to the Expression of Im/Politeness. In C. Cabrillana Leal (Ed.), *Recent Trends and Findings in Latin Linguistics. Vol. 2, Semantics and Lexicography. Discourse and Dialogue* (pp. 685–701). Berlin/Boston: De Gruyter.
Wharton, T. (2003). Interjections, language, and the 'showing/saying' continuum. *Pragmatics and Cognition*, *11*, 39–91.
Wharton, T. (2016). That bloody so-and-so has retired: Expressives revisited. *Lingua*, *175* (176), 20–35.
Wierzbicka, A. (1992). The semantics of interjection. *Journal of Pragmatics*, *18*, 159–192.
Wilkins, D. P. (1992). Interjections as deictics. *Journal of Pragmatics*, *18*, 119–158.
Windstedt (1912). Cicero, *Letters to Atticus*, vol. I. Cambridge, MA: Harvard University Press.

Elena V. Zheltova

Semantic Diversity and Conversational Potential of *faxo* in the Language of Roman Comedy

Abstract: The study aims to identify the semantic nuances, pragmatic functions and conversational potential of the sigmatic future *faxo* in the language of Roman comedy. The vast majority of its 89 occurrences demonstrate causative semantics, but there are at least seven cases in which a clear semantic shift can be observed. This shift resulted in a series of connotations that can be defined as either modal-epistemic or evidential. The author substantiates this assumption by means of in-depth linguistic and philological analyses of those contexts in which *faxo* does not have causative value, and by drawing on evidence from modern languages in which a similar semantic shift is attested. Since the relationship between epistemic modality and evidentiality has been a highly debated issue, it is also addressed in the paper. As a result, *faxo* is identified as an evidential parenthetical marker with inferential meaning in two of the seven cases considered, and as a modal marker with high epistemic support in the other five cases. Finally, the conversational properties of *faxo* in causative, epistemic, and evidential contexts are examined, and conclusions are drawn about the contribution of *faxo* to the inventory of linguistic means of conveying im/politeness.

Keywords: *faxo*, causative meaning, epistemic modality, evidentiality, conversational strategies, im/politeness

1 Introduction

The extraparadigmatic sigmatic future *faxo* has long sparked scholarly interest, in terms of both its origin and its semantic nuances (Lindsay 1936; De Melo 2002, 2008; Pinkster 2015; Novikova 2015; Bertocci 2017). The origin of *faxo* remains a subject of debate, and the suffix *-s-* has been attributed to both the sigmatic aorist (in which

Note: I thank my anonymous reviewers for their valuable advice and Dr. Steven Kaye for correcting the English.

Elena V. Zheltova, Saint Petersburg State University, Russia

https://doi.org/10.1515/9783111332956-011

case *faxo* is a reflex of an earlier aorist subjunctive) and the Indo-European desiderative mood.[1] *Faxo* was used intensively by Plautus and Terence and then, after a considerable time gap, by some later archaizing authors who probably used this extravagant form as a spectacular stylistic device rather than as a genuinely existing synchronic feature of the language. Out of 114 instances attested in Latin literature (Pinkster 2015: 470), 79 occurrences are found in Plautus and 10 in Terence, and since *faxo* occurs exclusively in the dialogue parts of Roman comedy and practically disappears in the post-Plautine epoch, we can consider it not only as an archaism but also as an element of colloquial language. This article continues my earlier research[2] and will be an attempt to identify the range of semantic nuances and to evaluate the conversational potential of *faxo* in the language of Roman comedy.

2 The Diversity of Syntactic Constructions with *faxo*

The variety of syntactic patterns and semantic connotations that *faxo* exhibits in the sub-corpus of early Roman comedy is truly remarkable and deserves a brief overview. Unlike *faxim, amassim,* and other similar forms, *faxo* occurs only in independent clauses, but in a range of quite different constructions. Sometimes it is used as a full-fledged verb in the simple future, alternating with the standard forms of the future (*faciam*), in combination with the first-person pronoun *ego* and the construction *accusativus duplex*, as in (1):

(1) *Ego te hodie* ***faxo*** *recte acceptum, ut dignus es.* (Plavt. Rud. 800)
'Today I will **honour** you (lit: "**make** you respectable") as you deserve.'[3]

In a couple of examples *faxo* occurs in combination with *ut obiectivum* (2):

(2) . . . ***faxo*** *ut scias*
quid pericli sit dotatae uxori vitium dicere. (Plavt. Asin. 897–898)
'I'll **make** you learn how risky it is to dishonour a wife who has a dowry.'

1 For an overview of opinions, see Novikova (2015: 728–731) and Bertocci (2017: 24–26).
2 See Zheltova (2022).
3 All translations are mine unless indicated otherwise.

But most often *faxo* occurs directly alongside another verb in the future (49 instances in Plautus and 5 in Terence) or the subjunctive (14 cases in Plautus and 2 in Terence), see (3) and (4):

(3) *Iam ego illic* ***faxo*** *erit.* (PLAVT. Men. 956).
'Now I will **bring** him there.' (lit. "I'll **make** him be there').

(4) *Quin venis quando vis intro?* ***Faxo*** *haud quicquam sit morae.* (PLAVT. Amph. 972)
'Why don't you come in as soon as you wish? I'll **make sure** that there won't be any delay.'

Faxo with the present subjunctive is thus found in both hypotactic and paratactic constructions (Lindsay 1936: 61), and it is hardly possible to see any tangible semantic differences between, for instance, *faxo ut scias* (2) and *faxo scies / scibis* (5):

(5) PY. *Vise amabo num sit.* PH. *Iam* ***faxo*** *scies.* (TER. Eun. 663)
'PY. Please, see if he is there. PH. I will **let** you know immediately.'

It is worth noting that two specific combinations predominate in numerical terms: *faxo* with *scies / scibis / scias* (13 cases) and *faxo* with *(ad)erit / (ad)erunt* (15 cases), which together make up almost a third of the total number of occurrences of *faxo* in the language of Roman comedy. It cannot therefore be ruled out that these two expressions functioned as special formulae or collocations, much like *certiorem facio*, which has almost the same meaning as *faxo scies / scibis / scias*.

3 *Faxo* as a Causative Verb

As can be seen from (2–5), *faxo* is most frequently used as a causative verb with the meaning "make sure, bring it about, cause it to happen (that)",[4] sometimes in emotionally neutral contexts, but much more often in promises (6–7) or threats (8–10):

(6) *illa hic cubabit, vir aberit* ***faxo*** *domo.* (PLAVT. Cas. 483–484)
'She'll sleep here and I'll **make sure** the husband is out of the house.'

(7) *nunc Amphitruonem volt deludi meus pater:* ***faxo*** *probe*
iam hic deludetur, spectatores, vobis inspectantibus. (PLAVT. Amph. 996–997)

4 See Glare (Ed. 1968: 668).

'My father wants to fool Amphitryon.
I'll **make sure** he's fooled, in front of your eyes, dear audience.'

(8) ***faxo** foris vidua visas patrem.* (PLAVT. Men. 113)
'I'll **make sure** you visit your father as a widow.'

(9) *Nescio quam tu familiaris sis: nisi actutum hinc abis,*
*familiaris accipiere **faxo** haud familiariter.* (PLAVT. Amph. 354–355)
'I don't know how familiar you are. If you don't leave right now,
I'll **make sure** you're not seen as an acquaintance here.'

(10) *Non enim ibis. Ego ferare **faxo**, ut meruisti, in crucem.* (PLAVT. Mos. 1133)
'For you will not get away. I will **make sure** you hang as you deserve.'

Although *faxo* shows causative meaning in most occurrences available in early Roman comedy, there are a few contexts where this value is not observed. We will focus on these in the next section.

4 *Faxo* in Non-causative Contexts

De Melo (2002: 83) has drawn attention to two cases in which *faxo* does not demonstrate its typical meanings, namely PLAVT. Curc. 586–587 and PLAVT. Men. 790–791.

In the passage from *Curculio*, the comic effect is created by the pun linking the proper name *Curculio* and the noun *curculio* 'breadworm', ex. (11):

(11) THER. *Ubi nunc Curculionem inveniam?* CAPP. *In tritico facillume,*
*vel quingentos curculiones pro uno **faxo** reperias.* (PLAVT. Curc. 586–587)
'THER. Where is he, the evil worm (Curculio)? CAPP. In the wheat, of course,
you will [***faxo***???] find five hundred breadworms instead of one.'[5]

It is unlikely that Cappadox plays the role of a causer stimulating (or facilitating) Therapontigonus' search for breadworms in this scene, as Therapontigonus is searching for a parasite with the charactonym Curculio rather than actual breadworms. Therefore, in this instance, *faxo* must have something other than causative meaning, which may be difficult to translate accurately.

5 In this section, I will intentionally leave *faxo* untranslated or question the generally accepted translation.

The second example is from *Menaechmi*, (12):

(12) MAT. *At enim ille hinc amat meretricem ex proxumo.* SEN. *Sane sapit,*
atque ob istanc industriam etiam ***faxo*** *amabit amplius.* (PLAVT. Men. 790–791)
'MAT. But he has fallen for a hetaera from the neighbourhood.
SEN. Well, he's got a knack for it! By your efforts, he'll [***faxo***???] fall for many more.'

The causative meaning of *faxo* is inappropriate in this context too. Translating *faxo amabit* as 'I'll make him fall in love' would be absurd, as a father-in-law would hardly encourage his son-in-law to have an affair on the side, much less openly confess such bizarre conduct to his own daughter.

De Melo (2002: 83) suggests two potential explanations of *faxo* in the examples above: 1) *faxo* has been reanalysed syntactically and has become an adverb similar to *forsitan* 'perhaps', and 2) *faxo* has been reanalysed semantically and has turned into a parenthetical expression with the meaning 'I assume'.

In addition to the cases highlighted by De Melo, I have found five other examples of non-causative *faxo*. Two of them are located close together in the dialogue between two old men in Plautus' *Trinummus*. Example (13) shows Megaronides persuading Callicles to exchange their annoying wives. Megaronides assures his friend that he will not lose out by such an action, as he considers his own wife much worse than his friend's wife. In this context, *faxo* seems to take on a meaning similar to 'I believe' or 'be sure', rather than its usual causative value:

(13) MEG. *Vin commutemus, tuam ego ducam et tu meam?*
Faxo *haud tantillum dederis verborum mihi.* (PLAVT. Trin. 59–60)
'MEG. Would you like to swap? You'll take mine,
And I'll take yours. [***Faxo***???] you won't have tricked me, not in the slightest.'

In example (14) which comes immediately after the previous one, *faxo* appears to behave in the same way: Megaronides does his best (*Ne . . . hercle*) to reassure Callicles that he will know in advance what is to be done:

(14) CAL. *Namque enim tu, credo, me imprudentem obrepseris.*
MEG. *Ne tu hercle* ***faxo*** *haud nescias quam rem egeris.* (PLAVT. Trin. 61–62).
'CAL. Well, I'm sure you'll sneak up on me.
MEG. I swear by Hercules, [***faxo***???] you won't be unaware of what you have done.'

Three additional instances of non-causative *faxo* can be found in the plays *Pseudolus*, *Poeniculus*, and *Asinaria*.

In example (15), Callidorus requests that his slave Pseudolus read Phoenicium's letter, from which he will learn why Callidorus needs money so desperately. Pseudolus is his last hope of rescuing his girlfriend from the Captain, so he can only plead with him, not force him to do anything. The causative interpretation is once again unsuccessful:

(15) CAL. *Recita modo: ex tabellis iam* ***faxo*** *scies*
quam subito argento mi usus invento siet. (PLAVT. Pseud. 49–50)
'CAL. Just read it! From the letter, you will [***faxo***???] realize at once
how urgently I need to find money.'

The next passage from *Poeniculus* is of special interest (16):

(16) AGOR. *Omnia faciet Iuppiter* ***faxo,***
[nam mi est obnoxius et me metuit.] (PLAVT. Poen. 1191)
'I'll **make sure** (???) that Jupiter will do it all,
for to me he is indebted, and stands in awe of me.'

Evidently, Agorastocles speaks of Jupiter in an unacceptably impious manner, especially if one interprets *faxo* as having its typical causative function, as Riley does. He translates this line as follows: 'I'll engage that Jove shall do it all; for to me he is indebted, and stands in awe of me.' On the basis of this reading, Riley (1912) considers "this impious expression out of character with Agorastocles, and the latter portion of the line to be spurious".

In my view, if we recognize the non-causative value of *faxo* here, it may sound less arrogant.

The last example (17) seems to be ambiguous and allows for both causative and non-causative interpretations:

(17) *Horrescet* ***faxo*** *lena, leges quom audiet.* (PLAVT. Asin. 749)
'The madam will [***faxo***???] shudder when she hears the terms.'

Parasitus is indeed the author of the terms to be read to the madam, which makes a causative reading of *faxo* quite possible. At the same time, the terms were written by Parasitus on behalf of his master Diabolus, who is ultimately the causer in this scenario, meaning that *faxo* need not have a causative connotation.

Obviously, in all the passages in question, *faxo* has lost its grammatical meaning of future tense, as well as its syntactic function as the verb governing the dependent predicate, and its lexical meaning "do, make". The question arises as to what value this verb has acquired to compensate for what has been lost.

Analysis of the syntactic structure of example (14) will presumably help us to identify the true meaning of *faxo* in all these non-standard cases. Let us take a closer look at this passage:

(14) CAL. *Namque enim tu, credo, me imprudentem obrepseris.*
MEG. *Ne tu hercle* ***faxo*** *haud nescias quam rem egeris.* (PLAVT. Trin. 61–62)

What catches the eye first and foremost is the remarkable and thoroughly elaborated parallel structure of lines 61–62, namely the alliteration of the particles *Nam* and *Ne* at the beginning, the homoeoteleuton in the words *obreps**eris*** and *eg**eris*** at the end, and parenthetical *credo* and *faxo* in the middle. Of particular interest is the deliberate parallelism of *credo* and *faxo*, which I think may shed light on the meaning of *faxo* in all the passages under consideration. Assuming that *faxo* in line 62 fulfils a similar pragmatic function to *credo* in line 61, we can suppose that *faxo* is a kind of parenthesis with the function of epistemic evaluation of the utterance. And if we compare all passages (11–17) with each other, the most likely meaning of *faxo* seems to be either 'certainly, definitely, without any doubt', which corresponds to the adverb *certe* / *certo*, or 'perhaps, possibly', which is in line with *forsitan*. In the first case, we are dealing with the lexicalization of *faxo* into a modal-epistemic adverb, and in the second case, the grammaticalization of the full-fledged verb into a parenthetical evidential marker.

5 Epistemic Modality and Evidentiality: What Do They Have in Common?

It is worth emphasizing that epistemic modality and evidentiality are partly overlapping categories, and their interaction has long been the subject of lively discussion. A detailed analysis of the literature on the topic is beyond the scope of this paper, but a few remarks may be helpful.

According to one commonly used definition, "epistemic modality is a conceptual domain pertaining to the speaker's assessment of the truth concerning some propositional content p (in logical traditions) or to the speaker's subjective evaluation of the degree of certainty that p holds true (in functional cognitive frameworks)" (Wiemer 2018: 87). The range of epistemic meanings includes knowledge, certainty, epistemic necessity, probability, likelihood, uncertainty, epistemic possibility, doubt, unlikelihood, and epistemic impossibility. As for evidentiality, this is “a linguistic category whose primary meaning is source of information” (Aikhenvald 2004: 3). Depending on the ways knowledge can be obtained, evidentials are divided into three groups, *viz.* direct (perceptual, visual, firsthand), indirect inferential (obtained by means of inferring, presumption or induction), and indirect reported.[6] In early studies of evidentiality, it was often treated as a subcategory of epistemic modality (Palmer 1986: 51; Willett 1988: 52, among others), whereas in later studies quite a few scholars consider evidentiality and epistemic modality to constitute two different categories which, however, are very close to each other and are often expressed by the same means (de Haan 1999; Cornillie 2009; Remberger 2010; Plungian 2010: 44–46; Haßler 2010: 239; Zheltova 2017; Wiemer 2018).

The affinity of these two categories is particularly understandable if evidentiality is reconsidered as encoding the *mode of access* to information rather than its source. What links evidentiality with epistemic modality is the speaker’s “attitude towards knowledge” (Givón 1982; Chafe 1986: 262; Willet 1988: 52), and it is no surprise that Chafe and Nichols (1986) subtitled their collective monograph on evidentiality *The linguistic coding of epistemology*. In recent works one can observe an intention to find new explanations why evidential and epistemic markers often coincide. Wiemer (2018) has put forward the notion of *reliability* as an intermediate layer between evidential and epistemic meanings. With reference to de Haan (1999: 85), he argues that epistemic modality and evidentiality both deal with evidence but differ in what they do with that evidence: epistemic modality *evaluates* evidence and on the basis of this evaluation assigns a confidence measure to the speaker’s utterance, while an evidential *asserts* that there is evidence for the speaker’s utterance but does not interpret the evidence in any way (Wiemer 2018: 99–103).

It should be stressed that the intertwining of epistemic modality with evidentiality concerns only one evidential type, *viz.* indirect inferential (presumptive). The fact that a question of probability arises at all indicates that the speaker has no direct knowledge of the situation (Plungian 2001: 354), which belongs to the realm of indirect evidentiality and is normally expressed by either grammatical or lexical tools with the meaning “perhaps, possibly, probably” corresponding to a weak or medium degree of reliability. The intersection of these two categories is successfully explained by Plungian (2010: 46):

> If we regard such values as modal, we stress one of the basic characteristics of modality, namely the assessment of a situation (as highly probable); regarding it as evidential, we stress

6 For more detailed classifications of evidential meanings, see Plungian (2001: 353; 2010: 37); a concise classification of evidential meanings is also given in one of Aikhenvald’s recent works as follows: “[Evidentials] cover a limited set of semantic parameters – visual, non-visual sensory, inference, assumption, speech report, and quotation” (Aikhenvald 2018: 30).

> one of the basic characteristics of evidentiality, namely the reference to logical conclusions as a source of information about a situation. This way, markers of presumptive evidentiality are the only evidential markers with inbuilt modal components and the only modal markers with inbuilt evidential components.

Importantly, epistemic markers can evolve into evidential ones, as happened with the Russian and Polish particle *jakoby* 'allegedly'. It is worth highlighting that in Polish this particle became a pure reportative (quotative) evidential, with its epistemic component entirely suppressed, while in Russian it has not lost its epistemic component but retains both epistemic and evidential potential: Russian *jakoby* — often translated 'as if, as though' — frequently occurs in contexts of reported speech, but, unlike its Polish cognate, it has not lost its strong connotation of doubt (Wiemer 2005: 117; 2018: 102–104). These observations on the correlation and intertwining of epistemic and evidential values will hopefully help us to identify the true meaning of *faxo*.[7]

6 Epistemic or Evidential *faxo*?

We now return to the question of what this remarkable verbal form turns into at the final stage of its evolution.[8] Does it become a modal-epistemic marker signifying "certainly, definitely, without any doubt" or an evidential marker with the meaning "perhaps, possibly"? In other words, what semantic nuances can be identified in the *faxo* of examples (11–17)?

It will hardly be possible to answer this question if we rely only on the seven examples at our disposal. But on the assumption that the same or similar phenomena could occur in other languages, we have the opportunity to draw on comparative data from elsewhere. Unceta Gómez and Berger (2022: 31) have rightly observed with regard to politeness that "ancient languages offer data and evidence that challenge theorization on politeness and offer new angles on phenomena that are documented in modern languages", but this statement can also be interpreted

7 The idea that *faxo* developed its evidential extension due to its pre-existing future tense value cannot be excluded: grammaticalized evidentials go back to future markers in some languages (Aikhenvald 2004: 111), and coinciding markers of indirect evidentiality and future tense are not uncommon (Forker 2018: 67). This may provide an additional argument in favour of an evidential interpretation of *faxo* in some contexts.

8 In my previous study (Zheltova 2022: 80–81), I analysed all stages of the grammaticalization of *faxo* and came to the conclusion that in this process, *faxo* has reached the penultimate stage (switch context) of the trajectory laid out by Heine (2002) and Hopper (1991).

the other way round: modern languages also provide us with data and evidence that allow us to better understand challenging phenomena in ancient languages.

Fortunately, a problem similar to ours has been successfully solved by Dendale and Kreutz (2019), who investigated in detail the whole array of connotations of the French modal adverb *certainement*. This adverb had traditionally been considered an expression of epistemic modality with the semantics of certainty, akin to "sûrement, bien sûr". However, on the basis of a corpus analysis that reflects the actual usage of this adverb in modern French, Dendale and Kreutz come to the conclusion that the traditional modal epistemic interpretation applies only to a limited number of contexts, whereas in the vast majority of cases *certainement* functions as a means of expressing an inferential/deductive conclusion (*probabilité, plausibilité*), which belongs to the domain of indirect inferential evidentiality. For this kind of evidential strategy, the scholars coin the terms "posture épistémique / posture de certitude". With this strategy, a speaker, despite not being entirely assured of the truth of his/her statement, is pretending to be sure and makes the addressee believe in the truth of what he/she says (Dendale and Kreutz 2019: 18).[9] The term "posture de certitude" seems to be part of a broader concept of *stance*, which in recent studies has increasingly replaced the familiar term "evidentiality". As Squartini argues with reference to Biber (2004: 109), "in some of the discourse-focused perspectives the relationship with the original grammatical notion is so loosened that the very term 'evidentiality' is dismissed in favour of the overarching notion of 'stance', which comprises 'the linguistic mechanisms used by speakers and writers to convey their personal feelings and assessments'. Within these 'linguistic mechanisms' Biber (2004) admits evidential (*apparently*) as well as epistemic adverbs (*certainly*) without distinguishing them from prototypical grammatical markers" (Squartini 2018: 275–276).

9 Among many others, Dendale and Kreutz analyse the example: "Mon interlocutrice était certainement plus âgée que moi, mais la confusion était telle que j'avais du mal à ne serait-ce que mettre un âge sur son visage" and come to the conclusion that "la présence de *certainement* a pour effet que l'énoncé ne s'interprète plus comme transmettant un savoir mémorisé (Mon interlocutrice était plus âgée que moi), que le locuteur a pris dans son stock d'informations. Il s'interprète, au contraire, comme communiquant une information que le locuteur (ou locuteur représenté) a générée par inférence (déductive), information ayant ainsi le statut d'une supposition, conjecture ou hypothèse. Par conséquent, l'information a peu de chances de paraître intrinsèquement « certaine » à l'interprétant. Toutefois, par l'emploi de *certainement* (plutôt que d'un adverbe comme *probablement, sans doute, peut-être. . .*), le locuteur se donne une posture de certitude, une assurance « jouée » par rapport à l'information communiquée : il se présente – de bonne ou de mauvaise foi – comme légitimement confiant en ces propos. Une telle posture peut évidemment être exploitée à des fins argumentatives" (Dendale and Kreutz 2019: 18).

A detailed overview of Dendale and Kreutz's arguments and an analysis of the whole body of examples at their disposal lie beyond the scope of this paper. However, it seems important to emphasize that the authors examined all the examples against the background of sufficiently broad contexts which described various situations *not directly accessible* to the speaker, but comprehended on the grounds of inference, "common knowledge" or other indirect sources. The lack of direct access to information provides the basis for conjecture and hypothesis (Dendale and Kreutz 2019: 21). From this perspective, in modern French the adverb *certainement*, despite its etymology, corresponds not so much to the adverbs 'certainly, precisely, for sure' (epistemic-modal interpretation), as to 'obviously, probably' (evidential interpretation). Consequently, Dendale and Kreutz identify a semantic-pragmatic shift in the evolution of *certainement* similar to that seen with Russian *jakoby* 'as though, allegedly':[10] *certainement* has developed a new evidential extension but without losing its original epistemic value. In addition to *jakoby*, I can point to one more example in Russian: the word *navernoe* 'precisely, surely' has transformed syntactically from a modal-epistemic adverb into a parenthetical expression, and semantically from an epistemic marker to an evidential one, cf. *On znal navernoe, chto…* 'He knew for sure that…' and *On, navernoe, znal, chto…* 'He probably knew that…'[11]

Unfortunately, with regard to Latin we do not have at our disposal the tools which are applied to the analysis of living languages; nevertheless, we can try to look at our examples (11–17) from the perspective of "posture de certitude".

In the seven passages under consideration *faxo* seems to admit of both epistemic and evidential interpretations. In two of them (11–12), *faxo* is closer to *forsitan* than to *certo*, and should be translated by evidential expressions such as "perhaps, I suppose, obviously, probably":

(11) *vel quingentos curculiones pro uno* ***faxo*** *reperias* (PLAVT. Curc. 587).
'You will **obviously** find five hundred breadworms instead of one'.

(12) *ob istanc industriam etiam* ***faxo*** *amabit amplius.* (PLAVT. Men. 791)
'By your efforts, **I suppose**, he'll fall for many more'.

10 See Wiemer (2005: 117, 2018: 102–104).

11 Interestingly, the shift in usage (from adverb to parenthetical expression) is reflected in the shift in punctuation.

In both examples, *faxo* has a clear semantics of guess/presupposition, though accompanied by the "posture de certitude (position of certainty)" which the speaker wishes to inspire in the addressee.

By contrast, in ex. (13), Megaronides is eager to convince his friend that there is nothing but mutual benefit in his offer. Therefore, *faxo* appears to be close to a modal-epistemic marker with a high degree of reliability, such as *certo* 'surely, certainly, definitely, no doubt':

(13) ***faxo** haud tantillum dederis verborum mihi.* (PLAVT. Trin. 60).
'**Be sure,** you won't have tricked me, not in the slightest!'

The same strategy of assurance is evident in Megaronides' remark in ex. (14). Both the formula of the oath (*Ne . . . hercle*) and the litotes *haud nescias* 'you won't be unaware', which reinforces the statement, favour the epistemic interpretation, which, in turn, is reinforced by the parallelism of *credo* and *faxo* that has already been discussed earlier:

(14) *Ne tu hercle **faxo** haud nescias quam rem egeris.* (PLAVT. Trin. 62)
'I swear by Hercules, **no doubt** you won't be unaware of what you have done'.

As regards the remaining examples, *viz.* (15–17), they seem to provide grounds for treating *faxo* as a modal-epistemic marker with a high degree of reliability rather than an evidential with low epistemic support. Therefore, I suggest the following translations:

(15) CAL. *Recita modo: ex tabellis iam **faxo** scies*
quam subito argento mi usus invento siet. (PLAVT. Pseud. 49–50)
'CAL. Just read it! From the letter, you will **definitely** realize at once
how urgently I need to find money.'

(16) AGOR. *Omnia faciet Iuppiter **faxo**,*
[nam mi est obnoxius et me metuit.] (PLAVT. Poen. 1191)
'**No doubt** Jupiter will do it all,
for to me he is indebted, and stands in awe of me.'

(17) *Horrescet **faxo** lena, leges quom audiet.* (PLAVT. Asin. 749)
'The madam will **certainly** shudder when she hears the terms.'

Thus, modal-epistemic cases of *faxo* appear to occur more often than evidential ones. The predominance of epistemic over evidential instances of *faxo* seems to be the result of the natural evolution of its semantics: it is only one step from the causative meaning "make sure that" to the epistemic meaning "be sure that". And just as the French adverb *certainement* and the Russian epistemic markers *jakoby* and *navernoe* have developed evidential extensions in some contexts, Latin *faxo* may well have followed the same path.

7 Conversational Potential of *faxo*

We are now in a position to try to understand how *faxo* contributes to the inventory of strategies used by comic poets to create the illusion of live conversation.[12] The conversational potential of *faxo* is determined at least by the fact that it is predominantly encountered in situations of highly emotional dialogue, which are somehow related to the pragmatic domain of im/politeness. These situations favour various strategies of im/politeness involving "a set of compensatory behaviours that try to avoid or mitigate face-threatening acts" (Brown and Levinson 1987: 65).

The semantic diversity of *faxo* presumably makes it appropriate in the context of quite diverse im/politeness strategies. Thus, *faxo* as a causative verb may have conveyed threats or warnings that, according to Brown and Levinson (1987: 65), "primarily threaten the addressee's (H's) negative-face want, by indicating (potentially) that the speaker (S) does not intend to avoid impeding H's freedom of action". Examples (8–10) in Section 3 seem to be of this type. By contrast, the non-causative instances of *faxo* which allow an evidential interpretation could be taken to show a hedging device used to mitigate assertions (ex. (11–12) in Sections 4 and 6).

As regards the five examples in which we identified epistemic-modal semantics, they could be placed in between, as part of "those acts that predicate some positive future act of S toward H, and in so doing put some pressure on H to accept or reject them, and possibly to incur a debt". According to the classification suggested by Brown and Levinson (1987: 66), they also belong to those acts that threaten the addressee's (H's) negative face, as exemplified in (13–17), see Sections 4 and 6.

To sum up, in the course of its evolution, *faxo* developed a whole array of connotations that could be used as different conversational strategies in talk-in-interaction.

12 It is no secret that the "comedies of Plautus and Terence, with their vivid colloquial style and socially diversified characters, have been a valuable source for pragmatic and sociolinguistic investigations of (early) Latin" (Berger 2021: 57).

8 Conclusions

We have analysed the syntactic behaviour, semantic diversity and pragmatic functions of the sigmatic future *faxo* in the language of Roman comedy. Alongside the large array of examples of causative *faxo*, there are seven instances of non-causative uses that can be identified as modal-epistemic and evidential. Our interpretation is based on in-depth linguistic and philological analyses of contexts in which *faxo* does not have causative meaning, as well as on data and evidence from modern languages in which similar semantic shifts are attested. Taking into account that "the lack of native speakers . . . undoubtedly hinders the access to the interpretation of a given utterance, both as intended by the speaker and as understood by the addressee" (Unceta Gómez and Berger 2022: 28), drawing on comparative data appears to be not only desirable but indispensable, because it lends more weight to our hypothesis. It is especially notable that the abundance of semantic nuances and pragmatic functions of *faxo* manifested itself particularly in the genre of Roman comedy, in the lively dialogues of comic characters. This gives us reason to assume that *faxo* made a major contribution to the set of colloquial techniques which could be used by comic poets to reproduce the colloquial speech of ordinary people, and from this point of view it can be considered as a special marker of orality in a written text.

Bibliography

Aikhenvald, A. Y. (2004). *Evidentiality*. Oxford: Oxford University Press.

Aikhenvald, A. Y. (2018). Evidentiality. The Framework. In A. Y. Aikhenvald (Ed.), *The Oxford Handbook of Evidentiality* (pp. 1–43). Oxford: Oxford University Press.

Berger, Ł. (2021). Interruptions in Roman Comedy: Gender, Status, and Power in Interaction. *Philologia Classica, 16* (1), 57–76.

Bertocci, D. (2017). Remarks on the type *faxō/faxim*. In P. Poccetti (Ed.), *Latinitatis Rationes* (pp. 22–37). Berlin/Boston: Mouton de Gruyter.

Biber, D. (2004). Historical patterns for the grammatical marking of stance: A Crossregister comparison. *Journal of Historical Pragmatics, 5*, 107–136.

Brown, P. & Levinson, S. (1987). *Politeness. Some universals in language usage*. Cambridge: Cambridge University Press.

Chafe, W. (1986). Evidentiality in English conversation and academic writing. In W. Chafe & J. Nichols (Eds.), *Evidentiality: the linguistic coding of epistemology* (pp. 261–272), Norwood, NJ: Ablex.

Chafe, W. & Nichols, J. (Eds., 1986). *Evidentiality: the linguistic coding of epistemology*. Norwood, NJ: Ablex.

Cornillie, B. (2009). Evidentiality and epistemic modality. On the close relationship between two different categories. *Functions of Language, 16* (1), 44–62.

Dendale, P. & Kreutz, Ph. 'Certainement': adverbe epistemico-modal ou évidentiel? https://www.researchgate.net/publication/336939220_%27Certainement%27_adverbe_epistemico-modal_ou_evidentiel (accessed December 29, 2022).
Forker, D. (2018). Evidentiality and its relations with other verbal categories. In A. Y. Aikhenvald (Ed.), *The Oxford Handbook of Evidentiality* (pp. 65–84). Oxford: Oxford University Press.
Frajzyngier, Z. (1985). Truth and the Indicative Sentence. *Studies in Language*, *9*, 243–254.
Givón, T. (1982). Evidentiality and epistemic space. *Studies in Language*, *6*, 23–49.
Glare, P. G. W. (Ed., 1968). *Oxford Latin Dictionary.* London: Oxford University Press; Clarendon Press.
de Haan, F. (1999). Evidentiality and Epistemic Modality: Setting Boundaries. *Southwest Journal of Linguistics*, *18*, 83–101.
Haßler G. (2010). Epistemic modality and evidentiality and their determination on a deictic basis: the case of Romance languages. In G. Diewald & E. Smirnova (Eds.), *Linguistic Realization of Evidentiality in European Languages* (pp. 223–248). Berlin/New York: Mouton de Gruyter.
Heine, B. (2002). On the Role of Context in Grammaticalization. In I. Wischer & G. Diewald (Eds.), *New Reflections on Grammaticalization* (pp. 83–101). Amsterdam: Benjamins.
Hopper, P. (1991). On Some Principles of Grammaticization. In E. C. Traugott & B. Heine (Eds.), *Approaches to Grammaticalization* (pp. 17–36). Amsterdam: Benjamins.
Lindsay, W. M. (1936). *Syntax of Plautus*. New York: G. E. Stechert & Co.
De Melo, W. D. C. (2002). The sigmatic future in Plautus. In M. Bolkestein, C. H. M. Kroon, H. Pinkster, H. W. Remmelink & R. Risselada (Eds.), *Theory and Description in Latin Linguistics. Selected Papers from the 11th International Colloquium on Latin Linguistics* (pp. 75–90). Amsterdam: Brill.
De Melo, W. D. C. (2008). *The Early Latin Verb System*. Oxford: Oxford University Press.
Novikova, M. I. (2015). Latin *faxo* and Venetian *vha. Indo-European Linguistics and Classical Philology, 19*, 727–736.
Palmer, F. R. (1986). *Mood and modality*. Cambridge: Cambridge University Press.
Pinkster, H. (2015). *The Oxford Latin Syntax. Volume 1: The Simple Clause*. Oxford: Oxford University Press.
Plungian, V. A. (2001). The place of evidentiality within the universal grammatical space. *Journal of Pragmatics*, *33*, 349–357.
Plungian, V. A. (2010). Types of verbal evidentiality marking: an overview. In G. Diewald & E. Smirnova (Eds.), *Linguistic Realization of Evidentiality in European Languages* (pp. 15–58). Berlin/New York: Mouton de Gruyter.
Remberger, E.-M. (2010). The Evidential Shift of WANT. In T. Peterson & U. Sauerland (Eds.), *Evidence from Evidentials. The University of British Columbia Working Papers in Linguistics, 28* (pp. 161–182).
Riley, H. Th. (Ed., transl.) (1912). *The Comedies of Plautus*. London: G. Bell and Sons. http://www.perseus.tufts.edu/hopper/text?doc=Perseus%3Atext%3A1999.02.0106%3Aact%3D5%3Ascene%3D4#note1 (accessed June 15, 2023).
Squartini, M. (2018). Extragrammatical expression of information source. In A. Y. Aikhenvald (Ed.), *The Oxford Handbook of Evidentiality* (pp. 273–285). Oxford: Oxford University Press.
Unceta Gómez, L. & Berger, Ł. (2022). Im/Politeness Research in Ancient Greek and Latin: Concepts, Methods, Data. In L. Unceta Gómez & Ł. Berger (Eds.), *Politeness in Ancient Greek and Latin* (pp. 3–44). Cambridge: Cambridge University Press.
Wiemer, B. (2005). Conceptual affinities and diachronic relationships between epistemic, inferential and quotative functions (preliminary observations on lexical markers in Russian, Polish and Lithuanian). In B. Hansen & P. Karlik (Eds.), *Modality in Slavonic Languages. New Perspectives* (pp. 107–131). München: Sagner.
Wiemer, B. (2018). Evidentials and Epistemic Modality. In A. Y. Aikhenvald (Ed.), *The Oxford Handbook of Evidentiality* (pp. 85–108). Oxford: Oxford University Press.

Willett, T. (1988). A cross-linguistic survey of the grammaticalization of evidentiality. *Studies in Language, 12*, 51–97.
Zheltova, E. V. (2017). Evidential Strategies in Latin. *Hyperboreus. Studia Classica, 23* (2), 313–337.
Zheltova, E. V. (2022). *Faxo* in Plautus revisited: Causativity vs. speaker's stance. *Philologia Classica, 17* (1), 77–84.

Section 6: **Epigraphy**

Catarina Gaspar

Fecit curavit: A Micro-Contextual Approach to Epigraphic *Formulae* and Textual Variation in Latin Inscriptions

Abstract: This study focuses on the role of Latin finite verbal forms that are part of the *formulae* of funerary Roman inscriptions. We aim to demonstrate that the final formula *fecit curavit* in one inscription, in Herdade da Camugem, Elvas, Portugal, is a substandard variant in the Latin language, as has been assumed by previous authors, and an epigraphic textual variation. However, this is a single example in *Lusitania* and ancient *Hispania*, which is otherwise known only from a monumental inscription in Corinth (AE 1947, n. 90). A micro-contextual approach explains the unusual sequence *fecit curavit* as a case of textual variation among the *formulae* in four other inscriptions in the same necropolis. Bearing in mind that the other epigraphic texts were found in the same place and the characteristics of the Roman epigraphic texts in the same region, we shall demonstrate that the usage of this *formula* might be explained on aesthetic grounds and the result of textual variation. Moreover, it signifies a cumulative rhetorical effect of finite verbal forms that express similar and correlated actions by the person who saw the erection of the epigraphic monument.

Keywords: Latin epigraphy, *Lusitania*, verbal forms, variation, epigraphic *formulae*

1 The Text and Its Archaeological Context

The inscription which is the starting point of this study was found with four other inscriptions in Herdade da Camugem, in Terrugem e Vila Boim, Elvas, Portugal. This rural area is not far from the modern city of Elvas and other archaeological sites where rural necropolises, in small farms and *villae*, were identified during the twentieth century (Rolo 2018). This strategic region connects Atlantic cities such as

Note: This work is financed with National Funds through FCT (Foundation for Science and Technology), through the project UIDB/00019/2020.

Catarina Gaspar, University of Lisbon, Portugal

https://doi.org/10.1515/9783111332956-015

Olisipo to the ancient *Augusta Emerita*,[1] with several *villae* and necropolises being identified along it (Almeida 2017). Their archaeological remains show evidence of prosperous rural economic communities (Encarnação 1977: 45–46; Largueiras 2018: 55–56), linked to the *territorium* of *Augusta Emerita*.[2] The epigraphic corpus of this area includes a high number of inscriptions in *tabulae*,[3] dating from the first and second centuries CE, that were part of funerary buildings, and mausoleums[4] that probably existed in these necropolises.[5] Recent studies on the archaeology and epigraphy of Elvas (Largueiras 2018) identified a corpus of forty-three inscriptions (of which thirty-three were funerary, eight votive, and two indeterminate);[6] among these are the five funerary inscriptions found in Herdade da Camugem and which are the subject of linguistic analysis in our study.

2 The Inscriptions Found in Herdade da Camugem

These five inscriptions are kept in Museu de Arqueologia e Etnografia António Tomás Pires (MAEE-AT)[7] in Elvas, Portugal. They are all written in white marble

1 The connections between the Atlantic area of *Olisipo* and *Augusta Emerita* can also be seen in the onomastic distribution of some *nomina*, such as the case of *Cominius*/*Cominia* that is attested in inscriptions in *Olisipo*, Elvas and *Augusta Emerita*. For more information, one can consult the *Atlas Digital Onomastique de la Péninsule Ibérique Antique* (ADOPIA): http://adopia.huma-num.fr/names/667.

2 The social relations between the city and the rural communities can be seen, for instance, in the epitaph of *Caius Axonius* (Encarnação 1984: 641–642) and the epitaph of the veteran *Gaius Iulius Gallus* (Encarnação 1984: 647–648).

3 We follow here the epigraphic corpus of Largueiras (Largueiras 2018: 53–57), which contains a total of forty-three inscriptions (of which thirty-three are funerary, eight votive, and two undetermined); among these, twenty inscriptions are *tabulae*, nine *arae*, three *arulae*, one *stela* and ten undetermined (Largueiras 2018: 55).

4 In the region of Elvas, a mausoleum is yet to be identified; however, we have examples in other regions in the south of Portugal, for instance, in the *villa* of Pisões, Beja (Pereira et al. 2013).

5 These necropolises were in use for several centuries until Early Christian times, and show evidence of the reuse of materials in later graves. Besides, some were partially known from the end of the 19th century by authors such as António Tomás Pires or were excavated by A. Dias de Deus and A. Viana, among others, in the middle of the 20th century (Largueiras 2018: 20–40). More recent authors who visited these places had difficulty identifying the necropolises (Rolo 2018: 129); this happened in Herdade da Camugem (Rolo 2018: 259).

6 See Largueiras (2018: 53) for a complete review of the previous references regarding the epigraphic corpus. See also Almeida (2000: 56), Carneiro (2014), Deus et al. (1955: 571), Encarnação (1977: 45–57) and Encarnação (1984: 650, 655, 656, 660–661).

7 I would like to thank the Museu de Arqueologia e Etnografia António Tomás Pires, especially Patrícia Cutileiro and Susana Teixeira, for their help and permission to study and photograph these inscriptions.

tabulae, with moulded frames similar to those we find in the other *tabulae* from the same region, as well as those we know in other areas of *Lusitania*, specifically in Mérida. They were not all found at the same time: some were found in 1906, and the others later, in 1949 (Rolo 2018: 260) and in 1986 (Encarnação 1988). The inscriptions (3) and (5) were reused in a later tomb with a cranium and a skeleton (Encarnação 1977: 47); they both had the text turned on the inside of the grave, which suggests that it was a later reuse of the funerary materials in the necropolis. The five epigraphic texts that will be analysed are the following:

(1) *Calaetica · Luci(i) · / f(ilia) · Severa · ann(orum) / XV · h(ic) · s(ita) · e(st) · s(it) · t(ibi) · t(erra) · l(evis) / Q(uintus) · Cornelius · / Vitulus · coniugi / suae · d(edicavit) · p(onendum) · c(uravit) ·*
'Here lies *Caelaetica Severa*, daughter of *Lucius*, aged 15; may the earth lie lightly on you! *Quintus Cornelius Vitulus* dedicated and saw to the erection (of this tombstone) for his wife.'[8]

Figure 1: Epitaph of *Calaetica*.

8 This inscription is in MAEE-AT (n. 6949) and was found in 1986, in a grave with bones, in Herdade da Camugem (Encarnação 1988; AE 1988, n. 688; Largueiras 2018: 158).

(2) *Maxsuma / Maxsumi*[9] · *f(ilia)* · *an(norum) / XXV· h(ic)* · *s(ita)* · *e(st)* · *s(it)* · *t(ibi)* · *t(erra)* · *l(evis) / Modesta* · *Gemini / f(ilia)* · *mater* · *f(aciendum)* · *c(uravit)* ·
'Here lies *Maxsuma*, daughter of *Maxsumus*, aged 25; may the earth lie lightly on you! The mother *Modesta*, daughter of *Geminus*, had this set up.'[10]

Figure 2: Epitaph of *Maxsuma.*

(3) *Sex(to)* · *Soio / Quartioni* · *et / Catiniae / Maxsuma<e> / Albanus* · *f(ilius)* · *p(onendum)* · *c(uravit)* ·
'The son *Albanus* saw to the erection (of this monument) for *Sextus Soius Quartio* and *Catinia Maxsuma.*'[11]

9 Both in *Maxsuma* and *Maxsumi* we have *xs pro x* (LLDB-17576 and LLDB-17577).
10 The epitaph of *Maxsuma* is in MAEE-AT (n. 4689) and it was offered to the Elvas Museum in 1906 (Encarnação, 1977: 6–7; Encarnação 1984: 656; AE 1977, n. 369; Largueiras 2018: 158).
11 This inscription is in MAEE-AT (n. 4941) and was found reused in a grave together with the inscription (5) (AE 2018, n. 788).

Figure 3: Epitaphs of *Sextus Soius Quartio* and *Catinia Maxsuma*.

(4) *Cn(aeo) Marcio Naso/ni • Cominia M(arci) • f(ilia) • / Maxsuma • uxsor*[12] */ et fili(i) • p(osuerunt)*
'To *Cnaeus Marcius Naso*, *Cominia Maxsuma*, daughter of *Marcius*, the wife, and sons have set (this monument).'[13]

(5) *Faleia • Avita • an(norum) • / XXX • h(ic) • s(ita) • e(st) • s(it) • t(ibi) • t(erra) • l(evis) • / L(ucius) • T(erentius?) • Rufinus / marite • sue / fecit cura/vitt [sic]*
'Here lies *Faleia Auita*, aged 30; may the earth lie lightly on you! *Lucius Terentius (?) Rufinus* had set and erected (this monument) for his wife.'[14]

These five inscriptions are related to the same necropolis and share formal features. They are *tabulae* moulded by similar frames, as can be seen in Figures 1–5, common in the epigraphy of that area of Lusitania. They are also consistent with the formal patterns of the first and second centuries CE that can be found, for instance, in the inscriptions of Mérida (Pando Anta 2016). In addition, they share the same type of

12 Both in *Maxsuma* and *uxsor* we have *xs pro x* (LLDB-17572 and LLDB-17573).
13 The epitaph of *Cnaeus Marcius Naso* is in MAEE-AT (n. 4744) and was offered to the Museum in 1906 (Encarnação 1977: 46–47; AE 1977, n. 368; Encarnação 1984: 655; Largueiras 2018: 158).
14 This inscription is in the MAEE-AT (n. 4944) and was found with inscription (2), also reused in the same grave (Encarnação, 1977: 47–48; Encarnação, 1984: 650; Largueiras 2018: 158).

Figure 4: Epitaph of *Cnaeus Marcius Naso.*

Figure 5: Epitaph of *Faleia.*

stone, white marble, that is common in funerary monuments. They have the same type of *ordinatio*, using interpunctuation marks, triangular strokes, commas, and round strokes; in line 3 of the first inscription (1), there is an unusual punctuation mark in the shape of a star. From a palaeographic viewpoint, there are differences between them relating to the regularity of the letters' carving. Inscriptions (1), (2), (3), and (4) are all *librariae*, whereas in the inscription (5) the letters were carved more irregularly with respect to their sizes and the space between them. In line 3, the final letter *s* is in a diagonal position.

The absence of the invocation to *Dis Manibus* is another characteristic common to all these five texts. This feature, combined with the formal features of the monuments and their palaeography, enable us to date these inscriptions to the 1st and 2nd centuries CE. Even taking into account all the features already mentioned, in the following we will focus on the differences between these five texts and how they exemplify the balance between formulaic repetition and variation in epigraphic texts that were probably made by the same atelier and could be seen side by side in the same necropolis.

3 The *formulae* in the Inscriptions of Herdade da Camugem

In this section, we will detail the *formulae* related to the monument's setting, specifically regarding the finite verbal forms and the gerundives. The epigraphic texts and, in particular, their *formulae* reflect a specific semantic and cultural context in their use of verbal forms, that can occur alone or side-by-side, creating a cumulative effect.

In this study, we will show how epigraphic *formulae* favoured the use of some verbs that designate the action of erecting the funerary monument. This implies the use of finite verbal forms, such as *posuit*/*posuerunt* and *dedicavit*, as well as *formulae* using the verbal gerundive, such as *faciendum curavit*/*curaverunt* and *ponendum curavit*/*curaverunt*, that are semantically linked in epigraphic contexts but are not synonymous. These uses of verbs were common to epigraphic texts all over the Roman empire; however, sometimes *formulae* had specific traits in different regions with respect to the word order, verbal form combination, and position in the epigraphic text. Texts (1) and (5) illustrate this phenomenon.

In the text (1), the abridged formula *D. P. C* can be interpreted as *d(edicavit) p(onendum) c(uravit).*[15] It has an unusual word order; however, the finite verbal forms, *curavit* and *dedicavit*, appear joined in the formulaic sequence *ponendum curavit sub ascia dedicavit*, which is prevalent in *Aquitania* and other regions in ancient *Gallia.*[16] Nevertheless, in the inscription (1) from Herdade da Camugem, we have a different word order, namely *dedicavit ponendum curavit*, which is less frequent than the inverse. There is only one other example (CIL XI, 246) in Ravenna, where the finite verbal form *dedicavit* stands before *ponendum curavit.*

We must also note that this inscription (1) is the only example known in *Hispania*, as noted by the editors of *L'Année Épigraphique* (AE 1988, n. 688): "La formule finale serait nouvelle dans la Péninsule". Still today it remains unique and relevant in attesting to a social milieu that can be seen as a new Romanised community ("des romanisées de plus fraiche date", according to Encarnação 1977) which uses Roman onomastics in a peculiar way,[17] namely by having single attested *nomina* in *Lusitania*, such as *Soius* (3) and *Faleia* (5).[18]

In texts (2) and (3),[19] we find the usual abbreviations for *faciendum curavit* and *ponendum curavit* with the gerundive (Kirk 1942; Poccetti 1980). The gerundive is related to obligation (Bauer 1993: 60), while it is also stated that "the gerundive is generally said to mark intention or purpose" (Bauer 1993: 66). Considering the distinction between the imperfective and perfective forms and the difference between gerundive and adjective forms in *-to-*, she says that "the difference is aspectual in nature. The gerundive, which is based on the present root is imperfective (*capi-endus*); the adjective in *-to-*, on the other hand, indicates that the process expressed by the verb is completed" (Bauer 1993: 66).

The notions of obligation and the purpose of making something is fundamental to the epigraphic *formulae faciendum curavit* and *ponendum curavit*. Both are attested in the epigraphic record since Republican times (Poccetti 1980) and remained in use for a long time and across the Roman empire. As I see it, the constructions with the gerundive are related to formal and legal language and count

---

15 It could also be *d(edit) p(onendum) c(uravit)*; however, we have not been able to find any other examples in other epigraphic texts or in epigraphic repertoires of epigraphic abbreviations. For these reasons, the option *d(edicavit) p(onendum) c(uravit)* is more plausible in this context.

16 This can be seen in inscriptions in CIL XIII. See also Sandys (1909: 80–81) on *ascia* in epigraphic texts.

17 On the onomastics of these inscriptions, José d'Encarnação has already concluded that we find a "filiation peu orthodoxe" made with *cognomina*.

18 Cf. *Atlas Digital Onomastique de la Péninsule Ibérique Antique* (ADOPIA); on *Soius* see http://adopia.huma-num.fr/names/1772 and on *Faleia* see http://adopia.huma-num.fr/names/850.

19 In this text, we must also note that, in line 4, *Maxsuma* stands for *Maxsumae, nominativus pro dativo* singular.

as what Poccetti called as "un formulario cancelleresco ed epigraphico, destinato a marcare l'ufficialità dell'espressione, che si distacca, per questo, dalla fraseologia del comune parlare" (Poccetti 1980: 179).[20] Bruun also defines *faciendum curavit* as the "traditional formula by which the magistrates and other officials denote public work they are overseeing" (2005: 23).

These formulaic expressions tended to be even more stable in their structure and position in the epigraphic text; meanwhile, local variations and *formulae* appear in specific linguistic and cultural contexts relating to the interference between Latin and other languages. We see this in the Oscan formula corresponding to the Latin *faciundum curavit idem probavit*: *upsannam dedet isidum prufatted* (Poccetti 1980: 182).

Moreover, the official tone of these *formulae* in public and monumental epigraphy spread to funerary epigraphy, extending from public texts to private contexts. Within the funerary inscriptional record, *faciendum curavit* and *ponendum curavit* were already disseminated all over the Roman empire and usually abridged as *F.C.*[21] and *P.C.* The high frequency of their occurrence has also led to the reinterpretation of the *formula* and its variation in Classical Latin (Adamik 2015: 650). Among the inscriptions of Elvas, we have a high frequency of *faciendum curavit* and fewer examples of *ponendum curavit*. A similar difference in the frequency of these two *formulae* can be found in the funerary inscriptions from *Augusta Emerita* (Pando Anta 2016).

Text (4) has the single verbal form *p(osuerunt)*. Both *posuit* and the plural *posuerunt*, abbreviated by the single letter *P*, were frequently isolated at the end of the text. Among these five inscriptions, it stands out as an example of variation with a regular *formula*.

Finally, in text (5), we have uncommon traits. The name *Faleia* is scarcely attested, and it was interpreted as an error due to the difficulties in reading the *minuta* by the stonecutters that carved *FALIIIA* for *VALERIA* (Tantimonaco 2016: 251).[22] However, another example of the name *Faleius* is a possibility in the inscription CIL V, 7185. Moreover, what is carved in the stone, *Faleia*, can be read easily,

20 The author also states that: "La formula *faciundum curare* viene così a sostituire negli atti pubblici, il semplice *facere*, che rimane vivo nei documenti privati per indicare, sia la realizzazione materiale di qualcosa («firma» d'autore), sia l'esecuzione indiretta («far fare»), ma sostituisce anche le più antiche e diffuse costruzione di *curare* con il congiuntivo e di *dare* con il gerundivo" (Poccetti 1980: 179–180).

21 The epitaph of *Cominia*, found in Herdade do Falcato, Elvas (MAEE-AT n. 4747; CIL II 5214; Encarnação 1984: 648–649), has the final *formula* in plural faciendum *curar(unt)* with the gerundive entirely written and the verb *curarunt* partially abbreviated.

22 See also LLDB-42370.

even if it is a hapax legomenon in Lusitania.[23] The word *curavitt* is the result of an orthographic error, or *littera superflua,* made by the stonecutter, probably due to the *hypercorrectio* to the falling of the final *-t*.[24] These linguistic aspects are consistent with the palaeographic traits due to the poor quality of the work done by the stonecutter. However, the use of *marite sue*, which stands for *maritae suae*,[25] is noteworthy, since it combines a Vulgar Latin spelling of the diphthong *ae* as [ɛ], being attested probably since the first century CE (Hermann 2000: 31) through the use of the feminine noun *marita*. This noun was related to a lexical choice that reflects the adoption of high-prestige cultural epigraphic models (Gaspar 2017).

As mentioned earlier in this study, the final formula *fecit curavit* is unusual but correct and possible in Latin. The use of *fecit* extended from specific kinds of epigraphic texts, stamps and *instrumenta domestica* to funerary inscriptions. Its use is regular and widespread in Latin epigraphic texts. However, the sequence *fecit curauit* is only known from a monumental inscription found at Corinth (AE 1947, n. 90[26]). The exact sequence can be found, but we cannot tell if it was in the same final position of the text, as the inscription is incomplete. Nonetheless, this is a problematic parallel because of the significant differences between a funerary text and a monumental one found in a different region and cultural environment in the Roman Empire.

In the Iberian Peninsula, no other examples of *fecit curavit* are attested. There is only one incomplete inscription, found in Herguijuela, Cáceres, also in *Lusitania* (Esteban Ortega 2017), in which the editor read the sequence *curavit fecit;* however, it still has a different word order. The author also accepts the possibility of reconstructing the abbreviation as *c(uravit) [s(ua) p(ecunia)?] / f(ecit?)*. Bearing this in mind, this is a problematic parallel to the final formula in text (5).

4 Formulaic Variation and Cumulative Effect

In the micro-context of the five inscriptions found in Herdade da Camugem, the sequence *fecit curavit* can be seen as a variation to *faciendum curavit*, in line with the different *formulae* and verbs used in the other inscriptions of this necropolis. Furthermore, the sequence of the two finite verbal forms is quite common in

23 It was also accepted as a *nomen* by ADOPIA: http://adopia.huma-num.fr/names/850.

24 See LLDB-17571.

25 See LLDB-17569 and LLDB-17570.

26 See also the record of this inscription in the Epigraphic Database Heidelberg, with images: https://edh.ub.uni-heidelberg.de/edh/inschrift/HD019472.

Roman epigraphy; usually, the sequence of verbs corresponds to a series of actions that someone has done, in this specific case, setting up the funerary monument. The unusual aspect is the association between *facio* and *curare*, both of which appear as finite forms in the past tense, without the copulative conjunction *et*. The consecutive use of *facio* and *curare* seems repetitive from a semantic point of view: *fecit* 'made it' and *curavit* 'had this set up'. However, the co-occurrence of these two verbs is also present in *faciendum curavit*, and this repetition can also be seen as an emphatic reiteration built into the cumulative expression of the actions, as is frequent in epigraphic texts.

This cumulative effect can be seen in other inscriptions in different regions of the Roman empire, for instance in one inscription from Capua (*Ephemeris Epigraphica* 1872: 126) that ends with *f(aciendum) c(uravit) fecit*. The same cumulative effect can also be found with other verbs, such as *donavit po/suit*, in one inscription from Bordeaux (CIL XIII, 878).

5 Conclusion

In the expression *fecit curavit*, we witness the cumulative actions of setting up the funerary monument using two finite verbal forms, without *et* or any other coordinate conjunction. Even though they seem redundant, they were used to create an alternative to *formulae* used in the same necropolis and region. Despite being an unusual juxtaposition of these two verbs, the formulation can be seen as a substandard variant of *faciendum curavit* that was used to create textual variation among the epigraphic *formulae*. Through this micro-contextual analysis of the inscriptions from Herdade da Camugem, the textual variation was shown to be unequivocal as we have four different *formulae* in five inscriptions.

Moreover, this textual variation and unusual combinations of verbs, such as the abbreviated *formula DPC* for *dedicavit ponendum curavit* and the cumulative semantic effect of these verbs, can be identified as characteristic of Classical Latin in this area of *Lusitania* as well as connected to other regions of the Roman empire, for instance ancient *Gallia*. The connections to other areas of *Lusitania* and the capital *Augusta Emerita* can also be seen by the distribution of the *formulae*, the formal and material features of the monuments, and by onomastic elements found in this small group of inscriptions. Bearing in mind that the expression of the causative relation by means of *facio* and infinitive is rare in the literary language[27] and later became a characteristic of Vulgar and Late Latin (Väänänen 1985: 225–226),

27 See TLL VI 115, 37ff.

fecit curavit should be understood as a substandard variant[28] that evolved from the random merging of *fecit curare* and *faciendum curavit*.

Bibliography

Adamik, B. (2015). The periodization of Latin. An old question revisited. In G. M. Haverling (Ed.), *Latin Linguistics in the Early 21st Century* (pp. 640–652). Uppsala: Uppsala Universitet.

Almeida, M. J. M. H. (2017). *De Augusta Emerita a Olisipo por Ebora: uma leitura do território a partir da rede viária, Tese de Doutoramento.* Lisboa: Universidade de Lisboa. http://hdl.handle.net/10451/29682

Bauer, B. L. M. (1993). The coalescence of the participle and the gerund/gerundive: An integrated change. In H. Aertsen, & R. J. Jeffers (Eds.), *Historical Linguistics 1989. Papers of the 9th International Conference on Historical Linguistics* (pp. 59–71). Amsterdam: Benjamins.

Bruun, C. (2005). Puzzles about Procurators in Rome. *Arctos, 39*, 9–24.

Carneiro, A. (2014). *Lugares, tempos e pessoas – Povoamento rural romano no Alto Alentejo*. Coimbra: Imprensa da Universidade de Coimbra.

d'Encarnação, J. (1977). Inscriptions mal connues du *conventus Pacensis*. *Conimbriga, 14*, 45–57.

d'Encarnação, J. (1985). *Inscrições Romanas do conventus Pacensis*. Coimbra: Universidade de Coimbra.

d'Encarnação, J. (1988). Epitáfio de *Calaetica*, de Vila Boim. *Ficheiro Epigráfico, 25*, n. 116.

Deus, A. D., Louro, H. S. & Viana, A. (1955). Apontamentos de estações romanas e visigóticas da região de Elvas (Portugal). In *III Congresso Arqueologico Nacional (Galicia 1953)* (pp. 568–578). Zaragoza: Secretaría General de los Congresos.

Gaspar, C. (2017). *Maritus/marita*: Notes on the Dialectal Variation in Relation to Lexical Choices. *Graeco-latina Brunensia, 22* (2), 143–154.

Kirk, W. H. (1942). The syntax of the Gerund and the Gerundive. *Transactions and Proceedings of the American Philological Association, 73*, 293–307. https://www.jstor.org/stable/283552

Largueiras, L. M. C. (2018). *Elementos da presença romana no atual concelho de Elvas: contributos para o retrato de uma sociedade. Dissertação de mestrado.* Évora: Universidade de Évora.

Esteban Ortega, J. (2017). Estela de Coria en Herguijuela, Cáceres, *Ficheiro Epigráfico, 153*, n. 612.

Pando Anta, M. T. (2016). *Las manifestaciones sociales proporcionadas por soporte y texto en las estelas y placas funerarias de Augusta Emerita en época altoimperial*. Santander: Universidad de Cantabria.

Pereira, C., Soares, A. M. & Soares, R. M. (2013). Os mausoléus da *uilla romana* de Pisões: a morte no mundo rural romano. *Revista Portuguesa de Arqueologia, 16*, 303–321.

Poccetti, P. (1980). Su una caratteristica del formulario epigrafico latino en età republicana. *Materiali e discussioni per l'analisi dei testi classici, 5*, 177–182. https://www.jstor.org/stable/40235756

Rolo, A. M. S. (2018). *O mundo funerário romano no nordeste alentejano (Portugal) – o contributo das intervenções de Abel Viana e António Dias de Deus. Tese de Doutoramento*. Lisboa: Universidade de Lisboa.

Sandys, J. E. (1909). *Latin Epigraphy. An introduction to the study of Latin inscriptions*. Cambridge: Cambridge University Press.

28 A *permixtio syntagmatum* (LLDB-152961).

Scranton, R. (1944). Two Temples of Commodus at Corinth. *Hesperia: The Journal of the American School of Classical Studies at Athens, 13* (4), 315–348. https://doi.org/10.2307/146700

Tantimonaco, S. (2016). *Vltra Anam flumen*. Apuntes sobre la alfabetización en la Lusitania Meridional. In J. Carbonell Manils & H. Gimeno Pascual (Eds.), *A Baete ad fluvium Anam: Cultura epigráfica en la Bética Occidental y territorios fronterizos. Homenaje al profesor José Luis Moralejo Álvarez* (pp. 243–264). Alcalá de Henares: Universidad de Alcalá.

Väänänen, V. (1985). *Introducción la Latín Vulgar*. Madrid: Gredos.

Lothar Willms

Divodurum Vulgare: Linguistic Change and Cultural Integration in the Vulgar Latin Inscriptions of Divodurum (Metz)

Abstract: This paper explores linguistic change and (De-)Romanisation as reflected in the non-standard inscriptions from Divodurum (modern Metz). Commensurate with their relatively small number in comparison with the three eastern metropoles Trier, Mainz, and Cologne, the non-standard inscriptions of Divodurum cover only a reduced range of non-standard basic features. Syncope and the loss of final consonants are over-proportionately present and find a match in Gaulish which is especially present in spelling, phonetic, morphology, syntax, and onomastic, often with features unrecorded in the metropolitan inscriptions (*Tau gallicum*, raising of short *e* before *s*, nom sg. *-os*, personal names) or firmer proof for their Celtic character (raising of long *e* in word forms that exist in Gaulish). The Romanisation of Celts operated via polytheism, the cult for the Imperial House, the presence of a Latin-speaking population, interethnic marriage, and commercial exchange and mobility that were favoured by the city's location at the Moselle-Rhine waterway system and the crossroad of two Roman highways. Due to Divodurum's western location and status as a provincial urban centre, the Greek and Germanic element is less present than in the eastern metropolitan inscriptions.

Keywords: Metz, Vulgar Latin, inscriptions, (De-)Romanisation, Celtic

1 Introduction: Divodurum (Metz)

In previous articles, I have explored how the historical processes that would determine the history of Europe (Romanisation of Celtic population, Christianisation of Roman and Germanic people, fusion of Roman culture, Germanic society and Christian religion) are reflected in non-standard Latin inscriptions from the three beacon metropoles Trier, Mainz, and Cologne. The main focus of my investigation was on linguistic change and the factors and features of (De-)Romanisation. In this paper, I shall apply the same approach to Divodurum (modern Metz), an urban centre of the province of Belgica, that was located at the Moselle upriver of the Imperial metropolis Trier in the rather safe – both more rural and less urbanised –

Lothar Willms, Humboldt-Universität zu Berlin, Germany

https://doi.org/10.1515/9783111332956-016

Gaulish hinterland west and south of the three eastern metropoles where Romanisation was not fostered by a large afflux of Latin-speakers through military and administrative institutions.

In the first part of this paper, I shall systematise the 109 entries (in 73 inscriptions) from the Budapest-based *Computerized Historical Linguistic Database of the Latin Inscriptions of the Imperial Age* (http://lldb.elte.hu/)[1] for Divodurum to a local grammar of Vulgar Latin. In the second, I shall discuss the role of Celtic substratum and Greek adstratum in the process of Romanisation. My working hypothesis is that Romanisation operated in Divodurum by a more organic coalescence, favoured by polytheism and commerce. The third part will be devoted to Late Antique and Merovingian inscriptions that offer, despite their small number, a wide range of innovative features and sufficient material for investigating prominent Vulgar Latin and Romance phenomena (nasalisation, palatalisation) and regional differentiation. All linguistic phenomena will be matched with those found in Trier, Mainz, and Cologne.

2 Pagan Inscriptions of the Early Empire

Divodurum was a regional centre. Only nine non-standard deviations stem from its vicinity. The vast majority of the inscriptions can be dated to the early Empire. The almost exclusive private origin of the inscriptions conforms to the picture of a pacified provincial city in the hinterland. The only official inscription was found outside the city and deals with the military.[2] It is like most private inscriptions engraved on stone. Only one private inscription appears on a gem and six on pottery. The vast majority is on tombstones. A few inscriptions document the sponsorship of building restoration or are dedicated to the Imperial House or pagan deities.

---

1 For the sake of economy of space, the LLDB numbers are only indicated if they offer an additional or divergent linguistic interpretation of the inscriptional text. The abbreviations of the inscription editions and their complete bibliographical references follow Clauss and Slaby (https://db.edcs.eu/epigr/hinweise/abkuerz.php?s_language=de). The last numbers mark the number within the inscription editions, not the page. All inscriptions are AD, pagan, private, prose, stone unless marked differently. *Ceteris paribus* epigraphical references are listed in a chronological order. From extensively attested phenomena only the most representative instances are included. The dating of the inscriptions follows the LLDB. If the LLDB indicates that the date is unknown, no date will be given at all.

2 ILTG 387, l. 4, AE 1920, 118, official, vicinity, 67–100.

2.1 Vocalism

Vowels undergo evolutions similar to those found at Mainz and Cologne. The lowering to *e*[3] or drop[4] (ubiquitous in the Cologne inscriptions[5]) of posttonic *i* before the ending are attested once each. We find almost the same picture with the contraction of *uu*[6] which is typical of Vulgar Latin[7] and *ii*[8] which persists in Christian inscriptions.[9] Archaising spelling is limited to *ii* instead of *i* in intervocalic position,[10] monophthongisation of *ae*, featuring only in pretonic[11] where it persists in Christian inscriptions[12] and posttonic position, always in feminine singular, once with a possessive pronoun,[13] at times with an appellative,[14] but chiefly with personal names.[15] One instance of monophthongisation of *au* stands out as it finds no match in the inscriptions from Trier, Mainz and Cologne.[16]

What stands out in the Metz corpus is the density of syncope which occurs both in posttonic[17] and in particular pretonic position[18] and is numerically compara-

3 VISVVEVS instead of *Vesuvius* (CIL 13.4406 l. 3, CAG 57.2 p. 338, 51–300).

4 CONCORDVS > *Concordius* (CIL 13.12734/2 l. 1, pottery).

5 Willms 2021: 202.

6 [I]NGENVS instead of *Ingenuus* (CIL 13.11407, l. 3 CAG 57.2 p. 270, 51–300).

7 Leumann 1977: 120.

8 VEXSILLARI| instead of *vexillarii* (ILTG 387 l. 4, AE 1920,118, official, vicinity, 67–100), FILI ET HEREDES instead of *filii et heredes* (CIL 13.4331, l. 6, CAG 57.2, p. 236).

9 Plur. nom. FILI instead of *filii* (RICG 1.247 l. 5, CIL 13.11440, Christian, 501–600).

10 EIIVSDEM instead of *eiusdem* (ILTG 387 l. 8, AE 1920,118, official, vicinity, 67–100), MAIIABVS instead of *Maiis* (CIL 13.4303 l. 4, ILS 4818).

11 EMILIIS instead of *Aemiliis* (CIL 13.4339 l. 1, CAG 57.2 p. 262), PREF instead of *praefecti* (LLDB-94526, CIL 13.4291 l. 3, CAG 57.2 p. 214).

12 PRESTARE instead of *praestare* (RICG 1.250 l. 2, CIL 13.4733 l. 2, Christian, vicinity, 480–600).

13 SVE instead of *suae* (CIL 13.11378, l. 4, CAG 57.2 p. 293, 51–300).

14 FILIE instead of *filiae* (CIL 13.4416 l. 4, CAG 57.2 p. 133, 51–300; CIL 13.4405 l. 4, CAG 57.2 p. 133, 51–300).

15 DECMILLE instead of *Decimillae / Decumillae* (CIL 13.4370 l. 2, CAG 57.2 p. 295, 51–300), PACATE instead of *Pacatae* (CIL 13,11400, l. 2, CAG 57.2 p. 266, 51–300), PRISCILLE instead of *Priscillae* (CIL 13.4416 l. 2, CAG 57.2 p. 133, 51–300). For foreign names, see Section 2.4 Language contact.

16 CLOSTRARIAE instead of *(artis) claustrariae* (AE 1976,484, CAG 57.2 p. 188).

17 DECMI instead of *Decimi / Decumi* (CIL 13.4441, l. 3, 51–300), ORICLAE instead of *Oriculae* (LLDB-94528, CIL 13.4293 l. 3, CAG 57.2 p. 181, 1–300).

18 DECM[A]NI instead of *Decumani* (AE 2003,1212 l. 3, AE 2017, +980, CAG 57.2 p. 194, 171–200), DECMANI instead of *Decumani* (AE 1976.480, l. 1, CAG 57.2 p. 187), DECMANO instead of *Decimano / Decumano* (AE 1906, +181, AE 1907, +189, CAG 57.2 p. 265; CIL 13.11359 l. 3, AE,1905,169, 51–300), DECMILLE instead of *Decimillae / Decumillae* (CIL 13.4370, l. 2, CAG 57.2 p. 295, 51–300), DECMIN[I instead of *Decimini / Decumini* (CIL 13.4320, l. 2, CAG 57.2 p. 228), MACLONO instead of *Maculono* (CIL 13.4397 l. 2, AE 1903,272, 51–300).

ble to the Cologne occurrence.[19] This hyper-proportionate attestation might reflect the influence of Gaulish where the same phenomenon in pretonic position can be observed,[20] and indeed, Gaulish influence has been identified for all the instances where this phenomenon occurs in the Roman personal names *Decumanus* and *Decimilla* in the Metz corpus.[21]

2.2 Consonantism

Consonants tend to be suppressed at the beginning, in the middle or at the end of a word. Initial suppression is limited to *h*.[22] In mid-position, *x* loses its occlusive element before another voiceless stop,[23] *v* is dropped before *u*,[24] a change well-attested in Vulgar Latin,[25] and de-gemination is firmly attested,[26] with one hypercorrect gemination.[27] In final position, consonant suppression is quite accentuated,

19 Willms 2021: 208. The contrastive foil of Cologne demonstrates that my focus on city corpora and the inclusion of social and ethnic factors (eastern metropoles with afflux of administrative and military personnel vs. Celtic hinterland) allow for more fine-grained results below the level and beyond the borders of selected provinces (Aquitania, Narbonensis, Venetia-Istria, Dalmatia), including Belgica, on which the highly meritorious regional analysis of syncope by Adamik 2016 is based. Even in his approach, Belgica has the highest level of syncope in the Early Empire whereas the non-documentation of this phenomenon in Late Antiquity might be accounted for by the dominance of the imperial capital Trier that attracted educated upper class people from the entire Empire.

20 De Bernardo Stempel 1994: 30, 2023: 74–93.

21 De Bernardo Stempel 2023: 92.

22 ELV|IVS instead of *Helvius* (CIL 13.4301 l. III 8–9, CAG 57.2 p. 335).

23 ESCIPE instead of *excipe* (AE 1912,293 l. 1). Both the phonetic and spelling of *x*, a letter that represents a combination of two consonants, is challenging. There is only another instance of phonetic change, this time a transposition of the two elements (VISCIT instead of *vixit* (CIL 13.4328 l. 4, CAG 57.2 p. 245, 51–300). As elsewhere, the biconsonantal character of *x* is clarified by an additional *s* in several instances: SAXSETANO| instead of *Saxetano*, VEXSILLARI| instead of *vexillarii* (ILTG 387 l. 3–4, AE 1920,118, official, vicinity, 67–100), VIXSIT instead of *vixit* (CIL 13.4362 l.7, CAG 57.2 p. 235), VXSOR instead of *uxor* (CIL 13.11406 l. 4–5, CAG 57.2 p. 267, 51–300; ICMetz 4 l. 1, AE 2017,979, Christian, 401–500), SAXSIS instead of *saxis* (RICG 1.258 l. 2, CIL 13.4733, Christian, vicinity, 480–600), VIXS instead of *vixit* (RICG 1.245 l. 3, CIL 13.11442, Christian, 470–550).

24 VIVS instead of *vivus* (AE 1976,477 l. 5, CAG 57.2 p. 186; CIL 13.4363 l. 4, CAG 57.2 p. 209, 51–300).

25 Leumann 1977: 138.

26 COMVNI instead of *Communi* (cf. Ital. *comune*) (CIL 13.10001/100oo, l. 1, pottery, vicinity), MARCELINO instead of *Marcellino* (AE 2004,951 l. 2, CAG 57.2 p. 192, 141–180), ANVLINO instead of *Anullino* (CCCA 5,446 l. 5, CIL 13.11352, AE 1913,243, 199).

27 EPPAXIAE instead of *Epaxiae* (CIL 13.4372 l. 2, CAG 57.2 p. 301, 51–300).

covering the full range of consonants regularly omitted in Vulgar Latin (-*m*,[28] -*s*,[29] -*t*[30]), mostly in endings.[31] The drop of -*s* and -*n* (< -*m*) in the later Gaulish[32] and, more specifically, Gaulish names in at least three of four instances where the loss of -*s* and -*m* occurs in the Divodurum inscriptions suggest an influence of Gaulish substrate.[33]

2.3 Morphosyntax

Like vowel spelling, morphosyntax yields an archaising tendency that unveils an effort for complying with the standard norm. It is manifest in etymologising spelling that brings about a hypercorrect folk etymology[34] or annuls internal sandhi. In this case, the grammatical conformism to linguistic standards goes along with political loyalty since this phenomenon features in a votive inscription for the Imperial House.[35] The restorative tendency in spelling and practice go hand in hand when the restoration of roads and bridges is documented.[36] An innovative tendency, the

28 SENONV TRIS instead of *Senonum tres* (CIL 13.4304 l. 1, CAG 57.2 p. 167), AI[3]NIA | ARA (|) REF C instead of *aram () reficiendam curavit* (LLDB-73054: / nom./abl. pro acc. in obiecto directo, CCCA 5,446 l. 5–6, CIL 13.11352, AE 1913,243, 199).

29 (CARADDOVNAE | DONNO |) MARCV | V instead of *Marcus vivus* (CIL 13.4355 l. 3, CAG 57.2 p. 300, 51–300), (DEO MERCVRIO ET ROSMERTAE | MVSICVS LILLVTI FIL ET) SVI EX VOTO instead of *suis ex voto* (LLDB-94540: / nom. pro dat., CIL 13.4311 l. 2, CAG 57.2 p. 182).

30 DONAVI | instead of *donavit* (CIL 13.4301, l. III 3, CAG 57.2 p. 335).

31 The only exception is E instead of *et*, cf. Ital. *e* (CIL 13.4445 l. 5, CAG 57.2 p. 255, 51–300; CIL 13.4329 l. 5, CAG 57.2 p. 262, 51–300).

32 Lambert 2003: 47.

33 The scarce evidence from Belgica for these phenomena provides no material basis for a numerical assessment, let alone by a comparison with other better documented provinces. Divodurum still provides two of four instances of the omission of -*m* and three of -*s* respectively in this province during the Early Empire (cf. Paulus 2020: 133).

34 OBTIMO instead of *optimo* (LLDB-94550, CIL 13.4353 l. 7, CAG 57.2 p. 299, 51–300), here remodeled after the preposition *ob*, actually to be derived from *ops*, *opis* f. 'power, resources' (de Vaan 2008: 430–431 who reports a genetic analysis that meets the reservation advanced by Leumann 1977: 318 about this derivation).

35 SCRIBTI instead of *scripti* (LLDB-94530, CIL 13.4301 l. I 6, CAG 57.2 p. 335).

36 CONL[APSAS (or *conlabsas*?, with form *con-*, instead of *collapsas* [CAG 57.2 p. 288, CIL 17.2.518, CIL 13.9054, AE 1983,710]). The etymological spelling of prefixes is more common in official texts than the assimilation (Leumann 1977: 194) and prevails in the database by Clauss and Slaby with a ratio of 247 (whence 1 *conlabs-* and 56 that are conjectured by the editor and not confirmed by identical formulas elsewhere) : 52 (whence 22 that are conjectured by the editor and not confirmed by identical formulas elsewhere) in *conlaps-* vs. *collaps-*.

erosion of case syntax,[37] is manifest in the use of an additional preposition[38] and in personal names that are not inflected in a nominal phrase where the other elements sufficiently indicate its function.[39]

2.4 Language Contact

2.4.1 Gaulish Influence

What singles Divodurum out from the Eastern metropolitan cities is the strong Celtic element which appears in six points and covers spelling, phonetics, morphology, syntax, and onomastics. Four of them are unique in this area and almost completely unparalleled in the inscriptions from Trier, Mainz, and Cologne despite the fact that these cities bear witness to firm and various Celtic influence.

The first point is a Celtic letter, the *Tau gallicum* 'Gaulish tau', as the Romans called it. This letter was a theta in Gallo-Greek inscriptions which was first used also in Gallo-Latin inscriptions as evidenced in an inscription from Divodurum.[40]

The Divodurum inscriptions offer a fascinating candidate for elsewhere undocumented Celtic phonetic influence, the raising of short *e* before *s* to *i*[41] which finds a pertinent parallel in contemporary Gaulish (*Ales-ia* > *Alisia*, **swesor-* > **swisor-* > *suior-* 'sister').[42]

Moreover, the Metz inscriptions provide an instance of possible phonetic and probable syntactic Gaulish influence in a votive inscription for the three Celtic *Matres* (SENONV TRIS instead of *Senonum tres*[43]). The form *tris* can be read as the archaic Latin accusative *tris* that features during the Early Empire in litera-

---

37 Cf. PRO SALV | TE MERCVRIALIS | FILIVS SECVND | IVS SECVNDINVS instead of *pro salute Mercurialis filii Secundius Secundinus* (CSIR-D 43 183, AE 1924,17, Trier).

38 EX IVS instead of *iussu* (CIL 13.4304 l. 4, CAG 57.2 p. 167).

39 [DO]M[IT]IA () COIVGI instead of *Domitiae () coniugi* (AE 1983,713 l. 2, AE 2001,1415, CAG 57.2 p. 196, 101–300), SANCTO (| |) E SA[NC] | TINIA C[ONIVGI instead of *Sancto () et Sanctiniae coniugi* (CIL 13,4329 l. 5, CAG 57.2 p. 262, 51–300).

40 CARAΘΘO[V]NVS instead of *Caraddounus* (ILTG 388 l. 1, vicinity). This frequent name is derived from the verb *car-* 'love'. Its further analysis is not certain. It is segmented either as **cara-sto-mno-* with a particle element *-mno-* (no certain sense) or *carat-souno-* (from *caratos* 'beloved') 'who likes sleeping' or rather 'who likes dreams, dreamer' (Delamarre 2003: 107, 279).

41 VISVVEVS instead of *Vesuvius* (CIL 13.4406 l. 3, CAG 57.2 p. 338, 51–300).

42 Lambert 2003: 43.

43 CIL 13.4304 l. 1, CAG 57.2 p. 167.

ture[44] and, albeit rarely, in inscriptions.[45] Although there is some hesitation about the inscription's syntax,[46] the most likely case is a dative since the numeral most probably refers to the Celtic *Matres*. However, only Late Latin started to use *tres* instead of *tribus*.[47] This makes a non-Latin origin of the deviant form more likely. The context provides clues for Gaulish background and linguistic influence since the *Matres* co-feature with Mercury whose epithet *Cosumi* is a hapax,[48] most probably of indigenous origin as often with this god's epithets in Roman Gaul.[49] Still, the form *tris* cannot be explained by Gaulish morphology or syntax. Scarce attestation makes the reconstruction of the Gaulish paradigm of 'three' fairly thorny, and the form *tris* finds no match here. Gaulish had a special feminine form for the numeral 'three' *(tiđres)*[50] and Old Irish like Latin (*tribus*) a dative in *b* (*trib*).[51] One could at best speculate about an influence of the form *treis* 'three' that features in a short and mutilated inscription which makes it hard to determine its precise morphosyntactic function.[52] Its phonetic value is likewise hard to determine: **trīs*, which is reconstructed for Proto-Celtic as well[53] and would provide bullet-proof evidence for Gaulish influence on our Latin form *tris*, is the most likely interpretation, yet Proto-Celtic **trīs* is not established and challenged by the alternative **trīns*.[54] The most plausible explanation for this unusual case in the Early Empire is thus an insufficient command of Latin by a non-native speaker who did not adapt the numeral to the bisyllabic form, required by Latin syntax, although an almost homophonous equivalent might have featured in their mother tongue, but instead used *tris* which was a rare monosyllabic Latin accusative and in addition homophonous with the datives of the *a/o*-declension. The form *tris* may additionally have been inspired by the compound form of this cardinal in Gaulish (*tri-*)[55] which is

---

44 Kühner and Holzweissig 1912: 635–636.

45 OLEAS [T]/[RIS (CIL 8.25943, Ain el-Djemela / Sustri, 15–16), REGNAVIT [sc. Aeneas] AN]NOS TRIS (CIL 10.08348, Pompei), TRIS PRO MULTIS ORBANT (CIL 3.4346, Komarom / Komorn / Brigetio (Pannonia superior), verse, 201–400).

46 Cf. the commentary on LLDB-94536 by the collector Vágási Tünde: "context is uncertain, the dedicator(s) may have been the civitas Senonum or its 3 members. Fortasse recte."

47 Kühner and Holzweissig 1912: 636. Cf. Custurulinga [3 viva] / SE CUMPARABIT S[IBI LOCUM A 3] / AURI SOL(IDIS) TRI(BU)S SI[MIS (ICUR 2,5172, Christian, Rome, 301–500).

48 CAG 57.2 p. 167.

49 C. Robert III. Philipps, art. Mercurius. DNP 8 (2000) 3–4.

50 Lambert 2003: 145, LEIA T-140.

51 LEIA T-139.

52 Lambert 2003: 143–144.

53 Matasović 2009: 390 s.v., LEIA T-140.

54 Delamarre 2003: 301.

55 Matasović 2009: 390.

solidly attested[56] since it is invariant as well, regardless of the case of the noun it modifies. The ultimate proof for Gaulish interference comes from another inscription, dedicated to the *Matres*, where *tris* features doubtless in the place of *tribus*, as warranted by the preceding *matribus*.[57] This parallel hence demonstrates that Gaulish influence in the Metz inscription is not limited to phonetics, but that the non-native authorship also affected syntax.

Gaulish origin has duly been suspected for the ending *-os* of *Bellos*,[58] a Gaulish name.[59] *-os* which is the nominative singular ending of the *o*-declension in Gaulish[60] later dropped its final *-s*[61] as evidenced by Gaulish potters' names in two potter marks from Divodurum.[62]

The fifth point of Celtic influence is most common, though still debatable in the Metz inscriptions. The dative in *-abus* which in Cologne appears in numerous epithets of the Celtic triadic goddesses *matres* or *matronae*[63] and thus might cover the dative plural in *-abo* of the Gaulish *a*-declension[64] is limited in Metz to one instance (DIS MAIIABVS instead of *Diis Maiis*)[65] which is far from unambiguous. Its linguistic presence is sufficiently justified by gender differentiation which is not guaranteed by the preceding *Dis*. The stone monument on which the inscription features depicts three standing female figures whose iconography (that in the middle presents unidentifiable objects, probably fruit) strongly suggests an identity with the *Matres*, an identification, which, however, has been contested in view of the epithet by a scholar who still identifies the goddesses as indigenous.[66] Still, the

---

56 Delamarre 2003: 300.

57 *Ma[t]ri[b]us / Tri(bu)s (?) Pom(peia?) / [Pullatis(?)] f(ilia) Paulla h(eredes) e(x) t(estamento)* (AE 2012,783, Navarro-2017,596,3, HEp 2012,723, Los Banales de Uncastillo / Tarraca, 71–130).

58 MARVLLINA BELLOS instead of *Marullina Bellus* (LLDB-101499: / substratum vel adstratum, "ethnic and / or linguistic background of persons involved in the inscription: Celtic name?", AE 1983, 707 l. 3, AE 2001,1416, CAG 57.2 p. 196, 101–200).

59 Not included in Holder 1896.

60 Lambert 2003: 51–52.

61 Lambert 2003: 47, 52.

62 LVGETO FF instead of *Lugetus fecit* (CIL 13.10010/1176n l. 1, pottery). Attested as a male personal name (Holder 2 (1904) 305). Probably derived from *lugus*, the name of a god that features prominently in *Lugu-dunum* (Delamarre 2003: 210), perhaps originally 'the shiny one' (Matasović 2009: 248 s.v.).

AVNEDO F instead of *Aunedus fecit* (CIL 13.10010/244d-e l. 1, pottery, 140–200). *Aunedo(n)* is attested as a male cognomen (Holder 1896: 1.294). Like other personal names, derived from *auni-* or *auno-*, it is of uncertain etymology (Delamarre 2003: 61).

63 Willms 2021: 210–211.

64 Lambert 2003: 56, 59.

65 CIL 13.4303 l. 4, ILS 4818, CAG 57.2 p. 239.

66 R. Peter, art. Maiae. Roscher 2 (1894–1897) 2240–2241.

Roman goddess Maia is the dedicatee of several inscriptions in the west bank of the Rhine and Gallia Narbonensis, often co-appearing with Mercure.[67] The *matres* are introduced as DIS and three and co-feature with Mercure on the aforementioned Metz inscription that is co-dedicated to Mercure and inspired by him.[68] This parallel provides a strong clue for identifying our DIS MAIIABVS as the Celtic *matres* who have been conflated with the Roman goddess Maia,[69] an intriguing instance of multi-layered cross-cultural syncretism in pagan polytheism. The alternative reading MAIRABVS[70] is a Celtic epithet of the *Matres*[71] and strongly supports a Celtic origin of this dative ending. Regardless of the epithet's and goddesses' precise identity, the inscription's dedication to the Imperial House offers an intriguing insight into the integrative power of ancient polytheism.

The sixth instance which finds a match in the inscriptions of Mainz[72] builds on the ubiquitous monophthongisation of *ae* which is abundantly attested in the genitive and dative of female names of the *a*-declension, thus bringing to the fore numerous Celtic names.

AGISILLE[73] instead of *Agisillae*[74]
BRIXE[75] instead of *Brixae*[76] < **brigo-* 'force, strength' (> *Brigius, Brigo-marus*)[77] or **brixta* 'magic' (theonym *Bricta, Brixtae*)[78]
C]ARANTIE[79] instead of *Carantiae*[80]

67 H. Link, art. 2) Maia. RE 14.1 (1928) 532–533.
68 CIL 13.4304 l. 1, CAG 57.2 p. 167.
69 Flotté 2005: 239.
70 Flotté 2005: 239.
71 De Bernardo Stempel 2021: 71.
72 BODICE instead of *Bodicae* (CSIR-D 2.14 70.5, *Finke* 224, 200), IBLIOMARIE instead of *Ibliomariae* (CSIR-D 2.14 70.5, *Finke* 224, 200), MELISSE instead of *Melissae* (AmphMainz 116/11.1, pottery, 201–300).
73 *Agisillus, Agisilus* (Holder 1896: 1.59). The alternation with the voiceless equivalent *c* in the variant *Acisilliae* from Metz (CAG 57.2 p. 264) provides an additional clue for Gaulish origin (cf. Lambert 2003: 47–48).
74 CIL 13.11364 l. 2, CAG 57.2 p. 270, 51–300.
75 *Brixa* (only present instance), *Bricca, Brixo, Briccio, Brictio* (Holder 1896: 1.612).
76 CIL 13.4401 l. 3, CAG 57.2 p. 263, 51–300.
77 Delamarre 2003: 88.
78 Delamarre 2003: 90.
79 *Carantius* and *Carantia* were used as Roman nomen gentile (Holder 1896: 1.768–769).
80 AE 2003,1212 l. 3, AE 2017, +980, CAG 57.2 p. 194, 171–200.

CARANTODIE instead of *Carantodiae*:[81] both frequent PN names, from *carantos* 'friend, beloved', derived by the active participle ending *-ant-* from the verbal base *car-* 'to love'[82]
CINTVS | ME instead of *Cintusmae*[83] < *cintus* 'first', *cintusmos* (formed with the superlative suffix *-s(a)mos*) 'very first' (PN)[84]
DIVIXTE instead of *Divixtae*:[85] PN *Divixta*,[86] *Divicta, Divixtus* 'avenger'[87]
[G]AV | V[E] instead of *Gauvae*:[88] *cauo-* 'hollow' (?) > (?) PN *Cauus, Cauius, Cauia*, Καουα (Delamarre 2003: 111–112), *Gavia* (?) (cognomen, f.).[89] Only neatly Roman names feature around her in the inscription, coalescence, but no identity with the Roman nomen gentile that features also in the feminine.[90]
IASSE[91] instead of *Iassae*[92] < (?) PN *Iantu-* 'desire, ambition'[93] or shortened form of PN *Ianussa*, built on the root *i̯ānu-, i̯āno-* 'just'[94]
MANAVE[95] instead of *Manavae*[96] < (?) *manos* 'good' (?) > PN *Sego-mannae, Manurus, Manus, Manutia, Mannius, Mannia*[97]
SAC | RANE[98] instead of *Sacranae*[99] < *sacro-* 'consecrated, cursed', extremely frequent in personal names, e.g. *Sacro-bena, Sacruna, Sacrinus, Sacrius, Sacro, Sacrotus, Sacrila, Sacratius, Sacronius*[100]

If any relatives co-feature on these inscriptions, their names are hardly genuinely Roman. Only one of these inscriptions yields a husband who bears a genuine

81 CIL 13.4359 l. 2, Mander 351, 51–300.
82 Delamarre 2003: 107.
83 AE 1903,272 l. 3–4; CIL 13.4397 l. 3–4, CAG 57.2 p. 218, 51–300.
84 Delamarre 2003: 116, Holder 1896: 1.1024–1025.
85 AE 2003,1211 l. 3, AE 2017, +980, CAG 57.2 p. 196, 171–200.
86 Lambert 2003: 58.
87 Delamarre 2003: 145. Many instances in Holder 1896: 1.1294–1295.
88 AE 1983,708 l. 3–4, AE 2001,1414, CAG 57.2 p. 195, 101–200.
89 Holder 1896: 1.1991.
90 E. Groag, F. Münzer, A. Stein, artt. Gavius, Gavia. RE 7.1 (1910) 866–872.
91 *Iassus, Iassa; Iassia, Iasso, Iassu* (Holder 1904: 2.13–14).
92 CIL 13.4382 l. 2, CAG 57.2 p. 302, 51–300.
93 Delamarre 2003: 32.
94 Delamarre 2003: 320.
95 *Manavi* (place name in Britannia), *Manavia* (Isle of Man) (Holder 1904: 2.401).
96 CIL 13.4343 l. 2, CAG 57.2 p. 299, 51–300.
97 Delamarre 2003: 214–215.
98 Cognomen, Crundale, Kent (Holder 1904: 2.1279).
99 CIL 13.4430 l. 2–3, CAG 57.2 p. 304, 51–300.
100 Delamarre 2003: 263.

Roman name (M(arco) Micioni Ma[tt]osso),[101] relegating inter-ethnic marriage to an inferior rank among the factors that drove Romanisation.

Two female names that at first glance look Greek turn out to be Celtic upon closer investigation:

EPPAXIAE instead of *Epaxiae*[102] might be the feminine of Ἐπάξων (Ἐπαξ(ί)ων?), attested once in Bithynia,[103] but its Celtic second name (or cognomen?) *Diviciae* (fem. of *Divicius* 'avenger'[104]) strongly suggests an etymology from the Gaulish word for 'horse' that features in many personal names, both with a suffix in *a* (*Epacus*, *Epasius*, *Epaticcus*) and in compounds (e.g. *Epo-redo-rix* 'king of horse racing'),[105] and favours an interpretation as *epo-* + *ago-* 'fight, combat',[106] whence 'fighting with / from horses'.

Melisse and its masculine equivalent *Melissi* which co-feature on a pottery stamp[107] are two most common Gaulish names which mean 'sweet' and are derived like their Greek homophone μέλισσα 'bee' from PIE **melit-* 'honey'.[108] The parallel appearance in the genitive on a pottery stamp from Mainz[109] suggests that this couple, either spouses or siblings, were running a pottery-making business.

2.4.2 Greek Influence

Divodurum's location at the crossroad of two Roman highways and its integration to the Roman road system that span the entire empire are reflected in Greek personal names that point to the presence of a Greek-speaking population that came from the Empire's south and far east. Greek personal names thus are limited to instances of sub-standard treatment of aspirates, which are a feeble category in Latin. They document the aspirates' spirantisation in Greek (*ph* > *f*)[110] or their loss[111] as well as their hypercorrect[112] or vicious appearance (CRHYSOPAES instead

101 AE 2003,1212 l. 3, AE 2017, +980, CAG 57.2, p. 194, 171–200.
102 CIL 134372 l. 2, CAG 57.2 p. 301, 51–300.
103 Fraser and Matthews vol. V.A [2010] 156.
104 Delamarre 2003: 145.
105 Delamarre 2003: 163.
106 Cf. Delamarre 2003: 35.
107 MELISSE instead of *Melissae* (CIL 13.10002/297c e, l. 1, pottery, vicinity).
108 Delamarre 2003: 320.
109 MELISSE instead of *Melissae* (AmphMainz 116/11.1, pottery, 201–300).
110 DELFICVS instead of *Delphicus* (CIL 13, 4291 l. 4, CAG 57.2 p. 214).
111 CLORON > *Chloron* (CIL 13.10021/191 l. II 2, ILS 8742, CAG 57.1 p. 443, gem, steatitis).
112 HEVTYCHIAE instead of *Eutychiae* (CIL 13.11378 l. 2, CAG 57.2 p. 293, 51–300).

of *Chrysopaes*).[113] The last element of this personal name could represent an early stage of monophthongisation[114] of Gk. παῖς,[115] be a Latin transposition of a hypercorrect spelling by an itacised eta (which is the most unexpected and complicated scenario), or be even of Thracian origin (PN Παιβης, *Paibes*, Παιβις, Παης),[116] as were many other slaves in Antiquity.[117]

3 Christian Inscriptions of Late Antiquity and the Merovingian Era

Inscriptions of Late Antiquity and the Merovingian Era are much more uniform than the earlier pagan ones. They are funerary inscriptions on tombstones, which are almost exclusively private and Christian, extremely formulaic, and chiefly more laconic and fragmentary than the contemporary metropolitan inscriptions from the Northeast. Despite their relatively low number, however, post-classical inscriptions cover a large post-antique chronological range (450–800) and document a high density of non-standard features (19 in 10 inscriptions), many of them previously unrecorded. Late Latin inscriptions offer the first certain instances of the nearby-merger which is less comprehensive than in the metropolitan inscriptions. The nearby-merger of *u* is limited to a single posttonic instance.[118] *i* is lowered to *e* twice in tonic position[119] and in posttonic position only in the verbal ending *-it* of *quiescit*[120] or *requiescit*.[121] The raising of long *e* and *o* to *i* and *u* which is frequent in the Gauls and Germanias remains marginal in the Metz inscrip-

113 CIL 13.11397 l. 7, CAG 57.2 p. 268.

114 Cf. αε in Boeotian (Thumb et al. 1959: 2.24–25).

115 χρυσόπαις is attested once in Phrygia (Fraser and Matthews vol. V.C [2018] 451), Asia Minor being a common source for slaves (Volker Grieb, art. Kleinasien. HAS 1638–1641, at 1638–1639).

116 Detschew 1976: 351.

117 Cf. Dilyana Boteva, art. Thrakien. HAS 3066–3069, at 3067.

118 VRSOLA instead of *Ursula* (RICG 1.246 l. 4, CIL 13.11443, Christian, 501–600).

119 TETV | [LVM instead of *titulum* (ICMetz 4 l. 2–3, AE 2017,979, Christian, 401–500), PRINCEPIV[S] instead of *Principius* (RICG 1.251 l. 2, CIL 13.4460, Christian, 450–600).

120 LLDB-8434: / -ET pro -it, RICG 1,252, l. 1, CIL 13.4461, Christian, 601–800; LLDB-8422: / -ET pro -it, RICG 1.242 l. 1, CIL 13.11441, Christian, 601–800.

121 [REQVIE]SCET instead of *requiescit* (LLDB-91982: / ET pro -it, ICMetz 12 l. 1, 401–600).

tions, affecting *e*[122] once in tonic and *o* twice in posttonic position.[123] A singular anaptyxis after *s*[124] would find a match in the Trier inscriptions[125] if we assume that *c* was still pronounced as stop and be compatible with its palatalisation as the additional vowel would have eased a hard to articulate cluster of two palatals. The drop of *u* after *q*,[126] matched in Trier[127] and Cologne,[128] suggests that this sound had lost its labial element at that late stage, as evidenced in all Romance languages before *i*.

The vicious appearance of *-m* at a former ablative in *-e* that was required by the preposition *in*[129] attests to far-reaching nasalisation or the total drop of final *-m* and to the blurring of the difference between ablative and accusative that had been initiated by the drop of accusative *-m* in Early Empire inscriptions after the same preposition.[130] This phenomenon is widely attested in the Trier Christian inscriptions.[131]

Despite their large post-antique chronological range, the Late Latin inscriptions contain chiefly Latin and Christian names[132] and only one which can be read as Germanic (*Aralainus*[133] < *ara-* [a compound form of *aran-* 'eagle'][134] + **laihna* 'property'[135] or **laiþaz* 'loathsome',[136] 'hostile'[137] or **laidjan-* 'to lead'[138]). The tiny

---

122 QVIISCET instead of *quiescit* (RICG 1.242 l. 1, CIL 13.11441, Christian, 601–800).

123 VIXIT ANNVS instead of *vixit annos* (LLDB-8428: / decl. IV pro II, RICG 1.247 l. 3, CIL 13.11440, Christian, 501–600), VIXS | ANNVS instead of *vixit annos* (LLDB-8425: / decl. IV pro II, RICG 1.245 l. 3–4, CIL 13.11442, Christian, 470–550).

124 REQVIE|SECIT instead of *requiescit* (RICG 1.246 l. 1–2, CIL 13.11443, Christian, 501–600).

125 DOMESITIGVS instead of *domesticus* (RICG 1.1/5, CIL 13.3682, 351–400).

126 QIEC[IT] instead of *quiescit* (RICG 1.251 l. 1, CIL 13.4460, Christian, 450–600), RECI[ESCIT] instead of *requiescit* (RICG 1.250 l. 1, CIL 13.11446, Christian, 501–600).

127 Willms 2019: 656.

128 Willms 2021: 203.

129 [IN P]|ACEM instead of *in pace* (LLDB-8423: acc. pro abl. / -ø > -m, RICG 1.242 l. 1–2, CIL 13.11441, Christian, 601–800).

130 IN | HONORE | DOMVS instead of *In honorem domus* (LLDB-97533: / abl. pro acc, CIL 13.4303 l. 2, ILS 4818, CAG 57.2 p. 239).

131 Willms 2019: 657–658.

132 *Aspasius* (RICG 1.242 l. 1, CIL 13.11441, CAG 57.2 p. 271, ILCV +03110b, Christian, 601–800), *Paulus* (RICG 1.245 l. 2, CIL 13.11442, ILCV 3068a, CAG 57.2 p. 271, Christian, 470–550), *Princepiu[s* (RICG 1.251 l. 2, CIL 13.4460, ILCV 3094a, CAG 57.2 p. 286, Christian, 450–600), *Vi]talis* (CIL 13.11444, RICG 1.255, CAG 57.2 p. 288); *Nice* (CIL 13.4733, ILCV 3416, CLE 1833, RICG 1258, CAG 54 p. 350, Christian, vicinity); *Ursol[a* (RICG 1.246 l. 4, CIL 13.11443, CAG 57.2 p. 271, ILCV +03543, Christian, 501–600).

133 CIL 13.11440, ILCV 3580a, RICG 1.247, CAG 57.2 p. 271, 501–600.

134 Förstemann 1900: 135–138, Kroonen 2013: 32.

135 Kroonen 2013: 323.

136 Orel 2004: 233–234.

137 Förstemann 1900: 998–1001.

138 Kroonen 2013: 323, Förstemann 1900: 998.

Germanic presence is a significant difference from the now German metropoles Trier, Mainz, and Cologne, and it conforms to the fact that Metz today belongs to the francophone part of Lorraine.

4 Overarching Trends

In three points, deviant spelling which in the past has been labelled as misspelling may rather reflect language change. The phonetic interpretation is more specific than the cautious epigraphical one, drawing on particular features that render the transition from one sound to another plausible as well as on parallels from neighbouring Trier and Cologne; still, this new and more specific argument sometimes stands on epigraphically shaky ground and duly invites further discussion.

The Metz inscriptions offer numerous instances of syncope, both in pretonic and posttonic position. This supports the idea that instances in which letters for vowels are missing, as well in pre-[139] and posttonic[140] position, reflect their loss or weak articulation. Two posttonic instances that do not conform to the classical scheme of syncope[141] might be accounted for by nasalisation[142] that goes along with weaker and less marked articulation than oral[143] or by a position between two sonorants (*r*, *l*, *m*, *n*) which were favourable for syncope[144] and the withdrawal of the accent to the preceding vowel, facilitated by the Vulgar Latin loss of vowel length distinction and the coexistence of two suffixes with a short and long vowel (*dīv-īnus* 'divine' vs. *fāgĭnus* 'of beech-wood') already in Classical Latin.[145]

Like in Trier (M before B),[146] the drop of a nasal before a stop of the same place of articulation (N before T[147]) may reflect nasalisation. In inscriptions from

139 DIV | CIANA instead of *Diviciana* (CIL 13,4306, l. 2–3, CAG 57.2 p. 311), NATLIC | IVM instead of *natalicium* (CCCA 5,446 l. 3–4, CAG 57.2 p. 238, CIL 13.11352, AE 1913,243, 199). The AE which offers the most faithful reproduction shows a ligature with the cross beam of the T above the A which could still be meant to represent ATA, still even the AE (and CCCA) reads this section as *at(a)*. The transcription as *a(t)a* in CIL (and CAG) neglects the ligature's cross beam. In the case of M | TVS instead of *maritus* (CIL 13.4412.5–6, CAG 57.2 p. 303) where three letters including the preceding tonic one are missing, an epigraphical explanation is preferable.

140 VIXT instead of *vixit* (CIL 13.11360 l. 3, AE 2011,781, CAG 57.2 p. 334).

141 Cf. Leumann 1977: 95–98.

142 SENONM | instead of *Senonum* (CIL 13.4304 l. 1, CAG 57.2 p. 167).

143 For parallels from Cologne, see Willms 2021: 207–208.

144 Leumann 1977: 95.

145 ANVLNO instead of *Anulino* (*Anulĭno* < *Anulīno*) (CCCA 5,446 l. 5, CIL 13.11352, AE 1913,243, 199).

146 NOVEB instead of *Novembres* (RICG 1.227, CIL 13.3949, 480–800).

147 FRO | TONE instead of *Frontone* (CCCA 5, 446 l. 5–6, CIL 13.11352, AE 1913,243, 199).

Cologne[148] and Metz,[149] the change of vowel quality provides an additional clue for nasalisation, as best evidenced in French that has only three nasal vowels.

My last point concerns palatalisation and mouillement, the palatal articulation of nasals and liquids which is warranted by modern Romance languages. The Trier inscriptions offer several instances,[150] those from Cologne few[151] in which, in all due epigraphical caution, the absence of *n* or *l* or the unexpected presence of *i* could be interpreted as a graphical reflection of this shift. In Metz, the absence of L in one instance might cover this phenomenon (F]IIVS instead of *filius*, cf. Lat. *filius* > Ital. *figlio*, Port. *filho*).[152] Palatalisation is less dubious. The drop of *s* before *c* in *quiescit*[153] is unmotivated if we assume an occlusive articulation of *c* in [sk] and makes phonetic sense only if we assume a palatalisation of *c* since [tʃ] has a propensity for assimilating and absorbing a preceding [s] (Russ. счастье 'luck', считать [ʃtʃ-] 'to assume, surmise', Germ. Rhenish dialect *Kreissparkasse* 'district savings bank' [-(ʃ)ʃ-]).

Abbreviations

DNP Cancik, H. & Schneider, H. (Eds.) (1996–2003). *Der neue Pauly. Enzyklopädie der Antike*. Stuttgart: Metzler.

HAS Heinen, H. (Ed.) (2017). *Handwörterbuch der antiken Sklaverei*. 3 vols. Stuttgart: Steiner.

L- Lambert, P.-Y. (Ed.) (2002). *Recueil des inscriptions gauloises. Vol. 2.2: Textes gallo-latins sur instrumentum*. Paris: Éditions du Centre National de la Recherche Scientifique.

LEIA Bachellery, É. & Lambert, P.-Y. (Eds.) (1959–1996). *Lexique étymologique de l'Irlandais Ancien de Joseph Vendryes*. Dublin: Dublin Institute for Advanced Studies.

RE Ziegler, K. (Ed.) (1893–1980). *Pauly's Real-Encyclopädie der classischen Altertumswissenschaft*. Stuttgart: Metzler.

148 *quondam* > OVANDAM (RSK 490 l. 4 and 7–8 (bis), CIL 13.8384, 176–300).

149 CIOCN|DIDO instead of *Candido* (CIL 13.4420 l. 3–4, CAG 57.2 p. 303, 51–300).

150 Willms 2019: 657.

151 Willms 2021: 209.

152 AE 2003,1211 l. 4, AE 2017, +980, CAG 57.2 p. 196, 171–200.

153 QIEC[IT] instead of *quiescit* (RICG 1.251 l. 1, CIL 13.4460, Christian, 450–600).

Bibliography

Adamik, B. (2016). The frequency of syncope in the Latin of the empire: a statistical and dialectological study based on the analysis of inscriptions. In P. Poccetti (Ed.), *Latinitatis Rationes. Descriptive and Historical Accounts for the Latin Language* (pp. 3–21). Berlin/Boston: de Gruyter.
de Bernardo Stempel, P. (1994). Zum gallischen Akzent: Eine sprachinterne Betrachtung. *Zeitschrift für celtische Philologie*, *46*, 14–35.
de Bernardo Stempel, P. (2021). *Muttergöttinnen und ihre Votivformulare. Eine sprachhistorische Studie*. Heidelberg: Winter.
de Bernardo Stempel, P. (2023). *The Accents of Celtic. New Light on the Older and Oldest Stages*. Heidelberg: Winter.
Delamarre, X. (2003). *Dictionnaire de la langue gauloise. Une approche linguistique du vieux-celtique continental*. 2nd ed. Paris: Éditions Errance.
Detschew, D. (1976). *Die thrakischen Sprachreste*. 2nd ed. Vienna: Verlag der Österreichischen Akademie der Wissenschaften.
Flotté, P. (2005). *Carte archéologique de la Gaule. Vol. 57.2: Metz*. Paris: Académie des Inscriptions et Belles-Lettres.
Förstemann, F. W. (1900). *Altdeutsches Namenbuch. Vol. 1: Personennamen*. 2nd completely revised ed. Bonn: Hanstein.
Fraser, P. M. & E. Matthews (Eds.) (1987 ff.). *A Lexicon of Greek Personal Names*. Oxford: Clarendon Press.
Holder, A. (1896, 1904, 1913). *Alt-celtischer Sprachschatz*. 3 vols. Leipzig: Teubner.
Kroonen, G. (2013). *Etymological Dictionary of Proto-Germanic*. Leiden: Brill.
Kühner, R. & F. Holzweissig (1912). *Ausführliche Grammatik der lateinischen Sprache. Part 1: Elementar-, Formen- und Wortlehre*. 2nd ed. Hannover: Hahn.
Leumann, M. (1977). *Lateinische Laut- und Formenlehre*. Munich: Beck.
Lambert, P.-Y. (2003). *La langue gauloise. Description linguistique, commentaire d'inscriptions choisies*. 2nd ed. Paris: Éditions Errance.
Matasović, R. (2009). *Etymological Dictionary of Proto-Celtic*. Leiden: Brill.
Orel, V. E. (2003). *A Handbook of Germanic Etymology*. Leiden: Brill.
Paulus, N. (2020). A study on the weakening of the word final *-s* compared to *-m* in the epigraphic corpus. *Acta Classica Universitatis Scientiarum Debreceniensis*, 56, 125–143.
Roscher, W. H. (Ed.) (1886–1937). *Ausführliches Lexikon der griechischen und römischen Mythologie*. 6 vols., 4 suppl. vols. Leipzig: Teubner.
Thumb, A., Kieckers, E. & Scherer, A. (1932, 1959). *Handbuch der griechischen Dialekte*. 2nd ed. 2 vols. Heidelberg: Winter.
de Vaan, M. (2008). *Etymological Dictionary of Latin and the Other Italic Languages*. Leiden: Brill.
Willms, L. (2019). *Augusta Treverorum Vulgaris*: Linguistic Change and Cultural Integration in the Late Antique and Early Medieval Inscriptions of Trier (Germany). In B. Adamik, A. Barta & E. Krähling (Eds.), *The Proceedings of 13th International Colloquium on Late and Vulgar Latin (Latin vulgaire – latin tardif XIII)* (pp. 651–661). Budapest: Akadémiai Kiadó.
Willms, L. (2021). *Colonia Agrippina Vulgaris*: Linguistic Change and Cultural Integration in the Vulgar Latin Inscriptions of Cologne. In A. M. Martín Rodríguez (Ed.), *Linguisticae Dissertationes. Current Perspectives on Latin Grammar, Lexicon and Pragmatics* (pp. 199–216). Madrid: Ediciones Clásicas.

Index

https://doi.org/10.1515/9783111332680-047